THE CAMBRIDGE HANDBOOK OF PRIVATIZATION

Some goods and services seem to be fundamentally public, such as legislation, criminal punishment, and fighting wars. By contrast, other functions, such as garbage collection, do not. This volume brings together prominent scholars from a range of academic fields – including law, economics, philosophy, and sociology – to address the core question of what makes a certain good or service fundamentally public and why. Sometimes, governments and other public entities are superior because they are more likely to get at the right decisions or follow fair procedures. In other instances, the provision of goods and services by public entities is intrinsically valuable. By analyzing these answers, the authors also explore the nature of the state and its authority. This Handbook explores influential arguments for and against privatization and also develops a number of key studies explaining, justifying, or challenging the legitimacy and the desirability of public provision of particular goods and services.

Avihay Dorfman is a professor of Law at the Tel Aviv University Faculty of Law. His research areas include private law theory, legal theory, and political philosophy.

Alon Harel is the Mizock Chair in Administrative and Criminal Law at the Hebrew University in Jerusalem and a member of Federmann Center for the Study of Rationality. He specializes in political and legal theory as well as constitutional law theory.

The Cambridge Handbook of Privatization

Edited by

AVIHAY DORFMAN

Tel Aviv University, Faculty of Law

ALON HAREL

Hebrew University, Faculty of Law

Shaftesbury Road, Cambridge CB2 8EA, United Kingdom

One Liberty Plaza, 20th Floor, New York, NY 10006, USA

477 Williamstown Road, Port Melbourne, VIC 3207, Australia

314–321, 3rd Floor, Plot 3, Splendor Forum, Jasola District Centre, New Delhi – 110025, India

103 Penang Road, #05–06/07, Visioncrest Commercial, Singapore 238467

Cambridge University Press is part of Cambridge University Press & Assessment,
a department of the University of Cambridge.

We share the University's mission to contribute to society through the pursuit of
education, learning and research at the highest international levels of excellence.

www.cambridge.org
Information on this title: www.cambridge.org/9781009295703

DOI : 10.1017/9781108684330

First published 2021
First paperback edition 2023

A catalogue record for this publication is available from the British Library

Library of Congress Cataloging-in-Publication data
NAMES: Dorfman, Avihay, editor. | Harel, Alon, editor.
TITLE: The Cambridge handbook of privatization / edited by Avihay Dorfman, Tel Aviv University
Faculty of Law; Alon Harel, Hebrew University Faculty of Law.
DESCRIPTION: Cambridge, United Kingdom ; New York, NY : Cambridge University Press, 2021. |
Series: Cambridge law handbooks | Includes index.
IDENTIFIERS: LCCN 2021000124 (print) | LCCN 2021000125 (ebook) | ISBN 9781108497145 (hardback)
| ISBN 9781108684330 (ebook)
SUBJECTS: LCSH: Privatization – Law and legislation.
CLASSIFICATION: LCC K1366 .C36 2021 (print) | LCC K1366 (ebook) | DDC 338.9/25–dc23
LC record available at https://lccn.loc.gov/2021000124
LC ebook record available at https://lccn.loc.gov/2021000125

ISBN   978-1-108-49714-5   Hardback
ISBN   978-1-009-29570-3   Paperback

Contents

Figures

Tables

Contributors

Shai Agmon (University of Oxford, Politics and International Relations)

Chiara Cordelli (University of Chicago, Political Science)

Brenda Cossman (University of Toronto, Faculty of Law)

Michael Fehling (Bucerius Law School)

Talia Fisher (Tel Aviv University, Faculty of Law)

Lisa Herzog (University of Groningen)

Louis-Philippe Hodgson (York University, Philosophy)

Israel Klein (Ariel University)

Jon D. Michaels (UCLA Law School)

Martha Minow (Harvard Law School)

Mariana Mota Prado (University of Toronto, Faculty of Law)

J. Mark Ramseyer (Harvard Law School)

Hans-Bernd Schäfer (Bucerius Law School)

Assaf Sharon (Tel Aviv University, Philosophy)

Yael Kariv Teitelbarum (The Hebrew University, Faculty of Law)

Jonny Thakkar (Swarthmore College)

Malcolm Thorburn (University of Toronto, Faculty of Law)

Ashwini Vasanthakumar (Queen's University, Faculty of Law)

Alexander Volokh (Emory University, School of Law)

Acknowledgments

We would like to acknowledge the superb administrative support of Noa Cohen of the Edward J. Safra Center for Ethics, Tel Aviv University as well as this Center's generous financial support. Special thanks to Noa Adivi whose substantive and technical editorial work during the early stages of this *Handbook* was enormously helpful. Finally, thanks to Daniel Schönpflug of Wiko and two anonymous readers for Cambridge University Press for their helpful insights.

Introduction

Avihay Dorfman and Alon Harel

Editing a volume, we have found out, requires much modesty on the part of the editors who discover that their own perceptions and convictions are not always shared by others and that the area they thought they are fully familiar with is much richer and more diverse than they expected. And yet, despite all of that, we are bound to analyze and systemize the subject matter of privatization with a particular emphasis on the contributions made in this volume. What we wish to do in this introduction is to both develop an exhaustive classification of the major approaches to the permissibility and desirability of privatization and identify their structural strengths and weaknesses. We then describe briefly the different contributions to the volume and conclude with some observations on the future of the study of privatization.

THREE APPROACHES TO THE VALUE OF PUBLIC PROVISION OF GOODS AND SERVICES

The primary (although by no means the only) question addressed in this volume is a normative one, namely, whether, and, if so, what, when, and why, to privatize. Addressing this inquiry gives rise to three approaches to the question of privatization: outcome-based, process-based, and agency-based approaches.

The outcome-based approach assesses the privatization of the provision of a good or a service by reference to the quality or quantity of its provision. Private provision is desirable when private entities make better – more efficient, more just, etc. – decisions with respect to the relevant good/service than public entities. The most influential outcome-based approach is the economic theory that typically considers the merits of privatization on efficiency-based grounds. Alternatively, it can be argued that public entities have valuable process-related properties; for instance, public institutions are more accountable, transparent, and answerable to their beneficiaries and other constituents. **A process-based** approach focuses its attention on the decision-making *procedures*, in particular the reasoning of the institution, rather than on outcomes. Finally, some theorists maintain that the identity of the agent itself may matter. For instance, it is claimed that being a private or a public entity is crucial for the very possibility of engaging in certain enterprises, for example legislation or the imposition of criminal punishment, as these are agent-dependent practices; their success hinges on the identity of the agent. An **agency-based approach**, then, challenges the permissibility or the desirability of shifting control from public to private entities (or vice versa) *simply as such*, that is, independently of the quality of the decisions or the procedures leading up to them. Typically, the first two approaches provide instrumental arguments relying on contingent conjectures concerning the different ways in which private and public institutions are likely to decide/act or reason. By contrast, the third approach provides a principled, non-instrumental argument that does not depend upon such contingent conjectures. It, therefore, challenges privatization as such.

This classification is useful not merely for aesthetic reasons. Its main value lies in setting a standard against which to evaluate the nature of any argument against (and for) privatization. As Alexander Volokh shows in Chapter 7,[1] some theories purporting to rest on claims about the intrinsic value of public institutions are, in truth, contingent or instrumental arguments, relying on empirical assumptions that should be subjected to empirical scrutiny. Bearing this classification in mind may contribute to greater clarity and caution on the part of theorists in developing their arguments.

In previous work, we defended an agency-based approach. We showed why privatization of certain goods may be impermissible and also established that large-scale privatization might be undesirable on principled grounds.[2] We will not repeat these arguments here. Let us, however, provide here an argument as to why instrumental arguments (which can be outcome-based or process-based) often fail. Establishing this point does not imply, of course, the soundness of non-instrumental ones, but it does at least motivate their pursuit.

It is often appealing to justify legal and political institutions on instrumentalist grounds, namely by understanding their value in terms of a technology designed to bring about desirable ends. For instance, it is claimed that legal or political rights are designed to realize preexisting values underlying these rights such as autonomy or equality; the state is designed to provide in the most efficient way public goods such as security; constitutions are meant to guide public officials to act in accordance with reason, etc. In our context, privatization is desirable because it is likely to bring about better outcomes or superior decision-making processes. There are, however, two main weaknesses in instrumental arguments.[3]

First, the task of establishing that an institution or a procedure is conducive to a worthy goal relies heavily on social-science analysis. But the kind of questions that are often asked in political theory are beyond the reach of empirical social science. Given the breadth and generality of such questions, even sophisticated social science methods are impotent. Perhaps economic theory could tell us that privatization of a particular industry under a specific set of simplifying assumptions and circumstances would be efficient. And even then, as contributions to this volume show, yielding a decisive prescription remains elusive. But evaluating the long-term consequences of large-scale privatization would be a daunting task that is far beyond the available tools of social science as we know it. Large-scale privatization not only affects the goods that are privatized; it may also transform the relations between the state and its citizens. Large-scale privatization may strip the state of its responsibilities and may erode public responsibility. It may transform the political system and the public culture from being characterized by robust shared responsibility and political engagement to being characterized

---

[1] Chapter 7 in this volume.
[2] Avihay Dorfman and Alon Harel, "The Case against Privatization," 41 *Philosophy & Public Affairs* 41 (2013): 67; Avihay Dorfman and Alon Harel, "Against Privatisation as Such," *Oxford Journal of Legal Studies* 400(36) (2016): 400; Alon Harel, "Why Privatization Matters," in *Nomos LX*, Melissa Schwartzberg and Jack Knight, eds., (New York University Press, 2018), ch. 3.
[3] Alon Harel, *Why Law Matters* (Oxford University Press, 2014), pp. 3–5.

by fragmentation and sectarianism.[4] The existence and the strength of these effects are not such as can be properly identified, and accounted for, by social scientists.

Second, instrumentalist arguments often stop short of scratching the surface. Instead of uncovering the considered judgments underlying people's embrace of political institutions, they often offer rationalizations of these institutions in consequentialist terms and these rationalizations fail to account for the sentiments underlying the judgements concerning these institutions. There is often a sense of incongruity between the official (allegedly rational and quasi-scientific) instrumentalist justifications and the underlying considered judgments in support of public institutions. In other words, there is a sense that the instrumentalist arguments provide ad hoc justifications but that, beneath the surface of empirical claims of means-ends rationality, there are deeper non-instrumental sentiments that move people to support certain institutions. To provide an illustration, it seems evident that a utilitarian argument against slavery is false not because slavery is not detrimental to utility but because slavery's effects on utility are simply irrelevant to its permissibility. In our context, we believe that the urge to maintain public institutions is (at least sometimes) grounded in their being *public*, rather than merely in matters concerning the quality of the decisions or in the virtues of the processes by which these decisions are made. Let us examine more thoroughly the three types of theories by drawing on examples from this volume.

Under the **outcome-based** approach, public control over the provision of goods and services is desirable if, and only if, the quality of decisions (and performance, more generally) of public institutions is superior or, at least, equal to that of private provision.[5] Famously, many economic theories regard public institutions as means to overcome market failures and collective action problems.[6] Such considerations also determine the level at which such goods should be provided. In Chapter 12, Mark Ramseyer argues that security is often a non-excludable public good that involves economies of scale. For this reason, efficiency requires that the government provides residents with basic security services. Yet, he also maintains that the level of demand for security tends to increase with people's income. If government investment in security is too high, citizens cannot select the level of security they want. Hence, efficiency requires that the government ought only to provide a minimal level of security and to allow those who wish better security to buy it directly from private firms.[7] In contrast, in Chapter 13, Schäfer and Fehling posit that the responsibility of public institutions such as the police is not to promote efficiency but rather to sustain equality in the provision of security. While private institutions provide an efficient level of security, public institutions can

---

[4] Dorfman and Harel, "Against Privatisation as Such."

[5] This is typically the way in which the public control of criminal prosecutions by the state is justified by economists. See, e.g., Chapter 12 in this volume. At the same time, private control of tort law is subject to the same consequentialist terms. Economic analysis of tort law explains private rights of action in terms of the privatization of attorney-general powers to pursue wrongdoers. A tort victim is, therefore, the proper plaintiff not because their rights have been infringed but rather because it would likely perform the task of pursuing the wrongdoer more efficiently. Guido Calabresi, "The Complexity of Torts," in *Exploring Tort Law*, M. Stuart Madden ed. (Cambridge University Press, 2005), p. 333, at p. 337; *Mathias v. Accor Economy Lodging*, 347 F.3d 672, 676 (7th Cir. 2003) (*per* Posner J.). This conclusion is contingent and indeed some have challenged this view on economic grounds. For instance, it has been argued that limiting the scope of the plaintiffs to those who have suffered harm or those whose rights were infringed is inefficient. See Ehud Guttel, Alon Harel and Shay Lavie, "Torts for Non-victims: The Case for Third Party Litigation," *University of Illinois Law Review* 3 (2018): 1049.

[6] See Michael J. Trebilcock and Edward M. Iacobucci, "Privatization and Accountability," *Harvard Law Review* 116 (2003): 1422; Ronald A. Cass, "Privatization: Politics, Law and Theory," *Marquette Law Review* 71 (1988): 449; Alon Harel, "Economic Analysis of Criminal law: A Survey," in *Research Handbook on the Economics of Criminal Law*, Alon Harel and Keith N. Hylton, eds. (Edward Elgar, 2012), p. 10.

[7] Chapter 12 in this volume.

mitigate disparities in the level of security between the rich and the poor.[8] Note that, in principle, public institutions may be designed to achieve other desirable goals that typically are not achievable (or, at least, less likely to be achieved) by private institutions. Both of these contributions to the volume are outcome-based as they both regard public institutions as means to achieve certain predetermined goals: promoting efficiency or distributive justice, respectively.

Outcome-based approaches figure prominently in discussions of privatization. Philosophically speaking, their appeal is closely associated with the view that regards the state and its legal system as a technology designed to realize valuable ends. The most influential and sophisticated theory of state authority that underwrites this view is that of Joseph Raz. Under his "service conception," law can be instrumentally valuable in setting out rules and institutions that help people comply with the demands of morality and right reason,[9] or, as John Gardner has put it, "the main point of . . . all law . . . is to help people to do what they ought to be doing anyway, quite apart from the law."[10] Hence the choice between public and private institutions rests on the overall quality of the decisions likely to be made by the respective institutions. Public institutions are desirable only if they are likely to bring about more (or better) convergence between behavior and the demands of right reason than would have been brought about by private ones.[11]

A primary task of outcome-based approaches is, therefore, to evaluate and compare the quality of the decisions likely to be made by private and by public institutions. Such evaluations depend on both moral convictions as well as empirical generalizations. For instance, to the extent that public institutions are more likely to pursue distributional goals rather than efficiency, then those who care more about just distribution may prefer public over private provision of the relevant goods. Hence, empirical considerations such as what incentives work best for public officials and what incentives work best for private entities are highly relevant to the decision whether to privatize or not. Unfortunately, however, as we argued earlier, the empirical conjectures necessary for establishing the soundness of outcome-based theories are inescapably contingent, and, further, they are often context-dependent, weak, and speculative. As a result, it is very difficult to evaluate the ways in which different institutions operate; it has been pointed out that the soundness of such claims differs from one society to another and from one generation to another, so that no general claims can be established.[12] Indeed, in Chapter 15, Mariana Prado shows the pitfalls of deriving general insights and prescriptions concerning privatization on outcome-based grounds.[13] She examines the literature on privatization and corruption and shows why, in some particular cases, privatization is a strategy to combat corruption while, in other cases, it facilitates corruption. Determining when it hinders and when it facilitates corruption depends on multiple factors such as the specific institutional framework in which decisions are made and the particularities of the sector(s) involved.

[8] Chapter 13 in this volume.
[9] Joseph Raz, *The Morality of Freedom* (Oxford University Press, 1988), ch. 3; Joseph Raz, "The Problem of Authority: Revisiting the Service Conception," *Minnesota Law Review* 90 (2006): 1003.
[10] John Gardner, "Dagan and Dorfman on the Value of Private Law," *Columbia Law Review Online* 117 (2017): 179, 197. See also Joseph Raz, *Between Authority and Interpretation* (Oxford University Press, 2009), p. 178.
[11] For a critique of this view, see Avihay Dorfman and Alon Harel, Law as Standing in *Oxford Studies in the Philosophy of Law*, Leslie Green & Brian Leiter eds. (forthcoming 2021).
[12] A good example of the unpredictability of the outcomes of privatization is the case of private prisons. The privatization of prisons has led to radically different outcomes in different countries. See, e.g., Malcolm M. Feeley, "The Unconvincing Case against Private Prisons," *Indiana Law Journal* 89 (2014): 1401. Harel, *Why Law Matters*, p. 4.
[13] Chapter 15 in this volume.

According to **process-based approaches**, public institutions are uniquely positioned to promote accountability, transparency, and other procedure-related values. The transition from outcomes to processes may seem to address the challenge faced by outcome-based approaches, namely, the difficulty of establishing the empirical conjectures necessary to assess the permissibility and desirability of privatization. Arguably, the distinctive and essential features characterizing public institutions are certain procedures that can be described in terms of accountability, transparency, impartiality, or some such. It is believed that, unlike outcomes, process-related values are intimately connected to public institutions and they cannot be replicated or realized by private entities, not even in principle. They are non-contingent features of public institutions.

But the soundness of this claim hinges on how one understands such concepts as accountability, transparency, and related procedural values. A meticulous examination of the literature indicates that such terms are understood in many different ways. At times, accountability is used as a way to promote better outcomes, in which case process-based arguments are ultimately reducible to an outcome-based approach.[14] At other times, accountability is reducible to agency-based approaches. Yet, we believe that procedural theories constitute an independent category, one that rests upon procedural values that often characterize public institutions.[15] We maintain, however, that there is no reason to believe that private institutions could not implement decision-making procedures that advance the process-related values currently associated with public institutions.

In her work, Elizabeth Anderson explores process-related concerns and especially those she associates with democratic egalitarianism. On her view, hierarchical private organizations such as commercial corporations cannot vindicate the egalitarian aspirations of public institutions, properly conceived.[16] In the legal context, Martha Minow developed a sophisticated process-based theory. Minow defended the importance of public institutions on the grounds that only they can realize process-based values, in particular public accountability. The concept of public accountability focuses on process-related values such as transparency, the taking of responsibility, answerability, and so on.[17] While practices that promote these values may be conducive to the quality of the resulting decisions, they are often deemed independently valuable.

In this volume, Jon Michaels's Chapter 9 develops a process-based theory.[18] Michaels maintains that the value of public institutions rests on the multiplicity and diversity of the voices and the inherent conflicts between different components of the civil society that participate in decision-making. This does not imply that the decisions made by public institutions are necessarily better, say, from the decisions made by an expert; rather, they will likely be more democratic, participatory, and so on.

That said, as some theorists have noticed, process-based approaches often face the same problem that outcome-based approaches do, namely, they rest on empirical assumptions that cannot be properly established. It is only contingently, rather than necessarily, the case that public institutions, and public institutions only, are accountable and transparent. As Jody

---

[14] Martha Minow, "Public and Private Partnerships: Accounting for the New Religion," *Harvard Law Review* 116 (2003): 1212, p. 1263.

[15] A familiar exposition of this approach can be found in the writings of Jeremy Waldron, especially in Jeremy Waldron, *The Dignity of Legislation* (Cambridge University Press, 1999); Jeremy Waldron, "Kant's Legal Positivism," 109 *Harvard Law Review* 109 (1996): 1535.

[16] See Elizabeth Anderson, *Private Government* (Princeton University Press, 2010).

[17] Minow, "Public and Private Partnerships," at p. 1260.

[18] Chapter 9 in this volume.

Freeman has observed, the procedural values commonly identified with public institutions can at least in principle be realized by private entities. Freeman argues:

> Instead of seeing privatization as a means of shrinking government, I imagine it as a mechanism for expanding government's reach into realms traditionally thought private. In other words, privatization can be a means of "publicization," through which private actors increasingly commit themselves to traditionally public goals ... So, rather than compromising democratic norms of accountability, due process, equality, and rationality – as some critics of privatization fear it will – privatization might extend these norms to private actors through vehicles such as budgeting, regulation, and contract.[19]

Freeman as well as other theorists point out that many of the procedural concerns that are perceived to be ones that can only be realized by public institutions can be replicated by private entities.[20] Similar arguments have also been raised by economists.[21] On this view, there is nothing in the nature of private entities to preclude the incorporation of procedures that are traditionally identified with public entities. Accountability, transparency, and answerability are values that can be more or less realized also by private institutions. On the basis of this, Freeman calls for the publicization of private entities, namely the infusion of practices that promote accountability, transparency, and answerability into the operation of private entities. If this is so, process-based approaches cannot overcome the difficulty faced by outcome-based approaches. They are equally vulnerable in the sense that both depend on (indefensible) empirical conjunctures concerning the way in which public and private institutions operate. Indeed, in Chapter 7, Alexander Volokh shows that purportedly non-instrumental arguments against privatization are fundamentally instrumental. Although they justify public institutions on the grounds that they are conducive to desirable procedural mechanisms, such procedural mechanisms can be implemented in private entities.

To defend the view that public institutions can be distinctively valuable, the justification must rest on principled considerations, ones that are integral to public entities only and, so, cannot be made private. The challenge is to establish that publicness itself, rather than its contingent consequences, is necessary for the realization of certain values. To do so, we need to identify what might be the distinctive features of public institutions. The ambition of agency-based approaches is to identify these features.

Agency-based approaches explain and justify public institutions on principled, non-instrumental grounds. Public institutions are necessarily, rather than contingently, required for the realization of certain goals and services. Such approaches, therefore, challenge privatization as such.

Note that we do not presuppose that such principled arguments are convincing. Our contention is that instrumental arguments developed by the outcome-based or the process-based approach often fail because of their dependence upon empirical conjectures, and that such a failure motivates the development of an agency-based alternative for justifying public institutions.

A straightforward case of a good that, in principle, cannot be privatized is legislation. As John Locke has already pointed out:

---

[19] Jody Freeman, "Extending Public Law Norms through Privatization," *Harvard Law Review* 116 (2003): 1285.
[20] The very same phenomenon has also been noticed by international lawyers. See Sabino Cassese, "New Paths for Administrative Law: A Manifesto," *I-Con* 10 (2012): 603.
[21] See Trebilcock and Iacobucci, "Privatization and Accountability."

The Legislative cannot transfer the power of making laws to any other hands. For it being but a delegated Power from the People, they, who have it, cannot pass it over to others . . . . And when the people have said, We will submit to rules, and be govern'd by Laws made by such Men, and in such Forms, no Body else can say other Men shall make Laws for them; nor can the people be bound by any Laws but such as are Enacted by those, whom they have Chosen, and Authorised to make Laws for them.[22]

Presumably, legislation cannot be privatized because its legitimacy depends on its being public, and this may also seem to characterize the role of courts in democratic societies. But while it is easy to see why legislation and, perhaps, adjudication cannot be privatized, it is more difficult to extend it to other activities. In a series of papers, we invoked the agency-based approach to develop several arguments against privatization.[23] The underlying intuition is that institutions are public insofar as they can speak and act in the name of all. To do so, such institutions must be capable of representing the people. Representation is, therefore, the abstract feature that makes public institutions genuinely public. As a matter of fact, one can define a public institution as an institution whose decisions and acts are attributable to the polity as a whole because they are made in the name of all.[24]

The notion of "speaking in the name of all" requires certain institutional settings. At times, it can be satisfied by democratic regimes whose political authorities act in the very same way that constituents would have acted had they held the power to do so. At other times, representation involves institutional reflection of deeper or fundamental values attributed to the people represented; it may also require institutional mechanisms in which decision-makers replicate certain objective features and traits of the represented people.

This volume contains several attempts to develop an agency-based theory. In Chapter 1, Chiara Cordelli maintains that privatization of the power to alter the normative situation of citizens violates citizens' freedom even if those decisions are rightful and even if they are authorized through contract because, on her view, such decisions count as unilateral imposition of power and coercion. Hence, it is privatization itself that violates freedom rather than any contingent consequences following privatization. In Chapter 4, Malcolm Thorburn develops a "public authority account" of criminal law, conceiving criminal punishment in terms of an essential incident of the relationship of justified public authority between state and subject. Thus, he maintains that criminal punishment is integral to the state's exclusive claim to political authority. Moreover, criminal punishment vindicates the right to rule and, so, cannot be outsourced.

In Chapter 7, Volokh challenges agency-based approaches, defending the view that only empirical considerations could matter. In his view, there is no inherently normatively relevant difference between goods and services provided by state employees and by independent contractors apart from empirical concerns, in particular the prospects of different institutions to decide rightly or justly. The state must use agents to achieve its goals. Both state employees and private contractors are private individuals who serve the state in return for consideration. A sound argument concerning privatization must, on Volokh's view, be rooted in empirical-instrumental considerations.

To conclude this subsection, we identified three ways of justifying public institutions: outcome-based, process-based, and agency-based. At this point, it should be noted that the boundaries between these three approaches are often blurred and, at times, theorists raise

---

[22]   John Locke, *The Second Treatise of Government*, Peter Laslett, ed. (Cambridge University Press, 1988), §41.

[23]   See the sources cited in note 2.

[24]   Dorfman and Harel, "Law as Standing."

arguments that belong to more than one category.[25] In fact, we believe that the proposed classification helps to understand what is at stake when considering the value of public institutions. The difficulty in classifying some theories into these categories may be an indication that the theory is vague and that it needs clearer articulation and deeper grounding. Hence, we deem this classification valuable not for aesthetic reasons but rather for developing systematic and coherent theoretical frameworks.

What is evident, however, is that the sentiment that public institutions matter and that there are, and should be, limits to what can be privatized is widely held. Most evidently, this sentiment finds its legal expression in many jurisdictions, as diverse as the USA's doctrine of inherently governmental functions, India's Supreme Court decision that certain police functions are essentially governmental, and the Israeli Supreme Court's decision that private prisons are per se unconstitutional.[26] Instrumental theories purport to explain this sentiment in instrumental terms, but such explanations often stand on shaky ground. To address these difficulties, theorists have sought to develop non-instrumentalist theories and those have also been subjected to criticisms. Many of the contributions to this volume cast new, and intriguing, light on the ground question of what normative approach (if any) may succeed in providing an adequate account of the value(s) of public institutions.

A BRIEF SUMMARY OF THE HANDBOOK CONTRIBUTIONS

We divided the chapters along the three-part classification proposed above: outcome-based, process-based, and agency-based. Classifying these chapters according to these categories is not always clear-cut. Certainly, the authors of the chapters may have had different and more important concerns in mind than conforming to our proposed classification. As a result, some chapters cannot always be neatly fit into a single category. In particular, it is evident that many authors develop both outcome-based and process-based arguments, in which case the decision to locate them in this or that category is somewhat arbitrary. Needless to say, there are many other ways of organizing the chapters. We provide a very brief description of each chapter so that readers can get a sense of its main themes. Unfortunately, our description may not always do full justice to some of the chapters.

Part I *On the Virtues of Public Provision (Agency-Based Approaches)*

Agency-Based Arguments Against Privatization

This section examines general, agency-based theories against privatization, that is, theories that do not focus on the privatization of any particular good but apply to various goods and services, providing principled arguments against privatization.

In Chapter 1, **Chiara Cordelli** develops an agency-based argument against privatization, drawing on the Kantian justification of legitimate, state authority. She argues that the "very same reasons that we have . . . to exit the state of nature" generate "a duty to constitutionally

---

[25] In her intriguing contribution to the normative assessment of privatization, Debra Satz develops several arguments against privatization, appealing to all the three approaches on our proposed classification. See Debra Satz, "Markets, Privatization, and Corruption," *Social Research* 80 (2013): 993.

[26] See Federal Activities Inventory 1998 Act and 48 Code Federal Regulation § 7.503 – Policy; *Sundar and Others* v. *Chattisgarh* (2011) 7 SCC 547, paras. 71–76 (India); HCJ 2605/05 *Academic Ctr. of L. & Bus.* v. *Minister of Finance*, 63(2) PD 545 (2009) (Isr), respectively.

limit privatization and to support, on normative grounds, a case for the republicization of at least certain functions." Her argument begins with identifying these reasons with the problem of private authority – how a private person can determine rights, duties, and other normative restrictions for other private persons. This is a problem, Cordelli argues, because private persons are free and equal agents and so cannot be subjected to the choices of one or more private persons. In Kantian parlance, private authority is illegitimate because it is a form of unilateral subjection.

The solution lies in constructing the "omnilateral" rule. Cordelli specifies two necessary conditions for a rule to count as omnilateral. First, the rule has to be able to guide decision-makers to make decisions regarding people's rights and duties that all could, in principle, accept. Second, these decisions can be attributed to a "unified juridical order," namely, a shared, unitary practice of law-making (and law-applying insofar as it involves legislation, rather than merely execution of existing laws).

Much of contemporary Kantian political philosophy focuses on the get-go question of why one ought to submit oneself to the authority of the state to begin with. Cordelli adds another dimension to this philosophical tradition by asking what state powers are inalienable, that is, in which case the state cannot pass these powers to nonstate actors. Her non-instrumental agency-based argument against privatization is, therefore, an argument against essentially reinstating the state of nature's condition of unfreedom and inequality. Outsourcing law-making powers to private entities is impermissible because, and insofar as, it brings about a state of unilateral subjection: subjection of one person to the will of another.

In Chapter 2, **Louis-Philippe Hodgson** argues that non-instrumental objections to private provision of *particular* goods and services are bound to fail. This is so because successful provision of these goods and services does not depend on the identity of the provider. Instead, it turns on the outcome or quality of the provision and so makes considerations of efficiency internal, rather than external, to the moral assessment of particular instances of privatization. Thus: "If private prisons really delivered a safer, more humane environment than public prisons at a given cost, then *of course*" we should not object to their existence.

That said, Hodgson argues that privatization is objectionable when viewed from a broader or "structural" perspective. A structural perspective does not take issue with specific instances of privatization as it concerns privatization's *cumulative* loss of direct public control over the lives of citizens. It focuses on the problem of privatization "on a massive scale."

Hodgson identifies several reasons why large-scale privatization should concern us even when the expected gains in efficiency are substantial. These reasons have to do with privatization's negative impact on the state's ability to contain (or even constrain) economic inequalities, provide access to employment for all, and construct a more democratic economic order for the workers. Thus, a robust public sector is all-things-considered valuable because it is conducive to the state's ability to deliver on its duties of distributive justice and democratic egalitarianism.

Objections to privatization may be outcome-based, considering whether the costs of private provision exceed its benefits cast in economic or other terms. Another line of objection is agency-based, considering the legitimacy of private provision of certain goods and services. In Chapter 3, **Jonny Thakkar** develops an objection to privatization that occupies a middle-ground between the former two. It is middle-ground in the sense that, with many outcome-based approaches, it takes seriously consequences and empirical considerations; but, on the other hand, it also follows some agency-based approaches by incorporating a priori considerations into the assessment of privatization.

Thakkar develops this approach by drawing on the philosophical tradition of ancient Greece and especially on the celebrated debate between Plato and Aristotle with respect to the merits of public ownership. On his account, a fundamental distinction is between craftsmanship or professionalism and moneymaking, a distinction that (according to Thakkar) shows why Plato has the upper hand in the debate with Aristotle. Although Plato's notion of craftsmanship is not distinctive of public officials, it nonetheless carries specific implications for the institutional arrangement of the public office held by the legislator, the administrator, the adjudicator, and so on. To begin with, all craftsmanship (broadly defined to include professionals such as physicians) ought to guide professional conduct according to a standard given by the demands of the common good, rather than personal profit. Public officials are craftsmen, too, in that their basic responsibility is the common good. However, part of their professionalism includes the function of guarding the guardian, namely, ensuring that all other craftsmen can and will meet their responsibility as professionals. To do so, public officials are tasked with setting the legal rules and the institutions to ensure that craftsmen will be working under suitable conditions, namely, conditions conducive to realizing the common good. For instance, fiduciary law is designed to address the conflict of interest between a corporate officer's private interest and professional responsibility.

Thakkar argues that Plato's argument from professionalism suggests that fiduciary law (and many other legal rules and institutions designed for some such purpose) depends on the existence of public officials acting for the common good, rather than their private interest. As he puts it, "those who are in charge of regulating, governing and educating society as a whole must be especially insulated from the logic of moneymaking." On this view, privatizing such public functions is impermissible because their professionalism – viz., their being solely oriented toward the common good – is essential to maintaining, and facilitating, the professionalism of craftsmen, more generally.

Specific Arguments Against Privatization

This section summarizes specific agency-based theories against privatization, that is, theories that focus on the privatization of a particular good such as the criminal law system, the provision of legal services and other goods.

Malcolm Thorburn examines the privatization of criminal punishment in Chapter 4. He maintains that "there is something in the nature of criminal punishment that makes it unsuitable for privatization." After examining and rejecting several traditional agency-based explanations, he develops the "public authority" account. This account conceives of criminal punishment as affirming the authority of the state.

The "public authority" account begins with a basic feature of modern legal orders: modern states claim a *right* to rule over their subjects. They do not merely assert that they have more effective power than we do, so it would be prudent to do as we are told. Instead, they claim that they are legitimate practical authorities.

Legal institutions and legal remedies provide mechanisms through which legal rights are vindicated. In the private law context, for instance, where you take my property from me, the private law remedy of *vindicatio* requiring you to return it to me does not simply provide an incentive to encourage you to respect my property. The central point of the remedy is not to bring about some new, desirable state of affairs; it is just a reassertion of the abiding normative salience of the plaintiff's claim of right.

Criminal sanctions are similar to the private law remedy. Where someone takes it upon themselves to act contrary to the demands of the state's laws because they are acting instead upon their own view of their rights and duties, powers and liabilities, they are directly challenging the state's claim to have the exclusive right to make the law around here. The remedy in this case – the criminal sanction – reasserts the state's claim of right and shows that the state's right to rule survives its violation by the offender. The state's claim of an exclusive right to rule has been transformed from an empty claim to an institutional reality.

In Chapter 5, **Assaf Sharon** and **Shai Agmon** look at how an expansive literature has analyzed the moral limits of markets in recent years, focusing on the question: what kinds of goods should not be bought and sold on the market? The salient goods under discussion are goods related to the body, and also to its sexual functions, like organs, surrogacy, and sex itself. Other kinds of goods that occupy theorists are goods with certain social significance, such as standing in line, naming one's children, or making blood donations.

In their contribution, Sharon and Agmon argue that legal representation should not be for sale. Legal services that are currently provided by lawyers should be severely regulated or even outlawed. Sharon and Agmon point out that an independent state-funded legal system, which applies the law impartially, consistently, and equally, is fundamental for a free society and also for the market itself.

Many commentators have pointed out (and criticized) the importance and the centrality of money in the legal system and even in the criminal law system. One commentator has said that money is the defining element of the modern American criminal justice system. In this chapter, Sharon and Agmon argue that the privatization of legal representation undercuts legal justice, at least in adversarial legal systems. As justice is the aim of the legal system, its operation should not be influenced by the parties' wealth. This entails that the quality of legal representation available to a person should not be determined by his or her financial ability.

To avoid its pernicious effects, the market of legal representation must be severely restricted, if not eliminated altogether. Reflecting on this argument, they propose a novel method for setting limits on markets, one that diverges from the current "moral limits of markets" arguments. More generally, Sharon and Agmon identify a distinct category of goods that ought not to be distributed by the market. These are goods whose social function (as opposed to social meaning) is incompatible with the market, particularly in light of the economic disparities it enables. These might be goods that are intrinsically egalitarian, that is, goods whose value and justification can only be realized if they are distributed equally. Or they might be goods that can only be obtained if other goods are distributed equally (like adversarial justice or democratic legitimacy).

The state is the paradigmatic example of a public entity. But is it indeed always a public entity? In Chapter 6, **Ashwini Vasanthakumar** argues that states, as they are currently constituted, cannot be properly considered public actors with respect to border control and, hence, that new institutions need to replace them in making decisions concerning migration.

In popular discourse, border control is often cast as a good provided by the state, the beneficiaries of which are its citizens. By these accounts, border control protects citizens from external threats and enables a measure of self-determination. But Vasanthakumar argues that, in the context of border control, citizens are not the only relevant subjects; those seeking entry also stand to have their normative position altered by border control practices. State institutions should not therefore count as genuinely public with respect to these questions.

What institutions or practices might enable a properly public view in this context? First, there should be mechanisms by which the interests and perspectives of all migrants enter into the deliberations of the properly public actor and inform its policy decisions. And second, there should be mechanisms by which migrants can hold accountable the properly public actor and its frontline agents, both for their policy goals and for the ways in which frontline agents implement them.

In reality, states have very broad powers with respect to border control, and migrants are subjected to, rather than the subjects of, the institutions and processes governing border control. Vasanthakumar suggests that, where the state is not a properly public actor, some nonstate actors may ameliorate institutional shortcomings *and* help to pave the way to the establishment of properly public institutions. He focuses on two types: *advocates*, who work within existing institutions to compensate for their defects, and *samaritans*, who thwart the decisions of these defective institutions.

In the context of border control, the state is not really a public entity as it speaks in the name of one party – the citizens – and ignores another – the immigrants. Hence, the analysis challenges the traditional view concerning what publicness means and establishes that publicness may mean different things in different contexts.

Objections to Agency-Based Approaches

In this section, we examine theories that challenge agency-based views and advocate the exclusive use of consequentialist considerations in determining whether a good or a service ought to be privatized.

In Chapter 7, **Alexander Volokh** provides a detailed and meticulous examination of what we labeled above process-based and agency-based arguments. His conclusion is that the only relevant considerations bearing on privatization are empirical considerations. There are no sound agency-based arguments for or against privatization.

Volokh argues that the state is an abstract entity – the sum total of a large number of relationships. The state cannot wage war, because war requires fingers to push buttons and pull triggers, and the state lacks fingers. The state cannot incarcerate, because incarceration requires guards, doctors, cooks, psychologists, and teachers; the state itself has no body with which to perform all these functions. To operate, the state can hire state employees, or it can use state contractors. The choice between the two is important for various empirical reasons because different contracts have different terms, are subject to different legal regimes, can be enforced in different ways or to a different extent, and therefore create different incentives – which, in turn, lead to different results in the real world. But these are, at bottom, *empirical* factors.

One class of process-based arguments examined by Volokh focuses on accountability. Volokh maintains that accountability-based theories cannot provide an argument against privatization *as such*. Another class of arguments focuses on the supposed symbolism, expressive value, or social meaning of private punishment. Volokh maintains that, at least under certain interpretations, these arguments also are empirical.

Volokh admits that there are some arguments that rest purely on principled rather than empirical arguments (of the type we labeled agency-based arguments). But he maintains that those often rest on functional rather than formal understanding of privatization. He concludes by arguing that there is no true objection to privatization *in itself* or privatization *as such*. In the end, both the public employee and the private contractor are just private individuals who agree to do the state's bidding for money.

Part II *On the Virtues of Publicness as a Means to the Realization of Procedural Values (Process-Based Theories)*

This section examines various arguments that rest on procedural values, most typically accountability. Under such theories, the value of public institutions rests on the quality of the procedures used in decision-making.

Privatization is often challenged in connection with the private provision of traditionally core governmental services such as criminal justice and national security. In Chapter 8, **Martha Minow**, by contrast, explores the privatization of social services such as schooling, financial assistance for vulnerable people, and social support to children and the elderly. She observes that the "private provision of social services raises particular questions when governments turn to for-profit companies, nonprofit organizations, and religious institutions to perform [social] functions that, at other times, have been undertaken by governments." Unlike many other services whose successful provision depends on instrumental considerations such as efficiency, Minow argues, the provision of social services reflects, and implicates, the dignity of individuals in need.

Accordingly, Minow argues that considerations of cost-saving and efficacy cannot exhaust the moral assessment of private provision of social services. She further argues that even nonwelfarist considerations such as fair process and checks and balances that are typically invoked against the privatization of core traditional governmental purposes (such as criminal justice) may not capture what is particularly objectionable about privatization in the context of social services provision. Minow argues that, owing to their profit-making or sectarian motives, private providers of social services may inevitably or typically fail to uphold public commitment to civic inclusion in the form of antidiscrimination norms and sectarian neutrality. More generally, the tension between private purposes – economic or sectarian – and social services undermines the possibility of genuine civic spaces as well as eroding governmental responsibility for treating individuals in need with care and respect.

In Chapter 9, **Jon D. Michaels** examines and defends on procedural grounds the modern administrative state, in particular, the US administrative system. The US administrative state is subject to two different criticisms. First, it is claimed by constitutional conservatives that the power of the administration violates constitutional principles as administrative agencies are not subject to democratic control. Hence the administrative state is ruled by administrators rather than by the people. Second, neoliberals wish to outsource and commercialize essential government responsibilities primarily for efficiency-based reasons. Michaels's defense of the administrative is particularly timely given the populist efforts to weaken or even eliminate the administrative apparatus of the state.

In addressing both arguments, Michaels develops a separation of powers argument: administrative separation of powers. In his view the modern administrative state combines three types of players. Specifically, power was – and often still is – triangulated among presidentially appointed political leaders atop the agencies, politically insulated career civil servants who carry out much of the day-to-day work of the agencies, and the public, which is empowered to participate meaningfully in administrative policy-making, implementation, and enforcement.

Understanding administrative power through this lens of an enduring, evolving separation of powers provides, in Michaels's view, an answer to both the constitutional conservatives and the neoliberals. To the former, one needs to underscore how disaggregated and rivalrous administrative agencies truly are – making them worthy decision-makers that reflect conflicting and diverse interests. And to the latter, one needs to explain that attempts to run administrative agencies like businesses will invariably subvert rivalries, weaken the checks and balances, and thus undermine the necessary structural safeguards.

Discussions of privatization often take up the transfer of responsibilities from public entities to either commercial or nonprofit organizations. It is then assessed instrumentally, that is, by reference to efficiency and expertise advantages. However, privatization can take other forms as well. **Brenda Cossman**'s Chapter 10 explores the case of the family as a provider of care services such as financial and psychological support of children. She dubs this form of privatization familialization.

Cossman further observes that privatization as familialization is often explained in two ways: first, by appeal to the naturalness in which the services in question are part and parcel of what it means to be a family; and, second, by emphasizing the responsibility that is built into the institution of the self-governing family. And she argues that the rise of both explanations noncoincidently corresponds with the resurgence of the neoliberal ideology among Western societies during the last several decades or so.

Familialization, Cossman argues, is used to justify a public policy approach of hands-off by state agencies and courts, often to the detriment of mothers who are being asked to shoulder greater burdens as the state retracts. Finally, Cossman finds that "there is no simple return to a social welfare state in sight." Hence, the case for greater public responsibility for child support would have to go beyond the somewhat nostalgic idea of the social welfare state. Cossman's contribution and the scholarship she discusses contribute to the understanding of the multiple meanings of privatization, including in particular the ways in which the sphere of the family has been made private.

Part III *Outcome-Based Theories: On the Virtues and Vices of Public Provision as a Means to Promote Efficiency and Justice*

These chapters regard privatization as a means to achieve desirable decisions, namely decisions that promote values such as efficiency, justice, democracy, etc.

Privatization of legal institutions takes two different forms: market-based and community-based. In Chapter 11, **Talia Fisher** analyzes both types and examines the different consequentialist grounds supporting privatization. Fisher devotes her chapter to a juxtaposition of these two distinct visions regarding the privatization of legal institutions.

The market-oriented approach to privatization of law advocates competition among legal entities and suppliers of legislative and adjudicative services that operate simultaneously within the same geopolitical unit. The market-oriented privatization model endorses a consent-based type of normativity. The normative foundations underlying the market-based model are premised on utilitarian (efficiency-based) grounds as well as on libertarian (autonomy-based) grounds. Under the utilitarian arguments, market forces are desirable because they are conducive to efficiency. Under the liberty arguments, privatization enhances choice in legal governance and allows individuals greater authorship over their life stories.

The community-based model of legal privatization is premised upon delegation of law-making powers to substate collectives, such as tribal, religious, or ethnic groups. State power is privatized and decentralized into multiple sources of law and authority that are linked to various group-forming and identity-forming affiliations that protect the relevant communities' social norms. Privatization of legal institutions under this community-oriented paradigm awards varying degrees of self-governance to religious, ethnic, tribal, and other identity groups.

Each of these models has virtues and vices that are analyzed by Fisher. Fisher concludes that not all nonstate legal entities are created equal, and that pitting these two archetypes against each other is crucial for proper understanding of the debate concerning privatization.

In Chapter 12, **J. Mark Ramseyer** examines from an economic perspective the provision of security and the interplay between private and public providers of security. To do so, he uses examples taken from Japanese history.

From an economic perspective, security is often considered a "public good," that is, a non-rivalous and non-excludable good. Providing it to one person does not reduce the provision to another (non-rivalry) and, in many circumstances, it is difficult for a person to opt out of the service (non-excludability). A guard who protects a neighborhood often provides the service to the whole neighborhood; further, it is not feasible for a neighbor who is reluctant to bear the costs to opt out of this service. Hence the concern that privatizing the provision of security would be inefficient because individuals would invest too little in security. For these obvious reasons, modern democracies provide their residents with basic security services.

Further, public security is also a normal good, namely a good whose demand increases as income increases. Because security services are a normal good, people do not necessarily want the same level of security. Instead, the welfare-maximizing level of protection rises with income. Ramseyer believes that this is the reason why democratic governments provide only a base level of police protection. Beyond that base, wealthier citizens buy extra protection out-of-pocket. But it would be inefficient to force all individuals to buy a high level of security. Ramseyer rejects the concern that some egalitarian commentators have, namely that it is unfair that the rich enjoy better protection than the poor. Demand for most goods and services rises with income (hence the term "normal good" as defined in economics). Given that it does, the rich consume more of most such goods and services. So too with security protection.

Although writing separately, **Hans-Bernd Schäfer** and **Michael Fehling** seem, in Chapter 13, to be directly responding to Ramseyer. Schäfer and Fehling reject the view that the public police are designed to promote efficiency and argue that the primary rule of public as opposed to private police is to promote equality of protection from crime. Efficiency-based police cannot achieve equal security for all residents. With regard to crimes against life, bodily integrity, or the security of public places, it leads to unequal protection based on the willingness to pay. The resulting inequality, which translates into unequal protection of rights, becomes more severe with a more unequal distribution of wealth.

The "equal security for all" mission of the public police is not without inconsistencies either. It conflicts with other objectives, such as the objective to guarantee effectiveness such that the total number of crimes is minimized, or the objective of nondiscrimination as sometimes equal protection would require investing more in the protection of some groups than others. To achieve equal security for all residents, including those targeted by hate crimes, might require concentrating public security spending on the targeted individuals or on members of a targeted ethnic or religious community. It is therefore inevitable that the goal of equal security for all – as the concept of efficient security – cannot override all other considerations but must be traded off against other principles and reasonable policy goals.

Schäfer and Fehling also analyze the costs of private police and the problems these create. A major shift from public to private police may jeopardize the rule of law and the fundamental rights of citizens – especially of suspects. With private police, there are fewer safeguards against the abuse of power. Private security personnel develop loyalty and responsibility first and foremost to the private principal who pays for their service, but not for the rights of suspects. The protection of suspects must come from outside, through the use of legal restriction and administrative controls. Private police lack democratic responsibility and accountability. This problem is growing as private police increasingly control the public sphere, replacing the state police.

The philosophical analysis of privatization mostly considers the possibility and the desirability of private provision of goods, including goods that are deemed inherently public goods. **Lisa Herzog**, by contrast, in Chapter 14 shifts attention to what may be viewed as inherently private goods, namely, personal data. In particular, Herzog explores the "privatization of the private," by which she means the appropriation of users' personal data by social media corporations. These commercial corporations, in turn, claim exclusive control rights over users' personal data, viewing themselves as having the entitlement to use such goods without attention to the general interest. This state of affairs calls for a critical reassessment as personal data can amount to a public good if massively collected and processed.

Herzog argues that the case for exclusive control rights over users' personal data is rather weak. She discusses arguments from consent and from intellectual property rights as potential grounds for such rights and finds them wanting. Herzog adds another line of critique to show that private rights of control over personal data, especially when these rights are held by unusually powerful social media and internet companies, undermine democratic ideas of accountability and public participation. Against the backdrop of these considerations, Herzog reaches a conditional conclusion, namely, that if the collection and the analysis of personal data are desirable, the information should be made publicly available, rather than being held as a privately controlled asset. She further gestures toward possible public arrangements for the organization of otherwise personal data.

In Chapter 15, **Mariana Mota Prado** explores how outcome-based assessment of privatization often identifies private provision of goods and services with efficiency. The basic idea is that (for-profit) private entities operate in a competitive environment and, moreover, typically face far less regulation than their public counterparts. The efficiency gains that arise under these circumstances presuppose relatively low levels of corruption. Furthermore, privatization is often viewed as a means to insulate the provision of goods and services from corruption's adverse consequences. What, however, should be the case if we relax the presupposition that corruption levels are low? Must the introduction of corruption as a self-standing factor change the analysis and, if so, in what ways?

Prado argues that it does, and that corruption affects the efficiency assessment of privatization in importantly different ways. She shows that there are particular circumstances in which privatization defuses corruption and other circumstances in which privatization enables or reinforces corruption. An adequate framework for assessing the question of privatization ought to consider the multiple phases of the privatization process, the unique institutional framework in which decisions are made, and the particularities of the sector(s) involved. Prado structures such a framework along three key stages: the decision to privatize, the privatization process, and the dynamics governing the privatized functions. In each of these stages, Prado shows how privatization could sometimes tackle whereas at other times embody corruption, thus making "simplistic views of privatization … untenable." That said, Prado does draw some general inferences, such as that privatization has enhanced social welfare in countries with robust institutional frameworks and low levels of corruption. By contrast, in countries with high levels of corruption, privatization is less likely to succeed and may even be detrimental to the efficient provision of goods and services. Finally, Prado looks at emerging trends among policymakers and recommends a "comprehensive risk assessment" framework that could incorporate as many considerations as needed to make informed decisions concerning whether to privatize and how to do so.

Traditionally, argues **Yael Kariv-Teitelbaum** in Chapter 16, states privatized the production and provision of goods and services but maintained the power of regulation. Regulation was therefore perceived as a core governmental function. Kariv presents the rise of private regulatory authority, roles, and responsibilities, and the blurring of boundaries between public and private regulation. She also classifies diverse regulatory practices, techniques, and regimes into three central modes of privatization: delegation, reregulation, and deregulation. By using numerous examples, she illustrates the complexity of the considerations bearing on the decision to privatize regulation.

Delegation is an active, overt, and formal version of privatization, where the state transfers the exercise of coercive regulatory power to private hands. *Reregulation* is a less visible form of privatization, where the state reshapes regulatory regimes in such a way as to reduce the number of public supervisors by relying on private actors, such as consumers or the regulated firms themselves. These increasingly popular regulatory regimes are often described as "market-driven regulation" and new "self-regulation." Finally, regulation can be privatized through *deregulation*. In this passive and often hidden version of privatization, the state privatizes regulation by withdrawal and omission. It can be carried out by cutting the budget of a public regulatory agency, narrowing its powers, or refraining from applying regulations in new areas that evoke similar social problems. What Kariv shows is that it is often complicated to determine what counts as privatization of regulation, as often it is done in ways that are not transparent.

Kariv explores the advantages and the disadvantages of privatization. She examines issues concerning efficiency and efficacy as well as legitimacy. The power to regulate private activity using rule-setting, rule-monitoring, and rule-enforcing is commonly perceived as being one of the central remaining roles of the state in the "post-privatizations" era. The privatization of regulation therefore prods us to rethink the roles of the state. It challenges the regulatory state's claim for a legitimate state monopoly over regulatory power.

Finally, in Chapter 17, **Israel Klein** examines critically the privatization of the creation of accounting standards. The practice of accounting employs professional standards to reflect and assess the financial condition of entities, private as well as public ones (such as municipalities). For both types of entities there arises a similar organizing question, namely, what transactions are considered of negative value, or of positive value, for the entity?

Klein observes that the underlying accounting considerations for these two types of entity might differ substantially. This difference is reflected in the distinction between the meaning of financial information for investors, on the one hand, and for citizens, on the other. For example, investors ultimately care about future cash inflows so that increased public investments in non-income-generating infrastructure, such as paving new non-toll highways, count for bond holders as negative spending. By contrast, the public may likely view investments in improving accessible infrastructure as a positive use of funds. Thus, a profit accounted and disclosed under the investors' perspective is not necessarily a profit under the general public's perspective, and vice versa.

Against this backdrop, Klein considers two basic questions: What are the appropriate accounting standards for public-sector entities and who gets to decide them? He argues that both questions are inextricably linked. On his account, delegation of the authority to set public-sector accounting standards to private accountants affects the content of such standards. In particular, it gives rise to standards that might be apt for the purpose of reflecting the financial condition of businesses, rather than public entities. Such delegation, Klein argues, results in financial reporting that "serves needs different from, and contradictory to, the desire for efficient, effective, and accountable governance of public entities." He therefore concludes that setting the right accounting standards for the public sector counsels against privatizing standards-setting. Instead, it requires a different, public arrangement, one that sufficiently insulates the process of setting accounting standards for public entities from the constant pressures of investors and opportunistic politicians.

THE FUTURE OF PRIVATIZATION

The past several decades have been characterized by a growing trend toward privatization of goods and services. The trend is partly ideological (consider the Thatcher and Reagan years) and partly a result of economic pressures as well as interest group influence. In addition, recent decades have been characterized by blurring the boundaries between the private and the public by creating diverse channels of interaction and cooperation between private and public entities. Populist movements have also contributed to this process by challenging the role of experts and expertise in the governance of the state and in political life, more broadly.

The way people think and talk about privatization has been predominantly governed by instrumental reasoning. What else can be said against (or for) privatization if indeed goods and services are better provided privately, or even if the process-related values are equally (or better) honored by the private provider? In recent years, it has become evident that there is a growing incongruity between the instrumental arguments used to justify, and criticize, privatization and the kinds of intuitions and sentiments underlying public discourse with respect to it. Part of our ambition in editing this volume has been to explore what lurks beneath the surface, namely to identify and articulate the sensibilities and convictions that ultimately govern the debate concerning privatization.

Indeed, if agency-based concerns – viz., regarding privatization as such – are brought to the fore, the debate about privatization could provide an opportunity for looking at fundamental questions concerning the powers and the role of the state in facilitating the representation of the people. On this view, what is really at stake is not only or primarily improving the quality of the privatized good or service, or even guaranteeing fair processes of decision-making, but, rather, facilitating, or even making possible, public control. Further, public control is intimately related to the public character of the entity in charge of the decision-making.

The debate concerning privatization is therefore a means to explore why the private/public distinction matters in the face of a prevailing ideology that can be labeled privatism – the thought that public institutions may at times be necessary, but that ultimately it is always better to narrow their scope as much as possible. To the extent that publicness is indeed, as we believe, deeply engrained in our sentiments and political convictions, the provision of a theoretical framework to express this conviction is valuable in that it can shape political action. More particularly, in our context, such a theoretical framework may be used as a way to tackle privatization as it articulates novel arguments for this debate. If we are right, and such anti-privatization intuitions lurk beneath the surface, the construction of a coherent theory of the public may both strike a reflective equilibrium between intuitions and theory and radically transform political discourse.

PART I

On the Virtues of Public Provision (Agency-Based Approaches)

1

The Wrong of Privatization: A Kantian Account

Chiara Cordelli

1.1 INTRODUCTION

Privatization – the outsourcing of public responsibilities to private actors – is a pervasive phenomenon across the world.[1] Welfare and healthcare delivery, military defense and prisons management are only some of the functions that governments increasingly contract out to private actors.

In this chapter, I will argue that even if privatization could facilitate the achievement of socially desirable goals, there would still be non-instrumental reasons to object to it (or, at least, to many of its instances). Importantly, my argument is meant to apply also to cases where the privatized function does not involve the direct exercise of force and where the private actor is a nonprofit organization, as opposed to a for-profit firm. Political philosophers have recently developed several powerful non-instrumental objections to privatization. Some locate its moral objectionability in the inherently problematic, because profit-maximizing, motives of private actors.[2] Others contend that privatization is wrong because it commodifies, thereby corrupting, the nature of the goods it privatizes.[3] For others again, the problem with privatization is that private actors conceptually fail to provide goods that government ought to secure and the nature of which is intrinsically public.[4] Although, for reasons of space, I will not provide a critical analysis of all these accounts, I find them partly unsatisfactory. I will thus suggest an alternative, broadly Kantian, account that positions the question of the moral objectionability of privatization within the broader and more fundamental question of why we need political and legal institutions in the first place.

The non-instrumental wrong of privatization, I will suggest, consists in the creation of an institutional arrangement that, by its very constitution, denies those who are subject to it

---

[1] For an empirical overview of the phenomenon, see Henry Farrell "Privatization as State Transformation," in *NOMOS LX*, eds. Melissa Schwartzberg and Jack Knight (New York: New York University Press, 2018), pp. 171–222.

[2] For a version of this argument, see James Pattison, "Deeper Objections to the Privatisation of Military Force," *Journal of Political Philosophy* 18 (2010): 425–447.

[3] Michael Walzer, *Spheres of Justice* (New York: Basic Books, 1983). See also Debra Satz, "Markets, Privatization, and Corruption," *Social Research* 80 (2013): 993–1008.

[4] Avihay Dorfman and Alon Harel, "The Case Against Privatization," *Philosophy & Public Affairs* 41 (2013): 67–102.

equal freedom. Along Kantian lines, I understand freedom as a relationship of reciprocal independence. To be free is not to be subordinated to another person's merely unilateral will. Building on Arthur Ripstein's recent analytic reconstruction of Kant's *Doctrine of Right*, I will argue that current forms of privatization reproduce, within a civil condition, the very same problem that Kant attributes to the state of nature, thereby making a rightful condition of reciprocal independence impossible.[5] Importantly, this is so *even if* private actors are publicly authorized through contract and subject to regulations, and *even if* they are committed to reason in accordance with the public good.

The reason for this, to wit, derives from the fact that private agents cannot rule omnilaterally, even if their actions are omnilaterally authorized by government through some delegation mechanism, for example a contract. The ability to act and rule omnilaterally, I will suggest, must be understood as a function of both (1) *rightful judgment* and (2) *unity*. By "rightful judgment," I mean the capacity to make just determinations regarding the rights and duties of citizens that the latter could accept or, at least, not reasonably reject. By "unity," I mean the capacity to make these determinations in a way that can be attributed to a unified juridical order and authoritative system of decision-making. The condition of unity is crucial insofar as there might be multiple interpretations compatible with rightful judgment, which would still problematically reproduce the problem of unilateral judgment, if separate authorities – rather than a unified one – were left with the discretion to come to different determinations. The institutional realization of the idea of omnilateral ruling in turn requires that relevant determinations concerning the demands of justice be attributable to a coherent and unified collective practice of law-making. The requirements of rightful judgment and unity are necessary (whether they are also sufficient is a different question) to render an otherwise unilateral decision an omnilateral act of a law, which has the authority to change the normative situation of individuals by determining the content and scope of their rights and duties in accordance with the equal freedom of all.

I will argue that, insofar as (i) private agents make decisions that fundamentally alter the normative situation of citizens, and insofar as (ii) their decisions, unlike the decisions of public officials, cannot be properly attributed to a unified collective practice of law-making, (iii) those decisions, even if rightful and authorized through contract, cannot count as omnilateral acts *of* law. They rather and necessarily remain merely unilateral acts of particular men and women. Hence, for the very same reasons that we have, following Kant, a duty to exit the state of nature, we also have a duty to constitutionally limit privatization and to support, on normative grounds, a case for the republicization of at least certain functions. I will conclude by briefly comparing my account to Avihay Dorfman and Alon Harel's non-instrumentalist case against privatization.[6]

1.2 THE KANTIAN STATE AND THE PROBLEM OF UNILATERAL SUBJECTION

As it is familiar, Kant sees the state not as an instrument needed to achieve valuable outcomes but rather as a constituent of a relationship of reciprocal freedom between subjects, and thus of justice.[7] Indeed, for Kant, freedom *is* an institutionally constituted relationship of equal

---

[5] Arthur Ripstein, *Force and Freedom: Kant's Legal and Political Philosophy* (Cambridge, MA: Harvard University Press, 2009).

[6] Dorfman and Harel, "The Case Against Privatization."

[7] See Ripstein, *Force and Freedom.*

freedom. But why, exactly, does freedom need the state, understood as a unified juridical order?

"Freedom," Kant argues, "is the only original right belonging to every man by virtue of his humanity."[8] To be free is to be independent, that is to say, not to be subordinated to another person's choice. A person is independent if they are able to pursue their own ends – to exercise their power of choice – without someone else deciding what ends they will pursue, or unilaterally setting the background normative restrictions against which they are free to act.[9]

But if freedom is an original, pre-institutional right, how is it possible that there cannot be freedom without a state? The answer lies in the connection between freedom as independence and acquired rights. The ability to establish purposes for oneself and pursue them, Kant argues, requires rights. At minimum, it requires that a person be able to acquire usable means, according to their own purposes, within the limits imposed on them by the equal entitlements of others to do the same.[10] Usable means include not only physical objects but also other people's performance of an act, as well as other people's status in relation to oneself.[11] The notorious problem is that rights to usable means can only be provisional, not conclusive, in the state of nature.[12] The reason for this rests on what we might call *the problem of unilateral subjection.*

As Ripstein points out, one first aspect of this problem emerges from the fact that acquiring rights over external objects necessarily entails imposing new obligations on others (i.e. to refrain from using those previously unowned objects) that they would not otherwise have. Now, for someone like Locke, I would be justified in imposing new obligations on you – to "legislate" the restrictions under which you can permissibly act – as long as my act of acquisition complies with valid principles, for example with the proviso that acquirers leave "enough and as good" for others. But, for Kant, the mere fact that the obligations I try to impose on you are not too demanding (because you have sufficient property left for your ends), or can be subsumed under valid principles, does not mean that I am justified in imposing those obligations on you.[13] Or, to be more precise, even if I could be justified in imposing those obligations on you, I would still lack the authority to do so. For if I, through my merely unilateral judgment, could place you under new obligations you did not previously have, this would effectively subject you to my will. This would in turn violate your "original right" to freedom, and this is so even if my claim is valid. The fundamental point is that, since all persons are moral equals, no private person has any more right than another to legislate (and enforce) the rights and duties of others.[14] Someone's unilateral will cannot be a binding law for anyone else.[15]

So we reach a state of contradiction internal to the very idea of freedom: while my innate right to freedom gives me provisional rights to exclude you from my acquired possession of usable means, because it is only by having these rights that I can form and pursue my ends, at the same time, I lack the authority, through my own merely unilateral action, to change your normative situation by imposing on you a new binding obligation to respect those rights.

[8]   Immanuel Kant, *The Metaphysics of Morals*, ed. and trans. Mary Gregor (Cambridge: Cambridge University Press, 1996), p. 30.
[9]   Ripstein, *Force and Freedom*.
[10] Kant, *Metaphysics of Morals*, p. 41.
[11] Ibid., at p. 48.
[12] Ibid., at p. 52.
[13] Ripstein, *Force and Freedom*, p. 150.
[14] Ibid.
[15] Kant, *Metaphysics of Morals*, p. 51.

The escape from this state of incoherence famously rests in an omnilateral system of rules. It is only when my act of appropriation is authorized by a public, omnilateral will – exercised on behalf of all of us, including you – that you can regard yourself as bound by it.[16] But what makes a will "omnilatreal"? For Kant, the omnilateral will is an ideal criterion of *rightful judgment* – the capacity to make universal laws that could be the object of everyone's (hypothetical) agreement. It follows that my unilateral act can have the authority to change your normative situation only if it complies with a system of laws the content of which meets the test of hypothetical consent.

Yet, the pre-political condition is characterized by a further problem – the indeterminacy problem. Rights, by conceptual definition, impose reciprocal constraints on freedom and must thus apply equally to all. But rights are indeterminate and both their definition and their enforcement necessitate judgment. A general principle – for example finders keepers – is too general to determine the contours of specific rights, and multiple schemes of rights are compatible with that principle. However, as Kant puts it, "the doctrine of right wants to be sure that what belongs to each has been determined (with mathematical exactitude)."[17] For if you and I have different understandings of what our respective rights entail, and cannot find agreement, neither of us can have a right, consistent with the freedom of others, no matter how reasonable our respective understandings are. After all, if, say, my right to property was subjectively determined according to my own understanding of the boundaries of this requirement, your obligations not to interfere with it would entirely depend on my unilateral will.[18] Since my judgment and your judgment are equally weighty, for we are moral equals, in case of disagreement neither of us is required to follow the other person's judgment. This means, effectively, that I would have a provisional right to coerce you into respecting my own rights (as subjectively determined through my own unilateral judgment), without, however, you having any obligation to respect those rights. This system is incoherent and fails to secure freedom as independence. To overcome this situation, the boundaries of rights need to be determined omnilaterally, not only in the sense of (i) in accordance with rightful judgment but also in the sense of (ii) through a unified juridical body, an arbiter, that can provide one clear, authoritative and coherent interpretation of these boundaries in the name of all. This is what I have called the requirement of unity.

In what follows I wish to demonstrate that privatization, as currently experienced in many liberal-democratic states, is a regression, albeit partial, to the Kantian state of nature, and thus to a condition of merely provisional justice. This is so even if the privatized function does not directly entail the exercise of force (as it is the case in the context of prisons, military defense, and policing), and even if private actors are disposed to act rightfully. Therefore, to succeed, my argument must demonstrate that (1) under privatized systems, private actors unavoidably make decisions that change the normative situation of citizens in relevant respects; and (2) even if private actors are publicly authorized through government contracts to make these decisions, and even if they exercise rightful judgment, their decisions fail to meet the condition of unity.

---

[16] Ripstein, *Force and Freedom*, p. 150.
[17] Kant, *Metaphysics of Morals*, p. 26.
[18] For an extensive discussion of the connection between indeterminacy and unfreedom, see Anna Stilz, *Liberal Loyalty: Freedom, Obligation, and the State* (Princeton, NJ: Princeton University Press, 2009).

1.3 PRIVATIZATION AS REGRESSION TO THE STATE OF NATURE

1.3.1 *How Private Actors Change the Normative Situation of Citizens*

The fact that my decision harms you – that is, it sets back some of your interests – or restricts your options does not mean that it changes your normative situation. For example, if I decide to open a shop next to yours and, due to the better quality of my products, you go out of business, we can say that my decision both restricts your options and harms you.[19] Yet, it does not change your normative situation insofar as it neither establishes the scope of your entitlements nor imposes upon you new obligations. It does not therefore legislate the limits of the normative space within which you are left free to act. Further, as Ripstein rightly points out, even decisions that do impose obligations on others cannot all be regarded as changing their normative situation in a way that raises the question of authority.[20] For example, my giving you a gift imposes on others obligations, for example not to use the object of the gift without your consent, that they did not previously have in that exact form. But my decision to give you a gift already presupposes my right to the object of the gift and thus the correlative obligations of others, given the existence of that right. This decision transfers certain entitlements from me to you, thereby changing the addressee of other people's obligations, but it does not establish new normative requirements (entitlements or duties) from scratch.[21] Unlike my decision to give you a gift, my decision to acquire previously unowned property in the state of nature changes your normative situation in a different sense for it purports to transform an object from something that others could freely use to something that I have the exclusive entitlement to use. In this way, it changes the very set of background normative conditions under which individuals are free to exercise their power of choice, compatibly with the same freedom for others. It "legislates" the conditions of freedom. It is because of this that my decision to appropriate in the state of nature can be compatible with your freedom only if it is authorized in everyone's name, including your own, while my decisions to give to you as a gift something that I already own, or, say, to sell you my house, within a civil condition, can be unilaterally made as long as the more fundamental system of property and contract rules upon which the practices of gift-giving and contract exchange are parasitic is itself omnilaterally authorized, and attributable to a unitary juridical order that acts on behalf of all of us.

With this distinction in mind, we can ask whether and when, in current cases of privatization, private actors make authoritative decisions that change the normative situation of citizens in a relevant sense. As cases of privatization are often described, this would not seem to be the case. Formally, while private actors are delegated the responsibility to implement state functions (e.g. the delivery of healthcare services or the administration of prisons), which in turn entails the power to execute rules that have been duly legislated elsewhere, the power to legislate and adjudicate what people are entitled to as a matter of right remains in the hands of elected officials or the courts. It follows that private actors' decisions do not change citizens' normative situation in any relevant sense.

Things appear, however, more complicated, once the separation between executive and legislative power is questioned on both empirical and normative grounds, within the context of modern administrative states. As legal scholars have long shown, within such context, "the

[19] Ripstein, *Force and Freedom*, p. 152.
[20] Ibid.
[21] Ibid.

power to implement and apply rules is inseparable from the power to set policy,"[22] and the exercise of administrative discretion acquires legislative aspects. Further, the transfer of significant discretionary authority to private agents very often cannot be limited through mere monitoring and regulatory oversight. As Gillian Merger explains: "Close government oversight or specification of policies and procedures can limit the extent of discretionary authority delegated to private actors but cannot eliminate it."[23] But is this discretionary authority of the kind that "legislates" the conditions of freedom in a relevant sense?

A concrete example might help answer this question. Consider the question of who determines the public entitlements to healthcare of American citizens.[24] Under the US healthcare system, recipients of publicly funded healthcare services typically enroll in "managed care organizations" (MCOs). The government pays MCOs a set amount for their services.[25] Since, given resource scarcity, it is impossible to cover all requests for treatment, an MCO must make decisions about what treatments to cover. To illustrate the indeterminacy of rightful judgment, suppose that two patients, A and B, both enrolled in the same MCO, claim access to different kinds of treatments, T_1 and T_2. Both patients advance reasonable claims and are *prima facie* owed the treatment, but because of resource scarcity only one treatment can be covered.[26] The MCO must then decide how to balance their claims. The government could try to reduce the MCO's discretion to a minimum by providing narrowly specified directives. First, it could require the MCO to adopt a prioritarian principle according to which priority ought to be given to those who are worst off in absolute terms. In this case, however, the MCO would still unavoidably retain discretion in establishing whether A's needs count as more urgent than B's or vice versa. More importantly, providing the MCO with this guidance would seem unreasonable. For it would seem that even if A's need is more urgent than B's, if, due to the particulars of the situation, treating B would result in a much higher net health benefit, then B's claim should be given priority. Alternatively, the government could require the MCO to adopt a maximizing principle and to prioritize the treatment with the highest chance of producing the greatest net health benefit per dollar spent, in which case, again, the MCO would have to establish what counts as the greatest net benefit. But, like in the previous case, this guideline would sometimes provide unclear, if not unreasonable, directives, such as in a case where A's claim is much more urgent and B would only benefit marginally more from the treatment. The government would then have to provide guidelines that specify, exactly, how much net health benefit the MCO would have to be willing to sacrifice in order to give priority to worse-off patients. Providing this kind of specification in a way that leaves no discretion to the MCO seems impossible, and perhaps not even desirable. Guidelines should then be designed in

---

[22] Gillian E. Metzger, "Privatization as Delegation," *Columbia Law Review* 103 (2003): 1367–1502, p. 1395.

[23] Ibid.

[24] I am here assuming that a commitment to freedom as independence can justify, at least under certain historical conditions, the (at least sufficientarian) public provision of certain in-kind goods, including health care. I cannot defend this claim here and I am aware that Kantians widely disagree on the extent to which freedom as independence can be interpreted as justifying more or less expansive forms of welfare provision. I can, however, say that the defense of my assumption would need to explain how certain kinds of provision are necessary to avoid objectionable forms of dependence among citizens, either directly or indirectly, by providing the conditions for appropriately functioning political institutions or the conditions of active citizenship.

[25] For an overview of the role of MCOs in healthcare delivery, see Jody Freeman, "Extending Public Law Norms through Privatization," *Harvard Law Review* 116 (2003): 1285–1300.

[26] For a discussion of a similar case, see Norman Daniels, "Limits to Health Care: Fair Procedures, Democratic Deliberation, and the Legitimacy Problem for Insurers," *Philosophy & Public Affairs* 4 (1997): 303–350.

a way that leaves the MCO with a reasonable amount of discretion and space for practical judgment.

One way in which the MCO could deal with such discretion is by exercising particularized judgment on a purely individualized basis, assessing each case according to the unique nature of the situation, and striking a particular balance between its various considerations. Although responsiveness to particular needs may be an important consideration, this approach would be impractical because excessively time-consuming. It would also be undesirable because individualized treatment is not the only value at stake. We also want equal treatment.

To reconcile these competing values, the MCO must then rely on a process of categorization. A process of categorization, to use Victor Thompson's definition, "requires that the raw data of reality be organized into classes or categories that often recur."[27] The MCO could develop something like the following categorization: most urgent treatment, with very low net benefit; least urgent treatment, with moderate health benefit; urgent treatment, with high net benefit. It then needs to establish priorities between different kinds of treatment accordingly. Through their routine application and continuous re-adaptation to new cases, these categories eventually acquire an institutionalized form. The more advanced the process of institutionalization, the more the resulting rules take the form of a coherent set of norms. These norms finally come to constitute in effect a presumptively authoritative new policy. The creation of a dominant pattern of decision-making through these classifications ends up determining the allocation of entitlements to particular goods and services. In the case of MCOs, it amounts to a policy for the allocation of entitlements to publicly funded medical treatment. Different classifications generate different allocative policies.[28]

This stylized reconstruction of the MCO's exercise of discretion is meant to show how the administrative discretion exercised by even "street-level" bureaucrats can often have a regulatory, or even legislative, rather than merely executive, character. The MCO's decision-making process purports to change the normative situation of citizens by developing presumptively authoritative rules, in the form of allocative policies, on the basis of which A's and B's justice-based entitlements to health care are ultimately determined. Unlike exercises of contractual private power, the MCO's exercise of power – similarly to acquisitive decisions in the state of nature – is public in a relevant sense. First, it purports to transform something others, including B, could use (collective resources) into something A has the exclusive entitlement to use. Second, it establishes some of the very background rules, in the form of allocative policies, according to which rights to certain resources ought to be distributed, rather than simply distributing certain rights in accordance with clear preexisting rules. Third, it determines not simply the addressee of certain entitlements but also the precise content or scope of such entitlements, for example, to what kind of care an agent is entitled. In these ways, the MCO has the public power and de facto authority to legislate some of the enabling conditions of freedom.[29]

---

[27] Victor Thompson, *Modern Organization* (New York: Knopf, 1961), p. 15.

[28] For an empirical analysis of how categorizations become allocative policies, see Michael Lipsky, *Street-Level Bureaucracy: Dilemmas of the Individual in Public Services* (New York: Russell Sage Foundation, 1980). See also Bernardo Zacka, *When the State Meets the Street: Public Service and Moral Agency* (Cambridge, MA: Harvard University Press, 2017).

[29] This is also the reason why privatization raises a problem that is different from the apparently similar problem raised by private ownership. While also the institution of private ownership is a case of omnilateral authorization of private persons to exercise unilateral powers over other individuals, the powers transferred by privatization

The MCO's exercise of discretion has the further feature of being partly *nonderivative*. By this I mean that the MCO's final determination does not automatically follow from the mere, instrumental specification of a more general and publicly authorized rule or mandate. Unlike in cases of purely derivative discretion (i.e. merely applying clearly defined standards to particular cases), the MCO does not simply apply independently developed standards. It rather develops, through the exercise of value-loaded judgment, new standards, to some extent independently from higher norms. Because of its quasi-legislative and nonderivative character, the MCO's exercise of discretion would seem to pose a genuine threat of unilateral subjection.

It could be argued that the threat of unilateral subjection disappears as soon as we take into account the existence of a judiciary with the final authority to adjudicate disputes between the MCO and those subject to its rulings, in case of conflict. There are, however, some reasons why this view may be excessively simplistic. Empirically, even when citizens have a right to sue a private organization for violating a state–provider agreement, the problem of information asymmetries often leads to widespread judicial deference.[30] Courts tend to defer to street-level bureaucrats because the latter are supposed to have better knowledge of particular circumstances and situations. Yet, when judicial deference becomes the default position, the distinction between the MCO having presumptive authority and their having final, adjudicative authority blurs.

Further, courts can often offer only *ex post* remedies. Yet the fact that a court will provide me with a remedy later on does not eliminate the original act of subjection. Remedies may be necessary to restore my rights, but they are not fully sufficient to cancel a wrong.

In sum, due to the indeterminate nature of entitlements – an indeterminacy that remains even *after* a system of general rules is in place – what people are entitled to is partly legislated by the discretionary and, to a certain extent, autonomous judgment of those administrators who seem to be merely applying general principles to particular cases at lower levels of government. Within a privatized system, many of these are private actors.

The often-unavoidable vagueness of original, authorizing mandates, together with the fact that the policies issued by delegated agents often develop to respond to new contingencies that could not have been anticipated originally by the authorizing agent itself, provides us with some reasons to at least question whether many exercises of discretion by private actors can be understood as being fully publicly authorized.[31] But let us assume, *arguendo*, that private entities are fully authorized to make whatever determinations they make and that they do so in a rightful way. The question remains whether the fact that a certain determination can be regarded as being publicly authorized is sufficient to confer to the determination in question the standing of an omnilateral act of law. In what follows I will argue that this is not the case.

---

contracts have a public (e.g. legislative) character that the power to acquire and sell property against the background of an already defined public system of rules does not have. Because of the public nature of such powers, it is not enough that private actors be omnilaterally authorized to exercise those powers; they must also *exercise* them omnilaterally, that is, as part of a unified juridical order that acts on behalf of all its citizens.

[30] Jerome Carlin, Jan Howard and Sheldon Messinger, *Civil Justice and the Poor* (New York: Russell Sage Foundation, 1967), pp. 46–59.

[31] Administrative law scholars have repeatedly noticed the quasi-autonomous character of administrative discretion and the problems in terms of legitimacy it generates. For a recent reiteration, see Jon Michaels, *Constitutional Coup* (Cambridge, MA: Harvard University Press, 2017).

1.3.2 *Privatization and the Problem of Unity*

Every individual decision, it appears, is necessarily unilateral in the following sense. Even if I do my best to set aside my private purposes and I reason publicly in my decision, I unavoidably decide according to *my* own interpretation of the public interest or the nature of the public good. It follows that, if the decisions made in the name of the state were simply reducible to the aggregation of decisions made by particular individuals *qua* individuals, these decisions would necessarily remain unilateral determinations of particular men and women, rather than omnilateral acts of law. This is why Kantians distinguish between, on the one hand, publicly constituted *offices* and, on the other hand, the *individuals* occupying them who might have their own private purposes.[32] We can regard the decisions of an office as omnilateral, and consistent with the right of everyone, only because even if concrete individuals do the ruling, it is the law – publicly authorized mandates exercised through state offices – that rules, not the unilateral wills of single individuals who might occupy those offices.

So the crucial question becomes: What does it take for laws rather than for individuals to rule, given the fact that necessarily individuals are the ones doing the ruling? It could be argued that so long as the discretion exercised by private agents is authorized through government contracts, and exercised within the relevant contractual boundaries, then that discretion is exercised on behalf of everyone, for citizens, understood as a collective body, can be regarded as having authorized its delegation. That exercise of discretion would then count as an omnilateral act of law, rather than as an instantiation of the unilateral will of particular men and women.

This is a powerful argument. Indeed, so powerful that the arguments of those who have attempted to reject it encounter some problems. For example, Dorfman and Harel argue that even if private actors are authorized through contract by the government, as well as committed to reason publicly, they cannot nevertheless act "in the name of" the state, and of its citizens. This is because only acts that are fully deferential to the principal can be said to be done in the name of the principal and only acts performed by agents who are integrated in an appropriate community of practice, to which private actors remain external, can count as deferential.[33] Yet, the problem with this argument is that it does not seem true that an agent's act must be deferential to the principal in order to count as being done "in the name of" the principal. To illustrate, suppose that I hire someone to write the content of my webpage and I grant them wide discretion in the choice of words and sentences to communicate my research interests. Suppose further that I waive the right to direct and redirect the content of the web designer's performance. I think that, as long as the web designer acts within the terms of my authorization and because of it, we could still say that the resulting content of the webpage and the messages it contains are communicated *in my name*, although they may not count, *stricto sensu*, as *my* messages. This is because the web designer's exercise of discretion is ultimately dependent on my authorization.[34] If this is correct, as long as private actors act within the terms of their duly authorized contracts or mandates, they do act in the name of all.

---

[32] See discussion in Ripstein, *Force and Freedom*, pp. 192–193.
[33] Dorfman and Harel, "The Case Against Privatization," pp. 88–89.
[34] For a more expansive defense of this point, see Chiara Cordelli, *The Privatized State* (Princeton, NJ: Princeton University Press, 2020), ch. 5.

And yet, I do agree that authorization through contract is not sufficient to transform a private discretionary decision into an omnilateral act of law, and I also agree, with Dorfman and Harel, that integration in a community of practice of a certain kind matters. However, as we shall see, integration matters not as a condition of *representative agency* – the ability to communicate messages or act in someone else's name – but rather as a condition of *proxy agency*, that is, as attributability to a unified agent.

Recall that for a decision or action to count as an omnilateral act of law it is then not enough that (i) the content of the decision be consonant to the idea of right so that it could be willed by all those subject to it; it must also be (ii) carried out *as part of a unified and authoritative practice of law-making*.

To demonstrate that private actors' contractually authorized decisions remain merely unilateral judgments, we must then explain under what conditions exactly an individual act or decision that "legislates" the conditions of freedom can be *attributed* to a unified, collective practice of law-making. If we assume, following many legal theorists, that the law can be regarded as a collective social practice – an instance of shared agency – the relevant question then becomes: how can the determinations made by separate individuals be regarded as instances of a unitary, collective social practice? In answering this question, we need a theory of collective action. Here I will build on Christopher Kutz's theory insofar as, unlike other theories of collective action, his theory can be extended to cases of large-scale and complex instances of shared institutional agency.[35]

Before proceeding, a clarification is in order. I will refer to all the parts of law-making that can be categorized as social practices with the term "legal institutions." These institutions are not reducible to courts and legislatures. As one scholar puts it: "In modern legal institutions, the officials are not only judges and legislators but also are lawyers, police officers, officers of the court, and *bureaucrats in administrative agencies that are created by legislation in order to apply policies* that have been duly legislated."[36] As I understand it, legal activity thus also encompasses part of the activity of governance, which defines entitlements and imposes obligations by de facto fixing their content, even at the last stage of policy implementation.

1.3.2.1 The Conditions of Attributability

To explain how we can *attribute* separate individuals' decisions to a shared, unitary practice of law-making, and thus to the state, I shall draw on Kutz's example of how discrete decisions get to be attributed to a smaller collective unit – an academic department. Suppose that members of the department are in the process of hiring a new member of faculty and disagree about the purpose of hiring. Some think that hiring provides them with the opportunity to increase the number of underrepresented groups in their university, while others seek the opportunity to strengthen their own field of research. In spite of these differences, we would still attribute the final hiring decision to "the department." Why can we say that "the department," as opposed to its individual members, has hired a new person? Two main conditions are essential for this attribution to hold: (C1) the action of the members of the department constitutes an instance of "collective" action, and (C2) a set of rules and procedures structuring the institution, which assigns roles (offices) and mandates to each member, must be in place.[37]

---

[35] Christopher Kutz, "Acting Together," *Philosophy and Phenomenological Research* 61 (2000): 1–31.
[36] Matthew Smith, "The Law as Social Practice," *Legal Theory* 2 (2006): 265–292, p. 272.
[37] Kutz, "Acting Together."

C1 is met when each member of the department acts with a "participatory intention." This is an intention to contribute to a collective end. When there is sufficient overlap among individuals' conceptions of the end – for example most members of the department are committed to making a hiring decision and agree on what "hiring" entails – and when all members (or the vast majority) share an intention to contribute to that end, the claim of collective authorship of the kind "*we* hired a new person" becomes justified. This can be captured by the following principle (P):

P: "A group intentionally acts (performs joint activity G intentionally) when its members do their parts of intentionally promoting G and overlap in their conception of G."[38]

Yet, P is insufficient to justify the *attribution* of the hiring choice to the department in a way that enables us to say that "the department" has chosen. This is because P fails to exclude decisions or acts by agents who may have the appropriate intentions but who do not count as members of the department. Imagine an agent, let's call him Peter, who always accompanies his wife to departmental meetings. Peter intentionally participates in the deliberations of the department, has great influence on those deliberations and is fully committed to hiring a good candidate. Because of his evident commitment to departmental life, the members of the department regard him as a colleague and a member. In spite of all this, what Peter does cannot be attributed to the department. The following membership qualifier (I) must therefore be added to P.

I: "A group intentionally acts (perform G intentionally) when (a) its members do their parts of intentionally promoting G and overlap in their conception of G," and when (b) its members satisfy the criteria of the institutions that identify them as members.[39]

The latter criteria can be both procedural and substantive. Only those who are formally appointed count as members of the department. But formal appointment may not be sufficient in order to qualify as a member of the department in the sense required so that one's actions can be regarded as actions *of* the department. As Kutz puts it, "someone whose behavior was so out of line with institutional norms would also be excluded from the inclusive 'we.'"[40] The notion of "being in line with institutional norms" is admittedly vague. Certainly, we want to regard as legitimate members of the department people who oppose existing institutional norms because they believe that they are unjust or inappropriate. At the same time, however, it is hard to see how the isolated decision of a formal member of the department who never attends meetings, fails to deliberate with their colleagues, and systematically fails to act with the identity of the department in mind could fully count as the department's action or decision.

But assume that all those making the hiring decision qualify as members of the department in the relevant sense and that they all share a participatory intention so that the requirements set out by both P and I are met. We can then say that we, as members of the department, have collectively chosen the new faculty members. But how do we get from "we" have chosen to "the department" has chosen a new member? Here is where the second condition (C2) becomes essential. Institutional rules define what a department is and prescribe specific mandates for members. They also establish a specific set of normative relations among the members of the collective – for example common procedures and shared "background

[38]   Ibid., at p. 28
[39]   Ibid., at pp. 28–29.
[40]   Christopher Kutz, "The Judicial Community," *Philosophical Issues* 11 (2001): 442–469, p. 460.

frameworks" – as well as a space of unified, collective action.[41] It is not only the participatory intentions of individuals but also the *institutionally framed relations* among them that transform an aggregate of individual actors into a unified collective agent. In order for our acting to count as the department's action, there must be a unified institutional space within which we can orient our actions, where this orientation consists in part (i) of our "acceptance of the norms constitutive of the institution,"[42] (ii) in being committed to the overall project of the collective and (iii) *in being related to the other members of the collective in a way that sustains that commitment*. Without a shared institutional space, there is no unified collective action that can be attributed to an organization made of different offices and members.

Now, what we have defined as "law-making" is a form of collective action. Legal institutions, like departments, consist of a set of individuals each contributing to the collective project of defining and applying norms in an appropriate way, that is, through rightful judgment. The unity of the legal system is unity through the participants' orientation toward a collective goal.[43] This orientation in turn consists of the agents' acceptance of the norms constitutive of the institution, including an acceptance of certain restraints with regards to what kind of reasons can be advanced in support of their decisions, as well as of the project of determining law *qua* a collective project. But this shared orientation cannot exist without an institutional space and web of normative relations capable of directing the behavior of different officials through its constitutive norms. Without this shared space, we cannot attribute separate actions of law-making to the collective practice of law-making. It is only when officials share an institutional space that provides them with a shared orientation that their decisions can count as acts of law, rather than of particular men and women.[44] They are acts of law *because* they result from a collective project.

The relevant question then becomes whether, in the implementation of policies, private actors, within political systems where privatization is widespread, inhabit the same institutional space of official members of the law-making community. My contention – and here I agree with Dorfman and Harel – is that they do not. They are not connected to official members through an appropriate web of relationships that serves to provide the necessary shared institutional orientation. It is because of *this* reason that their decisions, however rightful, cannot be attributed to that law-making community that is responsible for interpreting and applying norms on behalf of the entire political community. They are not omnilateral acts *of law* but rather remain unilateral acts of particular men and women.

1.3.2.2 Why Private Actors' Decisions Cannot Be Attributed to the Law-Making Community

The law-making community, including the system of public administration, is a sort of "department" whose main purpose is to collectively define and implement a scheme of entitlements and obligations. In a representative democracy premised upon a notion of

---

[41]   Michael Bratman uses the term "background frameworks" to identify shared policies or rules, often embedded in institutional relations, that structure and unify practical reasoning and deliberation by (1) shaping what options are to be considered in a decision or (2) what to count as a relevant consideration. Michael Bratman, *Structures of Agency* (New York: Oxford University Press, 2007).

[42]   Kutz, "The Judicial Community," p. 461.

[43]   Ibid.

[44]   Kutz limits this claim to judges: "When judges do share an institutional orientation, no matter how they disagree in their decisions, their decisions count as conclusion of law, not of men ... The normativity of the decisions consist[s] in their being product of the collective *project*." Kutz, "The Judicial Community," p. 463.

popular sovereignty, however exactly specified, the people are the ultimate head of the department.[45] Elected officials and representatives are department chairs whose purpose is to represent the public point of view. It is from this perspective that the content of norms and the public interest must be articulated in a unitary way, through a shared social practice of law-making. It is the task of elected officials to ensure that all participants in the law-making practice maintain the appropriate institutional orientation and commitment. Since the definition and the implementation of policies and norms are necessarily underspecified and always entail some discretion on the part of the people carrying them out, in order for these decisions to count as acts of the same "department" they must be made within an institutional authority structure that, through shared background frameworks, unifies practical reasoning and deliberation between individual decision-makers and political offices. This structure must (1) shape what options are to be considered in a decision, (2) determine what counts as a relevant consideration and (3) provide effective mechanisms and channels of communication for the circulation of information and the meshing of individuals' sub-plans.[46] Members of the law-making community must be responsive to one another's sub-plans and must all act with an institutional identity in mind, which orients their action toward a common purpose.

When the administration and the implementation of policies are at stake, what are the practical means that secure this unitary institutional space, which provides the possibility of collective agency oriented toward a common purpose? The answer points toward certain institutional, administrative procedures the purpose of which is to establish stable and integrated relationships between lower administrators and elected officials. Importantly, the purpose of administrative procedures is not reducible to securing fairness and accountability in decisions made by administrators. Administrative procedures should also be thought of as *unifying channels of public practical reasoning* that contribute to the very definition and justification of those rules through a collective, shared practice. Further, through administrative procedures, democratically elected officials retain control over the decisions and deliberations of administrative bureaucracies, so that the latter can orient their decisions according to the actions and decisions made by public officials. In all these ways, administrative procedures create that shared institutional space and sustained institutional orientation that are both necessary to *attribute* the actions of unelected actors to the democratic state as a whole.

Through which mechanisms do administrative procedures play this role? Beyond monitoring and regulatory functions, an important, if neglected, function of administrative procedures is to create integrated deliberative relations between administrators and elected representatives.[47] In many states, including the USA, administrative agencies commonly solicit comments and provide all interested parties with an opportunity to communicate their

[45]   Although I here focus on the case of democratic societies, my argument could arguably be extended to some nondemocratic societies, as long as they exhibit what John Rawls calls a "decent consultation hierarchy."

[46]   In his discussion of the judicial system, Scott Shapiro points out how certain mechanisms embedded in the authority structure of this system help create a mesh between the sub-plans of participants who disagree about the content of certain decisions. The legal concept of *res judicata* provides one such mechanism. Scott Shapiro, "Legal Practice and Massively Shared Agency" (unpublished manuscript), available at https://lists.cam.ac.uk /pipermail/phil-events/2013/pdft5nodakQp8.pdf. As far as the administration of policies is concerned, the authority structure of the administrative system should provide a similar function.

[47]   Judicial review of agency decisions includes an assessment of the conformity of an agency's decision to its mandate. The assessment is based not only on the actual legislation but also on committee reports, floor debates and other deliberative practices. Since judicial review is meant to apply to state actors only, private actors are often not subject to it. See Mathew McCubbins, Roger Noll and Barry Weingast, "Administrative Procedures as Instruments of Political Control," *Journal of Law, Economics, and Organization* 3 (1987): 243–277.

views, and must allow participation in the decision-making process. Agencies are required to deal with the evidence presented to them and to provide reasons, on the basis of that evidence, in justification of their decisions. The entire sequence of decision-making – notice, comment, deliberation, collection of evidence and construction of a record in favor of a chosen action – provides political principals with opportunities to respond when an agency seeks to move in a direction that goes against the judgment of public officials.[48] These procedures also ensure that relevant political information is available to form the basis of the agency's action. Through properly structured administrative procedures, then, the modern state's administrative apparatus becomes an institutional space for collective public practical reasoning oriented toward shared public goals. Democratically elected representatives can orient and structure the political environment in which an agency operates so as to lead the latter to adopt the political point of view and to interlock its participatory intention with the ones of political officials.

While the broader system of administrative rules secures an integrated institutional connection between the individual decisions of public administrators and the lawmaking community as a whole, so that we can see their actions as a part of a unified collective practice of governance, that system does not often frame the institutional space within which private actors operate.[49] This leaves these actors outside of the collective project of law-making. Ad hoc contractual agreements between government and private actors may include accountability requirements, but they fail to establish a systematic, continuous and shared web of appropriate institutional relationships between those actors and the law-making community.[50] Indeed, privatization contracts often have the very purpose of separating private actors' decision-making from the institutional constraints imposed by a bureaucratic structure. Only in this way, defenders of privatization argue, can cost-effectiveness, flexibility and innovation be achieved. This is why privatization is not merely a problem of accountability or of representative agency but is one of *attributability*. Private actors' decisions do not count as something that the law-making community has done *together*, for there is no shared institutional space in which private actors participate. Their actions cannot therefore be attributed to the state – "the department" – as omnilateral acts *of law*. They unavoidably remain unilateral conclusions of particular men and women.

But why cannot we bring private actors within the law-making community by simply extending to them relevant administrative procedures and requirements? The answer is twofold. First, this solution would be self-defeating, for the practical purpose of privatization is precisely to bring certain decisions outside of the constraints of public administration, characteristic of the modern state, so as to foster efficiency, flexibility and innovation. Second, as Dorfman and Harel also point out, if private actors were fully embedded within the procedural structure of public administration and the system of public offices, they would

---

[48] Ibid.

[49] "State actors are subject to the full panoply of congressional, executive and judicial oversight mechanisms. They must comply with all constitutional requirements, including procedural due process, and ... the procedural demands of APA [Administrative Procedural Act]. Private actors, by contrast remain relatively unregulated by procedural norms." Jody Freeman, "Private Parties, Public Functions, and the New Administrative Law," *Administrative Law Review* 52 (2000): 813–858.

[50] As Jody Freeman points out, "outsourcing services replaces command and control regulation with a contractual model of regulation in which the agency and private providers negotiate the terms of the contract .... The contract ... is meant to specify the terms under which the private party will implement the agency's policy decisions, but again, the divide between policymaking and implementation is suspect." "Private Parties, Public Functions," at p. 825.

cease to be "private" in the relevant, normative sense (although they may retain some descriptive features that are often taken to characterize private actors). This would make privatization a conceptually empty term.

1.3.3 *Privatization as Unfreedom*

If I am correct that (1) private actors, within privatized systems of governance, unavoidably make decisions that change the normative situation of citizens (and, at times, residents), insofar as they legislate what individuals can ultimately claim as a matter of right, and if it is true that (2) such determinations, no matter if contractually authorized, remain merely unilateral acts of particular men and women rather than being genuine acts *of law*, it follows that, for the reasons explained in Section 1.2, (3) *privatization is a condition of unfreedom*, which subjects the power of choice of some to the merely unilateral will of others.

When the MCO decides that a patient is not eligible for a certain treatment and cannot be reimbursed for it, the MCO is unilaterally determining the scope of certain individuals' entitlements that, at least under certain historical circumstances, can be plausibly regarded as necessary conditions of reciprocal independence. Similarly, when the managers of a private prison specify the rules according to which punishment should be inflicted on inmates in case of misbehavior, they unilaterally determine the restrictions under which inmates can permissibly exercise their freedom. The free pursuit of both the patient's and the inmate's ends, and the enjoyment of the very conditions that make this free pursuit possible, are made dependent on the merely unilateral will of others, whose moral status is by no means superior to that of those subject to those restrictions. This is a condition of unfreedom (as well as a violation of relational equality), structurally similar to that of the Kantian state of nature. It follows that (4) the very same reasons we have for exiting the state of nature are also reasons to limit the extent of privatization and to restore a more unified system of public administration. My argument therefore can be read as providing at least *pro tanto* reasons to support constitutional limits to privatization.

Before concluding, one clarification is in order. In this chapter I focused on private actors that have the power to "legislate" the conditions under which others can permissibly act, or the entitlements they can rightfully claim. My argument can, however, be extended to cases of privatization that do not involve this kind of power but do involve other kinds of freedom-restricting public powers, such as the power of enforcement. Consider, for example, the case of a private prison guard who, under government contract, enforces a rule that says that under certain conditions inmates should regress to their cell. The mere enforcement of such a rule may not change the inmates' normative situation. However, insofar as the guard's act constitutes an exercise of freedom-restricting public power that deploys state force to enforce citizens' obligations, and insofar as, in theory, different authorities could reach different determinations as to how the rule in question should be applied, the guard's act must be exercised omnilaterally – in a way that not only is rightful but can also be attributed to an authoritative and unified juridical order, charged with the responsibility to enforce those obligations on behalf of all citizens.

My argument shares important similarities with Dorfman and Harel's powerful case against privatization.[51] Dorfman and Harel have argued that privatization renders the provision of certain "inherently public goods" such as punishment conceptually impossible.

---

[51] Dorfman and Harel, "The Case Against Privatization."

Punishment consists, in their view, in the public condemnation of a public wrong. On the basis of this communicative conception of punishment, they claim that punishment is possible only if it emanates from an agent that can speak "in the name" of the political community on whose behalf the condemnation is conveyed. The only appropriate agent capable of performing this communicative act is the state. Dorfman and Harel then argue that private actors cannot communicate condemnation in the name of the state because their decisions are not appropriately deferential to the sovereign's point of view. In order to be so deferential, private actors would need to be integrated into a community of practice that brings together the political and the bureaucratic, but this would entail transforming private actors into public officials. Dorfman and Harel thus conclude that privatized punishment is not punishment; it is an act of violence that subjects some to the private condemning judgment of others. As such, it constitutes a violation of dignity.

Like Dorfman and Harel, I also stress the importance of an integrated practice between the political and the bureaucratic and locate private actors as being positioned outside of this practice. Further, like them, I also locate the non-instrumental problem with privatization in the agency of private actors, and how they relate to public actors, as opposed to the reasons for the sake of which they act. Yet while Dorfman and Harel concentrate on what privatization does to the provision of particular goods, by rendering this provision conceptually impossible I concentrate on how privatization compromises the freedom-constituting function, and thus the legitimacy, of political institutions.[52] More importantly, my argument is potentially able to condemn a broader range of cases, including the privatization of healthcare services and other welfare programs. This is because, whereas Dorfman and Harel's account focuses on the inherently public nature of particular goods, my account focuses on the power to determine the boundaries of those entitlements and constraints that are constitutive of a rightful condition. Further, while Dorfman and Harel seem at times to frame the problem as one of representative agency – private actors fail to act or speak "in our name" – I frame the problem as one of proxy agency – private actors' exercises of public power are not acts *of* the juridical community. Finally, while Dorfman and Harel regard privatization as a violation of dignity, I regard privatization as an infringement of individual independence. This difference is important because, it seems, there are cases where an agent's independence can be violated without this necessarily compromising the person's dignity. The fact that a private guard purports to unilaterally determine whether I should have a right to stay in or out of my cell at a given moment need not violate my dignity. This is so especially if the guard is well intentioned, willing to provide very good reasons in support of their decision and robustly disposed to treat me humanly. Yet, insofar as all this is insufficient to transform the guard's decision into an omnilateral act of law, my power of choice remains subject to a private person's unilateral judgment. Therefore, my freedom as independence is infringed, even if my dignity arguably remains untouched.

---

[52] To be fair, in a different article, Dorfman and Harel make the interesting claim that privatization is problematic as such, independently of the particular goods at stake, because, insofar as private actors, owing to their lack of deference, cannot act in the name of the state, privatization undermines citizens' public responsibility for their state's actions. See their "Against Privatisation As Such," *Oxford Journal of Legal Studies* 36 (2016): 400–427. For reasons previously explained, I am not convinced that deference is a necessary condition of representative agency, although it is, I believe, necessary for attributability or proxy agency. Further, I believe that citizens can retain responsibility for their state's actions, even if these are not done in their name. See Cordelli, *The Privatized State*, ch. 5.

2

Privatization, Efficiency, and the Distribution of Economic Power

Louis-Philippe Hodgson

2.1 INTRINSIC AND STRUCTURAL OBJECTIONS TO PRIVATIZATION

Proponents of privatization tend to rest their case on a strikingly simple line of argument. Compared to the mighty private sector, they maintain, the state is hopelessly inefficient at providing goods and services. Trains, hospitals, schools, and even prisons perform better when private corporations take charge, energized by the dynamic logic of competition, rather than the rigid, monopolistic state. We all do better by relying on the private sector whenever possible, they conclude, including for the provision of goods and services that were traditionally viewed as the state's exclusive responsibility.

Resting one's entire case on such a straightforward argument can seem unimaginative in some contexts, but here it mostly denotes confidence in the strength of the underlying considerations. And the confidence is understandable. If the state is inefficient compared to the private sector, then privatization promises the same quality of services at a lower cost – or, alternatively, a higher quality at the same cost. By privatizing, we free up scarce resources that can be used to improve other essential services (privatizing trains to fund schools, say) or, when needed, the very service in question (privatizing hospitals to improve the overall quality of health care, say). Who could be against *that*?

So powerful are these considerations, you may wonder how anti-privatization arguments ever get off the ground. Of course, it's possible to dispute the efficiency gains that privatization advocates prophesy. Whether the private sector would be more efficient than the state at providing a given service is, after all, a highly complex empirical question. Arguing from the armchair that it must be so doesn't suffice; hard work on the ground is required to establish when the claim actually holds. And note that the claim is interesting only if it's quite robust: the private sector must do better than the state not just for now but for the foreseeable future, and its performance must prove superior along all the relevant dimensions of assessment. We should therefore expect

Earlier versions of this chapter were presented at the 2019 Philosophy, Politics, and Economics Society annual meeting in New Orleans, at a workshop on "Political Philosophy and the Future of Capitalism" held at Waseda University, and at a practical philosophy workshop held at Sankt Oberholz, in Berlin. I am indebted to the audiences on these three occasions for extremely helpful suggestions, and endlessly grateful for a characteristically illuminating exchange with Stephen White on the day following the Berlin workshop, during a long streetcar ride to and from the abandoned children's hospital in Weissensee. Special thanks to Chiara Cordelli and to the editors of this volume for detailed comments on the penultimate version that led to major improvements. This chapter draws on research supported by the Social Sciences and Humanities Research Council of Canada.

many exceptions, both because of well-known problems with the long-term accountability of private corporations (especially in monopoly or oligopoly situations) and because of limits on what we can expect from actors that ultimately answer to market incentives.[1]

Empirical work questioning the alleged efficiency of private actors thus constitutes a crucial battlefront for opponents of privatization.[2] From a philosophical standpoint, however, the most interesting questions arguably arise when victory can't be secured on that ground. This is bound to happen: even if advocates of privatization tend to overstate their conclusions, few would deny that, for many types of goods and services, private production is considerably more efficient. In such cases, opposition to privatization can appear paradoxical, a perverse refusal to adopt measures that would improve everyone's lot. I want to ask what reasons there might be to resist the push for privatization *specifically in those cases* – when it promises substantial efficiency gains, and hence when the argument in its favour applies in full force.

I contrast two strategies that opponents of privatization might adopt. The first favours a sort of *inner retreat*. It starts by acknowledging that, when it applies, the efficiency argument dominates the field of instrumental considerations. It then goes on to suggest that the battle should be decided on different grounds: our focus should be on *intrinsic reasons* to oppose privatization, and on how such reasons can undercut any alleged gains in efficiency. The second strategy pushes in the opposite direction. It begins by noting that the efficiency argument and the inner retreat strategy have something important in common: both focus on the merits of particular instances of privatization. As a result, both tend to disregard the *scale* on which privatization has been carried out in recent decades and the transformational impact it has had on the economic structure of countless societies.[3] The idea is then to correct this oversight by considering what objections to privatization arise when we recognize its broader impact on society – that is, when we switch from a micro to a macro or *structural* outlook. To the extent that (as I suggest in Section 2.2) inner retreat arguments have roots in Kant's political philosophy, this second strategy can be viewed as advocating a Rawlsian turn.[4]

I maintain that the second strategy is the more promising one. The first is perhaps more ambitious philosophically, and it has certainly received impressive articulations in the recent literature. But, as I argue in what follows, it's unclear how the intrinsic considerations that its proponents invoke can trump substantial efficiency gains. To identify concerns about

---

[1] To take an example that is particularly salient as I write these lines, it has become painfully clear that private healthcare actors can't be relied upon to prepare for pandemics. Given the vital importance of such preparedness, an entirely privatized healthcare sector can't be efficient in the robust sense.

[2] For a sense of the complex questions that arise in this connection, see Johan Willner, "Privatization: A Skeptical Analysis," in *International Handbook on Privatization*, eds. David Parker and David Saal (Northampton, MA: Edward Elgar Publishing, 2003), pp. 60–79, at pp. 69–72.

[3] To be fair, the authors I associate with the inner retreat strategy also acknowledge the importance of considering the scale on which privatization takes place, although in works other than the ones I discuss here. Thus, in their recent "Against Privatisation as Such," Avihay Dorfman and Alon Harel argue that large-scale privatization has the effect of undermining political engagement and public responsibility (see Avihay Dorfman and Alon Harel, "Against Privatisation as Such," *Oxford Journal of Legal Studies* 36 (2016): 400–427). And in her forthcoming book *The Privatized State*, Chiara Cordelli argues that privatization on a massive scale undermines the possibility of meaningful self-determination through political institutions (see Chiara Cordelli, *The Privatized State* (Princeton, NJ: Princeton University Press, 2020)). These arguments would deserve a separate discussion, but here I simply note that they go in a different direction from the one I advocate. Their focus is on how large-scale privatization affects the political process; mine is on the impact that it has on the economic structure (although the points I make in Section 2.5 concerning the possibility of democratic control over the economic structure are closer in spirit to these more narrowly political arguments).

[4] I have in mind John Rawls's well-known claim that the primary concern of a theory of justice is what he calls the "basic structure" of society – a term that clearly encompasses the economic structure as I understand it here. See John Rawls, *A Theory of Justice*, rev. ed. (Cambridge, MA: Harvard University Press, 1999), pp. 6–10.

privatization that stand up to the efficiency argument, we do better by approaching the phenomenon at a structural level, as the second strategy enjoins. I focus on two pairs of objections arising from this standpoint: one pair stemming from concerns about preserving the state's ability to fulfill its duties of economic justice; another stemming from concerns about the extent to which the workings of the economy are responsive to the democratic process. In each case, I first consider an objection concerned with the outcome of production (how its benefits are distributed; who decides what gets produced), and then an objection concerned with production itself (what opportunity people are given to participate; how much democratic control there is over the development of new employment models). I don't claim that these exhaust the objections that could be formulated from a structural standpoint, but I believe that, together, they help explain how large-scale privatization can be problematic even when the expected gains in efficiency are significant.

I proceed as follows. In Section 2.2, I present two particularly sophisticated versions of the inner retreat strategy – one developed jointly by Avihay Dorfman and Alon Harel, the other by Chiara Cordelli. In Section 2.3, I argue that the intrinsic considerations on which these arguments rest can't stand up to the efficiency argument. I then turn to the structural strategy. In Section 2.4, I explain how the state's ability to deliver on two important duties of economic justice depends on a sufficient share of the economy's being under public control. In Section 2.5, I argue that maintaining a vibrant public sector allows for some segments of the economy to be more responsive to the democratic process, which may be needed both to produce outcomes that the people value and to deliver models of employment allowing all citizens to contribute to society in accordance with their conception of the good. I conclude in Section 2.6 with some brief remarks on how structural objections to privatization should be interpreted.

2.2 THE INNER RETREAT STRATEGY

The argument that Avihay Dorfman and Alon Harel develop in "The Case Against Privatization" provides a conspicuous illustration of the inner retreat strategy.[5] It starts from a distinctive claim: some of the goods provided by the state are "inherently public" – that is, they are *goods whose value essentially depends on their being provided by the state.*[6] Many of the goods that states are in the business of providing don't fall in that category (water, electricity, education, and health care don't have to come from the state to be valuable). But Dorfman and Harel focus on the infliction of punishment, which they take to be a paradigmatic instance of an inherently public good.[7] As they see it, when a sentence is carried out by a private contractor, it no longer constitutes punishment but violence, pure and simple.[8] Private prisons may appear efficient to the untrained eye, but this is illusory: they can't be efficient because they don't deliver the good we want from them, namely, justified punishment.

---

[5]   See Avihay Dorfman and Alon Harel, "The Case Against Privatization," *Philosophy & Public Affairs* 41 (2013): 67–102. See also Alon Harel, *Why Law Matters* (Oxford: Oxford University Press, 2014), chap. 3.

[6]   See Dorfman and Harel, "The Case Against Privatization," at p. 69.

[7]   Note that their claim concerns the *infliction* of punishment, not its meting out. Privatizing decisions regarding who should be punished, for how long, and under what circumstances would amount, on almost any view, to an outright dismantling of the state. Dorfman and Harel's position is distinctive because they think that *all aspects of incarceration* must be carried out by the state.

[8]   See Dorfman and Harel, "The Case Against Privatization," at p. 93. This isn't to deny that some of the goods associated with punishment – security or deterrence, for instance – can be provided by a private actor. But when private actors are involved, these goals are achieved through sheer violence, not through legitimate punishment.

This is a radical claim. Strikingly, it holds even when private contractors are subject to – and perfectly abide by – all the necessary state regulation. Even in such ideal circumstances, Dorfman and Harel maintain, private actors necessarily fail to inflict genuine punishment. You might have thought that, so long as hard treatment is inflicted by private actors only *by leave of* and *in accordance with directives of* the state, it's still punishment, since the state remains in the driver's seat. Dorfman and Harel disagree. To count as punishment, the treatment must be inflicted entirely *by the state* – that is, by individuals who are officials of the state and not merely contractors.[9] Why? Because those who inflict punishment are bound to make judgment calls about what prisoners should be allowed to do in specific circumstances.[10] Consequently, even if their acts are done *for* the state, they can't be doings *of* the state, since they inevitably reflect their own private judgments. Note that this remains true even if they act in accordance with what they sincerely hold to be the best interest of the country (or of the prisoners).[11] The problem isn't the *content* of the judgments in question; it's who makes them.

Why does it matter if those who inflict punishment act only *on behalf of* and not *as* the state? Here Dorfman and Harel borrow a familiar page from Joel Feinberg, according to which punishment essentially involves condemnation.[12] This is significant, they contend, because it means that those who inflict punishment must claim the standing to condemn, and hence a status superior to that of the criminal. This doesn't pose a problem when the agent inflicting the punishment acts as the state, since the state plainly has the standing to condemn criminals. But when a private contractor is in charge, the alleged difference in status fails to obtain, with the result that the treatment can't be compatible with the criminal's dignity.[13]

I won't go into the details of what Dorfman and Harel believe is required for a person to act *as* and not merely *on behalf of* the state. In outline, their thought is that the agent must defer "to a community of practice to which he or she belongs – a community that collectively determines what the public interest dictates."[14] Articulating this idea would require more space than I have here. For our purposes, let's just assume that the line they seek to draw (between acting on behalf of, and as, the state) can be drawn – as we must for the idea of privatization to make sense. And let's assume that it should be drawn roughly as they suggest. Even under such favourable assumptions, as I explain in Section 2.3, it's unclear whether the case they present can stand up to the efficiency argument.

As I hinted already, Dorfman and Harel's argument has the obvious weakness that its domain of application is extremely limited: it has nothing to say about education, health care,

---

[9] See ibid., at p. 68.

[10] Dorfman and Harel note that "the tasks dictated by the state are typically underspecified such that they leave broad margins of discretion" (ibid., at p. 80), but they recognize "the (theoretical) possibility that the state could provide the executor with comprehensive guidance as to how to proceed with the task in question" (ibid., at p. 80 n. 22), in which case their argument would not apply.

[11] See ibid., at p. 75.

[12] See ibid., at pp. 92–96. For Feinberg's discussion, see Joel Feinberg, "The Expressive Function of Punishment," in *Doing and Deserving: Essays in the Theory of Responsibility* (Princeton, NJ: Princeton University Press, 1970), pp. 95–118.

[13] See "The Case Against Privatization," at pp. 94–95. You may think that Dorfman and Harel make their argument rest on an unnecessarily contentious theory of the justification of punishment, but their point could be rephrased in terms of the hierarchy that the infliction of hard treatment itself presupposes. This may even strengthen the argument, since inflicting hard treatment arguably presupposes a special standing in a way that simply conveying condemnation on behalf of someone else doesn't (as Chiara Cordelli notes in *The Privatized State*). That Dorfman and Harel shouldn't harness themselves to the expressive justification of punishment is stressed by Malcolm Thorburn in "Judgment, Communication, and Coercion: What's Wrong with Private Prisons?," *Critical Analysis of Law* 2 (2015): 234–243.

[14] Dorfman and Harel, "The Case Against Privatization," at p. 81.

water distribution, car manufacturing, or countless other things that states were in the business of doing when the privatization wave hit. For all its inventiveness, then, the argument fails to engage with most forms of privatization that have taken place in recent decades. A more ambitious version of the inner retreat strategy is defended in Chiara Cordelli's recent work.[15] Cordelli contends that privatizing undermines legitimacy not just when inherently public goods are involved but *whenever the service in question is one that the state has a duty to provide.* This makes for a much wider focus, plausibly extending to services such as education, health care, and welfare in addition to the infliction of punishment (but still leaving out car manufacturing). This version of the argument thus seems, on its face, more in keeping with intuitive worries about privatization.

Cordelli deploys a form of reasoning that recent discussions of Kant's political philosophy have made familiar: she stresses the relation of *dependence* that obtains when citizens must rely on private actors for services to which they are entitled; and she goes on to claim that this dependence undermines freedom, and therefore, ultimately, state legitimacy.[16] The argument differs from Dorfman and Harel's, but worries about private discretion remain key. When hospitals are privatized, a private doctor gets to decide whether I really need a certain treatment. When welfare benefits are privatized, a private welfare agent gets to settle what my benefits will be. In both cases, the problem is that the discretion exercised by private actors makes me dependent on their will.

The move gives rise to an obvious objection: isn't this kind of dependence on the will of others inevitable? Even in a public hospital, after all, *someone* must make a judgment call about whether I should get a certain treatment. Why isn't dependence on that doctor's will equally problematic? On Cordelli's view, there is a crucial difference between the two cases. Because public providers are part of a bureaucratic structure that creates "integrated deliberative relations"[17] between private actors and elected officials, their decisions are attributable to the law-making community as a whole (and hence, in a democracy, to all citizens). By contrast, because private providers are not part of such a structure (even if they follow all the directives and regulations that apply to them), their decisions are *not* attributable to the law-making community. That's why these decisions undermine the freedom of those who are subject to them.

Note how this argument ultimately rests on a theory of agency. The state is a collective agent; when I seek a service to which I am entitled, it must be provided by that collective agent (that is, by an individual who, as a matter of agential theory, is part of that agent). The same holds for Dorfman and Harel's argument, which also entails – albeit on different grounds – that the nature of the agent providing certain goods and services matters. Such claims plainly have roots in Kant's political philosophy, although it is worth stressing that they go further than anything we find there. Kant's signal claim is that the *legislation, adjudication,* and *enforcement* of rights are fully legitimate only when they are carried out by the state.[18] When private actors adjudicate a dispute of rights and use force in support of their decision, something seriously defective is going on. But if the judiciary and the police force are clearly

---

[15] See in particular Chiara Cordelli, "Privatization without Profit?," in *Privatization: NOMOS LX,* eds. Jack Knight and Melissa Schwartzberg (New York: New York University Press, 2018), pp. 113–144, and Chapter 1, this volume.

[16] See "Privatization without Profit?," at pp. 117–119. As Cordelli acknowledges, her interpretation of Kant's position largely follows Arthur Ripstein, *Force and Freedom: Kant's Legal and Political Philosophy* (Cambridge, MA: Harvard University Press, 2009).

[17] Chapter 1, this volume, p. 33.

[18] See Immanuel Kant, *Doctrine of Right,* part 1 of *The Metaphysics of Morals,* in *Practical Philosophy,* trans. Mary J. Gregor (Cambridge: Cambridge University Press, 1996). For a fuller discussion of Kant's position on this point, see Louis-Philippe Hodgson, "Kant on Property Rights and the State," *Kantian Review* 15 (2010): 57–87.

part of the state, is it essential in addition that *every aspect of punishment* (to stick to that example) be carried out by individuals who are also, as a matter of agential theory, part of the state? That hardly follows. Prisons must be subject to appropriate regulations, of course, and prisoners must have full legal recourse when they deem their conditions unacceptable. But if all that is in place, it's not clear why Kant's argument would demand that all aspects of punishment count as something that the law-making community *does together* (to borrow Cordelli's phrase), rather than as something that is done *only by its leave* and *under its strict supervision*. And, of course, what goes for punishment goes (*a fortiori*, if anything) for other state services.

Inner retreat arguments are thus undeniably original, but they are also more contentious than the Kantian argument from which they draw their inspiration. This is noteworthy, since the ability of these arguments to stand up to efficiency considerations depends precisely on whether the problems they find with the private provision of services are sufficiently significant to trump substantial gains in efficiency. As I suggest in Section 2.3, there is room for doubt on this point.

2.3 TAKING EFFICIENCY SERIOUSLY

Consider how powerful the efficiency argument would be if it applied to private prisons. Leave aside the unpromising way in which the claim is often framed – basically, that private prisons can be operated at a discount.[19] Suppose we agree that conditions in prisons are woefully inadequate, and that the aim of privatization should be to improve those conditions while maintaining current spending levels. Unlike proposals that involve massive cost-cutting, this doesn't suggest a hidden agenda to dismantle government.

What does it mean concretely if private prisons are more efficient? It means that, while keeping our budget constant, we can have prisons that do as well or better than public prisons along all the relevant dimensions – including protecting the public, providing inmates with decent living conditions, and guaranteeing the safety of both inmates and guards. These are tremendous advantages. If private prisons performed measurably better on all these fronts, how sensible would it be to object, as the inner retreat strategy enjoins, that what they're inflicting isn't *really* punishment but sheer violence, or that inmates in private prisons are subject to a rarefied kind of unfreedom that is absent in public prisons? How sensible would it be to focus on the extent to which prison guards are integrated in the state's agential structure? Given the substantive advantages that greater efficiency promises, such considerations appear hopelessly formalistic. Certainly, when presented with a choice between a private prison that is clean and safe and a rather less clean and less safe public prison, it's hard to imagine anyone choosing the latter just because the employees of private prisons are not officers of the state.[20]

---

[19] The Heritage Foundation famously claimed in the 1980s that whereas governments in the USA spent on average $40 per day per prisoner, private prisons could be run at a cost of $30 per day per prisoner at most (see Dana Joel's report "A Guide to Prison Privatization" from May 1988, available at www.heritage.org/political-process/report/guide-prison-privatization). Since it seems likely that tightening budgets on such a scale would have a serious impact on the quality of service, and since such decisions are not easily reversed, this kind of claim will be met with justified skepticism by those who aren't already bent on dismantling government.

[20] This may seem unfair. If private prisons are more efficient, then why not say that the upshot of the inner retreat arguments is that safe and clean prisons can't be had that cheaply? For, surely, we want prisons that are safe and clean *and legitimate*; if running public prisons turns out to be more expensive, then we must spend the extra money to have well-functioning, legitimate prisons. A lot turns here on what we take inner retreat arguments to establish. Is it that private prisons are outright illegitimate? This would suggest that prison guards lack the moral license to use force against inmates, and possibly that inmates have the right to resist – conclusions that hardly

A comparison with a case in which considerations of legitimacy do seem to trump substantive considerations may help. Consider the possibility of privatizing not merely the infliction of punishment but criminal adjudication itself. In that case, we do want to say that even if a private firm could be more efficient at delivering substantive justice – even if it could deliver a higher standard of imperfect procedural justice than public tribunals – there would be a fundamental objection to this way of proceeding, namely, that only the state has the kind of institutional structure that allows for minimally legitimate adjudication of the criminal law.[21] It's hard to believe that anything similar could be said about private prisons that are applying the decisions of duly constituted public tribunals, that are subject to appropriate state supervision and regulations, and in which prisoners have full legal recourse when they feel that they are not treated adequately.

It seems correct that providers of state services shouldn't be too far removed from the state's bureaucratic structure, but for reasons much more mundane than what inner retreat arguments suggest. Lack of integration in the state's bureaucratic structure often means lack of accountability. Operators of private prisons are likely to be tempted to cut corners, giving priority to short-term profit over long-term quality. This is an important worry, but it doesn't track what inner retreat arguments were supposed to be about.[22] Whether agents who deliver state services are subject to sufficient oversight to ensure long-term quality is, at bottom, an instrumental consideration; it can't undercut efficiency considerations as the inner retreat strategy demands, since it is part of the efficiency argument properly construed.

It could turn out that, for complex and sensitive operations such as prisons, the *only* way for the state to achieve a sufficient level of oversight is to integrate the providers into its institutional structure, and hence to turn them into agents of the state.[23] But that result would also fail to support the inner retreat strategy. The worries we encountered in Section 2.2 about a lack of agential integration are meant to operate *even when the state takes full responsibility for what a private actor does* – that is, even when the state enforces appropriate standards on the delivery of the relevant service, remains ready to intervene if needed, and provides citizens with the necessary channels for legal appeal. The point isn't meant to turn on whether the state can succeed in holding a private provider fully accountable without thereby absorbing it into its agential structure.

follow from the arguments we considered in Section 2.2. Alternatively, we could interpret the arguments as establishing that private prisons are not *fully* legitimate – that they are defective from the point of view of legitimacy, even if they clear the bar for minimal legitimacy. This seems more plausible, but it's not obvious that this comparatively modest conclusion provides a solid bulwark against the efficiency argument. Unless we can show that, from the point of view of the prisoners and of the public, what matters most is that prisons not have the deficiencies in agential integration highlighted by inner retreat arguments – even if that integration must come at a significant cost in safety – it's hard to see how the efficiency argument is truly undercut. (The problem may be particularly intractable for Dorfman and Harel, since they ultimately ground their argument in an appeal to dignity (see "The Case Against Privatization," at pp. 95–96), and you would think that unsafe and squalid living conditions are themselves an affront to dignity. Why one appeal to dignity should trump the other is unclear.)

[21] Obviously, the claim would demand to be filled out, and how you'll want to do so will depend on your theory of the state. I propose a broadly Kantian reconstruction in my "Right and Justice in Kantian Political Philosophy" (unpublished manuscript), but I think that the claim is plausible on a broad range of views, in a way that the claims made by proponents of the inner retreat strategy are not. On the idea of imperfect procedural justice, see Rawls, *A Theory of Justice*, at pp. 74–75.

[22] As Dorfman and Harel point out; see "The Case Against Privatization," at p. 68 n. 2.

[23] Alternatively, it could be that the costs of assuming full responsibility for the actions of certain private providers are too great for privatization to make economic sense. Again, this would not support the inner retreat strategy. The point would simply refute the efficiency argument on its own terms by showing that, given the need for the state to hold private actors accountable to ensure long-term efficiency, privatization presents no efficiency gain overall.

These considerations are obviously not decisive. Trying to show that the conclusion of a certain kind of argument fails to hold up against the conclusion of another kind of argument inevitably makes appeal to judgments that are imprecise. It might help here if we can get a clearer sense of what arguments that *do* hold up against efficiency considerations look like. That is what I attempt to convey in Sections 2.4 and 2.5. I hope to show that, whereas inner retreat arguments end up at best in a stalemate with efficiency arguments, structural objections to privatization rise above the fray precisely because they operate at a different level.

2.4 STRUCTURAL OBJECTIONS, I: ECONOMIC JUSTICE

To grasp the problems that large-scale privatization poses, we must ask not just how it affects the provision of specific goods and services but also how it changes the economic structure of society. We must move beyond the focus on particular transfers of discretionary power from state employees to private contractors that characterizes inner retreat arguments and consider the societal impact of massive transfers of economic power from the public to the private sector. This allows us to cast a wider net. We saw that Dorfman and Harel's argument applies only to inherently public goods, while Cordelli's is restricted to goods that states are duty-bound to provide. By contrast, worries about massive transfers of economic power arise for all major instances of privatization, whatever the goods or services involved. This wider net should be welcome: many of the countless state-owned enterprises that were privatized since the 1980s produced goods – train transportation or cars, say – that aren't inherently public in the Dorfman-Harel sense, and that few would think the state has a duty to provide. Moreover, focusing specifically on the scale of the transfer brings out what seems most immediately troubling about the impact of privatization. It's not that privatization makes no sense in particular instances; perhaps privatized garbage collection does produce better results. It's that the economic structure of society is transformed in problematic ways when the private sector gains control over too great a share of economic activity.[24]

What we need is an account of the problems that arise when the balance of economic power shifts on a large scale. It is useful first to distinguish two ways in which the shift can occur.[25] In what we might call cases of *complete privatization*, ownership itself is privatized: there is a transfer of capital and (as a result) of decisional power from the public to the private sector. In cases of *partial privatization*, only governance is privatized: there is a transfer of decisional power, but ownership remains public. Unsurprisingly, structural objections are at their most compelling when privatization is complete; large-scale transfers of capital bring about the most significant shifts in the balance of economic power. But important objections apply to cases of partial privatization as well.

Let me begin with two objections that apply specifically to complete privatization. Both stem from the fact that the state's ability to deliver on its duties of economic justice often depends on a substantial share of the economy's being publicly owned; large-scale transfers of capital from the public to the private sector therefore tend to undermine this ability. The first objection is informed by recent work on economic inequality that has found its canonical

[24] One issue I leave aside here is the extent to which massive privatization can hinder the state's ability to ensure, through regulation, that fully adequate standards of provision are maintained (because keeping private contractors accountable will be harder when there are more of them and when they are more economically powerful). The worry is important, but it plainly belongs under the heading of efficiency. For an insightful discussion of the issue, see Cordelli, *The Privatized State*.

[25] I am grateful to Chiara Cordelli and Marco Meyer for pressing me to be explicit about this distinction.

expression in Thomas Piketty's *Capital in the Twenty-First Century*.[26] Consider the book's most celebrated claim: in free-market economies, the rate of return on capital tends to exceed the rate of growth of the economy as a whole (in the now iconic formula: $r > g$). If this is correct, then governments aiming to prevent privately owned capital from generating massive economic inequalities must battle powerful economic forces whose workings have been observed across a broad range of societies. This isn't to say that they can't succeed; in principle, the tendency toward inequality could be curbed entirely through progressive taxation. But the dizzying rate at which inequalities have grown across various societies in recent decades suggests that this is extremely unlikely. If the state is to conform to its duty to keep inequalities in check, then it needs to adopt policies that prevent massive pre-tax inequalities from arising in the first place.

This line of thought features prominently in James Meade's *Efficiency, Equality and the Ownership of Property*, a prescient discussion from the 1960s in which he worries precisely about the extent to which private ownership of the means of production constitutes a powerful inequality-generating force.[27] And Meade draws a conclusion that goes very much in the direction I have in mind: he argues that a significant part of the economy should be socialized. Indeed, it is striking how he seems to find it obvious that something along those lines must be at least part of the solution. His discussion is more concerned with *how* exactly this could be done – how the state could increase its share of revenues without distorting incentives in a counterproductive way, what it should invest in once the necessary capital has been raised, and so on.[28] These are certainly significant hurdles standing in the way of large-scale nationalization. But since we are focusing here on objections to *privatization*, we can fall back on a comparatively unproblematic claim: that when we ask whether capital that is *already* publicly owned should be privatized, we must take into account that doing so will increase the share of privately owned capital. This shift in the balance of economic power can be expected to feed the inegalitarian forces against which Meade and Piketty warn us, and hence to compromise the state's ability to keep inequalities in check.

This is not a decisive consideration. Its importance diminishes when the state's ability to curb inequality through redistributive taxation is greater. Moreover, given its structural nature, it doesn't count strongly against any particular instance of privatization – only against allowing privatization to obtain on a massive scale (a point to which I return in Section 2.6). At the same time, the objection displays a resilience that was wanting in inner retreat arguments. To see this, note that our reasons for objecting to rising economic inequality plausibly include concerns about the economic power that the very rich have over others, about the political influence that great wealth tends to afford, and also about the stigmatizing differences that large inequalities make possible.[29] Such concerns are not assuaged when privatizing the production of a certain good or service promises gains in efficiency; they may

---

[26]   Thomas Piketty, *Capital in the Twenty-First Century*, trans. Arthur Goldhammer (Cambridge, MA: Harvard University Press, 2014).

[27]   See James E. Meade, *Efficiency, Equality and the Ownership of Property* (London: George Allen & Unwin, 1964). Meade suggests that the problem he envisages will become more acute with increased automation, but he thinks that it already arises in the UK at the time of his writing, so presumably he views it as a general problem for modern free-market economies (see ibid., at pp. 25, 75).

[28]   See ibid., at pp. 71–74. Meade leaves out a further complication: if we are skeptical about the possibility of curbing inequality through redistributive taxation, then presumably we should also be skeptical about the prospects for using the political process to socialize the economy.

[29]   See T. M. Scanlon, "The Diversity of Objections to Inequality," in *The Difficulty of Tolerance* (Cambridge: Cambridge University Press, 2003), pp. 202–218, and T. M. Scanlon, *Why Does Inequality Matter?* (Oxford: Oxford University Press, 2018).

even be aggravated if the rich secure a disproportionate share of the gains. The objection thus provides grounds for favouring a relatively large public sector even when this comes at some cost in efficiency (on the assumption, once again, that containing inequalities exclusively through redistributive taxation will prove difficult or impossible).

The second objection I want to mention shifts our focus from the outcome of production to productive activity itself; it concerns an economic duty having to do not with distributive equality but with *opportunity*. Different views are possible about the extent of the state's duties in this domain. Here I simply assume that the state has a duty to act as an *employer of last resort*, in order to give those who can't otherwise find employment the option of engaging in remunerated productive activity.[30] This should be relatively uncontentious, at least for liberal egalitarians. As Rawls observes: "Lacking a sense of long-term security and the opportunity for meaningful work and occupation is not only destructive of citizens' self-respect but of their sense that they are members of society and not simply caught in it."[31] By acting as an employer of last resort, the state makes room for all citizens to take an active part in the productive activities that sustain society over time. This allows citizens to view themselves as full participants in society, and thereby provides crucial support to their sense of self-respect.

Assume that something along these lines is correct. Two further thoughts are required to establish the need for a robust public sector. First, that the state can't fulfill its duty by conjuring up dummy jobs – artificial forms of employment designed to make those who hold them feel better about themselves but contributing nothing to society. To act as an employer of last resort in a meaningful sense, the state must provide work that makes a real contribution. People hired to count blades of grass or to do useless administrative work would be right to think that their interest in being meaningfully employed wasn't fulfilled.

The other further thought is that the state's ability to create genuine positions of employment depends on its having direct control over a significant part of the economy. This is contentious, as there could be other ways to proceed. Most obviously, the state could demand of private employers that, for certain types of positions, they hire people who aren't fully competitive. But that approach presents significant challenges. Firms competing globally already struggle to pay decent wages to employees who contribute to their productivity. How they could survive if they were mandated to add comparatively unproductive employees to their payroll is far from obvious. Of course, the state could subsidize the positions in question.[32] Ascertaining the merits of such a system is a difficult matter (and one plainly exceeding the scope of the present discussion), but I do want to mention some grounds for thinking that it would be less than ideal. Asking for-profit private firms to hire employees whom they deem insufficiently productive is, to put it mildly, unlikely to make for a smooth integration. If anything, we should expect the incentives guiding decision-making in such firms to push in the direction of severely marginalizing these employees. "Look, just do your little things and try to stay out of everyone's way," you can almost hear the exasperated manager blurting out. Even if the effort was restricted to firms structured as nonprofits,

---

[30] Obviously, the idea is not to make welfare benefits conditional on the willingness to work, only to ensure that those who want to work are given the option.

[31] John Rawls, "Introduction to the Paperback Edition," *Political Liberalism* (New York: Columbia University Press, 1996), p. lix.

[32] Or it could restrict the demand to companies that enjoy natural monopolies (utilities or train carriers, say) since they are not subject to the same kind of external pressure (but see note 34).

concerns would remain about how well they could integrate less productive employees amid constant worries about their viability.[33]

All this suggests that the state's ability to act as an employer of last resort will be most secure when it maintains direct control over a significant part of the economy.[34] Massive transfers of capital to the private sector are thus criticizable because they tend to undermine the state's ability to fulfill this duty. The remarks I made about the previous objection apply here as well. Once again, the point doesn't count against specific instances of privatization – only against privatization on an excessive scale. And once again, crucially, the objection can stand up to efficiency considerations. Even if capital could be used more productively in the private sector, if it can be put to reasonably productive use in the public sector, and if keeping it there preserves the state's ability to act as an employer of last resort, then appeals to efficiency lose much of their bite.

2.5 STRUCTURAL OBJECTIONS, II: DEMOCRACY

I turn now to a pair of objections grounded not in considerations of economic justice but, rather, in the broader ideal of a democratic society. These objections apply to a potentially greater range of cases, since the concern here is primarily with the transfer of decisional power that accompanies privatization, a transfer that doesn't always require ownership to be privatized. The objections may apply with greater force when the transfer of decisional power stems from a transfer of capital, since decisional power is then most likely to be unfettered. But since I must leave aside the complex matter of what institutional conditions are necessary for private agents to acquire excessive decisional power through privatization, when I speak of public and private firms in this section, I mean to refer simply to firms whose *governance* is public or private.[35]

The objections I want to consider rest on a simple idea: in a democratic society, public firms are linked to the democratic process in a way that private firms are not. The exact extent of democratic control over public firms varies – it depends on how tightly a specific firm is integrated into the state bureaucracy, as well as on the quality of the democratic procedures that prevail in the society in question. But it shouldn't be controversial that public firms are normally more closely connected to the democratic process than private ones. Besides, it's good to remind ourselves that there is something fundamentally anti-democratic about the amount of economic power that large private firms wield, and about the outsized control over

---

[33] For a discussion arguing that private nonprofit firms are more efficient than government enterprises precisely because their survival is less certain, see Michael J. Trebilcock and Edward M. Iacobucci, "Privatization and Accountability," *Harvard Law Review* 116 (2003): 1422–1453, pp. 1428–1430. The flip-side of that argument is that nonprofit firms are poorly suited to fulfill the duty under discussion.

[34] Two other possibilities should be briefly mentioned. First, private nonprofit firms could be placed in charge of natural monopolies (such as utilities or train transportation). This would allow them to integrate noncompetitive employees more successfully, but the advantages of this approach remain elusive, since the efficiency argument is tied to private firms' exposure to competition. Second, the state could promote an ethos of full employment. Shin Osawa has suggested to me in conversation that such an ethos prevails in Japan, where private corporations tend to employ significantly more people than would be thought justified in other countries. This is an intriguing approach, but whether and how it could be replicated elsewhere is unclear.

[35] Although decisional power is likely to be greater when privatization is complete, it could be particularly unfettered if the state retains ownership but fails to provide adequate supervision. Decisions are then made with someone else's money, so they're not even subject to minimal market discipline. Once again, I leave these complications aside.

vast swaths of the economy that their leaders enjoy.[36] This isn't to say that such power differentials can never be justified (perhaps they are when they operate to the overall benefit of the worst-off, as Rawls's difference principle would have it).[37] But there remains a tension with basic democratic ideals.

The economic power of private actors is most obviously problematic when they have considerable discretion about how to wield it – when they can decide, from a broad range of options, what gets produced, what jobs get created, and so on. But even when there is little discretion to speak of, because decisions are severely constrained by fierce market competition, the logic guiding these decisions can remain at odds with the ideal of a democratic society, because market pressures often fail to track the values to which a society is democratically committed. When that happens, democratic principles may not be directly violated, but we still fail to live up to an important aspect of the democratic ideal, namely, that decisions shaping society at a deep level should be responsive to the shared values of citizens.

Imagine, for instance, a country whose electors care deeply about the environment. Their electoral choices reflect this, but, because they have a hard time resisting a good bargain, their consumer choices don't follow. What kind of responsiveness to the relevant shared democratic value can we expect from private firms in such circumstances? We can certainly expect some responsiveness if the value translates into tighter regulations, at least insofar as these regulations are enforced effectively. But it would be naïve to expect private firms to go beyond what's required of them – and not unduly cynical to suspect that some will invest considerable resources in trying to escape the regulations. Insofar as shared democratic values diverging from market incentives have any impact at all on their decision-making, it will probably have more to do with branding and advertising than with their production and research agenda.

The integration of public firms in the political process allows for greater responsiveness to shared values. This wouldn't necessarily be attractive for the economy as a whole – innovation may demand that certain firms be guided purely by market incentives. But it seems desirable that some segments of the economy be more closely aligned with shared values than private decision-making allows. A significant drawback of privatization is that it undermines the possibility of such an alignment. As I have been hinting, the problem is particularly glaring in the energy sector, because the looming environmental catastrophes that humanity confronts largely result from market failure, and hence from the gap between what market behaviour brings about and what we really want. It therefore makes perfect sense to prefer that enterprises with an outsized environmental impact be guided by a democratic rather than a market-based logic. And, going back to our main thread, this makes sense even if the private sector could produce energy more efficiently. Indeed, not only does efficient production fail to address worries about democratic accountability; insofar as it leads to lower prices and increased consumption, it compromises the very value that the democratic process would favour.

Since I am focusing on objections to privatization that hold even when it promises efficiency gains, I should note that delicate questions arise about how we should understand efficiency in the present context. You could say that the point I just made simply shows that private energy production isn't truly efficient because it fails to deliver everything we want.

---

[36] See Thomas Christiano, "The Uneasy Relationship between Democracy and Capital," *Social Philosophy and Policy* 27 (2010): 195–217.

[37] See Rawls, *A Theory of Justice*, at pp. 65–73.

Perhaps you could insist on construing almost anything as a problem of efficiency, provided you have a sufficiently broad conception of what counts as the outcome of a given productive activity. For instance, you could think that the point I made above regarding the state's duty to act as an employer of last resort really shows that private production isn't efficient after all, since it fails to provide something we want – employment for all who seek it.[38] That would be too quick, however. We want to distinguish between the efficiency of individual firms and that of the whole system. Claims about the efficiency of individual firms depend on what these firms can reasonably be expected to produce. The inability of certain persons to find gainful employment can't be blamed on any individual firm. The fault must lie instead with the economic and political structure, and hence ultimately with those who decide what shape that structure takes.

By contrast, there is little doubt that energy firms can be held accountable for how much they pollute; their failure to track shared values in this respect could therefore be construed as a problem of inefficiency. But this is an incidental feature of the case: not all situations in which we want the provision of certain services to be responsive to democratic input will involve market failure, and hence inefficiency. We may think that the provision of train travel should be determined democratically because we believe that quality of service should be more uniform across richer and poorer areas. The aim wouldn't be to correct a market failure but rather to dissociate quality of service from market inputs. This is something we may reasonably want to do even if equal provision requires some amount of levelling down, so long as this is what our publicly shared values demand. Concerns about how privatization makes it harder to align the outcome of certain productive activities with democratically shared values are thus genuinely distinct from – and can stand up to – efficiency considerations.

The aim of democratic input needn't be just to influence the outcome of production; the focus can also be on productive activity itself. We saw above that public ownership can be viewed as an enabling condition for the state to discharge its duty to act as an employer of last resort. I now want to signal an advantage that public ownership presents even when basic duties of justice aren't at stake, namely, that it allows for greater democratic input into the kinds of positions that are created. A corresponding objection to privatization is that it limits this input. Of course, in a well-functioning democracy, there will always be *some* democratic input into the kinds of positions that are created: laws and regulations pertaining to employment are adopted by representatives who are ultimately accountable to the electorate. But there are limits to what can be accomplished in this way: trying to lead a recalcitrant private sector to create desirable forms of employment through laws and regulations only gets you so far.

Keeping a robust public sector in place allows for a more promising approach by preserving a segment of the economy in which employment creation can be more directly responsive to democratic input. You may worry that citizens won't be particularly good at directing the public sector to create desirable positions of employment, simply because no one quite knows how to create such positions on a large scale (at least if minimal requirements of productivity remain in place). But democratic input could take a different form. The decision could be made to maintain a strong public sector to preserve space for *experimentation*. In the spirit of John Stuart Mill's famous claim that making room for "experiments of living"[39] is crucial to

---

[38] Thanks to Lucas Stanczyk for pressing me on this point.
[39] John Stuart Mill, *On Liberty*, ed. Elizabeth Rapaport (Indianapolis: Hackett, 1978), ch. 3.

allow each person to find a way of life suited to their personality, the aim would be to favour a structuring of the economy that encourages more diverse forms of employment, in the hope that each person will then find a way of contributing to society that is consistent with their conception of the good. Resisting the push to privatize already serves that end, since it ensures that the economic structure isn't all subject to the same private-sector logic. In addition, even if we don't know exactly what more desirable forms of employment might look like, we can decide democratically to demand of the public sector that it be open to experimenting with different employment models – by allowing more flexible schedules, for instance, or greater levels of job security without full-time employment.

The claim I am making here is modest. I am saying that it's important to preserve the possibility of democratic input into the forms of employment that are created by society, that keeping a robust sector in place is an important means to doing so, and that a push to promote experimentation with respect to employment models is one form that demo-cratic input might take. You may think that a stronger conclusion is warranted. You could contend that the private sector's record at creating minimally desirable forms of employ-ment is so dismal that a fundamental duty of economic justice is at stake here. The thought would then be that the interest that individuals have in contributing to society in accord-ance with their conception of the good demands not only that the state act as an employer of last resort but also that it provide a sufficient diversity of options for those who are ill-suited to the work environments that the private sector tends to create. This wouldn't mean that people have a right to their dream job, but it would entail that improving on the range of options provided by the private sector is a demand of justice, not merely something we may decide to do democratically.

We don't need to settle the matter here. The present objection holds so long as leaving room for direct democratic input into the forms of employment that society creates is important. If the demands of justice in this domain turn out to be more extensive than I have been assuming, then the scope for democratic input will be more restricted, but the general point will still hold. Either way, we have a further consideration in favour of maintaining a sizeable public sector – and, once again, a consideration that does not simply give way before the efficiency argument, since it is perfectly reasonable to prefer a greater diversity of employment opportunities even when that comes at a cost in efficiency.

2.6 INTERPRETING STRUCTURAL OBJECTIONS

By way of conclusion, I want to take stock of the considerations I discussed in Sections 2.4 and 2.5 and say more about how they contrast with inner retreat arguments. I first presented two objections to large-scale privatization stemming from the role that a robust public sector plays in enabling the state to deliver on its duties of economic justice. I suggested that having direct control over a significant share of the economy strengthens the state's ability to contain economic inequalities, and that it can be crucial to its ability to act as an employer of last resort. I then turned to objections grounded in the broader ideal of a democratic society. Here the key idea was that public firms are generally more responsive to the democratic process than private firms. They stay more closely aligned with shared democratic values (a point that is particularly important when these values fail to translate into consumer choices). And they make room for greater democratic input into employment models, thus opening up new possibilities to allow citizens with a broad range of aptitudes and views about the good to find fulfilling ways to contribute to society. My contention is that, together, these different considerations explain how large-scale transfers of economic power from the public to the private sector can be objectionable even if they bring about significant efficiency gains.

When discussing inner retreat arguments, I raised doubts about whether they truly undercut considerations of efficiency as their proponents intend them to do. I argued that when important substantive goods are at stake, efficiency considerations don't become outright irrelevant in the way they would if the strategy were successful. Now, as I have hinted already, the structural objections I articulated also fail to trump considerations of efficiency in such extreme cases. Does it follow that my misgivings about the inner retreat strategy also apply to the strategy I favour? Here it is crucial to note that the two strategies have different ambitions, and that their success conditions are accordingly different. The inner retreat strategy fails to accomplish what it sets out to do because it can succeed on its own terms only if it identifies intrinsic considerations that render efficiency gains irrelevant.

Structural objections reflect more modest aspirations. As I stressed repeatedly, the aim is to explain why privatization on a massive scale should concern us, not to provide decisive reasons against any specific instance of privatization. It is therefore entirely consistent with the arguments I presented to recognize that what we should think about specific cases depends on the importance of the goods that the private sector promises to deliver more efficiently. If private prisons really delivered a safer, more humane environment than public prisons at a given cost, then *of course* we would have to look elsewhere when seeking to ensure that the state can deliver on its economic duties or that the economy is sufficiently responsive to the democratic process. The stakes are simply too high. By contrast, a slight loss of efficiency in the provision of utilities or of train transportation would seem an acceptable cost to pay to serve the relevant purposes.

When the need for privatization is overwhelming because of the importance of the substantive goods at issue, structural objections simply give way. That is as it should be. The aims that underlie these objections (constraining inequalities; providing access to employment for all; making the economy more democratic) can be achieved in different ways. When choosing among these, we must be mindful of the importance of the goods whose provision is at stake. To say that structural considerations don't always prevail isn't to deny their importance; it is to recognize that orchestrating the productive activities of society is a complex matter that inevitably involves difficult trade-offs.[40]

[40] Earlier versions of this chapter were presented at the 2019 Philosophy, Politics, and Economics Society annual meeting in New Orleans, at a workshop on "Political Philosophy and the Future of Capitalism" held at Waseda University, and at a practical philosophy workshop held at Sankt Oberholz, in Berlin. I am indebted to the audiences on these three occasions for extremely helpful suggestions, and endlessly grateful for a characteristically illuminating exchange with Stephen White on the day following the Berlin workshop, during a long streetcar ride to and from the abandoned children's hospital in Weissensee. Special thanks to Chiara Cordelli and to the editors of this volume for detailed comments on the penultimate version that led to major improvements. This chapter draws on research supported by the Social Sciences and Humanities Research Council of Canada.

3

Public and Private Ownership in Plato and Aristotle

Jonny Thakkar

3.1 INTRODUCTION

The privatization of publicly owned and operated industries and services that has occurred in certain countries over the last forty or fifty years is routinely condemned on the political left, yet the grounds of that condemnation often remain unspecified. This is perhaps unsurprising, given the practical advantages of what Cass Sunstein has called "incompletely theorized agreements" in facilitating collective action.[1] But the advantage of distinguishing between different kinds of objections is that doing so allows us to assess their implications independently and therefore weigh and balance different factors in our practical reasoning. Sometimes we might want to object to privatization on straightforward economic grounds: when Chicago sold its parking meters on a seventy-five-year lease for just $1.15 billion, giving up a long-term revenue stream in order to balance the budget for just one year, it seemed less like selling the family silver than selling the family silver mine.[2] Other times we might want to object on more abstract lines: we might wonder, for instance, whether prisons run by profit-seeking private corporations can ever be legitimate.[3] Now we seem to be squarely in the realm of political philosophy, which from Hobbes onwards has often asked under what conditions, if any, coercion can be considered legitimate. In this chapter I want to outline an objection to privatization that occupies a middle-ground between practical concerns of the nickel-and-dime variety and abstract concerns that hold independently of consequences. Not coincidentally, my discussion will focus on the ancient Greek philosophers whose failure to distinguish between empirical and a priori considerations so horrified Kant, namely Plato and Aristotle.

In *The Republic*, Plato has Socrates ban private property for the guardians of his ideal state. This prohibition does not amount to a program of public ownership in anything

---

[1] Cass R. Sunstein, "Incompletely Theorized Agreements Commentary," *Harvard Law Review* 108 (1994): 1733–1772.

[2] For a broader critique, see Ivan Kaplan, "Does the Privatization of Publicly Owned Infrastructure Implicate the Public Trust Doctrine – Illinois Central and the Chicago Parking Meter Concession Agreement," *Northwestern Journal of Law and Social Policy* 7 (2012): 136–169.

[3] See Avihay Dorfman and Alon Harel, "The Case Against Privatization," *Philosophy & Public Affairs* 41 (2013): 67–102, and Chiara Cordelli, *The Privatized State* (Princeton, NJ: Princeton University Press, 2020).

like the modern sense: Socrates never argues that the property denied to guardians should be held by the polis as a whole, or that the polis should own the means of production. What I want to argue, however, is that the line of thought that underlies Socrates's prohibitions might offer *us* reasons for favouring public ownership in certain circumstances. The structure of this chapter is therefore as follows. I begin, in Section 3.2, by reconstructing Socrates's basic argument for preventing the guardians from owning property. Then, in Section 3.3, I show how that argument is grounded in Socrates's view of labour and in particular in his objections to what he calls "moneymaking." In Section 3.4, I argue that Socrates's position on personal property derives from a concern over whether citizens will reliably work for the common good in the absence of institutional restraints. In Section 3.5, I consider Aristotle's objections to Socrates's proposals, arguing that Aristotle's position is in some ways more utopian than Plato's, and then in the concluding Section 3.6, I suggest how all of this might bear on contemporary discussions regarding privatization.

3.2 THE LOGIC OF PLATO'S COMMUNISM

In Book III of *The Republic*, Socrates suggests that the rulers of an ideal city would be prohibited from owning any private property that is not "wholly necessary" (416d). They should receive a salary in the form of basic provisions fit for "temperate and courageous men, who are warrior-athletes," but beyond that they are to live and eat together like soldiers in a camp, their living quarters and storerooms are to be open for all to enter at will, and they will be forbidden to handle or touch gold and silver, to wear them as jewellery, to drink from cups made out of them, and even to enter buildings where they are present (416d–417a). These restrictions do not themselves amount to a program of public ownership, since there is no suggestion that the property denied to guardians on a personal basis is to be held in common by the polis as a whole. Some of it (such as the living quarters) will be held by the community of guardians, while the rest (such as the gold and silver) will remain with the ordinary citizens who are to be spared the predations of rapacious rulers. Still less is there any suggestion that ownership of the means of production should be transferred to the state. What I want to argue, however, is that the line of thought that underlies Socrates's prohibitions might offer *us* reasons for favouring public ownership in certain circumstances. To see why, we need to examine the logic of Plato's communism.

Socrates sets up a series of correlative binaries: depending on whether or not the rulers are allowed "private land, houses and money," they will become either wolves *or* sheepdogs toward their flock; savage, hostile masters *or* gentle allies; moneymakers *or* soldiers; farmers and household managers *or* guardians (415e–416b, 417a). This seems to imply a slippery-slope argument according to which there is no meaningful difference between different levels of private property to which guardians might have access, one drop of the polluting substance being enough to corrupt them entirely. This interpretation is corroborated in Book VIII, where we hear that Kallipolis will collapse when a few rotten apples find their way into the ruling class and "pull the constitution toward moneymaking and the acquisition of land, house, gold, and silver" (547b) with the result that soon the whole ruling class "will have an appetite for money just like those in oligarchies, passionately adoring gold and silver in secret, owning storehouses and private treasuries where they can deposit them and keep them hidden; and they will have walls around their houses, real private nests, where they can spend lavishly on their women or on anyone else they please" (548a). As in Book III, the result is a change in their relationship to the ruled: rather than guarding the other citizens "as free friends and providers of upkeep," they treat them as slaves, serfs and servants, and this means they need to be held down by force (547b-c).

Like any slippery-slope argument, this might be dismissed as melodramatic; we might think the challenge is just to find reliable safeguards and bulwarks to prevent things getting out of hand. We will come back to this thought at the end of the chapter, but for now the point is that if Socrates and his interlocutors reject – or at least fail to consider – such an approach, it is because in their view the stakes are simply too high: as Socrates puts it at the start of Book IV, "if the guardians of our laws and city are not really what they seem to be, you may be sure that they will destroy the city and, on the other hand, they alone have the opportunity to govern it well and make it happy" (421a). Here the binaries listed just now are resolved into a single one: either the rulers are genuine guardians (*phulakas hōs alēthōs*) or they are frauds who claim to be what they are not.

In what follows, Socrates presents three considerations that link this binary to the question of private property. The first is that a city in which the powerful are allowed to accumulate wealth will be one in which class conflict emerges, such that it is no longer really *one* city but rather contains two cities at war with one another, "the city of the poor and that of the rich," each of which in turn contains further cities (422e–423a, 547b-c, 551d). Given that there is no greater good for a city "than what binds it together and makes it one" (462b), it follows that the ruling class should not be allowed to accumulate wealth.[4] The second consideration derives from the one man, one job principle (370b-c, 423d). Like all craftsmen, guardians must devote themselves exclusively to their own profession if they are to do it well. If property turns guardians into "farmers" and "household managers," it is presumably because ownership brings with it the task of stewardship – those who own land have to cultivate it and those who own houses have to manage them – and therefore tears them away from the task for which the city most needs them (417a, 421b).[5] The third consideration is closely related. Wealth, Socrates says, makes craftsmen degenerate qua craftsmen: they are no longer willing to devote themselves to their crafts and therefore become idler and more careless than before (421d). Since guardianship is a craft (421c, 500d), it follows that wealth will make guardians degenerate qua guardians.[6]

The argument concerning social unity and the arguments concerning craftsmanship are more closely related than they might seem. What it means for a city to be *one* city is for its citizens to be pulling in the same direction. When a chasm opens up between rich and poor, the notion of a common good comes to seem quixotic since neither side of the divide can view its own flourishing as bound up with that of the other. Meanwhile, Socrates specifies what it means for citizens to aim at the common good in terms of performing their allotted roles in

---

[4]   This argument can be fleshed out by pairing Socrates' Book V remark that there is no "greater evil for a city than what tears it apart and makes it many instead of one" with his Book VIII observation that oligarchical regimes permit "the greatest of all evils," namely "allowing someone to sell all his possessions and someone else to buy them, and then allowing the seller to continue living in the city while not being any one of its parts – neither moneymaker nor craftsman, nor cavalryman, nor hoplite, but a poor person without means" (552a).

[5]   In this vein, consider Socrates' remarks on the evils that the guardians would escape thanks to his proposed living arrangements: "the flatteries of the rich by the poor; the perplexities and sufferings involved in bringing up children; the need to make the money necessary to feed the household – the borrowings, the defaults, and all the things people have to do to provide an income to hand over to their wives and slaves to spend on housekeeping" (465b-c).

[6]   Poverty would also cause such a degeneration, according to Socrates, but only insofar as it denies craftsmen the things they need for their craft; since the guardians are to be provided with just enough to enable them to carry out their tasks, this need not concern us (416d–e).

the division of labour to the best of their abilities. A city comes to exist, Socrates says, "because none of us is individually self-sufficient, but each has many needs he cannot satisfy" (369b). Mutual advantage is therefore the principle (*archē*) of the city, its guiding purpose, and this is what grounds the principle of specialization (370b–c). The thought that a city is well-ordered when united (462b) and the thought that it is well-ordered when its citizens are "the best possible craftsmen at their own work" (421c) are therefore one and the same, since the only unity that a city can aspire to is the complex harmony of a fully functional cooperative scheme for mutual advantage.[7] As Socrates puts it in Book IV, each citizen must be "assigned to what naturally suits him, with one person assigned to one job so that, practicing his own pursuit, each of them will become not many but one, and *the entire city thereby naturally grow to be one, not many*" (423d, my italics). And on Socrates's account, a city that is united by means of each citizen practicing his own pursuit is a just city.

Justice is a property that strictly speaking applies to the whole city or the whole soul, and not to their parts. But because justice is the property of being well organized or constituted, such that each part is doing the work appropriate to it, Socrates seems to allow that we can speak of justice in a derivative or secondary sense as applying to individual citizens insofar as they "do their own work in the city" (433a–434a, 443c–d). We could call this justice in the political sense. Another way of putting Socrates's argument regarding communism among the guardians is therefore to say that a ban on private property is required in order to ensure that guardians remain just in the political sense, playing their allotted parts in a division of labour aimed at the common good. The prohibition is therefore downstream from Socrates's reflections on labour, and it is these reflections that I take to be most relevant to contemporary debates regarding public and private ownership.

3.3 CRAFTSMEN AND MONEYMAKERS

Ina passage from Book One whose connections to the theme of justice have not often been noticed, Socrates asks Thrasymachus whether "a doctor in the precise sense" is "a moneymaker or someone who treats the sick" (341c).[8] The context is Socrates's attempt to refute Thrasymachus's claim that "justice is nothing other than what is advantageous for the stronger" (338c). Thrasymachus has just claimed that a ruler, insofar as he is acting as a genuine ruler, decrees only what is best for himself (340e–341a) and Socrates is attempting to persuade him that genuine rulers enjoin what is advantageous for their subjects rather than themselves (342e). In response to Socrates's question, Thrasymachus immediately concedes that a true doctor is someone who treats the sick, rather than being a moneymaker. This ought to surprise us. Surely it is possible for a doctor both to heal people and to make money?

To grasp Socrates's point here is to understand his vision of craftsmanship and hence, ultimately, his hostility to the ruling class – understood as a class of craftsmen – owning private property. He is asking after the property in virtue of which we can appropriately call someone one kind of craftsman rather than another (341c–d). His assumption is that crafts are distinguished by the goods they aim to provide. Each genuine craft aims to provide a distinct

---

[7] Aristotle is therefore wrong to imagine that Socrates is assuming such a degree of unity that homogeneity replaces harmony. See *Politics*, 1263b30–36.

[8] This section is largely drawn from two previous pieces of work – Jonny Thakkar, "Moneymakers and Craftsmen: A Platonic Approach to Privatization," *European Journal of Philosophy* 24 (2016): 735–759, and ch. 7 of Jonny Thakkar, *Plato as Critical Theorist* (Cambridge, MA: Harvard University Press, 2018) – but it arrives at a different conclusion concerning the exact nature of the distinction between craftsmanship and moneymaking.

good; the craft of navigation aims at making us safe while sailing, for example, whereas the craft of medicine aims to produce health (346a). Living as a navigator may be good for one's health, but this does not mean that navigators are practicing medicine; health is merely a by-product of navigation, utterly irrelevant to its constitutive aim (346b). If the notion of a constitutive aim seems vague, we can make it more precise by thinking in terms of standards of success and failure. If a navigator fails to become healthy through her voyages, she has not thereby failed qua navigator; if her boat runs aground, she has. A true craftsman – the craftsman in the precise sense, the craftsman qua craftsman – is therefore a worker who deliberates in light of standards of success constitutive of her craft, and hence with an eye to the function of that craft within a division of labour aimed at the common good. Socrates's argument regarding doctors and moneymaking is that wages stand to medicine as health stands to navigation: just as promoting health plays no role in making navigation what it is, and hence plays no role in the deliberations of the navigator qua navigator, so earning wages plays no role in making medicine what it is, and hence plays no role in the deliberations of the doctor qua doctor.

This might seem like an abstract concern with acting on the right reasons in order to manifest virtue or a goodwill. If that were the case, then it would have no practical importance for the consumer. As Aristotle observes in the *Nicomachean Ethics*, the quality of a craft object is in principle independent of the quality of the craftsman in a way that the virtue of an action is not independent of the virtue of the agent.

> For the things that come about by means of the crafts have their goodness internal to them, and thus it is enough if they come about in such a way as to be in a certain state. The things that come about in accord with the virtues, by contrast, are done justly or temperately not simply if they are in a certain state but if the one who does them is also in a certain state.[9]

From the user's point of view, it makes no difference whether a hammer has been produced by a craftsman who deliberates with an eye to the function of their craft or by one who has something else on their mind. The question is just whether it performs its function. But there is no need to interpret Socrates's concern with moneymaking as merely abstract. Given his vision of society as a division of labour aimed at the good life, the relevant unit of assessment is not one particular craft product but rather a whole life spent producing certain kinds of goods and services. And here the consumer – understood now to be society at large – does have reason to care about the reasoning of a given craftsmen. For over time the only way to reliably produce the goods for the sake of which a craft exists is to deliberate with the relevant standards in mind.

Imagine two dentists, a moneymaker and a craftsman. In deciding on a course of treatment, the craftsman is going to orient themselves toward the goal of relieving their patients' pain and restoring them to health. They will assess competing courses of action, to the best of their ability, with reference to their efficiency in promoting these goals. The moneymaker, by contrast, is going to view their patients' pain as an opportunity to profit. This means that they will assess competing courses of action with reference to their efficiency in bringing them profit. As political economists have pointed out, in an ideal market economy a rationally self-interested dentist of this sort will often decide that the best way to make money over the long run is to acquire a reputation for providing good service, and that the best way to do that is to actually provide such service. But generalizations of this sort are not robust. For one thing, moneymakers will not always act rationally over the long term. Cognitive failures may lead them to prioritize

---

9   Aristotle, *Nicomachean Ethics*, trans. C. D. C. Reeve (Indiana: Hackett Publishing, 2014).

short-term over long-term profit, but so might political insecurity and epistemic humility: a bird in the hand is better than two in the bush. For another, it is perfectly possible to acquire a reputation for providing good service without actually providing it. This is especially true in cases where there are important asymmetries of information between a provider and a customer, as with dentistry. How is the patient to know whether extracting a tooth is truly necessary? Patients' trust in dentists might track whether they appear caring and friendly and authoritative rather than the quality of their work, in which case a moneymaker ought to focus on the former rather than the latter. The likelihood that the monetary incentives align perfectly with the needs of the patient, such that moneymaking dentists consistently provide optimal service, is therefore low. If offered the choice between being treated by a moneymaker or a craftsman, patients would have reason to choose the latter.

An obvious response to this line of argument is that we ought to distinguish between the reasons that lead somebody to engage in a given activity in the first place and the reasons that they allow into their deliberations during the course of that activity. You might choose to become a dentist, or to continue being one, because you think it is the most efficient way to make money given your talents and the state of the market, and yet be determined to leave all moneymaking considerations at the door of the clinic, so to speak, acting only on reasons that are strictly medical. We might think that this is just what professionalism *is* – the ability to zone out considerations that are irrelevant to a given role while acting in that role, while nevertheless remaining sensitive to them when stepping outside that role.[10]

Socrates does accept that people will require wages to motivate them to engage in a given craft in the first place, suggesting that each craftsman of a particular kind also engages in a distinct craft of "wage-earning" (*misthōtikos*; 346a–d). It might therefore seem that he thinks that all craftsmen are moneymakers when it comes to choosing an occupation, with differences of professionalism emerging only within the activity itself. This is not the case, however. Strictly speaking Socrates concedes only that craftsmen are all wage-earners, not that they are all moneymakers when it comes to choosing an occupation. He goes on to observe that money is not the only kind of compensation for work. A second kind of wage is honour and a third is the avoidance of a penalty or punishment, as when the best people are motivated to rule by the fact that not doing so would lead to the disaster of being ruled by someone worse (347a–c). Socrates makes clear that the first and second wage are inferior to the third. Whereas "those who love honour and those who love money are despised, and rightly so," the "wage of the best people" (*ton tōn beltistōn misthon*) is the third (347b).

Socrates stops here because his dispute with Thrasymachus has centred on ruling. But in principle his argument might extend to other crafts as well. Every doctor is a wage-earner before he or she is a doctor, yet different kinds of people seek different kinds of wage. Some pursue medicine for money; others pursue it for honour; but the best pursue it because they don't want lesser people to carry out the task. This might seem like a strange motivation at first, but on reflection it makes perfect sense. The scheme of social labour will work better – and our needs will be better satisfied – to the degree that each performs the task for which he or she is best suited. The best kind of people are therefore motivated to engage in a particular craft by the desire to see citizens deploy their talents appropriately within a division of labour constituted for the sake of the common good. This reflects a combination of justice and wisdom.

---

[10]   See Joseph Raz's discussion of "exclusionary reasons" in *Practical Reason and Norms* (Oxford: Oxford University Press, 1975), ch. 1.

We concluded earlier that dental patients have reason to prefer being treated by a craftsman rather than a moneymaker, where those terms have to do with the standards that guide decision-making within the workplace. Do they also have reason to care whether their dentist is a moneymaker at the higher level? Our answer will depend on whether we believe that the Chinese wall between levels of reasoning can be maintained. If it can, then the ultimate motivation of workers will be irrelevant to the consumer and, by extension, to the proper functioning of the cooperative scheme.

By the logic of Socrates's argument, however, it seems that ultimate motivations should make a difference. For he thinks of wage-earning as a craft, and if one craft is engaged in for the sake of another, deliberation within the subsidiary activity will be governed by standards of success derived from the master activity.[11] What a craftsman counts as successful lace-cutting, for instance, will depend on what they count as successful shoemaking, and what they count as successful shoemaking will depend on their purposes. A true craftsman will measure success by the condition of the customer's feet, given the function of shoemaking within a division of labour aimed at the good life, but those who enter into the craft for the sake of money or honour will measure success differently. Where moneymaking or honour-seeking is the master activity, in other words, the subsidiary activity is likely to be distorted. To return to Socrates's own example, the goal of medicine is to restore patients to health. But what if an opportunity arises for a doctor to enrich themselves at the expense of the patient by prescribing needless and dangerous surgery? Qua doctor, they should resist; qua moneymaker or honour-seeker, they should weigh the prospective profit (and resulting prestige) against the chances of getting caught. We might imagine a disciplined moneymaker or honour-seeker who rejects this slide by committing in advance to a rule according to which they must always act as a genuine craftsman at the lower level – but if a case materializes in which there really were a great profit to be made with no chance of getting caught, they would either have to break the rule on pain of practical irrationality or revise their conception of their ultimate ends. In the end, then, the moneymaker and the honour-seeker can only ever masquerade as, or imitate, genuine craftsmen: producing a social good will only ever be an incidental goal for them, pursued just insofar as the incentives line up.[12]

3.4 INSTITUTIONALIZING CRAFTSMANSHIP

Given Socrates's view that a city is well-ordered when its citizens are "the best possible craftsmen at their own work" (421c), the question that naturally arises for his project of designing a "city in speech" is how a lawgiver might ensure that citizens become craftsmen rather than moneymakers. Yet there is no prospect of everyone magically becoming the "best

---

[11] It is unclear that wage-earning can in fact count as a craft, given Socrates' apparent understanding of crafts: it does not seem to be "set over" some object that is deficient, unless that object is one's wallet; and if its goal is to benefit the craftsman then it serves as a counter-example to Socrates' argument against Thrasymachus. See Rachel Barney, "Socrates' Refutation of Thrasymachus," in Gerasimos Santas (ed.), *The Blackwell Guide to Plato's Republic* (Oxford: Blackwell Publishing, 2006), p. 52.

[12] One might plausibly object that the subordination of medicine to wage-earning is destructive of the craft even when the wages in question are "the best people's kinds of wages" – after all, Socrates holds that in Kallipolis some people will be denied medical treatment (405c–408b). In my view, this merely illustrates a distinctive feature of crafts on Plato's account, namely that their proper bounds can be determined only by those with an understanding of the good of the city (and its citizens). So, on Plato's view a doctor who attempted to heal "naturally sick and intemperate people" would in fact be departing from, and corrupting, the craft of medicine properly understood. Asclepius "invented the craft of medicine for people whose bodies are healthy in nature and habit, but have some specific disease in them" (407c–d).

kind of people," those who engage in crafts out of a sense of justice and wisdom. The vast majority of people are motivated to engage in a given craft by the prospect of money or honour. This is true even within Kallipolis, where the entire productive class is characterized as moneymaking or acquisitive (*chrēmatistikon*; 441a).[13] This is primarily a psychological characterization: the productive class count as moneymakers because they are inclined to organize their lives around securing appetitive satisfaction and hence securing the all-purpose means to appetitive satisfaction, namely money (580e–581a).[14] But, as we have seen, the Chinese wall between second-order motivation and first-order decision-making is not robust; at some point moneymakers at the second level will become moneymakers at the first. The puzzle, then, is how Kallipolis can be the model of a well-ordered, united city, in which citizens are "the best possible craftsmen at their own work," while the majority of those citizens remain moneymakers. And the answer can only be institutions.

For the proposition that moneymakers in the psychological sense will tend to become moneymakers in their labours if left to their own devices inevitably leads us to the conclusion that they should not be left to their own devices. Socrates clearly envisages the institutions of Kallipolis generating a salutary culture whose myths, images and prizes generate honour- and shame-structures that regulate behaviour from within so as to promote just motivation. But such reorientation can only go so far, given the natural distribution of psychological propensities among humans. There will always be some who remain appetitive (or honour-loving); the key is for such people to be shepherded by the law, which both enjoins and enforces justice in behaviour, making citizens act *as if* they were ruled by reason (590c–591a).[15] This shows us the way out of our puzzle. For even if a large portion of citizens in Kallipolis remain moneymakers in the psychological sense, they might still organize their labours as craftsmen insofar as the logic of their institutions pushes them to orient their workplace deliberations toward social needs. Hence the reason that Plato believes Kallipolis can be a genuine society despite containing a majority of moneymakers is that he thinks institutions can make craftsmen of moneymakers.

How exactly Plato envisages this functioning is not entirely clear, since the discussion of Kallipolis is mostly centred on the rulers. The general picture is of an economy whose nerve centre is the ruling class, who assign each citizen to the craft or pursuit that naturally suits them (423d; 453e–457c) and supervise their work in order to ensure that they produce a healthy environment (401a–d).[16] This supervision would presumably have the effect of ensuring that workers deliberate with respect to the correct standards of success: as a general matter it is the user who informs the craftsman what makes a given object good or bad

---

[13] In this regard, it is worth noting that Socrates uses the term "craftsmen" (*dēmiourgoi*) not only in the sense that we have been considering so far, i.e. to denote all those engaged in structured activities aimed at satisfying particular social needs, but also in a different sense, to denote the particular subset of the lower class within Kallipolis that is engaged in the artisanal activities usually thought of as crafts (*technai*). And he makes clear that craftsmen in the latter sense are *all* moneymakers, speaking, for instance, of someone "who is by nature a craftsman or some other kind of moneymaker" trying to force his way into the class of soldiers (434a–b).

[14] Note that Socrates describes the appetitive element within the soul as "insatiable for money" (442a). For a useful discussion of moneymaking as a psychological term, see "Souls, Soul-Parts, and Persons" in C. D. C. Reeve, *Blindness and Reorientation: Problems in Plato's Republic* (New York: Oxford University Press, 2013), pp. 79–109. For a comprehensive account of appetitiveness, see Hendrik Lorenz, *The Brute Within: Appetitive Desire in Plato and Aristotle* (Oxford Philosophical Monographs) (Oxford: Oxford University Press, 2009).

[15] For an interpretation that sees this notion of "quasi-reasoning" as central to the whole structure of the *Republic*, and in particular to the Cephalus episode at the start and the myth of Er at the end, see Thakkar, *Plato as Critical Theorist*, pp. 125–128, 179–194.

[16] See ibid., at pp. 97–98, 157–162.

(601d–e); in the case of Kallipolis, the city as a whole might be seen as the user of craft products, with the rulers reasoning on its behalf; and so in Kallipolis the user might have coercive power over the craftsman.[17]

Apart from these general considerations, which are hardly fleshed out, there are also some specific remarks regarding the need to insulate producers (and so moneymakers in the psychological sense) from financial incentives. In Book VIII, Socrates attributes the decline of oligarchy to the failure of the ruling class to take appropriate action against moneymakers who "inject their poison of money" into the rest of the population (555e). He suggests two possible recourses against such poison: the second-best approach would be to pass a law that "compels the citizens to care about virtue" by prescribing that voluntary contracts are entered into at the lender's risk rather than the borrower's (556a–b); better still would be a law "preventing a person from doing whatever he likes with his own property." It seems reasonable to conclude that such a law would be in force in Kallipolis.[18] In Book IV, meanwhile, Socrates argues that craftsmen should not be allowed to become either too poor or too rich, since those who become too poor will not be able to buy tools and raw materials while those who become too rich will no longer devote themselves to their crafts, becoming idle and careless (421d–422a). The worry is that the presence or absence of money can corrupt (*diaphtheirō*) craftsmen – destroy them in their very being, render them no longer what they are.[19] This applies to all craftsmen in the sense of all those whose work aims to produce a specific good within the social division of labour, and therefore also to guardians and auxiliaries.

This brings us back to the topic with which we began, namely Socrates's prohibition on private property among the guardians and their auxiliaries. If the interpretation offered so far is correct, then among the things that the guardians are supposed to guard will be the institutions that make producers accountable to the city and therefore ensure that moneymakers at the motivational level deliberate as craftsmen. But who will guard the guardians? There is nobody with the power to prevent them from becoming moneymakers, even if their subjects would resentfully think of them as "hirelings" or "thieves" (347b). This is why, rather than simply being prevented from becoming too rich or too poor, like the other craftsmen, they must be subject to stronger "safeguards," including the ban on private property (416b–d). Socrates makes clear that the most important safeguard is the education system, which is supposed to both select for and cultivate the capacity of guardians to guard themselves, that is, to maintain their motivation of furthering the common good.[20] The ban on private property should therefore be seen partly as a failsafe, a tripwire that ought to alert the rulers to

---

[17] There is a sense in which the power of rulers over the division of labour is itself a form of public ownership. If we follow J. G. Fichte in thinking of "the right to property as a right to *acts*, not to *things*," then we might think of the economic organization within Kallipolis as transferring certain property rights from individuals to the polis. Something similar would follow on Lockean self-ownership views such as that of Robert Nozick. See J. G. Fichte, *The Closed Commercial State* (New York: State University of New York Press, 2012), p. 92 and Robert Nozick, *Anarchy, State and Utopia* (New York: Basic Books, 1974), ch. 7.

[18] It is possible that such legislation would not be necessary in a well-ordered society. Socrates says that a true lawgiver should not legislate about "all that marketplace business, the contracts people make with one another in the marketplace, for example, and contracts with handicraftsmen, and slanders, injuries, indictments, establishing juries, paying or collecting whatever dues are necessary in marketplace and harbors, and, in a word, the entire regulation of marketplace, city, harbor, or what have you" (425c–d). A fuller piece on this subject would have to take into account a text that I do not consider here, namely Plato's *Laws*.

[19] What wealth and poverty have in common, Socrates tells us, is that they engender social instability; they introduce *neōterismos*, the desire for novelty or revolution (422a; cp. 555d). I take it that this happens at least in part because they destroy genuine craftsmanship and hence the cooperative scheme that is society.

[20] On the notion of guarding oneself, see Thakkar, *Plato as Critical Theorist*, at pp. 92–97.

impending danger. Genuine rulers would not want to accrue property through their position, Socrates is saying – so as soon as a ruler advocates for removing the prohibition, their colleagues will know that something has gone wrong. By that point it may be too late, of course. But the ban also functions as part of the education system, in that, like all institutions, it habituates people and therefore shapes their beliefs and desires. For, as Socrates puts it in Book IV, "fine practices lead to the possession of virtue" (444e).

So although Plato's ban on private property for the guardians is often regarded as utopian, it in fact represents his solution to a feasibility objection. It is precisely because the vagaries of human psychology make it a standing possibility for citizens to be tempted away from craftsmanship and toward moneymaking that a society needs restrictions on property. And these restrictions will have to be most stringent for those with the most important jobs – for even if a combination of nature and nurture means that, left to their own devices, guardians would most likely be inclined to act virtuously, the risk of testing that proposition is simply too great to bear.

3.5 ARISTOTLE'S COUNTERARGUMENT

Before considering how Plato's arguments might apply to our own world, it is worth pausing to consider Aristotle's famous critique of those arguments in his *Politics*. Aristotle charges public ownership with generating inefficiency and impeding virtuous activity, but at the same time he is himself sensitive to the destabilizing effects of inequality and contemptuous of moneymaking. He therefore serves as an interesting counterpoint to Plato, since he shares some of Plato's premises while rejecting his conclusions. Although Aristotle's own proposals regarding property depend on a certain kind of utopianism regarding the power of education, his arguments nevertheless suggest the possibility of modifying Plato's view while retaining his core insights.

Like Plato, Aristotle combines aristocratic contempt for moneymaking – the citizens of the ideal state should have their own *agora* free of all commercial activity and they should not "live the life of a vulgar craftsman or tradesman," since "lives of these sorts are ignorable and inimical to virtue" – with reasoned objections that do not depend on such contempt.[21] His fundamental point is that property acquisition (*ktētikē*) is by nature – and hence, given his teleology, should only ever be – a subordinate component of the wider activity of securing the good life for individuals and communities, namely household or political management. In Book I of the *Nicomachean Ethics*, he explains that if humans are to flourish fully they require "external goods" such as money, good looks and fortune – for although these are less important than virtuous rational activity, they are sometimes a condition of it.[22] Property acquisition therefore helps to secure such goods (*chrēmata* – useful things) as are necessary for leading the good life. Properly understood, then, riches (*ploutos*) are merely tools (*organa*) for the use of household and political managers, and should be pursued only to the degree that they contribute to human flourishing.[23] Out of this natural practice of property acquisition there can arise a perversion, Aristotle thinks: the idea of accumulation as an end in itself, as a distinct craft (*chrēmatistikē*).[24] What makes this perversion possible is the nature of

---

[21] 1331a31–1331b3 and 1328b39–41.
[22] Aristotle, *Nicomachean Ethics*, I.8 (1099a31–4), VII.13 (1153b14–19) and X.8 (1178a23–31). For similar passages in the *Politics*, see VII.1 (1323b20–1324a1) and VII.13 (1331b41–1332a1).
[23] Aristotle, *Politics*, 1256b27–40 and *Nicomachean Ethics*, IV.1–2.
[24] Aristotle, *Politics*, 1256b40–1257b40.

exchange. Exchange, however healthy, will always require the use of a given good not as the good that it itself is but as an equivalent. For example, although the primary or proper (*oikeios*) use of a shoe – that for the sake of which it comes into being – is to protect the feet, in barter a pair of shoes might be used as equivalent to, say, half a pillow. In order to make exchange more convenient, Aristotle hazards, humans begin to use one particular commodity, such as silver or gold, as a general measure of the exchange-value of other goods. This commodity becomes the currency (*nomisma*).[25] At this point the possibility of a perversion arises: it becomes possible to think of currency as wealth itself. This is mistaken, conceptually speaking, because even the richest man can still die of hunger; properly understood, riches constitute wealth just to the extent that they help us achieve the good life.[26] But apart from being a mistake, it also perverts exchange itself. For if property acquisition becomes decoupled from the requirements of household and political management, it becomes a craft unto itself. Even if it makes use of the same articles as natural property acquisition, it disciplines them toward a new *telos*: accumulation. The means has become the end. And as an end in itself, the acquisition of money becomes a boundless task.[27]

This discussion of wealth acquisition (*chrēmatistikē*) forms part of a wider discussion of property acquisition (*ktētikē*) that itself occurs as part of a wider discussion of household management (*oikonomia*).[28] This might lead us – and indeed I believe that it leads Aristotle – to pass over its political implications. As we have seen, Aristotle explicitly states that the question of the proper nature and limits of property acquisition pertains directly to statesmen (*politikoi*) as well as to household managers (*oikonomoi*).[29] Yet the closest we come to any direct discussion of this is in Book VII of the *Politics*, where Aristotle criticizes the Spartan constitution as promoting only those virtues "held to be more useful and more conducive to acquisition (*pleonektikos*)," namely the military ones.[30] As Aristotle's discussion of wealth has already made clear, however, acquisition can happen through peaceful as well as military means. We could therefore imagine an Aristotelian critique of a society organized around the goal of accumulation. Just as unlimited property acquisition can be seen as perverse relative to a natural, bounded form of acquisition, so a society organized around accumulation would appear as perverse relative to the natural order hinted at by Aristotle at the start of the *Nicomachean Ethics*, where he implicitly draws a picture of a whole economy tied together by reflection on what it is for individuals and collectives to flourish. Every human activity seeks some good, and some activities control the ends of other activities. Bridlemaking falls under horsemanship; horsemanship falls under generalship; and generalship falls under the political craft, which is the expertise "that sets out which of the expertises there needs to be in cities, and what sorts of expertises each group of people should learn, and up to what point," with its guiding end being "the human good" (*tanthrōpinon agathon*).[31] A healthy society of

---

[25] Ibid., 1257a6–14, 1257a32–41.

[26] Ibid., 1257b8–31; Aristotle uses the Midas legend as a figure for this thought.

[27] To the objection that Aristotle has ignored the possibility of pursuing the craft of accumulation in moderation, only up to a point, the answer seems to be that if the art of accumulation (*chrēmatistikē*) were pursued in moderation it would no longer be what it is but rather the art of property acquisition tethered to an understanding of the good life (*ktētikē*). The complication is that Aristotle believes that although some who engage in accumulation do so out of a failure to direct their efforts towards the good life, as opposed to mere life, others do so out of a misguided understanding of the good life as consisted in bodily pleasure. For these people, it seems that *chrēmatistikē* and *ktētikē* must amount to the same thing. See 1257b41–1258a11.

[28] See the openings of *Politics* I.4, I.8 and I.9 for these divisions.

[29] 1256b38.

[30] 1333b10–11; see also 1271a41–b10, 1324b5–11 and 1334a2–b5.

[31] Aristotle, *Nicomachean Ethics*, I.1–I.2.

this kind would presumably require individual bridlemakers to deliberate as craftsmen rather than as moneymakers, both for the reasons mentioned in our discussion of *The Republic* and also because (according to Aristotle, at least) moneymaking is zero-sum in the sense that one person's profit entails another's loss.[32] Unlike Plato, however, Aristotle does not seem to draw the moral: he treats moneymaking as an individual phenomenon rather than a social one.[33]

Aristotle does advocate imposing some restrictions on the moneymaking freedoms of rulers. Strikingly, he agrees with Plato that *"the most important thing* in every constitution is for it to have the laws and the management of other matters organized in such a way that it is impossible to make a profit (*kerdainein*) from holding office."[34] This statement seems to be grounded in a concern for stability, since he goes on to stress how important it is for oligarchs to abide by the principle in order to avoid generating resentment among the masses. Unlike Plato, however, Aristotle's preferred mechanism for ensuring that it is impossible to profit from office is a gentle combination of carrot and stick:

> To prevent public funds from being stolen, the transfer of the money [from officials leaving office to their successors] should take place in the presence of all citizens, and copies of the accounts should be deposited with each clan, company and tribe. And to ensure that people will hold office without seeking profit, there should be a law that assigns honours to reputable officials. (1309a10–14)

In this passage Aristotle seems to assume a fairly flat-footed understanding of what it might mean to profit from office: it has to involve the kind of activity that a thorough audit would catch, such as embezzlement.[35] But this amounts to a petty form of corruption in the grand scheme of things. After all, rulers could behave transparently and honestly while nevertheless acting to feather their own nests at the expense of the city as a whole: indeed, such behaviour is literally constitutive of oligarchy on Aristotle's account, and he recognizes that it threatens to divide the city into two warring classes.[36]

It was precisely in order to stop the degeneration of a united city led by an aristocracy into "two cities" under moneymaking oligarchs that Socrates instituted his ban on rulers holding private property. Aristotle is willing to countenance restrictions on private property that go some way toward meeting Socrates's objectives. He argues that some land ought to be communally owned in order to provide for public religious rituals and to support the common dining messes so that no citizen wants for sustenance;[37] that in the ideal society each citizen would have one lot near the border and another near the city, since such a distribution "accords with justice and equality" and "ensures greater unanimity (*homonoia*)";[38] that, in democracies, surplus revenues should be "distributed in lump sums to the poor" so that the latter can achieve long-term prosperity by acquiring land or starting a trade; that the rich should be taxed to sponsor the poor to attend the assembly;[39] and that in the ideal democracy there would be prohibitions on owning more than a certain amount of land, lending against more than

---

[32] For the (vaguely expressed) idea that moneymaking is zero-sum, see 1258b1–2.

[33] In response to very different social conditions, Marx does draw the moral in Volume One of *Capital*, drawing on Aristotle in order to diagnose capitalism as a malfunctioning social form that is organized around accumulation. See Thakkar, *Plato as Critical Theorist*, at pp. 293–306.

[34] 1308b32–34, my italics.

[35] On the theory and practice of accountability in classical Athens, see Matthew Landauer, *Dangerous Counsel: Accountability and Advice in Ancient Greece* (Chicago: University of Chicago Press, 2019).

[36] 1279a26–b10 and 1295b14–24.

[37] 1330a9–14, 1263a38–39.

[38] 1330a14–18; cf. Plato, *Laws*, 745c–d.

[39] 1320a36–1320b4.

a certain portion of each person's land, and even buying and selling certain allocations of land.[40]

What Aristotle is not willing to countenance, however, are Socrates's prohibitions on private property. He raises three distinct objections. First, he offers a tragedy-of-the-commons-style argument, observing that "what is held in common by the largest number of people receives the least care … [since] the thought that someone else is attending to it makes them neglect it the more."[41] Second, he argues that if the goal is to engender unity among the guardians, it might be counterproductive, given that "those who own and share communal property have far more disagreements than those whose property is separate."[42] Although these two objections are the most famous, they seem beside the point in obvious ways. Socrates does not argue that his prohibition on private property will lead guardians to take better care of their lodgings and other collective property. If anything, his point is that they shouldn't concern themselves much with this collective property but, rather, attend to the needs of their subjects, whom they think of as "as free friends" (547b–c). And if the guardians do not care much about the property that they hold in common as a class, viewing themselves as wealthy in a more important sense (521a) and despising ordinary pleasures relative to those deriving from contemplation (581d–e), it seems unlikely that they will spend much time disagreeing over its use. Finally, Aristotle nowhere addresses Socrates's underlying argument for his prohibitions, namely that they are necessary in order to prevent the guardians becoming moneymakers (and hence oligarchs rather than aristocrats, in Aristotle's terms).

Ultimately, Aristotle's opposition to Platonic communism is best grounded in the third objection that he raises, which is that personal possessions are necessary for the good life. "It is evident that nature itself gives such property [as is necessary for self-reproduction] to all living things," writes Aristotle in Book I.[43] Nature sees to it that newborn animals come into the world with access to what they need to survive, and likewise "we must suppose in the case of fully developed things too that plants are for the sake of animals, and that the other animals are for the sake of human beings, domestic ones both for using and eating, and most but not all wild ones for food and other kinds of support, so that clothes and all the other tools may be got from them."[44] The art of property acquisition (*ktētikē*) is therefore the art of taking possession of what nature has already earmarked for our use: examples include hunting for wild animals and, shockingly, making war – "just war," as Aristotle calls it – against those naturally suited for slavery.[45] Aristotle's notion of natural property therefore encompasses whatever goods (*chrēmata*) are either necessary or useful to the city-state or

---

[40] 1319a6–19. It is unclear how exactly these provisions relate to Aristotle's praise in IV.11 for the "middle constitu-
        tion" in which there is a strong middle class, since there he seems to view the distribution of property as
        exogenous to lawgiving and statesmanship: "[I]t is the height of *good luck*," he says, "if those who are governing
        own a middle or adequate amount of property" (1295b39–1296a, my italics).
[41] Aristotle, *Politics*, trans. C. D. C. Reeve, 1261b34–37; cf. 1263a27–29.
[42] 1263b24–26. At 1263a9–20 Aristotle appears to say that conflict arises both from questions of how to distribute the
        benefits and burdens associated with common ownership and from excessive dependence on others more
        generally.
[43] 1256b8–9.
[44] 1256b15–20.
[45] 1256b20–26. As Fred D. Miller Jr. points out, Book I's account of slavery is therefore premised on an argument,
        partly implicit, justifying the existence of property as a collection of tools that are necessary parts of the household,
        where the household exists by nature. See Fred D. Miller Jr, "Property Rights in Aristotle," in Richard Kraut and
        Steven Skultety (ed.), *Aristotle's Politics: Critical Essays* (Lanham, MD: Rowman & Littlefield, 2005),
        pp. 126–128. This argument depends on combining passages in I.2, I.4 and I.8.

household – where "necessary" seems to mean "necessary for self-reproduction" and "useful" seems to mean "useful for human flourishing."[46]

Clearly, Socrates has no interest in denying the guardians whatever goods are necessary for daily self-reproduction: even if they are not allowed to own anything, they do receive payment in the form of sustenance and shelter (465d-e). Aristotle's claim against Plato has to be that Socrates denies the guardians the goods that are useful for human flourishing. This isn't obvious: once again, even if they are not allowed to own anything, the guardians are clearly supposed to have untrammelled access to whatever is required for leading the philosophical life that Socrates regards as blessed. The key claim is therefore that in the case of some goods, mere access is not sufficient for the good life. And this is in fact what Aristotle suggests in the third of his objections to Socrates's proposals in Book II of the *Politics*. He makes two separate arguments in this connection. The first is that personal property makes possible the pleasure that comes when one is able to "regard a thing as one's own" and the pleasure that comes from being able to help out "one's friends, guests, or companions" and to do them favours. The second is that personal property makes it possible to exercise the virtue of generosity, which consists precisely in "the use made of property."[47] This second argument is then pursued further in Book VII, where Aristotle argues that in an ideal society every citizen would have private property. His reasoning can be reconstructed as follows: the lawgiver should promote the happiness of the polis; a polis can only be happy if all of its citizens are happy; virtuous activity is constitutive of happiness (whether partly or fully); and personal possessions are necessary for virtuous activity.[48]

In the end, then, the debate between Plato and Aristotle on private property comes down to two questions. The first is whether private property is necessary for the good life. From a narrowly textual point of view, the Platonic position seems stronger on this question. Even if Aristotle is right that owning something "makes an enormous difference" to the pleasure that we get from it, it is not clear that human flourishing is impossible in the absence of such pleasures. Likewise, even if Aristotle is right that private ownership makes possible certain exercises of the virtue of generosity, it is not clear that generosity requires private ownership.[49] The second question is whether it is possible to allow the ruling class to own private property without thereby permitting them to use their power to feather their own nests. Here again Aristotle's position seems weak. He claims that the best arrangement would be "for property to be private and its use communal" throughout society.[50] In response to the obvious question concerning how the city can ensure that individuals make their private property available for common use, Aristotle merely states that it is "the legislator's special task to see that people are so disposed."[51] Institutional solutions such as mandating forfeiture for anyone who fails to permit their property to be used by others would presumably be rejected

---

[46] 1256b26–30.

[47] 1263a40–b14.

[48] Adapting the reconstruction in Miller, pp. 135–136. See 1329a17–26 and 1323b40–1324a21.

[49] It seems to me (a) that one can be generous with the provisions one receives from the common stock, e.g. by sharing one's meal with someone who is hungrier, and (b) that one's actions can be generous independently of any use of property, such as when we spend time with someone we know to be lonely. To the response that this is not what Aristotle means by generosity, the obvious question is, why not? See Terence Irwin, "Aristotle's Defense of Private Property," in David Keyt and Fred Miller, eds., *A Companion to Aristotle's Politics* (Oxford: Blackwell, 1991), pp. 222–224.

[50] 1330a1–2.

[51] 1263a39–41. Presumably he would give the same answer in response to the question of whether the common use element of his system would not generate disagreements that parallel those he expects to occur among those who own things in common.

by Aristotle on the grounds that the virtue of generosity requires that actions be voluntary.[52] Something similar goes for Aristotle's response to the possibility of material inequality destabilizing the polis. Although he recognizes that "equalizing the property of citizens is among the things that helps prevent faction," he rejects Phaleas of Chalcedon's proposal to do just that in favour of asking legislators to focus on education so that "naturally decent people are disposed not to want to be acquisitive (*pleonektein*), and that base ones cannot be."[53] This hands-off approach would enable noble individuals to voluntarily imitate the Tarentines, "who retain the goodwill of the multitude by giving communal use of their property to the poor."[54] Given that he criticizes moneymaking as a way of life, recognizes the need to ensure that rulers look out for the common good, and acknowledges the destabilizing effects of material inequality, Aristotle's emphasis on enabling elites to exercise voluntary generosity seems either naïve or ideological. After all, it was precisely as a safeguard against the failure of education that Plato's Socrates suggested his ban on private property for the rulers. In a certain sense, then, it seems that Aristotle was actually more utopian than Plato.

3.6 CONCLUSION

Transposing this discussion to the contemporary context is no simple matter. Socrates's proposals regarding private property do not seem to amount to a program of public ownership in anything like the modern sense of the "nationalization" of certain industries and services, in that they are focused on communal living arrangements for the rulers rather than economic and social functions more generally. And although Socrates does seem to call for some kind of centralized control of economic life, with philosopher-rulers assigning people to jobs and supervising their work, such control would surely look very different in the context of the ancient Greek polis than in today's nation states with their professionalized civil services. That said, the debate between Plato and Aristotle over private ownership does seem to offer important resources for thinking through contemporary proposals concerning public ownership.

Socrates's prohibition on private property for the guardians of Kallipolis is grounded in three fundamental propositions: that it is vital for each citizen to work toward the common good rather than aiming at personal profit; that institutions can shape individuals' choices in order to make this more likely; and that the most important work in the city is that of the guardians. Abstracting from the particular context of Kallipolis, and hence from the distinctive role given to guardians, we can see that from a Platonic perspective it is vital to create institutions that insulate workplace deliberations from the logic of moneymaking. Even in the case where individuals have entered into a given profession for the purpose of making money, the decisions they make within the profession should be governed by professional objectives alone. In our own world, we might think about this in terms of the importance of generating a certain kind of culture or ethos within an institution, and in the end that might lead us to think about ownership structures. In brief, the thought process might run as follows.[55]

---

[52] See Mayhew, "Aristotle on Property," at pp. 819–820.

[53] 1267b7–9.

[54] 1320b9–11. Aristotle also says that it is unjust for the poor to redistribute the property of the rich. His argument is not that the rich have rights that would thereby be violated, but rather that such actions would destroy the polis (by causing civil strife) and justice cannot be something capable of destroying the polis. It follows that if redistribution did not destroy the polis, e.g. because the rich agreed to it, it would not be unjust. See 1281a15–22.

[55] For a fuller treatment, see "Moneymakers and Craftsmen: A Platonic Approach to Privatization" (*supra* note 8), at pp. 748–750.

Workplace deliberations do not take place in a vacuum; they typically spring from a workplace culture that makes certain assumptions and practices seem natural. But the culture of a workplace does not arise in a vacuum either. It is the product, at least in part, of institutional architecture that shapes patterns of behaviour. A crucial element of this architecture consists in the mechanisms by which individuals are assessed and held accountable for their work. If these mechanisms incentivize craftsmanship as opposed to moneymaking, then ultimately that will feed down into individual deliberations. But, the argument would go, accountability mechanisms themselves do not exist in a vacuum. They are typically the product, at least in part, of ownership structures. In a private company, for example, standards of success tend to centre on contribution to financial profit. In a public service, by contrast, standards of success tend to be centred on contribution to the common good. If this is right, then it would follow that one reason for favouring public ownership would be to ensure that workers in a given sector deliberate as craftsman rather than moneymakers, that is, with the common good rather than financial profit in mind.

Following Aristotle, we can see that this reason is by no means definitive. First, private ownership might bring benefits of its own. Aristotle speaks of distinctive pleasures and opportunities for virtuous action, but we might also think of Hegelian recognition and republican freedom. Second, public ownership can itself lead to suboptimal results. Aristotle alerts us to perverse incentives that can arise through diffusion of responsibility, but we might also point to managerial inefficiency and bureaucratic rent-seeking. Third, private corporations can in principle organize themselves around the goal of public service. As we have seen, Aristotle thinks this can be achieved through education so that private actors are virtuous enough to use their resources for the common good – the modern analogue might be an emphasis on teaching business ethics in MBA programs. But Aristotle also recommends some institutional safeguards – such as accountability audits, redistribution from rich to poor, and restrictions on property transfers – whose tameness seems contingent. In our own world, we might think that the nonprofit corporate structure can generate fairly stringent accountability audits whereby officers have to demonstrate that they have not been acting in their private interest; that fiduciary law can likewise mandate officers to respect certain duties of loyalty and care towards their institutions; and that an aggressive framework of progressive taxation of income and wealth would dramatically reduce incentives for moneymaking behaviour in any case.[56] Insofar as these measures are in place, it might be that the goal of facilitating craftsmanship rather than moneymaking can be achieved without incurring the costs that can come with public ownership.[57]

The great merit of Plato's discussion is his recognition that it is more important to ensure craftsmanship in some cases than in others: those who are in charge of regulating, governing and educating society as a whole must be especially insulated from the logic of moneymaking. For even if we grant that an ethos of craftsmanship can be generated in the private sector, the institutional mechanisms that might support such an ethos – such as accountability audits, fiduciary law and highly progressive taxation – are themselves dependent on the existence of a state whose officials act for the common good rather than their own private interest. This suggests that privatization must stop somewhere: if the tax inspectors were privatized, for instance, who would hold them accountable? But this focus on the special

---

[56]   With regard to this last suggestion, see Joseph Carens, *Equality, Moral Incentives, and the Market: An Essay in Utopian Politico-Economic Theory* (Chicago: University of Chicago Press, 1981).

[57]   This is not to say, of course, that there are no additional benefits of public ownership – such as democratic control and legitimation – that might tip the balance in the other direction.

responsibilities of the state also opens up a line of reasoning that points beyond Plato and Aristotle. For if we assume a liberal framework for managing the tensions inherent in a modern pluralistic society, we might question whether an ethos of craftsmanship is sufficient to guarantee deliberation in terms of the common good, at least where matters of justice are concerned. After all, nonprofits are constitutionally permitted to rely on sectarian reasoning rather than being forced, as a condition of their legitimacy, to justify their actions in terms of "public reasons." However objectionable it might be for prisons, credit agencies and paramilitary groups to be run by profit-seeking corporations, it might be even worse for them to be run by the Catholic Church.

4

Privatizing Criminal Punishment: What Is at Stake?

Malcolm Thorburn

What, if anything, is lost when we privatize criminal punishment? The literature responding to this question is already vast and growing. But it would be a mistake to understand it as forming a single, coherent line of inquiry. Writers on this topic have raised concerns of at least three different sorts. Concerns of the first sort are specific to a particular legal order, suggesting that some legal doctrine in that jurisdiction prohibits the privatization of one sort of criminal punishment or another. In the United States, for instance, much of the literature in this vein has focused on specific constitutional and administrative law doctrines, as well as specific legislative obstacles to the privatization of criminal punishment.[1] There have been similar scholarly movements in many other countries, as well.

There is a second literature on privatization that has more universal ambitions. These writings argue that if we privatize criminal punishment, we will necessarily run afoul of many of our broader normative commitments. Some argue that private punishment will be costlier than the public alternative,[2] that it is more liable to corruption,[3] that private punishment is more likely to be harsher,[4] and more likely to be arbitrarily imposed.[5] These are vitally important concerns – any development that is likely to lead to waste, corruption, arbitrariness and the mistreatment of prisoners is deserving of condemnation for that reason – but they are all versions of objections one could raise against the privatization of almost anything. There is nothing about them that is particular to the practice of criminal punishment.

---

[1] The literature on this is voluminous. One example is Paul R. Verkeuil, *Outsourcing Sovereignty: Why Privatization of Government Functions Threatens Democracy and What We Can Do about It* (New York: Cambridge University Press, 2007), p. 105ff, where he cites due process in the fifth and fourteenth amendments, and the appointments clause of Article II of the United States Constitution, p. 122ff where he points out the limits inherent in the Subdelegation Act as grounds to object to privatization of prisons (and other public functions).

[2] Much of the literature on efficiency has been supportive of privatization. But see Alex Friedmann, "Apples-to-Fish: Public and Private Prison Cost Comparisons," *Fordham Urban Law Journal* 42 (2014): 503–568.

[3] Ahmed A. White, "Rule of Law and the Limits of Sovereignty: The Private Prison in Jurisprudential Perspective," *American Criminal Law Review* 38 (2001): 111–146, p. 141, arguing that "the confused juridical structure of the contemporary private prison is intrinsically connected to endemic corruption."

[4] Sharon Dolovitch, "State Punishment and Private Prisons," *Duke Law Journal* 55 (2005): 437–546, arguing that penal parsimony and a bar on inhumane treatment of prisoners is related to the public provision of punishment.

[5] Warren Ratliff, "The Due Process Failure of America's Prison Privatization Statutes," *Seton Hall Legislative Journal* 21 (1997): 371–424.

In this entry, my focus is on a third, quite distinctive set of concerns about private punishment that arise from the very idea of criminal punishment itself. In one way or another, proponents of this third sort of argument against the privatization of criminal punishment all insist that in addition to more general normative concerns, there is also another set of worries arising from a normativity internal to the idea of criminal punishment itself. When we try to make moral sense of the practice, they insist, we must take account of something beyond its good and bad consequences. Criminal punishment is a practice with its own internal structure (what we may call its constitutive principle) that both limits what sorts of practices count as instances of criminal punishment and that is tightly linked to the standards that make for more and less successful versions of the practice (what we may call its regulative principle).[6] When we pay careful attention to criminal punishment's constitutive principle, we find that it is an intrinsically relational idea that requires the party administering it to bear the right sort of relation to the one suffering it.

To make sense of these arguments about the idea of punishment and the normative constraints they impose on its privatization, we shall turn our focus toward an old and familiar idea: the nature of criminal punishment. In reexamining this old idea once more, I hope not only to advance the debates about the privatization of punishment; my aim is also to use the light cast by the discussion of privatization to illuminate these old debates about the nature of punishment, as well.

* * *

This entry is guided by the thought that there is something in the very nature of criminal punishment that makes it unsuitable for privatization. I consider four different conceptions of the "very nature of criminal punishment" that have dominated the criminal law theory debate over the past half-century. For ease of reference, I will refer to them as: (1) the "necessary burdens" account; (2) the "ordinary language" account; (3) the "legal moralist" account; and (4) the "public authority" account. The "necessary burdens" account is the philosophical embrace of nominalism about the nature of punishment. It understands criminal punishment as nothing more than the coercion necessary to enforce justified rules, subject to other important values such as distributive fairness, the minimization of suffering, social equality, and the like. Although it is a normative account of criminal punishment, all of the norms at work in the account are general ones that stand outside the idea of punishment itself.

The other three accounts of punishment all attempt to draw out something from the very idea of criminal punishment that may operate as a constraint on its privatization. The "ordinary language" account is a largely descriptive, rather than normative position; it relies on standard English usage to tell us what we mean when we talk of criminal punishment. On that account, it is simply a fact about the English language that the standard case of criminal punishment is state administered, and private punishment is (at best) a defective, non-standard case. This is a straightforward argument, but not a very convincing one. In contrast to the explicitly deflationary "ordinary language" position, the other two philosophical accounts of criminal punishment are clearly normative ones. The "legal moralist" view

---

[6]   The distinction between constitutive and regulative principles has a long philosophical pedigree. More recently, it has been invoked in understanding social reality (John Searle, *The Construction of Social Reality* (New York: Free Press, 1997) and in understanding a variety of legal phenomena (Arthur Ripstein, "Reclaiming Proportionality," *Journal of Applied Philosophy* 34 (2017): 1–18, and Jacob Weinrib, *Dimensions of Dignity* (Cambridge: Cambridge University Press, 2016).

conceives of criminal punishment more narrowly as a response to a certain kind of moral wrongdoing, either as retribution or as the communication of deserved censure. The "public authority" account is the one that I have championed elsewhere: it conceives of criminal punishment as an essential incident of the relationship of justified public authority between state and subject. In both the "legal moralist" and the "public authority" accounts, the understanding of criminal punishment turns crucially on the nature of the relationship between punisher and punished. I argue in what follows that the "public authority" account provides the more compelling understanding of criminal punishment.

The discussion in this entry is not complete until we have turned our minds more carefully to what it is we mean when we talk of "privatizing" anything, including criminal punishment. The state is not a separate entity, distinct from the natural persons who carry out its wishes. Accordingly, the distinction between public acts and private ones is always about how we characterize the acts of natural persons. Where acts are undertaken by public officials in their official capacity, their acts are clearly of a public nature. And when they are undertaken by private actors without any instruction or consultation with public officials, they are clearly private. The grey areas in between, however – where public officials engage private corporations to carry out specific tasks according to quite detailed contractual arrangements, for example – are much more difficult to categorize. Sorting out a final answer to that question is best left for another day once we have sorted out our initial worries about the rights and wrongs of private punishment more generally.

4.1 WHAT IS CRIMINAL PUNISHMENT? THREE FALSE STARTS

4.1.1 *The "Necessary Burdens" Account*

Many of those who advocate privatizing criminal punishment seem to assume a nominalist understanding of the thing they seek to privatize.[7] For them, there is no unifying and justifying idea of criminal punishment to guide our thinking; criminal punishment, on this understanding, is just a collection of burdens that courts happen to impose as criminal sentences in the given jurisdiction: prison time, house arrest, fines, and so on. To impose criminal punishment, on this view, is just to carry out the tasks that courts have ordered. The only interesting question, then, is who is best placed to carry out those tasks in a way that meets whatever broad normative criteria we apply to any policy initiative: that they be cheap, reliable, fairly administered, and so on. It would seem bizarre to most advocates of the privatization of criminal punishment to suggest that the very nature of criminal punishment itself might be a source of normative commitments that could constrain our privatization initiatives.

This nominalist understanding of criminal punishment is not only asserted by privatization advocates who are ignorant of debates of criminal law theory, however. It is also at the heart of the "necessary burdens" account of criminal punishment that is now one of the dominant positions in contemporary criminal law theory. This account takes its inspiration from Jeremy Bentham's nominalism about punishment. On this view, as Bentham famously insisted, "all punishment in itself is evil."[8] Since it is in itself evil, the only justification available for its

---

7 See, e.g., Alexander Volokh, "A Tale of Two Systems: Cost, Quality, and Accountability in Private Prisons," *Harvard Law Review* 115 (2002): 1838–1963, p. 1868.

8 "An Introduction to the Principles of Morals and Legislation" in Jeremy Bentham, *A Fragment of Government with an Introduction to the Principles of Morals and Legislation* ed. W. Harrison (Oxford: Basil Blackwell, 1960), p. 281.

continued existence must lie outside itself. That is why Vincent Chiao, one of the leading "necessary burdens" proponents, insists that the justification of punishment must lie (if anywhere) only in its role as a "generically coercive rule-enforcement mechanism."[9] Criminal punishment, on this account, can be redeemed only by showing it to be an effective instrument in the pursuit of our broader general normative commitments. Chiao calls this view a "public law" account of criminal law and punishment,[10] but this is only an accurate moniker if we take "public law" to consist in the regulation of a set of tasks each without any internal normativity, governed only by general principles external to each practice.[11] I refer to it instead as a "necessary burdens" account because of its core insistence that punishment is in itself merely a burden (or evil), and that any justification for it must turn on its role as a necessary means to some valuable extrinsic end.

The "necessary burdens" account is dominated by two questions: what rules should we enforce? And what measures may we take to enforce them? Under the "necessary burdens" account, the question of what rules we should enforce is wide open to debate by reference to norms of general application. One might favour the prohibition of morally wrongful conduct, that which causes social harm, or some more complicated policy formula that determines what forms of conduct should be coercively enforced. Advocates of the "necessary burdens" account would say the same when considering the question of how to distribute the coercive enforcement measures in response to rule violations. Some say we should try to reduce aggregate harm in our choice of punishments; others suggest that distributive considerations such as fair opportunity ought to play an important part; yet others insist that a panoply of distributive considerations, perhaps involving considerations of political egalitarianism, should inform the distribution of punishment. Indeed, once we throw off any concern for the internal normativity of punishment, the door is open to consider punishment in the light of almost any substantive political theory. So it is no surprise to see advocates of the "necessary burdens" account who are Rawlsian liberals, advocates of the Sen-Nussbaum "capabilities approach," followers of Philip Pettit's republicanism, and many more camps besides.[12] Notwithstanding their differences in how they would answer these questions, however, advocates of the "necessary burdens" account share a common approach: normative debates about criminal punishment are nothing more than the application of general norms to a new set of particulars. There are no norms special to the very idea of criminal punishment to give us pause.

These "necessary burdens" accounts of criminal punishment are unable to provide any principled argument against privatization that is specific to criminal punishment and the reason for this is quite plain to see. Because they treat criminal punishment as a generic form of state coercion, the only arguments they can help themselves to are ... generic arguments

---

[9] I take this helpful expression from Vincent Chiao, "What Is the Criminal Law For?," *Law and Philosophy* 35 (2016): 137–163, p. 139.

[10] Vincent Chiao, *Criminal Law in the Age of the Administrative State* (Oxford: Oxford University Press, 2018). The first three chapters of the book are entitled "criminal law as public law."

[11] By contrast, I have used the expression "criminal law as public law" to very different effect. See Malcolm Thorburn, "Criminal Law as Public Law," in *Philosophical Foundations of Criminal Law* (Oxford: Oxford University Press, 2011). I discuss this vision of criminal law at length as the "public authority" account, in Section 4.2.

[12] Much of the literature in the recent "political turn" in criminal law theory is of this sort. Erin Kelly, *The Limits of Blame: Rethinking Punishment and Responsibility* (Cambridge, MA: Harvard University Press, 2018); Ekow Yankah, "Republican Responsibility in Criminal Law," *Criminal Law and Philosophy* 9 (2015): 457–475; Chiao, *Criminal Law in the Age of the Administrative State*; Corey Brettschneider, "The Rights of the Guilty: Punishment and Political Legitimacy," *Political Theory* 35 (2007): 175–199, and many others.

about state coercion. In recent years, a number of very thoughtful political philosophers have turned their attention to the privatization of the state's coercive powers generally, and of its discretionary coercive powers in particular.[13] Several of them have come up with powerful arguments of general application against the privatization of such coercive powers generally, irrespective of whether they are in the context of criminal punishment. These are important, indeed essential arguments in the modern debate about privatization more generally. But they are not specific to the idea of criminal punishment.

4.1.2 *Ordinary Language*

In the mid-twentieth century, philosophical arguments against the privatization of criminal punishment, such as they were, were dominated by the leading philosophical movement of the time: "ordinary language" philosophy. According to that way of thinking, the best way to understand what words truly mean is simply to look carefully at how they are used by competent speakers of the language. Or, as Ludwig Wittgenstein put the point, "the meaning of a word is its use in the language."[14] Following that way of thinking, a number of philosophers tried to determine the paradigm case of punishment – what punishment "really means" – through the analysis of ordinary linguistic use. According to the ordinary language philosopher Anthony Flew, "direct action by an aggrieved person with no pretensions to special authority is not properly called punishment, but revenge."[15] Whenever we speak of punishment administered by someone other than a legally constituted authority for an offence against that legal system, the argument goes, we usually adjust our language to indicate that it is a non-standard case, specifying that it is a case of *private* punishment. That adjustment of our language is an indication that private punishment is, at best, a non-standard case.

One way of illustrating this intuition about the state-centred nature of criminal punishment is to consider what we would make of the conduct of private persons responding to wrongdoing. If we see people who have done something wrong, we might try to register our disapproval of their conduct in some way. We might choose not to talk to them, or not to do business with them, or not to engage in social relations with them. But when we act in this way – treating wrongdoers less favourably than others as a response to their wrongs – this isn't something that we would naturally refer to as "punishment," and the main reason is that it is not administered by the state. When third parties choose not to associate with someone because he committed a crime, we would usually refer to that as a "collateral consequence" of criminal wrongdoing, rather than as punishment for it.[16] And once we categorize these responses as "collateral consequences" rather than as punishment, a number of other important things follow. Many of the usual norms that apply to punishment – most importantly, the prohibition against being punished more than once for the same wrong – do not seem to apply to collateral consequences. We think of it as a great injustice to be punished

---

[13] See, e.g., Chiara Cordelli on the privatization of discretionary coercion in Chapter 1 of this volume. See also Arthur Ripstein, *Force and Freedom: Kant's Legal and Political Philosophy* (Cambridge, MA: Harvard University Press, 2009), on the same point.

[14] Ludwig Wittgenstein, *Philosophical Investigations*, trans. G. E. M. Anscombe (Oxford: Basil Blackwell, 2002), p.18.

[15] Anthony Flew, "The Justification of Punishment," *Philosophy* 29 (1954): 291–307, p. 294.

[16] Although many collateral consequences are themselves state-administered (such as deportation or felon disenfranchisement), the majority of such consequences arise from private action. Thus, those with a criminal conviction will find it more difficult to find work, housing, etc.

twice for the same offence;[17] by contrast, we don't usually think of the fact that others have shunned someone as any reason for us not to do so.[18]

In *Punishment and Responsibility*, H. L. A. Hart invokes this "ordinary language" understanding of punishment, agreeing with Flew and others that private punishment is a nonstandard case. But Hart's principal reason for invoking the distinction is in order to reject the larger way of thinking about punishment of which it is a part. Whatever our standard use of the word "punishment" might be, he insists, the meaning of the word alone cannot be enough to tell us how to design our institutions. The hard questions – which are also the interesting questions – are normative ones. At best, claims about standard word usage can only tell us that certain responses to wrongdoing don't count as what we refer to as "punishment" around here. But that should not be the interest of criminal law theorists. The hard and interesting question that should be their focus, Hart insists, is: "Why do we prefer [punishment] to other forms of social hygiene which we might employ ...? ... No account of punishment," Hart insists, "can afford to dismiss this question with a definition."[19]

Hart must be right on this. For when we ask whether there is something wrong with private punishment, we are not merely looking for someone to clarify the concepts we are already using. Instead, we are looking for someone to provide a normative argument to explain why it would be *a bad thing* to privatize criminal punishment. But instead of showing that it would be a *bad* thing for private actors to administer punishment, the ordinary language argument about the meaning of the word "punishment" – what Hart calls the "definitional stop" – shows only that it would be a *different* thing. The ordinary language argument ignores the question that most concerns advocates of privatization: whether it would be a *better* or a *worse* thing (whatever we might call that thing) if we replaced publicly administered punishment with a privately administered alternative.

A number of philosophers have pursued Hart's line of thinking, suggesting that we may profitably sidestep the conceptual argument simply by giving our alternative practice another name ("funishment," "telishment" and many others have been proposed).[20] By doing so, we can ignore the definitional worry and focus instead on the normative concerns that they take to be more important. The question that is of real interest is not whether we are using the expression "criminal punishment" in its standard sense when it is administered by private actors, but whether there is something lost, morally speaking, when we move from state-administered criminal punishment to an otherwise similar practice administered by private actors – whatever we might call it. The last two accounts of criminal punishment – the "legal moralist" and the "public authority" accounts – can be seen as two answers to this challenge. Each of them provides arguments for why criminal punishment (rather than telishment, funishment, etc.) is a morally significant practice and why it must have a certain structure in order to live up to its own ambitions.

---

[17] This is the core care of "double jeopardy," prohibited by most human rights documents such as the fifth amendment to the constitution of the United States and s. 11(h) of the Canadian Charter of Rights and Freedoms.

[18] We might think that someone has suffered enough if they have been universally shunned for a wrong of middling significance. But that is an argument more about disproportionate responses to wrongdoing, rather than the principle against double punishment.

[19] H. L. A Hart, *Punishment and Responsibility: Essays in the Philosophy of Law* (Oxford: Oxford University Press, 2008), p. 6.

[20] John Rawls coined the expression "telishment" for the conviction of and infliction of suffering on the innocent where it would promote the general welfare ("Two Concepts of Rules," *Philosophical Review* 64 (1955): 3–32, p. 11); Saul Smilansky uses the expression "funishment" to describe the practice of holding wrongdoers securely incarcerated in places of pleasure even though they lack moral responsibility for their acts ("Hard Determinism and Punishment: A Practical 'Reductio,'" *Law and Philosophy* 30 (2011): 353–367).

4.1.3 *Legal Moralism*

Hart's move away from the "definitional stop" has given rise to a very different sort of normative argument about criminal punishment that has dominated the criminal law theory scene for several decades. Rather than suggesting that the meaning of punishment is simply a product of the ways in which we use our language, moralists insist that punishment is a morally justifiable practice insofar as it is a morally appropriate response to moral wrongdoing. In saying this, they provide what they take to be answers to the two great challenges Hart posed: (1) what is the positive moral value of the practice of criminal punishment; and (2) what constraints does that idea of the moral point of punishment impose upon its administration? In answer to the first question, moralists of almost every stripe insist that there is something in the structure of moral life that demands some sort of answer to wrongdoing. In answer to the second question, many moralists insist that since the idea of criminal punishment is tied up with the idea of morally appropriate responses to wrongdoing, we must pay careful attention to the relational nature of moral wrongdoing and responses to it.

Interestingly, however, most moralists set out their account of criminal punishment in a way that severs any special connection between it and the state.[21] For some, this is because they simply do not share Hart's view about the correct use of the expression "criminal punishment." John Gardner sets out his disagreement with Hart in the following terms:

> I for one do not share Hart's conceptual intuition here, or even see where it gets its appeal. Friends, colleagues, spouses, siblings, and business partners regularly punish each other for actual or supposed wrongs that are not legal wrongs. They typically do so by withdrawing favours or cooperation, but there are many other possible ways, some of which are capable of involving the infliction of grave suffering.[22]

On the moralist understanding of punishment, it is not ordinary language that defines the meaning of punishment. It is, instead, a certain understanding of the structure of moral life, the nature of wrongdoing and the morally appropriate responses one might take to instances of wrongdoing. On this account, criminal punishment, to qualify as such, must be a response to *wrongdoing* of some sort and it must respond to it *as* wrongdoing. Oftentimes, advocates of this moralized understanding of criminal punishment point to the law's talk of culpability, wrongdoing, etc. and insist that such language is justifiable only if criminal offenders truly are *wrongdoers*. Thus, they insist that criminal prohibitions, to be legitimate, ought always to target genuine moral wrongdoing. Otherwise, they risk illegitimately tarring individuals who have committed no moral wrong as moral wrongdoers.

Moralists agree on the sort of thing to which criminal punishment should be a response – moral wrongdoing – but they differ widely on what they think the appropriate response to wrongdoing might be. Some moralists insist that retributive punishment is the appropriate response. Michael Moore, for one, insists that the imposition of hard treatment on moral wrongdoers is an intrinsic good.[23] Although the occurrence of moral wrongdoing may not always be in itself sufficient reason to impose criminal punishment, it is always a necessary

---

[21] John Gardner explicitly endorses a moralist conception of criminal wrongdoing while disowning any special connection between punishment and the state. See John Gardner, "Justification under Authority," *Canadian Journal of Law and Jurisprudence* 23 (2010): 71–98; John Gardner, "Criminals in Uniform" in R. A. Duff et al., eds, *The Constitution of the Criminal Law* (Oxford: Oxford University Press, 2013), p. 97.

[22] Gardner, "Introduction" to *Punishment and Responsibility* (*supra* note 19), at xlix.

[23] Michael S. Moore, *Placing Blame: A General Theory of the Criminal Law* (Oxford: Oxford University Press, 2010).

condition.[24] That is, even though we might sometimes have strong countervailing reasons not to punish wrongdoers in some cases, we would only ever have good reason to punish someone where they had, in fact, committed a wrong. Things get a bit more complicated when we also recognize that there are relevant reasons both for and against punishment that concern matters other than the offender's wrongdoing. Nevertheless, the fact of moral wrongdoing by the offender must at the very least be among the reasons why he or she is being punished. Once again, John Gardner puts the position most eloquently: "The criminal law (even when its responses are non-punitive) habitually wreaks such havoc in people's lives, and its punitive side is such an extraordinary abomination, that it patently needs all the justificatory help it can get . . . ."[25]

There is another group of moralists about the criminal law who go even further than Gardner: they deny that moral wrongdoing provides even *pro tanto* reasons to impose punishment on wrongdoers. For them, the fact of moral wrongdoing gives us strong reasons to communicate moral censure of the wrongdoer, but it does not give us any reason at all to impose coercive hard treatment. Any hard treatment that accompanies the message of censure, they insist, must by justified in some other way. Victor Tadros proposes an account of punishment uniting deterrence with a moral duty – the duty to protect others against wrongdoing by suffering punishment.[26] Andrew Ashworth and Andreas von Hirsch insist that any hard treatment that follows from criminal wrongdoing must be justified on deterrence or other grounds.[27] The core of what we usually think of as punishment – the imposition of coercive hard treatment – is reduced to a sort of prudential supplement.[28]

There is nothing distinctive in the nature of punishment under either Moore's retributivist account or Ashworth and von Hirsch's communicative theory that shows why it could not, in principle, be administered by private agencies. In large part, this is because their moralist accounts are focused on the offender and his or her desert: if the offender committed a moral wrong, then they are deserving of some sort of response (either retributive hard treatment for Moore or the communication of censure for Ashworth). That desert is a free-standing matter; it does not require that the response come from any actor in particular who bears a particular relationship to the wrongdoer.

There is at least one moralist account of criminal punishment, however, that challenges the exclusive focus on the offender and his or her desert: this is the account championed by Alon Harel.[29] Harel echoes Antony Duff's moralist communicative theory of punishment. Following Duff, he argues that criminal punishment "is an expressive or a communicative act of condemnation." Also like Duff, he insists that what distinguishes criminal punishment

[24] Ibid., at p. 739ff.
[25] John Gardner, "Crime: In Proportion and in Perspective," in *Offences and Defences* (Oxford: Oxford University Press, 2008), pp. 214–215.
[26] Victor Tadros, *The Ends of Harm: The Moral Foundations of Criminal Law* (Oxford: Oxford University Press, 2011).
[27] Andrew Ashworth and Andreas von Hirsch, *Proportionate Sentencing: Exploring the Principles* (Oxford/New York: Oxford University Press, 2005), p. 21ff.
[28] Ibid., at p. 23: "The explanation why, in punishment, hard treatment (instead of purely symbolic means) is used as the vehicle for censuring is that this provides him with a further reason, a prudential one, for resisting the temptation."
[29] Alon Harel, *Why Law Matters* (Oxford: Oxford University Press, 2014), pp. 96–97. See also Alon Harel and Avihay Dorfman, "The Case Against Privatization," *Philosophy and Public Affairs* 41 (2013): 67–102; Alon Harel, "Why Only the State May Inflict Criminal Sanctions: The Case Against Privately Inflicted Sanctions," *Legal Theory* 14 (2008): 113–133; Alon Harel, "Outsourcing Violence?," *Law & Ethics of Human Rights* 5 (2011): 396–413; Alon Harel, "Why Only the State May Inflict Criminal Sanctions: The Arguments from Moral Burdens," *Cardozo Law Review* 28 (2006): 2629–2659.

from other forms of response to wrongdoing is the fact that it is *public* in some important respect. Crimes, according to both Duff and Harel, are a proper subset of moral wrongs – *public* moral wrong – that violate the basic terms of our political association. Since crimes are wrongs against the terms of our political association, Harel argues, the condemnatory response must come from an agent who can speak in the name of the polity as a whole. Harel explains: "[P]ublic condemnation is possible in the first place only if it emanates from the appropriate agent. [It] is ineffective unless done by an agent ... whose judgments concerning the appropriateness of the behaviour is [*sic*] worthy of attention or respect. Otherwise, an infliction of 'a sanction' amounts to an act of violence ...."[30]

Harel's suggestion is very promising. Unlike most other moralists, he does not merely focus on the individual desert of criminal wrongdoers. Instead, he insists that criminal punishment is a fundamentally relational idea connecting the offender to the state. What makes punishment the valuable thing it is, on Harel's account, is (in part) that it occurs within a broader *relationship* between state and subject. Criminal punishment is a valuable practice insofar as it is a morally appropriate reaction *by the polity* to a wrong by a citizen against the polity's defining norms. In drawing our attention to the internal normativity of criminal punishment and to its intrinsically relational nature, Harel has moved the debate forward in a very important way. What is puzzling about Harel's account, however, is the idea of criminal punishment he has inherited from Antony Duff. It is an idea of morally appropriate responses to wrongdoing that are made up only of judgments, without any actual coercive sanctions attached. This is problematic for Harel because, as he himself notes, criminal punishment is not merely the communication of a judgment; it is essentially coercive – something that Harel calls "an act of violence." Unfortunately, Harel's account explains why the state has a special standing to communicate judgments of condemnation to criminal wrongdoers, but it has nothing to say about the state's standing to inflict the "acts of violence" that are the stock-in-trade of criminal punishment.

Alon Harel's account of why only the state may punish is a major advance in thinking about privatization. Unlike most of his moralist forebears, he makes clear that it is not merely the offender's individual desert that is necessary to justifying criminal punishment but also the *relationship* between offender and punisher. This, in itself, is a path-breaking advance. But he leaves unexplained how the imposition of criminal punishment – involving the imposition of coercive hard treatment and not just communicating a message of censure – is connected to the state in the same way. To find an account that seeks to connect the practice of coercive punishment to the fundamentally relational nature of criminal punishment, we will have to turn to the "public authority" account.

4.2 A FRESH START: THE PUBLIC AUTHORITY APPROACH

I have argued elsewhere[31] for an account of criminal punishment that is tied closely to the relationship of practical authority that obtains between state and subject.[32] In that account,

---

[30] Harel, *Why Law Matters*, p. 97.

[31] See my "Punishment and Public Authority" in Antje du Bois-Pedain, Magnus Ulväng and Petter Asp, eds., *Criminal Law and the Authority of the State* (Oxford: Bloomsbury, 2017); "Criminal Law as Public Law" in R. A. Duff and Stuart P. Green, eds., *Philosophical Foundations of Criminal Law* (Oxford: Oxford University Press, 2010), pp. 21–43. Much of this section is adapted from my "Criminal Punishment and the Right to Rule," *University of Toronto Law Journal* 70 (2019): 44–63.

[32] Alan Brudner (*Punishment and Freedom: A Liberal Theory of Punishment* (Oxford: Oxford University Press, 2009)) is another writer who connects punishment with the state's authority, but in a rather different way.

punishment – not just the communication of censure but the imposition of *coercive hard treatment* – is an essential part of the justified relationship of practical authority that obtains here. The basic thought is this: states not only claim to have the effective *power* to secure their subjects' compliance with their will; they also claim a *right* to rule their subjects. This idea of the state's right to rule involves at least three important normative claims.

First, it involves the claim that states exercise normative powers over their subjects, not just the effective power to coerce. As Hart made famous half a century ago in his critique of John Austin's theory of legal obligation,[33] an important difference between a state in charge of a legal system and a gunman who can oblige people to do his bidding is that whereas the gunman claims only effective power over others, a state in a functioning legal system claims a normative power to make law, thereby changing the legal rights, obligations, powers and liabilities of its subjects. A gunman may only oblige through his effective power, but a state may create obligations through the exercise of normative powers. To make sense of this distinction, Hart introduced the idea of "the internal point of view" on the normativity of law.[34] Although one might be able to predict when the law will impose coercion on us without considering its normative claims, there are many aspects of law (especially the operation of legal powers) that cannot be properly understood without taking seriously its normative claims "from the inside."

Second, in modern times – in the common law world, since the time when "the King's peace" was extended across England and across different subject matters[35] – states claim the *exclusive* right to determine the content of the law and, through it, the legal rights and obligations, powers and liabilities of their subjects.[36] They do not merely claim to be *a* source of legal norms within the jurisdiction; they claim the exercise of that normative power over the content of the law as a matter of exclusive right[37] – the right to rule – against all comers.[38] Two clarifications of this claim are in order.[39] First, states are not the only parties to exercise normative powers: private actors do so all the time by making contracts, making wills, welcoming visitors to their homes, engaging in consensual sex, and much more. But all these exercises of normative powers are legally binding because they are recognized by the state and its laws. Second, we should also clarify that even though states claim the exclusive right to set down legal norms, this is fully consistent with the possibility of people violating

---

[33] H. L. A. Hart, *The Concept of Law*, 3rd ed. (Oxford: Oxford University Press, 2012), p. 58: "Rex will not only in fact specify what is to be done but will have the *right* to do this; and . . . it will generally be accepted that it is *right* to obey him. Rex will in fact be a legislator with the *authority* to legislate, i.e. to introduce new standards of behaviour into the life of the group . . . ."

[34] Hart, *The Concept of Law*, p. 89.

[35] Sir Frederick Pollock, "The King's Peace in the Middle Ages," *Harvard Law Review* 13 (1900): 177–189.

[36] Of course, within the framework set out by the state, individuals may have powers to change the legal rights and duties of others. But those powers exercised by individuals are always subject to the superior power of the state to alter their normative powers.

[37] I will leave aside for now questions of how international law and the application of foreign law might be integrated into this picture. But the various accounts in public international law of how these are to be received within a jurisdiction point to the fact that this issue is one to which that field is alive – and the starting assumption of state monopoly on law-making within the jurisdiction is operative in the field.

[38] This is the crucial grain of truth in Max Weber's claim that "a state is that human community which (successfully) lays claim to the monopoly of legitimate physical violence within a certain territory" ("Politics as a Vocation," at pp. 310–311, in *Weber: Political Writings*, eds. Peter Lassman and Ronald Speirs (Cambridge: Cambridge University Press, 1994)). On one level, this claim is clearly false: private actors may sometimes legitimately use physical violence (for example, in self-defence). The deeper truth here is that the state successfully claims the exclusive right to determine the conditions under which any persons may act coercively within the territory.

[39] Thank you to the editors for pressing me to clarify my position on this point.

those norms from time to time. All that is required is that conformity be sufficiently prevalent that it remains plausible for us to say that the state's laws operate as norms within the jurisdiction.

If we wish to identify the political authority within a particular jurisdiction (say, to distinguish the British Parliament's claim of authority to make law from the claim of a madman standing on a soapbox at Speakers' Corner), we cannot rely only on Hart's idea of the "internal point of view." The "internal point of view" is helpful in making sense of the normative relationship between ruler and subject (the relationship of power and liability), but it does not help us to understand the relationship between the genuine ruler (who claims the exclusive right to be the one to make laws in the jurisdiction) and the many would-be rulers in a given jurisdiction (who are under a duty not to usurp the state's law-making power). For this, we need the idea of exclusive legal rights and their necessary connection to the availability of legal remedies.

The third normative claim at work in the state's exclusive right to rule is the possibility of some remedy to address violations of that right. According to the old equitable maxim, "ubi jus ibi remedium [est]"[40]: the very idea of a claim of right is that there must be available some remedy for the violation of that right. For a right is not just a matter of present fact, it is something to which we are *entitled* even when facts change. When we say that the state has the (exclusive) right to rule within the jurisdiction, we are interested in vindicating the claim that the state and *only* the state is entitled to make law within the jurisdiction. To make sense of the idea of the right to rule and its connection to a remedy for its violation, we need to make clear precisely what would constitute a violation of that right. As in private law, it is not usually enough to violate another's exclusive right to exercise a legal power merely to utter a verbal formula (such as "I hereby abolish all private property in Canada"). What is required is some recognizable effort actually to make it the case that one's decision changes legal relations in the world. This is precisely what we see in the case of intentional criminal conduct: a decision that legal relations should change in some way (that your property should become mine, say, or that your body should be open to my interference) and an attempt to make it the case that the world should conform to that decision. When we think of the state's right to rule as an exclusive right to make law within the jurisdiction in this way, it becomes clear that some sort of remedy must be available to vindicate that right in the face of its violation. What is required is a legal remedy that can vindicate the state's claim to be the exclusive holder of the right to rule in the jurisdiction.[41] Properly understood, I argue, criminal punishment is that remedy.[42] Criminal law and punishment, then, is not just another branch of the law with its own specialized subject matter and its own free-standing function;[43] it is, instead, an essential part

---

[40] Loosely: "wherever there is a right, there is a remedy." Lord Chief Justice Holt's judgment in *Ashby* v. *White* (1703) 14 St Tr 695, 92 ER 126, is usually cited as the classic statement of this maxim.

[41] And so it is not murders and assaults and thefts as such that are subject to criminal punishment but only those committed within the state's jurisdiction – *under the King's peace.* Even the most egregious wrongs, such as intentional killing, are no crime when committed in wartime simply because they were not committed under the King's peace. See my "Soldiers as Public Officials: A Moral Justification for Combatant Immunity," *Ratio Juris* 32 (2019): 395–414.

[42] This account of criminal law as the backstop of the law's authority sounds very unfamiliar to contemporary Anglo-American criminal law theory. But it was the received wisdom in nineteenth- and early-twentieth-century German criminal law theory. See Markus Dubber, *The Dual Penal State* (Oxford: Oxford University Press, 2019), pp. 18–19.

[43] Michael Moore famously described criminal law as a functional kind of this sort in Moore, *Placing Blame*, p. 19ff. But, as in many things, Moore was simply making explicit what a great many criminal law theorists of the time took for granted.

of the state's exclusive claim to practical authority over all within its territory.[44] The availability of criminal punishment for violations of the state's right to rule is a necessary part of that claim of practical authority.

The "public authority" account of criminal law and punishment takes a very different starting point from most of its rivals. The "necessary burdens" and "legal moralist" accounts alike assume that the key question in criminal law theory concerns a choice among the state's purposes. They ask: what should we *do* with the authority of the state? Ought we to minimize the incidence of harmful conduct through deterrence (and perhaps rehabilitation, incapacitation, etc.)? Or ought we to pursue the putatively intrinsic goods of retribution for moral wrongdoing or (more plausibly) calling wrongdoers to account? The "public authority" account, by contrast, insists that before we ask how to exercise the state's right to rule, we must first establish the conditions for the very *existence* of that right to rule. And when we look more closely, we find that criminal law and punishment are essential constituent elements of that right to rule. When we try to make sense of the institutions of criminal justice, our starting point, at least, should be to set out the necessary institutional arrangements for the state to claim a right to rule.[45]

The "public authority" account begins with a basic feature of modern legal orders: modern states claim a *right* to rule over their subjects. That is, they do not merely assert that they have more effective power than we do, so it would be prudent to do as we are told to avoid the coercive force of the state and its agents. Instead, they claim that they are legitimate practical authorities – that they have put in place a normative system concerned not merely with what its subjects *will* do (or will have or will decide) but with what they *are entitled to* do (or to have or to decide). Although the legal order that states put in place will, in fact, alter how we act in myriad ways (if it is an effective legal order at all), it does not do so merely by the direct threat of coercion – attaching threats of coercion to a series of commands. Instead, states in functioning legal systems guide our conduct indirectly, by putting in place a framework of rights and duties, powers and liabilities that, in turn, structure the coercive relations among their subjects. That means that we are not concerned here with the legal realist's "bad man" perspective on the state, concerned only with what *will* happen to us as a result of our conduct.[46] Instead, our focus is on the state's normative claim that it is entitled to change what it is that we are *entitled* to – our rights and duties, our powers and liabilities – merely by deciding to do so.[47] It is, in Hart's language, a claim that makes sense only from within the "internal point of view" on the legal system – the perspective of at least some participants in the practice of legal order who see the state as exercising a genuine law-making power and thereby giving rise to genuine rights, duties, powers and liabilities.[48] This is because the state's claim is one of right, rather than a merely descriptive claim of effective power: the state and only the state is *entitled* to exercise *normative* powers to change the basic rights and duties, powers and liabilities of subjects within the jurisdiction.

---

[44] Or, as Jean-Jacques Rousseau puts the same point, "criminal laws ... [are] at bottom ... less a specific kind of law than the sanction of all the others." *On the Social Contract* (Harmondsworth: Penguin Books, 2004), p. 99 (emphasis added).

[45] With emphasis on the expression "starting point." Once we have the basics of criminal law and punishment in place according to this account, we might have good reason to use those same institutions to carry out some of the valuable purposes proposed by other accounts as well. But it is essential to see that they are secondary uses of an institution the essential purpose of which is connected to its role in securing the state's right to rule.

[46] O. W. Holmes, "The Path of the Law," *Harvard Law Review* 10 (1910): 457–478.

[47] Andrew Halpin, "The Concept of a Legal Power," *Oxford Journal of Legal Studies* 16 (1996): 129–152.

[48] Hart, *The Concept of Law*, p. 89.

But the "public authority" account goes beyond Hart's insight. Of course, we cannot understand modern states' claims to have a right to rule unless we first recognize that their claim is being made from within the "internal point of view" where legal rights and duties, powers and liabilities are real and not mere tools for predicting when coercion may be imposed to force us to act in one way or another. But modern states' claim that they have a right to rule is a claim of exclusive right: it is the claim that the state – and *only* the state – has the power to make laws altering the rights, duties, powers and liabilities of those within its jurisdiction. (As we mentioned already, this exclusive right is consistent with the law's recognition of powers in private actors to make wills, contracts and the like. It is also consistent with the predictable fact that the law's norms will sometimes be violated.) Like many familiar claims of right, the right to rule is a claim to *exclusive* control over some particular set of something good against the world. We may speculate as to precisely why modern states claim the exclusive right to rule in this way. One explanation might be historical: over time, royal power grew, slowly but surely, to the point where the king claimed to be in a position not merely to adjudicate disputes between private parties but also to assert sole authority over the governing law. Another explanation might concern the state's claim to *justified* political authority. A common rule of law argument justifying the existence of state coercive power concerns its necessary role in setting in place a legal order in which we are not subject to the arbitrary will of any private persons. To put such a legal order in place, the state must necessarily claim an exclusive right to make laws for all its subjects. And so on. For now, though, we may simply note that the right to rule – the exclusive right to exercise normative powers to make laws setting out the rights and duties, powers and liabilities of subjects in its jurisdiction – is something claimed by all modern states.

The state's claim to have the exclusive right to rule is, of course, much more than a mere statement of fact or of moral right. The state's claim that it has the exclusive right to rule, like all claims of legal right, really concerns an institutional arrangement. For where we are concerned not simply with a state of affairs but with a matter of *legal entitlement*, we are concerned with a set of institutions that guarantee the existence of the right even in the face of specific violations of it. Contemporary republicans often refer to the role of institutions in showing how both freedom and slavery are constructed by legal institutions.[49] The wrongness of slavery, they point out, lies not merely in the fact of specific acts done to slaves by their owners. The deep, abiding wrong of chattel slavery – the wrong that persists irrespective of empirical conditions, no matter how kind or weak the owner might be – lies in the fact that legal institutions treat one person's mistreatment of another as incidents of his or her abiding legal *right* to do so.[50] The institutions that make slavery possible are not ones that actually inflict any particular harm onto slaves; rather, they make it a matter of legal rights that one person is subject to the absolute discretion of another in all things. More to the point, the institution of chattel slavery does all this by providing legal remedies designed to vindicate the slave-owner's claims of right: it is not merely that slaves do not have the effective power to

---

[49] Philip Pettit, *Republicanism: A Theory of Freedom and Government* (Oxford: Oxford University Press, 1997); Quentin Skinner, *Liberty before Liberalism* (Cambridge: Cambridge University Press, 1998). Both make essential use of the image of legal relationship of slavery as the central contrast to their conception of republican freedom, which is also an accomplishment of legal institutions.

[50] This is partly why it is so difficult to define "modern slavery" in contemporary legal instruments concerned with human trafficking. The concept of slavery is constructed through legal institutions. De facto slavery is a very different sort of entity. I discuss this issue in "Human Trafficking: Supplying the Market for Human Exploitation," in *What Is Wrong with Human Trafficking? Critical Perspectives on the Law*, eds. R. Haverkamp, E. Herlin-Karnell and C. Lernestedt (Oxford: Hart, 2019).

escape but that they shall be returned to the owners as a matter of legal right; it is not just a matter that slaves cannot resist the injustices done to them by their masters but that their masters are legally entitled to do so; and so on.

In these and other ways, legal institutions and legal remedies provide mechanisms through which legal rights are vindicated as the abiding normative structure governing our lives, notwithstanding the specific facts of our situation at the time. By returning a slave to their master *as a runaway*, we do not merely provide coercive power in support of the slave-owner; we also vindicate the slave-owner's claim of right over their slave: "You are being returned to my possession *because you belong to me.*" Or, to take a less objectionable private law example, where you take my property from me, the private law remedy of *vindicatio* requiring that you return it to me does not simply provide an incentive to encourage you to respect my property. Instead, the availability of a remedy to ensure that I may regain possession of my property is just part of what it means to have property rights in the thing in the first place. It is just what we mean when we say that we own a thing, that whatever anyone else might do to our property – take it, damage it, use it without our permission, etc. – it remains the case that it is we, and not they, who are entitled to decide the use to which it is put.[51] The point of private law remedies, then, is not merely to *support* claims of right by encouraging others to respect them; rather, the very idea of the claim of right itself is partly *constituted* by the availability of remedies for the violation of the right. Only where there are institutional mechanisms available for the vindication of a right can we say that the entitlement is legally meaningful.

Returning, now, to the state's claim to have a right to rule, we can see that its nature as a claim of right means that it is not merely a descriptive claim ("I have the effective power to make people do as I wish") or a free-standing moral claim ("it is morally right that others should act according to the rules I set down"). It is, instead, a distinctly *legal* claim, like the property-owner's claim to have the exclusive right to determine what shall happen to his property, that is partly constituted by a set of institutional arrangements – most importantly, a set of available remedies for any violations of that right. The question, then, is what sort of remedy might be appropriate to the vindication of the state's claim of right? In private law, the relationship of right to remedy is often fairly straightforward: where someone takes my property, he must return it; where he injures my property, he must provide me with the market cost of returning it to its prior state; and so on.[52] But not all cases are as straightforward as the return of a taken thing or damages for injury. One particularly pertinent example is the remedy for the unauthorized taking and profitable use of another's property.[53] In this sort of case, a defendant who takes it upon himself to take over another's property and make use of it as his own might not be liable for any of the usual sorts of remedies: he might have returned the property before the action began and he might not have caused any injury to the thing. Nevertheless, he has usurped the true owner's exclusive right to determine the uses to which his property may be put. In such a case, the appropriate private law remedy would be to treat the defendant's taking as though it were done at the plaintiff's behest. That is, if the defendant made a profit from the use of the thing, he must disgorge that profit to the plaintiff. Why would this be the appropriate remedy? Because by forcing the defendant to disgorge all

---

[51]   Larissa Katz, "Exclusion and Exclusivity in Property Law," *University of Toronto Law Journal* 58 (2008): 275–315.

[52]   I do not mean to minimize the complexity of fitting rights to remedies in private law. The debate on this issue is famously complex. See, for example, the decades-long discussion of the appropriate remedy for breach of contract following the publication of Lon L. Fuller and William R. Perdue, "The Reliance Interest in Contract Damages," *Yale Law Journal* 46 (1936): 52–96.

[53]   The case of *Olwell* v. *Nye and Nissen* 173 P.2d 652 is a classic example of this sort, discussed at length in E. Weinrib, "Restitutionary Damages as Corrective Justice," *Theoretical Inquiries in Law* 1 (2000): 1–37, p. 1.

profits, we would thereby treat the defendant's actions as consistent with the plaintiff's ongoing claim of exclusive right to determine the use to which his property may be put. No judicial remedy can make it so that the wrong never occurred; but the remedy can provide the institutional mechanism to vindicate the plaintiff's exclusive ownership right over the thing. Put another way, the central point of the remedy is not to bring about some new, desirable state of affairs; it is just a reassertion of the abiding normative salience of the plaintiff's claim of right.

I raise the somewhat recherché example of restitution remedies for private law wrongs because they share an important feature with criminal punishment under the "public authority" model. The state's exclusive right to rule, like the owner's exclusive right to determine the use of his property, may suffer a wrong even where there is no compensable injury or loss of property. The wrong in question is simply the wrong of *usurpation*. In the private law context, the point of the remedy is not to undo the harm done through a wrong; it is merely to follow through on the normative implications of a claim of right and vindicate the plaintiff's claim of exclusive ownership authority over the thing. (It is this focus on authority, rather than harm, that unites my account of criminal punishment with private law remedies – and puts both accounts at odds with standard harm-based accounts of each.)[54] In the criminal law context, we are concerned with something similar. Where someone takes it upon himself to act contrary to the demands of the state's laws because he is acting instead upon his own view of his rights and duties, powers and liabilities, he is directly challenging the state's claim to have the exclusive right to make the law around here. (Whether he flaunts his ability to make the rules or whether he tries to do it under cover of darkness, he challenges the state's exclusive right to rule, all the same. By acting with full *mens rea*, contrary to the law's demands, he has set himself up as sole arbiter of how the situation will be resolved, at odds with the state's claim to an exclusive right to rule.) Indeed, he is doing so in much the same way as the individual who takes another's property and uses it as he pleases (even though it causes no injury to the plaintiff's property). The nature of the wrong is simply that the criminal accused has attempted to usurp the state's role as sole law-maker in the jurisdiction. What, then, should be the appropriate remedy to vindicate the state's exclusive right to rule? From the point of the right to rule, we are not concerned with the particular goods we may bring about through a particular remedy. Rather, our concern is with what sort of remedy is required by the very idea of a state's exclusive right to rule. And the answer, it seems, is that there must be some remedy that re-asserts the normative implications of the state's claim of right, to show that the state's right to rule survives its violation by the offender.

The appropriate remedy through which to vindicate the state's right to rule is available only where the state threatens punishment for disobedience. For where the state only sets down rules of conduct (but does not also threaten punishment for their violation), it claims the normative *power* to change our legal rights and duties, but it does not yet do so *as a matter of exclusive right*. Where the state is confronted with individuals who show contempt for its authority by acting on their own view of their rights and duties, rather than on the legal relations set down in the state's laws, there is no remedy available through which we may show the state's right to rule to survive these attempts at usurpation. Where the state adds a threat of punishment for the violation of its rules, however, a new remedy is made available. Now, even in cases where offenders succeed in acting on their own view of things rather than the state's assertion of rights and duties, we have a further mechanism by which to vindicate the state's

---

[54] Thanks again to the editors for pressing me to clarify my position here.

right to rule. For now, it is open to the state to seek a conviction and administer punishment to anyone who has attempted to supplant its laws with their own. And when this is available, we are able to vindicate the state's right to rule as a claim of exclusive right. The state's claim of an exclusive right to rule has been transformed from an empty claim to an institutional reality.

4.3 CONCLUSION

There are arguments of at least three different sorts against the privatization of criminal punishment. In this entry, we have ignored the arguments of legal doctrine specific to particular jurisdictions and the broad arguments of political or moral theory that might apply to the case of punishment. We have focused only on those arguments that arise from an understanding of the nature of punishment itself. We found that, among these, the public authority account, unlike its alternatives, is able to show why the very idea of criminal punishment requires that it be administered by the state, and not by private actors. Unlike the "necessary burdens" account, it insists that there is a constitutive principle that animates criminal punishment. Unlike the "ordinary language" approach, it insists that the idea of criminal punishment is an important normative ideal, and not merely a matter of the meaning of words. And unlike Alon Harel's legal moralist account, it is able to show why criminal punishment is not only a normative practice that obtains between state and offender but also a practice that is necessarily coercive in nature. In this short treatment of the "public authority" account, we have not come close to establishing the soundness of its conclusions. To do so would require a much larger canvas upon which to sketch a theory of law and the state and the place of criminal punishment within them. Nevertheless, we have shown why it is that the "public authority" account, unlike its rivals, is at least *aiming* to draw a connection between the idea of criminal punishment and the requirement that it be publicly administered.

5

Justice and the Market

Assaf Sharon and Shai Agmon

Do not pervert justice; do not show partiality to the poor or favoritism to the great.

—Leviticus

If I didn't have some money, I would have no chance at all.

—O. J. Simpson

5.1 INTRODUCTION

Some things should not be for sale. One's body or one's children, to take the most glaring examples. But, arguably, more trivial things like the family heirloom or a citizen's vote should also not be bought and sold. Theorists differ both about the membership of this class (what things should not be for sale) and about the grounds for membership in it (why they should not be bought and sold). Yet there is virtual unanimity that it is not an empty set. Human beings, if nothing else, should not be sold on the market, not even by themselves (selling oneself into slavery).

In recent years, an expansive literature has been produced analyzing the moral limits of markets, focusing on the question just presented: what kinds of goods should not be bought and sold on the market.[1] The salient goods under discussion are goods related to the body, and particularly to its sexual functions, like organs, surrogacy, and sex itself. Another kind of good that occupies theorists is goods with certain social significance, such as standing in line, naming one's children, or blood donations.

One good is conspicuously absent from this burgeoning literature: legal representation. This absence is particularly glaring in light of the wide agreement that other legal functions, like prosecution and the judiciary, should not be commodified. Even staunch defenders of the market do not suggest extending it to the judicial system. In fact, they regard adjudication

---

[1] See, e.g., Elizabeth Anderson, *Value in Ethics and Economics* (Cambridge, MA: Harvard University Press, 1993); Michael J. Sandel, *What Money Can't Buy: The Moral Limits of Markets* (New York: Farrar, Straus and Giroux, 2012); Debra Satz, *Why Some Things Should Not Be for Sale: The Moral Limits of Markets* (New York: Oxford University Press, 2010); Michael Walzer, *Spheres of Justice: A Defense of Pluralism and Equality* (New York: Basic Books, 1983).

as the quintessential role of the state. A uniform law, Hayek claimed, "can only exist if it's enforced by government."[2] Milton Friedman wrote: "The basic rules of government in a free society" are "to provide a means whereby we can modify the rules, to mediate differences among us on the meaning of the rules, and to enforce compliance with the rules on the part of those few who would otherwise not play the game."[3] Nozick similarly argued that operating a legal system is one of the two necessary roles of the minimal state, since "only the state can enforce a judgment against the will of one of the parties ... [T]he parties who wish their claims put into effect will have no recourse permitted by the state's legal system other than to use that very legal system."[4] Even Ayn Rand did not hesitate to assign responsibility over the legal system to the state: "The proper functions of a government [are] ... the police, to protect men from criminals – the armed services, to protect men from foreign invaders – the law courts, to settle disputes among men according to objective laws."[5]

In fact, an independent state-funded legal system, which applies the law impartially, consistently, and equally is fundamental in their eyes not only for a free society but also for the market itself. As Hayek put it: "The relation between the character of the legal order and the functioning of the market system received comparatively little study ... [H]ow well the market will function depends on the character of the particular rules."[6] All of these market-enthusiasts apparently presuppose that the legal system is governed by a rationale which is markedly different from the market's. It must be complementary to the market, not part of it. They apparently share the Lockean observation that the fundamental role of the state, which cannot be reliably supplied by spontaneous coordination of the kind that exists in the market, is impartial adjudication according to set laws and fair procedures. At the same time, even the most extensive critiques of the market do not mention legal representation among the goods which ought not be commodified.[7]

This discrepancy is all the more striking in light of the unsettling implications of the legal market. As O. J. Simpson's trial was drawing to a close, legal scholar John Langbein wrote:

> Money is the defining element of our modern American criminal-justice system. If Simpson walks, as most lawyers think he will, what will have decided the outcome is not that O.J. is black, but that he is rich. He can afford to buy what F. Lee Bailey, Alan Dershowitz, Johnnie Cochran and the others have to sell: the consultants on jury packing, the obliging experts who will contradict the state's overpowering DNA and related evidence, and the defense lawyer's bag of tricks for sowing doubts, casting aspersions and coaching witnesses. By contrast, if you are not a person of means, if you cannot afford to engage the elite defense-lawyer industry—and that means most of us—you will be cast into a different system, in which

[2] Friedrich A. Hayek, interview by Tom Hazlett, UCLA Oral History Program and the Pacific Academy of Advanced Studies, November 12, 1978, http://hayek.ufm.edu/index.php/Tom_Hazlett.

[3] See Milton Friedman, *Capitalism and Freedom* (Chicago: University of Chicago Press, 2002), p. 25.

[4] Robert Nozick, *Anarchy, State, and Utopia* (New York: Basic Books, 1974), pp. 14–15.

[5] Ayn Rand, "The Objectivist Ethics," in *The Virtue of Selfishness* 34 (1964), p. 131.

[6] Friedrich Hayek, *The Constitution of Liberty* (Chicago: University of Chicago Press, 1960), p. 229.

[7] Michael Walzer is the only one, as far as we know, who makes a passing reference to the issue: "Criminal Justice is nor for sale. It is not that judges and juries cannot be bribed, but that the services of defense attorneys are a matter of communal provision – a necessary form of welfare given the adversary system" (see Walzer, *Spheres of Justice*, at pp. 100–101). Anderson mentions only the ethical concern: "Lawyers may act merely as hired guns for their clients, harassing those against whom their clients have no genuine legal case" (see Anderson, *Value in Ethics and Economics*, at p. 148). To the best of our knowledge, only Shai Agmon and Alan Wertheimer directly engaged with the subject, but not as a "limits of markets" issue. See Shai Agmon, "Undercutting Justice – Why Legal Representation Should Not Be Allocated by the Market," *Politics, Philosophy & Economics* 20 (2021): 99–123, doi:10.1177/1470594X20951886; Alan Wertheimer, "The Equalization of Legal Resources," *Philosophy & Public Affairs* 17 (1988): 303–322.

the financial advantages of the state will overpower you and leave you effectively at the mercy of prosecutorial whim.[8]

Though this concern is shared by many, its cause is rarely properly identified and, consequently, not adequately addressed. In this chapter we argue that the privatization of legal representation undercuts legal justice, at least in adversarial legal systems. To avoid its pernicious effects, the market of legal representation must be severely restricted, if not eliminated altogether. Reflecting on this argument, we propose a novel method for setting limits on markets, one that diverges from the current "moral limits of markets" arguments.

We begin in Section 5.2 with an intuitive picture of privatized legal representation's harmful effects. In Section 5.3 we examine the standard accounts of the moral limits of markets and show that they do not adequately capture these problems. Consistent with these accounts, legal theorists have focused on formulating ethical constraints for lawyers and on ensuring access to justice for everyone. Their importance notwithstanding, these ideas, we argue, aim to mitigate some of the legal market's pernicious effects, but do not treat their source. In Section 5.4 we analyze the rationale of adversarial adjudication and argue that the constitutive role of parity in legal adversity is inconsistent with the laissez-faire distribution of legal representation. Section 5.5 explains how this argument differs from 'moral limits of markets' arguments. Finally, in Section 5.6 we look at possible objections.

5.2 "DO EQUAL RIGHT TO THE POOR AND TO THE RICH"[9]

In December 2013, the local paper in Fort Worth Texas reminded its readers of a decade-old story:

> The night of Feb. 13, 2004, Eric Bradlee Miller coaxed $10 out of his grandfather, telling him he was going to rent a movie. Miller, then 16, instead bought vodka, got drunk and stole a pickup at a convenience store. With the lights turned off, he sped away. Soon after, a 19-year-old husband and father, Philip Andress, was dead, killed when Miller crashed the stolen pickup into his vehicle near River Oaks. Miller, whose blood-alcohol level was 0.11 – over the legal limit of 0.08 – was arrested on charges of murder and failure to stop and render aid. Because Miller was a juvenile, his case went before state District Judge Jean Boyd.

Miller was convicted of murder. At sentencing, Judge Boyd told Miller, whose father had abandoned him and his drug-addict mother: "The court is aware you had a sad childhood, but you are fortunate to have a grandfather who is so committed and loves you . . . I hope you will take advantage of the services [offered by the Texas Youth Commission] and turn your life around." She sentenced Miller to twenty years in jail.

What prompted the recounting of the forgotten accident was another car accident by another drunk Fort Worth teenager:

> On the night of June 15, another 16-year-old, Ethan Couch, got drunk and was speeding down a rural road in south Tarrant County when he crashed his pickup into an accident scene, setting off a chain of collisions that killed four people and injured 12. Couch, who had a blood alcohol level of 0.24 – more than three times the legal limit – also went before Boyd. He admitted responsibility – the adult equivalent of pleading guilty – to four counts of intoxication manslaughter and two counts of intoxication assault causing serious bodily injury. On

---

[8] John H. Langbein, "Money Talks, Clients Walk," *Newsweek*, April 17, 1995, https://law.yale.edu/system/files/documents/pdf/Faculty/Langbein_Money_Talks_Clients_Walk.pdf.

[9] From "Oath of Justices and Judges," 28 US Code §453.

Dec. 10, Boyd sentenced Couch, described in testimony as a spoiled teen from a dysfunctional but wealthy family, to 10 years' probation and intensive therapy.[10]

Presumably many factors are responsible for the different outcomes in these cases. But the financial disparity is glaring. Miller was represented by a court-appointed attorney since his grandfather "didn't have the $10,000 to $15,000 to retain legal help." Couch's affluent parents hired two leading local lawyers, who with the help of an expert convinced the court that he had suffered from the medically unrecognized condition "affluenza" – "a mental state of irresponsible and reckless behavior brought on by wealth." Reflecting on the two cases, one friend of the Millers remarked: "It was the same only different because Couch's family has all that money."[11]

This extreme example illustrates a familiar reality: wealth disparities entail inequalities in legal resources. This applies both to the professional level of lawyers one can hire and to the resources they can recruit: experts, private investigators, lab analyses, etc.[12] The implications of these disparities are hard to quantify, but even harder to deny. "The rich enjoy superior legal representation and therefore much better prospects for success in court than the poor," Glenn Greenwald, a litigator turned journalist, notes as if stating the obvious.[13] Unless a momentous yet undetected market failure plagues legal representation, the disparity in price is itself a credible indication of the difference between the representation available to the affluent and that to the indigent.[14]

This disparity itself is presumably unfair, especially in view of its consequences. Focusing on capital cases one scholar summarizes:

> Experts with whom I've spoken have generally agreed that the most important variable in determining whether a capital defendant will be sentenced to death is not the details of the crime, the locale in which the case will be tried or the race of the defendant but rather the

---

[10] Mitch Mitchell, "Fatal Crash in 2004 Drew Different Sentence from Tarrant Judge," *Star-Telegram*, December 21, 2013, www.star-telegram.com/news/local/community/fort-worth/article3840394.html.

[11] Laura Bult, "Family of Texas Man Who Got 20 Years for Fatal Drunk Driving Crash by Same Judge Who Sentenced Ethan Couch Outraged 'Affluenza' Teen Is on the Lam," *New York Daily News*, December 19, 2015.

[12] Marc Galanter, "Why the 'Haves' Come out Ahead: Speculations on the Limits of Legal Change," *Law & Society Review* 9 (1974): 95–160, pp. 97–98, 114; Gillian K. Hadfield, "The Price of the Law: How the Market for Lawyers Distorts the Justice System," *Michigan Law Review* 98 (2000): 953–1006, pp. 963–999; Robert A. Kagan, *Adversarial Legalism: The American Way of Law* (Cambridge, MA: Harvard University Press, 2009), p. 95. In a free market of legal representation, money naturally influences lawyers' career choices. According to an American Bar Association report from 2014, most graduates from elite universities are employed by top private firms, which seldom represent the poor. Few graduates of these schools work in organizations providing legal services for the poor. Consequently, the services of the most qualified lawyers are normally beyond the reach not only of the poor but of most people who lack excessive wealth. Sometimes even basic representation is not attainable. A Legal Services Corporation (LSC) report from 2009 shows that the proportion of self-representation in court among low-income citizens is disproportionally high. See Legal Service Corporation, *Documenting the Justice Gap in America: The Current Unmet Civil Legal Needs of Low-Income Americans* (2009).

[13] Glenn Greenwald, *With Liberty and Justice for Some: How the Law Is Used to Destroy Equality and Protect the Powerful* (New York: Metropolitan Books, 2011), p. 1.

[14] In fact, the usual pressures of the market are arguably amplified in the case of legal representation. Given the complexity of the law and the adjudication processes, clients are often unable to assess the quality of the service they receive. Because the stakes are frequently high, clients are willing to spend as much as they can, which gives rise to high – often excessive – fees that only a few can afford. Consequently, the quality of legal resources one can deploy is largely determined by financial ability. See Hadfield, "The Price of the Law," at pp. 963–999; Richard Moorhead, "Filthy Lucre: Lawyers' Fees and Lawyers' Ethics: What Is Wrong with Informed Consent?," *Legal Studies* 31 (2011): 345–371, pp. 349–350.

competence of the defendant's attorney in trying death cases. This opinion is shared by death penalty scholars as well.[15]

A survey conducted among federal judges, for example, indicates that decisions are significantly influenced by disparities in the quality of legal representation.[16] In 1967, a commission on law enforcement and criminal justice, appointed by President Johnson, concluded: "The offender at the end of the road in prison is likely to be a member of the lowest social and economic groups in the country."[17] More recently, Ruth Bader Ginzburg testified alarmingly: "I have yet to see a death case, among the dozens coming to the Supreme Court on eve of execution petitions, in which the defendant was well represented at trial."[18]

Disparities between the rich and the poor are even more pronounced in cases that end in plea bargain. Innocent defendants are more likely to plead guilty and receive harsher plea deals if they can't access good counsel, and public defenders lacking sufficient resources are more likely to recommend taking plea bargains. This is not a minor point considering that more than 90 percent of criminal prosecutions end with a guilty plea.[19]

These anecdotes and assertions attest to the wide awareness among theorists and practitioners of the unsettling effects of economic inequality within the legal system. But what do they entail? Intuitively, they suggest that the market in legal representation ought to be limited. But such a conclusion does not seem to be supported by the standard arguments for limiting markets.

5.3 THE LIMITS OF THE MORAL LIMITS ARGUMENTS

Arguments for limiting or prohibiting markets can be classified into three types. Criticism of some markets appeals to fundamental values like dignity and autonomy, which are claimed to rule out the commercial exchange of goods and services related (in some significant way) to these values. Thus, things that are taken to be part of one's person, like organs, labor, or sex, may not be bought and sold since rights to them are inalienable.[20] This is taken by many to follow from human dignity or individual autonomy.[21] The market of legal representation does not seem to have such implications, so we shall set such considerations to one side.

---

[15] Kagan, *Adversarial Legalism*, at p. 95.
[16] Richard A. Posner and Albert H. Yoon, "What Judges Think on the Quality of Legal Representation," *Stanford Law Review* 63 (2011): 317–349, pp. 343–346. See also James M. Anderson and Paul Heaton, "How Much Difference Does the Lawyer Make: The Effect of Defense Counsel on Murder Case Outcomes," *Yale Law Journal* 122 (2012): 154–217, pp. 188–197.
   The appointment of public defenders hardly mitigates the problem. Public defenders are paid less than private lawyers and have a greater workload and fewer resources to expend on each case. Consequently, they devote less time to preparation and consultation with their clients and tend to submit to plea bargains more readily. Their achievements are in accordance. Jeffrey Reiman quoted a study showing that public defenders got 11.3 percent of cases dropped, while 48 percent of cases litigated by private attorneys are dismissed. See Jeffrey Reiman and Paul Leighton, *The Rich Get Richer and the Poor Get Prison: Ideology, Class, and Criminal Justice* (New York: Routledge, 2015), p. 127. See also Rhode, *Access to Justice*, pp. 11–12.
[17] Quoted in Reiman and Leighton, *The Rich get Richer*, p. 109.
[18] Ruth Bader Ginsburg, "In Pursuit of the Public Good: Access to Justice in the United States," *Washington University Journal of Law & Policy* 7 (2001): 1–15, p. 10.
[19] US Sentencing Commission, "Overview of Federal Criminal Cases Fiscal Year 2017" (Washington, DC: United States Sentencing Commission, 2018), p. 5; Mark Motivans, "Federal Justice Statistics, 2014 – Statistical Tables," *Bureau of Justice Statistics*, March 2017, p. 17, www.bjs.gov/content/pub/pdf/fjs14st.pdf.
[20] Stuart M. Brown, "Inalienable Rights," *Philosophical Review* 64 (1955): 192–211; William K. Frankena, "Natural and Inalienable Rights," *Philosophical Review* 64 (1955): 212–232.
[21] As coined in Kant's famous dictum, some things have a dignity, not a market price (see Immanuel Kant, *Groundwork of the Metaphysics of Morals*, ed. and translated by Mary J. Gregor (Cambridge: Cambridge University Press, 1998), p. 42. On the connection to autonomy, see Anderson, *Value in Ethics and Economics*,

Another type of argument against commodification appeals to the market's corrupting effects. Michael Walzer famously argued that the distribution of some goods by the market corrupts their social meanings. For example, Walzer discussed a provision in the Enrollment and Conscription Act of 1863, an Act that established the first military draft in American history. According to the provision, any man whose name was drawn in a lottery, if he was willing and able to pay $300, was exempt from military service. This, according to Walzer, "seemed to abolish the *public thing* and turn military service (even when the republic was at stake!) into private transaction."[22]

Other authors describe the corruptive effect of markets in terms of crowding out certain norms. Sandel claimed: "Friendship and the social practices that sustain it are constituted by certain norms, attitudes, and virtues. Commodifying the practices displaces these norms – sympathy, generosity, thoughtfulness, attentiveness – and replaces them with market values."[23] According to Elizabeth Anderson, commercial surrogacy, for example, "substitutes market norms for some of the norms of parental love."[24]

Whether it is put in terms of social meanings that get distorted or in terms of norms which get displaced, the corrupting effects of commodification seem relevant to the case of legal representation. Charles Dickens's comment in *Bleak House* that "the one great principle of the English law is to make business for itself" is provocative only against the background assumption that legal processes ought not to be shaped by the profit motive. This thought, we take it, is quite intuitive, yet it is hard to determine what follows from it. Specifically, it does not seem to entail that there is something wrong with distributing legal representation by a market mechanism as such. It pertains to lawyers' motivations in providing their services, not to disparities in distribution. The idea that lawyers ought to be committed to norms and values other than maximizing profits leads to the idea that they should be held to certain ethical standards and even restrictions, not to the conclusion that the market of legal representation should be limited, let alone eliminated.

Although grounding the moral limits of markets in their corrupting effects captures something important (at least in some cases), it has severe limitations. For one thing, as Debra Satz stressed, the social meanings of many goods and institutions are rarely agreed.[25] A good example is labor, which for Marx was the quintessential good whose meaning was corrupted by the market. Others had a different view of labor and its meaning. Moreover, as Elizabeth Anderson wrote: "Shared understandings, if they exist at all, are often riddled with contradictions and confusions, are established in relations of domination that silence the perspectives of some members of society, and fail to meet the pragmatic demands, such as the preservation of social order, that people ask of them."[26]

Furthermore, the fact that market norms do not properly express the ways we value a particular good does not entail that buying and selling that good corrupts its value. Satz illustrates this convincingly: "A religious person can buy a bible without believing that its price expresses her view about its worth."[27] And, as illustrated by the Dickensian example with

at p. 142. For a discussion of self-respect, see Cecile Fabre, *Whose Body Is It Anyway?* (Oxford: Oxford University Press), pp. 28–29.

[22] Walzer, *Spheres of Justice*, at p. 99.

[23] Sandel, *What Money Can't Buy*, at p. 107.

[24] Elizabeth S. Anderson, "Is Women's Labor a Commodity?," *Philosophy & Public Affairs* 19 (1990): 71–92, p. 76.

[25] Satz, *Why Some Things Should Not Be for Sale*, at p. 81.

[26] Anderson, *Value in Ethics and Economics*, p. 143.

[27] Ibid., p. 82. This point is expanded in Jason Brennan and Peter Jaworski, *Markets without Limits: Moral Virtues and Commercial Interests* (New York: Routledge, 2015), p. 52ff.

respect to legal representation, even if value is corrupted, it does not follow that market exchange ought to be banned or severely restricted.

The third type of argument against commodification appeals to inequality. Like the arguments from corruption, these arguments also come in two standard forms. One focuses on inequality in status or, to put it more accurately, takes inequality in the distribution of certain goods as undermining the social status of the disadvantaged party. Debra Satz, for example, argues that "lurking behind many, if not all, noxious markets are problems relating to the *standing* of the parties before, during, and after the process of exchange [italics in original]."[28] Having a basic share of certain goods, like education and physical security, is, according to Satz, "a prerequisite for full inclusion in society."[29] The problem with the market in such cases is that it does not guarantee the necessary distribution and hence undermines individuals' equal standing as citizens.

It is not automatically obvious how this kind of consideration applies to the case of legal representation.[30] It might be suggested that subjecting legal representation to the market threatens to leave the less affluent with inadequate access to the legal system, thus undermining their standing as equal citizens enjoying equal protection. This line of argument seems cogent, but it does not support banning or limiting the market in legal services. The opposition it poses between goods and their distribution by a market is contingent – it happens to be the case that under normal conditions, etc., markets do not guarantee the socially desirable distribution of these goods. And it suggests a threshold notion of adequacy. Thus, once the minimum necessary for ensuring people's standing has been secured for everyone, distributing the rest of the good by the market is, on these grounds, not objectionable. Assuming that high-school education is necessary for full inclusion in society, for example, there is no problem with a market for university education. Or suppose the basic level of physical security has been provided; there is no reason to oppose a market in private security services. Similarly, applying this reasoning to legal representation would entail that basic representation must be made accessible to everyone. Rather than an argument against the legal market, it is an argument for its supplementation by nonmarket mechanisms.

The other argument from inequality sees unequal distribution itself as a problem of fairness:

> If the only advantages of affluence were the ability to buy yachts, sports cars, and fancy vacations, inequalities of income and wealth would not matter very much. But as money comes to buy more and more – political influence, good medical care, a home in a safe neighborhood rather than a crime-ridden one, access to elite schools rather than failing ones – the distribution of wealth looms larger and larger.[31]

The commodification of certain goods and services inevitably leads to an unequal distribution of these goods and services (or the benefits derived from them) and, the argument suggests, such inequality is unfair and therefore unjust. On this argument, unequal access to legal services is but an instance of the broader issue of distributive justice. It is not transparent why disparities in the availability of legal services should constitute unfairness. But even if

---

[28]   Satz, *Why Some Things Should Not Be for Sale*, at p. 93.
[29]   Ibid., p. 102.
[30]   Note that the disparity in standing in the legal case is between the haves and the have-nots, not between the two sides to the exchange (client and attorney).
[31]   Sandel, *What Money Can't Buy*, at p. 8.

they do, as with health or education, this presumably applies to some basic level which must be made available to everyone.

If the corruption arguments supported ethical restrictions on lawyers, the inequality arguments seem to support ensuring an adequate level of access to the legal system to all citizens. Indeed, these have been the two main remedies proposed for the problems created by the market in legal representation: *access to justice* and *ethics for lawyers*.

In her influential book *Access to Justice*, Deborah Rhode sets out from the premise that "[t]he role that money plays in legal, legislative, and judicial selection processes often skews the law in predictable directions."[32] Her concern is to mitigate this role by enhancing access to the legal system for the less wealthy by such means as legal assistance in civil matters, expanding legal aid, pro bono requirements, and other access-enhancing mechanisms. Felstiner, Able, and Sarat pushed the point further, arguing that access to justice should not only focus on people's financial inability to hire a lawyer but also address other prelitigation disparities that affect access to the judicial branch.[33] These ideas align with the two forms of argument from inequality. Lack of access to justice can undermine the equal standing in society of those who do not have sufficient access and can qualify as an unfair distribution of an essential resource.

The literature on ethics of lawyers addresses another set of worries.[34] It focuses, roughly, on lawyers' role morality and its justification, by asking questions such as: How can it be justified for a lawyer to zealously defend a guilty person? What are the limits of lawyers' role morality? What ethical obligations arise from the fact that lawyers are "officers of the court"? In the context of the market of legal representation, there's a worry that financial incentives might obstruct lawyers' ethical commitment to their clients, to the courts, and to the law.

Both "access to justice" and "ethics for lawyers" remedies are important means of addressing some of the problems caused by the legal market. Yet both remain within the paradigm of privatized legal services. They aim to mitigate some of the pernicious effects of the distribution of legal representation by a market mechanism without questioning or seeking to challenge the fact that it is allocated by this mechanism.

Given its focus on the corruption and inequality arguments, it is less surprising, perhaps, that the moral-limits-of-markets literature has not paid special attention to legal representation. It remains, on this line of thought, one more unhappy consequence of economic inequality produced by a market, which may have to be augmented but is not a reason to question the market itself. Yet, the worries raised in Section 5.2 suggest that the fundamental problem with the distribution of legal representation by the free market is not the erosion of lawyers' ethical standards, or insufficient access to the legal system, or even distributive justice; rather, it is a problem of justice itself. We proceed to establish this claim in greater detail. Examining the history and logic of adversarial adjudication, we argue that, under

---

[32] Deborah L. Rhode, *Access to Justice* (New York: Oxford University Press, 2004), p. 6.

[33] William L. F. Felstiner, Richard L. Abel, and Austin Sarat, "The Emergence and Transformation of Disputes: Naming, Blaming, Claiming . . .," *Law & Society Review* 15 (1980): 631–654, pp. 649–650.

[34] See Charles Fried, "The Lawyer as Friend: The Moral Foundations of the Lawyer-Client Relation," *Yale Law Journal* 85 (1976): 1060–1089; David Luban, *Lawyers and Justice: An Ethical Study* (Princeton, NJ: Princeton University Press, 1988); David Luban, "The Lysistratian Prerogative: A Response to Stephen L. Pepper," *Law & Social Inquiry* 11 (1986): 637–649; Daniel Markovits, *A Modern Legal Ethics: Adversary Advocacy in a Democratic Age* (Princeton, NJ: Princeton University Press, 2008); Murray L. Schwartz, "The Zeal of the Civil Advocate," *Law & Social Inquiry* 8 (1983): 543–563, p. 546; Stephen L. Pepper, "The Lawyer's Amoral Ethical Role: A Defense, a Problem, and Some Possibilities," *Law & Social Inquiry* 11 (1986): 613–635; Richard Wasserstrom, "Lawyers as Professionals: Some Moral Issues," *Human Rights* 5 (1975): 1–24; W. Bradley Wendel, *Lawyers and Fidelity to Law* (Princeton, NJ: Princeton University Press, 2010).

conditions of economic inequality, the distribution of legal representation by the market undermines its claim to justice.

5.4 THE MARKET OF LEGAL REPRESENTATION

Adversarial adjudication rests on parity. Historically, parity has had a central role both as a motivation and as a persistent challenge. The altercation system, which had been in place since the Middle Ages, prohibited representation.[35] As the law became more complex and legal procedures grew more sophisticated, many defendants were incapable of effectively advocating for themselves; for those who could, trials were often too hasty to make effective arguments. Pretrial processes of evidence gathering and argument construction were increasingly seen as unskilled and amateurish.

Following the volatile period of 1678–1688, the English Treason Trial Act of 1696 marked the first breach in the rule against defense counsel.[36] Many of those executed as a consequence of the trials, in which the crown *was* represented, were believed to be innocent, convicted only due to political rivalries. This spurred a movement calling for greater protection of the rights of defendants. A central argument was based on the inherent inequality of prohibiting representation for the accused while the prosecution is represented by professional advocates. As James Fitzjames Stephens described it: "A criminal trial in those days was not unlike a race between the King and the prisoner, in which the King had a long start and the prisoner was heavily weighted."[37] To maintain parity, the argument went, one-sided representation (of the crown) should be replaced with two-sided representation. A second argument was that treason cases are too complex to leave individual defendants to defend themselves.[38] To address these claims, the Treason Trial Act allowed representation in treason trials only. Later, in the Prisoner's Counsel Act of 1836, Parliament extended the right to counsel to felony trials. With time, the lawyer-free altercation trial became lawyer-dominated, and turned into the adversarial system with which we are familiar today.

Ironically, inequality soon emerged as a source of difficulty in adversarial systems as well, arguably worse than its predecessor. As John Langbein notes, many of the defendants in the treason trials were "persons active in high politics." Normally they were persons with great wealth, who could afford to hire counsel and pay for their legal needs. Hence, "the drafters of the Treason Trials Act of 1696 presupposed that paying for adversary justice was not going to be an obstacle for the clientele that the Act meant to benefit."[39] With the expansion of the Act and, consequently, the lawyerization of the legal system, the commodification of legal representation began to emerge as a source of grievance. Almost immediately, resentment grew among those who could not afford representation. Langbein mentions a number of anecdotes, among them a woman, prosecuted in 1757 for forging a bond, who grumbled at the

---

[35]   See John H. Langbein, *The Origins of Adversary Criminal Trial* (New York: Oxford University Press, 2003), pp. 51–56. It should be noted that only the defendant was prohibited from hiring professional representation. Nevertheless, under the altercation system, representation was rare for the prosecuting party as well.

[36]   The 1670s and the 1680s were a period of instability in England. A series of major treason trials took place from 1678 to 1688. Amongst them were the Popish Plot (1678), the Rye House Plot (1683), and the Monmouth Rebellion (1685). See Langbein, *The Origins of Adversary Criminal Trial*, pp. 68–69. See also Stephan Landsman, "A Brief Survey of the Development of the Adversary System," *Ohio State Law Journal* 44 (1983): 713–739, p. 730.

[37]   James Fitzjames Stephen, *A History of the Criminal Law of England*, Vol. 1 (Cambridge: Cambridge University Press, 2014), p. 397.

[38]   Langbein, *The Origins of Adversary Criminal Trial*, at pp. 98–102, 310.

[39]   Ibid., at p. 103.

court: "I have not a sixpenny piece left to pay a porter, much less to fee counsel ... If I must die because I am poor, I can't help it." She was convicted and sentenced to death. Another defendant complained that he was "[c]onvicted and condemned to die partly for want of money ... to employ counsel." Even some magistrates were not reluctant to observe that a criminal unable to "procure the aid of counsel to defend him, is often convicted," whereas the villain who can afford it "is acquitted and escapes justice."[40]

This remains true in contemporary Anglo-American adversarial systems, which are radically lawyer-dominated, as parity not only is rooted in the history of adversarial adjudication but is part of its logic. The adversarial procedure is structured as a competition constituted by three components: a passive impartial tribunal (a judge and/or jury); formal rules of procedure; and two or more competing parties, normally represented by lawyers who advocate for them with one-sided partisan zeal.[41] Patrick Devlin described the logic of adversarial adjudication as resting on the idea that "two prejudiced searchers starting from opposite ends of the field will between them be less likely to miss anything than the impartial searcher starting at the middle."[42] Thus, it is the parties themselves who are responsible for gathering the evidence and presenting it before the neutral and passive arbiter. The competition between them is assumed to be the best means for revealing the truth and the optimally fair decision procedure. The underlying idea is akin to the invisible hand rationale of free speech famously expressed by Justice Holmes: "The best test of truth is the power of the thought to get itself accepted in the competition of the market."[43]

But as with Devlin's prejudiced searchers, this assumes that the field is level.[44] Unless the conditions are equal, there is no reason to assume that competition will deliver the right result. Competition is a reliable mechanism only when the rules are fair and the arbiter is neutral. If the king gets a long start and the prisoner is heavily weighted, or if the judge is bought and paid for, the legal competition loses its credibility. But fair rules and neutral arbitration, though necessary, are not sufficient. The resources available to the contestants must also be on a par. If one runner can wear shoes while the other cannot, the race hardly qualifies as a reliable competition. This is why there are weight classes in boxing and why men and women compete in different contests in the Olympics. More akin to our case, many sports leagues (e.g. the NBA, NFL, NHL, MLB) impose salary caps on teams in order to maintain competitive balance. By the same logic, legal competition also requires that pertinent legal resources be roughly equal.

In a lawyer-based system such as ours, lawyers are clearly a vital legal resource. The institutionalized passivity of the tribunal leaves control over significant parts of the process in the hands of the lawyers. In addition to litigation during trial, lawyers are responsible for its preparation: collecting evidence; finding and deposing witnesses; constructing legal arguments; and summoning experts. The roles of the parties and the tribunal are severely limited in comparison. The parties are "silenced" in court, assumed to lack the ability to

---

[40] Ibid., at p. 317.
[41] Rudolph J. Gerber, "Victory vs. Truth: The Adversary System and Its Ethics," *Arizona State Law Journal* 19 (1987): 4–5; Luban, *Lawyers and Justice*, at p. 57.
[42] Patrick Devlin, *The Judge* (Oxford: Oxford University Press, 1981), p. 60.
[43] See *Abrams* v. *United States*, 250 U.S. 616, 40 S. Ct. 17, 63 L. Ed. 1173 (1919). For the truth-revealing account, see Luban, *Lawyers and Justice*, at p. 69; Deborah L. Rhode, *In the Interests of Justice*, at p. 53; Wertheimer, "The Equalization of Legal Resources," at pp. 309–311. For objections, see Luban, *Lawyers and Justice*, at pp. 68–74.
[44] This point has been raised in both Schwartz, "The Zeal of the Civil Advocate," at pp. 546–548, and Thomas M. Scanlon, "Equality of Opportunity: A Normative Anatomy," Third Uehiro Lecture, University of Oxford, December 2013; Thomas M. Scanlon, *Why Does Inequality Matter?* (Oxford: Oxford University Press, 2018), pp. 15–18.

properly represent themselves in a complex legal system, requiring professional representation to stand in for them; the impartial judge receives processed legal material, his role limited to enforcing the "rules of engagement" and assessing the arguments in reaching a decision.[45] It is not surprising that in such a system, where lawyers play an active and substantial role in the procedure, in producing and presenting the information on the basis of which the court makes its rulings, disparities in the quality of legal representation can be decisive. As Robert Kagan concluded in his study of adversarial legalism, "in a regime of adversarial legalism, the quality of justice is especially dependent on equality in the quality of the dueling lawyers."[46]

So this is one argument against privatized provision of legal representation under conditions of economic inequality: when the justifiability of outcome depends on it being the product of fair competition, relevant resources must be distributed equally. Since representation is a central resource in legal competition, an adversarial system must ensure parity with respect to it. In a free market, where access to legal representation is determined solely by economic ability, this is not the case. By its own logic, such a system is ill-equipped to issue the right results.

But the issue is not just the likelihood of correct outcomes. An adequate justice system is one that does not subject individuals to unfair procedures, not only because they are not likely to produce correct outcomes but also due to their intrinsic inadequacy. In a system of procedural justice, fair procedure matters independently of correct outcome. One can have a valid grievance if subjected to unfair procedures, even if the outcome was correct. Consider a defendant convicted correctly, but on the arbitrary basis of a coin-flip or, worse, on the basis of racial bias. Such defendants, it seems, have a valid grievance, not with respect to their conviction (which, per hypothesis, was correct), but for having been subjected to an unfair procedure. On the other hand, one can lay no blame at the foot of the court in the case of incorrect outcome produced by a fair procedure.[47] From a doctrinal perspective, the norms associated with due process embody the idea that fair trial is not merely an instrument for optimal decisions.

Fair competition requires not just fair rules and impartial referees but also equal opportunities. As Brian Barry put it, procedural fairness must be supplemented by what he calls background fairness: "Procedural fairness rules out one boxer having a piece of lead inside his gloves, but background fairness would also rule out any undue disparity in the weight of the boxers [or] sailing boats or cars of different sizes being raced against one another unless suitably handicapped."[48] Following Barry, Rawls argued for fair equality of opportunity, as opposed to merely formal equality of opportunity, because

> [t]hose who are at the same level of talent and ability, and have the same willingness to use them, should have the same prospects of success regardless of their initial place in the social system. In all sectors of society there should be roughly equal prospects of culture and achievement for everyone similarly motivated and endowed. The

[45] Luban, *Lawyers and Justice*, at p. 57; Langbein, *The Origins of Adversary Criminal Trial*, at pp. 311–314.
[46] Kagan, *Adversarial Legalism*, p. 95. For a more detailed account with regards to the incompatibility of the market in legal representation with the justifications for the adversarial legal system, see Agmon, "Undercutting Justice"; Wertheimer, "The Equalization of Legal Resources," at pp. 303–306.
[47] Although one might have a legitimate grievance in the case of false conviction, for example. This is a separate issue from whether the court is blameworthy.
[48] Brian Barry, *Political Argument: A Reissue with a New Introduction* (Berkeley: University of California Press), p. 99.

expectations of those with the same abilities and aspirations should not be affected by their social class.[49]

Fair equality of opportunity is necessary in order for the distribution produced by market competition, constrained by the difference principle, to be just.[50] Analogously, the expectations of individuals in the same legal position (in terms of crimes committed, criminal responsibility, available evidence, etc.) should not be affected by their class or financial resources. If fair equality of opportunity aims to establish similar life chances for people with similar talents and motivation, equal legal opportunity aims to establish similar legal prospects for individuals with similar legal circumstances.[51] Thus, equality of legal opportunity is not focused solely on intra-case justice, namely, parity between the parties within a single case in order to provide justice. Rather, it requires inter-case equality as well.[52]

Since legal resources cannot realistically be equalized, justice in adjudication requires equal access to legal resources, or *equal legal opportunity*. This is what the condition of parity entails for the institutionalization of justice. If access to legal resources, or legal opportunities, is unequal, the integrity of procedure is undermined. If one party gets only half the time to question witnesses relative to the other, or is allowed to call only half as many experts as the other, it is not only fairness that has been violated – on account of unjustified disparity in the distribution of some good. Such inequality in legal opportunity – access to witnesses, experts, and other legal resources – undermines justice. By the same token, unequal access to legal representation, a legal resource of no less and arguably greater significance, is equally subversive of justice.

Representation, as we have seen, not only contributes to the legal process but is a structural element of it, at least in adversarial systems. Lawyers are not mere spokespeople for the parties; they are central components of the adjudication mechanism. This mechanism, we have argued, requires – by its own logic – parity between litigants. Parity requires equal opportunity, which entails that equal access to representation of equal quality must be available, at least in principle (that is, by the design of the institution).

Yet, so long as legal representation is dispensed by the market, economic inequalities are inevitably allowed to translate into legal inequalities. Even if subject to ethical standards, once it is placed on the market, legal representation is a service governed by the laws of supply and demand.[53] Consumers (clients) expend their resources as they see fit in order to procure the legal representation they desire and can afford. Suppliers (lawyers) set their prices in accordance with market pressures and can choose which customers to serve. Like other

---

49 John Rawls, *A Theory of Justice*, revised ed. (Cambridge: Belknap Press, 1999), p. 63.

50 Ibid., at p. 76. Notice that the concern is not merely optimizing outcomes: "[T]he reasons for requiring open positions are not solely, or even primarily, those of efficiency. I have not maintained that offices must be open if in fact everyone is to benefit from an arrangement" (ibid., at p. 73). Restricting access to positions, Rawls argues, is a violation of equal treatment.

51 Notice that we are arguing here by analogy. One need not buy into Rawls's argument for fair equality of opportunity in order to endorse equal legal opportunity. For Rawls, fair equality of opportunity entails limitations on the accumulation of wealth and a public duty to provide education. Given the competitive nature of adjudication, the requirement of legal opportunity cannot be a sufficiency requirement, but is rather a comparative requirement: not sufficient opportunity, but equal opportunity.

52 This distinction was made first in Agmon, "Undercutting Justice," at p. 106.

53 Notice, however, that our argument applies differently to criminal and civil cases. Prosecutors, for instance, are not regular attorneys (at least on some conceptions), and thus equality of legal opportunity would look different in criminal cases. Here we focus only on a general point with regards to institutional limits of markets. For a full analysis of the differences between criminal and civil cases with regards to the market in legal representation, see Agmon, "Undercutting Justice," at pp. 107-118.

consumer goods, the quality of representation a person can enjoy is largely determined by that person's wealth. And, as Justice Hugo Black wrote: "There can be no equal justice where the kind of trial a man gets depends on the amount of money he has."[54]

5.5 THE FUNCTIONAL ARGUMENT FOR LIMITING MARKETS

Our case for limiting the market of legal representation rests on a distinct kind of argument, different from the standard moral-limits-of-markets arguments sketched before. It does not appeal to the inherent injustice of inequality, the corruption of social meanings, crowding-out norms, or violating basic values. In fact, it is not about moral limits at all, at least not in the sense of moral standards that are external to the practice or institution that constrains it. It appeals, rather, to the internal logic of adversarial adjudication. The rationale of its institutional design, or the way in which it is supposed to achieve its aim, namely justice, requires equal access to representation, which is compromised by placing it on the market.

Such a functional argument for limiting markets can apply to other goods. In fact, it seems to be the logic behind one of the paradigm cases of market inadequacy, namely voting, which, surprisingly, has received little attention so far.

Buying and selling votes is almost universally considered wrong.[55] But the standard moral-limits-of-markets arguments do not seem to adequately account for its wrongness.[56] Take the fairness argument. It is not immediately clear why selling one's vote is unfair. A common argument is that selling votes gives unfair advantage to the rich over the poor. But if giving advantage to the rich is in itself unfair, then every market is unfair. The question is why this particular material (as opposed to formal) advantage warrants prohibiting commercial exchange. Debra Satz argues: "If political, regulatory, judicial, and legal decision mechanisms were literally up for sale, this would concentrate political power in the hands of the few."[57] This is true. But the problem with votes being up for sale is not just the unequal distribution of power (or the unequal status it entails).[58] Legally, buying votes is regarded as a paradigm of election fraud. Voting is supposed to be an expression of citizens' preferences, values, choices, etc., not their economic capacity. "No body politic worthy of being called a democracy entrusts the selection of leaders to a process of auction or barter," Justice Brennan wrote.[59] Buying and selling votes runs counter to the rationale of democratic participation and thus undermines "the integrity of the electoral processes," as Justice Brennan put it, and with it the legitimacy of elected institutions.[60] Similarly, a procedure of adjudication influenced by money undermines the main function of the legal system, namely, providing justice. It is not just unfair; it is also unjust.

Presumably, too, it is not solely the corruption of the social meaning of voting that is troubling. On the standard corruption argument, some value, contingently associated with

---

[54] *Griffin v. Illinois*, 351 U.S. 12 (1956).

[55] For an exception to this generalization, see Brennan and Jaworski, *Markets without Limits*.

[56] Some have argued against vote buying on grounds of inefficiency (for a summary of the literature, see Richard L. Hasen, "Vote Buying," *California Law Review* 88 (2000): 1323–1371). Our focus here is only on arguments pertaining to the intrinsic wrongness of this practice.

[57] Satz, *Why Some Things Should Not Be for Sale*, at p. 103.

[58] Power is unequally distributed along many dimensions, between officials and lay citizens, celebrities and common folk, and also between rich and poor independent in various ways apart from their ability to buy votes.

[59] *Brown v. Hartlage*, 456 U.S. 45, 102 S. Ct. 1523, 71 L. Ed. 2d 732 (1982).

[60] Anderson grounds this in autonomy: "Prohibiting the sale of votes helps preserve collective autonomy by blocking one way the wealthy may try to control political outcomes" (Anderson, *Value in Ethics and Economics*, at p. 142). Our argument does not require this additional, potentially contentious claim.

the good, is said to be corrupted when the good is exchanged for money. And its corruption is explained in terms of the way that monetary interests modify people's motivations and intentions. For example, the value of friendship or an honorary degree is diminished when it is commodified because the motivation attached to it is partly constitutive of its value. A gift is a gift when it is motivated by (and thus expresses) love and concern for the recipient. An honorary degree is honorary when it is motivated by the desire to express respect for and appreciation of the recipient's achievements, not their financial contribution to the granting institution. It is motivation that sets the deep moral difference between the otherwise identical actions of the son tending to the needs of his ailing mother and of her hired caretaker doing it. What the latter does in exchange for monetary compensation, the son does from affection and obligation. Practically, this may not make much of a difference. Morally, it is all the difference in the world.

In many of the cases discussed in the limits-of-markets literature – organs, honors, sex, children – the values that are presumably corrupted and the norms that are displaced by commodification have to do with people's attitudes and intentions. This is the primary form in which "market values crowd out nonmarket norms worth caring about" – by changing people's attitudes and motivations.[61] When it comes to voting, however, the issue is not motivation but that permitting the exchange of votes for money will allow economic advantages to translate into advantages in political influence.[62] This undermines the very rationale of voting, not just its moral significance but its intended democratic function.

Similarly, if economic advantages are allowed to translate into legal advantages, the justice of the legal process is jeopardized. Michael Sandel is thus overlooking the obvious when he writes: "When a judge accepts a bribe to render a corrupt verdict, he acts as if his judicial authority were an instrument of personal gain rather than a public trust. He degrades and demeans his office by treating it according to a lower norm than is appropriate to it."[63] Deuteronomy clearly has a better grasp of the issue: "Bribe blinds the eyes of the wise and twists the words of the righteous." Bribery is first and foremost a perversion of justice, as the Bible says, not the degradation of an office. Legal proceedings ought to be shaped by the evidence and in accordance with law, not by the economic relations between the parties, just as democratic elections ought to be governed by the preferences of all citizens, not by their financial abilities.[64]

Thus, as in the case of voting, it is not the motivations that matter but the value underlying the practice. The point is not that lawyers, judges, or juries need to be motivated in the right way (by the desire to do justice) but that the institution ought to be devised in such a way as to promote justice. Unequal representation, just like biased law enforcement or tainted judges, undermines justice, regardless of motivations.[65] This is a functional or institutional argument

---

[61]   Sandel, *What Money Can't Buy*, at p. 113.

[62]   Even those who believe votes should not be distributed equally, who reject the "one person, one vote" principle, do not think they should be allocated on the basis of economic ability.

[63]   Ibid., at p. 46.

[64]   To be sure, paying for legal representation is not the same as bribing the judge. But, we argue, the normative effects of this practice, given significant and pervasive inequality, are akin to those of bribery, at least in adversarial legal systems.

[65]   This sets the present argument apart from Elizabeth Anderson's argument, according to which when markets "undermine important ideals such as freedom, autonomy, and equality, or important interests legitimately protected by the state ... the state may act to remove the good from control by market norms" (Anderson, *Value in Ethics and Economics*, at p. 144). Thus, if prostitution undermines women's autonomy or equality, the state can prohibit or restrict it. Presumably, these are objective interests, not contentious social meanings. Yet their precise meaning and scope, and in particular their relation to the distribution of some good by the market,

for limiting markets, not a moral argument. Although justice is a moral concern, the reasons for limiting the legal market are not directly moral but rather have to do with the purpose of the legal system as a social institution. Unlike the standard anticommodification arguments, the focus of the present argument is not on the good under distribution (legal representation) or its social meaning but rather on the institution within which it is embedded (the legal system) and on the value that this institution is designed to promote (justice). The reason we prohibit selling votes is because it would undermine the representative function of the democratic election system. The reason to limit the market in legal services is that its distribution by the market undermines the value that the legal system aims to realize, namely justice.

5.6 OBJECTIONS

Two potential objections to our argument should be addressed.[66] One is that parity might conflict with justice. For instance, obtaining some evidence might require excessive expenditure which could only be provided privately. Prohibiting such expenditure in the name of parity means presenting the court with less evidence than could be presented, raising the probability of errors in judgment.

On its face, this is a potent objection. But, we believe, it assumes the wrong perspective – looking at individual cases rather than the legal system. Our question is one of institutional design, so we must ask what the optimal arrangement is overall. Further, the rationale of the adversarial system is that justice is best served by legal competition, not by maximizing evidence, and, we have argued, competition requires parity. As to specific instances in which parity requirements risk impairing judicial outcomes, there are two things to be said: (1) exceptions can be made when needed; (2) more generally, no system is perfect and an imperfect legal system will inevitably sometimes deliver unjust results. As long as these remain a small enough minority of cases, their possibility is not an objection to the system as a whole.

In fact, this is an established, and probably inevitable, feature of our legal system as it is. Everyone agrees that in order to preserve the integrity and functionality of the legal system as a whole, some restrictions and rules have to be imposed that may come at the cost of perfect justice in particular instances. One example of such restrictions is the "fruit of the poisonous tree" doctrine, according to which illegally obtained evidence may be inadmissible even when its epistemic value is unquestioned.[67] If nothing else, we take this to be a strong "partners in crime response" to the first objection. But, once again, the rationale of adversarial systems is that better and fairer results are attained by competition rather than by maximizing evidence.

---

can be contested. Even if they undermine values "legitimately protected by the state," it has to be shown that they undermine them in the ways and to a degree that justifies coercive interference by the state (as Anderson says: "This argument shows that commodified sex is degraded and degrading to the prostitute. It does not show that the sale of sexual services should be prohibited" (ibid., at p. 154)). In any event, they are distinct from the goods being distributed (autonomy or equality are independently valuable, not an aim or a constitutive condition of sexual relations). By contrast, parity is intrinsic to justice. Legal inequality corrupts justice not in the sense of changing social meanings or crowding out "norms worth caring about," or other values legitimately protected by the state, but rather in the literal sense. It undermines the process as a process of justice.

66   We limit our remarks to philosophical objections, leaving many public policy issues for a separate occasion.

67   For further discussion of the doctrine, see Robert M. Pitler, "The Fruit of the Poisonous Tree Revisited and Shepardized," *California Law Review* 56 (1968): 579–651.

A different version of the objection might concede the systemic perspective and argue that limiting the legal market might corrode the system as a whole. By removing powerful financial incentives, the argument might go, the quality of lawyers is likely to depreciate and legal proceedings will deteriorate. For one thing, it's not clear that financial incentives are as definitive as this argument suggests (there's no evidence, for example, that medicine draws less competent individuals in countries where health is a public provision). In fact, there is good reason to assume the opposite. The quality of public goods allocated by a nonmarket mechanism, usually supported by the state, is strongly influenced by the ability of consumers to exercise what Albert Hirschman called "voice." As Hirschman demonstrated with respect to education, private schools provide the wealthy with an "exist" strategy: leaving the public system rather than exercising their voice in order to improve it.[68] Similarly, restricting the ability of more powerful citizens to procure their legal needs independently of the public system would incentivize them to advocate for its improvement.[69]

A second objection to our argument focuses not on its implications for the quality of legal proceedings but on its relation to justice as a matter of rights. It is a person's right to make the best legal case that she or he can make, especially in criminal justice: defending oneself against criminal accusations to the best of one's ability is a right. Restricting the market of legal representation would be an unjust violation of this right, so the argument would go. This rests on a false assumption. Citizens have a right to justice, not to defend themselves by any means possible. They have a right not to be subjected to arbitrary laws, they have a right to equal treatment, to due process, etc. This is what justice consists of in an inevitably imperfect legal system. Once again, this is neither novel nor radical. The right to limitlessly defend oneself is already off the table when one accepts living under a legal system that imposes restrictions, for instance, on procedure and on admissible evidence. The right to justice is realized in adversarial systems by fair competition, which requires parity. Allowing resources to be determined by financial ability, in other words, violates people's right to justice both inter-case (between litigants with different resources in the same case) and intra-case (between affluent and indigent across cases).

This objection highlights another element of the market that is not suitable to the allocation of legal representation. The market not only creates inequalities; it allocates goods in accordance with both the ability to pay for them and the desire to procure them. Justice, on the other hand, is not sensitive to preferences. Convicting a homeless person confessing to a crime in order to find shelter on a stormy night is not justice. Similarly, one party's stronger preference for winning a case (and consequent willingness to spend more on representation) should not influence outcomes. Justice is preference-independent, whereas the market is preference-based. This applies not only to buying and selling but also to philanthropy-based exchange. Charity or gift can undermine parity all the same. Thus, our argument targets not just buying and selling legal representation on the market but also their unequal provision by nonprofit charities or gifts.

---

[68] Albert O. Hirschman, *Exit Voice and Loyalty* (Cambridge, MA: Harvard University Press, 1970), pp. 50–53.

[69] Even if this Hirschman-inspired argument fails, market-based allocation conflicts with the adversarial rationale of parity. Within the framework of the adversarial system, it is better to have a slightly lower level of legal representation overall, than higher quality representation overall, which leads to a consistent obstruction of the system.

5.7 CONCLUSION: THE NONMORAL LIMITS OF MARKETS

We have argued that there are sound reasons to limit the market of legal representations, as there are to limit the commercial trade in votes. These reasons are of a distinct kind, appealing neither to fairness nor to social meanings, or equal standing. They do not appeal to values or considerations external to the practice or to the institution under consideration, either. Thus, unlike the corruption and inequality arguments, the present argument does not infer from the claim that a particular market has undesirable moral consequences that restricting this market is justified. Rather, it argues from the premise that something *cannot* be bought and sold to the conclusion that something else *should not* be distributed by the market. Justice cannot be bought because an outcome that is determined by the amount of money expended is by definition not just. As justice is the aim of the legal system, its operation should not be influenced by the parties' wealth. This entails that the quality of legal representation available to a person should not be determined by his or her financial ability. Can't, in this case, implies shan't.

Kenneth Arrow once wrote, somewhat cryptically, that the problems with certain forms of commodification "seem more concerned with the operations of the social system than with preservation of individual integrity,"[70] or, we would add, with social meanings and independent moral values. Certain markets ought to be limited not because they violate disputable moral values or social meanings but because they undermine the intrinsic aims of the social institutions within which they operate. This type of argument identifies a distinct category of goods which ought not to be distributed by the market.[71] These are goods whose social function (as opposed to social meaning) is incompatible with the market, particularly in light of the economic disparities it enables. These might be goods that are intrinsically egalitarian, that is, goods whose value and justification can only be realized if they are distributed equally.[72] Or they might be goods that can only be obtained if other goods are distributed equally (like adversarial justice or democratic legitimacy).[73]

---

[70] Kenneth J. Arrow, "Invaluable Goods," *Journal of Economic Literature* 35 (1997): 757–765, p. 765.

[71] This does not necessarily mean replacing the private practice of law with state provision of legal representation. Markets can be limited in a variety of ways, including: the imposition of a fee scheme (in Germany some fees are set by the Federal Lawyers' Fees Act (Bargo)), or restricting legal services to semi-private nonprofit institutions, funded and regulated by the state, but not directly managed by it (similar to the way some countries distribute health care). The latter seems the preferable model, as it preserves the benefits of competition and independence from the state while avoiding the problems created by the incentive of profit maximization under conditions of inequality, but we cannot explore these issues in the detail they deserve here.

[72] For the idea of egalitarian goods, see Assaf Sharon, "Equality, Fairness, and Egalitarian Goods: Revisiting the Anti-egalitarian Argument in the Morality of Freedom," *Jerusalem Review of Legal Studies* 14 (2016): 125–134.

[73] Other social goods to which this argument can be applied, besides voting and legal representation, include public discourse, education, culture, and political campaigns. We cannot pursue these extensions of the argument here.

6

Outsourcing Border Control: Public Agency and Action in Migration

Ashwini Vasanthakumar

6.1 INTRODUCTION

Non-state actors are ubiquitous in effecting border control. Private security companies (PSCs) are involved in deterring prospective irregular migrants from reaching a border, apprehending them when they enter, and then detaining and deporting them. PSCs provide not only agents of border control but also the increasingly sophisticated technologies of surveillance and deterrence. Treating irregular migration as a security concern lends itself to the expanding use of PSCs – arguably, a way of framing irregular migration that is itself encouraged by PSCs.[1] The global border security market is, by some estimates, expected to grow to 29 billion euros by 2022.[2] At the other end of the spectrum of organisational sophistication are civilian gatekeepers: individuals tasked, by law and upon pain of penalty, with monitoring and reporting on migrants they encounter in the course of their work – as doctors, university professors, and employers. In between are myriad other individuals and entities – airline agents, charities, and supranational organisations – that are independent of the state but pressed into its service, enforcing its borders and realising its migration policies. And then there are those who do not act at the behest of the state, such as charities and international non-governmental organisations (NGOs) providing critical assistance to migrants, as well as those who act in defiance of it, mounting rescues at sea when these have been criminalised or partaking in the lucrative business of moving people across borders.

As it has in other domains, privatization in border control raises serious misgivings. In public discourse these misgivings tend to focus on the *consequences* of privatization: on the

---

[*] I am grateful for helpful comments from Grégoire Webber and the editors of this volume.

[1] See, e.g., Daria Davitti, 'The Rise of Private Military and Security Companies in European Union Migration Policies: Implications under the UNGPs', *Business and Human Rights Journal* 4 (2018): 33–53; Gallya Lahav, 'Immigration and the State: The Devolution and Privatization of Immigration Control in the EU', *Journal of Ethnic and Migration Studies* 24 (1998): 675–94; Georg Menz, 'The Neoliberalized State and Migration Control: The Rise of Private Actors in the Enforcement and Design of Migration Policy', *Debate: Journal of Contemporary Central and Eastern Europe* 17 (2019): 315–32.

[2] Frost and Sullivan, *Global Border and Maritime Security Market Assessment* (2014), cited in Mark Akkerman, "*Border Wars: The Arms Dealers Profiting from Europe's Refugee Tragedy*" (Transnational Institute, 2018). Precise figures are difficult to ascertain because of a lack of transparency around commercial contract prices.

violence and the lack of due process in privately run detention centres;[3] the discrimination that requires private citizens to determine immigration status invites;[4] and the complex chains of command, responsibility, and liability that frustrate attempts to hold wrongdoers accountable.[5] Scholarly analysis replicates this focus.[6] In this chapter, I consider instead *intrinsic* arguments against privatization and apply these to border control. In brief, intrinsic arguments hold that certain goods can only be provided by a 'properly public actor',[7] and that public provision entails a particular relationship between the public actor that makes policy decisions and the frontline agents that implement these on the ground. Insofar as privatization severs the connection between the public actor and the frontline agent, the frontline agent is incapable of providing the public good. Intrinsic arguments thus preclude prominent forms of privatization, and do so even when these result in positive outcomes.

Typically, intrinsic arguments conflate public provision with state provision because they focus on goods – criminal justice and punishment, say – in which those subject to the public actor's policy-making can further be conflated with citizens. These conflations are unavailing in the context of border control which, by definition, includes those who are subject to the state's control without being its subjects. Instead, a properly public actor in this context must give due consideration to the interests of migrants in its policy-making as well as be accountable to them in its decision-making. This calls for *ex ante* inclusion and *ex post* accountability mechanisms for migrants. I argue that states, as they are currently constituted, cannot be properly public actors with respect to border control – and that non-state actors unconnected from the state can in fact play an ameliorative role in its institutional shortcomings. Far from reifying the state, intrinsic arguments provide the resources for critically re-evaluating the state and the international order within which it is situated.

My argument is structured as follows. In Section 6.2, I provide a more detailed overview of the non-state actors involved in any given state's border control and summarise the main criticisms that their use attracts. I then reconstruct recent arguments that advance intrinsic objections to privatization, focusing in particular on the account provided by Avihay Dorfman and Alon Harel (Section 6.3). These arguments establish the essential role of a properly public actor in providing certain goods. I outline the features of a properly public actor and demonstrate how the state is wanting (Section 6.4). I then briefly explore how some non-state actors can mitigate the state's institutional shortcomings and perform an ameliorative function in the provision of border control (Section 6.5). Although intrinsic arguments against privatization usually focus on the state, in the context of border control they point to

---

[3] See, e.g., Melanie McFadyean, '£... per incident', *London Review of Books* 28 (2006): 33–6; Thomas Gammeltoft-Hansen, 'Can Privatization Kill?', *New York Times* (1 April 2012).

[4] 'Landlord Checks on Illegal Immigrants Risk "Everyday Racism," says Labour', *The Guardian* (11 October 2015), www.theguardian.com/uk-news/2015/oct/11/immigration-checks-discrimination-labour.

[5] A. Sager, 'Immigration Enforcement and Domination: An Indirect Argument for Much More Open Borders', *Political Research Quarterly* 70 (2017): 42–54, pp. 43–5.

[6] For helpful overviews of recent normative scholarship of migration, see Joseph Carens, *The Ethics of Immigration* (Oxford University Press, 2016); David Miller, *Strangers in Our Midst* (Harvard University Press, 2017); Sarah Fine and Lea Ypi (eds.), *Migration in Political Theory: The Ethics of Movement and Membership* (Oxford University Press, 2016). There is a growing literature on the ethics of immigration enforcement, which focuses on substantive state policy but touches on its use of private actors. See, e.g., A. Sager, 'Private Contractors, Foreign Troops, and Off-Shore Detention Centers: The Ethics of Externalizing Immigration Control', *American Philosophical Association Newsletter on Hispanic/Latino Issues in Philosophy* 17 (2018): 12–15; S. Silverman, 'Detaining Immigrants and Asylum Seekers: A Normative Introduction', *Critical Review of International Social and Political Philosophy* 17 (2014) : 600–17; M. Lister, 'Enforcing Immigration Law', *Philosophy Compass* (online, December 2019).

[7] The 'properly' qualifier is to distinguish actors who are only formally public.

actors above and below the state as agents that can be, and can bring about, a properly public actor. Section 6.6 concludes.

6.2 BORDER CONTROL AND NON-STATE ACTORS

Border control refers to state-sanctioned restrictions and rights relating to the movement of individuals across their territorial boundaries. Migrants are individuals seeking entry into a state or who are already present within its territory but who are not citizens. Although border control most visibly arises at the territorial boundaries of states, it is increasingly disaggregated from these boundaries, extending within and without.[8] Territorial boundaries remain the focus of border control – extraterritorial efforts are aimed at preventing would-be migrants from arriving at a boundary, and once they cross that boundary, the borders they encounter therein are tied to the terms of their entry. From the perspective of migrants, border control does not take place at some line they cross once; rather, it is an ongoing series of encounters with the state, often indirect and often with little prior warning.[9]

A proliferation of borders is made possible by a proliferation of agents charged with their enforcement. States rely on a number of actors beyond their border agents to enforce their borders and their migration policies: for-profit corporations, charities, civilian gatekeepers, supranational agencies, international organisations, and the agents of other states. And this is only those actors to whom the state deliberately *delegates* enforcement. Privatization also arises through other means.[10] Volunteers *supplement* state provision, for example by assisting migrants, providing language assistance, or otherwise aiding in the integration of newcomers. Private actors may *compensate* for state inaction, for example by rescuing migrants on the high seas. And entrepreneurs can *usurp* the state's prerogatives. Vigilantes police the border and detain suspected unauthorised migrants, even when doing so is unlawful, and individuals enable unauthorised migration, as criminal traffickers or people smugglers, for reasons of profit or principle, or both.

There is not always a clear distinction between state and non-state actors, nor a ready correlation between those actors and the public and the private, respectively. This is true in terms of both the nature or composition of these actors as well as the roles they play: non-state actors may have close ties to state authorities, may be involved in the formulation of public policy, as advisers or consultants, and may be involved in the execution of policy in roles that range from direct providers to monitors. There is also a great deal of variety among non-state actors, a category that includes charities, profit-maximising enterprises, religious bodies motivated by sectarian commitments, and rights-promoting organisations – some of these are not obviously private organisations pursuing self-interested ends. For these reasons, I refer to non-state rather than private actors and use privatization to refer to action by non-state actors in those domains typically reserved for the state.

---

[8]   Thus, some have argued that a border arises at any 'site where a control takes place' of individuals' movements that is sanctioned or sought by the state. Elspeth Guild cited in Nick Vaughan-Williams, 'Borderwork beyond Inside/Outside? Frontex, the Citizen-Detective and the War on Terror', *Space and Polity* 12 (2008): 63–79, p. 63.

[9]   I focus on *immigration* rather than emigration because most enforcement, particularly in liberal democratic states, is on entry rather than exit.

[10] Although privatization through delegation is commonly the focus, it is useful to identify other non-state actors who either perform functions typically reserved for the state or act within the remit allowed by the state. Malcolm Thorburn, 'Reinventing the Night-Watchman State', *University of Toronto Law Journal* 60 (2010): 425–43, p. 428.

Within its territorial boundaries, there are two prominent sets of non-state actors to whom the state delegates enforcement, and who illustrate the range of actors and activities undertaken at the state's behest. Private security corporations (PSCs) are large for-profit enterprises involved in immigration detention, transporting migrants, and deporting them. The state also relies on more diffuse modes of monitoring by tasking, under penalty, civilian gatekeepers to monitor immigrants' compliance with the terms of their entry, detecting those whose presence is unauthorised, and making untenable this unauthorised presence.[11] Civilian gatekeepers are called upon to monitor immigration status in the course of their daily, often professional, lives. Employers must ascertain and monitor the migration status of their employees, medical practitioners those they intend to aid, and landlords those to whom they may rent out properties.

The externalisation of borders invites further actors into the state's border control efforts. The European Union (EU) exemplifies this strategy. Frontex, which coordinates the EU's external border management, has relied on neighbouring states to aid in its border enforcement since 1992; this accelerated in 2005, and then again in 2015. Through a number of instruments, such as the EU Emergency Trust Fund for Africa, the Migration Partnership Framework, and the Refugee Facility for Turkey, the EU provides billions in funding to secure borders beyond its territorial boundaries. Among other things, these funds are used to train border guards and police in other states, and to provide biometric systems, helicopters, patrol boats, other vehicles, and surveillance equipment.[12] In addition to PSCs, externalised borders involve three main actors other than the relevant state: other states; supranational organisations, such as the International Organisation for Migration (IOM); and semi-independent development agencies, such as GIZ, the German development agency, and Civipol, connected to the French Ministry of the Interior.

In principle, these forms of delegation are the least objectionable because they only contemplate outsourcing the delivery of border control whilst retaining provision and control in state hands. Even these forms of delegation, however, have been subject to mounting criticism and alarm.[13] The use of non-state actors faces three main types of criticism. The first focuses on the consequences of privatization for migrants who in general are taken to be more vulnerable to rights abuses: physical harm in private detention facilities, discriminatory behaviour from civilian gatekeepers, and grave rights abuses by regimes empowered by the state to enforce its borders.[14] A second set of criticisms worries about the consequences for the delegating state. Far from gains in efficiency, privatization is often accused of spiralling costs that unduly burden the taxpayer. More insidiously, the creation of powerful constituencies invested in border control may distort the state's policy-making.[15] A final set of criticism

---

[11] This was deliberately pursued in the UK to create a 'hostile environment' for unauthorised migrants. See, e.g., Colin Yeo, 'The Evidence-Free Origins of the Hostile Environment', *Prospect Magazine* (February 2019); Maya Goodfellow, *Hostile Environment: How Immigrants Became Scapegoats* (Verso Books, 2019).

[12] Mark Akkerman, *Expanding the Fortress: The Policies, Profiteers and the People Shaped by EU's Border Externalisation Programme* (Transnational Institute, November 2018).

[13] See, e.g. 'Concerns over States Contracting Private Security Companies in Migration Situations', Working Group on Mercenaries, United Nations Office of the High Commission for Human Rights (December 2019), www.ohchr.org/EN/NewsEvents/Pages/SecurityPrivatisationMigrationContexts.aspx.
A comprehensive report from the Working Group is due in 2020.

[14] See, e.g., Human Rights Watch, *No Escape from Hell: EU Policies Contribute to Abuse of Migrants in Libya* (31 January 2019).

[15] See, e.g., Sharita Gruberg, *How For-Profit Companies Are Driving Immigration Detention Policies* (Center for American Progress, 2015). This distortion extends beyond the policy domain of border control, and can thwart or hijack a state's other commitments, including its overseas development priorities. See, e.g., M. Vermeluen,

focuses on the consequences of enforcement for the non-state actors themselves. Involving charities, religious, and humanitarian organisations in the enforcement of migration policies can compromise the ends of these organisations and the values they seek to promote. Similarly, drafting civilian gatekeepers into the service of the state conflicts with the professional ethics and virtues associated with a number of roles, such as medical practitioners. And finally, tying substantial amounts of aid to foreign states' cooperation in border control, particularly when they have relatively weak institutions, can thwart *those* states' economic and social development goals, or, worse, entrench and strengthen authoritarian regimes.[16]

These varied criticisms are powerful and the harms they attend to, grave. They remain, however, contingent moral objections that focus on outcomes and that – in principle – can be remedied through better institutional design or avoided entirely by limiting privatization to certain non-state actors. That is, these objections focus on particular forms of privatization rather than on privatization as such. A focus on consequences, moreover, hardly tells in favour of state provision, given the several and systematic abuses occasioned by the state's enforcement of borders.[17] For the rest of this chapter, I focus on intrinsic arguments against privatization, which ostensibly provide a more searching critique of outsourcing border control.[18]

6.3 INTRINSIC ARGUMENTS AGAINST PRIVATIZATION

Intrinsic arguments against privatization have recently been advanced by Avihay Dorfman and Alon Harel, and Chiara Cordelli.[19] Both accounts take seriously the 'intuitive dislike' for privatization[20] and provide arguments that hold irrespective of its consequences. These arguments generally proceed as follows. First, they identify certain goods as intrinsically public, meaning that these goods must be provided by a properly public actor in order for their value to be realised. Second, they place constraints on what constitutes public provision, focusing on the processes and networks that connect frontline agents to the public actor. Policy-making is therefore in the hands of a public actor who also retains control over the particular decisions taken by the frontline agents that implement these policies.

G. Zandonini and A. Azmat, 'How the EU Created a Crisis in Africa – and Started a Migration Cartel', *The Correspondent* (10 December 2019).

[16] Human Rights Watch, *No Escape from Hell.*

[17] See, e.g., A. Speri, 'Detained, then Violated: 1, 224 Complaints Reveal a Staggering Pattern of Sexual Abuse in Immigration Detention. Half of Those Accused Work for ICE', *The Intercept* (11 April 2018).

[18] To be sure, these are not the only criticisms of privatization. Privatization is also criticised because it trades on inappropriate or unattractive motivations, especially mercenary ones, and because it is inapt for particular types of goods, and tends towards their corruption. See, e.g., James Pattison, 'Deeper Objections to the Privatisation of Military Force', *Journal of Political Philosophy* 18 (2010): 425–47, and ' Outsourcing the Responsibility to Protect: Humanitarian Intervention and Private Military and Security Companies', *International Theory* 2 (2010): 1–31, pp. 10–13; Michael Sandel, *What Money Can't Buy: The Moral Limits of Markets*, The Tanner Lectures on Human Values (1998); Chiara Cordelli, 'The Intrinsic Wrong of Privatization', pp. 6–14 (unpublished manuscript on file with the author). Cordelli critiques each of these, which she refers to as the motivation, corruption, and intrinsic arguments.

[19] Avihay Dorfman and Alon Harel, 'The Case Against Privatization,' *Philosophy & Public Affairs* 41 (2013): 67–102; Avihay Dorfman and Alon Harel, 'Against Privatisation as Such,' *Oxford Journal of Legal Studies* 36 (2016) : 400–27; and Alon Harel, *Why Law Matters* (Oxford University Press, 2014) (hereafter 'WLM'); Chiara Cordelli, 'The Intrinsic Wrong', and 'Privatization without Profit?' *NOMOS LX* (2018); see also Cordelli's contribution to this volume (Chapter 1). I focus on Dorfman and Harel's account.

[20] Dorfman and Harel, 'The Case Against Privatization', at p. 69.

6.3.1 'Inherently Public Goods'

Dorfman and Harel argue that there are 'inherently public goods': goods whose value can only be realised if they are provided by the state. For such goods, the argument in favour of state provision is not instrumental: it is not that public provision is likely to be *better*, but that the provision of the good is agent-specific and cannot be provided by agents other than the state.[21]

There are two rationales for why a good is inherently public. The first is ontological:[22] an enterprise is agent-dependent as a matter of conceptual definition whereby the enterprise and the agent are constitutive of one another.[23] Ontological arguments are largely stipulative.[24] They may be useful for identifying the constitutive and contingent features of particular practices and tracking changes in these practices, but they do not by themselves explain or justify these transformations. Even if there were broad agreement on the existence of a category of 'state practice', more is needed to tell us why particular practices and agents fall into this category.

This is supplied by the second, axiological rationale: it claims that performance by a particular agent is constitutive of the value provided by performance. Take criminal punishment. Dorfman and Harel argue that criminal punishment has a communicative function that can be performed only if the communicating agent is in a normatively superior position to the target.[25] Even if one doesn't subscribe to their communicative theory of punishment, the state is still the only appropriate actor given the *method* of communication: the hard treatment of punishment.[26] Punishment entails the infringement of important interests, and only the state, as a public entity, can ensure that such infringements are both impartial, in that they do not serve sectarian interests, and reasonable, in that they are narrowly tailored to achieve the relevant goal. These conditions not only restrain state action, particularly when it implicates important interests, but also establish equal freedom among citizens. Cordelli pursues this line of reasoning. She focuses on cases where the 'normative situation of citizens' is changed and argues that only the state can reason publicly, ensuring that these normative changes are compatible with the equal freedom of all.[27]

On the axiological argument, it is not that criminal punishment is a constitutive element of sovereignty but rather that only a properly public entity can act for the right reasons and guarantee that punishment is carried out in a way that recognises the equal standing of citizens, even when they are the targets of punishment. Again, absent such an entity,

---

[21] Dorfman and Harel are not opposed to privatization in all domains, or to private actors performing functions orthogonal to the provision of 'inherently public goods'. Thus, for example, private actors could provide electricity or provide food for prisons. The axiological rationale I discuss in this chapter can account for this distinction.

[22] I borrow Laura Valentini's helpful distinction between ontological and axiological claims. See Laura Valentini, 'On the Value of Constitutions and Judicial Review', *Criminal Law and Philosophy* (2016): section 2 (published online, 15 February 2016).

[23] Dorfman and Harel use the examples of blood feud and war. Harel, WLM, at pp. 70, 99–103.

[24] See, e.g., John Gardner, 'The Evil of Privatization', at p. 3.

[25] Dorfman and Harel argue that only the state is in such a position. When private individuals subject other private individuals to the hard treatment of punishment, this hard treatment is simply private violence incapable of realising the expressive good of punishment; it doesn't even count as punishment.

[26] Malcolm Thorburn, 'Judgment, Communication, and Coercion: What's Wrong with Private Prisons?' *Critical Analysis of Law* 2 (2015): 234–43.

[27] Cordelli, 'The Intrinsic Wrong', at pp. 3–4. According to Cordelli, this means that citizens are governed by the omnilateral rule of the state rather than the unilateral will of an individual; they are in a state of freedom in the former and a condition of un-freedom in the latter.

punishment degrades into private violence. Inherently public goods are those goods whose provision implicates individuals' important interests and, per Cordelli, changes their normative position. And only a properly public agent can provide these goods and perform these functions in a way that ensures the equal freedom of all. Now, proponents of privatization need not deny any of this; they deny only that public decision-making cannot be severed from execution, such that private actors cannot perform or execute publicly taken decisions. For intrinsic arguments against privatization to work, it has to be the case that inherently public goods must be provided by the state *all the way down*: a public actor must not only decide to wage war or punish or, in our case, enforce borders but must also execute these decisions. Their argument for this centres on the inevitable discretion that frontline agents exercise when they execute decisions, and the conditions under which this discretion is legitimately exercised.

6.3.2 *The Right Agents Acting for the Right Reasons*

When the state authorises a frontline agent to execute a decision, that agent is called upon to exercise his or her 'capacities to reason, intend, and judge'.[28] Discretionary decision-making is inevitable not only because directives, however well specified, require interpretation but also because the public reasons underlying these directives are themselves indeterminate.[29] Ultimately, the authorised agent acts for reasons that *he or she* comes to embrace, even if he or she is earnestly and even accurately pursuing the public interest. From the perspective of those subject to these decisions, they are subject to the reasons of a private individual and to their arbitrary judgement, however benignly motivated or ultimately justified.

In Dorfman and Harel's terminology, the frontline agent in this case shows 'fidelity by reason': fidelity by reason calls for the agent to execute the state's command in accordance with the state's purposes – the 'general good' – as the agent judges it to be.[30] However earnestly, impartially and accurately he or she reasons, he or she will inevitably proceed from his or her conception of what that consists in.[31] His or her actions are doings *for* rather than *of* the state. What is required instead is that the frontline agent demonstrate what Dorfman and Harel call 'fidelity by deference': he or she suppresses entirely her private judgements about the public interest and defers to the 'public point of view'. This can be achieved when frontline agents are embedded in particular networks or practices such that they have access to the deliberations of political actors and are subject to their control – an embeddedness precluded by most contracts of privatization. This 'integrative practice'[32] subjects frontline agents to the practical deliberation of political actors. Political actors' guidance is not limited to establishing the basic rules of conduct within which these agents freely operate, or to providing run-of-the-mill *ex post* accountability. Rather, an integrative practice empowers political actors to 'influence [frontline agents'] *ongoing* deliberations and everyday actions'[33] and ensures that frontline agents are embedded in 'channels of public

---

[28] Dorfman and Harel, 'The Case Against Privatization', at p. 73.
[29] Cordelli, 'The Intrinsic Wrong of Privatization', at p. 27.
[30] Dorfman and Harel, 'The Case Against Privatization', at p. 74.
[31] Ibid., at p. 75.
[32] Dorfman and Harel refer to this as an 'integrative practice'; Cordelli refers to a 'shared institutional space' and a 'web of relationships that serve to provide the necessary shared institutional orientation'. Cordelli, 'The Intrinsic Wrong', at pp. 35–6. For ease, I will refer to an 'integrative practice'.
[33] Harel, *WLM*, at pp. 90–1, my emphasis.

practical reasoning'.[34] Dorfman and Harel emphasise that this integration does not call for frontline actors to appeal perpetually to their superiors, which would be impracticable, nor does this integration rely on political actors actually intervening to guide the deliberation and conduct of frontline agents.[35] It is enough that political actors *can* intervene at any time. This integrative practice ensures, Dorfman and Harel insist, that 'fidelity of deference' is not incompatible with the discretion that frontline agents necessarily wield.[36] And in virtue of their inclusion in such an integrative practice, all actors – whatever their official designation – count as public officials whose actions carry the imprimatur of the state.[37]

For privatising border control to be per se precluded under these accounts, border control would have to be 'an inherently public good', and (at least some) forms of privatization would have to leave frontline agents improperly subject to an integrative practice. On its face, these two conditions are satisfied. The control of movement affects important individual interests. Depending on their reasons for movement, individuals' fundamental rights and life chances are affected by borders. Indeed, some have argued that there is a human right to migration;[38] others, that border control constitutes domination.[39] Prima facie, border control is an inherently public good that only a properly public entity can provide on the accounts canvassed here. Public provision, in turn, requires a bureaucracy, properly understood as an 'integrative practice' wherein frontline agents deliberate from the public point of view. This is more than run-of-the-mill *ex post* accountability in that political control directs the deliberative process *leading up* to a decision. PSCs, civilian gatekeepers, and foreign states, at least in their prominent forms, are necessarily excluded from such a practice: PSCs, by the instrument of contract; civilian gatekeepers, by their very dispersal through civil society; and foreign states, by their putative sovereignty. Without an integrative practice, migrants are subject to frontline agents' private reasons and vulnerable to their unilateral wills – it is *this* claim that precludes many current forms of privatization in migration enforcement. Applying this framework to the context of migration and border control raises two questions: first, what are the criteria for a properly public actor in this context and does the state meet these? And if there is no such actor, does this recast some non-state actors in an ameliorative function? I address these questions in Sections 6.4 and 6.5.

6.4 PUBLIC AGENCY AND ACTION IN THE CONTEXT OF MIGRATION

In popular discourse, border control is often cast as a good provided by the state, the beneficiaries of which are its citizens. By these accounts, border control protects citizens from external threats and enables a measure of self-determination. Recall that, under the axiological rationale, a good is inherently public because only a public actor can adjudicate conflicts in a way that secures the equal freedom of all. In the context of border control, however, citizens are not the only relevant subjects; those seeking entry also stand to have

---

[34] Cordelli, 'The Intrinsic Wrong of Privatization', at p. 38.
[35] Harel, *WLM*, at p. 93.
[36] Dorfman and Harel, 'The Case Against Privatization', at p. 79.
[37] Harel argues that this means it is in principle possible for employees of a private company to count as public officials, albeit in the 'fantastic' scenario where they are integrated into public deliberation.
[38] See, e.g. Kieran Oberman, 'Immigration as a Human Right', in *Migration in Political Theory: The Ethics of Movement and Membership* (Oxford University Press, 2016).
[39] See, e.g. Iseult Honohan, 'Domination and Migration: An Alternative Approach to the Legitimacy of Migration Controls', *Critical Review of International Social and Political Philosophy* 17 (2014): 31–48; Sager, 'Immigration Enforcement'.

their normative position altered by border control practices. Indeed, the good of border control might better be understood as a just migration regime, the beneficiaries and subjects of which are would-be migrants – citizens and non-citizens alike.[40]

In order to provide border control, an agent must be capable of adopting a properly public view with respect to the competing claims of citizens and migrants so as to act justly towards both. To be clear, a properly public view is not necessarily a cosmopolitan one that treats the interests of citizens and non-citizens identically, or that prescribes open or porous borders. I take no view on what a just migration policy would call for, except to stipulate that migrants have claims: in some cases, a substantive entitlement to enter, and at least a procedural entitlement to minimal fairness. These are claims that even migration restrictionists recognise.[41] What institutions or practices might enable a properly public view in this context? First, there should be mechanisms by which the interests and perspectives of all migrants enter into the deliberations of the properly public actor and inform its policy decisions. And second, there should be mechanisms by which migrants can hold accountable the properly public actor and its frontline agents, both for their policy goals and for the ways in which frontline agents implement them. Whatever the precise institutional arrangement, then, a properly public actor must have *ex ante* input and *ex post* accountability mechanisms available to all migrants.

Input mechanisms include the power to select policy-makers and channels by which to communicate preferences, which can also function as mechanisms of accountability when they allow subjects to remove policy-makers and frontline agents, and to communicate criticism and disagreement, including by challenging particular decisions. These mechanisms include voting rights, consultations, and judicial or administrative review. Importantly, they should be formally institutionalised so as to enable input and accountability to migrants in a guaranteed and systematic manner. Informal mechanisms, say, public awareness campaigns that sometimes put pressure on policymakers, are insufficient; as I detail in Section 6.5, they are variable and arbitrary, and so fail to secure the equal freedom of all.

In order for the state to qualify as a properly public actor in the context of migration, it must provide for such mechanisms of inclusion and accountability. It can do so directly; indirectly, by being embedded in a supranational institutional framework that incorporates these mechanisms and channels them down to the state; or through some combination of both. Thus, for example, input mechanisms might be more feasibly incorporated at the supranational or global level with processes for judicial appeal or administrative review beginning at the point of frontline decision-making at the state level or even below.

In reality, these input and accountability mechanisms are wanting or simply do not exist at either level. Even in liberal democratic states, which are the most plausible candidates for properly public actors, migrants have limited means of informing state policy and are excluded from virtually all *fora* for collective decision-making, especially decision-making related to their rights.[42] Legal redress is more availing but still far from adequate.

---

40 'Would-be migrant' could be understood capaciously, to include anyone with the potential to move across a border, in effect, everyone in the world; or it could be understood more restrictively, to include only those actively seeking exit or entry, to a range between. My argument does not turn on any particular conception of would-be migrant. Recall that by 'migrant' I refer to non-citizens seeking entry into a state or who are present in its territory.

41 See, e.g., Michael Walzer, *Spheres of Justice: A Defense of Pluralism and Equality* (Basic Books, 1983).

42 See, e.g., A. Abizadeh, 'Democratic Theory and Border Coercion: No Right to Unilaterally Control Your Own Borders', *Political Theory* 36 (2008): 37–65; U. Steinhoff, 'Border Coercion and "Democratic Legitimacy": On Abizadeh's Argument Against Current Regimes of Border Control', *Res Publica* 26 (2020): 281–92. In some

Domestically, migrants often do not have guaranteed legal representation in administrative or judicial processes, and what provision they do have available can be reduced by policymakers. Moreover, there are limited avenues for legal redress, even when legal representation is available, as well as limited rights for migrants to assert in these avenues – states enjoy wide discretion in determining what constitutes an adequate process for adjudicating migrant rights and what these rights consist of.[43]

This is true even when there are binding international legal obligations. For example, a complex and evolving network of legal instruments, international agreements, and agencies exists at the supranational and global level for the protection of refugees. For the most part, however, compliance with these obligations falls to individual states, who have varying interpretations of their legal obligations and are subject to little accountability from without.[44] International agencies often rely on states for their resources, and their operations often must be negotiated with relevant states. These agencies can monitor compliance, and protest and publicise non-compliance, but little else. In part, this patchwork system of rule-making, agreements, and agencies reflects an attempted 'reconciliation of an international order of sovereign states and a cosmopolitan order of human rights'[45] in which states remain the principal agents. But, even if states were bound to be more deferential to international bodies, this would not necessarily enhance *migrants'* access to either input or accountability mechanisms since these mechanisms are largely absent even in those bodies dedicated to their rights. As Alexander Aleinikoff and Leah Zarmore note, refugees have no formal representation at the Executive Committee of the United Nations High Commission for Refugees (UNHCR) and no regular informal role. Although the UNHCR maintains close connections with refugees in camps, and uses a network of 'elders' and other contacts, these are informal and ad hoc. As Aleinikoff and Zarmore conclude, 'refugees remain largely voiceless', supplicants rather than agents in the processes and institutions that govern them.[46]

In sum, migrants are subjected to, rather than the subjects of, the institutions and processes of border control. They have little formal influence over the substantive policy goals of state and international actors – for the most part, they have no formal rights to select policymakers, participate in consultations, frame public discourse, or reorganise priorities. And they have little means by which to counter or check these policies when they are being enforced. Absent mechanisms of influence and accountability, the state is not a properly public agent in the context of border control. It cannot be one. Even those states that satisfy justice, however conceived, in border control do so at their discretion, and any attentiveness to the interests of migrants or willingness to be accountable to them is similarly discretionary. From the perspective of migrants subject to their control, they are not governed by public rule but instead are subject to the arbitrary decision-making of a state, albeit one that treats them justly

---

jurisdictions, migrants with certain residency statuses may be able to vote in local, state, or general elections. Those seeking entry, however, are excluded from political decision-making.

43 See, e.g., *Department of Homeland Security* v. *Thuraissigiam* (cert. granted) (on the habeas corpus rights of a migrant in expedited removal proceedings) and discussion of the case in Garrett Epps, 'The Fragility of Immigrants' Constitutional Protections', *The Atlantic* (November 2019).

44 Legal redress from beyond the state may also be available. See, e.g., Communication to the Office of the Prosecutor of the International Criminal Court: *EU Migration Policies in the Central Mediterranean and Libya (2014–2019)*; D. Davitti, 'Beyond the Governance Gap: Accountability in Privatized Migration Control', *German Law Journal* 21(2020): 487–505; B. Çalı, C. Costello, and S. Cunningham, 'Hard Protection through Soft Courts? Non-refoulement before the United Nations Treaty Bodies', *German Law Journal* 21(2020): 355–84.

45 David Owen, *What Do We Owe to Refugees?* (Polity Press, 2020), at p. 46.

46 Alexander Aleinikoff and Leah Zarmore, *The Arc of Protection: Toward a New International Refugee Regime* (Stanford University Press, 2018), at p. 43.

some of the time. This is not to deny that states act within a norm-rich, rule-based environment, both domestically and globally, or that the international web of law, norms, agreements, and agencies does not provide some modicum of governance, however diffused. These fall short of constituting a properly public actor, however. They do not sufficiently subject individual states to their control and deliberation; moreover, even if they did, they do not themselves adequately attend to migrants and so are not a properly public actor with respect to at least some who are subject to them.

Although border control is widely regarded as an inherently sovereign function, I have argued that states cannot be properly public actors in this context so long as migrants are denied institutionalised access to their decision-makers – either directly, or indirectly through global or supranational bodies. This suggests that the harmful consequences of privatization I outlined in Section 6.2 may arise *because* non-state actors are too closely, as opposed to insufficiently, tethered to the state. Conversely, it may recast the role that some non-state actors can play in providing border control as a public good.

6.5 NON-STATE ACTORS AND PUBLIC ACTION IN BORDER CONTROL

In the absence of a properly public actor with institutionalised *ex ante* input and *ex post* accountability mechanisms, non-state actors may play an ameliorative role. Beyond the private actors to whom the state expressly delegates border control activities, contemporary debates focus on the role of advocates, migrant-rights groups, citizen-operated search-and-rescue missions in the Mediterranean, and people smugglers. I suggest that, where the state is not a properly public actor, some non-state actors may ameliorate institutional shortcomings *and* help pave the way to properly public institutions. If intrinsic arguments point to the need for an integrative practice that connects frontline agents to public actors, here, the ameliorative function of some non-state actors may rely precisely on their being untethered to the state. I focus on two types: *advocates*, who work within existing institutions to compensate for their defects, and *samaritans*, who thwart the decisions of these defective institutions. I do not exhaustively conceptualise or justify these roles, but aim only to show how intrinsic arguments can recast them, illuminating their ameliorative function and providing guidance on how these roles should be performed.

Advocates include legal representatives, advocacy organisations, and the media. They lobby states to change their migration policies; provide migrants with legal advice in judicial and administrative proceedings; challenge the very constitutionality of state law and policy; and publicise the harms caused by these laws and policies with a view towards increasing awareness and opposition among citizens. Advocates operate within existing institutions by using the rights and mechanisms already available to them. As such, their activities are countenanced and even enabled by the state – for example, through robust rights of free speech and assembly, an accessible legal system, and a free press.[47] Advocacy informally provides mechanisms of input and accountability, thereby mitigating shortcomings in the state's decision-making process. In no small part, the advancement of norms, rules, and legal obligations with regard to migrants' rights is due to the efforts of advocates.

[47]   Unlike formal mechanisms, which are created in order to provide for inclusion and accountability for migrants, informal mechanisms merely provide opportunities for input and accountability, and are not always available to migrants. And although individuals using these informal mechanisms are indirectly supervised by the state, they are not subject to their control. For example, the state may fund and regulate legal representation, but it does not control or seek to control individual lawyers' advocacy efforts.

Samaritans[48] aim to thwart the policies resulting from this defective process. They come to the aid of migrants out of principled opposition to migration policies and decisions. Samaritans include those who mount rescues at sea, smuggle people across borders, provide sanctuary to those avoiding detection and deportation, and subvert, sometimes through disruptive protest or vandalism, the state's capacity to execute its decisions. Because samaritans are motivated by principle, their activities are distinct from ordinary criminality.[49] Samaritans operate outside existing institutions and in defiance of the parameters for protest and dissent established by the state. Their activities are therefore usually clandestine and do not expressly seek to change the state's policy-making processes.

A few clarifications about these two roles. First, there is not always a stark distinction between the roles of advocate and samaritan. For one, individuals can occupy both; and although advocacy is preponderantly concerned with policy-making processes and samaritanism with immediate respite from frontline decisions, both roles effect long and short-term change. Some forms of non-state action would even seem to overlap, such as acts of civil disobedience and disruptive protest.[50] Second, even though both roles engage the state, non-state actors performing these roles are not subject to the control of the state; their independence is in fact essential to their ability to perform an ameliorative function, since they are not tainted by the defects they seek to correct. And finally, identifying these roles does not mean that the non-state actors putatively performing them are always justified in doing so. Non-state actors do not always set out to perform an ameliorative function, but are often pursuing particular ends and particular roles that only *incidentally* perform an ameliorative function. And even when they do, publicly minded non-state actors may nevertheless get it wrong. My aim here is only to demonstrate how intrinsic arguments that preclude non-state actors can, in the context of border control, render some non-state action prima facie permissible, if not desirable.

It is important to emphasise, therefore, that non-state actors perform only an *ameliorative* function; they are not a substitute public actor. Advocates and samaritans illustrate the ways in which non-state actors can approximate, however roughly, input and accountability mechanisms that provide some means for migrants to engage with the state, as well as some respite from the state's commands. These are, however, ad hoc and unauthorised. As ad hoc measures, they are contingent on the availability of, among other things, funding, interest, and awareness. Some migrants are unable to access advocates, their particular quandary does not attract media attention, or when it does, it fails to generate the public sympathy and outcry required to push government officials to act. The availability and allocation of these mechanisms can therefore be arbitrary; worse, insofar as migrants' access to these mechanisms is determined by priorities and interests that might not align with their own, these mechanisms might systemically exclude some so as to exacerbate pre-existing inequities.

---

[48] These actors could also be described as subversives and civil disobedients. I refer to them as samaritans because they act with a view principally towards aiding migrants, as opposed to challenging the law or subverting the state's authority more generally.

[49] As I discuss elsewhere, there are a range of permissible motivations, including mercenary ones. A. Vasanthakumar, 'Privatizing Border Control', *Oxford Journal of Legal Studies* 38 (2018): 411–29.

[50] Those who engage in disruptive protests to halt deportation flights, for example, aim not only at preventing immediate harm to individual migrants but also at alerting fellow citizens to the harms of the state's policy in order to prompt change. See, e.g., L. Tondo, 'O Captain, My Captain: Sailors Who Risk Jail to Save Migrants' Lives', *The Guardian* (5 July 2019) and P. Kingsley, 'To Protect Migrants from Police, a Dutch Church Service Never Ends', *New York Times* (10 December 2018).

Second, advocates and samaritans act on behalf of migrants. Informal or unauthorised representation is often necessary in contexts where some actors have little voice,[51] but it has limitations: advocates are not always authorised, they may not correctly ascertain and advance the interests of those they claim to represent, and they are not always held to account. Indeed, because of the inherent asymmetry between those with no institutional voice and those in a position to mimic one, migrants might be less likely to hold them to account. Non-state actors do not, therefore, provide a stable mechanism that grants migrants consistent access to decision-makers in the state, and because it involves principally the relationship between citizen advocates and the state, it treats migrants ultimately as objects rather than subjects. Advocacy and samaritanism aim to mitigate migrants' vulnerability to the arbitrary decision-making of the state, but in doing so, they can subject migrants to their own arbitrary decision-making.

To be sure, these concerns can themselves be mitigated – and advocates and samaritans will often be motivated to do so. Foremost, advocates and samaritans can seek the sorts of institutional reform that might make migrants less reliant on them in the first place, that is, they can seek to bring about a properly public actor. Second, these non-state actors could develop practices and norms among themselves that maximise input from migrants and minimise arbitrary or biased decision-making. This might preclude certain forms of preferential treatment on the basis of, say, religion or nationality, and also argues against the profitmotive in people smuggling.[52] And finally, this counsels against individual acts and in favour of organised efforts, which enables more rigorous decision-making, reduces the risks of harm, and provides alternative sources of accountability. In short, non-state actors should seek to become more institutionalised in order to more effectively perform their ameliorative function.

Such institutionalisation is not without its costs, however. It can come at a cost to non-state actors themselves, especially when it requires that they shed their sectarian commitments.[53] And insofar as it is these commitments that motivate non-state actors to perform this ameliorative function, institutionalisation can come at a cost to the ameliorative function itself. This tension – between the roles of advocate and samaritan that non-state actors take on and the ameliorative function they also end up performing – need not be resolved. To reiterate an earlier point, advocates and samaritans do not set out to be public actors; rather, they act for non-public reasons that, in particular contexts, can align with the requirements of public reason and ameliorate the shortcomings of state action.[54] Indeed, there may be instrumental and intrinsic value in protecting these roles and the non-public reasons they embody. Non-state actors can ameliorate the absence of a properly public actor, not by substituting for one but by calling attention to its absence.

[51] For a general discussion of informal representation and accountability, see, e.g. Jennifer Rubenstein, 'Accountability in an Unequal World', *Journal of Politics* 69 (2007): 616–32, and *Between Samaritans and States: The Political Ethics of Humanitarian INGOs* (Oxford University Press, 2015); Laura Montanaro, *Who Elected Oxfam? A Democratic Defence of Self-Appointed Representatives* (Cambridge University Press, 2017).

[52] J. Hidalgo, 'The Ethics of People Smuggling', *Journal of Global Ethics* 12 (2016): 311–26; E. Aloyo and E. Cusumano, 'Morally Evaluating Human Smuggling: The Case of Europe', *Critical Review of International and Social and Political Philosophy* (2018): 1–24; J. Muller, 'The Ethics of (Commercial) Human Smuggling', *European Journal of Political Theory* 20 (2018): 147488511875446.

[53] C. Cordelli, 'How Privatization Threatens the Private', *Critical Review of International Social and Political Philosophy* 16 (2012): 65–87.

[54] Vasanthakumar, *'Privatizing Border Control'*.

6.6 CONCLUSION

An Eritrean citizen seeking asylum in Europe encounters a number of state and non-state actors: networks of smugglers that help him evade Eritrean military patrols with 'shoot to kill' instructions; smugglers, who sometimes turn out to be traffickers, to move him onwards to North Africa, Europe, or the Middle East; forgers who can provide fake passports that will fool even the experts sent by Frontex; the airline steward who does a cursory check before boarding; the asylum official who rejects his claim; the harried lawyer who helps prepare his appeal; the employer who pays him less because he is undocumented, before reporting him; the private contractor who takes him to pre-removal detention; and the student volunteer from a refugee charity who visits him and will later protest outside the airport when he is deported.[55] A discussion about the morality of migration is impoverished without a discussion of the morality of the agents who enable, manage, and thwart the movement of individuals.

In this chapter, I have applied normative arguments about privatization to the context of migration. The outsourcing of border control attracts the same scrutiny and criticism it has in other domains. The state's delegation of border enforcement policies to non-state actors enables abuse and discrimination towards migrants, is inefficient and corruptive of the state, and compromises the integrity of non-state actors themselves. To these contingent moral criticisms, scholars have recently added powerful intrinsic arguments against privatization. These arguments point to the necessity of a properly public actor for those goods that affect important individual interests and alter individuals' normative position, and they illustrate the importance of an integrative practice that connects a properly public actor to the frontline agents tasked with implementing its policies.

Typically, these arguments are taken to point to the state as the properly public actor. In the context of border control, however, they provide the resources to critically reassess the state and the international order within which it is situated. To be sure, there is no shortage of laws, regulations, and agencies concerned with border control within most states. But when these do not include *ex ante* input and *ex post* accountability mechanisms for migrants, the state cannot be a properly public actor. Potentially, such mechanisms exist beyond the state and filter down to it – for example, through international agreements, regional authorities, and aid agencies. The enduring pre-eminence of state sovereignty, however, means that states are not in an integrative practice where they are subject to the control of these global governance mechanisms. And in any event, these global governance mechanisms do not adequately extend to migrants themselves. Migrants remain supplicants, denied the equal moral respect and freedom from domination that properly public institutions promise. Intrinsic arguments thus help us assess how well different agents can comprise a properly public actor, and diagnose institutional shortcomings at both levels.

Intrinsic arguments also help reassess the role of non-state actors. For one, they suggest that the contingent moral criticisms canvassed at the outset arise not because privatization severs the connection between the state and non-state actors but because it does not do so sufficiently. In many cases, the harms inflicted by non-state actors happen not in spite of the state but because of it. Intrinsic arguments also illuminate the role that non-state actors play in ameliorating these institutional shortcomings, and especially their role in bringing about a properly public actor where one does not exist. Indeed, if dispersed forms of global governance are coalescing into a public actor, it is in no small part due to the efforts

---

[55] See P. Tinti and T. Reitano, *Migrant, Refugee, Smuggler, Saviour* (Hurst & Co., 2016), for detailed analysis of people smuggling.

of non-state actors. These ad hoc efforts may be necessary to mitigate the immediate harms produced by defective institutions and to remedy these defects, but they can replicate some of the very defects they seek to remedy. In the context of border control, they highlight in particular the need to ensure that migrants' voice in the processes and policies of border control is institutionalised – echoing concerns raised by democratic theorists, migration scholars, advocates, and migrants themselves.

The Moral Neutrality of Privatization as Such

Alexander Volokh

7.1 INTRODUCTION

The debate over the privatization of government services usually concerns practical considerations like cost and quality. This is not to say that moral questions are absent: in the current controversy over private prisons, for instance, even a supposedly "practical" factor like the "quality" of a prison includes many morally relevant features – like whether private prison firms are more likely to overcrowd their prisons or skimp on necessities like medical care, whether private correctional officers are more likely to abuse prisoners, and whether inter-inmate violence is more likely at a private prison.[1]

The range of "practical" considerations that dominate the privatization debate is extremely wide: again, in the prison example, prominent factors include the safety of the outside world (i.e., the likelihood of escape or the probability that inmates will revert to crime[2]) and the extent to which privatization will distort the criminal law due to the possibility of private firms' pro-incarceration lobbying.[3] But these questions are necessarily empirical: the latest empirical study might show that private prisons are better at preventing recidivism, or that public correctional-officer unions are greater pro-incarceration lobbyists than private prison firms – and newer studies may always supersede the findings of older ones. And even if private providers turn out to be inferior, the solution is not necessarily to avoid privatization; the problem can potentially be solved through clever contract design, for example by making private prison firms' contract payments more responsive to the prison's outcomes in terms of violence, health care, or recidivism.[4]

Recently, though, a number of scholars have crafted critiques of privatization that purport to be non-empirical: that argue against "privatization as such," in the words of the title of

---

[1] Alexander Volokh, "Prison Accountability and Performance Measures," *Emory Law Journal* 63 (2013): 339–416, pp. 347–364.

[2] Ibid., at pp. 357–360.

[3] See, e.g., Alexander Volokh, "Privatization and the Law and Economics of Political Advocacy," *Stanford Law Journal* 60 (2008): 1197–1253.

[4] See Volokh, "Prison Accountability and Performance Measures," at pp. 364–392.

a recent article by Avihay Dorfman and Alon Harel.[5] These critiques reject an approach that focuses too strongly on empirical comparisons of performance, and stress broader philosophical considerations like "public responsibility and ... political engagement,"[6] "the inherently public nature of crime and punishment,"[7] and "the nature and justification of punishment in a liberal democratic policy."[8]

Courts, too, have articulated similar critiques: for instance, the Israeli Supreme Court struck down a prison privatization statute on the grounds that such privatization violated the inmates' constitutional liberty and dignity rights – regardless of how well or badly the inmates were treated.[9]

(These sorts of concerns are present in a number of areas, from privatization of water and sewer systems, to privatization of Social Security, schools, or hospitals,[10] but here I will concentrate on "privatization of force" areas where these "inherent" arguments seem to have greater relevance – using private prisons as my primary example.)

I argue here that these concerns are misplaced. Some of the critiques turn out, on examination, to be empirical after all, so that – even if one grants the force of the critique in principle – privatization might turn out to be superior by the critic's own standard. Other critiques turn out to be indictments of a particular practice – not inherently tied to privatization – that might also exist in the public sector and that a well-designed privatization might avoid. Either way, there is no general problem with "privatization as such."

7.2 THE FUNDAMENTAL NEUTRALITY OF PRIVATIZATION

Non-empirical arguments against privatization assert that, regardless of how well a private contractor might perform a particular service, privatization is nonetheless illegitimate because *the service, by its nature, must be performed by the state*.[11]

But what is "the state"? The state is not a place, a person, or even a group of people. The state is an abstract entity – the sum total of a large number of relationships. The state cannot wage war, because war requires fingers to push buttons and pull triggers, and the state lacks fingers. The state cannot incarcerate, because incarceration requires guards, doctors, cooks, psychologists, and teachers; the state itself has no body with which to perform all these functions. For the state to act, it requires agents.

Where does the state get these agents? It must call on people who know how to push buttons or treat patients or cook food – private people like you and me. Most tasks are not subject to conscription, so let us presume that no one must do these tasks unless they agree to do so. Somehow, the state (really, someone who works for the state) must find such people and convince them to perform the necessary tasks.

Such people might become "state employees." Their contract with the state might be very complex: the job description might be intricate; the discipline and firing of the employees

5   Avihay Dorfman and Alon Harel, "Against Privatisation As Such," *Oxford Journal of Legal Studies* 36 (2016): 400–427.
6   Ibid., at p. 401.
7   John J. DiIulio, Jr., "What's Wrong with Private Prisons," *The Public Interest* 40 (Summer 1988): 66–83, p. 79.
8   Mary Sigler, "Private Prisons, Public Functions, and the Meaning of Punishment," *Florida State University Law Review* 38 (2010): 149–178, p. 151.
9   HCJ 2605/05 *Academic Ctr. of Law & Bus., Human Rights Div.* v. *Minister of Fin.*, ¶ 33 [2009] (Isr.).
10 Alexander Volokh, "Privatization and the Elusive Employee-Contractor Distinctions," *UC Davis Law Review* 46 (2012): 133–208, pp. 136–137.
11 "The state," here, of course refers to the government as a whole, not to "states" of a federal union.

might be governed by civil service statutes or a collective bargaining agreement negotiated with a public employee union; and the wages, pensions, and benefits might likewise be regulated by public law. But at its base, public employees are parties to a contract with the state, by which they agree to do the state's bidding in exchange for money.

Or such people might become "state contractors." Either way, the state acts by making contracts; either way, someone agrees to do the state's bidding in exchange for money.

Does it matter what sort of contract is involved? Yes, it matters greatly, because different contracts have different terms, are subject to different legal regimes, can be enforced in different ways or to different extents, and therefore create different incentives – which, in turn, lead to different results in the real world. Perhaps public-sector contracts differ systematically from private-sector contracts. Perhaps these institutional differences are highly contingent, and statutory reform or clever contracting can replicate the features of one sort of contract in another sector; or perhaps these institutional details are fairly sticky. When all is said and done, these differences might give a good reason for preferring public to private provision, or the other way around.

But these are, at bottom, *empirical* factors – still very important, but empirical nonetheless, and so they will not ground a critique of privatization "as such." When the state acts, it acts through its contractual agents. When considering the act of a public employee or that of a private contractor, it makes sense to say that *both* are acts of the state, because in both cases the actors have agreed to do the state's bidding. It also makes sense to say that *neither* is the act of the state, because in either case the actors are incompletely controlled by their contract and might perform unapproved acts for their own purposes. But it does not make sense to say that *one* of them is the act of the state (and therefore legitimate) while *the other* is not (and therefore illegitimate).

7.3 ACCOUNTABILITY-BASED ARGUMENTS

Can one successfully distinguish between public employees and private contractors, so as to say that the one is legitimate and the other is not?

One class of arguments refers to the differences in accountability between the two sectors. Malcolm Thorburn, for instance – discussing private policing – writes that accountability and public scrutiny are the key to being able to "legitimately claim to be acting in the name of the state."[12] To be legitimate, policing must be "bound up with impartiality," and only "the state, if properly constructed, can both represent us collectively ... and yet speak for no private party in particular."[13] Acting in the name of the state requires meeting "the accountability standards set out in public law – roughly, reasonableness and fairness," as well as "the rights protections set out in constitutional bills of rights, to which private citizens and private action are not similarly subject."[14]

This is a powerful critique, but it is not a critique of privatization as such. It is a critique of *unaccountability*, coupled with an observation that accountability is lesser (or absent) in the private sector. Perhaps, as a contingent matter, those who choose to work in the public sector are personally more inclined to be accountable than those who choose to work in the private sector. But this is not *necessarily* so.

---

[12] Malcolm Thorburn, "Reinventing the Night-Watchman State," *University of Toronto Law Journal* 60 (2010): 425–443, p. 441.
[13] Ibid.
[14] Ibid., at pp. 442–443.

It is also true that private action is generally not subject to the Bill of Rights in US constitutional law, so some privatization will reduce constitutional accountability.[15] But this is conspicuously *not* the case for private prisons in the United States, which are bound to respect all the same prisoners' rights as public prisons – and, in some respects, private prison guards are even subject to greater constraints than public prison guards.[16] The Israeli regime (if it had ever been implemented) would have gone further and actually made private prison guards into civil servants.[17]

This is a broadly applicable point that goes beyond the institutional details of particular jurisdictions. Public-law constraints that apply to public actors can conceivably be extended to private actors – perhaps even in the same statute that authorizes privatization in a particular area. Even if the statutes are silent on the matter, public-law constraints that apply to public actors can be extended to private actors by contract. Jody Freeman calls this phenomenon "publicization"[18] and suggests that privatization can be used as a method for private actors to "increasingly commit themselves to traditionally public goals as the price of access to lucrative opportunities to deliver goods and services that might otherwise be provided directly by the state."[19]

Whether such a move is likely is beside the point: its mere *possibility* shows that, if one is accountability-minded, one can support "the proper sort of privatization" that is accompanied by whatever accountability mechanisms one supports. Thus, the accountability critique of privatization is really about *accountability*. Even if past privatization has lacked the necessary accountability, the proper solution might be to reform privatization, not abandon it – and so the critique is not about privatization *as such*.

7.4 "PRIVATE PURPOSES" ARGUMENTS

Another set of arguments focuses on the actor's purposes: public actors have public purposes while private actors have private purposes, and legitimate punishment must be motivated by public purposes.

Michael Walzer, for instance, argues that "the agents of punishment [must] be agents of the laws and of the people who make them."[20] "Police and prison guards are our representatives, whose activities we have authorized. . . . When [the policeman] puts on his uniform, he strips himself bare, so to speak, of his private opinions and motivations. Ideally, at least . . . he treats . . . all criminals in the same way, whatever his personal prejudices."[21] A private prison, on the other hand – illegitimately – "exposes the prisoners to private or

---

[15] *Rendell-Baker* v. *Kohn*, 457 U.S. 830 (1982); *Blum* v. *Yaretsky*, 457 U.S. 991 (1982).

[16] Specifically, they lack the defense of "qualified immunity" in federal civil rights lawsuits. This is only one dimension of accountability: comparing the full constitutional accountability of public and private prisons is tricky, given the complex web of ordinary tort law and "constitutional tort law" that governs public and private prisons in the United States. See Alexander Volokh, "The Modest Effect of *Minneci v. Pollard* on Inmate Litigants," *Akron Law Review* 46 (2013): 287–329, pp. 294–299.

[17] Barak Medina, "Constitutional Limits to Privatization: The Israeli Supreme Court Decision to Invalidate Prison Privatization," *International Journal of Constitutional Law* 8 (2010): 690–713, pp. 790–710.

[18] Pronounced "public-ization," with a hard "c," to show that it involves the extension of public-law norms.

[19] Jody Freeman, "Extending Public Law Norms through Privatization," *Harvard Law Review* 116 (2003): 1285–1352, p. 1285.

[20] Michael Walzer, "At McPrison and Burglar King, It's . . . Hold the Justice," *The New Republic* 192 (April 8, 1985): 10–12, p. 11.

[21] Ibid. (presumably also including the prison guard).

corporate purposes."[22] (The same argument is made in other contexts – for instance, hospitals.[23])

The phrase "Ideally, at least" is significant: if one cares about purposes, surely what matters is not the *ideal* but whether the actor is *actually* motivated by the public purpose. As a contingent matter, public purposes might be more pervasive in the public sector: perhaps public employment has attracted more public-interested people, or perhaps public values are more likely to rub off on public employees. But the civil servant is not *necessarily* idealistically minded (are there no public prison guards who use their job to satisfy their own brutality?); nor is the private employee *necessarily* mercenarily minded. (Or, if we stick to the realm of ideals, why shouldn't the ideal of a private prison provider likewise be to fulfill its contractual obligations in good faith, or to treat prisoners according to the dictates of justice without regard to private motivations?)

Walzer ultimately argues that the risk of private purposes is greater in the private sector – and gives a number of sound reasons to suspect this – but implicitly seems to grant that his point is fundamentally empirical.

The Israeli Supreme Court similarly stressed the "private purposes" argument in the portion of its opinion holding that private prisons violate inmates' liberty rights (regardless of how well or badly they are treated). In the Court's view, "the question whether the party denying the liberty is acting first and foremost in order to further the public interest . . . or whether that party is mainly motivated by a private interest is a critical question."[24] Making inmates "subservient to a private enterprise that is motivated by economic considerations . . . is an independent violation [of the right to personal liberty] that is additional to the violation caused by the actual imprisonment under lock and key."[25]

In the Court's view, the Israel Prison Service – a "bod[y] that answer[s] to" and "receives its orders from" and "is subordinate to" and "acts through" (and "by and on behalf of") and is a "competent organ[] of" the state or the government or the executive branch (which, in turn, is "the representative of the public")[26] – is fundamentally different from the prison firm, which is "an interested capitalist" and "a private interest," "a party that is motivated first and foremost by economic considerations – considerations that are irrelevant to the realization of the purposes of the sentence, which are public purposes."[27]

But it is unclear why all this is true. The private contractor also receives its orders from the state. A private provider is not *necessarily* motivated by profit, and there is likewise no reason why public employees might not be motivated by personal considerations that are irrelevant to the public purposes behind the sentence. (There is even "profit" in civil-service employment: to the extent that civil-service employees earn more than the minimum they require to stay on the job, they "profit" from their employment – and perhaps some civil-service employees treat their position as "merely a job" and can therefore be said to be profit-motivated.)

The same problems run through "public purposes" arguments generally. Let us take as given, for purposes of argument, that whether the actor has a public purpose is morally relevant. One can soundly argue that public purposes are *more likely* in the public sector – but

[22] Ibid.
[23] Robert Lekachman, *Visions and Nightmares: America After Reagan* (New York: Macmillan, 1987), p. 106.
[24] *Academic Ctr. of Law & Bus. v. Minister of Fin.*, ¶ 22.
[25] Ibid., ¶ 30.
[26] Ibid., ¶¶ 24, 25, 26, 29, 23.
[27] Ibid., ¶¶ 23, 26, 29.

this is now an *empirical* argument, which proponents of "public purposes" arguments usually purport to avoid. (And because it is empirical, it is vulnerable to the counterargument that perhaps future privatizations can be designed with better incentives that blunt the profit motive and promote public-interestedness – for instance, by contracting with nonprofits.) Or one can argue that public purposes are *inherently* present in the public sector and *inherently* absent in the private sector – but this seems clearly false.

7.5 SOCIAL MEANING: THE SUBJECTIVE VIEW

Another class of arguments focuses on the supposed symbolism, expressive value, or social meaning of private punishment.

This social meaning might be a purely subjective matter: perhaps people *believe* that private prisons are illegitimate because they have private purposes. Martha Minow writes that private prisons "may jeopardize the legitimacy of government action because the public may suspect that private profit-making – rather than public purposes – is being served."[28] Justice Arbel of the Israeli Supreme Court writes that prison privatization "creates the impression that irrelevant considerations are involved . . ., something that undermines the moral authority underlying the activity of that enterprise and public confidence in it, since even if justice is done, it is not seen to be done."[29] And Richard Lippke writes that "[p]rivate prisons may add insult to injury and thus fuel social discontent, since it may not go unnoticed that such facilities, in effect, turn offenders into raw materials for corporate profit"[30] – suggesting that a relevant perceiving community might be the community of inmates, not just the public at large. These sorts of arguments show up in other contexts as well, from private military contractors to for-profit hospitals.[31]

At first glance, this seems like the "private purposes" argument: private prisons are illegitimate because they are motivated by profit. I have argued already that, even if one believes that a provider's purposes are relevant, it is not necessarily true that private providers are less public-motivated than public providers. But this argument is different. One might believe that public perceptions of legitimacy are an entirely separate source of legitimacy: to be legitimate, perhaps institutions have to be perceived as legitimate. If this is so, then, hypothetically, if enough people believed the "private purposes" argument against privatization, privatization might be illegitimate *even if the argument were entirely incorrect.*[32]

This symbolism argument is infinitely malleable. The supposedly objectionable symbolism of private incarceration needn't be tied to the specific "public purposes" argument. The objectionable symbolism could stem from a view that public provision supposedly represents collective action while private provision supposedly represents individualism. Michael O'Hare and coauthors, for instance, write:

---

[28]   Martha Minow, "Public and Private Partnerships: Accounting for the New Religion," *Harvard Law Review* 116 (2003): 1229–1270, p. 1234.

[29]   *Academic Ctr. of Law & Bus.* v. *Minister of Fin.,* ¶ 5 (Arbel, J.).

[30]   Richard L. Lippke, "Thinking about Private Prisons," *Criminal Justice Ethics* 16 (Winter/Spring 1997): 26–38, p. 31.

[31]   Jon D. Michaels, "Beyond Accountability: The Constitutional, Democratic, and Strategic Problems with Privatizing War," *Washington University Law Quarterly* 82 (2004): 1001–1127, p. 1042.

[32]   To be sure, one might resist the notion that even irrational notions of legitimacy should be given independent credence in a theory of legitimacy. Perhaps morally legitimate institutions are legitimate regardless of how they are perceived. (Sociological legitimacy is a different matter.) But here I am agnostic about the theories themselves; I am merely arguing that theories that are apparently non-empirical or about privatization as such are in fact empirical or not about privatization as such.

Public and private production differ in two primary ways. The first is that public actions have the authority, mandate, and consent of society as the consequence of collective choice; they are the concrete manifestation of what we *want to do* as a group. The second is that public actions serve a symbolic purpose; they are what we want to *see ourselves choosing to do* as a group. They are a significant part of what it means to be a political collectivity rather than an atomistic plurality.[33]

This, too, is incorrect as a logical matter: society may collectively choose to do something and then contract with private corporations to get it done; this is no less a social choice than the choice that we label "public provision," which is just another form of contract. The same is true of what we see ourselves choosing to do as a group, and being a political collectivity rather than an atomistic plurality: it is difficult to see what is atomistic about a choice to incarcerate that is arrived at collectively, paid for with collective funds, and delivered by parties who contract with the state pursuant to a collective authorization of this particular contractual form.

However, incorrect or not, if enough people believe this argument, it can be an independent argument against privatization.

The trouble with this argument, though, is that it, too, turns out to be empirical. How do we know whether people ascribe any of these objectionable social meanings to privatization? Usually this is merely asserted, not proved – but it's the sort of thing that is amenable to testing and measurement. Maybe very few people care who delivers incarceration, as long as prisoners are treated humanely. Or maybe some people care, but it is a transitional concern that will wear off as prison privatization loses its novelty. Or perhaps the government could "imprint literally private acts with semantically public significance, as it has learned to do with private education (by accreditation, curriculum supervision, and the pledge of allegiance) and the private services of defense lawyers (by making them officers of the court)."[34] Perhaps people's perceptions of legitimacy will follow the reality, so that if private prisons do an actually better job (by whatever standard of legitimacy people find relevant), people will eventually come to see them as *more* legitimate; if so, we might as well just care about the fundamentals, and let perceptions take care of themselves.

In any event, these are all empirical issues, so this objection to privatization also turns out to be a contingent one.

7.6 SOCIAL MEANING: THE OBJECTIVE VIEW

But not every "social meaning" theorist takes the subjective view. Some argue that private prisons have an objective meaning – independently of whether anyone subjectively believes this – that makes the practice illegitimate.

Consider, for instance, the view of Mary Sigler. Sigler writes that criminal punishment is a dialogue between society and the offender, in which it is important that the society that is punishing is the same society to which the offender belongs. "It must be 'us against us' rather than 'us against them.'"[35]

---

[33] Michael O'Hare et al., "The Privatization of Imprisonment: A Managerial Perspective," in *Private Prisons and the Public Interest*, ed. Douglas C. McDonald (New Brunswick, NJ: Rutgers University Press, 1990), pp. 107–129, p. 121.

[34] Ibid., at pp. 121–122.

[35] Sigler, "Private Prisons, Public Functions, and the Meaning of Punishment," at p. 174.

The problem with private prisons, then, is that "by privatizing punishment . . ., we terminate the dialogue between offenders and their community in just the same way as if we privatized prosecutors and criminal courts."[36] It can "easily . . . scramble[]" the message of punishment by

> interpos[ing] a filter between the community and the offenders whom it calls to account. In particular, by transforming the institutions of punishment into commodities – fungible objects of economic exchange – privatization alters the character of punishment, reducing the punitive enterprise to a question of price point and logistics. . . . As we distance ourselves from the condemnatory practice, . . . we attenuate its message of censure, alienating offenders and ourselves from the meaning and value that constitute the liberal-democratic community.[37]

Initially, we can observe that this is not a critique of privatization as such. Instead, it is a critique of a particular way of thinking about prisoners – thinking about them in terms of "logistics" instead of the very solemn social message of punishment. Many private-prison officials are former public-prison officials, and presumably they do not shed their attitudes at the door of their new workplace. Conversely, some Department of Corrections officials may also be efficiency-minded, seeking the lowest-cost way to run public prisons and leaving the social message of punishment to other actors in the system. (This is similar to the "private purposes" argument against privatization, only recast to emphasize the social message rather than the subjective attitudes of the participants.)

Second, one might wonder whether this critique is truly objective, rather than subjective. Sigler argues that the social meaning of punishment is rooted in "conventional forms of condemnatory expression," "deeply rooted public understandings," and "conventional symbols."[38] Does this depend, then, on the public's subjective perception after all?

Sigler, however, denies that this is a subjective inquiry. To the extent that people's perceptions come to accommodate private prisons as just another form of incarceration, she says, such "cultural change" should be "resist[ed]" as inconsistent with "liberal-democratic values": "For punishment engages fellow citizens in one of the most serious and definitive enterprises of a liberal-democratic community – holding ourselves and one another responsible for our actions – and the voice of the community is clearest when it speaks for itself."[39]

The problem for Sigler, then, is that under privatization, the community does not "speak[] for itself." But this is, again, the fallacy of contractual form: the community supposedly *does* speak for itself through public employees but *does not* speak for itself through private contractors – even though both are just private individuals who have agreed, by contract, to do the state's bidding for money.

The Israeli Supreme Court made a variant of the social meaning argument. I have discussed already how, in its holding that private prisons violated the inmate's constitutional right to *liberty*, the Court relied on a private purposes argument. In its second holding – that private prisons violated the inmate's constitutional right to *dignity* – the Court made a social meaning argument: Private prisons violate human dignity because of "the social and symbolic significance of imprisonment in a privately managed prison."[40] Because there is

---

[36] Ibid., at p. 176.
[37] Ibid., at p. 176–177.
[38] Ibid., at pp. 173–174.
[39] Ibid., at p. 177.
[40] *Academic Ctr. of Law & Bus. v. Minister of Fin.*, ¶ 38.

a "social consensus" that private prisons "express disrespect," the practice violates human dignity – "irrespective of the empirical data ... (which may be the source of the symbolic significance), and irrespective of the specific intention of the party carrying out an act of that type in specific circumstances."[41]

Why is there such a social consensus? Because, in the Court's view, private imprisonment "expresses a divestment of a significant part of the state's responsibility for the fate of the inmates, by exposing them to a violation of their rights by a private profit-making enterprise."[42] The theme is that the government must recognize the gravity of what it's doing to the prisoner and respect him as a person, and that privatization is an impermissible distancing. Critics make similar points as to privatization in areas far removed from prisons, such as education or Social Security.[43]

The authors who take this position are often unclear on whether this variant of the social meaning argument is subjective or objective. If it is subjective, then (as discussed earlier) the argument can be valid (assuming that people's subjective views should be relevant to legitimacy), but then it is an empirical question as to whether such views exist. If it is objective, it is unclear why privatization implies such a moral distancing. Perhaps past instances of privatization might have been motivated by this view, but then again, people who run public prisons may also take an inhumane attitude toward their charges and run their prisons with an eye toward efficiency. Moreover, privatization advocates often argue in favor of privatization precisely on the ground that it will improve prison quality (including the treatment of inmates and the protection of their rights) – so that, from their perspective, privatization is a profoundly moral act, and it is the insistence on the status quo of public incarceration that amounts to moral distancing.

7.7 THE DEFERENCE ARGUMENT

Perhaps the most interesting argument is one that has been fleshed out in a series of papers by Alon Harel, sometimes coauthoring with Ariel Porat and most recently coauthoring with Avihay Dorfman.[44]

7.7.1 *Fidelity of Reason vs. Fidelity of Deference*

Harel begins with a hypothetical: suppose the state sentences a criminal defendant to suffer some sanction, and then seeks to recruit me, a random person, to impose that sanction. May I do so? Harel argues that I cannot simply trust the government's judgment that the sanction is justified: if I am to impose the sanction, I must come to an independent judgment on the matter. But if I then impose the sanction, the sanction – which I have imposed because of my own private judgment – is at least in part a private act, and does not count as criminal

---

[41]   Ibid., ¶¶ 38, 39.

[42]   Ibid., ¶ 39.

[43]   Paul Starr, "The Limits of Privatization," in *Proceedings of the Academy of Political Science*, ed. Steve H. Hanke, 36 (1987): 124–137, p. 135.

[44]   Alon Harel, "Why Only the State May Inflict Criminal Sanctions: The Argument from Moral Burdens," *Cardozo Law Review* 28 (2007): 2629–2645; Alon Harel, "Why Only the State May Inflict Criminal Sanctions: The Case Against Privately Inflicted Sanctions," *Legal Theory* 14 (2008): 113–133; Alon Harel and Ariel Porat, "Commensurability and Agency: Two Yet-to-Be-Met Challenges for Law and Economics," *Cornell Law Review* 96 (2011): 749–787; Avihay Dorfman and Alon Harel, "The Case Against Privatization," *Philosophy and Public Affairs* 41 (2013): 67–102; Dorfman and Harel, "Against Privatisation As Such."

punishment. It is therefore illegitimate, because "[i]t is demeaning to subject a person to the normative judgment of another citizen rather than to the normative judgment of the state."[45]

For criminal sanctions to be justified, then, they must be "inflicted by the same agent who issues the prohibitions" – or at least "by individuals who satisfy some formal requirements that affiliate them with the state."[46] The private citizen may not punish without illegitimately using his private judgment (Harel calls this "fidelity by reason"), whereas a public official is "entitled to rely on the state's judgments concerning the appropriateness of the sanctions"; he must "perform [his] task irrespective of his private convictions" and "obey blindly … the orders of the state" (Harel calls this "fidelity by deference").[47]

This raises a number of questions, including: Why can't these "formal requirements that affiliate [someone] with the state" include a prison management contract? If the public official may rely on the state's judgment, why can't a private person commit to do the same – or, conversely, if (as Harel argues) a private person could never trust the state's judgment, what justifies a public official's similar trust? In other words, why must the "fidelity by deference"/"fidelity by reason" distinction track the public/private distinction?

In later work, Dorfman and Harel explain that one can't just *choose* to adopt fidelity by deference. "A person cannot merely approach the performance of the task at stake from the point of view of the state – there is no such ready-made perspective lying out there."[48] Fidelity by deference requires an "institutional structure" and a "community of practice" within which, through "practical deliberation," agents determine the point of view of the state. It is not enough for the providers themselves to constitute such a community of practice by themselves: "The practice must be able to integrate the political offices into this community."[49] Deliberation should thus "span the entire range of governmental hierarchy, which is to say all the way up to the highest political office and all the way down to the lowest-level civil servant who happens to push the proverbial button."[50]

This, in Dorfman and Harel's framework, is what separates public from private provision. A private community of practice is unable to achieve the required deference, even when it is supervised by state officials. "This is so because the interaction of participants in a private practice with state officials is mediated through a contractual agreement the effect of which is the replacement of deference to the polity with reason that is unconstrained by the polity."[51]

The relevant difference is between *direct* political control over the activity and control that is *mediated through an agreement*: a "typical privatization agreement" sets particular ends, "usually in general and underspecified terms," and allows the contractor to achieve the desired ends within some "*arena of permissibility*."[52] This arena of permissibility "is not an accidental feature of privatization": "[r]ather, it is a prerequisite for realising the goals that privatization is designed to realise – in particular, efficiency."[53]

---

[45]   Harel and Porat, "Commensurability and Agency," pp. 781–786; Harel, "Why Only the State May Inflict Criminal Sanctions" (2007), p. 2641; Harel, "Why Only the State May Inflict Criminal Sanctions" (2008), pp. 128–129.

[46]   Harel, "Why Only the State May Inflict Criminal Sanctions" (2008), at p. 130; Harel and Porat, "Commensurability and Agency," at p. 783.

[47]   Harel, "Why Only the State May Inflict Criminal Sanctions" (2007), at p. 2642; Harel, "Why Only the State May Inflict Criminal Sanctions" (2008), at p. 117; Harel and Porat, "Commensurability and Agency," at p. 784; Dorfman and Harel, "The Case Against Privatization," at p. 73.

[48]   Dorfman and Harel, "The Case Against Privatization," at p. 80.

[49]   Ibid., at p. 84.

[50]   Ibid., at p. 87; see also Dorfman and Harel, "Against Privatisation As Such," at p. 417.

[51]   Dorfman and Harel, "Against Privatisation As Such," at p. 414.

[52]   Ibid., at p. 415 (emphasis added).

[53]   Ibid., at p. 416.

Within this protected sphere, politicians are prevented from intervening directly. "Privatization, insofar as it cuts political officials off from the community of practice, immunises the participants – for example, the employees of a private firm – from being obligated to defer to the relevant political officials. It is thus implausible to describe their efforts in executing laws or judicial decisions as the doings of the state."[54]

7.7.2 *Shared Responsibility and Political Engagement*

Why is it necessary to debate whether acts are public or private in Dorfman and Harel's sense, that is, whether they result from reason or deference? What difference does it make? Recall that, in the case of prisons, the argument that private contractors cannot be deferential implies that private prisons are unjust, since "[i]t is demeaning to subject a person to the normative judgment of another citizen rather than to the normative judgment of the state."[55]

This is a prison-specific point. But a version of this point can be generalized to other spheres as well. In a recent paper, Dorfman and Harel – without taking a strong general position on "what goods must be publicly provided" – nonetheless seek "to identify the values that are promoted by *public* provision of goods and services as such."[56] Thus, even when a service *may* be provided by the private sector, their analysis still provides reasons *against* privatization, even if those reasons are not dispositive in any particular case.

Dorfman and Harel's position is that "privatization as such erodes shared responsibility and political engagement." This follows fairly straightforwardly from Dorfman and Harel's definition of the public sector in terms of deference and the requirement that deference include continuous control rights by political officials. It is worth quoting this discussion at length:

> The control that citizens possess (in some measure) over the doings of the polity carries immediate normative implications, but only when public officials, rather than private entities, are in charge of providing the relevant goods. Private contractors enjoy the discretion to make decisions within the scope of what we have termed "arena of responsibility". As a result, the polity has no control over them, and therefore no responsibility for these decisions and the actions that follow therefrom. Privatization, therefore, signifies detachment of the polity from at least some of the decisions made by the private body. By granting (Hohfeldian) immunity to the decisions made by the private entity, the polity distances itself from the privatised activity, or at least from those decisions made by the private entity which fall within the scope of the arena of permissibility.
>
> By contrast, citizens are responsible for the decisions of their polity. Even if they may not be in direct control over these decisions, the rightness or justness of these decisions is, nonetheless, directly their business, for such decisions are done in their name. This is the by-product of the facts that (i) citizens in a "well-ordered society" have "a meaningful role in making political decisions" and that (ii) politicians are active participants in the "integrative practice" of public officials. Hence citizens also participate, albeit indirectly, in the integrative practices.[57]

Whether such political engagement is absolutely required is a matter to consider case by case, depending on the importance of collective undertaking[58] – but privatization will still

---

[54]   Ibid.; see also Dorfman and Harel, "The Case Against Privatization," at p. 87.
[55]   See text accompanying note 45 *supra*.
[56]   Harel and Dorfman, "Against Privatisation As Such," at p. 421.
[57]   Ibid., at p. 422.
[58]   Ibid., at pp. 423–425.

have an aggregate, systemic effect of reducing political engagement overall. Thus, even if privatization seems justified in a number of individual cases, one must still consider the systemic effect as a strike against the whole privatization agenda.[59]

7.7.3 *Objections to Dorfman and Harel's Public–Private Distinction*

Dorfman and Harel's efforts come closer than any of the other theories canvassed here to laying out an inherent objection to privatization. Nonetheless, this theory is still vulnerable on a number of grounds.

7.7.3.1 The Definition of "Privatization" Does Not Correspond to Actual Usage

Could a private organization choose to act deferentially by integrating politicians into its practice in the way that Dorfman and Harel demand? At one point, they grant that this is possible, though unlikely – it could happen if they "turn their backs on the private purposes that provide the grounds for their operations – ... withdraw from their basic commitment to maximize profits or [in the case of a non-profit] vindicate certain ideals ... – and display fidelity of deference to the judgment of state officials in all matters pertaining to the execution of the contracted-for task."[60]

Relatedly, it is possible that some groups of public employees are in fact practicing fidelity by reason instead of fidelity by deference – failing to create a community of practice that seeks to determine the public point of view, that is, consistently trying to implement their own private goals (and usually succeeding because of imperfect monitoring), following the government's orders only because, and to the extent that, they personally agree with them, and standing ready to quit or disobey whenever this ceases to be the case.

It turns out that Dorfman and Harel's definitions of "public" and "private" are functional, not formal. If the provider of a service is a private, publicly traded corporation under contract with the government, common usage would call this, definitionally, "privatization." Nonetheless, such an arrangement might still count as "public" under Dorfman and Harel's theory if the contract includes truly pervasive opportunities for ongoing governmental input and control.[61] "We acknowledge that our definition may sometimes be revisionary."[62] It is thus apparent that Dorfman and Harel's theory is *not actually an objection to privatization in principle*, but rather an insistence on a particular sort of deferential attitude and practice that could in principle exist in either sector.

7.7.3.2 The Distinction between de jure and de facto Control Is Not Significant

Dorfman and Harel put strong emphasis on the government's legal ability to control the actor's conduct. In their view, the government's mere de facto control – along the lines of "you're well advised to do what we say, despite what your contract allows, because otherwise we won't renew your contract" – isn't enough, regardless of how open and effective such control is. "[W]hat is crucial is the participants' Hohfeldian liability to the power of political officials to place them under a duty to act in certain ways and the willingness to exercise this

---

[59]   Ibid., at pp. 425–426.
[60]   Dorfman and Harel, "The Case Against Privatization," at p. 88.
[61]   See also Dorfman and Harel, "Against Privatisation As Such," at pp. 412, 417.
[62]   Ibid., at p. 418.

power whenever they are unsatisfied with the ways in which the practice operates."[63] And this is true regardless of how frequently the government actually intervenes.[64]

But it is unclear why this distinction is significant. If a public employee acts contrary to the government's wishes – indeed, acts contrary to his employer's direct orders – then he may be disciplined, fined, or possibly fired. But this is exactly what can happen to a private contractor.[65] The government's *de jure* control over its own employees thus comes down to its de facto ability to convince them to follow its orders lest they be fired. The distinction between theoretical and practical control may exist in theory, but not in practice.

7.7.3.3 Fidelity by Reason Is Ethically Required

Dorfman and Harel grant that deference by fidelity, while ordinarily virtuous in a public official, is not always so – serving the Nazi regime is one such example.[66] Soldiers should refuse to follow orders that violate the laws of war, and correctional officers should violate orders that violate the constitutional rights of inmates. But this recognition seems damaging to the theory of deference by fidelity. Even if such problematic cases arise only 1 percent of the time, public officials have to be on guard against such cases 100 percent of the time. Indeed, every order has to be scrutinized – according to the official's own judgment – to verify that it does not fall within the forbidden 1 percent of cases. (In other words, to the extent that there exists a community of practice, if that community has its own set of ethical norms that diverge from public norms, and if in some cases public norms lead to unethical acts, the community is always required to consider whether to ignore the public point of view in favor of their private point of view.) Thus, fidelity by reason seems to be an inescapable feature of ethical public work. This recognition undermines the claim that punishment is illegitimate when it stems from fidelity by reason instead of fidelity by deference.

7.7.3.4 The Case for Independent Public Agencies Cannot Be Distinguished from the Case for Private Contractors

What about independent public agencies, characterized by "practices or institutions that are aptly perceived as public even though they defy an integrative character," for instance independent election committees that enjoy "formal and substantive independence from political influence"?[67] These agencies seem to have an arena of permissibility, like the arena that supposedly exists for privatization. Are they perhaps "private" under Dorfman and Harel's functional definition, since political actors have limited input – in other words, the polity has chosen "to release the institution's agents from the requirement to defer to political officials"?[68]

No, say Dorfman and Harel: these agencies are still public, but nonetheless legitimate. They explain how deference by fidelity is consistent with the existence of such institutions: "[R]esort[ing] to [the] discretion [of these independent officials] is sometimes the best, and

---

[63] Dorfman and Harel, "The Case Against Privatization," at p. 87.
[64] Ibid., at pp. 87–88; see also Dorfman and Harel, "Against Privatisation As Such," at p. 417.
[65] Armen A. Alchian and Harold Demsetz, "Production, Information Costs, and Economic Organization, *American Economic Review* 62 (1972): 777–795, p. 777.
[66] Dorfman and Harel, "The Case Against Privatization," at p. 89 n. 35.
[67] Harel and Dorfman, "Against Privatisation As Such," at p. 418.
[68] Ibid.

perhaps the only, proxy for a bureaucrat or an expert to display fidelity of *deference* to the public interest."[69]

How is this not privatization, in Dorfman and Harel's terminology? Because, in their view, the "arena of permissibility" created here is "qualitatively different" from the one created by privatization:

> In contrast to public officials, private actors possess a valid claim-right against state interference insofar as they act within the designated arena of permissibility. In other words, instead of being liable to the power of the state to direct their conduct, private agents enjoy a form of immunity on the basis of which they can invoke their *right* not to follow the demands of the public interest (as viewed from the polity's point of view). Agents of apolitical public institutions, by contrast, enjoy no such immunity. Accordingly, they have no valid claim of their own against state intervention whenever the polity determines that the judgments of these agents disserve the public interest.[70]

There is something counterintuitive about this distinction: if anything, it is *more illegal* to control an independent public agency than it is to intervene in the private contractor's arena of permissibility. The public agency is protected by some statutes granting the agency some degree of independence, so if politicians violate that independence, they are actually violating the law. But the private contractor is merely protected by a contract, and (at least under US law) it is generally legal to breach a contract as long as one is willing to pay damages (which may sometimes be equal to zero).

But, say Dorfman and Harel, unlike the private contractor's arena of permissibility, the apolitical public official's arena "is exclusively designed to promote the public interest" and should be seen as "an exercise of self-constraint on the part of politicians grounded in their judgment that the public interest is better served by apolitical practices."[71] In the case of privatization, politicians should defer to the private contractor "*even when* [its] decisions run afoul of the public interest" – because the contractor has the contractual right to do what it is doing. But when public officials act contrary to the public interest, their arena of permissibility "should be revoked."[72] "Put affirmatively, whereas a public official of an apolitical institution holds a *mandate from* the polity, a private agent holds a *right against* the polity."[73]

But this supposed distinction does not succeed in distinguishing independent public officials from private officials. In both cases, independence from political control is advocated because (in the advocates' view) political control would bias decision-making in undesirable ways. It could be because political control would result in badly drawn electoral districts; it could be because political control would prevent beneficial innovation or efficiency. Either way, independence is advocated because of a view that the public interest demands it. Perhaps what is important is a set of apolitical professional standards – such standards can be mandated by statute in the case of independent agencies, and can be mandated by statute and/or by contract in the case of private contractors.

In both cases, once the entity (whether an independent agency or a contractual partner) achieves the desired independence, the polity is (temporarily) prohibited from intervening in certain ways. In both cases, if the polity decides that the independence is no longer serving the public interest, it can (and should) revoke that independence. In both cases, doing so involves

---

[69]   Ibid., at p. 419 (emphasis in original).
[70]   Ibid. (emphasis in original).
[71]   Ibid., at pp. 419–420.
[72]   Ibid., at p. 420.
[73]   Ibid.

some legally required steps (invoking the elaborate procedure to change the statute, or seeking to modify the contract or waiting until the contractual term runs out).

The supposed difference between these two sorts of independent actors seems to be illusory. (If anything, as noted earlier in this section, there may be a difference that cuts in favor of privatization, since breaching a contract may be easier than amending a statute.)

7.7.3.5 Citizens Do Not Truly Detach Themselves from the Acts of Private Contractors

A fifth objection is related to the previous one. When Dorfman and Harel argue that privatization reduces political engagement, they particularly stress that citizens are responsible for their polity's decisions because they can control those decisions, whereas – because the private contractor has a legally protected "arena of permissibility" – they (to some extent) cannot control the contractor's decisions and are thus not responsible for them.

As I suggested in Section 7.7.3.4, the acceptance of independent public agencies is damaging to this theory. If an independent public agency acts improperly, the polity is still responsible for such acts because it is citizens who have given the agency a limited mandate to pursue the public good – when that mandate turns out not to serve the public good, the polity must revoke the agency's independence. But this is exactly the same thing that the polity must do if private control turns out not to serve the public good because of improper acts by the private contractor: it must revoke the contractor's arena of permissibility, by amending the contract, rescinding the contract, changing contractors when the contractual term is up, or taking the service in-house. These steps may take time, but it also takes time to revoke an independent agency's mandate. Legislative procedure is often a cumbersome matter. Moreover, just as the government can negotiate contracts with pervasive rights of legal control over the contractor's behavior, so, too, can government negotiate contracts with quick and simple termination rights. The government's ability to terminate a contract can be even simpler than the government's ability to revoke the mandate of an independent agency.

But, even more generally, it is questionable whether citizens truly detach themselves from the doings of those over whom they have insufficient control. If privatization really were such a detachment, the polity could be rightly blamed for having relinquished such control. Citizens' ethical duties therefore involve continually monitoring both their public servants and their private contractual partners – everyone who has agreed to carry out governmental tasks, regardless of what sector they work in. Dorfman and Harel argue that we are morally responsible for our own actions and for those actions done in our name[74] – but I would argue that our moral responsibility is no less when we authorize others to act for us. Moral responsibility attaches when we in fact authorize actions; it does not hinge on whether that authorization can be labeled "in our name." Even if that authorization implies some arena of permissibility, we bear moral responsibility for bringing that arena of permissibility into being and for failing to appropriately monitor the contractor and revoke the arena of permissibility when necessary.

Dorfman and Harel would divide the condemnation of private prisons into two steps: (1) private prisons are not truly acting in our name because they have been given a legally protected arena of permissibility; (2) because they are not acting in our name, their actions are unjust because justice, in this context, requires political engagement (regardless of empirical results). I would merge all this into one step: (1) everyone who incarcerates,

---

[74] Ibid., at p. 424.

whether a public or a private actor, is equally "acting in our name" because they have agreed to perform this service by contract with the state; arenas of permissibility are potentially equally beneficial (or equally suspect) in either sector; it depends to what extent such protected spheres serve the public interest, and these spheres should be abolished if they do not serve it. Then I would add a second step: (2) all that matters is whether the incarceration (whoever performs it) empirically contributes to particular desired real-world effects; citizens have a moral duty to adopt whatever structure (public or private provision) best produces those real-world effects.

7.8 CONCLUSION

There is no true objection to privatization *as such*. There are many coherent objections to privatization grounded on its supposed real-world effects. These are empirical and contingent objections, but they are no less important for all that. In the end, the case for or against privatization depends on these empirical judgments.

As for the supposedly non-empirical views, either they turn out to be empirical after all or they turn out to be about something else, other than privatization. In the end, both the public employee and the private contractor are just private individuals who agree to do the state's bidding for money. They might *both* be the state, or *neither*; but to say that one is the state while the other is not is to improperly reify the public and private sectors – rather than seeing them as alternate contractual forms by which people may serve the public.

PART II

On the Virtues of Publicness as a Means to the Realization of Procedural Values (Process-Based Theories)

8

Privatizing Social Services

Martha Minow[*]

8.1 INTRODUCTION

The involvement of private entities in performing government functions, whether publicly financed or removed from public responsibility,[1] is hardly new. Accelerated with support from Prime Minister Margaret Thatcher in Great Britain and US President Ronald Reagan, the use of private companies is generally advanced in terms of efficiency and cost savings.[2] Special issues are posed when governments outsource duties closely related to core governmental functions, such as criminal justice (including policing, prosecuting, and punishing) and national defense (including intelligence gathering and analysis, interrogation of enemies and detainees, and war fighting); the absence of robust private markets and the departure from public values in these domains make reliance on private for-profit providers especially

[*] Thanks to Avihay Dorfman and Alon Harel for the invitation to write and for their valuable comments and to Rachel Keeler for editorial assistance.

[1] Privatization here refers to two concepts: the first involves removing certain responsibilities, activities, or assets from the collective realm, and the second involves retaining collective financing but shifting the tasks of delivery to the private sector. See John Donahue, *The Privatization Decision: Public Ends, Private Means* (New York: Basic Books, 1991), pp. 1–8. Accordingly, sometimes when governments privatize, they decide to contract with private providers for services that remain publicly funded, and at other times, governments privatize by shifting fiscal and decision-making responsibility from government to private actors, including families, religious organizations, nonprofit organizations, and corporations. In either context, at some fundamental level, public decisions significantly frame who is responsible for what. The basic allocation of responsibility for children to their biological parents or the rules granting homeowners considerable latitude in the uses of their property embody governmental choices, backed up by enforceable legal protections. Seeing the pervasive role of government in ratifying or setting up and enforcing societal arrangements should not prevent recognition and debate over decisions shifting provision and at times actual responsibility from government to private actors. Especially where government had taken on responsibilities, such shifts raise issues of public values, and may also risk bypassing otherwise prevailing public norms and regulations. Some nations, especially after the fall of Communism, have converted governmentally owned and operated factories and companies into private free market–based enterprises, as another kind of privatization, but here the focus is on contracting out services still authorized and financed by government. The primary focus here will be on shifting to private actors duties retained legally and financially by government, but both types of privatization will be addressed.

[2] Donahue, *The Privatization Decision*, pp. 4–5.

problematic.[3] Also, direct and indirect involvement of private interests could in fact distort public decisions about whether and how to conduct armed hostilities, and how much to incarcerate people for infractions of laws. But it is more difficult to find fault with government contracting with private providers of food or garbage collection, or to object to some role for private developers in infrastructure and information technology projects. When the government consumes goods and services just like those used in private settings, market pressures on price and quality plus government oversight – if done conscientiously – have potential for ensuring effective use of public resources.

What about privatization of social supports, such as schooling, financial assistance for people with disabilities or in persistent poverty, drug treatment for people with addictions, programs for returning military veterans, children, and the elderly? As this chapter explores, private provision of social services raises particular questions when governments turn to for-profit companies, nonprofit organizations, and religious institutions to perform functions that at other times have been undertaken by governments in many countries.[4] The provision of social services shares with provision of prisons and garbage collection concerns about cost and effectiveness, but diverges in a critical way: social services reflect additional goals of building stronger communities, respecting individual dignity, promoting equality and opportunity, and expressing in concrete ways care for those in need. There are reasons, and some evidence, to doubt claims of efficiency, potential clashes between the profit motive and social services, dangers of private priorities replacing public values, and potential for disguising or accelerating shifts from government responsibility.[5]

8.2 SOCIAL SERVICES: GOVERNMENT AND PRIVATE PROVISION

People have needs that often go beyond what they themselves or their immediate families can meet. For people with disabilities, chronic illnesses, and addiction issues; people navigating poverty or limited incomes; immigrants, veterans, the elderly, and people losing their spouses or other family members to death; "social services" offer economic and personal support. Often provided by religious or communal organizations, social services have become government activities in many countries over the past two centuries. With the growth of industrial and post-industrial economic development, governments have been actively involved in decisions affecting and at times exacerbating social needs.[6]

---

[3] Lauren Brook-Eisen, *Inside Private Prisons: An American Dilemma in the Age of Mass Incarceration* (New York: Columbia University Press, 2018); Shir Hever, *The Privatization of Israeli Security* (London: Pluto Press, 2017); Jody Freeman and Martha Minow, "Introduction," in *Government by Contract: Outsourcing and American Democracy*, eds. Jody Freeman and Martha Minow (Cambridge, MA: Harvard University Press, 2009), pp. 1, 2, 9–12; Martha Minow, "Outsourcing Power: Privatizing Military Efforts and the Risks to Accountability, Professionalism, and Democracy," in *Government by Contract*, ed. Jody Freeman and Martha Minow, p. 110.

[4] See "Symposium: Public Values in an Era of Privatization," *Harvard Law Review* 116 (2003); Martha Minow, *Partners, Not Rivals: Privatization and the Public Good* (Boston: Beacon Press, 2003); Gillian E. Metzger, "Privatization as Delegation," *Columbia Law Review* 103 (2003). Nations have pursued a more dramatic privatization process in converting governmentally owned and operated factories and companies into private free market–based enterprises.

[5] What, if any, social services should be supported by government is a question with political and moral dimensions, but disguising whether prior commitments are being fulfilled is a potential betrayal of public trust.

[6] Martha Albertson Fineman, "Introduction," in *Privatization, Vulnerability, and Social Responsibility: A Comparative Perspective*, eds. Martha Albertson Fineman, Ulrika Andersson, and Titti Mattsson (New York: Routledge, 2017), pp. 1, 4–5.

In the United States, between the Revolution and the Civil War, local and state governments built asylums for people who were elderly, poor, or physically or mentally ill. The Progressive era of the 1890s generated research and advocacy for a new round of governmental social service, including mandatory schooling, financial assistance for mothers, social insurance for workers, and juvenile courts, as well as coordination between governmental and private social services for orphans and immigrants.[7] In response to the Great Depression, governments dramatically expanded social insurance and subsidized housing, and over time, social services provided by governments have grown to include drug treatment programs, legal aid for low-income individuals, and education and retraining for those who drop out of school or become unemployed.

Social services in the United States have continued to change with ongoing government provision, periodic political reaction against government expenditures and dependencies, and parallel activities by private, often religious, organizations. Arguments about the energy and creativity of for-profit and nonprofit sectors at times press governments to invest in private providers or to step aside altogether.[8] Across Europe, Scandinavia, Australia, and Israel, governmental social services more consistently include medical care as well as support for the poor, the disabled, and others in need. Government policies offer some assistance, such as police protection and schooling, to the whole population but other programs for specific, vulnerable groups.

Government providers of social services and private providers can be competitors or partners; governments may contract with private providers or give individuals vouchers allowing choice among providers. Competition can spur innovation and improvement of quality or tailoring of services to individuals that differ in religion, language, or preferences about kinds of programs.

Especially during times of economic constraint, movements to curtail either public provision or public payment for social services grow and often include attacks on the moral character or worth of vulnerable groups. The pattern has recurred with economic and political cycles. As a result, more recent calls for privatization follow exposés of failures from past efforts to privatize services. For example, in 2013 Mississippi officials urged privatizing the collection of child support payments, despite a failed experiment between 1995 and 2000 performing the same services; the private firm had higher costs and collected less in payments than the state did in the same time frame.[9] In 2016, journalists reported both new interest in privatizing social services in Australia and evidence of past scandals and failures in prior privatization efforts.[10] Similar failures in privatization of foster care in Colorado, privatization of health and human services in Indiana, and privatized welfare-to-work programs in Wisconsin included excessive financial costs, harms to individuals in need,

---

7 Encyclopedia of Chicago, Social Services, www.encyclopedia.chicagohistory.org/pages/1160.html.

8 See Martha Minow, "Public and Private Partnerships: Accounting for the New Religion," *Harvard Law Review* 116 (2003).

9 Nick Surgey and Katie Lorenze, "Profiting from the Poor: Outsourcing Social Services Puts Most Vulnerable at Risk," *Center for Media and Democracy's PR Watch* (October 8, 2013), www.prwatch.org/news/2013/10/12264/profiting-poor-outsourcing-social-services-puts-most-vulnerable-risk.

10 Compare Rob Taylor, "Australia Eyes Privatization of Public Health and Welfare Payments," *Wall Street Journal* (February 8, 2016), www.wsj.com/articles/australia-eyes-privatization-of-public-health-and-welfare-payments-1454991351, with John Quiggin, "People Have Lost Faith in Privatisation and It Is Easy to See Why," *The Conversation* (August 9, 2016), https://theconversation.com/people-have-lost-faith-in-privatisation-and-its-easy-to-see-why-63198. See Freeman and Minow, "Introduction."

and corruption.[11] After Florida outsourced case management of child welfare, the stability of foster care placements declined and the percentage of children shifting across three or more placements within twelve months doubled.[12] An investigation in Texas revealed that taxpayers' dollars used in privatizing its food stamp eligibility program were spent on trying to fix problems the private system had created.[13] These and other privatization efforts led to cancellation of contracts, but not to a halt in the repeated waves of privatization efforts.[14] Underlying factors may be at work, including failures to design correct incentives and oversight, or insufficient priority given as a political, financial, or moral matter to beneficiaries of services. Hence, beyond the familiar debates over privatization in other contexts, distinctive arguments and evidence about opportunities and problems come with privatization of social services.

8.3 OPPORTUNITIES AND CHALLENGES IN PRIVATIZATION OF SOCIAL SERVICES

The dominant policy arguments in favor of privatization focus on cost savings and efficiency; some argue further that competition and private-sector ingenuity will not only save money but also generate innovations and improvement of quality.[15] Opposing arguments stress risks to public values including equal treatment, fair process, checks and balances, and separation of religion from both the state and professionalism.[16] In the context of social services provision, further issues come to the fore. There can be a mismatch in incentives affecting particularly for-profit private actors. Private providers may well by design or by default depart from public norms of antidiscrimination and neutrality toward religion.[17] Private providers can and do escape from other rules and the checks and balances that bind government actors, and may replace public values with private ones. Reliance on private contractors hollows out public institutions and civic spaces, and makes it easier to cut public commitments altogether.

8.3.1 *Mismatch of Incentives*

After legislation authorized the government to outsource much of the operation of a prison to a private company, lawyers on behalf of incarcerated individuals brought a challenge arguing that a for-profit organization risks abusing the constitutional rights of individuals in the face of insufficient state supervision. The Israel Supreme Court did not adopt that

---

[11] Surgey and Lorenze, "Profiting from the Poor." Risks of corruption can arise in government operations, as well, but with typically more chances of exposure and correction.

[12] AFSCME, "Outsourcing Social Services: Eliminating Public Watchdogs," www.afscme.org/news/publications/privatization/power-tools-to-fight-privatization/document/3-Outsourcing-Factsheet-.pdf.

[13] Ibid.

[14] Surgey and Lorenze, "Profiting from the Poor." See John Quiggin, "People Have Lost Faith in Privatization" (describing Australian experiences with privatized vocational education, human services, and health care).

[15] Michael Trebilcock and Ron Daniels, *Rethinking the Welfare State: The Prospects for Government by Voucher* (London: Routledge, 2005). Michael J. Trebilcock and Edward M. Iacobucci, "Privatization and Accountability," *Harvard Law Review* 116 (2003): 1422–1453 (reviewing Martha Minow, *Partners, Not Rivals* (2003)).

[16] Jon D. Michaels, *Constitutional Coup: Privatization's Threat to the American Republic* (Cambridge, MA: Harvard University Press, 2017); Paul Verkuil, *Valuing Bureaucracy: The Case for Professional Government* (Cambridge: Cambridge University Press, 2017).

[17] Legal rules can be crafted to extend public norms into the private actors, but any such efforts are also constrained by independent protections for the autonomy and freedom of especially religious actors.

rationale, but did rule privatization of a prison unconstitutional. The Court reasoned that an inmate has a right not to be subject to coercion by a private for-profit corporation regardless of the actual conditions; the harm to prisoners' rights and dignity imposed by incarceration in an institution motivated by economic interests outweighs expected budgetary savings.[18] This misalignment of rights and economic calculus violated constitutional rights, according to the Court, regardless of contractual features preserving public supervision. Even though budgetary considerations and biases also operate within government bureaucracies, the goals of a for-profit entity could not be compatible with the exercise of government-authorized coercion unless those governmental powers are awarded to a private actor.[19]

Similar concerns could well arise if profit-seeking organizations provide social services. The focus on bottom-line cost-cutting and short-term profits reflects metrics that could often diverge from the kind of attention, continuity, and care required for effective drug treatment or support for both children and parents following instances of child abuse. Reliance on competition to reduce costs is unlikely to work in rural areas or other places with populations too small to support multiple providers of social services. In general, using a market model has sharp limits where there are insufficient people, resources, or infrastructure to support a market. Primary motivations of economic efficiency also tilt toward short-term thinking that misses the qualities of relationship building associated with effective afterschool programs. Short-term financial targets, such as the number of individuals processed for each dollar spent, give businesses the incentive to concentrate welfare-to-work services on those most easily assisted rather than attending to the long-term outcomes for all in need.[20]

Nonprofit organizations attract employees motivated by goals of service and typically less concerned with financial considerations, although maintaining their organizations is an inevitable purpose as well. Is there a clash between privatization and the caring relationship between provider and recipient at the heart of any social services? Even government staff are paid; caring work that is paid for can still be caring work. Devotion to the mission and to recipients animates many people who provide social services and softens the effect of low wages and difficult working conditions.[21] Although service missions guide some for-profit as well as non-profit enterprises, outsourcing services especially to for-profit organizations injects managerial controls and accounting pressures that can impair the providers' motivations and relationships.[22]

[18] HCJ 2605/05 *Academic Ctr. of Law & Bus.* v. *Minister of Fin.* (November 19, 2009), Nevo Legal Database (Isr.); Hila Shamir, "The Public/Private Distinction Now: The Challenges of Privatization and of the Regulatory State," *Theoretical Inquiries in Law* 15 (2014). The decision was predicated on the Basic Law in Israel, and its focus on dignity does not have a direct analogue in the United States.

[19] Shamir, "The Public/Private Distinction Now," pp. 22–23.

[20] In the Public Interest, "How Privatization Increases Inequality" (September 2016), www.inthepublicinterest.org/wp-content/uploads/InthePublicInterest_InequalityReport_Sept2016.pdf; John B. Goodman and Gary W. Loveman, "Does Privatization Serve the Public Interest?," *Harvard Business Review* (November–December 1991), https://hbr.org/1991/11/does-privatization-serve-the-public-interest; Demetra Smith Nightingale and Nancy M. Pindus, "Privatization of Public Social Services: A Background Paper" (prepared at the Urban Institute for U.S. Department of Labor, Office of the Assistant Secretary for Policy, under DOL Contract No. J-9-M-5-0048, #15) (October 15, 1997), www.urban.org/sites/default/files/publication/67086/407023-Privatization-of-Public-Social-Services.pdf.

[21] Mimi Abramovitz, "Privatization in the Human Services: Implications for Direct Practice," *Clinical Social Work Journal* 43 (2015), www.researchgate.net/publication/281556421_Privatization_in_the_Human_Services_Implications_for_Direct_Practice.

[22] Mimi Abramovitz and Jennifer Zelnick, "Privatization in the Human Services: The Impact on the Front Lines and the Ground Floor," in *Privatization, Vulnerability, and Social Responsibility*, eds. Fineman, Andersson, and Mattsson. A contrary view maintains that even government employees work for payment under contracts, and all

Shrinking the quality of relationships and the caring motivation of social service providers poses risks not only to the direct recipients of care but also to their families and communities. Community-based care strengthens social cohesion.[23]

Businesses organized to make profits are likely to shift to short-term financial targets and processing the highest numbers of clients rather than serving even the most difficult clients and improving quality.[24] Only if the government erects incentives and requirements elevating quality and service to time-consuming, difficult cases will this pattern be prevented. As corporations gain public contracts to deliver human services, they also explore ways to make more money on the expected income streams while rationing resources for services.[25] The shift to private provision may also open new opportunities for corruption as political leaders give out contracts.[26] A New York State directive forced families and friends to use exploitative commercial vendors to send packages to incarcerated loved ones until advocacy efforts exposed and ended the requirement that was simply a boon to private companies.[27]

8.3.2 *Departure from Public Norms of Antidiscrimination and Neutrality toward Religion*

When provided by the government, social services must avoid discrimination on the basis of race, national origin, gender, and religion. Such norms may not clearly apply to private providers, especially if they are faith based and have an exemption allowing them to discriminate on the basis of religion and in consonance with their religious commitments. Researchers found through a field experiment in Belgium that for-profit nursing homes were much less likely to provide enrollment instructions to someone identified as "Mohammed" than to someone identified as "Kenney."[28] Perhaps the difference reflects statistical models used by the for-profit providers; more research comparing governmental, nonprofit, and for-profit alternatives would clarify whether the risk of discrimination is greater in the for-profit settings.[29]

Outsourcing to religiously affiliated organizations may helpfully mobilize economic, communal, and spiritual resources, but may also impose religious messages that are not wanted by some recipients. Faith-based providers of homeless services in Texas, for example,

---

providing social services – whether employed by public or private employers – are agents, so the form of the organization is unimportant. Alexander Volokh, "Privatization and the Elusive Employee-Contractor Distinction," *University of California–Davis Law Review* 46 (2012). For a response, see William Paul Simmons and Leonard Hammer, "The Human Right to Dignity and Commodification of Prisoners: Considering Worldwide Challenges to Prison Privatization," in *Privatization, Vulnerability, and Social Responsibility*, eds. Fineman, Andersson, and Mattsson.

[23] Ian Burbidge, "What Makes a Social Movement Successful?," RSA (October 24, 2017), www.thersa.org/discover/publications-and-articles/rsa-blogs/2017/10/what-makes-a-social-movement-successful (describing social benefits of home health care).

[24] Pierre Koning and Carolyn J. Heinrich, "Cream-Skimming, Parking and Other Intended and Unintended Effects of High-Powered, Performance-Based Contracts," *Journal of Policy Analysis and Management* 32 (2013): https://doi.org/10.1002/pam.21695/.

[25] Surgey and Lorenze, "Profiting from the Poor."

[26] Harriet Diana Musoke, "What Does Privatization Mean for Women in Uganda?," in *Privatization, Vulnerability, and Social Responsibility*, eds. Fineman, Andersson, and Mattsson.

[27] Vivian Wang, "Cuomo Halts Controversial Prison Package Policy," *New York Times* (January 12, 2018), www.nytimes.com/2018/01/12/nyregion/prison-package-policy-suspended.html.

[28] Sebastian Jilke Wouter Van Dooren and Sabine Rys, "Discrimination and Administrative Burden in Public Service Markets: Does a Public-Private Difference Exist?," *Journal of Public Administration Research and Theory* 28 (2018): 423–439, https://doi.org/10.1093/jopart/muy009.

[29] See ibid.

use religious images, language, and ideas that are not permitted in governmental agencies.[30] For individuals who do not want such religious dimensions, there may well be no other choices, for providing more options would be more costly.[31] Ensuring the availability of public options serves civic purposes and could, alongside some private alternatives, promote pluralism, but would impose additional oversight and fixed costs.[32] Outsourcing to private providers also risks depleting public institutions, like schools, and civic spaces where people of different backgrounds can encounter one another. Communities that rely on charter schools and private social services providers divert public dollars from public institutions shared across the whole community.[33]

8.3.3 *Bypassing Other Rules Binding Government Actors/Purposes Subject to Checks and Balances*

Jon Michaels shows how executives can use contracting-out for "workarounds" that carry out objectives relatively free from judicial and legislative checks.[34] Constitutional provisions assuring freedom of speech, preventing establishment of religion, and guaranteeing equal protection of the laws may be bypassed when the government services are offered by private actors who are not bound by those constitutional provisions.[35] Even in a state forbidding the use of public social service dollars in contracts with for-profit companies, nonprofits can and do subcontract their work to for-profit companies, contrary at least to the spirit of the law.[36] Because so many contracts for social services are with faith-based providers, the services may include religious messages that government agencies could not use, even if private as well as governmental providers must avoid coercion in their programs.[37] Or the private provider may be outside of statutory duties – such as data privacy – that apply to government actors but not to the private sector.[38] Legislative oversight is less likely to occur and less likely to be effective when the providers are private, multiple, and able to assert their own rights, whether constitutional or proprietary.[39]

Contracts with private providers can also bypass public restrictions on the use of personal data that would not be available to government actors without individual consent. Informational privacy issues increase as information about individuals can be gathered, retained, and distributed without much personal awareness or conscious consent. Government agencies may be able to buy personal data collected by private companies and

---

[30] Helen Rose Ebaugh, Paula F. Pipes, Janet Saltzman Chafetz, and Martha Daniels, "Where's the Religion? Distinguishing Faith-Based from Secular Social Service Agencies," *Journal for the Scientific Study of Religion* 42 (2003): www.jstor.org/stable/1387743.

[31] Minow, *Partners, Not Rivals*, pp. 101–103.

[32] See ibid.; Ganesh Sitaraman and Anne L. Alstott, *The Public Option: How to Expand Freedom, Increase Opportunity, and Promote Equality* (Cambridge, MA: Harvard University Press, 2019).

[33] See Martha Minow, "We're All For Equality in U.S. School Reforms: But What Does That Mean?," in *Just Schools: Pursuing Equality in Societies of Difference*, eds. Martha Minow, Richard A. Shweder, and Hazel Markus (New York: Russell Sage Foundation, 2010).

[34] Jon D. Michaels, "Privatization's Pretensions," *University of Chicago Law Review* 77 (2010): 717, pp. 719, 735.

[35] Ibid., at p. 735.

[36] Mimi Kirk, "Does Privatized Foster Care Put Kids at Risk?," CityLab (June 15, 2018), www.citylab.com/life/2018/06/does-privatized-foster-care-put-kids-at-risk/562604.

[37] A religious provider may even claim constitutional freedom to include prayer or Bible study in its programs as a matter of its own rights and the rights of its employees. See also David Saperstein, "Public Accountability and Faith-Based Organizations: A Problem Best Avoided," *Harvard Law Review* 116 (2002).

[38] Michaels, "Privatization's Pretensions," pp. 738–739.

[39] See ibid., at pp. 770–772.

use it to develop profiles and to analyze patterns as part of law enforcement and security activities – even if the purchased information would not have been available to the government without the consent of the individual subjects, who remain largely unaware that the government now has their information. State and federal legislatures have developed health privacy protections to limit public and private uses of personal data in marketing drugs, making insurance decisions, and otherwise affecting individuals, but such rules, absent close governmental oversight, can be avoided by private providers.[40] Government uses of subcontracting, vouchers, and other techniques of privatization similarly water down or bypass legal restrictions that attach to public action. Once performed by private entities, functions such as policing, schooling, and elder care fall outside protections assured to individuals for freedom of speech, free exercise of religion, freedom from unreasonable searches or seizures, and cruel and unusual punishment.[41] Government contractual provisions and oversight could remedy such exclusions – but the supply of private alternatives itself may reflect the freedom from the obligations attached to the public sector.

8.3.4 *Shrinking Public Commitments*

One form of privatization removes the fiscal oversight as well as service provision once performed by government to the private sector, and hence directly shrinks public commitments. Leaving social services for those in need entirely to private actors – especially if they are under-resourced – may undermine loyalty and respect for the nation. Even when the form of privatization retains government responsibility and financial obligation but shifts service delivery to private actors, public commitments can gradually or sharply diminish. When a for-profit company has a contract for providing welfare services, it can easily be rewarded by the government for moving recipients off of the welfare rolls or otherwise curbing people's uses of services.[42] This is simply one of many ways that outsourcing can contribute to shrinking public provision and even the basic collective commitment to address social needs. Privatization often arises in the midst of political fights over whether to curtail public commitments. Welfare reform in the United States curtailed means-tested public assistance, cutting the percentage of those in poverty served from 68 percent to 27 percent between 1996 and 2012.[43] The same welfare reform supported state contracts with private entities that in turn threatened responsiveness to clients and assistance to individuals with special needs.[44] Scholars have identified reduction of social safety nets and greater social acceptance of inequalities with a stage of privatization.[45] Privatization of elder services in Sweden is associated with fewer

---

[40] See, e.g., Regulations issued pursuant to Health Insurance Portability and Accountability Act of 1996, 67 Fed. Reg. 52, 182 (August 14, 2002).

[41] In the United States, constitutional doctrine concerning what counts as "state action" sufficient to trigger constitutional protections is particularly muddled in areas affecting social services. Sacha M. Coupey, "The Subtlety of State Action in Privatized Child Welfare Services," *Chapman Law Review* 11 (2007).

[42] Michaels, "Privatization's Pretensions," at p. 741.

[43] Peter Edelman, *So Rich, So Poor: Why It's So Hard to End Poverty in America* (New York: The New Press, 2012). See Kathy Abrams, "Three Faces of Privatization," in *Privatization, Vulnerability, and Social Responsibility*, eds. Fineman, Andersson, and Mattsson.

[44] Mary Bryna Sanger, *The Welfare Marketplace: Privatization and Welfare Reform* (Washington, DC: Brookings Institution Press, 2003).

[45] Si Kahn and Elizabeth Minnich, The Fox in the Henhouse: How Privatization Threatens Democracy (Oakland: Berrett-Koehler, 2005); Abramovitz and Zelnick, "Privatization in the Human Services"; Mirjam Katzin, "Freedom of Choice over Equality as Objective for the Swedish Welfare State? The Latest Debate on Choice

employees per client, but also with more menu options – indicating that private contractors may offer more choices to clients while weakening the structural elements of quality care.[46] Reliance on private providers can veil changes in programs while initiating larger steps toward offloading collective duties to private groups and to individuals. Moreover, even if the private providers match the same level and quality of services previously offered by public entities, the shift to private settings can contribute to a diminished sense of commonality and public concern.[47]

8.4 REFLECTIONS

Using private providers is a long-standing and inevitable method for governments to meet at least some of their commitments, because governments often lack capacities and flexibilities that the private sector features. Special issues arise when governments turn social services over to private providers, whether for-profit of not-for-profit, religiously affiliated or secular. Government decision-makers may prefer the incentives affecting for-profit private actors, but doing so can undermine public purposes. Government officials may not intend to bypass public norms of antidiscrimination and neutrality toward religion by using private contractors – or the intent may be to do just that; either way, departure from public norms comes with the territory of privatization. Private providers can and do diverge from other rules such as those governing individual privacy and freedom of speech, and also bypass the checks and balances that bind government actors. Private providers may replace public values with private ones. Reliance on private contractors makes it easier to cut public commitments altogether. These are reasons to be especially wary of privatization in the context of social services.

in Education," in *Privatization, Vulnerability, and Social Responsibility*, eds. Fineman, Andersson, and Mattsson. On challenges to social safety nets and the contrast between universal and targeted programs, see Eduardo Porter, "Patching Up the Social Safety Net," *New York Times* (March 18, 2015), www.nytimes.com/2015/03/18/business/patching-up-the-social-safety-net.html.

46 Ragnar Stolt, Paula Blomqvist, and Ulrika Winblad, "Privatization of Social Services: Quality Differences in Swedish Elderly Care," *Social Sciences & Medicine* 72 (2011), https://doi.org/10.1016/j.socscimed.2010.11.012.

47 For a critique of private prisons along these lines, see Sharon Dolovich, "How Privatization Thinks: The Case of Prisons," in *Government by Contract*, eds. Freeman and Minow.

9

Privatization, Constitutional Conservatism, and the Fate of the American Administrative State

Jon D. Michaels[*]

9.1 INTRODUCTION

The American administrative state has, of late, been under siege, attacked on two fronts. The war on one front is somewhat parochial – a pitched battle over US constitutional law. It is waged largely by conservative movement lawyers who view the modern administrative state as an affront to the constitutional separation of powers.

The war on the other front has much greater transnational relevance. This second fight pits defenders of modern bureaucratic governance against those who see public administration as hopelessly inefficient, rigid, and unaccountable. This latter group of critics present themselves as more or less comfortable with the constitutionality of the administrative state – and thus claim to raise only technocratic objections. At bottom, many of these critics wish to see government run more like a business.

Both sets of challengers appear to be gaining ground, slowly but surely undermining the administrative state's personnel, procedures, and powers. The first group, composed of what I'll call *constitutional conservatives*, is transforming academic debates and, increasingly, American jurisprudence. Over the past several years, influential professors[1] and jurists (including those on the Supreme Court)[2] are evidencing an unprecedented willingness to demolish the whole administrative edifice, brick by brick, if not via a wrecking ball.

[*] Thanks are owed to Avihay Dorfman, Alon Harel, and their colleagues at the Edmond J. Safra Center.

[1] See Phillip Hamburger, *The Administrative Threat* (New York: Encounter Books, 2017); Phillip Hamburger, *Is Administrative Law Unlawful?* (Chicago: University of Chicago Press, 2014). See also Richard A. Epstein, *The Dubious Morality of Modern Administrative Law* (London: Rowman & Littlefield, 2020); Joseph Postell, *Bureaucracy in America: The Administrative State's Challenge to Constitutional Government* (Columbia, MO: University of Missouri Press, 2017). Cf. Gillian E. Metzger, "The Supreme Court, 2016 Term – Foreword: 1930s Redux: The Administrative State Under Siege," *Harvard Law Review* 131 (2017): 1–95 (describing constitutional conservative academic movement); Jack M. Beermann, "The Never-Ending Assault on the Administrative State," *Notre Dame Law Review* 93 (2018): 1599–1651.

[2] See *City of Arlington v. FCC* (2013) 133 S. Ct. 1863, 1878 (Roberts, C. J., dissenting); *Dep't of Trans. v. Ass'n of Am. R.R.* (2015) 135 S.Ct. 1225, 1242–1252 (Thomas, J., concurring); *Gundy v. United States* (2019) 139 S. Ct. 2116, 2130–2131 (Alito, J., concurring); *Gutierrez-Brizuela v. Lynch* (2016) 834 F.3d 1142, 1149 (10th Cir.) (Gorsuch, J., concurring); *PHH Corp. v. Consumer Fin. Prot. Bureau* (2016) 839 F.3d 1, 6 (D.C. Cir.) (Kavanaugh, J.).

   The Trump administration has prioritized appointing conservative jurists, particularly those that share the White House's commitment to "deconstruct[] the administrative state." Philip Rucker and Robert Costa, "Bannon Vows a Daily Fight for 'Deconstruction of the Administrative State,'" *Washington Post* (February 23, 2017), www .washingtonpost.com/politics/top-wh-strategist-vows-a-daily-fight-for-deconstruction-of-the-administrative-state /2017/02/23/03f6b8da-f9ea-11e6-bf01-d47f8cf9b643_story.html; Carl Hulse, "Trump and Senate Republicans

The second set of challengers, whom I'll refer to as *neoliberals*,[3] have been incredibly successful in transforming the way we think about and administer the American welfare state. Insisting they're merely wonks and tinkerers, the neoliberals couch their critiques of bureaucratic governance as nonlegal and apolitical when, in fact, neither is true. In the process, over the span of a couple of decades, they've managed to quietly reconfigure major components of the administrative state along businesslike lines by privatizing, outsourcing, and commercializing essential government responsibilities.[4]

All too often, defenders of the modern administrative state have responded to these attacks blithely or apologetically. When it comes to the challenges mounted by constitutional conservatives, these defenders tend to rely on the long-standing and still-capacious judicial decisions upholding the constitutionality of the administrative state. In brief, they've been telling the conservative critics to get over it: your battle was waged and lost in the 1930s.[5]

And when it comes to the attacks by neoliberals, these and other defenders of the administrative state are often quick to take a different but perhaps no less shortsighted tack. They rush to compromise, agreeing (too readily) that bureaucracy is indeed problematic and allowing that businesslike reforms such as government privatization are okay, at least in some contexts and under the right circumstances. Instead of propounding constitutional or normative defenses of modern public administration, they're apt to fall back on empirical arguments, pointing to the waste, fraud, and abuse that privatization and outsourcing initiatives have engendered. In the process, they are implicitly conceding that *good* privatization – free of waste, fraud, and abuse (and possibly bolstered by assurances that contractors already are or can be induced to be public spirited[6]) – is likely acceptable.[7]

Each of these responses is sensible and prudent. Yet neither seems to be working very well. As noted, the constitutional conservatives are making headway, decision by decision and

Celebrate Making the Courts More Conservative," *New York Times* (November 6, 2019), www.nytimes.com/2019/11/06/us/trump-senate-republicans-courts.html.

3   I appreciate that neoliberal is a freighted term and may be used in different ways in different settings. For my purposes, neoliberalism valorizes and prioritizes market practices and goals. Neoliberalism does so to such an extent that it prompts the state not simply to advance the interests of business but also to reconstitute itself along businesslike lines.

4   Paul R. Verkuil, *Valuing Bureaucracy: The Case for Professional Government* (New York: Cambridge University Press, 2017); Jon D. Michaels, "Running Government Like a Business . . . Then and Now," *Harvard Law Review* 128 (2015): 1152–1182; Jon D. Michaels, "Privatization's Progeny," *Georgetown Law Review* 101 (2013): 1023–1088; Jon D. Michaels, "Deputizing Homeland Security," *Texas Law Review* 88 (2010):1435–1473; Martha Minow, "Outsourcing Power: How Privatizing Military Efforts Challenges Accountability, Professionalism, and Democracy," *Boston College Law Review* 46 (2005): 989–1026.

5   This view is perhaps best summarized by Cass Sunstein's oft-cited remark that "the conventional [nondelegation] doctrine has had one good year, and 211 bad ones (and counting)." Cass Sunstein, "Nondelegation Canons," *University of Chicago Law Review* 67 (2000): 315–343, p. 322; cf. Metzger, "*1930s Redux: The Administrative State Under Siege*"; Richard Epstein, among others, takes scholars to task for assuming that nondelegation challenges are the only, or even primary, constitutional claims against administrative governance. Epstein, *The Dubious Morality of Modern Administrative Law*, pp. 51–58.

6   See, e.g., Jody Freeman, "Extending Public Law Norms through Privatization," *Harvard Law Review* 116 (2003): 1285–1352; Nina Mendelson, "Six Simple Steps to Increase Contractor Accountability," in *Government by Contract: Outsourcing and American Democracy*, eds. Jody Freeman and Martha Minow (Cambridge, MA: Harvard University Press, 2009), p. 241.

7   I present this argument in fuller detail in Jon D. Michaels, *Constitutional Coup: Privatization's Threat to the American Republic* (Cambridge, MA: Harvard University Press, 2017). There are, of course, some important and noteworthy exceptions, wherein scholars have challenged privatization (writ large) on normative grounds. See, e.g., Avihay Dorfman and Alon Harel, "Against Privatisation As Such," *Oxford Journal of Legal Studies* 36 (2015): 400–427. There are, additionally, any number of trenchant normative challenges to *specific* privatization practices. See, e.g., Sharon Dolovich, "State Punishment and Private Prisons," *Duke Law Journal* 55 (2005): 439–546.

appointment by appointment. In the past few Terms, the Supreme Court – buoyed by the confirmations of administrative-state-skeptics Justices Gorsuch and Kavanaugh – has chipped away at several important administrative law doctrines and practices. As a result, there is new and growing uncertainty over the legitimacy and legality of any number of administrative structures and powers.[8] The same is true vis-à-vis the neoliberal movement, increasingly strong and increasingly bipartisan.[9] What's more, these responses do little to deepen our constitutional or normative commitment to the project of modern administrative governance. That is to say, even if resting on seemingly settled precedents in order to rebuff the constitutional conservatives worked, and even if questioning the comparative efficiencies of neoliberal privatization proved persuasive, the defenders would still be lacking an affirmative philosophical and legal vision of the modern American administrative state. And without such a vision, the administrative state will remain legally, politically, and culturally vulnerable, particularly at a moment such as this amid White House calls to "deconstruct[] the administrative state"[10] and broadside attacks on a federal bureaucracy accused of constituting the vanguard of a traitorous, subversive "Deep State."[11]

In a volume devoted to the study of privatization, a windup of the sort just proffered may seem entirely misplaced. But this chapter aims to situate privatization, at least American privatization,[12] in the crosshairs of two of the most consequential legal and political debates of our time: constitutional conservatism and neoliberalism. These debates are important not only within US borders but also around the world, given the impact of American regulatory policy (or lack thereof) on such things as climate change, immigration, trade, and antitrust, and given the fact that American troops *and thousands upon thousands of military contractors* are, at any given time, deployed around the world.[13]

Furthermore, for those concerned principally about the privatization of government responsibilities and hopeful that compelling, persuasive anti-privatization-specific arguments will suffice to restore modern *truly public* public administration, it is essential to remain mindful of the other wave of attacks mounted by the constitutional conservatives. Thus, if one objects to privatization because it undermines that which is virtuous, accountable, and expertly adroit about public administration, discrediting privatization is only half the battle.

---

[8]   *Lucia* v. *SEC* (2018) 138 S. Ct. 2044; *Gundy* v. *United States*, at 2116; *Kisor* v. *Wilkie* (2019) 139 S. Ct, 2400; Elbert Lin, "At the Front of the Train: Justice Thomas Reexamines the Administrative State," *Yale Law Journal Forum* 127 (2017): 182–195, www.yalelawjournal.org/forum/at-the-front-of-the-train; Nicholas Bagley, "Most of Government Is Unconstitutional," *New York Times* (June 21, 2019), www.nytimes.com/2019/06/21/opinion/sun day/gundy-united-states.html.

[9]   Michaels, *Constitutional Coup*, at pp. 98–110.

[10]   Rucker and Costa, "Bannon Vows a Daily Fight for 'Deconstruction of the Administrative State.'"

[11]   Jon D. Michaels, "The American Deep State," *Notre Dame Law Review* 93 (2018): 1653–1670.

[12]   Privatization often has different meanings outside of the United States. In the United States, privatization and outsourcing are often used interchangeably, as governments at the federal, state, and local level are generally assigning public responsibilities to private actors. And it is this type of privatization that I discuss herein. Elsewhere, privatization may also include the selling off of state assets such as various utility companies. For a discussion of the many meanings of privatization, see Daphne Barak-Erez, "Three Questions in Privatization," in *Comparative Administrative Law*, eds. Susan Rose-Ackerman et al. (2nd ed., Cheltenham, UK: Edward Elgar, 2017), p. 533. Even in the United States, privatization is taking on new flavors and stripes. Michaels, *Constitutional Coup*, at pp. 106–110. But for these purposes, I focus on the core of American privatization – namely, outsourcing.

[13]   At the height of the United States's involvement in Iraq and Afghanistan – a little more than a decade ago – military contractors numbered in the hundreds of thousands. T. Christian Miller, "Contractors Outnumber Troops in Iraq," *Los Angeles Times* (July 4, 2007); Moshe Schwartz, "Department of Defense Contractors in Iraq and Afghanistan: Background and Analysis," *Congressional Research Service* (August 13, 2009), p. 13, www.fas.org /sgp/crs/natsec/R40764.pdf.

The affirmative theory propounded herein aims to be sufficiently robust to thwart both the neoliberals' and the constitutional conservatives' efforts to dismantle the administrative state.

This affirmative theory, which I term *the administrative separation of powers*,[14] takes as a given that the engendering of the modern American administrative state involved the collapsing of the traditional separation of powers. The theory further concedes that combining legislative, executive, and judicial powers all under one (administrative) roof is, for that very reason, highly disconcerting. After all, an animating fear of the constitutional framers was abusive or tyrannous government, which they associated with consolidated, concentrated state power.

But the story of modern administrative governance is not a static one. Early federal agencies may well have been dangerously concentrated. But, in fairly short order, government officials began disaggregating administrative agency power among three sets of rivalrous, diverse stakeholders. Specifically, power was – and often still is – triangulated among presidentially appointed political leaders atop the agencies, politically insulated career civil servants who carry out much of the day-to-day work of the agencies, and the public writ large empowered to participate meaningfully in administrative policymaking, implementation, and enforcement. Thus, modern expressions of federal regulatory power involve the interplay of these three rivals – just as traditional expressions of federal constitutional power involve the interplay of the three great branches.

This administrative triangulation is not a thin reproduction of, or a weak nod to, the familiar (*old*) separation of powers central to the framers' design. Rather, the old and new separations of powers are very much interconnected; and those connections bespeak a faithful dynamism wherein constitutional power can be delegated (for purposes of comparative expediency and expertise) to administrative agencies provided those agencies are likewise enmeshed within a robust system of checks and balances.

Understanding administrative power through this lens of an enduring, evolving separation of powers provides an answer to both the constitutional conservatives and the neoliberals. To the former, one needs to underscore how disaggregated and rivalrous administrative agencies truly are – making them worthy (and safe) recipients of delegations of constitutional power. And to the latter, one needs to explain that attempts to run administrative agencies like businesses – through various streamlining measures that replicate corporate hierarchies – will invariably subvert rivalries, weaken the checks and balances, and thus undercut constitutionally necessary structural safeguards.

In what follows, I first advance the theory of administrative separation of powers and explain how it maps onto the modern American administrative state (Section 9.2). I then show how the modern administrative state's enduring fidelity to checks and balances renders various privatization schemes (regardless of how efficient they may be) constitutionally suspect (Section 9.3).

9.2 ADMINISTRATIVE SEPARATION OF POWERS AS LEGITIMIZING THE AMERICAN ADMINISTRATIVE STATE

The basic structural tenet of American constitutional government is one of separating, checking, and balancing.[15] Most foundationally, we divide state and federal power – and,

---

[14] For a fuller articulation of the administrative separation of powers, see Michaels, *Constitutional Coup*.

[15] Separation of powers, not a Bill of Rights, was prescribed in the original constitutional and, for some, that structural framework seemed to serve as a sufficient safeguard of liberty. See, e.g., *The Federalist*, No. 51 (Madison); *The Federalist*, No. 84 (Hamilton).

within the latter sphere, we divide legislative, executive, and judicial powers.[16] It was, after all, James Madison who described concentrated power, even concentrated democratic power, as "the very definition of tyranny."[17] Two hundred years later, jurists are still celebrating Madison's constitutional blueprint of separated powers, which Justice Antonin Scalia called "the absolutely central guarantee of a just government."[18]

The challenge, especially in modern times, is that the framers' structure is incredibly unwieldy, so frustrating that in 1938, as America was working its way out of the Great Depression, then-future Justice William O. Douglas called the requirements of bicameral legislating "our great public futility."[19] Given the new and different demands placed on the government (as a result of industrialization and democratization, wherein women and people of color were only belatedly granted the franchise), the "constitutional mold," according to Judge Richard Posner, "had to be broken and the administrative state created."[20]

Modern administrative agencies combined heretofore disaggregated legislative, executive, and judicial powers. This was the great innovation of twentieth-century American public administration. With the advent of a new administrative state, novel, challenging, and urgent regulatory and welfare problems could be dealt with more expertly and expeditiously, as law-like agency rules could be promulgated, enforced, and even adjudicated all under one roof.

However helpful and, perhaps, necessary to meet the demands of modernity, this concentration of powers nonetheless posed a great threat to our constitutional system precisely because, in Justice Robert Jackson's words, it "deranged our three-branch legal theories."[21] But, in due time, government officials redeemed and refashioned the constitutional commitment to checking and separating state power. They did so not by reverting to the old, staid premodern system of *legislative* primacy, abandoning newfangled agency rulemaking and returning to what Chief Justice Warren Burger called the "finely wrought" system of bicameralism and presentment.[22] Rather, they did so by disaggregating *administrative* power, harmonizing the architecture of this new manifestation of state authority and coercion with the structural commitments to checks and balances set forth in the Constitution. Specifically, these officials separated administrative power among three sets of rivalrous, diverse stakeholders.

Consider this disaggregation and triangulation of administrative power in the case of rulemaking. Congress routinely delegates some of its constitutional authority to agencies, to make and enforce US public policy. Congress does so, more often than not, by issuing broad legislative mandates, tasking agencies to convert those broad mandates into concrete,

---

[16]   See generally Jon D. Michaels, "Separation of Powers and Centripetal Forces: Implications for the Institutional Design and Constitutionality of Our National Security State," *University of Chicago Law Review* 83 (2016): 199–220 (describing the US constitutional system as having layers upon layers of rivalrous separation).

[17]   *The Federalist*, No. 46 (Madison).

[18]   *Morrison v. Olson* (1988) 487 U.S. 654, 697 (Scalia, J., dissenting). Even more recently, then-Judge Brett Kavanaugh echoed this very sentiment, directly quoting Scalia in an important case invalidating the leadership structure of the new Consumer Financial Protection Bureau. See *PHH Corp. v. CFPB*, at p. 28. So did then-Judge Neil Gorsuch, in his Supreme Court confirmation hearing. See Sen. Hrg. 115–208, Confirmation Hearing on the Nomination of Hon. Neil M. Gorsuch to Be an Associate Justice of the Supreme Court of the United States, Sen. J. Comm. (March 2017), www.congress.gov/115/chrg/shrg28638/CHRG-115shrg28638.htm (referring in two instances to the "genius" of the separation of powers to promote liberty and guard against government abuse).

[19]   William O. Douglas, "Administrative Government in Action, Speech to the Lotus Club, New York" (November 1938), www.sechistorical.org/collection/papers/1930/1938_1100_Douglas_AdmGov.pdf.

[20]   Richard A. Posner, "The Rise and Fall of Administrative Law," *Chicago-Kent Law Review* 72 (1997): 953–963, p. 953.

[21]   *FTC v. Ruberoid Co.* (1952) 343 U.S. 470, 487 (Jackson, J., dissenting).

[22]   *INS v. Chadha* (1983) 462 U.S. 919, 951.

generally applicable, and legally binding rules.[23] Indeed, so much American lawmaking today is done not only through but also by agencies.[24] For instance, Congress directs the Department of Labor to set occupational safety and health standards that "most adequately assure[], to the extent feasible, on the basis of the best available evidence, that no employee [facing certain workplace risks] will suffer material impairment of health or functional capacity."[25] And Congress directs the Administrator of the Environmental Protection Agency to "prescribe (and from time to time revise) ... standards applicable to the emission of any air pollutant from any class or classes of new motor vehicles or new motor vehicle engines, which in his judgment cause, or contribute to, air pollution which may reasonably be anticipated to endanger public health or welfare ...."[26] That's often as specific as Congress gets, with the understanding that the House and the Senate lack in-house expertise, have limited institutional capacity, and, by design, move slowly such that they cannot quickly correct for rapidly changing industrial or scientific practices. Thus, Congress delegates the real work to agencies to promulgate law-like rules, furnishing the texture, specificity, and clarity that the legislature really cannot supply.

Once Congress delegates, it is generally up to the agency heads to set the agenda. Under the American system, these leaders are appointed by the president and serve at his or her pleasure.[27] Agency leaders usually do not remain in their positions for very long, often under two years.[28] For that reason, among others, agency leaders may lack in-depth expertise and institutional knowledge[29] – and consequentially are fairly heavily reliant on the career staff.[30] Still, agency leaders wield considerable power. They brainstorm with their leadership team (whose numbers include other political appointees) and decide: let's give meaning and effect to this new law Congress just passed. Or, let's update an existing rule that's based on outdated understandings of, say, toxicity levels. They may further decide: consistent with the president's overarching agenda, let's pay special attention to how the rule advances environmental priorities, employment numbers, business interests, or national security. Needless to add, each of these points of emphasis will affect the shape and forcefulness of the rule differently.

Next, the civil servants, those with the expertise and staffing resources, get to work.[31] Civil servants – lawyers, social workers, scientists, economists, nutritionists, and the

---

[23] See, e.g., Kenneth Culp Davis, *Administrative Law Treatise* (St. Paul, MN: West Publishing, 1971) (1970 supp.), §6.15, p. 283 (referring to agency rulemaking as "one of the greatest inventions of modern government"); J. Skelly Wright, "The Courts and the Rulemaking Process," *Cornell Law Review* 59 (1974): 375–397.

[24] This is a fact not lost on those most concerned with the rise of the administrative state and its displacement of Congress as the primary lawmaking venue. Christopher J. Walker, "Restoring Congress's Role in the Administrative State," *Michigan Law Review* 116 (2017): 1101–1121, pp. 1101–1102. Of course, it bears underscoring that it is Congress that establishes agencies, delegates power and discretion to those agencies, and provides the funds those agencies need to operate.

[25] See The *Benzene* Case, at p. 612 (quoting from the Occupational Safety and Health Act).

[26] See *Whitman* v. *Am. Trucking Ass'ns*, at p. 1447 (quoting from the Clean Air Act).

[27] There are exceptions for commissioners of so-called independent agencies. For a treatment of the administrative separation of powers as applied to independent agencies, see Michaels, *Constitutional Coup*, at pp. 194–196.

[28] Anne Joseph O'Connell, "Vacant Offices: Delays in Staffing Top Agency Positions," *Southern Californian Law Review* 82 (2009): 913–999, pp. 919–920.

[29] Jon D. Michaels, "Of Constitutional Custodians and Regulatory Rivals: An Account of the Old and New Separation of Powers," *New York University Law Review* 91 (2016): 227–291, p. 236 and n. 21.

[30] ibid. at p. 236 and n. 22; Peter L. Strauss, "The Place of Agencies in Government: Separation of Powers and the Fourth Branch," *Columbia Law Review* 84 (1984): 573–669, pp. 578, 586.

[31] To be sure, some of these folks are likely to come in at an earlier stage as well. Senior career staffers may be included in leadership meetings. Others may, on their own initiative, advise (and even lobby) agency heads, urging them to update an old or poorly conceived rule.

like – constitute much of the federal civilian workforce,[32] though, as will be discussed, privatization and outsourcing initiatives have of late reduced their numbers and cut into their professional prerogatives. Nevertheless, even after decades of privatization, civil servants continue to play important roles. By convention, culture, and law, they serve across political administrations, prioritizing fidelity to congressional directives and adherence to professional norms over, say, partisan presidential agendas. These bureaucrats conduct research, communicate with affected parties, and engage in other forms of due diligence, including at times resisting agency leaders' attempts to overly politicize administrative governance.[33] Their effectively tenured positions within the civil service give them the job security to, in effect, speak truth to power. And, again, their experience and competence ensure, if nothing else, a prized seat at the table.[34] Ultimately, after some give-and-take with agency chiefs (themselves at times distrustful of the career bureaucrats), they often take the lead in drafting a notice of a proposed rule, outlining what the agency tentatively intends to do and alerting the public to a probable new rule or rule change.[35]

It is at this stage when the public formally weighs in. Again, surely some members of the public have already been consulted; but now the doors are wide open for everyone to comment – in support, to contest, or to urge a shift in focus or emphasis.[36] Long-time experts on a given problem or controversy and first-time lay commentators may chime in, offering anything from a few sentences to detailed scientific reports, surveys, or testimonial accounts – with the understanding and expectation that agency officials must take any and all material comments seriously. (Failing to do so may prompt courts to invalidate the rules as arbitrary or capricious.) Thus, before any rule makes it into the Code of Federal Regulations, the administrative analog to Congress's US Code, all three sets of disparate, potentially rivalrous stakeholders have ample space and opportunity to participate, contradict one another, and – ideally – reach some consensus. After all, strong objections from any of the stakeholders are likely, if not certain, to derail the rulemaking exercise.

Triangulated administrative power isn't a perfect reproduction of the framers' checks and balances. As a matter of history and intentionality, efforts to disaggregate administrative power were, seemingly, arrived at incrementally and somewhat haphazardly, if ultimately ingeniously. By contrast, from the very outset, the framers clearly mapped out (and explained) the division among Congress, the president, and the courts. And, as a matter of form and function, the new administrative rivals themselves look and operate somewhat differently from the old constitutional rivals. Yet despite these quite real and often obvious

---

[32] David E. Lewis and Jennifer L. Selin, *Sourcebook of United States Executive Agencies* (Washington, DC: Administrative Conference of the United States, 2012), pp. 68–69, https://permanent.access.gpo.gov/gp037402/ Sourcebook-2012-Final_12-Dec_Online.pdf.

[33] Bruce Ackerman, "The New Separation of Powers," *Harvard Law Review* 113 (2000): 633–725, pp. 709–710 (describing presidents and their agency heads as "tempted to achieve" programmatic and ideological objectives "by politicizing" the administrative state).

[34] Michaels, "Of Constitutional Custodians and Regulatory Rivals," at p. 239 and nn. 34–36; see also Strauss, "The Place of Agencies in Government," at p. 586 ("[T]he bureaucracy constitutes an independent force ... and its cooperation must be won to achieve any desired outcome.").

[35] To simplify this account, I leave out the important, sometimes heavy-handed role played by the powerful Office of Information and Regulatory Affairs (OIRA), located with the Office of Management and Budget. I address OIRA's at times problematic involvement in the rulemaking process in Michaels, *Constitutional Coup*, at pp. 192–193. For discussions of what ought to be contained in an agency's notice of a proposed rule, see, e.g., *Long Island Care at Home, Ltd. v. Coke* (2007), 551 U.S. 158; *Chocolate Mfrs. Ass'n of United States v. Block* (1985) 755 F.2d 1098 (4th Cir.).

[36] See *Long Island Care at Home, Ltd. v. Coke*, at p. 158; *Chocolate Mfrs. Ass'n of United States v. Block*, at p. 1098.

differences, the old and new separations of powers share some crucial commonalities and connections.[37]

Specifically, the new (administrative) stakeholders individually and collectively channel many of the characteristics and rivalries we commonly associate with the old (framers') triad.[38] The closest analog is between agency heads and the president. Agency heads are almost invariably apt stand-ins for the president. After all, these agency leaders are hand-chosen by the president, usually because the president understands those leaders (and needs them) to be political and ideological allies – and expects them to implement his or her agenda through the levers of the administrative state.[39] And, to the extent that the president guesses incorrectly, or chooses unwisely, he or she can summarily remove them from office. For these reasons, we are often encouraged to think of a responsibility vested in the president or in his or her agency head as one and the same.[40]

The public writ large shares commonalities with Congress, in more or less flattering ways. The public's participation in administrative governance is direct, populist, multi-polar, pluralistic, and at times scattershot. We can say similar things about Congress, which is multipolar, with different geographical and ideological caucuses, and often scattershot, with varying degrees of coordination, preparation, and, say, party discipline. Public participation may be expert, just as some members of Congress are professionally trained doctors or scientists, industry executives, or the like – but it need not be. Participation may be organized or disorganized. At any given time and on any given question, some segment of the public will favor a given proposal or initiative while other groups will oppose it. This is, again, what we are likely to encounter in Congress, where only the rarest and most anodyne of legislative proposals invites no opposition. Organized, moneyed interest groups may intervene strongly and aggressively in the rulemaking notice-and-comment process, placing into doubt how truly populist or demo-cratic public participation really is. But even here the similarities to Congress are uncommonly strong, as that institution is hardly a stranger to the corrupting, democracy-distorting effects of money in politics.

For its part, the civil service acts as the administrative counterpart to the federal judiciary. Like the judiciary, the civil service is effectively tenured and politically insulated. Its mem-bers cannot be fired or demoted for good-faith disagreements with legislators or agency heads.[41] And, like the judiciary, the civil service is well positioned and professionally (and culturally) disposed to function as a counter-majoritarian check, resisting overly populist or

---

[37] I am indebted to Bruce Ackerman for, among other things, his important essay on other approaches to separating and checking power beyond the framers' specific scheme. See Ackerman, "The New Separation of Powers," at pp. 688–689; see also Bruce Ackerman, "Good-bye, Montesquieu," in Comparative Administrative Law, eds. Susan Rose-Ackerman and Peter L. Lindseth (Cheltenham, UK: Edward Elgar, 2010), p. 128.

[38] For a fuller treatment of what is discussed in the next several paragraphs, see Michaels, *Constitutional Coup*, at pp. 63–68.

[39] See Bruce Ackerman, *The Decline and Fall of the American Republic* (Cambridge, MA: Harvard University Press, 2010), pp. 33, 37.

[40] As with so much else about the Trump administration, this long-standing pattern of affinities between presidents and top appointees does not seem to apply. See, e.g., Madeline Joung, "Trump Has Now Had More Cabinet Turnover Than Reagan, Obama and the Two Bushes," *Time* (July 12, 2019), https://time.com/5625699/trump-cabinet-acosta/; Tina Nguyen, "No Wonder Trump's White House Is a Dumpster Fire," *Vanity Fair* (June 24, 2019), www.vanityfair.com/news/2019/06/trump-white-house-vetting-process.

[41] Note that what we're seeing today vis-à-vis Trump administration officials' attacks on the civil service is exceptional, if not unprecedented in the modern era. See, e.g., Jon D. Michaels, "The War on Federal Employees," *American Prospect* (December 11, 2017), https://prospect.org/article/war-on-federal-employees.

partisan endeavors that lack grounding in law or reason. And precisely because of its distance from the people, the civil service – like the judiciary – must do extra work to justify its central role in the American republic. The civil service does so through careful and robust engagement, through a clear explanation of an issue's importance and how it may be addressed, and through a demonstrated commitment to consistent, nonpartisan interventions, over time and across political trends.[42]

It is, again, the interplay among this set of rivalrous actors, some democratic, others further removed from the political fray, that ensures that administrative governance is the product of broad-based and pluralistic buy-in by stakeholders sharing considerable commonalities with the three constitutional stakeholders specified in the first three articles of the Constitution. As a result, the administrative state is not a runaway train of coercive power, precisely because there are multiple veto points. It is not a tool of naked presidentialism, precisely because agency heads by and large need the support of civil servants and the public writ large. And it is not a coven of unaccountable, untethered "Deep State" conspirators precisely because, conversely, the unelected, politically independent bureaucracy cannot accomplish much, if anything, without considerable support from agency heads and public participants.[43] Instead, the administrative state roughly reproduces what happens – or, often, what does not happen (because of all of the checking and balancing) – under traditional constitutional governance.

This is of little comfort, of course, to constitutional originalists, who don't cotton to what's commonly referred to as functionalist claims and give no quarter to those making structural arguments in service of justifying a modern reformulation of the old separation of powers. Yet for those committed primarily to the principles and purposes underlying the separation of powers – because they genuinely prize liberty and fear an arbitrary, abusive, or tyrannous government – the administrative separation of powers offers plenty of reassurance, redeeming the original architecture and refashioning it to suit the demands, obligations, and expectations of modernity.[44]

If state power morphs and evolves (and it has), and if state power flows through instruments new and different from those expressly mentioned in the Constitution (as it has), one means of ensuring constitutional fidelity between the old and the new is to insist that the instruments are themselves democratically informed and subject to substantially similar institutional checks and balances. And, indeed, administrative separation of powers represents a faithful restaging in which the disaggregated administrative architecture is tethered to the structures, personalities, and substantive content of the United States's underlying constitutional scheme.

---

[42] There is a large and important literature on the professionalism of the American civil service. See, e.g., Charles T. Goodsell, *The Case for Bureaucracy* (Washington, DC: CQ Press, 2004); Verkuil, *Valuing Bureaucracy*; see also Harold H. Bruff, *Balance of Forces: Separation of Powers in the Administrative State* (Durham, NC: Carolina Academic Press, 2006), p. 408 ("By training and inclination, bureaucrats seek legal authority for their actions. Accordingly, they constitute an often unappreciated bulwark to the rule of law in its everyday application to the citizens."); David E. Lewis, *The Politics of Presidential Appointments* (Princeton, NJ: Princeton University Press, 2008), p. 30 (remarking that civil servants "often feel bound by legal, moral, or professional norms to certain courses of action and these courses of action may be at variance with the president's agenda").

[43] Michaels, "The American Deep State," at pp. 1657–1666.

[44] One might draw insight and inspiration from Thomas Merrill, who posits that constitutional structure can be understood as "more than the sum of the specific clauses that govern relations among the branches." Thomas W. Merrill, "The Constitutional Principle of Separation of Powers," *Supreme Court Review* (1991): 225–260, p. 225.

9.3 PRIVATIZATION AS A CONSTITUTIONAL AFFRONT
TO THE AMERICAN ADMINISTRATIVE STATE

Administrative separation of powers not only addresses the concerns raised by constitutional conservatives unnerved by the prospects of concentrated, unilateral regulatory and welfare power; this triangulated system also responds to the neoliberal, businesslike-government crowd, whose privatization agenda (rather than the modern administrative state) is actually what's on shaky constitutional footing.

Adherents of businesslike government seek to effectively gut the bureaucracy. Civil servants are to be replaced by private contractors, deemed to be more efficient and responsive.[45] Such proposals to bypass the civil service – proposals championed, I hasten to add, by members of both major political parties[46] – are routinely framed as nonideological, wonkish fixes to speed up and streamline administrative governance.

Their arguments typically proceed along the following lines. Bureaucratic government is pathologically torpid and costly. Bureaucracies lack the proper incentives to run efficiently and accountably. So long as bureaucracy is necessary – and so long as it is immune from competition from would-be rivals (such as we find among firms in a competitive market-place) – agencies will do subpar work, slowly, and in a wasteful fashion.

Businesslike-government proponents view an analogous set of pathologies operating at the individual employee level. Career civil servants generally receive lock-step compensation and, as discussed earlier, enjoy what amounts to job tenure. They thus lack incentives that apply to workers in the private sector – the incentive to avoid being fired or demoted for inefficiency or obstinacy and the incentive to go the extra mile to receive bonuses or promotions. Again, all the benefits of industry and labor competition, as businesslike-government types understand them, are lost in the realm of bureaucracy. Hence the preference for private firms and actors, responsive in ways that bureaucracies and bureaucrats aren't.[47]

Starting in earnest in the 1980s and advancing further and further each decade, government outsourcing has become ubiquitous, permeating just about every government agency and government task. Among the things that are outsourced are prison administration, policing, intelligence gathering and analysis, and military responsibilities ranging from maintenance work in the motor pool to counterinsurgency efforts at the proverbial tip of the sphere. Jobs requiring personnel to inspect dangerous workplaces, to research and draft environmental rules, and to determine eligibility for welfare benefits are also routinely privatized.[48]

Indeed, privatization has become so commonplace and, in most sectors, so entirely unremarkable that those keen on running government like a business have pushed the envelope further. Rather than go through the hassles and expenses of contracting out government jobs to private firms, they've altogether revamped some agencies, refashioning them to look and operate as if they were commercial outfits. They've done so by enacting laws that expressly or effectively reclassify tenured civil servants as at-will employees, thus subject to dismissal or demotion not only for substandard work but also for obstinacy or resistance to agency leaders' hyper-partisan initiatives. Thus, in dozens of states and in many

---

[45]   See, e.g., Jon D. Michaels, "Running Government Like a Business ... *Then and Now,*" *Harvard Law Review* 128 (2015): 1152–1182.

[46]   Michaels, *Constitutional Coup,* at pp. 101–106.

[47]   Michaels, "Running Government Like a Business ... *Then and Now.*"

[48]   Michaels, *Constitutional Coup,* at pp. 105–114.

federal agencies, these state and federal efforts to reclassify, or deregulate, the civil service can be seen as privatization-lite, with its backers expecting the newly marketized employees to respond to cost and managerial pressures in the same way that at-will employees at Google, Boeing, or Walmart would.[49]

It is at this point when most skeptics of businesslike government point out how routinely unsuccessful privatization has been. They document fraud and waste. Armed with ample evidence, they insist that the promises of privatization fall far short in reality.[50] First, competition is often not all that it is cracked up to be, thus making contractor firms (and individual contractor employees) far less diligent and responsive than predicted. As a result, work quality and cost-efficiencies may both suffer.[51]

Second, even with hearty competition, the costs associated with privatizing a given responsibility, vetting would-be providers, and evaluating the work of the chosen firm are themselves high. Thus, in order to truly save money, those private firms must, by some accounts, be not just a little bit better but, rather, greater than 20 percent better.[52]

Third, even assuming that there are cost-savings, one still needs to ask where those savings are coming from. Are the private firms better motivated, more innovative, and more leanly staffed – thus providing a true benefit of the sort that privatization's proponents promise? Or are the firms "cheaper" because they pay lower wages to their employees than the government pays to its employees – and because they skimp on such benefits as pensions and health insurance? The latter cost savings say nothing about comparative efficiencies and everything about privatization being little more than a means to subtly undercut government labor policies.

For many, these concerns are more than sufficient to draw negative conclusions about the privatization agenda. Other privatization skeptics, by contrast, may be less focused on questions of efficiency and more interested in the fact that privatization entails the delegation of broad policymaking and policy-implementing responsibilities to private firms and individuals. The worry here, of course, is about an abdication of government power, resulting in private actors exercising state responsibilities arbitrarily or abusively – going off on what we might in other contexts refer to as frolics and detours.[53]

Private delegation concerns are, for some, sufficiently damning in their own right.[54] But both the economic arguments and the arguments sounding in abdication and abuse rest on discrete cases and contestable claims. That is to say, they are vulnerable to responses of the following sort: the fact that privatization has failed in the past (or in these particular settings) ought not be a reason for condemning all outsourcing initiatives going forward. Partly

---

[49] Verkuil, *Valuing Bureaucracy*; Michaels, "Privatization's Progeny," at pp. 1040–1050.

[50] Paul Chassy and Scott H. Amey, "Bad Business: Billions of Dollars Wasted on Hiring Contractors," *Project on Government Oversight* (September 13, 2011), https://docs.pogo.org/report/2011/bad-business-report-only-2011.pdf?_ga=2.47365927.1617185256.1566114174-226327644.1566114174; Ron Nixon, "Government Pays More in Contracts, Study Finds," *New York Times* (September 12, 2011), www.nytimes.com/2011/09/13/us/13contractor.html.

[51] David A. Super, "Privatization, Policy Paralysis, and the Poor," *California Law Review* 96 (2008): 393–469, pp. 414–427.

[52] John D. Donahue, *The Privatization Decision* (New York: Basic Books, 1989), p. 109.

[53] See, e.g., HCJ 2605/05 *Academic Ctr. of Law & Bus. v. Minister of Fin.*, 63(ii) PD 545 [2009] (Isr.), English translation at https://versa.cardozo.yu.edu/sites/default/files/upload/opinions/Academic%20Center%20of%20Law%20and%20Business%20v.%20Minister%20of%20Finance.pdf (holding the privatization of government's sovereign power to incarcerate to be per se unconstitutional); Laura A. Dickinson, *Outsourcing War and Peace: Preserving Public Values in a World of Privatized Foreign Affairs* (New Haven, CT: Yale University Press, 2011).

[54] See *Academic Ctr. of Law & Bus. v. Minister of Fin.*, 63(ii) PD 545 [2009]; *Dep't of Trans. v. Ass'n of Am. R.R.*, at pp. 1237–1238 (Alito, J., concurring).

because these responses have merit (and are voiced so frequently), there are strong reasons for grounding one's objections to privatization in the constitutional theory of administrative separation of powers.

Recall that administrative separation of powers understands administrative agencies to be constitutional precisely because they redeem and reproduce the framers' structural safeguards, specifically by triangulated administrative power among three rivalrous, contentious stakeholders. Viewed through this jurisprudential lens, privatization appears unconstitutional even (and perhaps especially) when privatization initiatives work as intended.

Adherents to the administrative separation of powers can assume that contractors are faithful and efficient stewards; that contractors are surrounded by market competitors ready and willing to take on the government's work if the incumbent firms fall short; that there is close monitoring of individual employees; and that there is a robust labor market, meaning that any single worker, if he or she isn't sufficiently diligent, can and will be readily replaced.[55] That is, we can put privatization in its ostensibly best light.

Given all those stipulations, it is hard to argue that privatization, in its ideal state, runs a high risk of fraud, waste, or abuse. Really well-drafted contracts and really well-orchestrated efforts to reclassify civil servants as at-will employees may blunt the efficiency and accountability concerns noted in this chapter. But consider what really well-drafted contracts and really well-orchestrated efforts to reclassify civil servants do to the structure of administrative governance – specifically to the separating and checking of state power. Simply stated, the reasons why the businesslike-government crowd likes contractors and at-will government employees (over civil servants) are the very same reasons why privatization is so constitutionally dangerous.

Civil servants are rivalrous with agency heads in ways that contractors and at-will government employees usually cannot be. Contractors and at-will government employees serve at the pleasure of agency heads. They are also more likely to be eligible for performance-based bonuses (as determined by agency leaders). Given these powerful carrots and sticks, contractors and at-will employees have every incentive to be "yes" men and women, highly solicitous of the political leaders atop the agencies.

Tenured, salaried civil servants, by contrast, are servants of the state, not any particular administration. As such, and as discussed already, they are well positioned to provide a meaningfully rivalrous check, resisting, challenging, moderating, redirecting, refining, and of course regularly lending independent credibility to the policy directives of the political leadership.[56] And lest one is tempted to think otherwise, civil servants act as rivals in both Republican and Democratic administrations. After all, it isn't just liberal bureaucrats checking conservative presidential administrations; Democratic administrations, too, run into all sorts of conflicts both with more conservative and with more left-liberal civil servants, let

---

[55] The same story applies with the reclassification of civil servants as at-will, commercialized workers. I take it as a given that those intent on commercializing the bureaucracy are successful. That is to say, they are able to exert greater control over the newly reclassified (at-will) government employees and, as a corollary, readily replace any obstinate at-will employees with more compliant or subservient ones. Michaels, *Constitutional Coup*, at pp. 126–134.

[56] See ibid., at pp. 60–61, 66–67. For recent discussions of bureaucratic resistance, see, e.g., Rachel Augustine Potter, *Bending the Rules* (Chicago: University of Chicago Press, 2019); Jennifer Nou, "Civil Servant Disobedience," *Chicago-Kent Law Review* 94 (2019): 349–381; Adam Shinar, "Dissenting from Within: When and How Public Officials Resist the Law," *Florida State University Law Review* 40 (2013): 601–657, pp. 622–624, 630.

alone those simply uneasy with any hyper-partisan or unsubstantiated directive.[57] Among other things, it was civil servants from the Department of Homeland Security who challenged President Obama's DACA and DAPA immigration initiatives.[58]

In short, the use of contractors or reclassified government workers weakens one of the important dimensions of rivalrous administrative separation of powers. And that's surely what the pro-privatization crowd wants to happen, as rivalries produce friction, interfere with top-down CEO-style managerial control, and invite extended discussions, debates, and negotiations regarding how best to proceed. Such friction, interference, and debate, to be sure, is costly and time-consuming.

The impulse to streamline may make sense in an entirely commercial sector, where there is a singular goal of profit maximization and where the decisions of firms do not carry with them much moral weight, let alone the force of law. But that same impulse to streamline, in the name of efficiency, doesn't translate well into the public domain, where goals are multitudinous, variegated, and highly contestable, where the decisions or actions of state actors decidedly do carry moral force and coercive effect, and where presidents and agency heads have strong political and ideological incentives to monopolize administrative power.[59] Thus, we ought to want, and I would argue *need*, broad, rivalrous engagement to ensure democratic and expert buy-in and guard against abusive or capricious government power. We ought to countenance, even welcome, messy, time- and resource-intensive, and costly public administration, even knowing that these clunky administrative checks occasionally stymie vital welfarist programs or impede the pursuit of justice. That messiness and that investment in time and resources are not bugs in the regulatory system to be rooted out. Rather, they are design features; they're what lend legitimacy, legal and political accountability, and expert guidance to the project of American public administration. Again, this is why separating and checking administrative power is constitutionally important – and why privatization, even when efficient, expedient, and well-intentioned, is constitutionally unsettling.[60]

But that's not even the whole story – just the part of the story that relates the collapsing of one dimension of rivalry: between agency leaders and civil servants. In addition, the outsourcing of policymaking and policy-implementing responsibilities to contractors shifts the locus of public governance into private corridors. When responsibilities are outsourced, decisions about policy design and administration are more likely to be formulated off-site. Those private spaces are not amenable to public input, nor are they subject to the same transparency and accessibility requirements that Congress imposes on

---

57 See Michaels, "The American Deep State," at pp. 1661–1662; Chris Cornillie and Mark Lee, "Government Executive 2016 Presidential Poll," *Government Executive* (August 13, 2015), www.govexec.com/insights/govern ment-executive-2016-presidential-poll-august-13-2015/119144/; David E. Lewis, "'Deep State' Claims and Professional Government," *Regulatory Review* (December 5, 2017), www.theregreview.org/2017/12/05/lewisdeep-state-professional-government/; Eric Katz, "There Are More Republicans in Federal Government Than You Might Think," *Government Executive* (August 14, 2015), www.govexec.com/oversight/2015/08/thereare-more-republicans-federal-government-you-might-think/119138/.

58 Alex Hemmer, "Civil Servant Suits," *Yale Law Journal* 124 (2014): 758–803; Carol Cratty, "Ten ICE Agents Target Obama Deportation Policy with Lawsuit," CNN.com (August 23, 2012), www.cnn.com/2012/08/23/us/ice-agents-lawsuit/index.html.

59 See Ackerman, *The Decline and Fall of the American Republic*, at pp. 37, 47; Ackerman, "The New Separation of Powers," at pp. 709–710.

60 To be sure, the privatization of non-policymaking and non-policy implementation responsibilities is unlikely to subvert the administrative separation of powers in a meaningful way. In such cases, there is no power or discretion that can be amassed or consolidated, let alone concentrated in a constitutionally troubling fashion. See Michaels, *Constitutional Coup*, at p. 130 (describing such custodial or ministerial contracting).

government agencies. What's more, contractors' working materials – plans, proposals, protocols, and the like – may further be withheld from public scrutiny as proprietary. In a world of competition for government contracts, it is only reasonable to expect firms to closely guard those materials that give them a leg up. But, in the process, public participation is limited and thus blunted, thereby subverting yet another dimension of the administrative separation of powers.[61]

Note, too, that the conventional tools we currently rely on to make government contracting more accountable are unhelpful when it comes to the phenomena I just described. Accountability, as commonly understood, is all about rooting out contractor abuse. Thus, resources are directed at empowering and compelling agencies (and external watchdogs) to more closely monitor contractors, thereby guarding against waste and abuse. Presumably, with or without external prodding to oversee the contracting process, agency heads already have adequate incentive to police fraud and abuse, as instances of contractor malfeasance not only make the agency look bad but also run the risk of interfering with the presidential administration's programmatic agenda.[62]

Not so when it comes to the converse problem, the one I argue is both more likely to occur when privatization is done "right" and more constitutionally troubling. When the administrative separation of powers is subverted, those best positioned to see it happening are not at all distressed. Outsiders – legislators, fiscal watchdogs, etc. – are looking for contractor misdeeds. What they see when contracting is done "right" is robust competition, scandal-free administration, and a close alignment between the agency leadership's goals and agency policies. They will thus have insufficient reasons to be alarmed. Insiders – principally, agency leaders – will see highly solicitous, perhaps even obsequious, contractors and at-will employees eager (or pressured) to do the presidential administration's bidding, if for no other reason than because they want to keep their jobs. These insiders will, of course, rejoice as outsourcing helps eliminate opportunities for bureaucratic dissent and resistance.[63]

Precisely because contractors (and commercialized employees) may appear to be particularly efficient and dutiful, it is doubly important to be sensitive to the dangers that underlie ostensibly "good" contracting and to appreciate the ways in which friction, resistance, and give-and-take among the administrative rivals is a true, indeed necessary, component of constitutional governance.

9.4 CONCLUSION

Privatization is a real and powerful force. It has fully insinuated itself into American law and policy. Many Americans have an innate (or at least deeply instilled) appreciation of the lures and logic of the market, and a corresponding distrust of the state. Thus, it is understandable why they may want to infuse bureaucracy with market values and virtues. But this is a profound mistake. Governments and firms have different agendas, responsibilities, powers, and constituencies. The different systems we use to organize – and control – state power and market power bespeak the different understandings, expectations, and fears we associate with

---

[61] ibid., at pp. 81, 133.
[62] See Jon D. Michaels, "Privatization's Pretensions," *University of Chicago Law Review* 77 (2010): 717–780, pp. 765–767.
[63] Ibid.

government agencies and commercial firms. Just as the administrative separation of powers justifies the refashioning of state power to befit the regulatory and welfarist demands of modernity, that same structural commitment proscribes the refashioning of state power to befit either the efficiency goals prized by neoclassical economists or the political and partisan goals prized by presidential administrations.[64]

[64]   There is, of course, an arguably important third option besides state and market provision – namely, provision by the nonprofit sector. For many, the difference between for-profit and nonprofit contractors is quite significant. For adherents to the administrative separation of powers, however, the distinction between for-profit and nonprofit is of little moment. This is because the true concern with privatization from a checking and balancing perspective is not contractor greed but rather bureaucratic independence.

   Nonprofit organizations do not typically provide civil service-like workforce tenure protections, nor do those workforces constitute a distinct corps of public servants trained and rewarded for being vigilant stewards of the state. See *supra* note 42. Private sector workers may well be principled, passionate, and conscientious, but their commitments are to their particular institutional missions, whether those are advocating for a particular cause or maximizing shareholder profits. Either way, they may be quite vulnerable or susceptible to pressure from agency leaders to go along with the president's agenda. Indeed, specially selected mission-oriented nonprofits may be particularly eager to carry the president's water. This is, again, potentially quite advantageous from an efficiency standpoint, but troubling if we remain committed to rivalrous, multipolar, and contentious administrative governance.

Privatization and the Intimate Sphere

Brenda Cossman

10.1 INTRODUCTION

What does privatization mean in the context of domains that have long been considered quintessentially private? Family, marriage, sexuality: each of these spheres of intimate life has been cast as private. Feminist and sexuality scholars have sought to reveal the artificiality of the public/private distinction and the many ways that intimate life is deeply political. Family, marriage and sexuality are spheres of life constituted through cultural, political and legal discourses. Each is deeply implicated in governance, past and present. Yet, the ideology of the private is enduring, and the idea of privatizing the private tautological. Indeed, the intimate sphere of family and sexuality has not featured prominently in the privatization literature, which has tended to focus on reconfiguring the relationship between the market and the state. In this chapter, I focus on scholarship that has sought to highlight the ways in which privatization has implicated and transformed the intimate sphere, focusing particularly on the ways in which the family has been reconfigured under neoliberalism. I explore the question of what it means to privatize that which is prefigured as private.

The scholarly interrogations of this question have changed over time. In the 1990s and 2000s, a feminist literature on privatization addressed the changing role of the family in the emergence of neoliberal governance, arguing that through the ideas of reprivatization and familialization, once-public goods and services were being reconstituted as private. A second and related literature on responsibilization explored the ways in which neoliberal governance has demanded that citizens self-govern, to manage their own risk, and take responsibility for their lives. Some scholars specifically sought to demonstrate the ways in which family was implicated in this responsibilization. Since that time, others have continued to develop analyses of the reconfiguration of the family under neoliberalism. Some have explored the discourse of "responsibility" within the family, interrogating the multiple meanings and political commands of responsibility, including its role in providing solutions to a broad range of once social problems. More recently, scholars have begun to explore the psychic life on neoliberal governance, interrogating ongoing privatization within the intimate sphere as a psychological project. In this chapter, I review these changing approaches, highlighting some of the important contributions and debates in thinking about reconfiguration and regulation of intimate life under neoliberalism. I also track the transformations in my own thinking about the privatization of intimate life.

It is worth noting that the broad range of literatures addressing these questions of privatization within the family that I review in this chapter share a deeply critical take; they see privatization and neoliberalism as a retreat from a more inclusive form of social citizenship. As a result, the literature is overwhelmingly critical of the ways in which privatization has played out in the context of the family. Normatively, these critiques are premised on the idea that the state should have a greater role in the collective well-being of its citizenry; that a commitment to social citizenship is required to promote greater social equality and inclusion. It is not an argument against the values of individual and collective responsibility and resilience, per se, although at times the tone suggests otherwise. Rather, it is an exploration of the particular political deployments of these concepts to support the retraction of the state from the well-being of its citizens. While, normatively, there are arguments to be made in favour of promoting autonomy, responsibility and individual choice, the feminist and critical literatures of privatization within the family have by and large not engaged these themes. Some of the literature on responsibility and resilience attempts to distinguish between the normativity of these concepts and their particular political deployment under neoliberal governance. I seek to highlight these themes – and the absence thereof – in my review.

10.2 PRIVATIZATION AND FAMILIALIZATION

Privatization is a broad term that is intended to capture the transition from the Keynesian welfare state (KWS) to the neoliberal state. At its most general, it involves a broad policy impulse to change the balance between public and private responsibility in public policy.[1] Privatization is often associated with the selling off of government operations, the deregulation of some sectors of the economy and the commercialization of government services. But the process of transition includes a broader range of strategies. It involves a fundamental renegotiation in the relationship between the public and private spheres that characterized the KWS,[2] whereby once-public goods and services are being reconstituted as private, that is, as more appropriately, efficiently and naturally located in the private spheres of market, family and/or charity. Much privatization literature has focused on the marketization of goods and services. But privatization has also included familialization. The concept builds on the basic idea of transferring goods and services from the public to the private sphere. Marketization (transfer to the market) and familialization (transfer to the family) share the intention of shrinking the state and reducing public spending. But the concept of familialization is intended to focus on the particular ways in which responsibility for the once-public goods and services is transferred to the realm of the family, rather than the market. It explores how responsibility for a range of goods and services is transferred, and the discourse through which this process is justified and naturalized.

A feminist literature, emergent in the 1990s, sought to explore the gendered implications of privatization and restructuring. Janine Brodie explored the changes to the narratives of

---

[1]   Steven Rathgeb Smith and Michael Lipsky, *Nonprofits for Hire: The Welfare State in the Age of Contracting* (Harvard University Press, 1993), p. 188, as cited in Donald McFetridge, *The Economics of Privatization* (C.D. Howe Institute, 1997), p. 3.

[2]   See Alan Sears "The Lean State and Capitalist Restructuring: Towards a Theoretical Account," Studies in Political Economy 59 (1999): 91–114, p. 104.

government and citizenship under neoliberalism.[3] These narratives entailed a new set of assumptions about the role of government and the rights of citizens, in which government responsibility and social citizenship were being displaced in favour of marketized and self-reliant citizens, in which the role of government was restricted to helping citizens help themselves. "Familialization" is one such narrative, whereby once partially public goods and services are being reconstituted as located within the family in particular: "[I]t is up to families to look after their own and it is up to the state to make sure that they do."[4] Brodie argued that "the Canadian experience is replete with examples of this movement, for example, the exemption of unemployed youth from welfare rolls, the defunding of women's shelters, declines in length of hospital stays, the privatization of child care and elderly care and the severe cutbacks to persons with disabilities."[5] Each of these changes places greater demand on the unpaid work of women within the sphere of family. It is a reprivatization of the costs of social reproduction; costs that were partially and intentionally socialized under the Keynesian welfare state, in the name of social citizenship.

The idea of families being responsible for the economic support of their members is hardly unprecedented: the male breadwinner family was a central site of support for economic dependency under the KWS and the costs of social reproduction were only ever partially socialized. But, even within the context of this partial public support of the costs of social reproduction, privatization through the strategy of familialization entailed significant legal and normative transformations of the regulation of the family. The retraction of the social welfare state has been accompanied by the normative claim that families are naturally responsible for taking care of their own.[6] The demise of social citizenship involves an even greater demand on families to meet the needs of their members, from health care to education to childcare. Familialization, as a concept, explores the political discourse and legal reforms through which these transfers of once-public goods and services are achieved. It also pays attention to who bears the costs of these transfers within the family, focusing in particular on the increased demands on women's unpaid labour within the family.

A number of feminist legal scholars took note of the changes afoot in various areas of the law. From health care[7] to tax law[8], these scholars explored the particular ways in which responsibilities were being transferred to the family, and how the discourse of privatization is "currently infusing law and social policy in Canada."[9] One focus is on the ways in which this privatization is playing out in the context of family and welfare law. "Increasingly ... courts and administrative arms of the Canadian state are reinforcing certain private familial responsibilities for women's poverty, in the name of feminist values and in part in response

[3] Janine Brodie, "Meso-discourses, State Forms and the Gendering of Liberal-Democratic Citizenship," *Citizen Studies* 1 (1997): 223–242.
[4] Ibid.
[5] Ibid.
[6] Ibid. See also Judy Fudge and Brenda Cossman, "Introduction: Privatization, Law and the Challenge of Feminism," in Judy Fudge and Brenda Cossman, eds., *Privatization, Law and the Challenge of Feminism* (University of Toronto Press, 2002).
[7] See Joan Gilmour, "Creeping Privatization in Health Care: Implications for Women as the State Withdraws Its Role," in Fudge and Cossman, eds., *supra* note 6.
[8] See Lisa Philipps, "Tax Law and Social Reproduction: The Gender of Fiscal Policy in an Age of Privatization," in Fudge and Cossman, eds., *supra* note 6; Susan B. Boyd and Claire F. L. Young, "Feminism, Law and Public Policy: Family Feuds and Taxing Times," *Osgoode Hall Law Journal* 42 (2004): 545–582.
[9] Susan Boyd, *Child Custody, Law and Women's Work* (Oxford University Press, 2002), pp. 215–218;

to feminist struggle in the courts, while diminishing public societal commitment to alleviating that poverty."[10]

My scholarship explores this expanding role of family law under neoliberalism. From broader definitions of spouse to more robust support obligations, I argue that family was becoming a more important regulatory instrument for the enforcement of private support obligations for economically dependent family members.[11]

In the Canadian context, I look at expanding definitions of spouse to include same-sex couples for the purposes of spousal support as an example of this normative shift. In the transformational case of *M. v. H.*, the Supreme Court of Canada, for the first time, held that the exclusion of same-sex couples from extended definitions of spouse was unconstitutional.[12] The case involved the definition of spouse for the purposes of spousal support, and included unmarried, opposite sex couples. The plaintiff, M. challenged the definition as discrimination on the basis of sexual orientation because it precluded any entitlement to claim spousal support from her ex-partner. Much of the Supreme Court analysis was conducted within section 15 equality discourse, displacing the hold of conservative and heteronormative visions of the family, and recognizing the equal dignity of same-sex relationships. But the Court explicitly gestured to the privatization of dependency within the family in observing that one of the crucial objectives of the spousal support legislation was the alleviation of "the burden on the public purse by shifting the obligation to provide support for needy persons, to those parents and spouses who have the capacity to provide support to these individuals."[13] According to Iacobucci, J., these objectives would only be furthered if same-sex couples were included within the definition of spouse. The court placed considerable emphasis on the goal of "reducing the strain on the public purse" by "shifting the financial burden away from the government and on to those partners with the capacity to provide support for dependent spouses."[14] This explicitly privatizing objective, that is, of ensuring that same-sex partners could claim spousal support from their ex-spouse instead of having to turn to the state for support, was used by the Court to support its conclusion that there was no legitimate government objective justifying the exclusion.

The expansion of spousal support obligations by the Supreme Court of Canada stands in stark discursive contrast to the Court's assertion, only ten years earlier. In *Pelech* v. *Pelech*, the Court considered whether a spouse should be entitled to spousal support, in the face of a separation agreement that had precluded any further support. While the case was intricately tied to questions of contract and private choices, the Court made broader statements about the nature of spousal support. In particular, the Court held that a spouse who found herself in economic need following the breakdown of her marriage, should, unless it fit a very narrow category of exception, look to the welfare state for support: "[T]he obligation to support the former spouse should be, as in the case of any other citizen, the communal responsibility of

---

[10]   Susan Boyd, "(Re)Placing the State: Family, Law and Oppression," *Canadian Journal of Law and Society* 9 (1994): 39–73. See also Boyd and Young, "Feminism, Law and Public Policy"; Mary Jane Mossman, "Child Support or Support for Children? Rethinking 'Public' and 'Private' in Family Law," *University of New Brunswick Law Journal* (1997): 46, pp. 63–85; Mossman and Morag MacLean, "Family Law and Social Assistance Programs: Rethinking Equality," in Patricia Evans and Gerda Wekerle, eds., *Women and the Canadian Welfare State* (University of Toronto Press, 1997).

[11]   Brenda Cossman, "Family Feuds: Neo-liberal and Neo-conservative Visions of the Privatization Project," in Fudge and Cossman, eds., *supra* note 6, at 169; Brenda Cossman, "Contesting Conservatisms, Family Feuds and the Privatization of Dependency," *American Journal of Gender, Social Policy and the Law* 13 (2005): 415–504.

[12]   *M. v. H.* (1999) 2 S.C.R. 3.

[13]   Ibid., para. 106.

[14]   Ibid., para. 98.

the state."[15] The case was decided at a very different time, under very different understandings of public versus private responsibility for dependency. In the face of private choices limiting spousal support (and the reasoning of the case was extended to cases not involving private contracts), dependency was placed squarely within the public realm of the state. Ten years later, the Court adopted a very different stance, namely, that dependency should now reside first in the private realm of former spouses.

My work also explores the expansion of child support obligations in the late 1990s as an example of the normative transformations of privatization, in both Canada and the United States.[16] The introduction of the federal Child Support Guidelines in 1997 had been preceded by a period of heightened public anxiety about the rates of child poverty and parents evading their obligations, aka, "deadbeat dads." Child poverty was being recast as an individual problem of fathers who failed to take responsibility for their children. They were not only castigated for abandoning their children but also "demonized as bad citizens for their flagrant abuse of the Canadian taxpayer, who must subsidize the resulting welfare dependency."[17] The Child Support Guidelines were in turn cast as a solution to these problems, with governments subtly and sometimes less subtly connecting the intensification of child support obligations with the privatization of welfare costs.[18]

A similar privatization of dependency is apparent in the United States, although less pronounced, in large part due to the fact that it never had a particularly robust welfare state or an ethic of collective responsibility of its citizenry.[19] Many legal scholars have explored this process, arguing that "privatization is increasingly seen as the solution to complicated social problems reflecting persistent inequality and poverty."[20] The discourse of public policy reform identified the privatization of support obligations as an explicit objective of welfare reform, and many commentators observed the extent to which this reform constituted a privatization of public responsibility.[21] Welfare reform in the 1990s both "expanded governmental presence into the private sphere" while sharply reducing "the sphere of public

[15] *Pelech* v. *Pelech* (1987) 1 SCR 801.

[16] Cossman, 2002, 2005, *supra* note 11.

[17] Cossman, 2002, *supra* note 11, at p. 193, citing Brodie (1997).

[18] Cossman, id. For example, an Ontario government backgrounder expressly linked child support with welfare: "Currently, close to $1 billion in child support payments is out-standing. This forces many recipients onto social assistance and denies children the support they need … About 95 per cent of recipients of child support are women. When child support isn't paid, women and children are forced into poverty and onto social assistance" (Ontario Ministry of the Attorney General, Backgrounder: "Tougher Family Support Enforcement," July 18, 1996).

[19] Cossman, 2005, *supra* note 11; Grace Ganz Blumberg, "The Regularization of Nonmarital Cohabitation: Rights and Responsibilities in the American Welfare State," *Notre Dame Law Review* 76 (2001): 1265–1310, pp. 1270–1271.

[20] On the role of family law in privatizing dependency in the USA, see Martha L. A. Fineman, "Masking Dependency: The Political Role of Family Rhetoric," *Virginia Law Review* 81 (1995): 2281–2215, pp. 2181, 2205 ("In the societal division of labor among institutions, the private family bears the burden of dependency, not the public state. Resort to the state is considered a failure. By according to the private family responsibility for inevitable dependency, society directs dependency away from the state and privatizes it."); see also Martha Albertson Fineman, "The Inevitability of Dependency and the Politics of Subsidy," *Stanford Law & Policy Review* 9 (1998): 89; Martha Albertson Fineman, "Contract and Core," *Chicago-Kent Law Review* 76 (2001): 1403, p. 1405. Fineman also recognizes the extent to which dependency is prefigured as the responsibility of the family: "Therefore, the public nature of dependency is hidden, privatized within the family, rendering decisions about public responsibility unnecessary, except for those stigmatized families that 'fail' in meeting their responsibilities." Ibid. at pp. 1405–1406.

[21] See Tonya L. Brito, "The Welfarization of Family Law," *University of Kansas Law Review* 48 (2000): 229; David L. Chambers, "Fathers, the Welfare System, and the Virtues and Perils of Child-Support Enforcement," *Virginia Law Review* 81 (1995): 2575; Deborah Harris, "Child Support for Welfare Families: Family Policy Trapped in Its Own Rhetoric," *N.Y.U. Review of Law & Social Change* 16 (1987/1988): 619; Roger J. R. Levesque, "Targeting

responsibility."[22] In the 1960s, a limited welfare state took greater responsibility in supporting poor, single mothers. But, beginning in the 1970s and intensifying through the 1990s, this limited public responsibility was cut back, as welfare reform sought to privatize the once-public responsibility of supporting poor families. Federal efforts to strengthen child support enforcement were very explicitly animated by the goal of reducing federal spending of welfare.[23] From the Child Support Act of 1974, through to the enactment of the Personal Responsibility and Work Opportunity Reconciliation Act (PRWORA),[24] Congress has sought to reduce its Aid to Families with Dependent Children (AFDC) spending. The 1974 Act, for example, created a federal Office of Child Support Enforcement and required states receiving AFDC funds to establish child support offices to assist parents in establishing and enforcing child support obligations.[25] The objective was very explicitly about reducing federal AFDC spending by privatizing dependency: "Clearly, Congress was seeking to shift the burden of support from the public to the private sphere, and would do so through massive enforcement mechanisms."[26] Fast forward to the 1996 PRWORA – the so-called end of welfare as we know it – and the connections between child support and cutting welfare through the privatization of dependency were even more explicit.[27] While PRWORA is best known for its restructuring of welfare, eliminating AFDC entitlements and replacing them with a block grant program known as Temporary Aid to Needy Families, it included significant provisions to strengthen child support enforcement.[28] "[I]t was the intent of Congress, by enacting PRWORA to eliminate, so far as it could, the public support of the family."[29] In the context of the paternity provisions in particular, the argument is that "[t]he motivating factor here is simply the state's fiscal concerns. Whereas in the past it was a private matter, now the state is much more involved in ensuring that paternity of nonmarital children is established. States want to establish paternity to identify a child support obligator so that they can collect support payments to offset the costs of welfare."[30]

The underlying critique of these privatizing strategies is ultimately one of the demise of the social citizen and its promise of greater social inclusion. It is not that individuals and families should not be responsible for themselves and their family members; it is rather that, under the limited KWS, there was a greater social commitment for the state to help them to be so. The critique is attentive to the ways in which underlying social inequalities are accentuated through these strategies, and the ways in which poorer populations are disproportionately impacted by the withdrawal of the state from a more collective responsibility for its citizens. Moreover, it is a process in which the private choices of individuals are overridden by state

'Deadbeat' Dads: The Problem with the Direction of Welfare Reform," *Hamline Journal of Public Law and Policy* 15 (1994): 1; Laura W. Morgan, "Family Law at 2000: Private and Public Support of the Family: From Welfare State to Poor Law," *Family Law Quarterly* 33 (1999): 705; Anna Marie Smith, "The Sexual Regulation Dimension of Contemporary Welfare Law: A Fifty State Overview," *Michigan Journal of Gender & Law* 8 (2002): 121.

[22]   Smith, *supra* note 21, at p. 211.
[23]   See Harry Krause, "Child Support Reassessed: Limits of Private Responsibility and the Public Interest," *Family Law Quarterly* 24 (1990): 1–34 (stating that Congress's primary goal in strengthening the enforcement of child support obligations was to reduce the federal funds allocated for the AFDC program).
[24]   42 U.S.C. § 1305 (1996).
[25]   Cossman, *supra* note 11, 2005, at pp. 447–448.
[26]   Cossman, ibid.
[27]   Cossman, ibid.
[28]   Cossman, ibid., at p. 452.
[29]   Morgan, *supra* note 21, at p. 712.
[30]   Brito, *supra* note 21, at p. 259.

interference; in the name of privatizing dependency, the state assumes a much stronger position in enforcing these now private responsibilities.

Scholarship on the privatization of dependency within the family, in both Canada and the USA, has argued, persuasively in my view, for the fundamental transformations in the governance of the family, particularly but not exclusively through the restructuring of family and welfare law. But this idea of the reprivatization of dependency within neoliberal restructuring has been subject to criticism. One objection is that dependency actually remained deeply privatized within the patriarchal family, under the welfare state.[31] This argument warns against the overstatement of reprivatization and the familialization of dependency.[32] In its strongest form, it is an argument that the claim is wrong, rejecting the idea that privatization is a useful concept. "The discourse of privatization simply does not allow one to analyze the ideological nature of the 'private' family or the 'public/private' split, and the very real fact that primary responsibility for family and childcare has *always* been primarily 'private' and gendered."[33]

These critics offer important reminders of the feminist critique of the Keynesian welfare state, and the extent to which dependency was only ever partially socialized. Yet I would argue that privatization remains meaningful in describing the transformations that occurred at the beginning of the 1980s and continued through the 2000s. The abandonment of the ideal of an inclusive social citizenship, and its replacement with a marketized and responsible citizenship, has had broad-ranging impact on dominant understandings of the role of the family. As Brodie argued, "privatization involves more than simply removing things from the public basket and placing them on the market or in the domestic sphere. The things moved are themselves transformed into something qualitatively different .... As services and responsibilities are shifted from the public to the private, they become differently encoded, constructed and regulated."[34]

The argument around the privatization of dependency within the family is not intended as a descriptive claim of a dollar for dollar transfer of responsibility from social welfare support to family law obligations. Rather, it was intended to be a more normative claim, justifying the simultaneous retraction of limited welfare rights and the expansion of family law support obligations. It was not that the plaintiff in *M. v. H* would have qualified for welfare on the breakdown of her relationship and is instead to be supported by her ex-spouse. It is rather that the legal discourse that supported the expansion of the definition of spouse in the case explicitly relied on neoliberal discourse of reducing the burden on the public purse. More liberal notions of choice and individual autonomy on the breakdown of a spousal relationship have been replaced with broader state-enforced private responsibilities. The retraction of the limited welfare state and the reprivatization of dependency have recoded the meaning and appropriate location of dependency as residing exclusively within the family, including for same-sex couples, where it never existed before.

---

[31] Shelley A. M. Gavigan and Dorothy E. Chunn, "From Mothers' Allowance to Mothers Need Not Apply: Canadian Welfare Law as Liberal and Neo-liberal Reforms," *Osgoode Hall Law Journal* 45(4) (2007): 733–771.

[32] Dorothy Chunn, "Book Review: Privatization, Law, and the Challenge to Feminism, by Brenda Cossman and Judy Fudge," *Osgoode Hall Law Journal* 41 (2003): 711–719.

[33] Shelley Gavigan, "Something Old, Something New? Re-Theorizing Patriarchal Relations and Privatization from the Outskirts of Family Law," *Theoretical Inquiries in Law* 13 (2012): 271–301, p. 286.

[34] Janine Brodie, *Politics on the Margins: Restructuring and the Canadian Women's Movement* (Fernwood Press, 1995).

10.3 RESPONSIBILIZATION AND PERSONAL RESPONSIBILITY

A second important literature and theme relevant to the privatization of intimate life is that of responsibilization. "The concept of responsibilization is most often used to refer to the increasing divestiture of obligations from the state onto individuals who are under growing pressure to formulate themselves as independent, self-managing, and self-empowered subjects."[35] It is a term developed in the governmentality literature, as part of the transformation of governance under neoliberalism. Nicholas Rose, for example, building on the work of Michel Foucault, has argued that neoliberalism involves a transition to increasing modalities of self-governance. As governments retract from the provision of public goods and services, individuals are called upon to become responsible for themselves and their families. He argues that "it has become possible to govern without governing society – to govern through the 'responsibilized' and 'educated' anxieties and aspirations of individuals and their families."[36] Thomas Lemke argues:

> [N]eo-liberal forms of government feature not only direct intervention by means of empowered and specialized state apparatuses, but also characteristically develop indirect techniques for leading and controlling individuals without at the same time being responsible for them. The strategy of rendering individual subjects 'responsible' (and also collectives, such as families, associations, etc.) entails shifting the responsibility for social risks such as illness, unemployment, poverty, etc., and for life in society into the domain for which the individual is responsible and transforming it into a problem of 'self-care.'[37]

Responsibilization, then, refers to the ways in which individuals are called to become responsible for themselves and their families, to manage their own risk and become self-reliant. It is a process of individualizing social problems; once-public goods and services from health care to education to poverty alleviation are being recast as the responsibility of individuals. It is a critique that goes beyond the way in which financial responsibilities are reallocated to and within the family, through support obligations. Rather, it is both material and expressive in nature. The concept of responsibilization is used to describe the ways in which the retraction of the KWS and its promise of social citizenship has placed greater pressures on families to provide for their own well-being, across a range of social registers. It is not that responsibility is a bad thing – individually or collectively. Rather, it is a critique that tries to illuminate the ways in which the discourse of responsibility has been used politically to justify the retraction of the promise of social citizenship and inclusion.

While much of the self-governance literature directs attention away from explicit forms of legal regulation, in its focus on less state-centered forms of governance, these transformations have been produced through a broad range of regulatory interventions. The rise of the neoliberal state, and its increasing reliance on self-governance, has changed, but not vacated, legal regulation. Moreover, it is important to recognize that the increasing reliance on self-governance has in no way led to the demise of the more coercive and authoritarian deployments of law. These more authoritarian forms of law are deployed against those who fail to self-govern. "Those who refuse to become responsible and govern themselves ethically have also refused the offer to become members of our moral community. Hence for them, harsh

---

[35]   Susanna Trnka and Catherine Trundle, eds., *Competing Responsibilities: The Politics and Ethics of Contemporary Life* (Duke University Press, 2017), p. 2.

[36]   Nicholas Rose, *Powers of Freedom: Reframing Political Thought* (Cambridge University Press, 1999), at p. 88.

[37]   Thomas Lemke, "'The Birth of Bio-politics': Michel Foucault's Lecture at the Collège de France on Neo-liberal Governmentality," *Economy and Society* 30 (2001): 190–207, p. 201.

measures are entirely appropriate."[38] There is a focus on the more coercive practices of government through the criminal justice system, which becomes increasingly important in policing poor, urban communities.[39] The continued expansion of the carceral state under neoliberal governance[40] demonstrates all too well the uneven nature of legal regulation, with self-governance for some, and coercion for others.

While responsibilization calls on individual citizens to self-govern, it is not inherently individualistic. It is a process that also intersects with familialization. It is a process with gendered implications, as women are called upon to take responsibility for the many challenges facing their families: "[R]esponsibility is not only construed in financial terms, but in terms also of providing solutions to all manner of problems . . . Myriad social problems, it seems, can be solved by people simply taking their family responsibilities seriously."[41] It is not a critique of the idea of responsibility per se, but rather an analysis of the ways in which the language of responsibility is deployed politically to "facilitate[] the privatization of responsibility for many social ills."[42]

Some of my scholarship has explored dimensions of responsibilization within the family. For example, I have explored how women have been called upon to self-govern the work/family balance.[43] I have argued that the so-called "opt out revolution," wherein professional women were choosing to leave the workforce to care for children, was a project of responsibilization:

> Individual women are being called upon to take responsibility for their lives and their families, for negotiating the competing and conflicting demands of work and family by choosing one over the other. It is the very existence of choices in relation to the work/family conflict that are to be managed, negotiated, and balanced that produces motherhood as a project of self governance and reconstitutes the identities of women as mothers through their chosen child rearing projects.[44]

In other work, I have explored the responsibilization of marriage.[45] It is a response to the instability of relationships and the rise of divorce. Marriages are said to be fragile, and therefore require hard work. It is the responsibility of individual spouses to "do the hard work of saving their marriages. They must take responsibility for their actions and for their marriages. They must learn to become better, more responsible risk managers in the project of maintaining fragile relationships."[46]

At one level, this emphasis on responsibility can be seen as a logical extension of the liberal values of choice; choice requires that individuals take responsibility for the consequences of their actions. In the context of marriage and divorce, and particularly the recognition of the

---

38 Nicolas Rose, "Community, Citizenship, and the Third Way," *American Behavioral Scientist* 43(9) (June/July 2000): 1395–1411, at p. 1047.

39 See Barry Hindess, "The Liberal Government of Unfreedom," *Alternatives: Global, Local, Political* 26(2) (April–June 2001).

40 See Elizabeth Bernstein, "Carceral Politics as Gender Justice? The 'Traffic in Women' and Neoliberal Circuits of Crime, Sex, and Rights," *Theory and Society* 41 (2012): 233–259, on the carceral state.

41 Alison Diduck, "New Ways of Thinking about Family Law," in Jo Bridgeman, Heather Keating and Craig Lind, eds., *Responsibility, Law and the Family* (Ashgate, 2008), at p. 257.

42 Ibid., at p. 258.

43 Brenda Cossman, "The 'Opt Out Revolution' and the Changing Narratives of Motherhood: SelfGoverning the Work/Family Conflict," *Journal of Law and Family Studies* 11 (2008–2009): 407–426.

44 Ibid., at p. 418.

45 Brenda Cossman, *Sexual Citizens: The Legal and Cultural Regulation of Sex and Belonging* (Stanford University Press, 2007).

46 Ibid.

precarity of marriage in light of the divorce revolution, the push to consider responsibility can simply be seen as a cautionary tale for individuals within marriages. Divorce is now largely an individual choice – and, in some registries, a choice that is too easy to make. Accordingly, individuals should take greater responsibility within their marriages, and make choices that consider the consequences.

Yet there is also a way in which the language of responsibility is being deployed politically to make marriage and family a site of more responsibility, including responsibilities that were once considered more public in nature. "Responsibility" has become a regulatory ideal, as that which governments should promote and individuals should become; "[C]alls to be responsible pervade contemporary life."[47] Baronese Hale has labelled responsibility a "buzzword amongst politicians and parliamentarians." The responsibility scholarship explores how this regulatory ideal is put to work in neoliberal governance. While the literature focuses on individual responsibility across a broad range of social domains, from health to education, some focuses on responsibility within the family. Family law reform in the UK has increasingly sought to promote a new ideal of "divorcing responsibly."[48] The law encourages divorcing couples to divorce well, by settling their own affairs and respecting their responsibilities to one another.[49] The language of parental responsibility increasingly appears in post-divorce parenting.[50]. While it is obvious that parents should do their best to be responsible for their children, this literature addresses the political use of the language of responsibility and the ways it is being used to justify the withdrawal of collective or public responsibility.

Along very similar lines, others have examined what they refer to as "austerity parenting."[51] Jensen and Taylor have explored how the discourses of neoliberalism from the 1990s, of individualizing welfare dependency, have intensified in the UK since the financial recession of 2008, with increasing demands on parenting. "'Bad parenting' and the 'problem families' it is attached to are increasingly blamed for social and economic ills. At the same time, 'good parenting' is increasingly positioned as the solution to an ever-broadening range of social and economic inequalities, and heralded as having the capacity to compensate for economic disadvantages."[52] It is not that responsibility is itself a bad thing, but, rather, how a host of social problems are being recoded as the responsibility of individual parents, with particularly damaging results for poorer parents.

The role of responsibility in the legal regulation of the family has become a central concern in much recent family law scholarship, particularly in the UK.[53] Despite its often elusive meaning, there is a concern that its political deployment is often a regulatory ideal of

---

[47] Trnka and Trundle, *supra* note 35, at p. 1.

[48] Helen Reece, *Divorcing Responsibly* (Hart, 2003).

[49] Ibid.

[50] Helen Reece, "From Parenting Responsibility to Parenting Responsibly," in Michael Freeman, ed., *Law and Sociology* (Oxford University Press, 2006), pp. 459–484; Helen Reece, "The Degradation of Parental Responsibility," in Rebecca Probert, Stephen Gilmore and Jonathan Herring, eds., *Responsible Parents and Parental Responsibility* (Bloomsbury, 2009), pp. 85–102.

[51] Tracey Jensen and Imogen Tyler, "Austerity Parenting: New Economies of Parent-Citizenship," *Studies in the Maternal* 4 (2012): 1.

[52] Ibid. See also Esther Dermott, "Poverty vs Parenting: An Emergent Dichotomy," *Studies in the Maternal* 4 (2012): 1–13; Sara de Benedictis, "Feral Parents: Austerity Parenting under Neoliberalism," *Studies in the Maternal* 4 (2012): 1–21.

[53] See Craig Lind, Heather Keating and Jo Bridgeman, eds., *Taking Responsibility, Law and the Changing Family* (Routledge, 2016); Jo Bridgeman, Heather Keating and Craig Lind, eds., *Responsibility, Law and the Family* (Ashgate, 2008); Jo Bridgeman, Heather Keating and Craig Lind, eds., *Regulating Family Responsibilities* (Routledge, 2016) (all three edited collections appear to have been published first by Ashgate, then by Routledge).

neoliberalism: "[U]nderlying all discussions of greater family responsibility is the suspicion that the more responsibility we place on families, the less responsibility the state will have to take for people who cannot look after themselves."[54] Responsibility, as it is being used politically and legally, is part of the retraction of the promise of social citizenship and public commitment to the well-being of citizens.[55] As the language of responsibility becomes pervasive in government policy documents, it is associated not only with the privatization of economic dependency but "in terms also of providing solutions to all manner of social problems."

> The political, social and economic problem of child poverty, for example, could be solved by families if non-resident parents acted responsibly and paid child support and resident parents earned income from employment outside the home. The problems of youth crime and disaffected youth generally similarly can be solved by families if all parents are employed outside the home and also take responsibility for their children's criminal, anti-social and truanting behaviour. The problems of an underfunded legal aid system and even the personal emotional difficulties of relationship breakdown can be solved by families if divorcing partners and their children take responsibility for arranging their own post-divorce families.[56]

A broad range of social problems can, according to this political discourse, be solved by "people simply taking their family responsibilities seriously."[57]

Some scholars have taken pains to point out that promoting responsibility is not exclusive to neoliberal governance. Trnka and Trundle have argued that "projects of inculcating self-responsibility in and of themselves are not necessarily linked to any particular form of governance."[58] The neoliberal vision of responsibility is not the only possible vision, and it is possible to find other ways to conceptualize the relational nature of responsibility, through the idea of competing responsibilities.[59] Responsibility to the Other remains an important ethical ideal, worthy of pursuit, including the responsibilities of individuals to one another within the intimate sphere. Other scholars have similarly argued against a reductionist and individualistic approach to responsibility, suggesting instead that "responsibility can be demanded of collective entities" and that it is "inherently relational ... it entails a set of obligations towards others."[60] This is a call for a deeper, more nuanced analysis of responsibility: "[T]he difficult questions concern the analysis and evaluation of who is being held responsible by whom for what, in relation to what, in what ways, and with what consequences."[61] The discourse of responsibility may be deployed to operationalize and legitimate the privatization of once-public goods and services, offloading responsibility from the state. But it may not be so operationalized, and critical scholars of responsibility seek to draw attention to the particular ways in which this regulatory ideal is being deployed.

---

54 Bridgman, Keating and Lind, eds., *Responsibility, Law and the Family, supra* note 53.
55 Diduck, *supra* note 40, "New Ways of Thinking about Family Law." See also Alison Diduck, "Family Law and Family Responsibility," in Jo Bridgeman, Heather Keating and Craig Lind, eds., *Responsibility, Law and the Family* (Routledge, 2016).
56 Diduck, "Family Law and Family Responsibility," *supra* note 55, at p. 257.
57 Ibid.
58 Trnka and Trundle, *supra* note 35.
59 Ibid.
60 Nicholas Rose and Filippa Lentos, "Making Us Resilient: Responsible Citizens for Uncertain Times," in Trnka and Trundle, eds., *supra* note 35, at p. 33.
61 Ibid., at p. 34.

10.4 THE PSYCHIC LIFE OF NEOLIBERALISM: ANXIETY AND RESILIENCE

More recently, scholars have begun to explore the psychic life of neoliberalism. While the governmentality literature has focused on the production of subjects and practices under neoliberalism, less has been said about its affective dimensions; about "the ways in which neoliberalism is lived out on a subjective level."[62] Gill and Kanai describe it as taking seriously neoliberalism's "affective and psychic registers, as an increasingly central means of governing and producing people's desires, attachment, modes of 'getting by.'"[63] There are shifts not only in the ideal subjects – responsible, enterprising subjects – but also in the investments and desires of these subjects, with "new 'structures of feelings.'"[64] Some track the unique affect produced through neoliberalism, with its increasing economic uncertainty and the proliferation of precariousness.[65] Hall and O'Shea argue that the structural consequences of forty plus years of neoliberalism have been "paralleled by an upsurge in feelings of insecurity, anxiety, stress and depression."[66]

This scholarship on the psychic life of neoliberalism explores the psychic aspect of the transformed subjectivities and regulatory ideals. It investigates the "psychosocial effects" of the disavowal of dependencies and the emphasis of personal responsibility.[67] This focus on affective life is not synonymous with the intimate sphere, but it has deep implications for it as a central site of affective life and of the processes of privatization and responsibilization. How do individuals subjectively experience and internalize self-governance and the demands of responsibilization within the family? Some scholars have focused on the particular affective demands placed on mothers in the current phase of neoliberalism. There has been an intensification of the demands on mothers to care not only physically for their families but also for their families' psychological well-being:[68] "Mothering becomes ever more rife with anxiety and impossibility, as social responsibility for family life comes to rest ever more squarely on mothers. Indeed, privatizing happiness entails a double movement composed of both the widening of what it takes to be a 'good' mom and the condensation of responsibility onto mothers and their women's work."[69] Women, as mothers, have long been constituted as responsible for the care of their family members, and it is of course impossible to measure the relative amounts of anxiety of mothers, in pre-KWS, KWS and post-KWS eras. But the point of this critique is to explore the particular political role of anxiety in the post-Keynesian moment, as mothers are asked to take responsibility for once-public goods and services. It is not only that the scope of care has been broadened as the state has retracted; it is also its self-reflexive nature: mothers are to

---

[62] Christina Scharff, "The Psychic Life of Neoliberalism: Mapping the Contours of Entrepreneurial Subjectivity," *Theory, Culture & Society* 33 (2016): 107–122.

[63] Rosalind Gill and Akane Kanai, "Mediating Neoliberal Capitalism," *Journal of Communication* 68 (2018): 318–326. See also Yvonne Ehrstein, Rosalind Gill and Jo Littler, "The Affective Life of Neoliberalism: Constructing (Un)reasonableness on Mumsnet," in Simon Dawes and Marc Lenormand, eds., *Neoliberalism in Context* (Palgrave Macmillan, 2019), pp. 195–213.

[64] Gill and Kanai, "Mediating Neoliberal Capitalism."

[65] Keith Woodward, "Affective Life," in Vincent J. Del Casino, Jr., Mary Thomas, Paul Cloke and Ruth Panelli, eds., *Companion to Social Geography* (Blackwell, 2011), ch. 19.

[66] Stuart Hall and Alan O'Shea, "Common-Sense Neoliberalism," *Sounds: A Journal of Politics and Culture.* DOI: 10.3898/136266213809450194.

[67] Gill and Kanai, *supra* note 63, citing Layton 2013, Binkley 2011a and McNay 2009.

[68] J. A. Wilson and E. Chivers Yochim, *Mothering through Precarity: Women's Work and Digital Media* (Duke University Press, 2017).

[69] Ibid., at p. 33.

care for their families, physically and affectively, while also self-reflexively self-governing as good mothers.[70]

Some of my work focuses on the role of anxiety in this self-governance – what I call anxiety governance – in the context of motherhood and the family.[71] I argue that discourses of anxiety produce anxious subjects who undertake a range of self-governing projects to manage and mitigate the experience.[72] I explored these processes in relation to the environment anxieties and the controversy over Bisphenol A in baby bottles. I focused on how the production of anxiety in mothers in relation to the toxic hazard of plastic baby bottles led to maternal self-governance: individual mothers took responsibility for the environmental health of their children through better consumer choices. The regulatory failure of the neoliberal state – the failure to prohibit Bisphenol A in products consumed by infants – operated to reinforce this self-governance; governments cannot be trusted to protect children from the toxins that are poisoning them, so mothers must do it themselves. The psychosocial state of anxiety, itself a product of neoliberalism, and circulated through mainstream and social media, operated to mobilize a specific instantiation of responsibilization. Part of the promise – real or imagined – of the KWS was that it would act in the public good, protecting its citizens from collective peril, from the provision of safe drinking water to the regulation of toxic substances. The failure of the state to prohibit this toxin in a consumer product designed for its youngest and most vulnerable citizens, in the face of scientific evidence of the harms, led to a new kind of self-governance amongst mothers, namely taking matters into their own hands. Anxiety about their children's health, in the light of apparent regulatory failure, was a powerful motivator. Mothers have stepped up to take responsibility for their children's health and safety, in an arena once considered to be the responsibility of the state.[73]

Many scholars have turned their critical attention to the increasing role of resilience as a regulatory ideal and affective state in the current stage of neoliberalism.[74] Resilience is broadly defined as adaptation to adversity, as "the capability to 'bounce back' from adversity."[75] Resilience has emerged as a central discourse in managing uncertainty and precarity. From its role as a regulatory ideal in government policy to its promotion in popular culture, scholars are exploring the particular ways in which resilience is being put to work as part of the psychic or affective life of neoliberalism. Gill and Orgad observe:

---

[70]　Ibid., at p. 39. Wilson and Yochim observe, at pp. 49–50: "Neoliberalism therefore touts a social world held together by self-actualizing citizens (as opposed to a social welfare state). For mothers, this means that family autonomy is to be guaranteed by their own 'active practices of self-management and identity construction.' Of course, good mothers have long been responsible for family autonomy, but now they must actively produce their own regimes of family government by honing their 'mom gut' and disembedding themselves from reliance on public authorities and resources through heightened self-reflexivity and gender empowerment."

[71]　Brenda Cossman, "Anxiety Governance," *Law and Social Inquiry* 38 (2013): DOI: 10.1111/lsi.12027.

[72]　The objects of anxiety have no doubt changed over time. Modernity has brought benefits, such as advanced sanitation systems and medical advances, leading to less daily worry over a range of once common illnesses. The bar of parental anxiety may be lower than it was a century ago. However, the critique focuses on the ways in which the discourse of anxiety is also now playing a distinctive role in the call for self, rather than public governance.

[73]　The role of privatization in this process is complicated. On one hand, the regulation of toxins is still very much within the scope of government responsibility. There has not been a material transfer of this service to the private sphere. However, at the discursive level, the regulatory failure was immediately taken up by a call towards individual self-governance and maternal responsibility.

[74]　Rosalind Gill and Shani Orgad, "The Amazing Bounce-Backable Woman: Resilience and the Psychological Turn in Neoliberalism," *Sociological Research Online* 23 (2018); Dorothy Bottrell, "Responsibilized Resilience? Reworking Neoliberal Social Policy Texts," *M/C Journal* 16(5) (2013): https://doi.org/10.5204/mcj.708.

[75]　E. Harrison, "Bouncing Back? Recession, Resilience and Everyday Lives," *Critical Social Policy* 33 (2012): 97–113, at p. 98.

Much ... recent interest in resilience has focused on policy, showing how the promotion of resilience is intimately related to cutting back, closure and privatization of public services, working as part of an individualizing and blaming strategy in which people are made responsible for their own well-being, always already at risk of being recast as "failing" or "non-resilient".[76]

The promotion of resilience, like the promotion of responsibility, is seen as related to the processes of the privatization of once-public goods and services.[77] While resilience is often framed in economic terms, as a response to changing labour markets and increasingly precarious employments, where market citizens are implored to be more flexible and quicker to recover, it is also evident across a broad range of domains, from climate change to security.[78] Bottrell has argued that resilience and responsibility are increasingly twinned within neoliberal social policy.[79] She observes that although "management of privatized risk has become the core responsibility of neo-liberal citizenship .... centered on economic contribution in the paid workforce," it also "extends to self management of health, education, child care and other social goods that are increasingly marketized."

Resilience has appeared in the intimate sphere, supporting the processes of privatization and responsibilization, as a regulatory ideal and affective state for the management of dependency and vulnerability within the family. Harrison describes the ways in which resilience has significant gender implications within the household, where it is deployed "euphemistically" to discuss "increased unpaid work, particularly the work of social reproduction."[80] Some of the literature focuses on the discourse of resilience in the context of poor and vulnerable populations; single mothers, for example, who continue to rely on social welfare, are cast as "lacking in resilience."[81] Their failure to privatize and responsibilize is seen through the individualizing character lens of resilience, rather than broader structural obstacles. Other scholars have extended the analysis of resilience to middle-class women.[82] Gill and Orgad, for example, have explored some of the ways that women are being called upon to become resilient in media and popular culture. Through the lens of affective neoliberalism, they examine the centrality of resilience in self-help literature, lifestyle magazines and social media in producing what they call the "bounce-backable woman."[83] They argue that the discourse of resilience is producing a new subject:

---

[76] Gill and Orgad, *supra* note 74, at p. 479. See also Harrison, *supra* note 75; Bottrell, *supra* note 74; B. Evans and J. Reid, *Resilient Life: The Art of Living Dangerously* (Polity Press, 2014).

[77] Pat O'Malley, "Resilient Subjects: Uncertainty, Warfare and Liberalism," *Economy and Society* 39 (2010): 488–509, p. 506.

[78] See also, e.g., Chris Methmann and Angela Oels, "From 'Fearing' to 'Empowering' Climate Refugees: Governing Climate Induced Migration in the Name of Resilience," *Security Dialogue* 46(1) (2015): 51–68; B. Evans and J. Reid, "Dangerously Exposed: The Life and Death of the Resilient Subject," *Resilience: International Policies, Practices and Discourses* 1 (2013): 83–98; Evans and Reid, *supra* note 76.

[79] Bottrell, *supra* note 74.

[80] Harrison, *supra* note 75.

[81] Harrison, *supra* note 75. Tracey Jensen, "Against Resilience," in R. Garrett, T. Jensen and A. Voela, eds., *We Need to Talk about Family: Essays on Neoliberalism, the Family and Popular Culture* (Cambridge Scholars Publishing, 2016), pp. 76–94.

[82] See, e.g., Gill and Orgad, *supra* note 74; L. Favaro, "'Just Be Confident Girls!': Confidence Chic as Neoliberal Governmentality," in A. S. Elias, R. Gill and C. Scharff, eds., *Aesthetic Labour: Rethinking Beauty Politics in Neoliberalism* (Palgrave Macmillan, 2017), pp. 283–300; Scharff, "The Psychic Life of Neoliberalism."

[83] Gill and Orgad, *supra* note 74.

(1) the 'bounce-backable' self (*women's magazines*) – the subject who is demanded agilely to bounce back unscathed from an experience of catastrophe; (2) the injured self who repudiates her injuries and invests in resilience as a lifelong project (*self-help/advice manuals*); and (3) the positive self who disavows and self-polices negative feelings and dispositions, favouring positive affect and, specifically, self-love, self-belief, confidence optimism, and living in the moment (apps).[84]

Building on scholarship that has critically examined the self-help genre as promoting the values of neoliberalism, Gill and Orgad explore the affective tone of texts directed at women. For example, in a close reading of Sheryl Sandberg's bestselling *Plan B: Facing Adversity, Building Resilience and Finding Joy*, they reveal the narratives of resilience directed toward women. Quoting Sandberg and Grant: "'[R]esilience is not a fixed personality trait. It's a lifelong project' – a notion that resonates with the idea of the entrepreneurial self as being in a constant mode of becoming."[85]. Women must consistently struggle to turn the negative into the positive; adversity into opportunity. With precarity and uncertainty as the new normal, women are counselled to roll with the punches "and harness[] individual resources to survive in neoliberalism with resilience."[86]

As with the idea of responsibility, a number of scholars have cautioned against reducing resilience to its neoliberal vision, and its wholesale rejection. Rose and Lentos suggest that resilience deserves a more nuanced analysis, recognizing that the future is indeed unpredictable.[87] Philippe Bourbeau, in precisely such a nuanced analysis, argues in favour of more multiple understandings of resilience[88]. He rejects the linear historical analysis of resilience by scholars such as Walker and Cooper, who have drawn a direct line between the resilience as a concept that emerged in system ecology in the 1970s to neoliberalism.[89] Bourbeau explores multiple political approaches to resilience, including resilience as maintenance (the one most closely associated with the neoliberal vision), resilience as marginality and resilience as renewal and transformation.[90] This more cautionary and ambivalent approach to resilience needs to extend to the analysis of resilience in the intimate sphere.

The particular ways in which these affective dimensions of neoliberalism and privatization are implicated in legal regulation remain largely uninterrogated. In contrast to earlier scholarship on the legal implications of privatization and responsibilization, the role of law in shaping and promoting these affects has not yet been explored within legal scholarship.

---

[84] Ibid., at p. 41.

[85] Ibid., at p. 486, citing Sandberg and Grant, at p. 111.

[86] Gill and Orgad, *supra* note 74. As I was writing this chapter, I got an email inviting me to "boost my resilience," from an organization called Aspire, targeting the demographic of professional women. As if on cue, I was offered "[a] tool kit to empower you to pick yourself up and bounce back quickly from unexpected challenges" and an understanding of "how women specifically need to be resilient and how this plays out in the workplace and at home." Resilience is in the ether, and women in particular are being schooled in it.

[87] Rose and Lentos, *supra* note 60, at p. 34.

[88] Philippe Bourbeau, *On Resilience: Geneology, Logics and World Politics* (Cambridge University Press, 2018).

[89] Bourbeau, ibid., citing Melinda Walker and Jeremy Cooper, "Genealogies of Resilience: From Systems Ecology to the Political Economy of Crisis Adaptation," *Security Dialogue* 42 (2011): 143–160. According to Bourbeau, resilience scholars have repeatedly cited Walker and Cooper as "the genealogy" of resilience, rather than interrogating its more complex history and contemporary instantiations.

[90] Bourbeau, *supra* note 88. See also Philippe Bourbeau and Caitlin Ryan, "Resilience, Resistance, Infrapolitics and Enmeshment," *European Journal of International Relations* (2007, online), arguing that resilience and resistance are not mutually exclusive.

10.5 CONCLUSION

Privatization of the intimate sphere has taken many forms. From the literal offloading of once-public goods and services to the sphere of the family, to the recoding of these goods and services as naturally the responsibility of families, the processes of neoliberalism have restructured the relationship between the public realm of the state and the private realm of the family. The range of goods and services for which families are responsible has expanded as the state has retracted. Deeming services to be private within the realm of the family further operates to justify the absence of the state; it is not just that the family can provide the service more effectively, it is rather that the state does not belong within the realm of the family, precisely because it is private. Family privacy is used to bolster the normativity of non-intervention. While there have been explicit policy discussions about the appropriate location of economic dependency welfare and family law reform, with the argument that individual families are best responsible for the financial support of their members, other areas have been more opaque. In the areas of health care, education and environmental well-being, it is unclear that families are being asked to do more because they can do it better than the state. But families – and, in particular, the unpaid labour of mothers therein – are being asked to shoulder greater burdens as the state retracts – because the family is constructed as a natural site of care.

Critical attention to these processes of privatization within the family, particularly through the strategies of familialization and responsibilization, is helpful in highlighting the many different modalities of privatization and the many different meanings of "the private." The market and the family are two very distinct sites of the private, and transferring once-public goods and services to the one is very different from transferring them to the other. Familialization is generally justified not in the name of efficiency but in the more amorphous language of promoting responsibility. Moreover, even within the realm of the family, there are often very different concepts of the private at play. The private choices of individual families, free from state intervention, sit awkwardly with relatively coercive welfare and child support laws. Private here speaks to the public enforcement of private financial responsibility, regardless of individual choice. In contrast, familialization and responsibilization have operated in tandem to encourage families to make better private choices to care for their members, precisely because it is their natural responsibility to do so.

Scholars have been investigating these changes since the 1990s and continue to trace the twists and turns in neoliberal's governance of and through intimate life. There has been a generally negative tone to much of this scholarship, which, as noted, is a critique of the demise of the KWS and its promise of social citizenship. Some of the earliest literature was characterized by a kind of nostalgia for the era of the social welfare state, and seemed to gesture yearningly toward its return. Three decades later, there is no simple return to a social welfare state in sight. Calls for greater collective responsibility need to find alternative registers. But the scholarship that has been generated, particularly in relation to transformations in the regulation of the family, has made important contributions to the understanding of the multiple meanings of privatization, and to understanding the ways in which the private sphere of the family has been made differently private.

PART III

Outcome-Based Theories: On the Virtues and Vices of Public Provision as a Means to Promote Efficiency and Justice

11

Privatization of Legal Institutions

Talia Fisher[*]

11.1 INTRODUCTION

The state and the law seem to be inextricably intertwined: The state is often identified with its legislative and adjudicative capacities.[1] Law and legal institutions are likewise associated with public authority, conjuring the image of public courts and state law.[2] But technological and social transformations, characterizing the modern age, pose a growing challenge to the connection between these two institutions. One type of challenge is posed by globalization, especially in this age of new information, which paves the way for legal transactions that traverse territorial boundaries and/or that occur in the stateless realm of cyberspace. Legal institutions whose jurisdictions are delineated according to geopolitical lines cannot adequately regulate behavior in a world in which physical-geographic location is gradually becoming irrelevant. Another type of challenge to the state–law model is posed by the multicultural state: A product of the liberal ethos and its rejection of coerced cultural assimilation and increased mobility, the multicultural state has led to internal disintegration into distinct legal communities and to alienation toward the legal agencies of the state.[3] Illustrative examples of such legal disintegration include the establishment of religious, tribal, and ethnic courts, as well as the evolvement of nonstate legal orders, like those of the farmers of Shasta County and of the dealers in the diamond industry.[4] From a slightly different angle, one can also mention the privatization of the proceedings for resolving (a significant portion of) civil disputes throughout the Anglo-American world in

---

[*] My thanks go to Leora Bilsky, Hanoch Dagan, Tsilly Dagan, Avihay Dorfman, Alon Harel, Roy Kreitner, Menny Matuner, Ariel Porat, Danny Statman, and the editorial team. This chapter is a consolidation of my previous writing on the topic of the privatization of legal institutions, including: Talia Fisher, *Separation of Law and State*, 43 U. MICH. J. L. REFORM 435, 464–478 (2010).
[1] MIRJAN R. DAMAŠKA, The Faces of Justice and State Authority: A Comparative Approach to the Legal Process 75 (1986).
[2] The positivist school of thought expresses this approach most incisively, in holding that "law" is devoid of any meaning without the state. See, e.g., JOHN AUSTIN, The Province of Jurisprudence Determined (1995) (1832); Hans Kelsen, The Pure Theory of Law and Analytical Jurisprudence, 55 HARV. L. REV. 44 (1941).
[3] See Carrie Menkel-Meadow, The Trouble with the Adversary System in a Post-Modern, Multi-cultural World, 38 WM. & MARY L. REV. 5, 29 (1996); JEROLD S. AUERBACH, Justice Without Law? 69 (1983).
[4] ROBERT C. ELLICKSON, Order Without Law: How Neighbors Settle Disputes (1991).

the past five decades – namely, the thriving of the arbitration industry and the proliferation of alternative dispute resolution (ADR) proceedings as well as self-regulation and private "soft law" mechanisms.[5] These manifestations of resort to nonstate legal agencies, as well as the challenges posed by cross-boundary legal transactions, all call for a reassessment of the state–law connection. One object of this chapter will be to engage in such reassessment of the state–law connection.

But the question of state versus nonstate supply of legislative and adjudicative services and the reassessment of the state–law model are only one part of the issue underlying the privatization of legal institutions. Framing the debate as state versus nonstate supply of legal services may actually mask the fact that the privatization of law is not a cohesive or unitary phenomenon. In fact, there are distinct and conflicting versions of privatization of law and of nonstate supply of legal services, which diverge on fundamental questions relating to the ontology of law, of social life, and of the human subject. These disparate versions of privatization of legal institutions also conflict with regard to the types of nonstate legislative and adjudicative agents that ought to replace the state's legal system, and pose different kinds of challenges to both proponents and opponents of the privatization of law. This chapter will, therefore, also be devoted to a juxtaposition of two distinct visions regarding the privatization of legal institutions – namely, the market-oriented nonstate archetype versus the community-oriented archetype. It will demonstrate that the market-oriented archetype is more susceptible to the underprovision of the public goods associated with the legal enterprise than the community-based model, and that it runs a higher risk of corrupting the prevailing understanding of law as a collective, meaning-creating enterprise. The community-oriented model, it will be shown, is more prone to political failures and to public choice fallacies, and it poses a greater threat to autonomy.

The chapter will proceed as follows: Section 11.2 will outline and juxtapose two archetypes of legal privatization: the market-oriented version and the cultural community-oriented version, demonstrating that the discrepancy between them derives from conflicting ontological premises regarding law, social life, and the human experience. Section 11.3 will survey the implications of these differences for the privatization of law debate, and list the shortcomings associated with each of these archetypes of legal privatization vis-à-vis state supply of legal institutions and services. It will show that the two modes of privatization pose fundamentally different kinds of challenges to both proponents and opponents of the privatization of legal institutions. Section 11.4 will conclude.

---

[5] MICHAEL TAYLOR, COMMUNITY, ANARCHY, AND LIBERTY 61 (1982); Neus Torbisco Casals, Legal Pluralism: Beyond Unity and Coherence: The Challenge of Legal Pluralism in a Post-National World, 77 REV. JUR. U. P.R. 535, 538 (2008). A parallel trend of legislative decentralization is emerging also on the federal plane, manifested in the transfer of legislative powers to the states. See William W. Bratton and Joseph A. McCahery, The New Economics of Jurisdictional Competition: Devolutionary Federalism in a Second-Best World, 86 GEO. L.J. 201 (1997). There is a clear ideological link between the decentralization of legislation in the federal context and the cancellation of the state's monopoly in law, with the central overlapping point rooted in interjurisdictional competition. The ideological basis to this is, amongst other things, Tiebout's classic model of the supply of local public goods, Charles M. Tiebout, A Pure Theory of Local Expenditures, 64 J. POL. ECON. 416 (1956). Yet, despite their similarities, there is a clear distinction to be made between the matter of decentralization of legislation in the federal context and the proposed model for privatizing law: under the federal structure, a legal monopoly is still preserved in any given geographical jurisdiction (even if smaller in scope), whereas the model proposed here in this chapter rejects the notion of monopolistic law in a given territorial expanse.

11.2 ARCHETYPES OF PRIVATIZATION OF LEGAL INSTITUTIONS

11.2.1 *Privatization of Legal Institutions under the Market-Oriented Approach*

In his renowned 1776 essay *An Inquiry into the Nature and Causes of the Wealth of Nations*,[6] Adam Smith asserted that in the free market economy, the invisible hand will convert individual competing interests into social well-being. The classical liberal thinker Gustave de Molinari was the first to apply these insights to the legal realm, by explicitly advocating competition in the legal arena.[7] In his 1849 essay *The Production of Security*, he articulated the claim that the free market logic is as valid with regard to the law as it is with regard to other economic goods and services.[8] According to this approach, privatization of the legislative and adjudicative services, and the adaptation of the legal product to consumer demand will lead to a legal order that is more efficient and of a higher quality than state-produced law, for the same fundamental reasons that market competition leads to efficient results in general.

The market-oriented approach to privatization of law is premised upon the provision of legal services by market institutions[9] and based on processes of the market economy – supply and demand, competition and bargaining.[10] Such a market-oriented model advocates competition among legal entities and suppliers of legislative and adjudicative services that operate simultaneously within the same geopolitical unit, thereby revoking the a priori conception of a uniform legal system in a geopolitical unit. In its most radical form, the authority to create legal rules and determine disputes according to those rules would be fully privatized and dispersed among the population, detached from the state apparatus altogether.

The market-oriented privatization model endorses a consent-based type of normativity. Legal rules would ultimately crystallize as the result of the willingness of individuals to subordinate themselves to them: the parties subject to the duty would create the duty themselves through voluntary agreement, and any such agreement would be a potential source of law. In the broad sense of the matter, all legal issues in such a market-based legal regime would, therefore, be reducible to the law of contracts, where one's basic rights are the upshot of others' contractual consent. In the narrower sense, competing legal regimes would offer different means of resolving disputes over property, torts, business transactions, and even events currently characterized as "criminal" in nature (which would be classified as "intentional torts"). The normative variety that would emerge in a private market for law would enable simultaneous accommodation of the needs of many submarkets. Individuals would be able to arrange their relations with their neighbors according to Legal Regime A, their relations with their co-workers under Legal Regime B, their conduct vis-à-vis other drivers according to the standards applied by Legal Regime C, and so on and so forth. They would be able to subject themselves to partial segments of the legal corpus offered by any given legal agency. The possibility of the parallel consumption of a number of normative regimes (by the same consumer) and the provision of an unlimited number of legal regimes (by each producer) would create

---

[6] ADAM SMITH, AN INQUIRY INTO THE NATURE AND CAUSES OF THE WEALTH OF NATIONS (Richard D. Irwin Inc. 1963) (1776).

[7] Edward Stringham, Introduction, *in* Anarchy and the Law 1, 10 (Edward P. Stringham ed., 2007).

[8] GUSTAV DE MOLINARI, The Production of Security (1977) (1st ed., 1894).

[9] Taylor, *supra* note 5.

[10] Roy A. Childs, *The Invisible Hand Strikes Back*, 1 J. LIBERTARIAN STUD. 23, 23 (1977).

an almost infinite number of potential normative variations in the framework of a polycentric legal structure.[11]

Likewise with regard to the adjudicative function: Under the market-oriented privatization model, the dispute-resolution function in society would be carried out by a multiplicity of competing suppliers of judicial services. Some judicial bodies may supply legislation or be affiliated with legislative agencies, while others would offer only dispute resolution services. Some judicial entities might stress certainty or adherence to strict formalistic rules in conducting the judicial process. Other private courts may focus on speediness or boast procedural lenience. We can expect to find tribunals that seek a judicial determination as well as bodies seeking consensual resolutions of disputes. Certain judicial bodies would likely specialize in narrow areas of dispute and would offer professional services to a defined clientele. Other judicial bodies may appeal to a wide range of clientele, offering adjudication services in an array of areas and disputes.

The network of relations that would be established among the private suppliers of legislative and adjudication services in such a polycentric legal regime would be similar to that currently existing among states in the international arena. Legal agencies seeking to reduce transaction costs for their consumers would establish choice of law rules to arrange "cross-boundary" interactions with members of other agencies. In this sense, the legal agencies would operate both as producers of rules and as intermediaries for social conventions. Legal conventions and confederations would be established to contend with conflicts of law and instances of "cross-jurisdictional" legal disputes. Concurrently, the legal agencies may choose to apply one set of rules to arrange inter-agency interactions and another set to handle intra-agency interactions.

The market-oriented version of legal privatization relies on market logic and on the superiority of the capitalist order of production:[12] the normative foundations underlying the market-based model are premised on utilitarian (efficiency-based) grounds as well as on libertarian (autonomy-based) grounds. According to the former, the assumption is that, under conditions of perfect competition, placing the power to create and supply the adjudicative and legislative services in private hands would lead to superior legal orders that are better tailored to consumer demand in both their procedural and their substantive characteristics. Exposing legal services to the effect of market forces would create incentives among private legislators to develop successful legal rules, in order to expand their customer bases and increase profits. A legislative agency that fails to provide legal regimes suited to consumer demand would not survive for long: its customers (both private and institutional, e.g. judicial agencies) would turn to other legislative agencies. Market forces would operate so that only legal systems that meet quality and efficiency standards (and other objectives set by the consuming public) prevail. The same holds true with respect to the adjudicative function: in a competitive adjudication market, fairness and neutrality of judges would be ensured by the

---

[11]   The described market-based privatization process can be expected to impact the material substance of the legal rules that will be established. The focus is likely to swing from the political–public dimension of the law to the private dimension. The most pronounced shift is likely to occur on the criminal law plane, a sphere that feeds on the state-and-law link. In the framework of a private legal market, tort law is likely to subsume the criminal law and the central legal remedy would be compensation for the victim. An additional presumable outcome of the focus on the private dimension of the law is that constraints on the individual's freedom of action would most likely be limited to conduct that involves a concrete victim, thus excluding "victimless" offenses, such as prostitution and gambling.

[12]   See Hans Hoppe, Capitalist Production and the Problem of Public Goods, *in* Anarchy and the Law 107 (Edward P. Stringham ed., 2007).

market forces' internal control mechanisms – the voluntary nature of the resort to private courts. The autonomy-based case for market-based legal institutions rests upon the assumption that granting individuals enhanced choice in legal governance allows them greater authorship over their life stories. Moreover, a body of law that is the by-product of market institutions – namely, institutions that are consent-based and that evolve in a spontaneous and decentralized manner – may exhibit a greater propensity to gravitate toward freedom-enhancing substance.[13]

The requirement of contractual formation of legal orders, set at the heart of the market-based privatization model, essentially invokes the political theory associated with contractarianism.[14] It is premised upon the notion that the basic social unit is composed of individuals "whose attitude toward the world is one of instrumental rationality."[15] The model has a consumer-oriented[16] perception of social interaction and ordering. Society is viewed as a locus for cooperation and competition between agents pursuing individual goals, and exit is conceived of as an essential component of the individual–community interaction.[17] The fundamental role of law in such a world is to enforce consensual transfers.[18] These features of the market-based privatization model combine to form a model of privatization of law that is strikingly different than that endorsed and promoted by the community-based privatization ideal. The following sections provide a brief outline of the community-based strand of the privatization of law.

11.2.2 *Privatization of Legal Institutions under the Cultural Community-Oriented Approach*

The community-based model of legal privatization is premised upon delegation of law-making powers to substate collectives, such as tribal, religious, or ethnic groups.[19] State power is privatized and decentralized into multiple sources of law and authority that are linked to various group-forming and identity-forming affiliations, and that allow for protection of the relevant communities' social norms. In light of the extensive literature on multiculturalism, I will only briefly sketch the general contours of this model of privatization of law: Like nationalism, multiculturalism is based upon the rationale that cultural belonging is a legitimate basis for the design of public policy.[20] Privatization of legal institutions under this community-oriented paradigm refers to awarding varying degrees of self-governance to

---

[13] Randy E. Barnett, The Structure of Liberty: Justice and the Rule of Law (1998); Bruce L. Benson, The Enterprise of Law: Justice Without the State (1990); Murray N. Rothbard, For a New Liberty (1978); Robert Nozick, Anarchy, State and Utopia (1974).

[14] The sort of contract envisioned by the privatization of law model refers to the discrete transaction contract, as opposed to the relational contract. For the distinction between discrete transaction contracts and relational contracts, see Ian R. Macneil, Contracts: Adjustment of Long-Term Economic Relations under Classical, Neoclassical and Relational Contract Law, 72 NW. U. L. REV. 854 (1978).

[15] Menachem Mautner, Contract, Culture, Compulsion, or: What Is So Problematic in the Application of Objective Standards in Contract Law?, 3 THEORETICAL INQUIRIES L. 545, 546 (2002).

[16] Charles Taylor, Philosophical Papers: Philosophy and the Human Sciences 187 (1985).

[17] For a discussion of such classification in the corporate context, see Paul N. Cox, The Public, the Private and the Corporation, 80 MARQ. L. REV. 391, 401 (1997).

[18] For further discussion of the link between contractual formation and social atomism, see Charles Taylor, The Ethics of Authenticity 118 (1991).

[19] See also Isaak Dore and Michael T. Carper, Multiculturalism, Pluralism, and Pragmatism: Political Gridlock or Philosophical Impasse?, 10 WILLAMETTE J. INT'L L. DISP. 71 (2002).

[20] Xavier Landes, Neither Multiculturalism nor Nationalism, www.politika.1v/topics/social_integration/16736/.

religious, ethnic, tribal, and other identity groups.[21] Ayelet Shachar broadly distinguishes between two versions of this multicultural privatization model, which she terms "the strong version" and "the weak version": Under the strong version, cultural communities and identity groups are given wide formal and legal standing that will allow them to self-govern their members in accordance with their customs and worldviews. The strong version is essentially based on the notion that the state constitution and the individual rights it protects cannot cater to culturally diverse citizenry. Distinct ethnic, cultural, and religious groups should, accordingly, be freed from the injustice of an alien form of rule, both through the creation of islands of self-governance for such groups, as well as through inclusion of the plurality of voices that such groups offer within the public deliberation process.[22] The central agent of the strong multicultural model is not the individual or the state but rather the minority group itself.[23]

Under the weak version, cultural rights and communal norms are construed merely as a supplement to (rather than a replacement of) the universal rights assigned to the citizens of the state,[24] with the underlying objective being the striking of a normative and institutional balance between the interests and needs of three entities: the minority cultural group, the individual, and the state.[25] Will Kymlicka advocates such a vision, in which "the multicultural state will include both universal rights, assigned to individuals regardless of group membership, and certain group-differentiated rights or 'special status' for minority cultures."[26] The normative premises underlying the weak version of multicultural privatization range from autonomy and choice-based considerations[27] to diversity rationales.[28] They are rooted in the underlying assumption that minority cultures "are not sufficiently protected by ensuring individual rights of their members and as a consequence should also be protected with special group rights or privileges."[29]

Either way, under both the strong and the weak versions of multiculturalism and of the community-oriented privatization approach, individuals would concurrently be subjected to – and derive their rights and obligations from – multiple, and competing, legal systems of state and community law. In order to accentuate the differences between the community-oriented and the market-oriented models of legal privatization, the discussion will chiefly refer to the strong version of multiculturalism.

11.2.3 *Discrepancies between the Privatization Archetypes*

While both the market-oriented and the community-oriented archetypes of the privatization of law envision a seemingly similar legal landscape, comprising a plurality of fragmented, overlapping legal jurisdictions operating within a single territorial and political framework, and while both challenge the monism of the legal institutions of the state, there is more

[21] [21]Ayelet Shachar, Group Identity and Women's Rights in Family Law: The Perils of Multicultural Accommodation, 6(3) J. POL. PHILO. 285, 286 (1998).
[22] Ibid., at 289.
[23] Ayelet Shachar, The Puzzle of Interlocking Power Hierarchies: Sharing the Pieces of Jurisdictional Authority, 35 HARV. C.R.-C.L. L. REV. 385, 391 (2000).
[24] Shachar, *supra* note 21, at 286.
[25] Shachar, *supra* note 23, at 391.
[26] WILL KYMLICKA, Multicultural Citizenship: A Liberal Theory of Minority Rights 6 (1995); Jeff Spinner, The Boundaries of Citizenship: Race, Ethnicity and Nationality in the Liberal State (1994).
[27] See, e.g., Joseph Raz, Multiculturalism: A Liberal Perspective, *in* Ethics in the Public Domain 170 (1994).
[28] Chandran Kukathas, Are There Any Cultural Rights? 20 POLITICAL THEORY 105 (1992).
[29] Susan Moller Okin, Is Multiculturalism Bad for Women? (1999).

separating the two than is shared by them. It is on the essence of law, of social life, and of the human subject that these two visions of legal privatization fundamentally diverge. In what follows I turn to briefly highlight some of the distinctions between the market-oriented and the community-oriented privatization schemes:

11.2.3.1 Ontology of Law

The market-oriented privatization archetype promotes a contractual vision with respect to legal institutions, conceptualizing them as the object of preference and individualistic choice about whether "to consume or not to consume." Law (or the portion of the legal corpus subject to privatization) is conceptualized as a realm for the expression of subjective particularistic visions of the good life, however idiosyncratic. Legal institutions are conceived of as "facilitative" and the infusion of "value" into them is viewed as solely transactional. The legal realm is not considered a sphere for the collective elucidation of conflicting notions of justice.[30] It is end-neutral in the sense that it does not seek to promote collective conceptions of the good life. In choosing a legal regime or an adjudicative system, each individual is guided by his or her own preferences or subjective morality. In other words, under the market-based archetype, legal institutions are perceived as an embodiment of individual "sovereignty" or control.

Under the community-oriented paradigm, in contrast, law is conceived of not only as an institution delineating or demarcating the lives of individuals together but also as a locus of collective moral judgment.[31] It is regarded as intrinsically valuable, and not simply as instrumental for other purposes. The enterprises of adjudication and legislation – the creation of a normative world – are considered collective processes for the communal elucidation of conflicting visions of the good life. This, of course, is not to say that the community-oriented privatization of law demands that jurisgenesis necessarily result from a democratic, deliberative, and reasoned decision-making process by community members (or by their vast majority). The source of law, under this model, may very well be tradition, but the collective nature inheres in the ontology of legal institutions. In addition to its innate collective quality, law is also conceived by the community-oriented approach as an object of value. The sine qua non of law is the fact that it expresses the community's constitutive morality. Again, the assertion that infusion of value is a constitutive feature of law is a normative, rather than descriptive, claim. The argument is not that legal institutions necessarily reflect communal moral standards, but that such reflection is a central feature in the ontology of law. Put differently, under the community-based paradigm, legal institutions are ultimately viewed as an embodiment of the community's "sovereignty" or control.

Another respect in which the community-oriented privatization model rejects the notion of law as a product of individual choice refers to the fact that, under its vision, legal institutions conceptually precede such choice. The underlying assumption is that without legal institutions there could be no meaningful categories of choice.[32] Law creates categories of meaning such as "theft" or "breach of contract" and categories of identity such as

---

[30] Of course, the choice with respect to legal institutions under the market model can also express an individual preference for belonging to a particular cultural group, but it ultimately remains an object of preference and individualistic choice.

[31] ROBERT NOZICK, The Examined Life: Philosophical Meditations 286 (1989).

[32] See C. Edwin Baker, Property and Its Relation to Constitutionally Protected Liberty, 134 U. PA. L. REV. 741, 778 (1986) ("people exist and have substantive liberty only within collective structures – legal, linguistic, and cultural structures to which people . . . conform").

"husband–wife" and "landlord–tenant." By asserting significance with regard to certain human and social interactions (and by disregarding others), law creates a conceptual framework within which human consciousness and categories of choice are formulated. Law defines the individual subject and serves as a prerequisite for the intelligibility of individual choices.[33] From a wider perspective, it can be argued that, within the community-oriented archetype, beyond being a system of rules, law is conceptualized as a system of meaning. Legal institutions serve as mechanisms for merging sporadic, diverse, occasionally conflicting fragments of narratives and normative schemes into a meaningful comprehensible nomos. Legal institutions organize the complexity of normative commitments and integrate them into a coherent voice, thereby endowing them with meaning.

Under the market-oriented privatization archetype, on the other hand, law is conceived of as merely a system of rules to be observed, not as a normative world that one inhabits. The market-based model rejects the very assumption underlying the "law as meaning" argument, according to which human ordering can be reduced to any sort of unity. It promotes modes of social interaction in which people may simultaneously be subject to conflicting norms under similar contexts (but vis-à-vis different individuals, for instance). For example, a possible scenario is that a woman is affiliated with one law agency allowing her to terminate her pregnancy with regard to A's fetus, and at the same time is affiliated with another law agency prohibiting the abortion of B's fetus. Likewise, the market-based paradigm allows for one set of rules that relate to intra-jurisdictional interactions and for another to regulate inter-jurisdictional interactions. This ability to effectively choose each legal rule and dismantle the bundles of social ordering negates the meaning-creating capacity of law. The debundling mechanisms embedded in the law, under the market-oriented privatization scheme, relieve of the need to prioritize – to create a clear hierarchy between different sets of normative commitments. Law remains fragmented and pluralistic in nature, irreducible to a single, consolidated meaningful discourse.

11.2.3.2 The Essence of the Legal Community

Another essential difference between the community-oriented privatization archetype and the market-based model refers to the characterization of the legal community. While the former model endorses a thick understanding of "community as identity," the latter adopts a thinner "community as purpose" conceptualization of communal life. The prototype legal and social agency of the community-oriented model is the cultural/ethnic/religious community, also termed "the stateless nation."[34] Such communities are conceived of as representative of "a people," as intergenerational entities comprising individuals who are homogeneous and distinct from others. They share a collective consciousness founded on a common history, a joint language, and a shared culture. Communities of these types are "paideic,"[35] in Robert Cover's terms, that is, constituted by a common narrative that is embedded in their members' internal, normative worlds. Community members share common understandings of the meanings of the normative aspects of their common lives and are united by a set of

---

[33] Social institutions (notable among them, law) provide the context for choice among diverse and valuable options, thereby allowing individuals to become the authors of their lives through their successive decisions. See JOSEPH RAZ, THE MORALITY OF FREEDOM 369 (1986).

[34] Neus Torbisco Casals, Legal Pluralism: Beyond Unity and Coherence: The Challenge of Legal Pluralism in a Post-National World, 77 REV. JUR. U.P.R. 535, 536 (2008).

[35] Robert Cover, Foreword: Nomos and Narrative, 97 HARV. L. REV. 14 (1983).

beliefs and artifacts, above and beyond the promotion of particular enterprises or the realization of specific goals. In this sense, community serves as a population-screening mechanism.

The market-oriented archetype of privatization of law, in contrast, presents a thin and diffuse version of communal life, perceived as a necessary mechanism for the provision of public goods, such as dispute resolution or the lowering of transaction costs. It is constituted for the purpose of ameliorating collective action problems, by preventing otherwise atomistic individuals from free-riding on the efforts of others. The prototype legal agency under this paradigm can be characterized as a nexus of contracts: a "network of social relationships marked by mutuality and reciprocity." The market-based community serves a screening function targeted at behaviors rather than populations: in terms of population composition, the market community's parameters are erratic and ever-changing. Market community members are itinerant and rootless: They are mobile both within a particular legal association and across market agencies. Furthermore, the prototype market association is premised not on common associational worlds or shared normative beliefs but, rather, on the converged preferences of its members. These members need not have a shared purpose in life beyond the immediate enterprise for which the agency was established.

Another feature that distinguishes between market legal associations and the legal institutions under the community-oriented model refers to the extent of their containment of the associational and normative worlds of their members. The cultural community typically aspires to constitute an all-encompassing *nomos*,[36] containing the most significant dimensions of its members' lives[37] and reflecting their most important normative commitments. Cultural and religious communities – such as the Amish, ultra-Orthodox Jews, early Mormons, Mennonites, and groups who form communes in urban surroundings – have holistic normative and ethical systems[38] aimed at addressing all the central aspects of human existence.[39] Such groups are more likely to demand exclusivity from their members and are typically less tolerant of cross-cutting legal affiliations.[40] They tend to view alternative *nomoi* (and especially the state) as "alien, redundant and potentially threatening."[41] In this respect, it can be claimed that the community-based model ultimately endorses a singular ethos regarding law and the legal enterprise. Despite being premised upon the coexistence of a plurality of normative regimes within one geopolitical unit, this model essentially views each of these systems as a cohesive whole in itself – as a single type of object unified by its distinct foundation.[42]

The market-based model, for its part, is premised upon limited-purpose affiliations. Bundling remains a viable option but is not conceived of as a normative ideal.[43] Market legal associations may be formed for specific enterprises and can supply a partial ordering of

36 Leslie Green, Rights of Exit, 4 Legal Theory 165, 168 (1998).

37 Will Kymlicka termed this a "societal culture": a society that "provides its members with meaningful ways of life across the full range of human activities, including social, educational, religious, recreational and economic life …" Will Kymlicka, Multicultural Citizenship: A Liberal Theory of Minority Rights 76 (1995).

38 Eduardo M. Penalver, Property as Entrance, 91 Va. L. Rev. 1889, 1946 (2005).

39 Of course, there are other sorts of cultural communities, such as the Francophone community in Québec, whose normative systems are narrower in scope. However, even in such communities, normative precepts are typically bundled together.

40 Hanoch Dagan and Michael Heller, The Liberal Commons, 110 Yale L.J. 549, 571 (2001).

41 Stephen A. Gardbaum, Law, Politics and the Claims of Community, 90 Mich. L. Rev. 685, 741 (1991).

42 For further discussion of the singularity ethos, see Margaret Davies, The Ethos of Pluralism, 27 Sydney L. Rev. 87, 88 (2005).

43 Under the market-based model, the barriers to cross-cutting affiliations are solely economical, emanating from the transaction costs involved.

narrow spectrums of human interaction. The market-based model thus advocates a plurality ethos in the deepest sense of the word, for, from a conceptual point of view (as opposed to what occurs in practice), there is no objective of totality or coherence in the legal regime one is subject to. Of course, as a practical matter, the difference in this regard is one of degree rather than kind. Under the market-oriented privatization model, transaction costs are likely to limit the viability of endless cross-cutting membership. But cultural communities are more likely to offer all-embracing *nomoi* (and the privatization model on which they are premised tends toward such a conceptualization of communal life), whereas the market-based model tends to envision legal associations that are relatively limited in scope (and are constituted by reciprocal normative commitments among members who simultaneously commit to a plurality of legal regimes).

Finally, the market-based paradigm and the community-based model also vary with respect to the nature of the interface they envision between individual members and the community at large. While the market-based associations are premised on contractual interactions, the cultural community is premised on status-like relations.[44] This divergence is manifest at both the entry and the exit levels of the interaction. Under the market-based model, entry into the association is contingent upon explicit contractual consent.[45] The market community is formed through the express mutual agreement of all members to associate with each other and is maintained strictly by contract.[46] The ideal association is one that is freely entered into and easily abandoned.[47] In contradistinction, under the community-based model, the notion of entry is less material.[48] Most cultural communities are bound together by shared charac-teristics that are essentially not chosen or that are elected in only a very weak sense. The paradigmatic way of joining most cultural or identity communities is by virtue of birth, as is the case with many ethnic and religious groups, families, and linguistic communities.[49] Joining such groups during adulthood may entail high costs[50] and, in certain cases (such as the ethnic community), may be utterly impossible. Beyond the fact that cultural communi-ties are not constructed contractually, they are also not sustained by contractual means. The relations between community members and the community resemble, in this sense, a status-based relationship.

The same holds true for the exit level. The market-based model fosters open boundaries: It places strong emphasis on exit, on each individual's ability to dissociate themselves from a relationship with other members and to leave the effective jurisdiction of the group.[51] The libertarian strand of the market-based model attributes intrinsic value to exit and views social mobility as a crucial component of individual freedom and autonomy. The utilitarian strand of the market-based model regards the ability to exit as a vital component in the liquidity of the market for law, insofar as it ensures market efficiency. The market-based model thus

---

44   Of course, the contract–status dichotomy is not clear-cut: market institutions may create status relations (CEO, for instance) whereas cultural and religious communities may lack distinction of status (the kibbutz in its ideal form). This may hold true for legal corporations and communities as well. I would like to thank Avihay Dorfman for highlighting this point.

45   FRED FOLDVARY, Public Goods and Private Communities 97 (1994).

46   Gregory S. Alexander, Dilemmas of Group Autonomy: Residential Associations and Community, 75 CORNELL L. REV. 1, 3 (1989).

47   Eduardo M. Penalver, Property as Entrance, 91 Va. L. Rev. 1889, 1894 (2005).

48   Leslie Green, Rights of Exit, 4 LEGAL THEORY 165, 172 (1998).

49   BRIAN BARRY, Culture and Equality: An Egalitarian Critique of Multiculturalism 148 (2001).

50   Amitai Aviram, A Paradox of Spontanoeus Formation: The Evolution of Private Legal Systems, 22 YALE L. & POL'Y REV. 1, 1 (2004).

51   See Albert Hirschman, Exit Voice and Loyalty (1970).

stresses the role of exit as a benefit-generating mechanism that enhances the utility that individuals can derive from communal affiliation. Members' unencumbered ability to exit their community's jurisdiction is considered the central incentive-creating mechanism for such communities to comply with consumer demand and ultimately enhances the benefits that members can derive from membership in the various legal associations.

Under the community-based paradigm, on the other hand, the commitment to effective exit is significantly weaker. The community-based model stresses the tension between easy exit and the benefits of community life – its underlying assumption being, that those communities that are easiest to discard are of the least value to their members and vice versa, with the family unit serving as an acute example.[52] The community-based model, in other words, views *barriers to exit* as a weighty factor in the unique goods and benefits derived from communal affiliation. Again, the difference described here is one of degree or emphasis rather than kind. The market-based model acknowledges the role that restrictions on exit play in preventing opportunistic behavior. But at its core it is exit, rather than barriers to exit, that operates as a mechanism for generating benefits.

11.3 IMPLICATIONS FOR THE PRIVATIZATION OF LEGAL INSTITUTIONS

The discussion has hereto attempted to draw the central distinctions between market-based and community-based nonstate legal orders, and to ground the claim that they represent two radically different ontologies, insofar as their fundamental conceptions of legal institutions and legal communities are concerned.[53] The contrast between the two models shifts the course of the privatization of law debate, highlighting the fact that the relevant question is not only one of state versus nonstate supply of legal institutions but also the question of which sort of agent ought to replace the state in its legal capacities. Who should be vested with such law-generating and dispute-resolving powers? The discussion now turns to highlight the distinctive set of considerations that each archetype of legal privatization raises with respect to the debate over privatization of law. It will develop a rough taxonomy of the different types of challenges posed by the market-based and the community-based versions of legal privatization. It begins with the market-based privatization scheme, and surveys its central virtues as well as the focal concerns associated with it – namely, failure in the adequate supply of legal public goods and the corruption of legal institutions.

11.3.1 *Virtues and Vices of the Market-Oriented Privatization of Legal Institutions*

The case for the market-oriented approach to the privatization of legal institutions is anchored in utilitarian and libertarian considerations. From the utilitarian perspective, the contention is that market institutions foster economic efficiency and may therefore lead to a higher quality legal order, one that is better suited to fit consumer demand. Others stress the liberating effect of the market for law – their claim being that subjecting adjudication and legislation to the market can depoliticize social ordering and limit the state's "power to control the behavior of

---

[52] Eduardo M. Penalver, Property as Entrance, 91 Va. L. Rev. 1889, 1911 (2005). For a critique of this view, see Hanoch Dagan and Michael Heller, The Liberal Commons, 110 Yale L.J. 549, 556 (2001).

[53] Of course, one can argue that the market model of privatization may theoretically accommodate a community-based form of legal privatization in those cases where individuals exhibit a preference for being part of the community, resorting to traditional legal institutions by choice. I would like to thank Alon Harel for highlighting this point.

people."[54] But both strands of justification for the dispersion of the legal functions to market-based associations can be contested. From the efficiency perspective, privatization of the law can be challenged on grounds of failures in the markets for adjudication and legislation. The liberating effects of the market for law, deriving from the enhancement of individuals' choice-making capacity, can also be challenged in light of the reductive effect that marketization may have on legal institutions and legal subjects. I will address both types of challenges, starting with the failures in the markets for adjudication and legislation.[55]

11.3.1.1 Underprovision of Public Goods in the Market for Law

Legal institutions are typically classified as first order public goods, in light of the fact that the allocation of contract and property rights constitutes a precondition for the functioning of any market.[56] The case for state intervention is especially potent with respect to the provision of such public goods and services: Starting with the adjudicative function, alongside the private utility generated to the parties to the dispute, as a result of its peaceful resolution,[57] there are also public benefits to legal adjudication:[58] When two parties consume private judicial services in order to resolve the dispute between them by peaceful means, the fruits of the peace that prevails between them are also reaped by third parties.[59] Resolving disputes without resort to force fosters social peace and stability. Moreover, the dispute-determining function promotes social peace not only in ending the enmity between the two parties to the actual dispute but also, in a broader fashion, by creating a general deterrence effect.[60] Bringing rights violators to justice deters potential injurers from acting similarly, the outcome being a general – non-rivalrous and inexcludable – prevention of harms and disputes.[61] The public goods associated with the adjudicative function refer not only to public *peace* but also to public *justice*: Thus, another public good supplied by the judicial process is the legal precedent, which guides behavior *ex ante* and assists in dispute resolution *ex post*.[62] Legal precedents also feature the public good's defining characteristics of nonrivalry and inexcludability: The marginal cost of supplying the legal precedent to an additional consumer is

[54]   Baker, *supra* note 32, at n. 29.
[55]   For an elaborate discussion of additional market failures relating to the "network industry" features characterizing the enterprise of law, as well as to cartelization tendencies in the market for law, see Talia Fisher, Separation of Law and State, 43 U. MICH. J. L. REFORM 435, 464–478 (2010).
[56]   Language and currency are additional public goods that can be deemed preconditions to the existence of the market. See JAMES C. SCOTT, Seeing Like a State: How Certain Schemes to Improve the Human Condition Have Failed 351 (1998).
[57]   *See* William M. Landes and Richard A. Posner, Adjudication as a Private Good, 8 J. LEGAL STUD. 235 (1979). Landes and Posner distinguish between the resolution of the dispute, which they classify as a private good, and the creation of legal precedent – a public good.
[58]   David Luban, Settlements and the Erosion of the Public Realm, 83 GEO L.J. 2619, 2622 (1995); Lawrence B. Solum, Alternative Court Structures in the Future of the California Judiciary: 2020 Vision, 66 S. CAL. L. REV. 2172 (1993).
[59]   Andrew P. Morriss, Miners, Vigilantes & Cattlemen: Overcoming Free Rider Problems in the Private Provision of Law, 33 LAND & WATER L. REV. 581, 582 (1998).
[60]   For an extensive discussion of the enforcement aspect of this phenomenon, see RICHARD A. EPSTEIN, Takings: Private Property Eminent Domain 5 (1985); A. Mitchell Polinsky, Private Versus Public Enforcement of Fines, 9 J. LEGAL STUD. 105 (1980).
[61]   Albert W. Alschuler, Mediation with a Mugger: The Shortage of Adjudicative Services and the Need for a Two-Tier Trial System in Civil Cases, 99 HARV. L. REV. 1808, 1813 (1986).
[62]   See JAMES M. BUCHANAN, The Limits of Liberty 108 (1975); KENNETH J. ARROW, The Limits of Organization 23 (1974); Jules Coleman and Charles Silver, Justice in Settlements, 4 SOC. PHIL. & POL'Y 102 (1986); William M. Landes and Richard A. Posner, Adjudication as a Private Good, 8 J. LEGAL STUD. 235 (1979); RODNEY H. MABRY ET AL., Nat'l Inst. L. Enforcement & Crim. Just., An Economic Investigation of State and Local Judiciary Services 78 (Law Enforcement Assistance Administration, Dept. Justice 1977).

negligible,[63] and any attempt to limit the consumption of the legal precedent solely to those who have participated in its supply process would be directly at odds with the very essence of the legal precedent as a tool for minimizing transaction costs and guiding social behavior.[64] For these reasons, and as claimed by Landes and Posner, the legal precedent will be under-supplied in the settlement arena. Moreover, even where the legal issues at stake are insignificant, and where the trial essentially revolves around the ascertaining of the factual claims, adjudication plays a central public role. For, similar to the case of the legal precedent, judicial fact finding is also a public good, and plays a role in succeeding litigation.[65] The trial serves as a public epistemological sphere – as a means of conveying messages to political actors, prospective litigants, and the public at large.[66] Other public goods associated with the judicial procedure emanate from its expressive function, and from the fact that the judicial verdict serves as a means of conveying messages of moral condemnation.[67] In her well-known article "Whither and Whether Adjudication?," Judith Resnik discusses the role of adjudication in the context of democratic governance, and raises another important public good associated with adjudication – namely, the publicizing of information regarding the imposition of state power. Privatization of adjudication to market institutions may undermine all of these public functions.[68]

The legislative component of law (including judicial law-making) is also considered a classic public good, for reasons similar to those discussed with respect to the legal precedent.[69] Players in a competitive legislation market may thus also refrain from allocating enough resources to the development of the law, and may be incentivized to free-ride on the law-making efforts of others.[70] Optimal development of the law may, thus, be possible only based on nonmarket motivations.[71]

---

[63] John R. Haring and Kathleen B. Levitz, The Law and Economics of Federalism in Telecommunications, 41 FED. COMM L.J. 261, 285 n.43 (1989).

[64] James M. Buchanan, The Bases for Collective Action 2 (1971).

[65] Ibid.

[66] See Samuel Bray, Not Proven: Introducing a Third Verdict, 73 U. CHI. L. REV. 1299, 1308 (2005).

[67] Dan Kahan, The Secret Ambition of Deterrence, 113 HARV. L. REV. 414, 419 (1999); Cass R. Sunstein, On the Expressive Function of Law, 144 U. PA. L. REV. 20, 21 (1996); Erik Lillquist, Recasting Reasonable Doubt: Decision Theory and the Virtues of Variability, 36 U.C. DAVIS L. REV. 85, 137 (2002).

[68] Judith Resnik, Whither and Whether Adjudication?, 86 B.U.L. REV. 1101, 1102 (2006) (discussing the public goods associated with adjudication).

[69] William M. Landes and Richard A. Posner, Adjudication as a Private Good, 8 J. LEGAL STUD. 235 (1979).

[70] Clayton P. Gillette, Rules, Standards, and Precautions in Payment Systems, 82 VA. L. REV. 181, 217 (1996) (claiming that the drawbacks associated with legal entrepreneurship in a competitive market for legislation arise in the federal context as well: "Essentially, the risks of innovative laws are borne asymmetrically: the benefits of successful legal innovations are shared with non-innovating, free-riding states, whereas the consequences of failed innovation (sunk research and development costs, migration of constituents out of the jurisdiction, and diminished reputation and goodwill) are shouldered by the innovating state alone."). See also Ronald J. Daniels, Should Provinces Compete? The Case of Competitive Corporate Law Market, 36 McGILL L.J. 130, 149 (1991). The flawed incentive for legislative initiative is likely to be exacerbated in private markets in which the supply of legislative services is intertwined with the supply of judicial services. Landes and Posner maintain that in a competitive market for adjudication, the exposure of the rules at the foundation of the judicial verdict is likely to guide potential litigators with regard to the line the particular private judge will take in similar cases in the future thereby deterring (at least one of) the sides from litigating before that judge. Due to the need to attract future customers, judges in the private sector are likely, therefore, to refrain from judicial law-making and to instead wrap a cloak of ambiguity around the normative considerations that guide them in their decisions. See William M. Landes and Richard A. Posner, Adjudication as a Private Good, 8 J. LEGAL STUD. 235, 239 (1979).

[71] Edward J. Brunet, A Study in the Allocation of Scarce Judicial Resources: The Efficiency of Federal Intervention Criteria, 12 GA. L. REV. 701, 706 (1978); RICHARD A. POSNER, The Federal Courts: Crisis and Reform 10 (1985);

The community-based privatization scheme may be better equipped to overcome the public good failures associated with the market provision of adjudication and legislation. As argued by Michael Taylor in *Community, Anarchy, and Liberty*, small and stable communities, characterized by reciprocal and many-sided interactions between members who hold shared beliefs and values, are more likely to overcome the free-rider tendencies in the provision of the public goods associated with the legislative and adjudicative functions.[72] In his well-known study of Shasta County, Robert Ellickson described this close-knit community utilitarianism in the following manner: "Members of a close-knit group develop and maintain norms whose content serves to maximize the aggregate welfare that members obtain in their workaday affairs with one another."[73] Empirical studies from the fields of social psychology, behavioral economics, and evolutionary biology support the tendency of close-knit communities to develop efficient rules for cooperation among their members.[74] Moreover, as these studies demonstrate, once people view themselves as part of a group, they alter their behavior not only because of fear for their reputation but also because of a transformation in their conception of their own welfare. Their own identity and welfare become integrated with the identity and welfare of the group. Individuals are more likely to exhibit other-regarding preferences toward fellow members when they think of themselves as part of a community than when they think of the aggregate as a random collective of individuals who seek to promote a particular enterprise.[75] In sum, since cultural communities are likely both to facilitate durable relations and repeated interactions between group members, as well as to alter the self-conception of individual members – by linking their welfare and identity with those of the community – they are more likely to induce cooperative behavior and facilitate the supply of the public goods associated with legal ordering. The public good concerns associated with legal privatization are thus expected to be less significant, when the social agents to which law-making powers are dispersed consist of cultural communities, as opposed to for-profit associations.

11.3.1.2 Corruption of the Prevailing Understanding of Legal Institutions in the Market for Law

A second type of concern that is more pronounced under the market-oriented privatization model refers to the possible *corruption* of the prevailing understanding of law as a collective, meaning-creating enterprise. The commodification of law poses, in other words, the risk of having a reductive effect on the way that legal institutions are construed and on human flourishing: Thus, as claimed by Radin, "many kinds of particulars – one's politics, work, religion, family, love, sexuality, friendships, altruism, experiences, wisdom, moral commitments, character, and personal attributes [are] … integral to the self. To understand any of these as monetizable … is to do violence to our deepest understanding of what it is to be

---

Geraldine Szott Moohr, Arbitration and the Goals of Employment Discrimination Law, 56 WASH. & LEE L. REV. 395, 436 (1999).

[72] MICHAEL TAYLOR, Community, Anarchy, and Liberty 28 (1982).

[73] ROBERT C. ELLICKSON, Order Without Law: How Neighbors Settle Disputes 167 (1991).

[74] Elizabeth Chamblee Burch, Litigating Groups, 61 ALA. L. REV. 1, 16 (2009); Nancy R. Buchan et al., Let's Get Personal: An International Examination of the Influence of Communication, Culture and Social Distance on Other Regarding Preferences, 60 J. ECON. BEHAV. & ORG. 373, 374 (2006); Kelly S. Bouas and S. S. Komorita, Group Discussion and Cooperation in Social Dilemmas, 22 PERSONALITY & SOC. PSYCHOL. BULL. 1144, 1145 (1996).

[75] Arjaan P. Wit and Norbert L. Kerr, "Me versus Just Us versus Us All": Categorization and Cooperation in Nested Social Dilemmas, 83 PERSONALITY & SOC. PSYCHOL. BULL. 616 (2002).

human."[76] The normative world one inhabits may be included among the list of attributes that Radin raises. Those who treat legal norms and institutions as constitutive of identity may object to their marketization on the basis of the claim that construing them as objects of market transactions and viewing them through the prism of the market mechanism are inconsistent with personhood and human flourishing.[77] Another possible source of corruption of the meaning of law that may be brought about by the infiltration of market logic into the legal arena derives from the fact that, under the market paradigm, law becomes the object of individual choice, thereby ceasing to function as constitutive of choice. Legal institutions can no longer effectively function as a background against which individuals can choose or judge, nor can they effectively create the conceptual framework within which human consciousness and categories of choice are formulated. Lastly, another possible source of corruption of the conceptualization of law under the market decentralization scheme stems from the debundling effect. As described already, the market-based model fosters the plurality ideal, with the ability to debundle social ordering set at its very heart. The inherent market ethos allows for modes of social interaction in which people are simultaneously subject to conflicting rules for the regulation of their social interactions. As a result, one cannot draw a coherent set of beliefs or artifacts from the juris-generative process. The plurality ethos underlying the market-oriented privatization archetype is thus another factor in the corruption of the understanding of law.

11.3.2 *Virtues and Vices of the Community-Oriented Privatization of Legal Institutions*

The community-oriented privatization model views cultural belonging as a legitimate basis for the design of legal institutions.[78] It seeks to enhance individual and collective welfare by protecting the normative worlds that marginalized communities and their members inhabit, and by allowing them to acquire jurisdictional autonomy over the various legal domains regulating their lives. At the same time, this paradigm of the privatization of legal institutions raises concerns about both infringement upon the choice-making capacities of community members and a host of public choice problems and rent-seeking tendencies within community walls.

11.3.2.1 The Coercive Nature of Legal Institutions of Cultural Communities

While concerns about consent and free choice may arise in any setting of private ordering, they have greater bearing within the context of cultural groups and communities.[79] The propensity for coerciveness is rooted, inter alia, in the fact that cultural communities are bound together by shared characteristics that are essentially not chosen, or that are elected in only a very weak manner. As has been claimed, cultural communities are not constructed by

---

[76]   Margaret J. Radin, Market Inalienability, 100 HARV. L. REV. 1849, 1905–1906 (1986).

[77]   According to Glenn Cohen, the corruption critique can be divided into conventionalist claims that determine the appropriateness of the commodification of the resource according to prevailing social conventions, and essentialist claims, that determine the appropriateness by inquiring into the essence of the good being traded. See I . Glenn Cohen, The Price of Everything, the Value of Nothing: Reframing the Commodification Debate, 117 HARV. L. REV. 689, 693 (2003) (drawing a typology of the corruption claims and dividing between arguments in which marketability of the resource stands in contrast to the established perception of the resource and claims relating to the ontology of the resource).

[78]   Landes, *supra* note 20.

[79]   Eduardo M. Penalver, *Property as Entrance*, 91 VA. L. REV. 1889, 1913 (2005).

contractual means, nor are they sustained contractually. In certain cases, individuals can never leave the effective jurisdiction of the group and are considered members irrespective of their personal will to exit. For instance, under Jewish Law, one cannot convert out of Judaism. Moreover, in certain cases, one's ability to exit is rejected not only within the community but also outside the community walls. Such was the case with converted and secular Jews in Nazi Germany, who discovered that their attempts to exit their religious community were regarded as irrelevant by the Nazi regime.[80] Exit's weaker role is also reflected in the constraints on exit in the cultural community, by means of cultivating group solidarity and loyalty. Loyalty mechanisms constitute a deliberate external interference in individuals' lives, whose object is to bind them more closely together. The presence of loyalty mechanisms alters the character of exit and transforms it from the legitimate rational mode of behavior of the alert individual to illegitimate and dishonorable defection.[81] The social costs placed upon exit also include sanctions aimed at harming the reputation of the individual as a social agent.[82]

In addition to the direct social costs of exit, the cultural community typically imposes indirect costs upon exit, by impairing the individual's ability to derive benefits from potential affiliation with competing communities. Prolific examples in this regard refer to the Amish or to Jewish ultra-Orthodox communities, whose members are raised in secluded environments, communicate in German dialects, and acquire a limited secular education. Such individuals' ability to support themselves and lead high-quality lives outside of their community – should they choose to leave it – is dramatically impaired. These indirect costs exist above and beyond the direct familial and social costs entailed in separation from the ultra-Orthodox community. While the scope of infringement upon the autonomy and choice-making capacities of community members may vary from one community to another, the essential thrust of this phenomenon remains the same, for this is one of the cultural community's central mechanisms of survival. In light of these effects, many have come to debate whether subjection to the community and its legal norms can be portrayed as an act of free choice "or is an end result of complex and subtle social processes of coercion that eventually restrict the agent's free will."[83] The barriers to exit and the potential for coercion under the cultural community paradigm may be even more acute with respect to the marginalized groups within the cultural communities, such as women. And this brings us to another type of concern with respect to the community-based privatization model – the problem of public choice.

11.3.2.2 Public Choice Problems

The community-based privatization paradigm is prone to political failures, made possible, in part, by the stability underlying cultural communities and their central institutions. Thus, as Landes and Posner point out, a critical factor for interest group activity and for the striking of legislative bargains, characterized by nonsimultaneous performance, is their prospective durability.[84] Durability enhances the chances of future performance and thus increases the prospect of striking legislative deals as well as raising the "price" that could be extracted for

---

[80]   Leslie Green, Rights of Exit, 4 Legal Theory 165, 173 (1998).

[81]   See Gregory S. Alexander, Dilemmas of Group Autonomy: Residential Associations and Community, 75 Cornell L. Rev. 1, 29 (1989).

[82]   Leslie Green, Rights of Exit, 4 Legal Theory 165, 172 (1998).

[83]   Ayelet Shachar, Privatizing Diversity, 9 Theoretical Inq. L. 573, 588 (2008).

[84]   William M. Landes and Richard A. Posner, The Independent Judiciary in an Interest-Group Perspective, 18 J.L. & Econ. 875 (1975)(discussing the role that an independent judiciary plays in ensuring durability of legislation).

a given legislation.[85] As discussed in Section 11.2.3.2, cultural communities are intrinsically stable. They are grounded on and defined by the constancy of social and political roles and by rigid internal hierarchies. The stability in the allocation of powers within the community (including law-making powers) as well as the inherent inclination toward conservatism all allow rent-seekers to derive greater utility over time from imposition of their policy preferences upon the community at large. These characteristics pave the way for the community-oriented privatization scheme's vulnerability to interest group legislation, and lay at the heart of what Ayelet Shachar terms "the paradox of multicultural vulnerability." Shachar argues that under potentially disproportionate allocation of burdens among community members, the multicultural model may reinforce intragroup power asymmetries.[86] In her words, "[w]henever a minority group's traditional practices produce intragroup power asymmetries, well-meaning accommodation policies that transfer a degree of authority and jurisdiction from the state to the group may, in fact, sanction and perpetuate the maltreatment of disproportionately burdened group members within their own minority community."[87]

Contrary to cultural communities and their *nomoi*, market institutions are less prone to capture: The fact that political currency in market associations can essentially be translated into monetary currency makes them more erratic and flexible – enabling easier formation of ad hoc coalitions by temporary aggregation of monetary resources. Such mobility at the heart of the market-oriented privatization archetype as well as the forces of competition decrease confidence in the enforcement of legislative deals and make rent-seeking initiatives less beneficial for special interest groups.[88]

11.4 CONCLUDING REMARKS

The object of this chapter was to introduce and enrich the discourse on the privatization of legal institutions by delineating the contours of two distinct archetypes of privatization: private legal orders that are market institutions and the private legal orders of cultural groups and communities. As was shown, the two schemes of legal privatization represent antithetical ontologies regarding legal institutions and association with them. It was also demonstrated that these distinctions have a bearing on the virtues and vices that each of the privatization models generates vis-à-vis the state–law model: The market-oriented privatization model, it has been claimed, is more susceptible to market failures and to the underprovision of public goods associated with the enterprise of law than the cultural community-based paradigm. The market-based model also runs a higher risk of corrupting the prevailing understanding of

---

[85] See also Donald J. Kochan, State Laws and the Independent Judiciary, 66 ALB. L. REV. 1023, 1034 (2003).

[86] This is further exacerbated by the fact that communal norms are susceptible to different interpretations, and by the lack of neutral bodies to adjudicate between these interpretations. Under such conditions, dominant segments within the community are often assigned the role of providing the official interpretation (or considered better equipped to do so). This proved to be the case in tribal legal systems when the British assigned the task of interpretation to the chiefs and not, for instance, to women. See further Okin, *supra* note 29. I would like to thank Alon Harel for bringing this to my attention.

[87] Ayelet Shachar, The Puzzle of Interlocking Power Hierarchies: Sharing the Pieces of Jurisdictional Authority, 35 HARV. C.R.-C.L. L. REV. 385, 406 (2000).

[88] Economic inequality can be self-perpetuating, of course, and dominant market players often use their leverage to extort further gains. However, power asymmetry in cultural and religious communities is often grounded in the DNA of communal life, in its very structure. Market players, on the other hand, are not inhibited by such structural restrictions. They can discard nonmarket roles in their capacities as market players and can form ad hoc coalitions. While these do not eradicate inequality, they may be regarded as qualitatively different and less potent, perhaps.

law under the state–law model as a collective and meaning-generating enterprise. The community-based model, on the other hand, may be more prone to infringing upon autonomy and choice-making capacities, and may be more susceptible to public choice problems and to capture by privileged groups from within the cultural group or community. Not all nonstate legal entities are created equal, and pitting these two archetypes against each other is crucial for proper formation of the privatization of law debate.

12

On Privatizing Police, with Examples from Japan

J. Mark Ramseyer[*]

12.1 INTRODUCTION

Security is often a non-excludable public good. On the one hand, it benefits the people who buy it; on the other, it also benefits those who live near the people who buy it. It benefits those neighbors even if they refuse to share in the cost of the security themselves. Security also entails economies of scale. In part because of the positive externalities involved, people economize when they purchase security together. Rather than each pay to protect him- or herself, they save resources if they purchase their security together.

Unfortunately, a firm (or person) who can protect can often also prey. The technology and organization entailed in preserving public security are often also the technology and organization by which a firm can extract benefits for itself. As a result, in dysfunctional societies the public police often exploit their power – either for those who control them or for themselves. Citizens then sometimes buy private security services in part to protect themselves *from* the public police.

Security is also a "normal" good (as economically defined): the level of security that people demand tends generally to rise with their income. Consequently, in modern democracies wealthier citizens often buy private security services to supplement the public police. Their need to do so becomes particularly acute under centralized (as opposed to federal) regimes – as the Tiebout sorting principles will not apply. In this chapter, I illustrate these simple principles with examples from Japan.

12.2 PUBLIC GOODS

In the course of keeping order and deterring crime, police officers face economies of scale. Through their investigations, their intervention and their sheer presence, they reduce the number of people who might otherwise take property or harm others. I could hire a team of private guards to do the same. So could my neighbors. Inevitably, however, we would spend

[*] I gratefully acknowledge the helpful suggestions of Frank Upham and the editors of this *Handbook*, and the generous support of Harvard Law School and the University of Tokyo Law Faculty.

more when doing so separately than if we cooperated at the outset and hired one team that simultaneously protected all the homes on our street.

In doing all this, police officers supply a service from which they cannot readily exclude someone who refuses to cooperate. We can take as an example guarding services: When a team of guards collectively protects several residents on a street, they supply a benefit (an externality) that redounds (that spills over) to the benefit of everyone else. Suppose one resident refuses to contribute to the cost of the guards. He still enjoys much of the security that the guards provide. Thanks to their presence, a thief has fewer homes on the street to rob, fewer cars to steal, fewer residents to mug, and hence faces lower returns to committing crime on the street. Necessarily, he or she is more likely either to travel elsewhere to steal or to opt for a lawful career instead.

Even the smaller steps that a resident takes to prevent crime produce positive externalities. Suppose I install an alarm. Although it covers only my house, it still reduces the aggregate take a thief can expect from my street. To be sure, if the thief is already on the street, my alarm (provided I post a credible sign on my lawn) may cause them to rob my neighbor instead. But to the extent that my alarm deters rather than diverts a criminal (a question that is outside the scope of this chapter), my alarm confers a positive externality on my neighbor.

Note that the same logic applies to military force. Although by convention we often analyze military protection separately from police work, many of the same principles apply to both. Police officers protect us from domestic predators. Military forces protect us from foreign predators. Both jobs involve economies of scale and supply non-excludable public goods.

12.2.1 *Functional and Dysfunctional Governments*

This logic straightforwardly fits wealthy democracies. In countries like Japan, the USA or those in Western Europe, it explains why citizens opt to fund basic security services through the government. And, for the most part, they purchase roughly similar levels of protection. Table 12.1 gives standard numbers for police, murders, and general population levels in the early 2000s, and rates per 100,000 population. Germany employs more police than the others; Japan hires fewer. The USA has a much higher murder rate than the others; Japan enjoys a lower rate.

Because this logic presupposes a reasonably honest and effective state sector, it carries less relevance for societies with dysfunctional governments. If an autocratic regime controls its police tightly, it may choose to use its police to keep itself in power. If it does not control its police, those officers may choose to use their power to extract revenue for themselves.

That said, democratic governments are not the only regimes that use police to preserve order. If a state protects its residents from outside predators, it enhances its opportunity to prey on its residents itself. It can use its monopoly on the use of force (as Max Weber and Douglass North put it) to exclude foreign predators and silence domestic predators. Necessarily, it increases its own ability to extract wealth for itself.

By some accounts, the relatively benign police and military forces in modern democracies have their roots less in the democratic process than in interstate competition. In medieval Europe, military predators (call them feudal lords) competed with each other for territory, and from their territories extracted private returns (tax payments, however denominated). Farmers on the periphery, however, could move. Rather than pay tribute to one sovereign, they could switch loyalties and pay tribute to a neighboring one instead. In effect, that competitive pressure tended to push incumbent lords toward keeping their extractions at competitive levels.

TABLE 12.1 *Public police and private security services, selected countries*[1,2]

	Police	Private security		Murders			Population
	No.	Rates	No.	Rates	No.	Rates	
Belgium	37,900	350.0	15,400	142.2	198	1.83	10,840,000
Bulgaria	28,200	372.4	57,100	755.5	128	1.69	7,564,000
France	220,000	340.0	147,800	228.4	743	1.15	64,714,000
Germany	308,400	377.0	168,000	205.4	662	0.81	81,802,000
Japan	251,900	199.6	543,000	430.2	442	0.35	126,220,000
Switzerland	17,800	228.9	17,700	227.9	46	0.59	7,786,000
UK	151,000	243.5	364,600	588.0	655	1.06	62,008,000
USA	807,000	245.3	1,133,900	344.7	14,612	4.44	328,994,000

12.2.2 *Nineteenth-Century Japan*

Military officers in late-nineteenth-century Japan saw their competition in the West. As the US Navy began to pressure the Tokugawa government to open its ports, military officers associated with several outlying domains ousted the government in a coup. Nominally, they returned the Kyoto-based emperor to power – hence the term "Meiji Restoration." In fact, they returned nothing to the emperor. He had served as titular head of the country before; he remained titular head now. The military officers toppled one military government and replaced it with their own.

Over the course of the next two decades, the new leaders steadily consolidated their power. They did not install a democracy or run a charity. They arrogated control to themselves, and rewarded themselves handsomely for the effort. They understood, however, that offering their countrymen stability and prosperity would increase their domestic support. And they understood that this stability and prosperity would also help provide the resources necessary to keep foreign threats in check.

To consolidate their power, the new leaders created a military. In 1871, they dissolved the rival domanial governments, and began to try to force the domanial leaders to disband their armies. They found it a hard process, and succeeded only after a civil war in 1877. Out of their own domanial armies, they then created the nucleus of a national military force. To staff the officer corps, they recruited heavily from their home domains. To staff the general soldiers, in 1873 they instituted a draft.

To further their control, the new leaders also created a national police force. By 1881, they had put in place its basic organizational structure. In the same year, they also created a special police (the kenpei) to maintain order within the military (and enforce the draft). And after several anarchists and socialists plotted to assassinate the emperor in 1910, they created a separate police force (the tokko) to watch groups that might threaten the national political structure.[3]

---

[1] Numbers for most recent years are available, but, because of differing sources and reliability, they should be taken only as rough approximations.

[2] CoESS and APROSER, "The Socio-Economic Added Value of Private Security Services in Europe," (Wemmel, Belgium: CoESS General Secretariat, March 14, 2013); U.S. Department of Labor, Bureau of Labor Statistics, "Occupational Outlook Handbook" (2019); United Nations Office on Drugs & Crime, "Intentional Homicide, Count and Rate per 100,000" (n.d.); Claire Provost, "The Industry of Inequality," *The Guardian*, May 12, 2017; general sources on internet. For Japan, see sources given elsewhere in the text.

[3] Ritto Yoshida, *Guntai no nainaiteki kino to kanto daishinsai* ["The Internal Function of the Military and the Great Kanto Earthquake"] pp. 53–59, 78–81 (Tokyo: Nihon keizai hyoron sha, 2016); Hiroshige Tsuchida, *Teito boei* ["Protecting the Capital"] pp. 8–33 (Tokyo: Yoshikawa kobunkan, 2017).

12.3 PROTECTION AND PREDATION

When a government creates an organization that protects its citizens, it necessarily also creates an organization that can prey on its citizens. After all, the structure and the technology of protection overlap heavily with the structure and the technology of predation. Dysfunctional governments are often dysfunctional precisely because they cannot constrain that public predation.

The same problem plagues private security forces. Suppose a person (or firm or group) maintains an organization to protect his or her family and its assets. On the one hand, the organization may provide a public good: to the extent that it deters rather than diverts crime, it confers a positive externality on other citizens. As several scholars noted about modern Australia, the modern private security industry has been "a major contributing factor to reductions in crime since the 1990s."[4] On the other hand, it also creates a threat: that security industry now enables the person (or firm or group) to prey on other citizens itself.

Over time, people have used private security services for what have seemed morally ambiguous ends. In the late nineteenth century, US firms famously hired the Pinkertons to break strikes. In the early twentieth century, firms hired Bugsy Siegel and Meyer Lansky. Because of Prohibition, those in the alcohol distribution chain could not turn to the police to enforce their contracts. Within that legal vacuum, Siegel and Lansky supplied contract-enforcement services. Note the obvious overlap between protection and predation: over time, the Siegel-Lansky firm would evolve into the entity that eventual presidential candidate Thomas Dewey would attack as Murder, Inc.

In modern democracies, we tend to believe (or hope) that we can use electoral pressure to keep the public police in check. But we read about the Pinkertons in Arthur Conan Doyle's *Valley of Fear.*[5] We watch Moe Greene (modeled on Siegel) and Hyman Roth (modeled on Lansky) in *The Godfather.*[6] Inevitably, we find ourselves less confident that anyone will keep private police forces in check.

12.3.1 *Dysfunctional Governments*

For obvious reasons, private security services thrive in societies with weak governments. Residents hire men to protect themselves and their family. They hire men to guard their property. They hire men to enforce their contracts (as New Yorkers hired Siegel and Lansky). Were the state to offer effective police protection, they might do without the private services. Absent that protection, they hire their own.

When Sicily lacked a strong government in the nineteenth century, the Mafia famously arose to take its place.[7] But more modern history offers its own analogues. With a population of only 57 million, for example, South Africa maintains 152,000 public police; its citizens, however, hire an additional 8,700 security firms and their 489,000 employees.[8]

---

[4]   Tim Prenzler, Rick Sarre and Dae Woon Kim, "Reforming Security Industry Training Standards: An Australian Case Study," *International Journal of Comparative & Applied Criminal Justice* 41 (2017): 323.

[5]   Arthur Conan Doyle, *The Valley of Fear* (New York: George H. Doran, 1915).

[6]   *The Godfather* (USA: Paramount Pictures, 1972).

[7]   Diego Gambetta, *The Sicilian Mafia: The Busines of Private Protection* (Cambridge, MA: Harvard University Press, 1996).

[8]   Julie Berg and Simon Howell, "The Private Security Complex and Its Regulation in Africa: Select Examples from the Continent," *International Journal of Comparative & Applied Criminal Justice* 41 (2017): 276.

Contemporary civil security services can introduce much the same ambiguity as the Pinkertons and Siegel-Lansky. As the chaos from the Soviet collapse spread through Eastern Europe, "trained professional soldiers ... switched to private security companies" (see note 9). As they did, "the private security sector became its own political, criminal and social force" (see note 9). The men who run these private firms in places like Eastern Europe are not all trained soldiers. They also include simple "[k]illers, drug dealers and racketeers" (see note 9). Many of them prey on their own behalf. In Bulgaria, they "force their way into the very companies they are hired to protect, taking shares and money from owners."[9]

In these dysfunctional states, sometimes those in the public regime manipulate the private security firms to their own private advantage. Sometimes, that advantage can be political. In Moldova, a minister threatened to drop security firms from government contracts unless they intimidated residents into voting communist. Sometimes, it can be financial. In Swaziland, the state serves as the principal client of the private security services. In Liberia and Senegal, government and police officials own the primary security services. In Tanzania, army officials own them.[10]

12.4 SECURITY AS A NORMAL GOOD

Security is a public good and a normal good, and the juxtaposition presents a problem. On the one hand, because security service is a non-excludable public good subject to economies of scale, we provide it through the state. Were everyone to buy his or her own security individually, we would collectively lose the economies of scale involved. We would also present people with a potential prisoner's dilemma, and find ourselves with suboptimal levels of service. Rather than leave each person to buy his or her own security, we provide it from the public fisc.

On the other hand, because security services are a normal good, people do not necessarily want the same level. Instead, the welfare-maximizing level of protection rises with income. Wealthy people spend more to protect their own security and, having more property to protect, they earn greater returns from protecting their property as well.

Modern democracies finesse this mismatch by limiting public security to a minimum (however defined). The government provides a base level of police protection. Beyond that base, wealthier citizens buy extra protection out-of-pocket. When doing so, they tend to focus on those services with the least spillover. Most home owners, for example, do not hire private guards for their houses. If they do hire guards, they hire them collectively as a neighborhood association. Instead, private individuals invest in technology. They purchase alarm systems, motion detectors, video cameras, higher quality locks – all of which do relatively less to help their neighbors.

Some democracies, like that of the USA, also limit the mismatch between public provision and private demand by hiring police at the local level. Given that people tend to segregate by income everywhere, this lets residents buy public security services closer to their private preferences. Richer citizens live in municipalities that hire police protection at levels that

---

9   OCCRP, "Security Chaos: Crime and Politics Mix in Security Industry" (2010), www.reportingproject.net /security/index.php/stories/1-stories/3-crime-and-politics-mix-in-security-industry.
10   Ibid.; Berg and Howell, "The Private Security Complex and Its Regulation in Africa," at p. 280.

ensure relatively low levels of crime. Poorer citizens make do with homes in higher crime areas.

Egalitarian commentators understandably complain about this, of course. The rich live in communities where the public police keep crime to low levels, they note. The rich buy private security services besides. All this is true, but it is also true for any other normal good. Demand for most goods and services rises with income (hence the term "normal" as defined in economics). Given that it does, the rich consume more of most such goods and services. So too with security protection.

12.5 PRIVATE POLICING IN JAPAN

12.5.1 *Introduction*

Security services form a large industry in modern Japan. The national government itself supplies 251,900 police officers. But, as befits a wealthy country with a range of tastes for security services, many Japanese augment this basic protection with private security contracts. As of 2016, 9,400 private firms employed 543,000 employees. These firms primarily offered traffic management and security services for homes and commercial establishments.[11]

Americans buy less private security. With roughly three times the Japanese population, the various governments in the USA provide roughly 810,000 police officers. Americans supplement this public service with 1.13 million of what the Labor Department calls "security and gaming surveillance officers" in 2017. They hire another 100,000 IT security officers and 40,000 private detectives.[12]

Table 12.1 offers some comparisons to a few other countries. Switzerland also enjoys low crime levels (though still higher than Japan), but uses only half the private security officers. The UK, France and Germany have more crime and more police. The UK has a larger market for private security; France and Germany have smaller markets.

The largest of the Japanese security firms is Secom. Founded in 1962, it boasts sales of 971 billion yen (as of May 2019, 1.00 US dollar traded for about 110 yen) and a workforce of 54,600. The next largest is Alsok, with sales of 436 billion yen and 37,500 employees. The typical Japanese security firm is much smaller. As of 2016, only 49 firms had 1,000 employees or more; 2,300 firms had 1 to 5.[13]

The industry does many things, of course, but it particularly seems to offer low-paid and non-demanding jobs to elderly men forced out of work before they had planned to retire. About 110,000 of the Japanese security workers in 2016 were aged 50 to 59 – the modal age decade. The most publicly visible of the security workers wave traffic around construction sites. Others guide elementary school children across traffic intersections, tell them grandfatherly jokes and encourage them to continue home carefully.[14]

That said, the growth in the modern Japanese security industry coincides with a growth in crime. Over the course of the 1990s, crime – especially thefts – soared. In 1992, police reported 1.74 million Criminal Code crimes (mostly thefts). By 2002, they reported 2.85 million. The

[11] Keisatsu sho, Heisei 28 nen ni okeru keibi gyo no gaikyo [The General Circumstances of the Security Industry in 2016] pp. 1, 4 (2016).
[12] U.S. Department of Labor, Bureau of Labor Statistics, "Occupational Outlook Handbook" (2019).
[13] Keisatsu sho, *supra* note 24, at pp. 2–3; Nihon keizai shimbun, Gyokai chizu [Industry Map] 247 (Tokyo: Nihon keizai shimbun shuppan kai, 2019).
[14] Keisatsu sho, *supra* note 24, at pp. 2–3.

number of private security employees followed quickly – from 291,000 in 1992 to 437,000 in 2002. After peaking in 2002, however, crime began to fall. By 2007 the Criminal Code violations had fallen to 1.91 million, and by 2017 to 915,000. Private investments in security stayed high: in 2007, private security firms employed 494,000, and in 2016 they still had 543,000.[15]

12.5.2 *The Criminal Overlap: Misora*

Of course, the investments that protect resemble the investments that enable a person to prey. For an effective guard (a real guard, not a grandfather helping grade school children over a crosswalk), one of the qualifications is a facility for violence. As a result, the security and criminal industries have often overlapped – as the Mafia, Siegel and Lansky, and the Pinkertons exemplify.

Japanese history illustrates the same overlap. Take Hibari Misora, the most wildly popular Japanese singer of the 1950s, and perhaps for the entire second half of the twentieth century. With a deep and throaty alto, she specialized first in jazz and then in a retro-traditional Japanese genre known as enka. In the days before television, she toured the country with her songs.

Singers lived vulnerable lives in the late 1940s. Arriving in a new town as entertainers, they worked at the mercy of the local mob. Often, the mobs controlled access to the local stage. From entertainers they demanded a protection tax.

In 1948, Misora's parents took their eleven-year-old daughter to meet Kazuo Taoka, the don of what would become the largest of the Japanese mobs, the Yamaguchi gumi. Misora sang for Taoka, and he apparently loved her voice. He promptly took her under his wing. For the rest of her career, she traveled with guards from the Yamaguchi gumi.[16]

In 1963, the city of Kobe (where the Yamaguchi-gumi has its headquarters) began building a retail arcade near the Sannomiya railroad station. For that work, Kobe hired the large, mainstream construction firm of Kajima. Yet Sannomiya lay in a mob-dominated part of the city. Anticipating trouble, Kajima contracted with the Yamaguchi gumi for security services. But the line between protection and extortion being as vague in Japan as anywhere else, the police called it extortion. They charged Taoka, and the court eventually sentenced him to four years in prison. Taoki died before serving time. Misora spoke at his funeral.[17]

12.5.3 *Iijima as Entrepreneur*

Isamu Iijima had anti-communist tastes. Born in 1921, he had served as a captain in the imperial army. In 1960, he organized a brigade to fight the far-left during the riots over the

---

[15] Yasuo Endo, Nihon keizai to keibigyo [The Japanese Economy and the Security Industry] p. 49 (Tokyo: Norin tokei shuppan, 2017); Keisatsu sho, Keisatsu hakusho [Police White Paper] (various years), www.npa.go.jp /publications/whitepaper/index_keisatsu.html.

[16] Misora Hibari to Yamaguchi gumi [Misora Hibari and the Yamaguchi gumi], http://misorahibariza.jp/hibari/ yamaguchi.html; Shigeki Yamadaira, "Ojo," "Ojisan" to yobiatta . . . [Who Called Each Other "Daughter" and "Uncle" . . .], Zakzak, March 23, 2016, www.zakzak.co.jp/entertainment/ent-news/news/20160323/ enn1603231140012-n1.htm; Buraku mondai [The Buraku Problem], in Hatena blog, June 14, 2015, http://mira00 .hatenablog.com/entry/2015/06/14/000332.

[17] Yakuza soshiki shoshi . . . [Concise History of the Yakuza Organization . . .], Doka to haijo no Nihon no rekishi, http://kasutorizassshi.blog.jp/blog-entry-579.html.

US–Japan defense treaty. And from that history, Iijima created a business. Primarily, he specialized in attacking student activists, labor unions and citizen protest groups.[18]

In 1969 and 1970, Iijima transformed his brigade into the Special Defense & Assurance firm (Tokubetsu boei hosho). As staff, he hired graduates of the martial arts teams at third-tier universities. Iijima had a memorable criminal history himself (eleven violations), and willingly hired men with similar records. He maintained about 200 core employees, and hired on another 2,000 as necessary.[19]

Iijima and his men played prominent roles in 1970s violence. Time and again, firms hired Iijima and his staff to break strikes. When victims of the Minamata mercury poisoning attended the general shareholders meeting of the polluting Chisso fertilizer firm, Chisso hired Iijima. His employees beat the shareholders, and closed down the protests.[20] When leftist groups fought plans to build an international airport at Narita, the firms involved hired Iijima. Again, his men left the protestors badly injured.

About this all, Iijima was nothing if not forthright:[21]

> When a security firm has a contract with a firm, it breaks the strikes at that firm . . . . And if we have a security contract with a university, we have police powers within the school precincts. . . . Lynching should be tried at law, to be sure. But if the other side fights back, and in order to clear them out a few skulls have to crack . . . . Well, that can't be helped. Sign a security contract, and we can enter fully into battle.

The unions retaliated by demanding industry regulation. Faced with their pressure, the government investigated, and counted 321 security firms with 27,000 employees. Of the managers, branch officers and directors, seventy-seven had criminal records and four were former members of the mob. Of the firm presidents, twenty had criminal records.[22]

Given the union pressure, the Diet passed a regulatory statute in 1972.[23] Through it, the government introduced a variety of measures that would let it exclude from the industry men with recent criminal histories or syndicate ties. The unions ran Iijima out of business, it seems. Today, security officers are more often genial grandfathers joking with grade-school children than they are Iijima's martial arts graduates.

12.6 TIEBOUT POLICING

That security is a non-excludable normal good complicates its public provision. Richer citizens would prefer more security than the poor (a normal good), but cannot buy more for themselves without buying it for the poor (a non-excludable good) as well. Poorer citizens would not themselves buy high levels of security, but will happily enjoy any security bought by the rich.

Federalism offers one way out of this dilemma. Suppose a municipal rather than national government supplies the security service. People can now choose the level of security that

---

18 Hiroyasu Iwasaki, Keibi gyosha ji yoru rodo sogi kainyu jirei i oeru ukeoi keiyaku no shokino [The Various Functions of the Contract by Security Firm to Become Involved in Labor Disputes], 14 *Core Ethics* 11, 13–14 (2018).

19 Iwasaki, *supra* note 18, at p. 14.

20 Kumamoto nichi nichi, Chisso kanbu tsuikyu mo [Targeting Chisso Management as Well], Kumamoto nichi nichi shimbun, May 30, 1971; see generally Frank K. Upham, *Law and Social Change in Postwar Japan* (Cambridge, MA: Harvard University Press, 1989).

21 Iwasaki, *supra* note 18, at p. 15.

22 Iwasaki, *supra* note 18, at pp. 18–19; Masayoshi Sato, Keibi hosho eigyo wo meguru mondaiten [Problems Relating to the Security Protection Industry], 24 *Keisatsu gaku* (1971): 107.

23 Iwasaki, *supra* note 18, at p. 11.

more closely matches their private preferences. They do this by moving. As Charles Tiebout classically put it, each "consumer-voter may be viewed as picking that community which best satisfies his preference pattern for public goods."[24]

Consider the USA and Japan. The USA illustrates the federalist approach. American communities organize and pay for their own police. Wealthier communities hire police to the point where crime falls to very low levels. Poorer communities have higher base rates of crime, and (given their more severe budget constraints) choose to hire enough police to lower those rates only to levels that remain quite high (exogenous differences in the base crime rate prevent my using simple sample statistics to illustrate the point). By contrast, Japan takes the centralized approach. The national government structures and controls the police. The prefectural governments maintain some modest control over police within their jurisdiction, and the municipal governments have none.

As Tiebout noted, US residents can sort themselves into communities in part on the basis of the local public goods offered. They can choose where to live, in other words, in part on the basis of the public services the community offers – and, necessarily, for which they will need to pay. They sort themselves in part by public school quality. And they sort themselves in part by police protection. Japanese residents cannot do so. They can sort themselves on the basis of the ambient crime, but not over the number of police officers who will fight that crime. Over the level of local police protection, they simply have no control.

All this suggests – other things being equal – that wealthy voters may buy more security services on the private market in countries that provide centralized national police than in those with a federal approach to police service. Under a federal regime, residents can vote to raise their own protection without having to raise it everywhere else. Under national policing, they cannot do this. Instead, they can raise their level of police protection only by raising it for all voters.

Rather than vote to raise police protection for everyone, rich voters in a centralized regime do best privately to supplement their policing with private security. Were they to raise the level of policing across the nation, they would pay for higher policing for other people. Better for them to keep public policing levels low, and buy extra private security for themselves on the side.

Wealthier Japanese do exactly that: they buy supplementary private security on the market.[25] In doing so, most of them contract for wired services. Although they could hire private guards for their homes, few do. Instead, they install alarm systems, post prominent Secom or Alsok signs, and connect the alarms to the relevant security service. On this much at least, upper-middle-class Japanese with centralized police match their counterparts in the federalized USA.

Two wealthy Tokyo wards, however, have gone further. Blocked by national policy from hiring additional police officers on staff, they contract with Secom to rent extra police officers by contract.[26] The wards are Minato, with a population of 243,000 and a mean household

---

[24] Charles M. Tiebout, "A Pure Theory of Local Expenditures," 64 *Journal of Political Economy* (1956): 416, 418. The literature on point is of course massive. See generally, e.g., Patrick Bayer and Robert McMillan, "Tiebout Sorting and Neighborhood Stratification," NBER Working Paper 176364 (2011); William A. Fischel, "Municipal Corporations, Homeowners, and the Benefit View of the Property Tax," Conference Paper for Property Taxation and Local Government Finance (2000).

[25] As of course do wealthy Americans in the federalist USA. Given the large differences in the exogenous baseline crime rates, the demand for private security obviously turns on many factors other than the federal–central divide.

[26] Minoru Yasuda, Itsudemo, dokodemo, darenidemo anzenwo teikyo suru [Anytime, Anywhere, Providing Safety to Anyone], Nikkei (2019), https://messe.nikkei.co.jp/ss/column/securitytrend/65592.html; Chiiki shakai no [anzen, anshin] ni kiko suru Sekomu no "bohan patorooru" [The Secom Crime Prevention Patrol that

income of 7.6 million yen, and Setagaya with its 930,000 residents and a 6.5 million yen mean income. The national income mean is 4.4 million yen per household.

Minato has relatively few residents, but those it has are wealthy. It lies downtown, and, as one might expect for a rich urban community, it has significant crime.[27] Of the 21 central Tokyo wards, the ward with the highest crime rate (Criminal Code violations per 100,000 population) is the downtown business district of Chiyoda: a rate at the end of 2018 of 5,053.4. With its convoluted network of alleyways packed with bars, brothels and strip clubs, Shinjuku had a crime rate of 1843.2. But at 1490.2, the sedate Minato had a rate close to Shinjuku's. Among the twenty-one core wards of Tokyo, Shinjuku had the third-highest crime rate. Minato ranked fifth.

Setagaya provides the more interesting case for this discussion. With nearly one million residents, it is the most populous of the Tokyo wards, more populous even than seven of the forty-seven Japanese prefectures. The ward lies west of Tokyo, immediately beyond the Hermes-and-Chanel retail center of Shibuya. It is a solidly upper-middle-class professional bedroom suburb.

As befits a wealthy bedroom suburb, Setagaya has low crime rates. Bunkyo (home of the University of Tokyo) has the lowest rate of the 21 wards: 545.3. With a rate of 648.7, Setagaya is the fifth safest. Among the Criminal Code crimes, Japanese police group together murder, arson, rape and violent robberies as the most serious of crimes. For this category, Shinjuku had the highest rate at 30.7, and Koto had the lowest at 1.9. Minato had a rate half as high as Shinjuku: 15.2. Setagaya's rate was the third lowest: 2.7.

Minato was rich, but, given its urban location, it suffered high rates of crime. As a wealthy bedroom suburb, Setagaya had no substantial crime problem but wanted more police anyway. Given Japanese political structure, neither ward could hire extra public police on its own. To this legal constraint, the two communities responded by contracting with a private firm. In both wards, Secom squad cars now circulate on a twenty-four-hour basis.

Note that this private augmentation will affect the voting choices that Setagaya and Minato residents will make. When Setagaya residents buy extra police protection through Secom, they pay for the protection only for themselves. Should they vote for additional protection through the national government, they (given Japan's graduated income tax) will vote for policies by which they will pay for security protection for poor communities as well. Necessarily, the higher the level of protection Setagaya residents can buy through Secom, the less support they will likely give to more protection through the national government.

12.7 CONCLUSIONS

Modern democracies provide security protection out of the public fisc. They do so both because the protection involves a non-excludable public good and because it is subject to economies of scale. Simultaneously, however, security protection is also a normal good. The demand for security tends to rise with income levels. In some countries (as in the USA), citizens decide the level of public security at the local level – facilitating Tiebout

Contributes to the Safety and Security of Regional Societies], August 16, 2012, Secom, www.secom.co.jp /flashnews/backnumber/20120816.html.

[27] To calculate these crime rates, I take population data from <u>Kokusei</u>; the data are available on the Tokyo municipal website. I take the crime data (Criminal Code violations) from the website of the Tokyo metropolitan police department.

competition. Other countries (e.g., Japan) find the resulting inequalities politically unpalatable and centralize policing instead.

Private citizens can augment their public security with private services bought on the market. These private services, however, carry with them the potential for extortion as well as protection. In the less developed world, citizens who hire private security to protect themselves from others sometimes find themselves victimized by the very people they hired to protect them.

13

Privatization of the Police

Hans-Bernd Schäfer and Michael Fehling

13.1 INTRODUCTION

This chapter deals with civilian private security in relation to public police. It first elaborates, in Section 13.2, on the specific legal norms that govern public and private security personnel and shows that the rise of private security is not the outcome of privatization in the usual sense of the term. It proceeds, in Section 13.3, to present some facts on private security, a large and fast-growing industry in many countries. Sections 13.4 and 13.5 deal with the sources of the demand for private security and its impact on security. We show that this impact is conceptually different from that of public police in a constitutional rule of law state. Private security aims at achieving efficient levels of losses from crime. Public police aim at an equal protection of citizens against crimes. The different objectives have different consequences for security and for the wealth distribution of citizens. Furthermore, private security usually does not create general deterrence. Also, deployment of security personnel generates crime diversion, which the public police take into consideration, whereas private security has no incentive to do so. We then elaborate, in Sections 13.6–13.8, on the diverging effects of private versus public security services on the rights of criminal suspects, on the rule of law and on democratic accountability. The chapter concludes, in Section 13.9, with a review of empirical findings on the effectiveness of private security for reducing crime levels, which show significant effects. Finally, Section 13.10 contains the appendix.

13.2 WHAT IS PRIVATIZATION OF THE POLICE?

13.2.1 *Specific Legal Restrictions on Privatization*

The police are subject to more restrictions on privatization than most other sectors because to ensure the safety of its citizens is a core duty of any state.[1] This applies to the prevention of crime and other threats to public security and order, and even more so to criminal

---

[1] See David A. Sklansky, "The Private Police," *UCLA Law Review* 46 (1998): 1165–1287, pp. 1165–1168; on criminal justice see Debra Satz, "Some (Largely) Ignored Problems with Privatization," in *Privatization*, ed. Jack Knight and Melissa Schwartzberg (New York: New York University Press, 2018), 9–29, pp. 9–11.

prosecution. Although private security may serve to protect private property, the rule of law in a broader sense limits the scope for the privatization of public security and in particular of criminal prosecution. Nearly all states under the rule of law respect the state monopoly on the legitimate use of violence, although the scope differs.[2] Some countries have even more restrictions on privatization for such governmental core functions.[3] For example, in Germany there is a broad discussion not only on essential state functions but also on the so-called "civil service reservation" (Article 33 (4) *Grundgesetz* [Federal Constitution]) with regard to police functions.[4] Even countries without such a concrete constitutional provision subscribe to the idea that "public officialdom is a *sine qua non* for [certain] acts to be carried out in the name of the state."[5] Therefore, a real transfer of functions to the private sector,[6] also called "substantial or material privatization," is not legally possible in the field of police. The international consensus seems to be that the state must not altogether give up police functions or even entrust them to the private sector.

In the police sector, privatization (in a broader sense) typically works more indirectly. Private security services supplement the state or local police. However, these private security efforts may simultaneously encourage the state to reduce its own police force and its funding for public security.[7] Real outsourcing of police functions, where private security is endowed with powers that are normally reserved for state actors, is quite limited for the reasons already mentioned. Many countries have seen some degree of police privatization in the area of airport security (for which Germany has a special legal basis in the constitution). However, state actors employ private civilian security in many other areas, though without assigning them core police powers. In several countries, legal doctrine discusses constitutional constraints on privatizing various police tasks.[8] In principle, reducing governmental involvement[9] or even replacing public police by private security is less problematic under constitutional law if the outsourcing affects only very specific services that are closely connected to the protection of economic activities of both the state and private actors.

---

[2] Short remarks, with a lot of skepticism, by David A. Sklansky, "Private Police and Democracy," *American Criminal Law Review* 43 (2006): 89–105.

[3] For India, see the Indian Supreme Court in *Nandini Sundar* v. *Chattisgarh* (2011) 7 SCC 547, concerning the appointment of special police officers for a short period of time: "These are essential state functions, and cannot be devested or discharged through the creation of temporary cadres with varying degrees of state control. They necessarily have to be delivered by forces that are and personnel who are completely under the control of the state" (cited by Avihay Dorfman and Alon Harel, "Against Privatisation As Such," *Oxford Journal of Legal Studies* 35 (2016): 400–427, at p. 410.

[4] See, e.g., Christoph Gramm, "Schranken der Personalprivatisierung bei der inneren Sicherheit," *Verwaltungsarchiv* 90 (1999): 329–360, pp. 329ff.

[5] Alon Harel, "Why Privatization Matters," in *Privatization*, ed. Jack Knight and Melissa Schwartzberg (New York: New York University Press, 2018), 52–78, at p. 63.

[6] This is the most common definition of privatization; see, e.g., Melissa Schwartzberg, "Introduction," in *Privatization*, ed. Jack Knight and Melissa Schwartzberg (New York: New York University Press, 2018), 1–6, at p. 1.

[7] Cf. Sklansky, "Private Police and Democracy," pp. 97ff.: "augmentation" and "displacement" of public police by private civilian security.

[8] In the USA the legal discussion centers on the Non-Delegation Doctrine; see, e.g., David M. Lawrence, "Private Exercise of Governmental Power," *Indiana Law Journal* 61 (1968): 647–695; Jody Freeman, "The Private Role in Public Governance," *New York University Law Review* 75 (2000): 543–675, pp. 543–580; relying heavily on a reconsideration of the State Action Doctrine, Gillian E. Metzger, "Privatization as Delegation," *Columbia Law Review* 103 (2003): 1367–1502, p. 1369ff.

[9] Some authors use this term as a broader definition of privatization, see, e.g., Ronald A. Cass, "Privatization: Politics, Law, and Theory," *Marquette Law Review* 71 (1988): 449–523, pp. 449–451.

13.2.2 *Diverging State Powers versus Private Police Entitlements as an Obstacle to Privatization*

Privatization in general implies that the tasks and the means available for them remain more or less the same during the transition to the private sector. This does not apply, however, to police functions and the legal entitlements to serve these functions.

First, public police have a much wider range of tasks than civilian private security agents can legally have. The law of criminal prosecution and related constitutional guarantees protecting suspects apply only to the public police. Private security workers are never entitled to trace and investigate suspects in criminal prosecution; they may only collect facts to help the state police prepare the official investigation. As every private person, private security workers may temporarily keep criminals who are caught red-handed in custody but must hand them over to the state police without delay. If an employer wants to avoid bad publicity from an official prosecution (e.g. in the case of insurance fraud or minor theft by employees), private security can rely on internal civil sanctions including restitution and, in the case of employees, suspension without pay.[10] Large differences also exist in the area of prevention. Although both public police and civilian security workers seek to prevent crime, the concept of public security is much broader. The public police must enforce the law and protect both private rights and public interests, with the latter including, for example, the enforcement of traffic rules and safeguarding the freedom of expression and assembly, even in cases where the violation of rules does not amount to a crime. These tasks of the public police which cannot be transferred to private security constitute a large part of all public police work. This implies that a requirement to hire private security in order to get a permit for a political demonstration would be unconstitutional in most states, which protect the freedom to assemble in their constitution.[11] Of course, details differ even among countries that have a strong rule of law. Furthermore, only the public police may under certain conditions act preemptively, for example in the context of terrorism, which includes the right to gather information from the citizens that would otherwise be considered off limits. In the context of routine street-level police work, checking the personal documents of people in hot spots and such being suspects for other reasons is essential. Private security workers are normally not entitled to do so, except on private property in some countries. In general, private civilian security is legally restricted to patrolling, observing and protecting the client from dangers to life, liberty and property. Video surveillance may only be used on private property. On the other hand, the public police face restrictions on operating on private property against the owner's will if only the owner's property but not the public interest is at stake. Only in this respect is private civilian security broader in scope than public security.[12] Unlike public police, private security may also protect rights whose encroachment triggers only a civil claim.

Second, there are major differences in the instruments that are available to fulfill these tasks. Because the public police represent the state and its monopoly on the use of violence, special legal provisions give them unique powers, including the use of force. By contrast, private security workers only have the rights shared by every individual under private law, most prominently the rights to self-defense and to defend others against imminent threats to life, health and property, as

---

[10]   With a critical analysis, John Hugh Colleran, "The Growth of Private Security and Associated Criminological Concerns," *Trinity College Law Review* 5 (2002): 104–125, pp. 103–114; Sklansky, "The Private Police," at p. 1276.

[11]   In Germany the Federal Administrative Court (BVerwGE Vol. 80, 158–164) decided that even cleaning up costs can be shifted to the organizers of political demonstrations only in specific narrow cases because of the potential chilling effect.

[12]   Colleran, "The Growth of Private Security and Associated Criminological Concerns," at p. 119.

well as the domiciliary rights. Private security workers are not entitled to searches or to arrests, except briefly until the state police arrive. Only in very limited areas can special laws entitle private security to some of the powers that are normally reserved for state officials.

Major differences also exist regarding the nature and comprehensiveness of the applicable substantive legal norms. State police are heavily regulated by constitutional law, public police law, criminal procedural law and the general laws regulating the duties of public servants to pursue the public good and to protect fundamental rights and special subjective public rights against infringement by the state. Some countries have an elaborate body of public police law dealing with the prevention of crimes and other dangers to public security; other countries deal with the task of crime prevention mainly as an annex to criminal prosecution. Naturally, all legal restraints on the police are more meaningful in countries with a strong rule of law than in autocratic systems. The public police are also subject to supervision and critique by ministries and, in democratic states, also by parliaments and parliamentary committees. By contrast, the work of private security is based on a different set of legal norms and regulated much more lightly, though large differences across countries exist. In the USA, the regulation consists of snippets from the law of torts, contracts and property. Only some countries have established minimum requirements for training and character checks for private security workers.[13]

Because of these totally different entitlements, the public police and private security firms are not on a level playing field. This is mainly (but not solely) why state and private police are not exchangeable – indeed, it is misleading to speak of "police" in both cases. This again shows that "privatization" is not quite the correct term in the context of private security officers to some extent supplementing public police.

13.2.3 *Existing Modes of Privatization*

Private actors may assume police functions in a number of fashions, which may be classified according to different aspects.

A first distinction can be made according to the different tasks and objectives which the police pursue (Table 13.1). As already shown, private police deal only with the prevention of crime, not directly with criminal prosecution. Within the prevention of crime, the domain of private police is the protection of individual interest as life, liberty and property in private areas.

Second, a distinction can also be made according to different forms of privatization and state responsibility (Table 13.2). Even if private civilian security acts completely independently and more so if there is a contracting-out arrangement, the state retains a responsibility to ensure that the private police is organized in such a way that it does not violate the rule of law and individual rights.[14] The range of this responsibility and the legal means to fulfill it very much vary between the different jurisdictions.

13.3 SOME FACTS ON CIVILIAN PRIVATE SECURITY

More than half of the world's population live in countries that have more private security workers to protect people and property than public police officers.[15] This applies to more than

---

[13]   Cf. ibid, at p. 119f. In Germany, for instance, private civilian security is regulated in detail in section 41a of the Commerce and Industry Regulation Act (Gewerbeordnung); for a short overview, see Wolf-Rüdiger Schenke, *Polizei- und Ordnungsrecht*, 9th ed. (Heidelberg: C.F. Müller, 2016), pp. 473–474.

[14]   In Germany this responsibility has an elaborate doctrinal structure, called *Gewährleistungsverantwortung*.

[15]   Claire Provost, "The Industry of Inequality," *The Guardian* (12 May 2017): statistical appendix.

TABLE 13.1 *Systematization according to different tasks and objectives which the police have to pursue*

Prevention of crime and other violations of law (*preventative*)		Criminal prosecution (*repressive*)
Mostly: Protection of individual interests as life, liberty and property in private areas (protection policing and intelligence policing)	Rarely: Protection of public interests in the public sphere (publicly contracted policing)	Only some support: - Temporarily keeping criminals in custody who are caught red-handed - Collecting facts to help the public police prepare investigation

TABLE 13.2 *Systematization according to different forms of privatization and state responsibility*

Acting independently from the state	Contracting-out arrangements	Police–private partnership	Acting similar to the public police
Without special legal entitlements, restricted to the rights of every private individual - State "guarantees responsibility" ("*Gewährleistungsverantwortung*") to ensure that the private police is organized in a way that does not violate the rule of law and individual rights - Legal means to meet this responsibility: e.g. minimum requirements for qualification and/or training of private security workers, checks on good character		Clear demarcation of responsibilities of both partners	Entrusted with special police powers by law ("*Beleihung*") Governmental supervision

forty countries, including China, the USA, India, Brazil, South Africa, Germany, Canada, Australia and the UK. Private security guards patrol shopping malls, fun parks, universities, gated communities and public streets and districts. They often wear uniforms that resemble police clothing. In some countries private guards carry handguns. They also guard the premises of companies, airports, railway stations and hotels. They provide cash solutions for banks and shops, cash-in-transit solutions, gate controls and executive personal protection packages, including protection for homes, royal families and diplomats. The total number of civilian private security workers is estimated at 20 million globally.[16] The total market amounted to around $180 billion in 2017 and is growing at the rate of 6 percent annually.[17]

Private security firms come in all sizes. Registered in the UK, G4S is one of the biggest private security corporations, with 546,000 employees in 44 countries,[18] more than twice the size of the public police force in Germany. Kötter GmbH, a German family business, has

[16] Ibid.
[17] Freedonia, "Global Security Services Market, 12th Edition – Industry Study with Forecasts for 2020 & 2025, Study 3451" (January 2017).
[18] G4S Directors Report 2018.

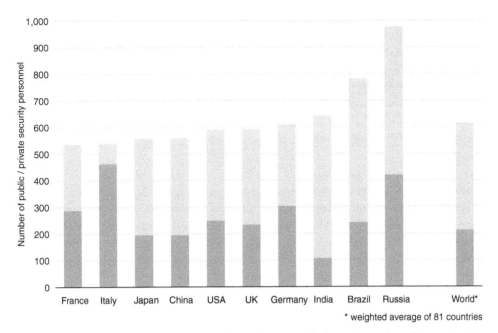

FIGURE 13.1 Private security (light gray) and public police (dark gray) in selected countries (per 100,000 inhabitants)
Sources: Various sources comprising data from 2011 to 2017 including Eurostat, SAS, Statcan, OAS and DCAF, compiled by Claire Provost (2017).

18,500 employees.[19] Demand for private security does not derive solely from private sources. In Europe, the share of total demand for private security that comes from public authorities is about 30 percent on average and rising.[20]

13.4 A BASIC DIFFERENCE BETWEEN PRIVATE SECURITY AND PUBLIC POLICE: EFFICIENT LOSS REDUCTION FROM CRIME VERSUS EQUAL SECURITY FOR ALL

13.4.1 *Loss Reduction versus Equal Protection against Crime*

Among economists, police services are a standard example of a public good, which the state must provide to prevent undersupply due to the missing demand from free riders, thus leading to a market failure. Correcting a market failure leads to public regulation and state financing and usually to mimicking a well-functioning market.[21] We show, however, that despite its merits – especially with regard to general crime deterrence – the public good theory of state police obscures the fact that a modern tax-financed public police provides a service that even a perfect market for police forces could not offer as its objectives differ from wealth maximization or economic efficiency. Also, the literature on the history of the police shows that public police are, in historical perspective, a relatively recent development and

---

[19] www.koetter.de/unternehmen/ueber-uns.
[20] CoESS, "Facts & Figures – Private Security in Europe 2015," www.coess.org/newsroom.php?page=facts-and-figures.
[21] Kevin Morrell and Ben Bradford, *Policing and Public Management* (London: Routledge, 2019), ch. 2.

closely related to the growing scope of police tasks under the modern concept of the rule of law with a state monopoly on the use of violence. Until well into the nineteenth century, police in England, for example, were mainly privately organized and financed.[22] Even if the public good problem did not exist at all, public police with their specific goals would be necessary because a rule of law state wants to achieve the result of equal security for all, which even a perfect market for private security cannot deliver.

Equal security for all as the mission of public police is now widely and internationally accepted not only among constitutional lawyers but also among practitioners and in the political arena.

In Germany, a constitutional "right to security" does not exist in the wording of the constitution, even though this has been proposed in the literature. But the constitutional court derives from several constitutional rights together with Art. 1 (1) of the constitution, which orders the state to protect human dignity, a state duty to protect basic rights such as life and health (Art. 2 (2) of the constitution) and property (Art. 14). From this doctrinal concept derives not only an objective responsibility of the state to organize protection and security against criminals but also an individual constitutional right to such protection. Because there exists also a general constitutional right to equal treatment (Art. 3 (1) of the constitution), the "right to security" is – in general – a right to equal protection. It supplements the traditional concept of preserving law and order as a function of the state, which is not right based.[23]

The UN security council urged (2004) "promotion of . . . equal security . . . for all inhabitants of Kosovo."[24] In the coalition agreement of the grand coalition (2018) in Germany one can read: "We do not want zones of unequal security in Germany."[25] These are two examples from a long list of authoritative political statements on the policy goal of public police.[26]

Public police do not mimic a perfect market for private police but reduce numbers of crimes weighted with the severity of a crime, and the severity weight is – in principle – equal for each citizen leading ideally to an equal state protection of equal fundamental rights. We call this the equal security approach of public police. This concept is a raw approximation because, even in democratic rule of law states, the constitutional rules relating equal fundamental rights for all citizens to police law differ across countries. It is, however, undisputable that the state does not follow the efficiency criterion and the

---

[22] "By the eighteenth and nineteenth centuries in Britain and America, volunteer groups using private funding complemented, supplemented, or supplanted the mandatory systems of community protection. In Britain, felons associations posted rewards to apprehend criminals, assisted their members in prosecuting criminals, and sometimes hired private patrols. Victims hired private thieftakers to retrieve stolen property. In colonial America, Boston established a night watch in 1636, and watchmen became commonplace throughout the colonies. Crime control administered by a centralized government did not exist, and responsibility for protection was thrust upon the people themselves" (M. Rhead Enion, "Constitutional Limits on Private Policing and the State's Allocation of Force," *Duke Law Journal* 59 (2009): 519–553, at p. 533).

[23] The same fundamental difference between public and private police is mapped out by Clifford D. Shearing and Phillip C. Stenning, *Private Policing* (Newbury Park: SAGE, 1987); Colleran, "The Growth of Private Security and Associated Criminological Concerns," at p. 114; Enion, "Constitutional Limits on Private Policing and the State's Allocation of Force," at p. 550. Enion argues that the security and welfare aspects of policing in the USA derive from the twelfth, thirteenth and fourteenth amendments of the US constitution.

[24] Security Council, Press Release, SC 8082, April 30, 2004.

[25] Koalitionsvertrag zwischen CDU, CSU und SPD, 19. Legislaturperiode, 2018, at p. 126.

[26] Harel and Parchmovoski make a similar argument and argue that fair protection against crime "imparts a duty on the state to equalize individuals' vulnerability to crime." This would imply more police efforts or higher punishment of crimes against those who are particularly vulnerable, like crimes related to race, gender, religion, and sexual orientation. Alon Harel and Gideon Parchmovoski, "On Hate and Equality," *Yale Law Journal* 109 (1999): 507–539.

related willingness to pay as a starting point for defining the mission of public police. The rationale of public police is not reducing losses from crimes based on the willingness to pay for loss avoidance. Public police often do not even have the information they need to reduce losses, as public crime statistics, on which police planning is based, seldom include information on losses from crime, let alone on the willingness to pay for the reduction of such losses. It concentrates police forces where crime rates are relatively high. Observed public police activity is not in line with an economic theory of public police, which maintains that such an entity corrects the public good market failure. Public police in democratic rule of law countries with good governance ideally achieve an equal state protection of those constitutional rights, for which an identical endowment of all citizens exists, like life or bodily integrity. It does not achieve an efficient reduction of the losses – including non-monetary and psychic damages – from crimes. Ideally, everybody should have the same perception of safety and security so that the fear of crimes does not have a chilling effect on his or her daily life or on the exercise of political rights like the right to assemble. This is important for individual freedom and necessary for a free and equal use of rights in a democratic society. A public police force should therefore be understood as a twin sister of fundamental and equal human rights and not as a public organization for the correction of a market failure. The measure of equality for a market-driven private police force or a market mimicking public police is the marginal loss reduction of a dollar spent on crime prevention across all police districts and all crime categories in a state. For the public police, it is an equal safety level for all residents. The state provision of security therefore differs categorically from economic regulation, which corrects market failure and tries to establish or mimic workable markets, as in antitrust law, regulation of capital markets, natural monopolies, networks or in tort law.

13.4.2 *Inconsistencies of the Two Approaches to Security*

Efficiency-based police cannot achieve equal security for all residents. With regard to crimes against life, bodily integrity or the security of public places, it leads to unequal protection based on the willingness to pay in different police districts with different incomes of residents. The resulting inequality, which translates into unequal protection of equal rights, becomes more severe with a more unequal distribution of wealth. Two other problems will be dealt with in more detail in Section 16.5.3. Private security, unlike public police, cannot distinguish between crime reduction and crime diversion. It is confined to the protection of a small territorial zone or of a person. This might lead to overinvestment if policing causes crime diversion. Also, under particular conditions, private crime prevention might cause general deterrence. This can lead to underinvestment in crime prevention, as will be shown in Section 16.5.3.

The "equal security for all" mission of the public police is not without inconsistencies either. In market-based private security, the police budget is derived automatically from the willingness to pay. On the contrary, the equal security approach does not determine the police budget. It seems to be the general opinion among constitutional lawyers that the size of the budget is subject to a final and exclusive democratic decision in parliament if it is not obviously much too low. This combination of two social decision mechanisms poses questions of justice and consistency, too. "Equal security" with almost any budget size cannot categorically stand alone as a definite normative concept. It can violate other important principles of justice and public policy:

(1) Effectiveness. The marginal spending for police should have the same effect on crime reduction in every police district. Effectiveness guarantees that the total number of crimes in a state is minimized with a given police budget.

(2) Inclusive benevolence. With public police, no resident should be less secure than without public police. A stronger form of inclusive benevolence relates this policy goal to any increase of the police budget.

(3) Nondiscrimination. Police activities against offenders must be nondiscriminatory with respect to gender, race or religion.

(4) Balance between rights. The police budget must not be increased above a level at which an additional unit of public police spending increases security less than it would improve the realization of another human right.

(5) Minimal efficiency. The police budget per resident in a state should not be lower than the average willingness to pay in the police district with the lowest per capita income and should not be higher than the average willingness to pay in the district with the highest per capita income.

Public police, which try to establish equal security for all, are likely to violate one or more of these principles. An easy illustrative case is this. Assume that a municipality has two police districts, a low-income district with a high crime rate (hot spot) and a high-income district with half of this crime rate if no police exists. Assume also, for the sake of argument, that in the low-income district all offenders are black and in the high-income district they are all white. This implies that a third of all crimes are committed by whites. Then equal security in both districts requires the concentration of police in the hot-spot area until crime rates are the same in both districts. This violates (3) because all arrested and convicted criminals are blacks. It also violates (2) because concentrating the police force in the hot spot leads to crime diversion, which makes residents in the rich district less safe than they would be without the existence of public police. If one wants to avoid this by evenly spending the budget in both districts, this violates (1) and the principle of equal security for all residents itself. If the police budget is increased to such a high level that the police can substantially reduce crimes in both districts and racial discrimination does not happen, this might not violate (1), (2) or (3) but it might violate (4).

Achieving equal security for all residents, including those targeted by hate crimes, might require concentrating public security spending on the targeted individuals or members of a targeted religious community. Assume that the victims of hate crimes are rich and live in the district with the highest incomes. Then achieving equal security across all police districts might require a level of police spending in favor of the potential victims of the hate crimes, which is higher than their own willingness to pay for police. This would violate minimal efficiency (5).

Equal security in all police districts can violate the principle of effectiveness (1). The latter guarantees that public police minimize the number of crimes in the state, given the police budget. Depending on the relation between police spending in different police districts and crime rates, effectiveness can imply to zones of unequal security in a state.

It is therefore inevitable that the goal of equal security for all – as the concept of efficient security – cannot be categorical but must be traded off against other principles and reasonable policy goals.

13.5 CRIME LEVELS UNDER EFFICIENT AND UNDER EQUAL SECURITY

The economic analysis requires several simplifications. Although police functions are much more diverse, we will concentrate on the prevention of crime through the presence of security workers because the tasks of the public police and of private civilian security are roughly comparable only in this regard. Therefore, we will not focus on criminal prosecution as such, bearing in mind, however, that prevention and prosecution are quite often closely linked in police practice. Although private security officers are not entitled to – and barely interested in – the punishment of crime, criminal prosecution indirectly serves the prevention of crime through the general deterrence effect and incapacitation. Furthermore, we ignore information collection as a preventive measure because, though it is part of crime prevention in a broader sense, it is the business only of the public police and therefore not suitable for comparison. Furthermore, we disregard political economy and public choice problems at different levels of the state, such as privileging and discriminating particular parts of the population, which differ across countries and would require further analysis.

We primarily focus on rational behavior and the level of security as an outcome of investment in public police or private security officers. However, we will also keep in mind that there is a public value of the "perception of security" which – also because of its psychological elements – goes beyond the mere tangible results of crime prevention.

13.5.1 *Efficient Spending on Crime Prevention*

In this section we show in an analytical way how much demand for private security would arise if there were no undersupply due to a public good market failure or – if there were – if the public police were to mimic the outcome of a perfect market for private police. Without the public good problem and the resulting market failure, the demand for police would depend exclusively on the willingness to pay for the reduction of crime. We then show how crime rates would differ if the public police force were to allocate its staff across zones or neighborhoods in line with a policy of equal security for all citizens. Next, we show that, without a public good problem for crime prevention, the political rationale for public police might cause demand for private security workers. We then find that private demand for security can generate underinvestment and overinvestment in security. These effects result from positive and negative spillovers of police activities, which lead to reactions of public police but not for privately financed security.

Let N be the number of crimes, v be the (constant) loss from one crime including nonfinancial and psychic damage, and x the expenditure on police services. We assume that the number of crimes depends on police expenditures, so the loss L from crime is

$$L = N(x) \cdot v \text{ with } N \geq 0, N'(x) < 0 \text{ and } N''(x) > 0 \qquad 1$$

The number[27] of criminal offenses is non-negative and declines as more is spent on the police, but it declines at a decreasing rate, so the law of diminishing returns applies. Losses from crime fall into two categories: firstly, the value of illegal transfers of wealth, and secondly, the monetarized value of any damage to the victims' personal well-being. If more police spending (x) reduces crime rates, the risk of being victimized declines for every individual. v is the amount a citizen is willing to pay for a one-unit reduction in crime and

[27] Note our simplification that there is only a single (representative) category of crime. Strictly speaking, N is a vector of the numbers of crimes in all categories, and v is a vector of the associated losses.

thus reflects this reduced risk. Rich citizens are willing to pay more for the reduction of illegal transfer because they have more wealth to lose, and they are also willing to pay more to reduce the risk of crime against their life, bodily integrity and other nonfinancial losses. Private police forces in a well-functioning market or public police forces that mimic a market for private security forces would be organized on the basis of efficient cost–benefit considerations, which translates into minimizing the total loss (*TL*), that is, the sum of the monetarized financial and nonfinancial losses from crime plus the cost of crime prevention.

$$TL = N(x) \cdot v + x. \tag{2}$$

Notice that, in this total loss function, the gains from crime are not included and set as zero. This is in line with what Usher (1986) calls a "democratic objective," where gains from illegal activities are not included in the social objective.[28] Also, the function implies that all other factors determining crime rates, like the punishment of criminals or the effectiveness of the criminal justice system, are held equal.

The first order condition for TL is $N'(x) \cdot v + 1 = 0$ and yields an efficient spending of x^* on crime prevention by police forces based on the willingness to pay. This result would not be different from the normative efficiency criterion used in the economic analysis of other types of market failure in which regulation tries to mimic a functioning market.

If public police were to follow the efficiency criterion, private demand for police could not exist. A loss-minimizing private person with complete information (including all relevant functions and parameters) would not spend money on private security, which at the margin is costlier than the resulting reduced loss from crime, which includes the willingness to pay for a reduction of nonfinancial damages. This would, however, be the case if the state police had already reduced crime levels to the economically efficient level of $N(x^*)$.

13.5.2 *Optimal Demand for a Market-Oriented Private Security and Public Police with an Equal Security Goal*

13.5.2.1 Private Security

We now introduce a simple model of two police districts with equal population but different wealth levels. The index 1 shall denote the high-income district; index 2 marks the low-income district. Within each district, wealth is distributed evenly, and offenders are fully informed about the conditions in both districts.[29] These model districts may be more representative of suburbs than of downtown areas, which tend to be more heterogenous.

The loss from crime in district $i = \{1, 2\}$ is

$$N_{i,max} \cdot (v_i/x_i) \tag{3}$$

where $N_{i,max}$ is the number of crimes in district i if the spending on police reaches a minimum value $x_{i,min}$, which is close to zero but positive.[30] Throughout the analysis we assume that $N_{1,max} \geq N_{2,max}$, so with the same level of police spending in both districts, the richer district experiences at least as much crime as the poorer district because more wealth

---

[28] Dan Usher, "Police, Punishment, and Public Goods," *Public Finance* 41 (1986): 96–115; Nuno Garoupa, "The Economics of Organized Crime and Optimal Law Enforcement," *Economic Inquiry* 38 (2000): 278–288.
[29] We relax this assumption in the next section.
[30] Given our simple formula, this assumption excludes that crime rates become infinitely high.

might attract more crime.[31] v_i is the loss per criminal offense in district i, and it is equal among all residents in the same district. A crime committed in the rich neighborhood ($i = 1$) causes greater loss, firstly, because more wealth is illegally transferred per crime and, secondly, because the richer citizens value the nonfinancial value of their personal security more highly in monetary terms ($v_1 > v_2$).

The total combined costs of crimes and police efforts are

$$TL = \frac{N_{1,max} \cdot v_1}{x_1} + \frac{N_{2,max} \cdot v_2}{x_2} + x_1 + x_2 \qquad\qquad 4$$

From this we can derive the efficient expenditures for police forces, x_1^* and x_2^* as

$x_1^* = \sqrt{N_{1,max} \cdot v_1}$ and $x_2^* = \sqrt{N_{2,max} \cdot v_2}$ (see Section 13.10).

Further, $v_1 > v_2$ implies that $x_1^* > x_2^*$ because by assumption $N_{1,max} \geq N_{2,max}$. Optimal spending on the police in the high-income district is higher than in the low-income district because of the greater willingness to pay in the rich district. Therefore, the optimal amount of police spending differs between the districts, even if the crime numbers are equal and even if more wealth did not attract more crime. The difference increases if one assumes that richer districts attract more crime at any level of police spending, that is, if $N_{1,max} > N_{2,max}$. This economically efficient result reflects neither police practice nor the legal norms on public police. The police aim for equal security for all citizens.

13.5.2.2 Optimal Public Police Spending versus Private Demand for Security

We now assume that the public police will try to protect each citizen in such a way that their probability of becoming a victim is tolerably low and equal, irrespective of their wealth. Clearly, for equal protection against crime, the optimal amount of police spending must be the same in both districts if greater wealth in a district does not attract more crime.

Equal security in all districts would then require that the number of crimes is the same in both districts, that is, $N_1 = N_2$, or

$$\frac{N_{1,max}}{x_1} = \frac{N_{2,max}}{x_2}. \qquad\qquad 5$$

Also, the budget constraint ($x_1 + x_2 = b$) must be met.

This allows the resources to be allocated in such a way that crime rates become equal in both districts. Expression 5 shows that the police forces must be allocated equally in both districts $(x_1 = x_2 = \frac{b}{2})$ if the districts attract the same number of crimes, that is, if $N_{1,max} = N_{2,max}$.

With the same total amount of police expenditures as in the market solution case, police expenditures exceed the willingness to pay in the low-income district. In the high-income district, the reverse holds, which creates a private demand for additional protection, provided that the public good problem leading to free riding can be overcome. Public police therefore under these conditions entails a redistribution of wealth – a consequence that is not attributable to intentions of distributive justice but that is a side effect of the equal protection policy.

The result changes, however, if we assume that the rich district attracts more crime than the poor district: $N_{1,max} > N_{2,max}$. If greater wealth leads to more crime, the equal protection

---

[31] This assumption is made for illustrative reasons only. It is often observed that crimes concentrate in poor regions. This assumption could also be made. Under both assumptions, private and public police fight crimes differently.

must lead to more police in the rich as compared with the poor district. This consequence follows not from equal marginal reduction of loss from crimes based on the willingness to pay for crime avoidance but, rather, from the equal security approach of state protection against crime. To reach the policy target of equal protection, the distributional effect in favor of low-income citizens is then smaller. If there were more crimes in the poor district – think, for example, of drug trafficking or gang violence – public police expenditure would have to be concentrated there to achieve the policy goal of equal safety for all. The redistribution effect in favor of the poor would then be greater compared to the situation in which all districts would suffer equal amounts of crime without police forces.

An outcome is also conceivable where the rationale of the public police obliges them to devote more resources to protecting rich people than private police would, based on willingness to pay. This arguably rare constellation may at times apply to particularly wealthy citizens or celebrities who are vulnerable to kidnapping or hate crimes. The protection of minorities can also lead to public police spending that exceeds the potential victims' willingness to pay for protection, even if they belong to the high-income group. As a general observation, abandoning the efficiency criterion in favor of equal protection against crimes typically entails a redistribution of welfare toward low-income citizens. But, under exceptional circumstances, the rationale of equal protection can also lead to regressive distribution effects if potential victims are both rich and more vulnerable than others.

13.5.2.3 Public Police Policy Creates Demand for Private Security Workers

If the state's spending on public police falls short of the rich citizens' willingness to pay for protection, they will demand private security. Such private demand need not indicate state failure in the form of underinvestment in security. Instead, it can be a corollary of a well-functioning state and good governance, which follows the equal security rationale and spends more than the willingness to pay for the residents in poor districts and less for the residents in the rich districts.

The existence of private police also shows that the departure from efficiency is partly offset by market forces when coordination problems, as familiar from public good theory, can be overcome, as is often the case. Freedom of contract allows wealthier citizens to raise their personal security above the state's equal protection standard in accordance with their higher willingness to pay. Airport security is often privately financed (through surcharges on ticket prices) by customers, whose willingness to pay is much higher than that of customers in bus terminals, which are less protected. With financing of private security, university campuses and adjacent neighborhoods are often better protected than the rest of the city. Private demand for security protects high-end shopping malls often better than the public police do in inner cities.

13.5.2.4 Numerical Examples

Using the above expressions and the results from the appendix (Section 13.10), we present some illustrative figures for security expenditures x_1 and x_2 and the crime rates N_1 and N_2 in the two districts if demand either is driven by the potential victims' willingness to pay or follows the public police policy of equal security for all citizens.[32]

---

[32]   Real-life crime figures must of course be integer numbers, but the examples provided in the table shall suffice for illustration.

TABLE 13.3 *Security spending and number of crimes under two alternative standards*

$v_1 = 10$ $v_2 = 5$ $b = 38.2$		Private security demand (willingness to pay standard)		Public security spending (equal protection standard)	
		District 1	District 2	District 1	District 2
$N_{1,max} = 50$	x	22.4	15.8	19.1	19.1
$N_{2,max} = 50$	N	2.2	3.2	2.6	2.6
$N_{1,max} = 60$	x	24.5	14.4	22.9	15.3
$N_{2,max} = 40$	N	2.4	2.8	2.6	2.6

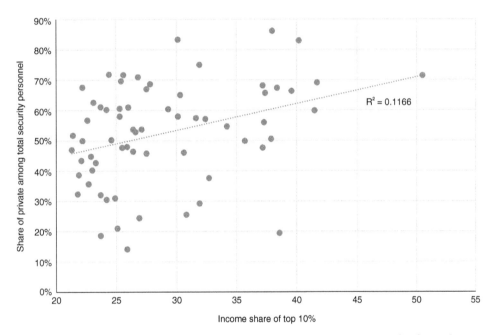

FIGURE 13.2 Income share (2013) of top 10 percent of income recipients versus the share of private police among total security personnel
Sources: See Figure 13.1.

If public police forces follow the described rationale for allocating their services, the demand for private police services should rise with greater inequality of income and wealth (which often coincides with a clearer separation of wealthier and poorer residential areas). One should expect more demand for private police protection in countries with a high concentration of wealth and income than in countries with a more balanced distribution. The available data tentatively support this hypothesis, as there is a positive correlation between income inequality and the number of private security workers.

13.5.3 *Inefficient Private Expenditures for Security Due to Crime Diversion and General Deterrence*

Police services like patrolling or video surveillance can prevent crime, divert crime to other areas, or both. They can also generate general deterrence in other areas, if offenders do not know how police expenditures are distributed between different districts and have knowledge only about the average expenditures across districts. Diversion and deterrence are both spillover effects, which entail a risk of market failure if the service is provided privately. In Sections 13.5.3.1 and 13.5.3.2, we deal with these market failures. We draw on previous literature by Shavell, Hylton, Hui Wei, Png, Baumann and Friehe, which is not on private police but on private physical investment in security.[33]

13.5.3.1 Private Overinvestment Resulting from Crime Diversion

If offenders know how well protected different police districts are, an increase of police spending in one district can divert crime to other districts.[34] Some of the crimes are not reduced but merely redistributed elsewhere.[35] It is straightforward that crime diversion leads to more than efficient police expenditure as long as the rising expenditures do not increase police expenditures in the affected district. For private police protecting a neighborhood, expenditures would be privately profitable, even if they resulted only in crime diversion and therefore socially in a waste. If these expenditures cause both crime prevention and crime diversion, their private benefit remains higher than their social benefit, which again leads to inefficiently high police expenditure.

However, there exists an interdependency between police expenditures in different districts. Reactions and counterreactions make the analysis of crime diversion less simple. Consider again the two different districts. To focus on the crime diversion effect, we now assume for convenience that both districts have the same income levels and willingness to pay for avoiding a crime. This implies that $v_1 = v_2 = v$ and $N_{1,max} = N_{2,max} = N_{max}$. More police spending in district 1 increases crime rates and losses from crime in district 2 and vice versa. Under this condition there can be no crime diversion (in effect) as long as police expenditures in the two homogeneous districts are equal, that is, if $x_1 = x_2$. Crime diversion from district 1 to district 2 increases with police expenditures in district 1 and decreases with police expenditures in district 2. The equivalent holds for crime diversion in the other direction. The following formula captures these interdependencies.

Crime losses diverted from district 1 to district 2 are assumed to be $\frac{x_1-x_2}{x_2}$ and crime losses diverted from district 2 to district 1 are $\frac{x_2-x_1}{x_1}$. The total losses from crime, which include crime diversion (TL), are then:

[33] Charles T. Clotfelter, "Private Security and Public Safety," *Journal of Urban Economics* 5 (1978): 388–402; Steven Shavell, "Individual Precautions to Prevent Theft: Private versus Socially Optimal Behavior," *International Review of Law & Economics* 11 (1991): 123–132; Keith N. Hylton, "Optimal Law Enforcement and Victim Precaution," *Rand Journal of Economics* 27 (1996): 197–206; Koo Hui-Wen and Ivan P. L. Png, "Private Security: Deterrent or Diversion?," *International Review of Law & Economics* 14 (1994): 87–101; Florian Baumann and Tim Friehe, "Private Protection against Crime When Property Value Is Private Information," DICE Discussion Paper No. 91 (April 2013), www.dice.hhu.de/fileadmin/redaktion/Fakultaeten/ Wirtschaftswissenschaftliche_Fakultaet/DICE/Discussion_Paper/091_Baumann_Friehe.pdf.

[34] David Weisburd, Laura A. Wyckoff, Justin Ready, John E. Eck, Joshua C. Hinkle and Frank Gajewski, "Does Crime Just Move Around the Corner? A Controlled Study of Spatial Displacement and Diffusion of Crime Control Benefits," *Criminology* 44 (2005): 549–592.

[35] Mark Grady and Francesco Parisi, *The Law and Economics of Cybersecurity: An Introduction* (Cambridge: Cambridge University Press, 2006), pp. 1–13.

$$TL = \left(\frac{N_{max} \cdot v + x_2 - x_1}{x_1}\right) + \left(\frac{N_{max} \cdot v + x_1 - x_2}{x_2}\right) + x_1 + x_2. \qquad 9$$

Differentiating the total loss function with respect to x_1 and x_2, the first order conditions yield the efficient expenditure on security based on the willingness to pay. Is this efficient combination x_1^* and x_2^* also a Nash equilibrium? It is not. Were police forces privately financed and initially to have the efficient size in both districts, it would pay for every district to invest more in crime prevention, moving beyond the efficient level provided that all others would remain at the efficient level of expenditures. As some of the crime reduction is crime diversion at the expense of other districts, however, the loss reduction from crime within a district would then exceed the additional costs incurred. This rationale applies for all districts.

Total losses in districts 1 and 2 are:

$$TL_1 = \frac{N_{max} \cdot v + x_2 - x_1}{x_1} + x_1; \qquad 10$$

$$TL_2 = \frac{N_{max} \cdot v + x_1 - x_2}{x_2} + x_2. \qquad 11$$

Differentiating 10 will give the reaction function determining the level of private police spending in the first district at any level of police spending in the second district. Similarly, differentiating 11 will give the reaction function for district 2. The private loss functions 10 and 11 yield the privately but not socially optimal demand for private security (see Section 13.10 Appendix). Neither district takes the negative effects of its security investment into account. The privately optimal security demand (x_i^P) in both districts exceeds the efficient demand:

$$x_1^P > x_1^* \text{ and } x_2^P > x_2^* \text{ with } x_1^P = x_2^P \text{ and } x_1^* = x_2^*.$$

Under socially optimal conditions as well as in market equilibrium, no crime diversion occurs as, in equilibrium, police expenditures are equal in both districts, which by assumption makes crime diversion disappear. But this result is reached with inefficiently high police expenditures in the private police market. If districts are not homogeneous, the market equilibrium might include crime diversion (not analyzed here). By contrast, there is no overinvestment problem with state funding of the public police if the state acts as a benevolent social planner.

It could be argued that the districts should coordinate their investments in private police to avoid overspending. Yet the free rider problem makes coordination difficult. The larger the number of districts, the greater the incentive to spend beyond the efficient level, contrary to the agreement, and thereby to shift one's losses from crime to others.[36] Like cartels, agreements to avoid overinvestment in private security would then be unstable.

Baumann and Friehe have shown that overinvestment in private security need not ensue if potential offenders have precise information about the distribution of private investment but not about the wealth of their potential victims: Knowledge of the concentration of private police workers provides strong clues about the wealth of potential victims, which attracts

---

[36] Ibid., pp. 1–13.

TABLE 13.4 *Private overinvestment in security due to the crime diversion effect*

$N_{1,max} = N_{2,max} = 50$	Privately optimal demand		Socially optimal (efficient) demand	
$v_1 = 10$ $v_2 = 10$	District 1	District 2	District 1	District 2
Investment into security (x)	22.87	22.87	22.36	22.36
Loss from crime (L)	21.87	21.87	22.36	22.36

crime. This offsetting effect can even outbalance the effect of crime diversion on the private demand for security.[37]

For political reasons, the state can deviate in numerous ways from its policy goals. These deviations are not analyzed here, though they must be taken into account for a normative institutional comparison between private and public security services. This is not part of this chapter.

Table 13.4 provides a numerical example of overinvestment in private security as compared to efficient investment. We assume here that both districts are homogenous to isolate the effect of crime diversion (see Section 13.10 Appendix).

13.5.3.2 Underinvestment Due to General Deterrence as a Side Effect of Crime Prevention

If potential offenders do not know which neighborhoods are well protected and which targets are wealthy, demand for private police has a comparable effect to unobservable physical investment in the protection of private property. If offenders cannot know which individuals made additional investments to protect their property, that investment not only protects the investor's private property better but also creates general deterrence as a side effect.[38] This type of general deterrence comes not from punishment, in which private security often has no interest, but from increasing investment in crime prevention. The offender knows only that more homes (but not which ones) are better protected, so the chances of a successful break-in, for example, are reduced, leading to less crime at the margin. Thus, across districts, everyone benefits from everyone else's investment in crime prevention. As in Section 13.5.3.1, in the present scenario private demand for security need not equal the efficient demand.

13.6 ORGANIZATIONAL CHANGES IN THE PRIVATE SPHERE INCREASE PRIVATE DEMAND FOR SECURITY

Much of the demand for private security services arises from changing patterns within the private sphere, where the public police have only a subsidiary role. Civil law gives individuals the right to protect their lives, bodily integrity, property and wealth against criminal offenses, including the right to self-defense, to temporally arrest aggressors and to use violence when the public police are not immediately available. These rights are alienable and can be delegated to private security. If private organizations are small, delegation is improbable. As they grow, the demand for private security is a consequence of the division of labor within organizations and an extended form of self-protection. Large firms employ private security

---

[37]   Baumann and Friehe, "Private Protection against Crime When Property Value Is Private Information."
[38]   Shavell, "Individual Precautions to Prevent Theft," at p. 130.

against offenses by employees and customers. New forms of mass private property such as shopping malls, sports stadiums, airports or fun parks (and in some countries also business improvement districts[39]) essentially amount to a privatization of what was formerly the public sphere and thereby contribute substantially to the rising demand for private security workers,[40] whose duties often extend beyond patrolling or gatekeeping. When acting on private ground, in some countries private security work resembles that of the public police, even though it is usually not performed by sworn-in policemen but by agents who are subject to a different set of rules, as shown earlier. This development is not the result of privatization in the usual sense. It is accompanied by the transfer of competences not from the state to private actors but from private actors to other private actors.

13.7 LOWER COST OF PRIVATE SECURITY

The demand for private police is partly cost-driven. Private security firms often specialize in services that they can provide more cheaply than state police officers. Public police officers are qualified for many police activities. Some of these require sophisticated training and skills; others – like patrolling and surveillance – much less so. Private security workers are mostly trained internally, for an average of 140 hours across 19 European countries, ranging from 320 hours in Hungary to less than 10 hours in Austria and Poland.[41] Accordingly, wages are relatively low. The low level of training limits the scope of civilian private security, which makes it therefore one of the very few industries that demand more public regulation of their services, especially more mandatory training and job certificates.[42] Cost differences thus explain why the state often outsources patrolling and security duties. Private security workers guard airports and sometimes, as in Germany, even military camps, often as part of a private–police partnership. The Confederation of European Security Services provides data on a number of European countries, showing that a sizeable part of total demand for private security services comes from the state (see Figure 13.3).

An important reason why private policing is relatively cheap is its concentration on patrolling and surveillance (sometimes even together with public police officers in so-called publicly contracted policing), which prevents crimes in the protected areas. Private security workers can deter but cannot check documents outside of their private employer's property. Most importantly, private security workers are generally not entitled to incapacitate suspects as part of criminal prosecution, that is, to arrest them and put them on trial. Under the rule of law, the requirements on proper criminal procedure and imprisonment make incapacitation and general deterrence relatively costly. Vigilant patrolling may achieve the same level of deterrence for the protected area at lower cost.[43]

---

[39] For the USA, Colleran, "The Growth of Private Security and Associated Criminological Concerns," at p. 108.

[40] United Nations Office on Drugs and Crime, "State Regulation concerning Civilian Private Security Services and Their Contribution to Crime Prevention and Community Safety" (April 2014), www.unodc.org/documents/justice-and-prison-reform/crimeprevention/Ebook0.pdf, at p. 1.

[41] CoESS, "Facts & Figures – Private Security in Europe 2015"; United Nations Office on Drugs and Crime, "State Regulation concerning Civilian Private Security Services and their Contribution to Crime Prevention and Community Safety," at p. 72.

[42] www.lendex.de/news/strengere-regeln-fuer-die-sicherheitsbranche.

[43] Weisburd et al., "Does Crime Just Move Around the Corner?."

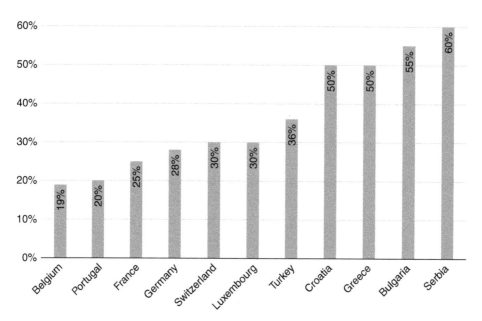

FIGURE 13.3 Public demand for private security as a share of total demand (2015)
Source: Confederation of European Security Services (CoESS; 2017), "Private Security in Europe,
Facts and Figures 2015," www.coess.org/newsroom.php?page=facts-and-figures.

13.8 GENERAL UNDERSUPPLY OF PUBLIC POLICE

Some authors[44] hold that the demand for private police arises mainly from a general undersupply of public police and public security. The UK, for example, has one of the smallest
public police forces and simultaneously features one of the largest numbers of private security
workers in Western Europe (see Figure 13.1). If public police presence is reduced and
replaced with private security, but only in areas with sufficient willingness to pay, large
parts of the population are left vulnerable to crime. A United Nations Development
Programme (UNDP) report on security in Latin America has found severe underfunding of
public security and public police, and a resulting surge in private security for those who can
afford it.[45]

A different but related view is that where the legal system is weak and the civil service is
perceived as corrupt, private police forces are in high demand because they are thought to
provide more reliable services than the state. Private firms may be better at solving principal-
agent problems between the subject of protection and the security workers than public police
forces whose integrity is doubtful, when they operate in a weak state with weak institutions
and control mechanisms.

So far, there is little, if any, econometric research on these hypotheses, but, according to the
available data, the share of private security workers among all security workers is not correl-
ated with the Corruption Perceptions Index, neither for all countries nor for developing
versus OECD (Organisation for Economic Co-operation and Development) countries. If the
demand for private police were to be explained by a general undersupply of public police

---

[44] Sklansky, "The Private Police," at p. 1221.
[45] UNDP, "Human Development Report (HDR) 2013."

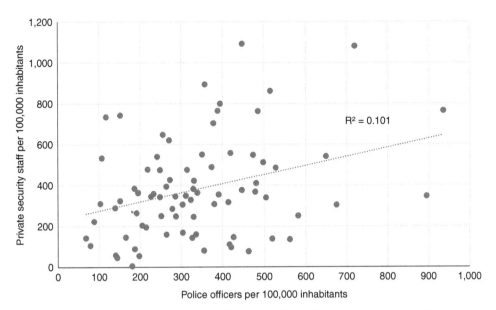

FIGURE 13.4 Number of private security staff versus police officers per 100,000 inhabitants
Sources: see Figure 1

forces, one would expect a negative correlation between the sizes of the two groups of security workers. Yet the available data show a positive correlation: Many countries have larger numbers of both public police officers and private security workers in relation to their population. However, the hypothesis of private security being driven by a neglect of public security may yet bear out in more elaborate empirical research. Also, the available statistics have nothing to say about the distribution of public police deployment within a state and about which groups it protects most.

13.9 SCOPE AND EFFECTIVENESS OF PRIVATE SECURITY

13.9.1 *Protection of Victims*

The rapid rise of the demand for private security shows that the public good characteristic of police protection often does not prevent effective protection through the market for those who can afford it. Some functions of the police are, however, most unlikely to be replaced by private services. For instance, victimless crimes cannot generate demand for private security. Public areas are unlikely to be protected based solely on private demand. Private security can cause general deterrence of crime only in special circumstances, because private investors have no incentive to invest into crime prevention and deterrence outside the privately protected area. And, unlike the public police, private security cannot incapacitate the perpetrators. Also, some functions of the state cannot be delegated without eroding its authority.[46] The arrest of violent and armed offenders, the response to hostage taking, combating the most serious crimes, or dangerous and violent rescue operations arguably

---

[46] Avihay Dorfman and Alon Harel, "The Case Against Privatization," *Philosophy & Public Affairs* 41 (2013): 67–102.

cannot be outsourced, regardless of how well the potential substitutes for the state police are trained.

How effective are private security workers? Many scholars are generally skeptical of the crime-reducing effect of police,[47] though this skepticism is not borne out by thorough empirical studies. "Boots on the ground" make a difference to reducing crime.[48] If security workers are vigilant, their numbers matter.[49]

A growing body of empirical literature affirms the effectiveness of civilian private security. The role of private police in crime reduction is especially pertinent for colleges and universities in high-crime neighborhoods that are concerned about the safety of their employees and students. MacDonald, Klick and Grunwald found large effects in an empirical study on the University of Pennsylvania, which employs 100 full-time sworn-in police officers.[50] Tripling the police presence led to an estimated 60 percent reduction in violent and property crime, which suggests an elasticity of crime with respect to police presence of about -0.3. Liu and Fabbri found similar results in a study on privately financed, unarmed security workers in an Oakland (CA) neighborhood.[51] Other findings likewise indicate that a 1 percent increase in spending on private police reduces crime by 0.3 per cent in the protected areas.[52] Surveys of the recent literature on police and crime by MacDonald, Klick and Grunwald, as well as by Chalfin and McCrary, report these estimated elasticities.[53] Significant effects of private police on crime are also found by Brooks[54] and Ayres and Levitt.[55] Little is known, however, regarding the deterrence effect that accrues outside of the protected areas, and how much crime diversion private security causes in comparison to the public police.

An UN report on private security qualitatively reviews experience with private security projects and private–public partnerships and arrives at positive conclusions.[56] In England and Wales, the state has actively encouraged cooperation between private security services and the

---

[47] Michael R. Gottfredson and Travis Hirschi, *A General Theory of Crime* (Stanford: Stanford University Press, 1990).

[48] John M. MacDonald, Jonathan Klick and Ben Grunwald, "The Effect of Privately Provided Police Services on Crime," University of Pennsylvania Law School, Institute for Law and Economics, Research Paper No. 12–36 (2019), http://ssrn.com/abstract=2171038.

[49] Ibid.

[50] Ibid.

[51] Paul Liu and Marco Fabbri, "More Eyes, (No Guns,) Less Crime: Estimating the Effects of Unarmed Private Patrols on Crime Using a Bayesian Structural Time-Series Model" (2016) http://hdl.handle.net/1765/99972.

[52] Philip J. Cook and John MacDonald, "Public Safety through Private Action: An Economic Assessment of BIDS," *Economic Journal* 121 (2011): 445–462.

[53] MacDonald, Klick and Grunwald, "The Effect of Privately Provided Police Services on Crime," at 21; Aaron Chalfin and Justin McCrary, "Criminal Deterrence: A Review of the Literature," *Journal of Economic Literature* 55 (2017): 5–48.

[54] Lea Brooks, "Volunteering to Be Taxed: Business Improvement Districts and the Extragovernmental Provision of Public Safety," *Journal of Public Economics* 92 (2008): 388–406; John M. MacDonald, "The Effectiveness of Community Policing in Reducing Urban Violence," *Crime and Delinquency* 48 (2002): 592–618; Lawrence W. Sherman and David Weisburd, "General Deterrent Effects of Police Patrol in Crime Hot Spots: A Randomized Controlled Trial," *Justice Quarterly* 12 (1995): 625–648; Jihong Zhao, Matthew C. Schneider and Quint Thurman, "Funding Community Policing to Reduce Crime: Have COPS Grants Made a Difference?," *Criminology & Public Policy* 2 (2002): 7–32.

[55] Jan Ayres and Steven D. Levitt, "Measuring Positive Externalities from Unobservable Victim Precaution: An Empirical Analysis of Lojack," *Quarterly Journal of Economics* 113 (1998): 43–77.

[56] United Nations Office on Drugs and Crime, "State Regulation concerning Civilian Private Security Services and Their Contribution to Crime Prevention and Community Safety."

police, especially in parks, shopping malls and hospitals. The state of South Africa considers private security so important that it has carried out legal reforms to strengthen its role for community services. Tightly regulated private security in cooperation with public police also exists in Spain.[57] Experience from these and other countries suggests that private security is more effective if intense cooperation and fast communication between private and public security personnel exist. Effectiveness also increases when cooperation with the state is tightly regulated and the competences and training requirements are clearly defined. In some countries, private security services are required to support the public police in cases of catastrophe, which mitigates their regressive distributional effect.[58]

13.9.2 *Protection of Suspects: The Accountability, Regulation and Control of Private Police Workers*

So far we have discussed only the protection of victims, but the protection of suspects and the public interest in the rule of law and accountability are equally important in a democratic state. A major shift from public to private police may jeopardize the rule of law and the fundamental rights of citizens – especially of suspects. With private police, there are fewer safeguards against the abuse of power. In theory, this is offset by the fact that the private police have fewer legal powers, which do not extend beyond the rights of any individual. One can argue that the problem cannot arise as long as private security services concentrate on patrolling, surveillance and gatekeeping, and generally abstain from arrests and the use of violence. One can also argue that private police are not interested in crime deterrence and the related search and interrogation anyway, as they incur cost but almost no benefit for the principal of the private security workers. This argument of rational apathy of private security, however, does not apply if private security protects employers against employees or customers with the consequence of dismissal, stay away order, damage compensation and/or private punitive damages. Cases of misuse of powers in this relation exist in many countries.[59] There is often little state control to ensure that the private security officers adhere to their legal limits – which in turn are often far from clear. The risk of illegal violence against suspects increases further if the private police are also allowed to use (fire) arms, as in several jurisdictions, including the USA. In addition, private security officers are generally less well trained than public police officers, which again exacerbates the risk of illegal violence.

Private security personnel develop, first and foremost, loyalty to and responsibility for the private principal who pays for their service and wants to pay for their own security but not for the rights of suspects. In the private principal–agent relationship, therefore, the preservation of the rule of law plays no intrinsic role when the law protects criminals. The protection of suspects must come from outside, by legal restriction and administrative controls. By contrast, the public police must protect suspects and victims alike and are therefore significantly constrained in their actions, not only by the law and outside controls but also by the mission of police as the guardians of the law and the resulting

---

[57] Andrea Giménez-Salinas, "New Approaches Regarding Private/Public Security," *Policing and Society* 14 (2004): 158–174.
[58] United Nations Office on Drugs and Crime, "State Regulation concerning Civilian Private Security Services and Their Contribution to Crime Prevention and Community Safety," pp. 9–20.
[59] For the USA, see especially Sklansky, "The Private Police," at p. 1231.

internal as well as democratic controls. The competences of private security should be delimited as much as possible with precise legal rules rather than imprecise standards, because private police have no reason to use their discretionary power in favor of suspects and to the detriment of their client. In this principal–agent relationship, the interests and constitutional rights of potential offenders tend to be neglected, unlike in the more complex principal–agent relationships of public police in a democratic rule of law state.

Private police lack democratic responsibility and accountability.[60] Even if their employer is the state itself, the principal–agent problem is more severe than with the public police. Political action and the civil engagement of citizens usually cannot change the "safety policy" or the "operational strategy" of the private police. This problem is growing if private police increasingly control the public sphere, replacing the state police.

13.10 APPENDIX

13.10.1 *Different Protection Levels from Private and Public Demand for Security*

There exist two police districts 1 and 2, each with an equal number but unequal wealth of residents. Wealth is higher in district 1 than in district 2. All individuals in the same district are homogeneous and have the same wealth.

The loss from crime is $N_{1,max} \cdot v_i / x_i$. with $i = \{1, 2\}$. $N_{1,max}$ is the number of crimes in a district if the spending on police is at a minimal but positive level. $v_{1,2}$ is the loss per crime and the willingness to pay for the reduction of one crime by the citizens in districts 1 and 2, respectively, is $v_1 > v_2$. The number of crimes at the same level of police protection in district 1 is either equal to or higher than that in district 2, the latter reflecting that more wealth can attract more crimes.

$\frac{N_{1,max}}{x} \geq \frac{N_{2,max}}{x}$. Total losses from crime (which do not include the gains from crime) are

$$ TL = \frac{N_{1,max} \cdot v_1}{x_1} + \frac{N_{2,max} \cdot v_2}{x_2} + x_1 + x_2. $$

Differentiating TL with respect to x_1 and x_2 and forming the first order condition yields the efficient expenditure for police, x_1^* and x_2^*, in districts 1 and 2:

$$ x_1^* = \sqrt{N_{1,max} \cdot v_1} \text{ and } x_2^* = \sqrt{N_{2,max} \cdot v_2}. $$

As $N_{1,max} \geq N_{2,max}$ and $v_1 > v_2$ this implies for the efficient private demand for security that $x_1^* > x_2^*$.

Equal protection of every citizen with a public police force requires $\frac{N_{1,max}}{x_1} = \frac{N_{2,max}}{x_2}$ subject to the budget constraint $x_1 + x_2 = b$.

$\frac{N_{1,max}}{x_1} = \frac{N_{2,max}}{b - x_1}$, so the publicly best police demand in district 1 is then

$x_1^{P*} = \frac{b \cdot N_{1,max}}{N_{1,max} + N_{2,max}}$. If crime rates with equal protection are equal in both districts, the publicly optimal demand for police is b/2 in both districts. If $N_{1,max} > N_{2,max}$, the share for the high-income district increases above b/2 but remains lower than the efficient demand

---

[60] For a broad concept of accountability in the context of privatization, cf. Laura A. Dickinson, "In Defense of Accountability as a Lens to Perceive Privatization's Problems: Some Examples from Military and Security Privatization," in *Privatization*, ed. Jack Knight and Melissa Schwartzberg (New York: New York University Press, 2018), 30–51, pp. 30–32ff.

because the state disregards the higher willingness to pay to avoid a crime in the high-income district (v_1).

13.10.2 *Private Overinvestment in Case of Crime Diversion*

With crime diversion, losses from crime in district 1 increase with police spending in district 2 and vice versa. Total losses from crime and police forces are

$$TL = \frac{N_{max} \cdot v + x_2 - x_1}{x_1} + \frac{N_{max} \cdot v + x_1 - x_2}{x_2} + x_1 + x_2.$$

For a numerical example, we assume that $N_{max} \cdot v = 500$. We show that the private police expenditures are strictly higher than the optimal investment, which a social planner would choose. Setting $N_{1,max} \cdot v$ at 500 and differentiating with respect to x_1 and x_2 yields the two first order conditions and the solution gives efficient security expenditures.

The first derivative of the total loss (TL) function is

$$\frac{\partial TL}{\partial x_1} = 1 + \frac{1}{x_2} - \frac{x_2 + 500}{x_1^2}.$$

The first order condition determines the optimal amount of expenditures in both districts:

$$\frac{\partial TL}{\partial x_1} = 0 \overset{yields}{\to} x_1 = \sqrt{\frac{x_2^2}{x_2 + 1} + \frac{500 x_1}{x_2 + 1}}; \text{ similarly, } \frac{\partial TL}{\partial x_2} = 0 \overset{yields}{\to} x_2 = \sqrt{\frac{x_1^2}{x_1 + 1} + \frac{500 x_1}{x_1 + 1}}.$$

The two functions yield the socially efficient police expenditures in both districts: $x_{1,}^* = 22.36$, with a crime loss of 22.9. As both districts are homogeneous, the same value is obtained for $x_{2,}^*$:

Total private losses in district 1 and 2 are

$$TPL_1 = \frac{N_{max} \cdot v_1 + x_2}{x_1} + x_1 \text{ and } TPL_2 = \frac{N_{max} \cdot v_2 + x_1}{x_2} + x_2.$$

The two first order conditions for the total private loss in districts 1 and 2 lead to the privately optimal demand for police protection in district 1. Setting $N_{1,max} \cdot v$ at 500 and differentiating TPL_1 with respect to x_1 and x_2 leads to

$$\frac{\partial TPL_1}{\partial x_1} = 0 \overset{yields}{\to} x_1 = \sqrt{x_2 + 500} \text{ and } \frac{\partial TPL_2}{\partial x_2} = 0 \overset{yields}{\to} x_2 = \sqrt{x_1 + 500}; \; x_1^p$$

$$= \sqrt{\sqrt{x_1 + 500} + 500} = 22.86.$$

As the formula for district 2 is symmetrical, the optimal expenditure for district 2 is the same: $x_1^p = x_2^p = 22.86$. Crime losses are 23.3.

14

Privatizing Private Data

Lisa Herzog

14.1 INTRODUCTION

Privacy seems to belong to the past. The dating website OkCupid asks its users whether they occasionally use illegal drugs, selling that information in real time to marketers.[1] Commercial data brokers hold thousands of data points about individuals.[2] The problem concerns not only apps and websites but also the "Internet of Things" (IoT) that increasingly surrounds us.[3] In *The Age of Surveillance Capitalism*, Shoshana Zuboff cites the example of a bed that uses "smart technology" to capture data on "heart rate, breathing and movement," allegedly to improve the quality of sleep.[4] The company reserves the right to use these data, including audio signals, even after customers have canceled their contracts, and also to share them with third parties. With households being equipped with more and more "smart" devices that communicate with each other, the weakest link in the chain with regard to privacy becomes the gateway for data collectors.[5] The deal with the Devil of "data against comfort" can now be built into the very infrastructure of our homes.[6]

---

[1] Rebecca Lipman, "Online Privacy and the Invisible Market for our Data," *Penn State Law Review* 120 (2016): 777–807, at p. 778, quoting Daniel Zwerdling, "Your Digital Trail: Private Company Access," NPR (October 1, 2013), www.npr.org/blogs/alltechconsidered/2013/10/01/227776072/your-digital-trail-private-company-access.

[2] Federal Trade Commission, "Data Brokers: A Call for Transparency and Accountability" (2014), www.ftc.gov/system/files/documents/reports/data-brokers-call-transparency-accountability-report-federal-trade-commission-may-2014/140527databrokerreport.pdf, at p. 47.

[3] Stacy-Ann Elvy, "Commodifying Consumer Data in the Era of the Internet of Things," *Boston College Law Review* 59 (2018): 423–545, p. 426, quoting AIG, "The Internet of Things: Evolution or Revolution?," pp. 6–7 (2015), www.aig.com/content/dam/aig/america-canada/us/documents/business/casualty/aigiot-english-report.pdf [https://perma.cc/BA7X-Y9VV], at p. 2.

[4] Shoshana Zuboff, *The Age of Surveillance Capitalism. The Fight for a Human Future at the New Frontier of Power* (London: Profile Books, 2019), pos. 4265.

[5] Elvy, "Commodifying Consumer Data," at p. 454.

[6] For earlier discussions on privacy and surveillance, see, e.g., Philip E. Agre, "Surveillance and Capture: Two Models of Privacy," *Information Society* 10(2) (1994): 101–127; or Spiros Simitis, "Reviewing Privacy in an Information Society," *University of Pennsylvania Law Review* 135(3) (1987): 707–746; or for more recent accounts, e.g., Helen Nissenbaum, *Privacy in Context: Technology, Policy, and the Integrity of Social Life* (Stanford: Stanford University Press, 2010); Jens-Erik Mai, "Big Data Privacy: The Datafication of Personal Information," *Information Society* 32(3) (2016): 192–199. On the "Internet of Things" and the data collection it enables, see, e.g.,

In the age of "big data" and IoT, the mainstream business models for online services and "smart technologies" build on the appropriation of data.[7] Zuboff describes this as a form of "rendition," in which data about all kinds of features of individuals' private lives are collected and turned into "prediction products."[8] These products are meant to increase profits, by creating differentiated products (or advertisement for them), or by inserting ever more individualized clauses into contracts, for example in insurance contracts.[9]

Zuboff's account, probably the most thorough-going description of these phenomena to date, is a sociological one. While there are some normative arguments, turning around the notions of a "home" and a "right to a future," she does not provide an explicit account of the "privatization of the private," as one might call it, that happens in such processes. This is the task of this chapter: it aims at asking what happens when something "private" (as in "privacy") is "privatized" (as in "controlled by a private company"). For reasons of simplicity, these two forms of privacy are here called "private (I)" and "private (II)." "Privatization (II)" of the "private (I)" thus means that something that belonged to the sphere of personal privacy – more concretely, personal data[10] – is appropriated, that is, made private in the sense of exclusive control rights by a profit-oriented entity. In addition to distinguishing these notions of privacy in more detail, the chapter aims at providing arguments for why shifts from "private (I)" to "private (II)" can be problematic. In many cases, "private (I)" information, *if* it is collected at all, should be made available, suitably aggregated and anonymized,[11] for *public* purposes that can serve society as a whole.

The philosophical debate about privatization has, so far, mostly turned around the privatization of public goods, public tasks, or public spaces.[12] In this chapter, the focus is different: What happens when data are shifted from "private (I)" to "private (II)"? The difference between these two meanings of "private" has not been given much attention so far. Historically, they often went hand in hand, and for many items – but not necessarily data – there are indeed non-accidental reasons for this. But new technological developments have created a situation in which "private (I)" and "private (II)" come apart more often. Standard arguments against the privatization of what has previously been public, for example about the "inherently public" nature of certain goods or tasks,[13] cannot easily be applied in such cases,[14] but there are nonetheless arguments that speak against it.

Scott R. Peppet, "Regulating the Internet of Things: First Steps toward Managing Discrimination, Privacy, Security, and Consent," *Texas Law Review* 93 (2014): 85–176, or Elvy, "Commodifying Consumer Data."

[7] Elvy, "Commodifying Consumer Data," at p. 435, quotes one prediction that holds that by 2020 "companies will be able to earn more profits transferring and disclosing IoT data than by selling IoT devices to consumers," quoting Matt McFarland, "Your Car's Data May Soon Be More Valuable Than the Car Itself," CNN: TECH (February 7, 2017), https://money.cnn.com/2017/02/07/technology/car-data-value/index.html [https://perma.cc/HM82-LPQR].

[8] Zuboff, *The Age of Surveillance Capitalism*, especially chs. 8 and 9.

[9] Ibid., especially ch. 10.

[10] I use the terms "data" and – where appropriate – "information" largely interchangeably, and in a non-technical sense.

[11] For reasons of space, I cannot here discuss the issues that arise because of the difficulties of protecting data from being de-anonymized. See, e.g., Elvy, "Commodifying Consumer Data," at pp. 446–448 and 461–462; Peppet, "Regulating the Internet of Things," at pp. 128–131.

[12] See, e.g., Avihay Dorfman and Alon Harel, "The Case Against Privatization," *Philosophy & Public Affairs* 41(1) (2013): 67–102, and the contributions in Jack Knight and Melissa Schwartzberg (eds.), *Privatization: Nomos IX* (New York: New York University Press, 2018).

[13] Dorfman and Harel, "The Case Against Privatization," at p. 68.

[14] See also Chiara Cordelli, "Privatization without Profit?," in Jack Knight and Melissa Schwartzberg (eds.), *Nomos LVII: Privatization* (New York: New York University Press, 2018): 113–144, for some reflections on privatization as

In Section 14.2, these two senses of "private" are distinguished in more detail, and arguments for the value of each are discussed. Section 14.3 defends the claim that if data that were previously "private (I)" change status, they should be turned into publicly available information, rather than into "private (II)" information. I first show that arguments based on the alleged consent of consumers for companies to appropriate their data cannot carry the normative weight ascribed to them (Section 14.3.1). Then I argue that arguments that follow the logic of intellectual property rights (IPR) to justify the exclusive appropriation of such data by profit-oriented companies are not sufficient either (Section 14.3.2). Lastly, I argue that concerns about democratic accountability provide further reasons against a "private (II)" appropriation of such data (Section 14.3.3). The conclusion (Section 14.4) briefly discusses which institutional form the public organization of such information could, in principle, take.

14.2 TWO SENSES OF "PRIVATE"

When we use the word "private," two different sets of ideas can be evoked.[15] "Private (I)" is used, for example, in the phrase "one's private life" or in the notion of "privacy." "Private (II)" refers to exclusive control that allows use for one's own goals, without attention to the public good, typically granted through forms of legal ownership that allow the exclusion of others.[16] For many issues, these two senses overlap; arguably, for many historical periods, "private (I)" was only a possibility for those who owned certain items in the sense of "private (II)": items such as diaries, family photo albums, and, most of all, houses. "The private home" is often understood as epitomizing privacy, and in many countries, it is standardly the case that a "private home" is also "privately owned" and hence comes with exclusive control rights. This may have contributed to the impression that the two notions coincide. Nonetheless, they can be distinguished, and doing so is important for grasping what happens in the current age of "big data."

"Private (I)" concerns items over which individuals have the authority to share them with others or to refuse to do so.[17] Without their consent, neither specific others, nor the broader public, nor the state, have access to what is "private (I)." The clearest case of an item that is "private (I)" is, maybe, one's "private thoughts." They are legally protected by various freedoms, such as freedom of expression or of assembly (so that one can share one's thoughts with chosen others). Other "private (I)" items are closely related to "private thoughts": private letters, private communication, the privacy of the home, etc. They are protected by legal principles that go far beyond questions of control in the sense of property rights: postal privacy, the right to informational self-determination, or the inviolability of the home.

---

concerning not commercial enterprises but other institutions. However, the cases she considers do not involve issues that are "private (I)" in the sense of this chapter.

[15] I do not claim that they are the only ones, but they seem to be central cases. For other categorizations and discussions, see, e.g., Nissenbaum, *Privacy in Context*, or Herman T. Tavani, "Informational Privacy: Concepts, Theories, and Controversies," in Kenneth E. Himma and Herman T. Tavani (eds.), *The Handbook of Information and Computer Ethics* (Hoboken, NJ: Wiley, 2008), pp. 131–164. The first canonical statement of privacy can be found in Samuel D. Warren and Louis Brandeis, "The Right to Private Property," *Harvard Law Review* 4(5) (1890): 193–220. I here draw mainly on the philosophical account provided by Beate Rössler, *Der Wert des Privaten* (Frankfurt am Main: Suhrkamp, 2001).

[16] But see Avihay Dorfman, "When, and How, Does Property Matter?," *University of Toronto Law Journal* (forthcoming 2021). for arguments as to how the notion of property could also be understood differently, and for arguments about why different forms of exclusion need to be distinguished.

[17] See also Rössler, *Der Wert des Privaten*, at p. 23.

Various families of metaphors try to capture what is specific, and specifically valuable,[18] about "private (I)." One set of metaphors is spatial: it draws on the image of secluded spaces, walls that protect individuals from the gazes of nosy neighbors, hedges that separate private gardens from public parks.[19] Other forms of figurative language use the contrast between light and darkness. This is a recurrent theme in Arendt's description of the public realm: it is one of light and mutual visibility, in contrast to the private realm of darkness.[20] The private realm is also associated with bodily needs and the intimacy of love and care. It is where bodies can be naked, deprived of all the things that clothing brings: the signaling of status and belonging, and a certain degree of disguise, for example covering up scars or diseases.

While "privacy," in this sense, comes in different forms and degrees, there are specific reasons for why it has value.[21] Privacy is connected to *autonomy* in the sense of the ability to reflect about the question of who one wants to be, and to decide about the life one wants to live. Rössler distinguishes three dimensions of privacy: decisional, informational, and local.[22] Because the topic of this chapter is data, I here focus on the informational dimension. The core of Rössler's argument here is that individuals need to have a certain degree of control over information about themselves.[23] Drawing on accounts of privacy by Fried and Westin, Rössler argues that violations of a person's informational control over their life can under-mine the conditions of autonomy.[24] If a voyeuristic neighbor, for example, observes them without their knowledge in what they took to be their "private" space, the relationship to this person changes, and they cannot control how they present themselves to the eyes of others. One may, after all, behave differently when one thinks that one is not being watched, whether by specific others, such as the nosy neighbor, or by unspecific others, as in the case of the surveillance cameras. If one is being watched without knowing it, one acts on the basis of wrong assumptions about one's situation.[25] This argument is particularly powerful for plural-istic societies, in which individuals with different worldviews and lifestyles live side by side. Many practices, e.g. religious practices, change their character if they take place in the harsh light of the public, where they can be watched by individuals who disagree fundamentally about their value.

Privacy also has an important connection to the kinds of *social relations* we can have with other people. It is a mark of intimacy to share one's thoughts, but also one's body, with others. If one learns that ideas or facts that were shared on the assumption of a protected private relation are spread to others, this can be perceived as a form of betrayal that cuts deep. Many forms, acts, and dimensions of intimacy would lose their specific value if they could not be protected from the gaze of third parties. This contributes to making a constant state of surveillance, as in Bentham's infamous *panopticum*, such an insidious form of

---

[18] This is not to deny that there can also be problematic aspects of "private (I)" arrangements, for example a lack of accountability for morally questionable forms of behavior. While this issue is potentially relevant for issues about data privacy, I here omit a discussion for reasons of space.

[19] For an extended discussion of spatial dimensions of privacy, see Rössler, *Der Wert des Privaten*, ch. IV.3.

[20] Hannah Arendt, *The Human Condition* (Chicago: University of Chicago Press, 1958), ch. II and *passim*. Her description also includes other elements, e.g. freedom vs. necessity, male vs. female, and the rise of "the social," which I do not endorse here.

[21] For reasons of space, I cannot discuss here the question of whether these are specifically "Western" values; if so, my arguments may not be valid, or not in the same way, for other cultures.

[22] Rössler, *Der Wert des Privaten*.

[23] Ibid., at p. 201.

[24] Ibid., ch. IV.2.

[25] Ibid., at p. 208.

punishment.[26] Importantly, surveillance, or even just the possibility of surveillance, change the character not only of intimate relations but also of other social relations, such as friendships.

This leads to a third, *political* role of privacy in the sense of "private (I)." A first connection runs from autonomy to democracy. As Rössler emphasizes, democracies need citizens who are autonomous, who are aware of their autonomy, and who cherish their autonomy.[27] The private realm provides the space in which individuals can prepare themselves for the light of the public: they cannot only take care of their physical and emotional needs but also share intellectual and ideological insecurities with trusted friends. The "private (I)" realm stands in a complex relationship to "the public" when it comes to citizens' ability to form political opinions. The boundaries are porous, and there are in-between-spaces, such as local pubs.

While one could say much more about this form of privacy, and the forms it takes in contemporary societies, it should have become clear that "private (I)" is different from "private (II)," which focuses on control over objects, and the right to do whatever one wants with them. This right usually includes the right to exclude others, allowing the creation of "privacy (I)," but it need not include it, and it goes much further in other dimensions. It includes, for example, the right to sell an object, or to modify or even destroy it. What is crucial for "private (II)," as I here understand the term, is the right to pursue one's own goals, without attention to the public good.

A typical form that "private (II)" takes is property rights, especially if these are understood as far-ranging, unified, and as carrying no moral obligations.[28] The justification for such "private (II)" control usually stems from assumptions about efficiency: exclusive control is taken to avoid the overuse of "commons,"[29] and, via the alleged "invisible hand" of markets, to contribute *indirectly* to the public good.[30] In Section 14.3.2, I explore some of these arguments in relation to "intellectual property rights."

"Private (II)" control can also take place without legally recognized property rights, as a matter of factual control that is accepted by the state. This is the case for data that are collected by companies, and scholars disagree on whether or not there *should* be property rights in them.[31] Nonetheless, consumer data are de facto treated as if they were the companies' private property, understood in the sense of almost unlimited control and the license to use items in a purely self-interested way. As Elvy puts it: "Despite this scholarly debate, companies are currently commodifying consumer data as it has significant value for such entities."[32]

---

[26] For a discussion see also ibid., ch. IV.2.2.

[27] Ibid., at pp. 218 and 234.

[28] Honoré's classical theory understands them as bundles of rights; interestingly, he includes a notion of responsibility that can come with rights that is often neglected (Anthony M. Honoré, "Ownership," in Anthony G. Guest (ed.), *Oxford Essays in Jurisprudence* (Oxford: Oxford University Press, 1961), pp. 107–147). For an overview of the philosophical debate, see, e.g., Jeremy Waldron, "Property and Ownership," *The Stanford Encyclopedia of Philosophy* (Winter 2016 edition), Edward N. Zalta (ed.), https://plato.stanford.edu/archives/win2016/entries/property/.

[29] The classic account here is Garreth Hardin, "The Tragedy of the Commons," *Science* 162 (1968): 1243–1248.

[30] For a critical discussion of this Smithian metaphor, see Lisa Herzog, *Inventing the Market: Smith, Hegel, and Political Theory* (Oxford: Oxford University Press, 2013), ch. 2 and *passim*.

[31] For a summary of the debate about whether or not there should be ownerships rights in data, see, e.g., Elvy, "Commodifying Consumer Data," at pp. 463–466, or Max-Planck-Institut für Innovation und Wettberb, "Argumente gegen ein 'Dateneigentum'. 10 Fragen und Antworten," www.ip.mpg.de/fileadmin/ipmpg/content/forschung/Argumentarium_Dateneigentum_de.pdf.

[32] Elvy, "Commodifying Consumer Data," at p. 466.

Such property rights, or comparable forms of control, are neither necessary nor sufficient for something to be "private (I)." They are not necessary because they typically go much further than the rights needed to secure "privacy (I)"; for example, a family can enjoy "privacy (I)" in a rented apartment, even though they have no right to modify or sell it. They are not sufficient because one could also imagine a situation in which agents have far-reaching control rights over an item, but need to publicly document everything they do, thus ruling out "privacy (I)." Or individuals may have property in a piece of land, with far-ranging control rights, but also with a requirement to give the right of way to whoever wants to pass, which means that it cannot function as a "private (I)" garden in which one would be protected from the gazes of others.

Importantly, such control rights can be held not only by human persons but also by legal persons, for example corporations. In such cases, the typical justifications for "private (I)" cannot be applied, because legal persons have no body, no intimate relationships, and no human autonomy that would require protection. There might be other reasons for granting legal persons something akin to "privacy (I)," but they would have to be based on different considerations.

In what follows, I will focus on data that are private in sense (I) or (II). In this area, much has changed in recent years, thanks to the "onlife"[33] we are now leading: the mutual penetration of offline and online activities. This is why the distinction between private (I) and (II), which may have appeared a sophistication applicable only to marginal cases in the past, gains relevance. Many of our activities that were traditionally "private (I)" are now fields from which data can be reaped. When we write "private" messages to others, these can be collected and analyzed by the companies through whose networks we send them. When we walk through cities, our smartphones can chart our movements. Credit card companies collect the data of what we buy. Fitness and health apps collect information about our breathing rate, heartbeat, and body temperature. When we read books on digital devices, they register how long it takes us, and which passages we ponder over. Each single data point may seem all too harmless when considered by itself, but taken together, they allow drawing worryingly detailed portraits of individuals.

14.3 PRIVATIZING THE PRIVATE?

The philosophical debate about privatization has mostly addressed questions about the privatization of previously public goods, tasks, or spaces. What happens in the realm of data collection, in contrast, is a "privatization of the private": issues are moved from the status of "private (I)" to that of – someone else's! – "private (II)," from individuals' privacy to the control by companies. Zuboff, in her account of this phenomenon, likens it to the appropriation of seemingly "uninhibited" land by colonial settlers.[34] She quotes Page, one of the founders of *Google*, as saying: "The places you've seen. Communications. ... Sensors are really cheap. ... Storage is cheap. Cameras are cheap. People will generate enormous

---

[33] Luciano Floridi (ed.), *The Online Manifesto: Being Human in a Hyperconnected Era* (Dordrecht: Springer International, 2015).

[34] In fact, this kind of data collection is not always automatic, but can also involve rather dehumanized forms of work. For a report of a worker who had to measure the floors of shops, with a smartphone app, see Frank Odenthal, "Entfremdete Arbeit. Aus dem Bauch der Digitalisierung," *Deutschlandfunk Kultur*, February 2, 2019, www.deutschlandfunkkultur.de/entfremdete-arbeit-aus-dem-bauch-der-digitalisierung.3682.de.html?dram:article_id=433701.

amounts of data. ... Everything you've ever heard or seen or experienced will become searchable. Your whole life will be searchable."[35]

In what follows, I develop some arguments about what is problematic about this "privatization of the private," which, in sum, lead to the conclusion that *if* data that were previously "private (I)" change their status at all, they should not be made "private (II)" in the sense of exclusive and far-reaching control by profit-oriented companies but should be made available for *public* use, for the benefit of society as a whole.

I develop this argument indirectly, by first replying to the objection that consumers consent to their data being appropriated (Section 14.3.1), then showing that the logic of IPR cannot be applied to consumer data (Section 14.3.2), and finally arguing that concerns about democratic accountability add weight to the conclusion that most forms of consumer data should *not* be controlled exclusively by profit-oriented companies.[36]

14.3.1 *Objection: Consent?*

Many business models, whether apps, websites, or "smart technologies," follow the logic of "data against service": they are made available without payment, or at a lower price, in return for the permission to collect data. At first glance, it may seem legitimate for grown-up individuals to give up some of their "privacy (I)" in exchange for services they like to use. For reasons of space, I here leave out cases in which there has been no explicit consent, such as Google's infamous collection of "street view" data,[37] cases in which companies violate their own terms and conditions,[38] or cases in which individuals are minors or otherwise incapable of meaningful consent.[39] Instead, let me focus on the harder, and more frequent, cases, in which grown-up persons have given what seems to be their "free" consent to the appropriation of their data by companies.

A first problem with such forms of consent is that individuals often do not realize what they agree to when they click on the "I agree" button of a terms-of-service agreement.[40] These texts are often formulated in a legalese that most people can hardly understand. The *extent* of data collection, the *use* of the data, and the *value* generated by the use of these data are usually anything but clear.[41] Empirical studies show that people hardly read these texts.[42] When clicking on the terms of services, consumers often "enter into essentially blind bargains."[43]

---

[35] Zuboff, *The Age of Surveillance Capitalism*, pos. 1748, quoting Edward Douglas, *I'm Feeling Lucky: The Confessions of Google Employee Number 59* (Boston: Houghton Mifflin Harcourt, 2011).

[36] I do not claim that these are the only arguments one could bring forward to support that conclusion. For example, one can also develop *economic* arguments about the possibility of competition between different companies that use certain datasets (see, e.g., Elvy, "Commodifying Consumer Data," at p. 515), or one might develop arguments that start from the danger of data companies gaining too much *political* power.

[37] See, e.g., Zuboff, *The Age of Surveillance Capitalism*, ch. 5.

[38] See Elvy, "Commodifying Consumer Data," at p. 443.

[39] Cases in the latter category fall under the broader category of youth protection issues; while they are highly relevant in practice (see, e.g., Josh Constine, "Facebook Pays Teens to Install VPN that Spies on Them," *TechCrunch*, January 29, 2019, https://techcrunch.com/2019/01/29/facebook-project-atlas/), analyzing them from a philosophical perspective is rather straightforward.

[40] See also Elvy, "Commodifying Consumer Data," at p. 442.

[41] In fact, Elvy holds that "there may be risks associated with the collection and disclosure of consumer data that consumers may never become aware of or fully understand" (ibid., at p. 449).

[42] See, e.g., Yannis Bakos, Florencia Marotta-Wurgler, and David R. Trossen, "Does Anyone Read the Fine Print? Consumer Attention to Standard-Form Contracts," *Journal of Legal Studies* 43(1) (2014): 1–35; Victoria C. Plaut and Robert P. Bartlett, "Blind Consent? A Social Psychological Investigation of Non-readership of Click-Through Agreements," *Law and Human Behavior* (2011): 1–23.

[43] Lipman, "Online Privacy," at pp. 780, 784; see similarly Mai, "Big Data Privacy," at p. 193.

However, one might nonetheless hold that individuals *could* read the terms of service if they wished; the fact that they do not read them might indicate that they trust companies, or do not care about privacy. But this assumption seems problematic, at least for certain kinds of markets. Many markets for online services are characterized by monopolies or quasi monopolies.[44]

This holds in particular for social networks, where individuals often have no real alternative to joining the predominant networks, a fact that makes arguments about their consent questionable. Given that a majority of individuals, at least below a certain age and in countries with a developed digital infrastructure, are active online, social expectations on individuals to participate in social networks and to use tools for online communication are high.[45] At the same time, there are few alternatives that would *not* rely on the collection of data, for example messenger services that use cryptography and do not collect data. Often, social dynamics are at play, creating real costs for individuals who prefer not to use data-collecting services. Take, for example, the parents who arrange play dates or shared rides for their children in social media groups.[46] Parents who do *not* want to take part in such arrangements might try to convince all others to switch to different forms of communication, but this is likely to be difficult and long-winded. Most individuals will simply go along, because the disadvantages of a lack of communication would be too large. As some commentators have argued, many online platforms have taken on the character of a public infrastructure, which operates in the background and on which individuals have to rely to lead their daily lives.[47]

One can explain the lack of pluralism with regard to many online services as a form of market failure. Social media are networked structures: their value is greater for users the more individuals are on the same network. And as long as profiles are not portable and networks not interoperationable – features that regulators could, in theory, impose on them, but which they have not imposed so far – there is a lock-in effect: once a critical mass of individuals uses a certain social network, single users do not have a choice but to join in as well. Having a large user base, in turn, can provide established companies with cost advantages, based on economies of scale. This, in turn, makes it harder for new companies to compete with them.

It might be objected that not all companies that use a "data against service" business model are social networks, and that there might well be opportunities for companies with better privacy protection to enter markets for, say, smart household appliances. Individuals with a genuine appetite for privacy might be willing to pay a premium, thus covering the additional costs of companies that do not, for example, sell customer data to third parties. Individuals who are not willing to pay this premium, it might be said, want to have their cake and eat it, too: they want lower prices *and* privacy, without seeing that this might not be feasible.

For some markets, this argument seems valid, but its force and scope should not be overstated. To repeat: it does not apply to social media, which are among the most powerful data collectors – and individuals may well have given up hopes for privacy, given that their

---

[44] See similarly Nancy S. Kim and D. A. Jeremy Telman: "Internet Giants as Quasi-governmental Actors and the Limits of Contractual Consent," *Missouri Law Review* 80 (2015): 723–770, at p. 732.

[45] See also Elvy, "Commodifying Consumer Data," at pp. 442–443, on the role of social norms for consumer consent, referring to Lior Jacob Strahilevitz and Matthew B. Kugler, "Is Privacy Policy Language Irrelevant to Consumers?," *Journal of Legal Studies* 45(2): 69–95.

[46] See also Lipman, "Online Privacy," at p. 799, about the social pressure to join one's friends on Facebook.

[47] See, e.g., Jean-Christophe Plantin, Carl Lagoze, Paul N Edwards, and Christian Sandvig, "Infrastructure Studies Meet Platform Studies in the Age of Google and Facebook," *New Media & Society* 20(1) (2018): 293–310.

data are collected by social media companies *anyway*. Moreover, individuals may have an insufficient understanding of what it means that their data are being appropriated by companies. They may not consider the possibility that they might have a *duty towars themselves* to protect their privacy.[48] And last but not least, they may simply lack the purchasing power to choose more expensive options that offer higher privacy – it is, after all, not too far-fetched a scenario that in the future, the "standard" model of many products is one that *does* collect data.[49]

In fact, pursuing this line of thought further leads to a scenario in which privacy, in sense (I), becomes a luxury item only available to individuals who have sufficient cash to spare on the premium versions of products and services.[50] The business model for many premium versions is to rely on fees, rather than on the income from the sale of data. If rich individuals have rich friends, all of them might switch to platforms and communication tools that keep their data "private (I)." This does not imply, however, that the consent of other users, who "agree" to have their data used by companies, can be understood as normatively sufficient. Their choices might simply express a (potentially unjust[51]) lack of purchasing power, combined with the role of many online platforms as infrastructures that individuals can hardly avoid using.[52]

It is telling which options individuals can usually *not* choose, not even for higher fees. They can seldom choose between different *levels* of privacy, with, for example, only part of their data being used, or sold, or only for particular purposes.[53] Nor can they opt for their data to be collected for *public* purposes instead of the profit maximization of private firms. In the context of medical data, the notion of "data donation" is used to describe the idea that sensitive data are voluntarily shared for the sake of medical research.[54] Such an option is not available for most other products or services. What is on offer is usually "all-or-nothing": complete handing over of the sovereignty over one's data, or blocked access to the relevant service. While such a choice may nonetheless allow for normatively meaningful consent when what is at stake are services that individuals can easily forgo, this is not the case when there are strong social pressures to use them.

In summary, the kind of consent that is currently used to transfer control rights over data to companies is normatively deficient: for many individuals and many online services, it cannot carry the full weight that it is supposed to carry. This means that an important argument *for*

---

[48] On a possible duty to protect one's own privacy, see Anita L. Allen, "An Ethical Duty to Protect One's Own Information Privacy?," *Alabama Law Review* 64(4) (2013): 845–866.

[49] Zuboff, *The Age of Surveillance Capitalism*, especially ch. 13.

[50] For a discussion, see, e.g., Stacy-Ann Elvy, "Paying for Privacy and the Personal Data Economy," *Columbia Law Review* 117 (2017): 1369–1454.

[51] In fact, many individuals would have *more* purchasing power if the value generated by the use of their data were, at least partly, paid back to them. This is how Jaron Lanier (*Who Owns the Future?* (London: Penguin Books, 2014)) envisages a better digital future, in which micropayments flow back to those who provide online content. This line of thinking is particularly plausible for *content* that individuals upload, e.g. video clips with songs they wrote. From a philosophical perspective, it is less clear that such payments are a plausible approach for "data exhaust." From a pragmatic perspective, higher taxes on data corporations, and redistribution to the public, would probably be a more feasible approach.

[52] Elvy, "Commodifying Consumer Data," at pp. 443–444, also mentions the problem that consumers "may become exhausted with having to implement or comply with numerous measures to ensure their privacy and security." See also Brian Stanton et al., "Security Fatigue," *IT Professional* 18 (2016): 26–32.

[53] As Lipman ("Online Privacy," at pp. 786–787 and 802) notes, this also means that the true taste, and willingness to pay, for privacy cannot become known.

[54] See, e.g., Jenny Krutzinna and Luciano Floridi (eds.), *The Ethics of Medical Data Donation* (Springer Open Access, www.springer.com/de/book/9783030043629).

the legitimacy of "privatizing the private" falls apart: when the data of one's social media account or smart bed are commodified by companies, this is *not* like letting a friend enter one's bedroom! But this leads to a follow-up question: What if the alternative to data sharing as we currently experience it is *not* to have any of these services available, or only at a considerably higher price? This is an argument based on economic efficiency, which can best be discussed by exploring the parallels with arguments for IPR.

14.3.2 *The Logic of Intellectual Property Rights?*

It is a basic feature of information, often commented upon, that it does not get less by being shared: in this respect, it is a public good.[55] The same holds for data: a dataset does not "get less" by being analyzed by more than one company. But this public nature of information has a well-known dark side: there might be a lack of incentives to *provide* information in the first place if one can anticipate that it will be used by everyone. This is one of the basic rationales for IPR: without them, certain forms of immaterial content would not be produced at an optimal level. Although data are not standardly treated as private property, it is worth asking whether a parallel case can be made for allowing companies to acquire their exclusive usage.

IP scholars are divided between those who justify it in "Lockean" terms, as a question of the moral rights of the creators of intellectual content, and those who take a utilitarian approach, which emphasizes the impact of different rights regimes on overall welfare.[56] The "Lockean" approach has its greatest plausibility for artistic creations; in the case of other forms of knowledge or information, it has rightly been criticized for privileging the interests of current owners over those of other potential users.[57] But for the current context, it is not necessary to take a general stance on the Lockean theory; it is sufficient to ask whether it makes sense to apply it to consumer data.

Data are not "created" in the sense in which a piece of art is created. Rather, the value of "big data" comes from a constellation in which the producers and the collectors of data *together* create something of value. Thus, from a Lockean perspective, what would follow would have to be *joint* rights. And they would have to be joint rights not only between one company and one user but between companies and large numbers of users – it is, after all, the "big" in "big data" that makes all the difference. The Lockean paradigm, apart from its general weaknesses, has problems – arguably, insurmountable ones – when it comes to constellations of complex forms of divided labor, by multiple agents.

In what follows, I thereby pursue the utilitarian line, and ask whether a rationale that runs in parallel to that in favor of IPR could be used for justifying the exclusive control rights of companies over data. From this perspective, a key question is whether it is necessary to create such exclusive control rights in order to provide *incentives* for information to be created in the first place, and how extensive these rights should be in order to maximize overall welfare.[58] At

---

[55] See, e.g., Axel Gosseries, "How (Un)fair Is Intellectual Property?," in A.Gosseries, A. Marciano, and A. Strowel (eds.), *Intellectual Property and Theories of Justice* (Basingstoke: Palgrave Macmillan, 2008): 3–26.

[56] On the Lockean approach, see, e.g., Justin Hughes, "The Philosophy of Intellectual Property," *Georgetown Law Journal* 77 (1988): 287–366; H. M. Spector, "An Outline of a Theory Justifying Intellectual and Industrial Property Rights," *European Intellectual Property Review* 11(8) (1989): 270–273; or more recently Adam Mossoff, "Saving Locke from Marx: The Labor Theory of Value in Intellectual Property Theory," *Social Philosophy and Policy* 29(2) (2012): 283–317.

[57] See, e.g., Peter Drahos with John Braithwaite, *Information Feudalism: Who Owns the Knowledge Economy?* (New York: Earthscan, 2002), ch. 2.

[58] See, e.g., Richard A. Posner, "Intellectual Property: The Law and Economics Approach," *Journal of Economic Perspectives* 19(2) (2005): 57–73. An overview of the debate – from a rather critical perspective – can also be found

first glance, it might seem that an analogous argument could be made for data: would they be provided in the first place if they could not be exclusively appropriated? To answer this question, we can distinguish between the *production* of data by consumers and the *collection* of data by companies.

For consumers, the answer is straightforward: the data in question are generated as a *by-product* of other activities, therefore there is no need to provide incentives. Individuals walk around in cities, write emails, or make noise in beds – and, meanwhile, data flows are generated. The argument that IPR would protect an object "that would not exist if not for the inventor"[59] does not make sense here. The terms "data exhaust" or "digital breadcrumbs"[60] have sometimes been used to describe the nature of these data, and they make clear, at the same time, that there is no need to incentivize individuals to produce these data.

What about *companies* – do they need to receive exclusive rights, comparable to IPR, as incentives for creating the products and services they offer? This is, in the final analysis, an empirical question, but there are good reasons to doubt that the answer would justify *exclusive* rights for companies in *all* cases. The matter is not one of production costs: sensors have become extremely cheap, and integrating them into "smart" products is often a matter of a few cents. More to the point is the question of whether companies would not even develop certain products or services if they had no chance to appropriate customer data (and then often also sell them to third parties).

Several answers can be given. One is that if companies did *not* have the option to appropriate data, they might develop *other* kinds of products and services, and it is not a priori clear that this scenario would be worse for customers. If companies are allowed to fully appropriate data, they may develop products or services with the *primary* goal of collecting data, while there are no genuine benefits for customers (other than the perceived status increase of using a "smart" product). One would have to carefully go through different cases to see what would actually be lost if data-collecting models were *not* possible.

A second objection, however, goes even further. It is not at all clear that companies need *exclusive* control rights over data for producing the goods and services they currently produce.[61] One could, for example, imagine that companies would have a right of *first* usage of data, for a limited amount of time, after which the data are transferred to a public data pool and opened up for use by other companies, researchers, and public authorities. Or companies could be required to provide access to some or all of the data, with or without compensation, by providing licenses to other companies or to public institutions. The sale of data to data brokers and other companies, or their use as collateral, could be limited or banned, which might make *some* business models no longer worthwhile, but would, presumably, keep many others in place.[62] We can imagine a broad variety of solutions, depending on the kinds of data and the kinds of business models in question. There may *occasionally* be

---

in James Boyle, *The Public Domain: Enclosing the Commons of the Mind* (New Haven, CT and London: Yale University Press, 2008), ch. I.

[59] Robert Nozick, *Anarchy, State, and Utopia* (New York: Basic Books, 1974), at 182, quoted in Gosseries, "How (Un)fair Is Intellectual Property?," at p. 13.

[60] Zuboff, *The Age of Surveillance Capitalism*, pos. 1648.

[61] See similarly (albeit from a slightly different perspective) Josef Drexl, "Designing Competitive Markets for Industrial Data: Between Propertisation and Access," Max Planck Institute for Innovation and Competition Research Paper No. 16–13 (2016), https://papers.ssrn.com/sol3/papers.cfm?abstract_id=2862975, at p. 31.

[62] See, in general, Elvy, "Commodifying Consumer Data."

cases in which *only* a right to exclusive control over data creates sufficient incentives for the provision of services, but these would probably be few and far between.

In fact, if one wants to put weight on the parallel with IPR, it is worth emphasizing that, according to the utilitarian approach, it is only the *use* of intellectual content that is, for a limited amount of time, protected. The social contract between society and inventor or artist is a reciprocal one: knowledge is *made public*, for example when filing a patent, in exchange for a temporary monopoly on its financial exploitation.[63] The analogy would thus require a similar form of reciprocity with data-collecting firms: they would have to make data publicly available, in exchange for a temporary monopoly on usage.

Thus, we can conclude that the attempt to draw on analogies to IPR fails to justify exclusive control rights for companies. Rather, reflecting on this analogy leads to the insight that insofar as "private (I)" data should be collected *at all*, the rules for collecting them need not, and probably often should not, prioritize the profit-oriented goals of companies. Arguably, our societies have been far too willing to let companies go ahead with the collection of "private (I)" data, instead of installing mechanisms for making sure that certain kinds of data are *not* collected, and that other kinds of data are used in ways that serve the public good.

14.3.3 *Democratic Accountability*

A third line of argument relies on the need for *democratic accountability* for organizations that have power over the data of individuals. As recent scandals around Facebook[64] and Google[65] have shown, the potential for culpable negligence and even active abuse in the data economy is enormous. Accountability for protecting data that should remain "private (I)" is only one aspect of this broader need for accountability: there are also questions about the use of data that could, for example, be analyzed to improve public welfare. As Zuboff writes about the way companies currently act: "They accumulate vast domains of new knowledge from us, but *not for us*."[66]

It is at this point that one can draw a connection to arguments about the genuinely public function of certain government tasks that the philosophical debate about privacy has discussed.[67] Many of the data in question seem to be public in character, in the sense that they concern all members of society, or large subgroups, and therefore should be used "for us," in Zuboff's words. Population-wide data concerning eating behavior, medical issues, or traffic can be of great benefit if they can be used by researchers and public institutions. The current regime of "private (II)" appropriation leaves much of this potential untapped.

The time-honored slogan of the "primacy of politics"[68] expresses the idea that public policy can set the rules by which actors with far-ranging control over certain items, in the sense of "private (II)," have to play. This may be difficult in times in which many corporations have gone global, while politics have, to a great extent, remained national. But countries can

---

[63] This is emphasized in particular in Boyle, *The Public Domain*, ch. 1.

[64] See, e.g., Carole Cadwalladr, "'I Made Steve Bannon's Psychological Warfare Tool': Meet the Data War Whistleblower," *The Guardian*, March 18 (2018), www.theguardian.com/news/2018/mar/17/data-war-whistleblower-christopher-wylie-faceook-nix-bannon-trump.

[65] See, e.g., Safiya Umoja Noble, *Algorithms of Oppression: How Search Engines Reinforce Racism* (New York: New York University Press, 2018).

[66] Zuboff, *The Age of Surveillance Capitalism*, pos. 245, emphasis added.

[67] Harel and Dorfman, "The Case Against Privatization."

[68] Sheri Berman, *The Primacy of Politics: Social Democracy and the Making of Europe's Twentieth Century* (Cambridge: Cambridge University Press, 2006).

coordinate their activities; the recent implementation of the EU's General Data Protection Regulation (GDPR), despite all its problems, shows that it is not impossible to rein in even the most powerful transnational corporations. Of course, big data companies keep repeating that regulation would hamper their innovativeness.[69] But firstly, we do not know to what extent this is really true, and secondly, if innovation is driven by an exclusive desire to make profits, rather than to serve the public good, and especially if it comes at the price of more and more ruthless data extraction, it is not clear that it would be desirable for societies to have such innovations.

To be sure, public authorities are not *necessarily* better at dealing with data; the US National Security Agency (NSA) scandal, uncovered by whistleblower Edward Snowden, is sad testimony to this fact.[70] *All* institutions that deal with sensitive data, whether public or private, need appropriate accountability structures to prevent abuse and to make sure that the data that *should* be used are used in the right way, while data that should *not* be used are not collected in the first place.

It should probably not surprise us that most societies are currently not yet very good at providing such structures. When new technologies open up the possibility of gaining access to new kinds of resources, we can expect inventive agents to claim this access.[71] In the case of data collection, political inaction has allowed the emergence of extremely large and powerful corporations that can crush (or simply buy up) most competitors. Democratic states urgently need to take steps to wrestle control back from them.

If "digital exhaust" is understood as a public good, and those who deal with it are held democratically accountable – whether by setting strict public rules about which data "private (II)" companies can control, or by collecting such data in public data pools – meaningful decisions can be taken about which data to collect, in what form, and for which purposes. Some forms of data should probably simply *not* be collected, because of "privacy (I)" considerations (audio files from individuals' bedrooms might be a case in point).[72] Other kinds of data could be collected, with fully informed consent, for the sake of public-oriented endeavors, but not for the sake of making profits (e.g. medical data,[73] or traffic data for city planning[74]). A third category of data could be made available, carefully anonymized, for profit-maximizing enterprises, but not necessarily as monopolized by specific companies (e.g. data about click-behavior on websites).

If such a (legal and technical) infrastructure for the age of "big data" were to be developed, the *connection* of different kinds of data points for single individuals – which contributes to the threat to privacy, because individuals can be easily identified– could probably be prevented, while data could still be used for various kinds of analyses. Researchers and public institutions could use "big data" to help societies to become more aware of patterns of behavior. For example, the CO_2 footprint of different activities could be understood in

---

[69] E.g. Zuboff, *The Age of Surveillance Capitalism*, at pos. 1110.

[70] See, e.g., Lipman, "Online Privacy," at p. 779.

[71] See similarly Katharina Pistor, *The Code of Capital: How the Law Creates Wealth and Inequality* (Princeton: Princeton University Press, 2019).

[72] See also Elvy, "Commodifying Consumer Data," at p. 501, who argues that certain data might be "rendered inalienable," referring to Walter W. Miller, Jr. and Maureen A. O'Rourke, "Bankruptcy Law v. Privacy Rights: Which Holds the Trump Card?," *Houston Law Review* 38 (2001): 777–854, at p. 847.

[73] See also Elvy, "Commodifying Consumer Data," at p. 438, and Sarah Kellog, "Every Breath You Take: Data Privacy and Your Wearable Fitness Device," *Washington Lawyer*, December 2015, https://old.dcbar.org/bar-resources/publications/washington-lawyer/articles/december-2015-data-privacy.cfm.

[74] See, e.g., Stamatina Th. Rassia and Panos M. Pardalos (eds.), *Smart City Networks: Through the Internet of Things* (Cham: Springer, 2018).

much more detail, which could help move environmental policies forward. Patterns of discrimination against minorities could be made visible, to support antidiscrimination policies. Forms of implicit social power, for example through the use of language, could be opened up for public deliberation.[75]

Such measures could and should go hand in hand with efforts to increase data literacy. As Noble notes, one of the problems of the current situation is that many individuals fundamentally misunderstand the nature of profit-oriented data companies.[76] For example, they take the rankings in a Google search to be authoritative sources of information, and do not even know that there might also be alternative, and alternatively structured, forms of access to information, such as public libraries. But the Google algorithms operate according to a specific rationale: that of selling advertisement; as such, they are not necessarily the best guide to what information is available, in what order. To help avoid such confusion, different kinds of data, delivered from different sources, and presented according to different logics, should be clearly demarcated as what they are. Citizens need to learn, from childhood onwards, what it means to draw on these different sources, and also how their own data are treated when using different services. If they are better informed, and have various options available to them, their consent could become normatively meaningful in ways that it currently cannot be.

14.4 CONCLUSION

In this chapter, I have discussed a specific case of privatization: the privatization, in the sense of "private" appropriate, of data, much of which should be "private" in a different sense, namely the sense of privacy and private autonomy. I have argued that this form of "privatization" is highly problematic not only because information is a public good and special justifications are required for its private acquisition (which current practices of consent rarely provide) but also because of the need for democratic accountability of the use of such data. The vast amounts of data that are currently being collected should be understood as, first and foremost, a public good. As with other public goods, there can be reasons for allowing "private (II)" actors to play a role in their provision and management. But this should be understood as a concession, which can always be recalled, and which needs to be carefully delineated.

What could be institutional arrangements for treating such data as a public good? In addition to legally banning the collection of certain kinds of data, one possibility, for data that it is in principle legitimate to collect, would be to introduce statutory or compulsory licensing, that is, to force companies to give other entities, for example public research entities, access to their data.[77] This is part of the toolkit of IPR, and its logic could also be applied to data. A second – and complementary – approach would be to hold certain kinds of data in publicly oriented institutions, with suitable accountability mechanisms. These could, for example, be public trusts or nonprofit foundations, similar to the Wikimedia Foundation, a nonprofit foundation that stands behind the various crowd-sourced and crowd-funded Wikipedia services. For more specific kinds of data, for example medical data, new

---

[75] Some commentators even envisage a form of "digital socialism" that would use "big data" for economic planning. For reflections on the need to make sure that the "feedback infrastructure" of the internet remains publicly accessible, see Evgeny Morozov, "Digital Socialism? The Calculation Debate in the Age of Big Data," *New Left Review* 116/117, Mar/Jun 2019, pp. 33–67.

[76] Noble, *Algorithms of Oppression*, chs. 5 and 6.

[77] A related regulatory step would be to make certain standardized interfaces mandatory, to allow portability of profiles to consumers and to allow benign forms of data sharing.

organizations could be founded, to collaborate closely with those who use these data, namely researchers, and those for whose benefit they are used, namely patients. For all institutions, whether public or private, careful institutional analysis would be needed to design suitable accountability mechanisms.

The kinds of institutions that are most suited for handling "big data" probably need to be as varied as the kinds of data that can be collected and put to good use. My claim is not that "private (II)" companies – ideally less powerful ones – could not play some role in such an institutional ecosystem. But, as I have tried to show, there is no reason to think that the silent privatization of data that we are currently witnessing is normatively justified. Many kinds of data, and of the knowledge that can be generated from them, should be *either* "private (I)" *or* public; maybe only a fraction should be held under exclusive control by profit-oriented companies in the sense of "private (II)." Democratic politics need to wrestle control back from data companies; a task that is certainly not easy but that is worth every effort, given what is at stake.

15

Political Connections, Corruption, and Privatization

Mariana Mota Prado

15.1 INTRODUCTION

The relationship between corruption and privatization[1] is a complex one. In some cases, they are conceived as polar opposites, with privatization touted as a strategy to combat corruption. In others, they are synonyms: privatization is perceived as a product of or a mechanism to enable corruption. In this chapter, I argue that there are particular circumstances in which each of these hypotheses may prevail, suggesting that the answer to the question "who gains from privatization?" is largely dependent on context. An accurate picture needs to consider the multiple phases of the privatization process, the unique institutional framework in which decisions are made, and the particularities of the sector(s) involved. To develop this argument, I organize the vast literature on the political economy of privatization according to three key moments: the decision to privatize (before privatization), the privatization process (during privatization), and the dynamics governing the privatized structures (after privatization). In each of these moments, concrete experiences show that privatization can be conceived as the opposite of corruption or its embodiment. The conclusion is that simplistic views of privatization (assuming it is either the solution to or the cause of corruption) are untenable.

15.2 CORRUPTION: IDENTIFYING THE PROBLEM AND ITS CAUSES

Corruption is often defined as the use or abuse of public office for private gain.[2] Traditional forms of corruption, such as embezzlement and bribes, involve financial benefits; but corruption could also include more intangible benefits, such as status.[3] The concept of

---

[1] The term privatization lacks a single definition (see Chapter 16 in this volume). For present purposes, I define privatization as "the deliberate sale by government of state-owned enterprises (SOEs) or assets to private economic agents." William L. Megginson and Jeffry M. Netter, "From State to Market: A Survey of Empirical Studies on Privatization," *Journal of Economic Literature* 39 (2001): 321–389.

[2] John Gardiner, "Defining Corruption," in *Political Corruption: Concepts and Contexts*, eds. Arnold J. Heidenheimer and Michael Johnston, 3rd ed. (Routledge, 2017), pp. 25–40.

[3] J. S. Nye, "Corruption and Political Development: A Cost-Benefit Analysis," *American Political Science Review* 61 (1967): 417–427, p. 419 (defining corruption as "behavior which deviates from the formal duties of a public role

institutional corruption expands the concept of "private gains" to include actions that benefit individuals in their official capacities rather than in their personal life.[4] This includes clientelism or patronage, which takes place when an elected official ("patron") offers high-ranked and well-paid jobs in the bureaucracy in exchange for political support, rather than hiring based on merit.[5] Lawrence Lessig has advanced an even broader concept – dependence corruption – which expands the concept beyond "the sale by government officials of government property for personal gain."[6] According to Lessig, the problem occurs "when individuals within that institution become dependent upon an influence that distracts them from the intended purpose of the institution. The distracting dependency corrupts the institution."[7] For example, certain forms of campaign financing and lobbying that are legal in the United States are defined by Lessig as dependence corruption.[8] This form of corruption, he argues, shows how money can impair institutional independence without involving quid pro quo, bribes, or any form of private gain. The challenge here is to determine which branch of government should be in charge of determining "the intended purpose of an institution," and to distinguish between political activity that will be classified as dependence corruption and acceptable practices in a democratic system.[9]

In most countries, anticorruption laws capture situations that fit into the traditional definition, prohibiting bribes, embezzlement, etc.[10] However, resorting solely to the law to determine what is corrupt behaviour may fail to capture instances that would be undesirable for other reasons. An act may be not classified as corruption by the law, despite being perceived as such by citizens, or despite not advancing the public interest.[11] Such discrepancies suggest that relying solely on legal definitions of corruption may not be advisable. On the other hand, a broad definition of corruption may dilute its value and may not be enough to spark the complex institutional reforms required to tackle them.[12]

In this chapter, I focus primarily on the traditional forms of corruption: the use or abuse of public office for private gain (e.g. bribery and embezzlement). While acknowledging the limitations of using a strictly legal concept of corruption, my analysis will focus on practices that were illegal where and when they took place.

In line with influential works in the specialized academic literature, in this chapter, corruption will be analyzed according to a political economy framework.[13] Assuming a rational-actor model, this framework suggests that corruption is the result of a system of

because of private-regarding [personal, close family, private clique] pecuniary or status gains; or violates rules against the exercise of certain types of private-regarding influence").

[4] Dennis F. Thompson, *Ethics in Congress: From Individual to Institutional Corruption* (Brookings Institution, 1995), p. 124; Gardiner, "Defining Corruption," p. 26.

[5] James Robinson and Thierry Verdier, "The Political Economy of Clientelism," *Scandinavian Journal of Economics* 115 (2013): 260–291.

[6] Andrei Shleifer and Robert W. Vishny, "Corruption," *Quarterly Journal of Economics* 108 (1993): 599–617.

[7] Lawrence Lessig, *Republic, Lost: How Money Corrupts Congress – and a Plan to Stop It* (Twelve, 2011), p. 15.

[8] Ibid.

[9] Deborah Hellman, "Defining Corruption and Constitutionalizing Democracy," *Michigan Law Review* 111 (2013): 1386–1422; Yasmin Dawood, "Classifying Corruption," *Duke Journal of Constitutional Law & Public Policy* 9 (2014): 103–134.

[10] Raymond Fisman and Miriam A. Golden, *Corruption: What Everyone Needs to Know* (Oxford University Press, 2017), pp. 26–29.

[11] James C. Scott, *Comparative Political Corruption* (Prentice-Hall, 1972); Gardiner, "Defining Corruption," pp. 30–31.

[12] Susan Rose-Ackerman, "Corruption & Purity," *Daedalus* 147 (2018): 98–110.

[13] Susan Rose-Ackerman, *Corruption: A Study in Political Economy* (Academic Press, 1978); Susan Rose-Ackerman, *Political Economy of Corruption: Causes and Consequences* (World Bank, 1996).

incentives and is likely to exist whenever the benefits of engaging in it exceed the expected costs.[14] Conceptualizing corruption as a political economy problem has significant implications. One is that no country, no government, no society is immune to corruption, challenging the idea that corruption is embedded in the informal rules and norms of "uncivilized" societies.[15] Another is that institutional reforms may limit opportunities *ex ante* (prevention) and increase costs *ex post* (deterrence), thus reducing the likelihood of public officials and private parties engaging in corrupt activities.

From this perspective, privatization may be conceived as a strategy to reduce corruption. The assumption is that by reducing the size of the state, reformers can minimize the opportunities for public officials to engage in wrongdoing. However, this assumption ignores the fact that privatization processes are designed and implemented by public officials. More specifically, these officials need to decide: whether, what, how, and when to privatize. For each of these decisions, there is a risk that some officials will see privatization as an opportunity for private gain. And, even assuming that the privatization process was not corrupt, if it is followed by any form of regulation of the private sector (as it often is in some sectors, such as infrastructure), the risk of corruption remains present.

In summary, privatization may not be a solution to corruption and, depending on the circumstances, it may be the source of the problem. This chapter provides an overview of the literature exploring the circumstances under which privatization may help or hinder the fight against corruption.

15.3 THE PRIVATIZATION DECISION: SOLUTION OR PROBLEM?

In the late 1970s, the Thatcher government (1979–1990) began a widespread program of privatization.[16] Similar programs were taken up in Western Europe and North America during the 1980s,[17] Eastern European and Latin American countries in the 1990s, and, to a lesser extent, South Asia (China and India) in the 2000s.[18] Sub-Saharan Africa had waves of privatization: some countries started in the late 1970s, others in the 1990s, and later starters only in the 2000s.[19]

These privatizations had both ideological and economic motivations.[20] They were linked with a neoliberal agenda supporting smaller governments, freer markets, and fiscal responsibility. Specifically, privatization was seen as a strategy to promote economic growth by reducing inefficiency while raising revenues. These revenues could, in turn, be used to fund new programs, tax cuts, or any number of other politically favourable ends.[21]

---

[14]   Susan Rose-Ackerman, "The Economics of Corruption," *Journal of Public Economics* 4 (1975): 187–203 (for public contracts); Susan Rose-Ackerman and Bonnie J. Palifka, *Corruption and Government: Causes, Consequences, and Reform*, 2nd ed. (Cambridge University Press, 2016) (for a broader analysis of governmental functions).

[15]   Nye, "Corruption and Political Development" (calling this the moralist view).

[16]   John Burton, "Privatization: The Thatcher Case," *Managerial and Decision Economics* 8 (1987): 21–29.

[17]   Gérard Roland, ed., *Privatization: Successes and Failures* (Columbia University Press, 2008).

[18]   Saul Estrin and Adeline Pelletier, "Privatization in Developing Countries: What Are the Lessons of Recent Experience?," *World Bank Research Observer* 33 (2018): 65–102.

[19]   Ibid.

[20]   Megginson and Netter, "From State to Market," pp. 322–324.

[21]   Harvey B. Feigenbaum and Jeffrey R. Henig, "The Political Underpinnings of Privatization: A Typology," *World Politics* 46 (1994): 185–208, p. 188. Privatization also provided an opportunity to eliminate politically powerful groups of state employees (e.g. British coal-miners). See Andrei Shleifer, "State versus Private Ownership," *Journal of Economic Perspectives* 12 (1998): 133–150, p. 142.

The case for privatization was built on the assumption that state-owned enterprises (SOEs) were inefficient, for at least three reasons. First, SOEs are inherently less effective than private enterprises at addressing principal–agent problems. This is primarily due to absence of market-imposed incentives such as the threat of failure, soft budget caps that do not impose fiscal discipline, the difficulty of specifying and monitoring performance that is not solely defined by the maximization of profits (e.g. the fulfilment of social goals), and the diversity of ownership (which creates a collective action problem vis-à-vis the monitoring of managers' behaviour).[22] Second, production/strategic decisions are driven by political rather than consumer preferences.[23] Third, in many countries, governance structures did not create incentives to maximize efficiency.[24] For example, a major source of SOE inefficiency in former communist countries was the fact that local managers and bureaucrats held the control rights for various SOEs but lacked incentives to maximize efficiency because cash flow rights – and thus the benefits of becoming more efficient – were held by a central authority.[25] The push for privatization was preceded by internal governance reforms in SOEs between 1960 and 1980 that tried to modify incentive structures without change of ownership; these earlier reforms generated only modest success, supporting the view that privatization was a superior option.[26] Initial support for privatization focused primarily on the ownership effect; but some experiences later showed that the competition effect, that is, exposing SOEs to a competitive market environment, also has a significant impact on their performance.[27]

There were also concerns that political oversight of SOEs created opportunities for rent-seeking. This was largely based on the assumption that corruption is likely to flourish in circumstances where public officials have monopoly and discretion combined with lack of accountability.[28] Thus, in most cases, the level of discretion in political appointments to SOEs, associated with the level of discretion granted to managers, the lack of an entrenched code of professional ethics regarding serving the public interest, and ineffective corruption monitoring or enforcement systems created the ideal conditions for corruption to thrive.

From a political economy perspective, the efficiency and corruption concerns are inter-connected as opportunities for rent-seeking reduce incentives for efficiency-enhancing

[22] Michael J. Trebilcock and Mariana Mota Prado, *Advanced Introduction to Law and Development* (Edward Elgar, 2014), pp. 167–169; Michael J. Trebilcock and Edward M. Iacobucci, "Privatization and Accountability Symposium: Public Values in an Era of Privatization," *Harvard Law Review* 116 (2003): 1422–1453, pp. 1427–1430.

[23] Andrei Shleifer and Robert W. Vishny, "Politicians and Firms," *Quarterly Journal of Economics* 109 (1994): 995–1025, pp. 995–997.

[24] This is known in the specialized literature as the split between control rights and cash flow rights. The distinction is built on the work of Grossman, Hart, and Moore on contract and property rights that was subsequently extended to the case of post-Soviet Russia by Boycko, Shleifer, and Vishny. Sanford J. Grossman and Oliver D. Hart, "The Costs and Benefits of Ownership: A Theory of Vertical and Lateral Integration," *Journal of Political Economy* 94 (1986): 691–719; Oliver Hart and John Moore, "Property Rights and the Nature of the Firm," *Journal of Political Economy* 98 (1990): 1119–1158; with respect to the latter, see Maxim Boycko, Andrei Shleifer, and Robert W. Vishny, *Privatizing Russia* (MIT Press, 1995).

[25] Daniel Kaufmann and Paul Siegelbaum, "Privatization and Corruption in Transition Economies," *Journal of International Affairs* 50 (1997): 420–458, pp. 429–430, referencing, generally, Boycko, Shleifer, and Vishny, *Privatizing Russia*.

[26] José A. Gómez-Ibáñez, "Alternatives to Infrastructure Privatization Revisited: Public Enterprise Reform from the 1960s to the 1980s," Policy Research Working Paper No. 4391 (World Bank, 2007); Timothy Irwin and Chiaki Yamamoto, "Some Options for Improving the Governance of State-Owned Electricity Utilities," Energy and Mining Sector Board Discussion Paper No. 11 (World Bank, 2004).

[27] D. Andrew C. Smith and Michael J. Trebilcock, "State-Owned Enterprises in Less Developed Countries: Privatization and Alternative Reform Strategies," *European Journal of Law and Economics* 12 (2001): 217–252.

[28] Robert E. Klitgaard, *Controlling Corruption* (University of California Press, 1988), p. 75 (proposing the now famous equation that corruption equals monopoly plus discretion minus accountability).

decisions. For instance, bribes could be requested by managers to guarantee employment at SOEs, preventing the hiring of the most qualified professionals. Alternatively, politicians and managers may rig tendering processes in exchange for bribes, awarding contracts to providers that may not be the most competitive in the market.[29] The government can also use SOEs for patronage, using the company to transfer resources to political supporters in the form of employment, contracts, or location of businesses.[30] Patronage can also be harmful if it involves inflated contracts and excess employment and wages.[31] Another concern is that governments are generally unable to refrain from drawing on the treasury to cover the cost overruns of SOEs.[32] Anticipating this, SOE managers have little incentive to cut costs and will under-invest resources into finding efficiencies. Allowing such transfers to occur also creates opportunities for collusion between politicians and public sector managers to siphon money from the treasury to promote private interests.

Although most economists now argue for a relatively limited role for SOEs,[33] the evidence to support the idea that privatization increases efficiency and reduces corruption is, at best, mixed.[34] Empirical studies show that privatization may offer substantial social welfare improvements to middle- and upper-middle-income developing countries, but these results are much less significant in low-income and lower-middle-income countries.[35] While one of the primary rationales for privatization was to foster economic growth, many countries have faced harsh economic recession and increased inequality in the aftermath of the reforms. In the infrastructure sector (especially telecommunications), some studies indicate efficiency gains from privatization.[36] However, the findings may be unrepresentative as there is a consistent pattern in both developed and developing countries of privatizing the most-profitable and easiest to sell state monopolies first: telecommunications then electricity and then, if ever, water and sewage.[37] This has the effect of leaving the state in control of the least profitable ones, which in turn is likely to bias the results of SOE/private comparisons.[38]

The evidence is also not robust on whether these privatizations help promote good governance and "abate corruption by eliminating rent-seeking opportunities."[39]

[29] See, e.g., Monica Arruda de Almeida and Bruce Zagaris, "Political Capture in the Petrobras Corruption Scandal: The Sad Tale of an Oil Giant," *Fletcher Forum of World Affairs* 39 (2015): 87–99.
[30] Shleifer, "State versus Private Ownership," at p. 142, citation omitted.
[31] Shleifer and Vishny, "Politicians and Firms," at pp. 995–997.
[32] János Kornai, "The Soft Budget Constraint," *Kyklos* 39 (1986): 3–30.
[33] Shleifer, "State versus Private Ownership," at p. 133.
[34] Sunita Kikeri and John Nellis, "An Assessment of Privatization," *World Bank Research Observer* 19 (2004): 87–118.
[35] Megginson and Netter, "From State to Market"; Ahmed Galal et al., "Welfare Consequences of Selling Public Enterprises: An Empirical Analysis" (World Bank, June 30, 1994), pp. 22–23; Clifford Zinnes, Yair Eilat, and Jeffrey Sachs, "The Gains from Privatization in Transition Economies: Is 'Change of Ownership' Enough?," *IMF Staff Papers* 48 (2001): 146–170; Kjetil Bjorvatn and Tina Søreide, "Corruption and Privatization," *European Journal of Political Economy* 21 (2005): 903–914; Estrin and Pelletier, "Privatization in Developing Countries."
[36] Agustin J. Ros, "Does Ownership or Competition Matter? The Effects of Telecommunications Reform on Network Expansion and Efficiency," *Journal of Regulatory Economics* 15 (1999): 65–92; Scott J. Wallsten, "An Econometric Analysis of Telecom Competition, Privatization, and Regulation in Africa and Latin America," *Journal of Industrial Economics* 49 (2001): 1–19; Bernardo Bortolotti et al., "Privatization and the Sources of Performance Improvement in the Global Telecommunications Industry," *Telecommunications Policy, Corporate Control and Industry Structure in Global Communications* 26 (2002): 243–268.
[37] Emmanuelle Auriol and Stéphane Straub, "Privatization of Rent-Generating Industries and Corruption," in *International Handbook on the Economics of Corruption*, vol. 2, eds. Susan Rose-Ackerman and Tina Søreide (Edward Elgar, 2011), p. 226; see, more generally, Bernardo Bortolotti and Domenico Siniscalco, *The Challenges of Privatization: An International Analysis* (Oxford University Press, 2004).
[38] Estrin and Pelletier, "Privatization in Developing Countries," at pp. 74–76.
[39] Bernhard Reinsberg et al., "Bad Governance: How Privatization Increases Corruption in the Developing World," *Regulation & Governance* (2019), https://doi.org/10.1111/rego.12265, p. 2.

Privatization is thought to accomplish these goals by eliminating or mitigating the effects of patronage networks as well as political interference and inefficiencies in the operation of SOEs. However, the decision to privatize may be tainted by corrupt motives. For instance, asymmetries of information may allow corrupt officials to misrepresent the performance of SOEs to the public, selling them for a reduced price and pocketing the difference.[40] Nobel Prize winner Joseph Stiglitz, reflecting on a number of failed privatization experiences, states: "Perhaps the most serious concern with privatization, as it has so often been practiced, is corruption. . . . Not surprisingly the rigged privatization process was designed to maximize the amount government ministers could appropriate for themselves[,] not the amount that would accrue to the government's treasury let alone the overall efficiency of the economy."[41]

Examples of corrupt privatizations abound. While in some cases interest groups (civil servants in state bureaucracies and SOE employees) simply halted the privatization process to continue benefiting from the status quo,[42] in others they conceived of privatization as a new opportunity for rent-seeking. This problem has manifested itself in a number of privatizations in Latin America.[43] For instance, in Argentina and Brazil, Presidents Menem and Collor were directly involved in corruption scandals related to the transfer of state assets to private hands.[44] Similar problems have been reported in other countries transitioning to market economies, such as former members of the Soviet Union, as well as Central and Eastern European countries.[45]

The economic consequences of corruption have been well mapped in the literature: it negatively affects the costs of doing business, ability to attract investments, and economic growth.[46] While there is no direct empirical evidence of the level of corruption in privatizations, or the impact of corruption in privatized sectors,[47] indirect measures suggest that corrupt privatizations are likely to undermine the potential benefits of the sale of SOEs, that is, increasing efficiency, attracting investments, and promoting development.[48] In addition, the privatization of SOEs may reduce a country's capacity to combat corruption in the long run. Using panel data for 141 countries over a period of 32 years (1982–2014), Reinberg et al. argue that privatization creates opportunities for insiders to obtain favourable treatment in the bidding process in exchange for bribes to those with decision-making authority. Those involved in these corrupt deals have incentives to weaken accountability institutions that are likely to uncover and punish wrongdoing, creating a vicious circle.[49]

---

[40]   Rose-Ackerman and Palifka, *Corruption and Government*, p. 35.
[41]   Joseph E. Stiglitz, *Globalization and Its Discontents* (W.W. Norton, 2003), p. 58.
[42]   Kaufmann and Siegelbaum, "Privatization and Corruption," at p. 429 (discussing the case of Cameroon).
[43]   Luigi Manzetti and Charles H. Blake, "Market Reforms and Corruption in Latin America: New Means for Old Ways," *Review of International Political Economy* 3 (1996): 662–697; Judith A. Teichman, *The Politics of Freeing Markets in Latin America: Chile, Argentina, and Mexico* (University of North Carolina Press, 2001).
[44]   Luigi Manzetti, *Privatization South American Style* (Oxford University Press, 1999).
[45]   Patrick Hamm, Lawrence P. King, and David Stuckler, "Mass Privatization, State Capacity, and Economic Growth in Post-Communist Countries," *American Sociological Review* 77 (2012): 295–324.
[46]   Paolo Mauro, "Corruption and Growth," *Quarterly Journal of Economics* 110 (1995): 681–712; Cheryl W. Gray and Daniel Kaufmann, "Corruption and Development," *Finance and Development* 35 (1998): 7–10.
[47]   There is an extensive literature dealing with effects of privatization on economic efficiency, which often include metrics of corruption in one form or another. They acknowledge that corruption is, almost by definition, next to impossible to accurately measure. For this and other reasons, empirical assessments of corruption tend to rely on perceived corruption, generally derived from surveys of the public or businesses, as well as expert assessments.
[48]   Charles Kenny, "Is There an Anticorruption Agenda in Utilities?," *Utilities Policy* 17 (2009): 156–165.
[49]   Reinsberg et al., "Bad Governance," at p. 2.

By the early 2000s, the long list of failed privatizations, and the recurring corruption scandals in these processes, challenged the neoliberal policy consensus that private ownership is a superior policy option.[50] Privatization processes came under close scrutiny and these analyses revealed that only countries with robust institutional frameworks (i.e. strong systems of accountability as well as robust mechanisms of checks and balances) had the pre-existing conditions to benefit from privatization processes.[51] While most OECD countries have these conditions, developing countries often did not have the institutional apparatus to prevent wrongdoing, and were less able to benefit from privatization. This included countries with weak institutional frameworks, such as Argentina, India, and Mexico, and was especially true for former Soviet countries transitioning from centralized to market economies.[52]

The neoliberal consensus around privatization has been now replaced in international development circles with a consensus around "good governance" that includes promoting rule of law to foster development.[53] Along with this process, infrastructure sectors have seen a surge of public–private partnerships (PPPs).[54] Over the past two decades, developing country governments have increasingly turned to PPPs to build and operate infrastructure.[55] They have gained prominence on the development agenda by offering a compromise between the two solutions previously proposed.[56] On the one hand, SOEs may provide social and political benefits to a country, but these may come at significant economic and fiscal costs because of operational inefficiencies. On the other hand, private companies may be able to deliver essential and basic services, such as electricity or telecommunications, but there are significant challenges in ensuring that these companies will provide universal service and foster other social and political goals. Reducing the inefficiencies of state-owned companies can provide infrastructure for other economic activities, thus fostering economic growth. However, this goal cannot be decoupled from alleviating poverty and providing universal access to essential services. This is especially true in developing countries.[57] In trying to accomplish these competing goals, PPPs have faced challenges, as I will discuss in Section 15.5.

Outside infrastructure sectors, the number of SOEs has grown. Since the economic crisis of 2008, the global economy has seen an increase in the number of multinational companies (MNCs) controlled by governments, as well as the rise of new forms of interaction with private investors, where the government is either a majority or a minority shareholder in

[50] Kikeri and Nellis, "An Assessment of Privatization"; Dani Rodrik, "Goodbye Washington Consensus, Hello Washington Confusion? A Review of the World Bank's 'Economic Growth in the 1990s: Learning from a Decade of Reform,'" *Journal of Economic Literature* 44 (2006): 973–987.

[51] See *supra* note 35 and accompanying text.

[52] Michelle Celarier, "Privatization: A Case Study in Corruption," *Journal of International Affairs* 50 (1997): 531–543; Kaufmann and Siegelbaum, "Privatization and Corruption."

[53] For an overview of the literature, see Trebilcock and Prado, *Advanced Introduction*, chs. 3 and 4; see also David M. Trubek and Alvaro Santos, eds., *The New Law and Economic Development: A Critical Appraisal* (Cambridge University Press, 2006).

[54] OECD, *Public-Private Partnerships: In Pursuit of Risk Sharing and Value for Money* (OECD Publishing, 2008).

[55] Roberto de Michele, Joan Prats, and Isaías Losada Revol, "Effects of Corruption on Public-Private Partnership Contracts: Consequences of a Zero Tolerance Approach," Discussion Paper (Inter-American Development Bank, 2018).

[56] Trebilcock and Prado, *Advanced Introduction*, ch. 11.

[57] Michael Trebilcock and Michael Rosenstock, "Infrastructure Public–Private Partnerships in the Developing World: Lessons from Recent Experience," *Journal of Development Studies* 51 (2015): 335–354.

publicly traded corporations.[58] In some cases, policymakers have recommended trading SOE shares on public stock markets as an alternative to full privatization (known as partial privatization) or as a step in that direction.[59] Widely traded stocks introduce stock prices (and changes thereto) as a benchmark of an SOE's performance, and are expected to create a private constituency with a direct stake in SOE efficiency. In some cases, governments have sold a minority interest to a single commercial partner who has a direct stake in enhanced SOE performance. While some fear that the rise of SOEs is a return to the problems of inefficiency and rent-seeking that prompted the call for privatization in the late 1970s,[60] others argue that these companies are operating under more constrained and disciplining conditions.[61] While some of these constraints are imposed through internal governance structures, others are external, that is, they are dependent on the broader institutional framework in which these SOEs are operating (e.g. an effective securities regulator or legislator).[62] Interestingly, the robust institutional frameworks that can prevent wrongdoing during privatization processes are generally the same that are capable of mitigating the risk of rent-seeking and preventing inefficiencies in the SOEs.[63] In fact, SOEs with publicly traded shares can still be involved in corruption, as recently illustrated by the scandal involving the Brazilian state-owned oil company Petrobras.[64]

In summary, privatization has been touted as a solution to corruption, but in many cases it became an opportunity for bribes, embezzlement, and rent-seeking. This has shaken the neoliberal consensus that prevailed in international policy circles in the 1980s and 1990s, but it also generated the false assumption that privatization and corruption are inherently linked. Further investigations revealed that countries with robust institutional frameworks were better able to prevent corruption in privatization processes. The lack of a robust system of accountability and checks and balances explains the failures (and corruption scandals) often observed in privatizations in developing countries and transitional economies.[65] While the existence of a strong institutional framework may preserve the integrity of the decision to privatize, this alone does not provide an explanation for all privatization failures. Even assuming a noncorrupt motive, at least two other conditions need to be present for positive

---

[58] Joshua Kurlantzick, *State Capitalism: How the Return of Statism Is Transforming the World* (Oxford University Press, 2016); see also Aldo Musacchio and Sérgio G. Lazzarini, *Reinventing State Capitalism: Leviathan in Business, Brazil and Beyond* (Harvard University Press, 2014); Chen Ding, *Corporate Governance, Enforcement and Financial Development: The Chinese Experience* (Edward Elgar, 2013); Curtis J. Milhaupt and Benjamin L. Liebman, eds., *Regulating the Visible Hand? The Institutional Implications of Chinese State Capitalism* (Oxford University Press, 2016); OECD, *Privatisation and the Broadening of Ownership of State-Owned Enterprises* (OECD Publishing, 2018).

[59] Curtis J. Milhaupt and Mariana Pargendler, "Governance Challenges of Listed State-Owned Enterprises around the World: National Experiences and a Framework for Reform," *Cornell International Law Journal* 50 (2017): 473–542; World Bank, "Corporate Governance of State-Owned Enterprises: A Tool Kit" (World Bank, 2014); OECD, *A Policy Maker's Guide to Privatisation* (OECD Publishing, 2019).

[60] William L. Megginson, "Privatization, State Capitalism, and State Ownership of Business in the 21st Century," *Foundations and Trends in Finance* 11 (2017): 1–153.

[61] Aldo Musacchio and Francisco Flores-Macias, "The Return of State-Owned Enterprises: Should We Be Afraid?," *Harvard International Review*, April 4, 2009, www.hbs.edu/faculty/Pages/item.aspx?num=36235.

[62] Milhaupt and Pargendler, "Governance Challenges of Listed State-Owned Enterprises"; OECD, *OECD Guidelines on Corporate Governance of State-Owned Enterprises* (OECD Publishing, 2015).

[63] Aldo Musacchio, Sergio G. Lazzarini, and Ruth V. Aguilera, "New Varieties of State Capitalism: Strategic and Governance Implications," *Academy of Management Perspectives* 29 (2015): 115–131. See also Charles Kenny, "Infrastructure Governance and Corruption: Where Next?," Policy Research Working Paper No. 4331 (World Bank, 2007).

[64] Almeida and Zagaris, "Political Capture in the Petrobras Corruption Scandal."

[65] Estrin and Pelletier, "Privatization in Developing Countries," at p. 92.

outcomes: an appropriate process and adequate regulatory infrastructure.[66] I will explore these in Sections 15.4 and 15.5.

15.4 THE PRIVATIZATION PROCESS: COMPLEX TRADE-OFFS

The decision as to whether to privatize is often complex and frequently multifaceted.[67] It may be motivated by an evidence-based assessment of circumstances suggesting it as the most viable option for achieving a relatively well-specified set of generally agreed-upon goals. It may also be ideologically motivated insofar as it is seen as "the inevitable consequence of neoclassical truths that dictate the retraction of a bulky, intrusive, and parasitic welfare state."[68] From a more overtly "political" perspective, it may also be undertaken tactically, as a means of achieving short-term goals such as re-election, or raising revenue in a fiscal crisis. It can also be strategic, as part of a longer-term plan to fundamentally restructure citizens' expectations of government vis-à-vis the provision of goods and services, reducing public sector oversight of the economy, and altering the balance of power among interest groups. Some combination of these motivations may also be at work in a given case. It should also be recognized that many countries – particularly developing countries – have had little choice as to whether they ought to privatize SOEs, being compelled to do so by international financial institutions such as the World Bank and the International Monetary Fund.[69]

Even when privatization is not a free choice, there are still options regarding what, when, and how to privatize, which may create different corruption opportunities. As Chong and Lopez-de-Silanes argue, "the design of the privatization process, the contracts ultimately written, the restrictions attached to the sale of state-owned enterprises, and the restructuring measures adopted before privatization should be understood as opportunities for politicians to extract rents and hand out favors."[70] Along the same lines, Shleifer notes that "the process of privatization is itself susceptible to corruption. In exchange for campaign contributions or bribes, politicians may award contracts or sell whole firms to inefficient providers, overpay these providers, fail to make them accountable for quality, and even fail to enforce those contracts."[71] In other words, regardless of what is driving privatization in a particular case, there is a risk that corruption may infiltrate the process.

The privatization in the former Soviet Union offers an illustrative example of this problem. As Kaufmann and Spiegelman argue, "there was no considered decision to privatize by democratically weighing the pluses and minuses and carefully formulating an efficient strategy. The decision was thrust upon these new countries' leaders by the breakdown of the discipline of the old system and the absence of new institutions to replace it."[72] The lack of

---

[66] Ibid.; David Martimort and Stéphane Straub, "Infrastructure Privatization and Changes in Corruption Patterns: The Roots of Public Discontent," *Journal of Development Economics* 90 (2009): 69–84, pp. 69–70.

[67] See, generally, Feigenbaum and Henig, "The Political Underpinnings of Privatization."

[68] Harvey B. Feigenbaum, Jeffrey R. Henig, and Chris Hamnett, *Shrinking the State: The Political Underpinnings of Privatization* (Cambridge University Press, 1999), p. 38.

[69] E.g., Mahmud I. Imam, Tooraj Jamasb, and Manuel Llorca, "Sector Reforms and Institutional Corruption: Evidence from Electricity Industry in Sub-Saharan Africa," *Energy Policy* 129 (2019): 532–545, pp. 532–533; Reinsberg et al., "Bad Governance."

[70] Alberto Chong and Florencio Lopez-de-Silanes, eds., *Privatization in Latin America: Myths and Reality*, Latin American Development Forum Series (Stanford Economics and Finance; World Bank, 2005), p. 51.

[71] Shleifer, "State versus Private Ownership," at p. 143.

[72] Kaufmann and Siegelbaum, "Privatization and Corruption," at p. 424.

robust institutional frameworks to contain wrongdoing in this context led to significant problems.[73] The process was characterized by rigged bids and massive self-dealing by controlling shareholders and managers.[74] While the corrupt nature of the process did not come as a surprise to many, there were hopes that the privatization would generate demand for protection of property rights and rule of law; but such demand never materialized.[75] On the contrary, the new controlling shareholders used their wealth to prevent reforms that would curtail wrongdoing and self-dealing, further entrenching corruption in the country.[76]

There are at least three factors that may affect the risk of corruption during the privatization process: the existence of an institutional framework to insulate the process from corrupt officials; the speed with which SOEs are transferred to private hands; and the methods of privatization. Based on the idea that those best-placed to corrupt a privatization process ought not be in charge of it, a number of countries have tried to secure an independent administration of the privatization process, creating specialized agencies that were temporarily constituted to oversee the sale of SOEs. Some, but not all, appear to have been successful.[77]

A second variable that contributes to the risk of corruption is the speed with which privatization takes place. Economists argue that fast privatization processes present fewer opportunities for backend deals, since these take time to be negotiated and structured.[78] However, it also takes time to set up an independent agency to manage the privatization process.[79] Therefore, countries may be confronted with the choice of having an expeditious process without independent management, or the other way around. In addition, other considerations may come into play in determining the speed at which a country should move away from an economy dominated by SOEs. "Gradualists" caution that rapid liberalization will be impractical to implement because privatization requires a broad social consensus, and generating such consensus is a long-term process.[80] Gradualists tend to favour gradual privatization and nurturing of the institutional infrastructure of a market economy, including competition, entrepreneurship, regulation of financial markets, social capital, and a strong legal system.[81] China is often cited as a successful example of this strategy.[82] In contrast, rapid reform advocates ("shock therapists") argue that economic reforms create

---

[73] Thomas Weisskopf, "Russia In Transition: Perils of the Fast Track to Capitalism," *Challenge* 35 (1992): 28–37; see also Stephen Kotkin and András Sajó, eds., *Political Corruption in Transition: A Skeptic's Handbook* (Central European University Press, 2002).

[74] Bernard Black, Reinier Kraakman, and Anna Tarassova, "Russian Privatization and Corporate Governance: What Went Wrong," *Stanford Law Review* 52 (1999): 1731–1808.

[75] Karla Hoff and Joseph E Stiglitz, "The Creation of the Rule of Law and the Legitimacy of Property Rights: The Political and Economic Consequences of a Corrupt Privatization," Working Paper (NBER, November 2005).

[76] Black, Kraakman, and Tarassova, "Russian Privatization and Corporate Governance: What Went Wrong"; see also Mark Levin and Georgy Satarov, "Corruption and Institutions in Russia," *European Journal of Political Economy* 16 (2000): 113–132.

[77] Kaufmann and Siegelbaum, "Privatization and Corruption" (citing the GKI in Russia, the Privatization Agency in Estonia, the Hungarian Privatization and State Holding Company, and the Treuhand in Germany); see also Josef C. Brada, "Privatization Is Transition – Or Is It?," *Journal of Economic Perspectives* 10 (1996): 72ff.

[78] Kaufmann and Siegelbaum, "Privatization and Corruption," at pp. 430–431.

[79] Alberto Chong and Florencio Lopez-de-Silanes, "The Truth About Privatization in Latin America," in *Privatization in Latin America: Myths and Reality*, ed. Alberto Chong and Florencio Lopez-de-Silanes, Latin American Development Forum Series (Stanford Economics and Finance; World Bank, 2005), 51ff.

[80] E.g., Joseph E. Stiglitz, "The Insider," *The New Republic*, April 17, 2000, https://newrepublic.com/article/61082/the-insider; Joseph Stiglitz, "Whither Reform? Ten Years of the Transition," *Voporsy Economiki* 7 (1999); Stiglitz, *Globalization and Its Discontents*; Kenneth Arrow, "Economic Transition: Speed and Scope," *Journal of Institutional and Theoretical Economics* 156 (2000): 9–18, p. 9.

[81] Stiglitz, "Wither Reform?."

[82] Joseph E. Stiglitz, "Transition to a Market Economy," in *The Oxford Companion to the Economics of China*, ed. Xiaobo Zhang et al. (Oxford University Press, 2014), pp. 36–41.

pressure for political and legal reforms that in turn lead to the establishment of market institutions. Poland, Kyrgyzstan, the Czech Republic, and the Baltic states, as radical liberalizers, they argue, have grown faster than "go-slow" countries such as Belarus and Ukraine because of their expediency.[83] Interestingly, Russia's economic decline in the period following the break-up of the Soviet Union is cited by both sides to prove their point: gradualists argue that the Russian experience proves that shock therapy was seriously misconceived; shock therapists contend that Russia was a go-slow reformer.[84]

A third factor to consider is how to privatize, that is, the method of privatization.[85] Building on Josef C. Brada's widely cited taxonomy,[86] it is possible to identify seven different types of privatization:[87]

(1) Restitution: returning land or other property that was expropriated by the state to the original owners or their heirs.

(2) Voucher or mass privatization: distributing vouchers for free, or at a nominal cost, that enable eligible citizens to bid for shares of SOEs or other assets that are being privatized.

(3) Management and employees buy-outs (MEBOs): transferring the rights of ownership of industrial or commercial facilities to those who are employed in them (employees and/or managers).

(4) Direct sale of state property: directly selling an SOE, or one of its component parts, to an individual, a corporation, or a group of investors.

(5) Share issue privatization (SIP): selling some or all of the government's holding in an SOE through a public share offering.

(6) Partial privatization: making a partial public offering (if the stock is publicly traded) or selling a minority interest to a single commercial partner or joint venture partner.

(7) Concession contracts: signing an agreement to transfer to the private operator the responsibility for managing the services and all necessary investment for the length of the concession (e.g. twenty years or more). Ownership of assets can remain public or be transferred back to the state when the agreement comes to an end.

Restitution, voucher-based mass privatization, and MEBOs were common in the former Soviet Union and Central and Eastern Europe.[88] Along with Organisation for Economic Co-operation and Development (OECD) countries, other transition economies and Latin America nations also used direct sale of assets or shares to strategic investors and via public share offerings.[89] In Latin America, where there has been large-scale infrastructure privatization, countries have also resorted to liquidation of SOEs, concession contracts and partial

---

[83] Andrei Shleifer and Robert Vishny, *The Grabbing Hand: Government Pathologies and Their Cures* (Harvard University Press, 1998), ch. 11.

[84] Stiglitz, "Wither Reform?"; John Nellis, "Time to Rethink Privatization in Transition Economies?" (World Bank, May 31, 1999).

[85] The literature on methods of privatization ranges significantly in focus, from largely descriptive, typology-oriented accounts to theory-oriented, prescriptive approaches, to empirical assessments of the subsequent productivity of privatized SOEs. It is beyond the scope of this chapter to provide an overview of this vast literature. Instead, the chapter will focus on how different methods of privatization present different opportunities for corruption.

[86] Brada, "Privatization Is Transition?."

[87] For a more detailed discussion, see Michael J. Trebilcock and Mariana Mota Prado, *What Makes Poor Countries Poor? Institutional Determinants of Development* (Edward Elgar, 2011), p. 208ff.

[88] Brada, "Privatization Is Transition?," p. 72ff; Kaufmann and Siegelbaum, "Privatization and Corruption."

[89] Megginson and Netter, "From State to Market."

privatizations.[90] In Asia, partial privatizations and direct strategic sales tend to be employed.[91] African countries, given the number of jurisdictions and the length of time in question, appear to have made use of all of the methods noted here.[92]

The risk of corruption is not solely determined by privatization methods; it also depends on other circumstances, such as the robustness of the institutional framework and the strength of the accountability network in a particular country. Yet, it is possible to identify features in each method of privatization that are generally associated with higher risk of corruption. For instance, methods that give public officials a high level of discretion but provide little in the way of transparency, such as MEBOs, create significant opportunities for rent seeking.[93] They have been advocated as a way to draw upon a substantial pool of "privatization demand" from the very people who work in the enterprise.[94] However, the method is vulnerable to corruption as SOE managers, given their information advantages and political influence, may be able to purchase their SOEs for less than fair market value.[95] While some methods are generally perceived to be more transparent than others, the details of institutional design also influence the risk of corruption. For example, the sale of controlling shares to strategic investors is considered less discretionary and more transparent than MEBOs. It was success-fully used in Chile and the UK with public tenders attracting foreign investors, but its Russian version ("loan for shares") ended up being a self-dealing scheme that largely benefited insiders, mostly bankers.[96]

In addition to the risk of corruption, different privatization methods offer other advantages and disadvantages: some are effective in attracting foreign investment (e.g. direct sales to strategic investors), while others are stronger in building political support for the process (e.g. MEBOs). There are, therefore, complex trade-offs in the choice of each of these methods. In some countries, combating or preventing corruption may be less of a priority than other pressing goals (e.g. raising revenues). In such cases, decision-makers may be tempted to adopt the method that most effectively addresses immediate priorities, even if the chosen method may involve a higher risk of corruption. These complex trade-offs illustrate that there may be decisions that, despite being driven by public interest and with the goal of increasing social welfare, are not the ones that are most likely to reduce the risk of corruption. Finding a privatization method that can satisfy the multifaceted goals of privatization, attend to often conflicting economic, political and social demands, and still reduce the risk of corruption is a tall order.

15.5 PRIVATIZED STRUCTURES AS CORRUPTION OPPORTUNITIES

The end of the privatization process does not mean the end of the risk of corruption. The complex interactions between the public and private sectors in the aftermath of privatization

[90] Chong and Lopez-de-Silanes, *Privatization in Latin America: Myths and Reality*; W. Rand Smith, "Privatization in Latin America: How Did It Work and What Difference Did It Make?," *Latin American Politics and Society* 44 (2002): 153–166.

[91] Estrin and Pelletier, "Privatization in Developing Countries"; Ding, *Corporate Governance: The Chinese Experience.*

[92] Ibid.; John R. Nellis, "Privatization in Africa: What Has Happened? What Is to Be Done?," Working Paper (Fondazione Eni Enrico Mattei, 2005), p. 21 (table 5).

[93] Kaufmann and Siegelbaum, "Privatization and Corruption."

[94] Harald Sondhof and Markus Stahl, "Management Buy-Outs as an Instrument of Privatization in Eastern Europe," *Intereconomics* 27 (1992): 210–214, pp. 210–211.

[95] Kaufmann and Siegelbaum, "Privatization and Corruption"; Brada, "Privatization Is Transition?," at p. 72ff.

[96] Kaufmann and Siegelbaum, "Privatization and Corruption."

also create opportunities for rent-seeking. Corrupt politicians may actively use regulation to extract rents from privatized firms.[97] Even assuming a noncorrupt privatization process and a regulatory framework that has enhanced efficiency and attracted investments, corruption may not be necessarily reduced. In some cases, the aftermath of privatization seems to have created even more opportunities for wrongdoing.[98] This section provides an overview of three instances in which this problem materialized: regulation, concession contracts, and public–private partnerships.

Regulation is one way in which the public officials continue to interact with private companies after the sale of SOEs. This is especially true in infrastructure sectors, where there are complex sectoral regulations. Electricity, water, telecommunications, and roads are essential services and natural monopolies, which demand some form of discipline. The importance of these regulatory frameworks cannot be overstated: the absence of effective regulation has been a major cause of mediocre post-privatization performance in lower-income developing countries.[99] Along with the recommendation to adopt robust regulations, creating specialized regulatory agencies became a recipe for legal reform during privatization processes.[100] The result was a global diffusion of these agencies:[101] by 2018, there was a total of 799 agencies in 115 countries, spread around 17 policy sectors.[102] They are prominent in infrastructure sectors, but can be found dealing with a variety of other matters such as sanitation, product safety, and consumer protection.

Regulatory agencies can be subject to corruption at all levels of their hierarchical structures.[103] At higher levels, corruption may affect rule-making and adjudication processes. In such cases, corruption will include board members, chairpersons, and other officials occupying high-level positions.[104] Corruption may also impact the administration of regulatory processes (e.g. permits) or oversight and compliance procedures and involve low-level

---

[97] Shleifer and Vishny, "Politicians and Firms," at p. 1007 ("The result with politician control might shed light on the large amount of corruption in countries like Italy or the Philippines, where firms are privately owned and then pay enormous bribes to politicians who control them through regulation.").

[98] Martimort and Straub, "Infrastructure Privatization," at p. 69.

[99] Narjess Boubakri and Jean-Claude Cosset, "The Financial and Operating Performance of Newly Privatized Firms: Evidence from Developing Countries," *Journal of Finance* 53 (1998): 1081–1110; Colin Kirkpatrick, David Parker, and Yin-Fang Zhang, "An Empirical Analysis of State and Private-Sector Provision of Water Services in Africa," *World Bank Economic Review* 20 (2006): 143–163; Luis A. Andrés, José Luis Guasch, and Stephane Straub, "Does Regulation and Institutional Design Matter for Infrastructure Sector Performance?," in *Corruption, Development and Institutional Design*, ed. János Kornai, László Mátyás, and Gérard Roland (Palgrave Macmillan, 2009), pp. 203–234.

[100] Susan Rose-Ackerman, "The Regulatory State," in *The Oxford Handbook of Comparative Constitutional Law*, ed. Michel Rosenfeld et al. (Oxford University Press, 2012), pp. 670–686.

[101] Jacint Jordana and David Levi-Faur, "The Diffusion of Regulatory Capitalism in Latin America: Sectoral and National Channels in the Making of a New Order," *ANNALS of the American Academy of Political and Social Science* 598 (2005): 102–124.

[102] Jacint Jordana, Xavier Fernández-i-Marín, and Andrea C. Bianculli, "Agency Proliferation and the Globalization of the Regulatory State: Introducing a Data Set on the Institutional Features of Regulatory Agencies," *Regulation & Governance* 12 (2018): 524–540.

[103] Independent Broad-Based Anti-Corruption Commission, "Corruption Risks Associated with Public Regulatory Authorities" (State of Victoria, July 2018), www.ibac.vic.gov.au/docs/default-source/intelligence-reports/corruption-risks-associated-with-public-regulatory-authorities.pdf.

[104] At this level, there is also the risk of regulatory capture, which is explored by an extensive literature, but it is beyond the scope of this chapter. For a careful discussion of the fine line that sometimes divides regulatory capture from regulatory corruption, as well as the instruments and strategies to combat both, see: Antonio Estache and Liam Wren-Lewis, "Anti-Corruption Policy in Theories of Sector Regulation," in *International Handbook on the Economics of Corruption*, eds. Susan Rose-Ackerman and Tina Søreide, vol. 2 (Edward Elgar, 2011); Jean-Bernard Auby, Emmanuel Breen, and Thomas Perroud, eds., *Corruption and Conflicts of Interest: A Comparative Law Approach* (Edward Elgar, 2014).

bureaucrats such as managers, inspectors, and compliance personnel.[105] Regulatory corruption can involve large sums of money (grand corruption) as well as small payments to bureaucrats in exchange for the (non)performance of their duties (petty corruption).

The causes of such corruption are manifold.[106] In some cases, there is direct political control of regulators by corrupt politicians, who use the regulatory agency to extract rents. Liberia under President Samuel Doe is one example.[107] In other cases, the industry may use its connections with corrupt politicians to influence the regulator.[108] For instance, local politicians in Brazil seem to influence bureaucratic discretion, as evidenced by the approval of a higher number of environmental licenses in the years in which there are municipal elections.[109] Independent regulatory agencies (IRAs) have been touted as a solution to this problem, since they insulate regulators from politics. In addition to corruption, IRAs tend to be seen as effective mechanisms for addressing other forms of undesirable governmental interference in regulated sectors and for creating stability for investors.[110] However, there is no robust evidence to indicate that these IRAs have contributed to reducing corruption.[111] If one defines corruption broadly, IRAs seem vulnerable to undue influence by special interest groups and asymmetries of information between themselves and the regulated industry.[112]

Measuring the impact of regulatory corruption is methodologically troublesome.[113] Some economic models hypothesize that, under certain circumstances, corruption may not undermine efficiency, although there is no direct evidence to support this.[114] Studies focusing on perceptions of corruption tend to find that privatized firms operating in countries with high levels of corruption are less efficient and have higher prices and lower quality than their counterparts in countries with lower levels of corruption.[115] One possible conclusion is that privatization does not reduce corruption, but simply alters who bears its burden. When ownership is public, taxpayers bear the brunt of the costs. When ownership is private, it is mostly consumers.[116]

[105] Saad Al-Mutairi, Ian Connerton, and Robert Dingwall, "Understanding 'Corruption' in Regulatory Agencies: The Case of Food Inspection in Saudi Arabia," *Regulation & Governance* 13 (2019): 507–519.

[106] Frédéric Boehm, "Anti-Corruption in Regulation – A Safeguard for Infrastructure Reforms," *Competition and Regulation in Network Industries* 10 (2009): 45–75; Frédéric Boehm, "Is There an Anti-Corruption Agenda in Regulation? Insights from the Colombian and Zambian Water Sectors," in *International Handbook on the Economics of Corruption*, eds. Susan Rose-Ackerman and Tina Søreide, vol. 2 (Edward Elgar, 2011), pp. 207–230.

[107] Estache and Wren-Lewis, "Anti-Corruption Policy," at pp. 269–270.

[108] Ibid., at p. 276.

[109] Claudio Ferraz, "Electoral Politics and Bureaucratic Discretion: Evidence from Environmental Licenses and Local Elections in Brazil," Working Paper (January 2007) (on file with author).

[110] Giandomenico Majone, "The Rise of the Regulatory State in Europe," *West European Politics* 17 (1994): 77–101; Mariana Mota Prado, "Bureaucratic Resistance to Regulatory Reforms: Contrasting Experiences in Electricity and Telecommunications in Brazil," in *The Rise of the Regulatory State of the South: Infrastructure and Development in Emerging Economies*, eds. Navroz K. Dubash and Bronwen Morgan (Oxford University Press, 2013).

[111] Saul Estrin et al., "The Effects of Privatization and Ownership in Transition Economies," *Journal of Economic Literature* 47 (2009): 699–728.

[112] Estache and Wren-Lewis, "Anti-Corruption Policy," at pp. 269–270; for a detailed discussion of information asymmetries, see Martimort and Straub, "Infrastructure Privatization," pp. 69–70.

[113] Kenny, "Is There an Anticorruption Agenda in Utilities?."

[114] Martimort and Straub, "Infrastructure Privatization," at pp. 69–70.

[115] Ernesto Dal Bo and Martin A. Rossi, "Corruption and Inefficiency: Theory and Evidence from Electric Utilities," *Journal of Public Economics* 91 (2007): 939–962; Antonio Estache and Lourdes Trujillo, "Corruption and Infrastructure Services: An Overview," *Utilities Policy* 17 (2009): 153–155; Liam Wren-Lewis, "Do Infrastructure Reforms Reduce the Effect of Corruption? Theory and Evidence from Latin America and the Caribbean," Policy Research Working Paper Series (World Bank, August 1, 2013).

[116] Martimort and Straub, "Infrastructure Privatization," at p. 69.

Does competition reduce corruption? In competitive sectors, consumer demand should discipline firms, responding to higher prices with reduced consumption and/or migration to competitors.[117] This, in turn, should lead to a decline in revenues for the corrupt entity as consumers migrate to other providers. Therefore, it is possible to reduce corruption by introducing competition in some sectors.[118] Indeed, some successful cases of privatization are associated with regulatory reforms that introduced competition. In the case of electricity generation, researchers found that competition increased service penetration, capacity expansion, and labour productivity. At the same time, the effect of privatization alone was statistically insignificant except for capacity utilization.[119] The challenge is that countries with high levels of corruption have high market concentration, and it is not clear whether such concentration is caused by corruption or is a consequence of it.[120]

Another form of post-privatization corruption is associated with renegotiation of contracts, especially concession contracts. These are often long-term contracts, where a private company becomes responsible for the asset of an SOE (e.g. a highway, a water treatment plant, or a bus route) for a period of time. The private company is entirely responsible for managing the services and all necessary investment for the length of the concession, which can be for twenty years or more. Consumers are directly charged by the private operator, while the public authorities determine service terms and all key decisions related to charges. Renegotiation often happens behind closed doors, leading to a perception that they are a way for corrupt politicians to extract rents.

Using panel data on over 300 water and transportation concession contracts in Latin America, Guash and Straub found that the likelihood of renegotiation was influenced by the level of corruption in a jurisdiction.[121] One of the most effective solutions to this problem is having a specialized regulator at the time that the contract is signed.[122] Such regulators would be able to formulate better contracts and act as a barrier against opportunistic behaviour.[123] While these regulators could reduce the incidence of renegotiations, it is not possible to affirm that they would reduce corruption in these sectors. In the presence of a regulator, it is possible that corrupt politicians would resort to other means (e.g. favouring a particular company in the selection process) in order to extract rents. In fact, countries with high levels of corruption are more likely to directly award concession contracts, rarely using bids.[124]

---

[117] These possibilities are more limited in infrastructure sectors. In some cases (e.g. water), it is hard for consumers to reduce consumption, since these are essential services. Moreover, for certain services (e.g. electricity distribution) often there is no competition, since these are natural monopolies.

[118] Cf. Christopher Bliss and Rafael Di Tella, "Does Competition Kill Corruption?," *Journal of Political Economy* 105 (1997): 1001–1023 (arguing that a corrupt official can force companies out of the market to maintain the status quo).

[119] David Parker and Colin Kirkpatrick, "Privatisation in Developing Countries: A Review of the Evidence and the Policy Lessons," *Journal of Development Studies* 41 (2005): 513–541, p. 514.

[120] Alberto Ades and Rafael Di Tella, "Rents, Competition, and Corruption," *American Economic Review* 89 (1999): 982–993.

[121] J. Luis Guash and Stéphane Straub, "Corruption and Concession Renegotiations: Evidence from the Water and Transport Sectors in Latin America," *Utilities Policy* 17 (2009): 185–190, p. 185.

[122] Ibid., at p. 186.

[123] J. Luis Guash, Jean-Jacques Laffont, and Stéphane Straub, "Renegotiation of Concession Contracts in Latin America," *International Journal of Industrial Organization* 26 (2008): 421–442; J. Luis Guash, Jean-Jacques Laffont, and Stéphane Straub, "Concessions of Infrastructure in Latin America: Government-Led Renegotiation," *Journal of Applied Econometrics* 22 (2007): 1267–1294.

[124] Guash and Straub, "Corruption and Concession Renegotiations."

The problems with concession contracts generally manifest themselves with other kinds of PPPs. While PPPs may offer a compromise between direct state intervention (SOEs) and privatization, they, too, require robust institutional capacity to achieve their objectives.[125] PPP contracts pose special problems of contractual design, monitoring, and enforcement. Typically, they involve large investments in durable, transaction-specific assets, raising a bilaterally dependent contractual relationship between the parties.[126] That is, while governments may have some choice among competing consortia *ex ante*, once they "lock into" a long-term relationship with a single consortium, there are significant risks of mutual opportunism or "hold-ups." This may give a consortium an incentive to bid low to win a contract and then exert undue leverage in subsequent contract renegotiations to secure better terms. As discussed earlier, these renegotiations can also involve corruption. Indeed, corrupt officials may make use of incomplete PPP contracts that will allow them to extract rents in the future via the (re)definition of terms.[127] Similar prevention strategies to concession contracts (specialized agencies, transparency, better-designed contracts) have been suggested to address corruption in PPPs.[128] Punishment and deterrence have also been discussed. For instance, there is controversy around the annulment of PPP contracts that involve corruption, as these can have substantial economic, social, and political costs, and may undermine a country's ability to attract future investors.[129] Alternative sanctions that do not invalidate the contract have been implemented in Colombia, Panama, and Peru in the aftermath of the revelation of bribes paid by the Brazilian construction company Odebrecht.[130]

Much of the literature on post-privatization corruption has emphasized the difficulties of implementing reforms in countries with weak institutional frameworks, echoing concerns raised in Sections 15.3 and 15.4. However, some of the documented failures in regulatory agencies, concession contracts, and PPPs were the result of legal transplants that did not account for the unique realities of developing countries.[131] More research is needed to explore institutional solutions and reform proposals that consider the unique challenges of privatization in developing countries.

15.6 CONCLUSION

In the 1980s and 1990s, transferring SOEs to the private sector was touted as a solution to reduce inefficiencies, and as a strategy to tackle corruption. The results of two decades of privatization experiences, however, are mixed. Generally, privatization has enhanced social welfare in countries with robust institutional frameworks and low levels of corruption. In countries with high levels of corruption, privatization has proven less likely to be able to address inefficiency or corruption and may even have exacerbated these problems. To

[125] Trebilcock and Rosenstock, "Infrastructure PPPs in the Developing World."

[126] Oliver E. Williamson, "The Logic of Economic Organization," *Journal of Law, Economics, & Organization* 4 (1988): 65–93, p. 71.

[127] Elisabetta Iossa and David Martimort, "Corruption in PPPs, Incentives and Contract Incompleteness," *International Journal of Industrial Organization* 44 (2016): 85–100, p. 85.

[128] Kevin E. Davis, "Civil Remedies for Corruption in Government Contracting: Zero Tolerance versus Proportional Liability," Working Paper (Institute for International Law and Justice, 2009), www.iilj.org/publica tions/civil-remedies-for-corruption-in-government-contracting-zero-tolerance-versus-proportional-liability/.

[129] Ibid.

[130] de Michele, Prats, and Revol, "Effects of Corruption on PPPs."

[131] Mariana Mota Prado, "Diffusion, Reception, and Transplantation," in *The Oxford Handbook of Comparative Administrative Law*, 2nd ed., eds. Peter Cane, Herwig C. H. Hofmann, Eric C. Ip, and Peter L. Lindseth (Oxford University Press, 2020).

illustrate this, this chapter discussed the lack of a robust institutional framework in transition economies in Central and Eastern Europe and challenges encountered in the Latin American infrastructure sector.

Part of these lessons has been incorporated in policy circles, where there is now more awareness of the need to reduce the risk of corruption in privatization processes. Yet, many of these policy recommendations focus on "getting privatization right," which assumes that (i) those making most of the privatization decisions are not corrupt and that (ii) there are robust institutional mechanisms ("good governance") in place to ensure the transparency and accountability of the process.[132] Yet, in some countries, these two conditions may not be present. Moreover, reforms to promote good governance are often long term and their results are frequently uncertain. Therefore, more than guidance as to how to reduce the risks of corruption in the actual process, countries may need a comprehensive risk-assessment framework that can indicate whether the three phases of the process (the decision to privatize, the process of selling assets, and the aftermath of privatization) can be safely (and easily) insulated from corruption risks. Such comprehensive risk assessment will need to consider both national levels as well as sectoral levels of corruption, which can vary significantly. Considering that privatization is a multifaceted decision, this information should be added to the long list of considerations that will likely come into play in deciding whether to go ahead with the process and the different options (and trade-offs) on how to do so. Such a comprehensive framework could also serve as a guide to international institutions, so that they refrain from pushing developing countries to implement privatization processes without duly considering the corruption risks involved in such prescriptions.

While a comprehensive risk-assessment framework may help determine the risks involved in a particular sector and/or country, it is unlikely to be able to determine whether privatization will reduce corruption or not. Such determination would require measuring the level of corruption with no sale of assets, and comparing it with corruption associated with each stage of the privatization process. The measure of corruption, however, is an indirect and imprecise exercise. As an illegal activity, most corrupt transactions are never caught or reported. Attempts to capture the phenomenon generally rely on perceptions indexes or use concrete experiences as a proxy to estimate how rampant corruption is. While these indicators can provide useful comparators across countries, they are not fine-tuned and detailed enough to guide a complex policy decision such as this.

The lack of indicators, however, is not a reason for paralysis. The "good governance" agenda offers general guidance and principles that can inform many of the decisions in this process.[133] The trick is to acknowledge that good governance cannot be acquired overnight, and therefore privatization decisions need to take into consideration the environment in which the process will be implemented and the privatized company will be operating. As shown in this chapter, the evidence available shows that the institutional context matters for privatization. However, this has yet to be incorporated into a framework that provides guidance for policymakers.

Recently, the support for privatizations has been largely replaced by PPPs and a renewed tolerance for SOEs, which now operate as multinationals, partially disciplined by capital markets. While this new focus seems to chart a less polarized view of the public–private dichotomy, it also involves the risk of corruption. Policy circles have been resorting to the

---

[132]   See, e.g., Mathilde Menard, "Cutting the Risk of Corruption out of Privatisation," Blog: OECD On the Level (2019), https://oecdonthelevel.com/2019/03/21/cutting-the-risk-of-corruption-out-of-privatisation/.

[133]   Kenny, "Is There an Anticorruption Agenda in Utilities?."

"good governance" agenda to respond to these challenges,[134] but they provide very little guidance for countries where the larger institutional framework is dysfunctional. Also, it is not clear that this "good governance" discourse for SOEs and PPPs has incorporated one of the most important lessons learned during the privatization experiences: developing nations are unlikely to benefit from solutions designed and tested in developed countries.[135] If PPPs and disciplined SOEs are to succeed in developing nations, instead of simply becoming opportunities for rent-seeking, scholars and policymakers should account for the particular needs of these countries and design novel strategies to tackle their unique challenges.

[134] OECD, *OECD Guidelines on Corporate Governance of State-Owned Enterprises* (OECD Publishing, 2015).
[135] Milhaupt and Pargendler, "Governance Challenges of Listed State-Owned Enterprises"; Trebilcock and Rosenstock, "Infrastructure PPPs in the Developing World."

16

Privatization of Regulation: Promises and Pitfalls

Yael Kariv-Teitelbaum

16.1 INTRODUCTION

When we think about "regulation" – that is, a sustained and focused control mechanism over valuable activities, using rule setting, rule monitoring and rule enforcement – the first image that comes to mind is a public administrative agency. However, over the past three decades, private entities have gradually assumed greater and greater regulatory roles. When we send our children to schools, the quality of education as well as their safety and health are often monitored by private auditors. When they are sick and must be taken to an emergency room, the standards of treatment are in many hospitals determined by a private organization. When we buy them a toy, it is usually a product made by workers in developing countries whose labor conditions are evaluated by a nonprofit organization, and in factories whose environmental standards are defined by a private industry association. When we open a mutual fund for our children, we rely on private professional entities to verify annual reports, assess the exposure to risk and even set the accounting standards by which they report.

Hence, the past three decades have seen a new trend of private entities that are becoming central actors in various regulatory regimes, filling diverse regulatory roles. This ongoing diversification of regulation is primarily viewed by scholars of regulation as an expansion of regulation[1] that does not threaten the state's regulatory capacity but rather increases it.[2] Two decades ago, the concept of sharing public regulatory responsibility with private entities was enthusiastically promoted as a promising way to increase the effectiveness, efficiency and legitimacy of regulatory regimes.[3] However, the financial crisis of 2008 somewhat dampened

---

[1] David Levi-Faur, "The Global Diffusion of Regulatory Capitalism," ANNALS *of the American Academy of Political and Social Science* 598 (2005): 12–32.

[2] Jacint Jordana, David Levi-Faur and Xavier Fernandez Marin, "The Global Diffusion of Regulatory Agencies: Channels of Transfer and Stages of Diffusion," *Comparative Political Studies* 41 (2011): 1343–1369.

[3] Orly Lobel, "The Renew Deal: The Fall of Regulation and the Rise of Governance in Contemporary Legal Thought," *Minnesota Law Review* 89 (2004): 342–470; Martha Minow, "Public and Private Partnerships: Accounting for the New Religion," *Harvard Law Review* 116 (2003): 1229–1270; Julia Black, "Decentring Regulation: Understanding the Role of Regulation and Self-Regulation in a 'Post-Regulatory' World," *Current Legal Problems* 54 (2001): 103–146; Colin Scott, "Regulation in the Age of Governance: The Rise of the Post-Regulatory State," in *The Politics of Regulation*, eds. Jacint Jordana and David Levi-Faur (Cheltenham: Edward Elgar, 2004), pp. 145–174.

this enthusiasm and stirred various discussions over the limitations and pitfalls of assigning regulatory missions to private entities. Recent experience has underlined the need to reconceptualize this diversification of regulation as "the privatization of regulation," amidst growing concerns about failing to meet regulatory goals and a diminution in the state's regulatory capacity. Privatizing regulation indeed offers the promise of advancing public goals by private measures, but it also raises concerns about promoting private interests through public means.

Looking back at the initial rationales of privatization policy in general, one may argue that the mere idea of privatizing regulatory functions is an oxymoron.[4] The move from "rowing" to "steering"[5] was originally advanced to free the state from the burden of providing public services, thus transforming the civil service into a small and efficient body that mainly focuses on and specializes in regulating the market and setting priorities.[6] Regulation was therefore perceived as a core governmental function that would remain in the hands of the state in the "post-privatization" era. Moreover, regulation was acknowledged as an essential governmental tool for minimizing the possible damage incurred by privatizing public services and products.[7] The privatization of regulation is therefore a puzzling phenomenon. However, to date, the research on privatization has focused mainly on privatization of the provision of public services and assets and not on the privatization of regulation. The scant research conducted from the lens of privatization has mainly studied specific cases of outsourcing regulatory functions or renting private regulators.[8]

The purpose of this chapter is to unpack this widespread phenomenon, reconceptualizing it as the privatization of regulation. Section 16.2 presents the rise of private regulatory authority, roles and responsibilities, and the blurring of boundaries between public and private regulation. It introduces various regulatory regimes, techniques and practices and the emergent regulatory theories that address them. Section 16.3 suggests reconceptualizing this phenomenon as the privatization of regulation. It classifies diverse regulatory practices, techniques and regimes into three central modes of privatization: delegation, reregulation and deregulation. Section 16.4 proposes assessing private regulation by first identifying the

---

[4] Yael Kariv-Teitelbaum, "The Privatization of Regulation in Israel," in *The Privatization of Israel: The Withdrawal of State Responsibility*, eds. Amir Paz-Fuchs, Ronen Mandelkern and Itzhak Galnoor (London: Palgrave Macmillan, 2018), pp. 225–254.

[5] David Osborne and Ted Gaebler, "Catalytic Government: Steering Rather than Rowing," in *Reinventing Government: How the Entrepreneurial Spirit Is Transforming the Public Sector* (Reading, MA: Addison-Wesley, 1992), pp. 25–48.

[6] Harvey Feigenbaum, Jeffery Henig and Chris Hamnett, *Shrinking the State: The Political Underpinnings of Privatization* (Cambridge: Cambridge University Press, 1998); Demetrius S. Iatridis, "A Global Approach to Privatization," in *Privatization in Central and Eastern Europe: Perspectives and Approaches* (Connecticut: Greenwood, 1998), pp. 3–25, 6.

[7] Robert R. Alford and Roger Friedland, *Powers of Theory: Capitalism, the State, and Democracy* (Cambridge: Cambridge University Press, 1985); John A. J. Ernest, *Whose Utility? The Social Impact of Public Utility Privatization and Regulation in Britain* (London: Open University Press, 1994).

[8] Sidney A. Shapiro, "Outsourcing Governmental Regulation," *Duke Law Journal* 53 (2003): 389–434; Dara O'Rourke, "Outsourcing Regulation: Analyzing Nongovernmental Systems of Labor Standards and Monitoring," *Policy Studies Journal* 31 (2003): 1–29; Miriam Seiftei, "Rent-a-Regulator: Design and Innovation in Privatized Governmental Decisionmaking," *Ecology Law Journal* 33 (2006): 1091–1149; Sophie Tremolet, *Outsourcing Regulation: When Does It Make Sense and How Do We Best Manage It?* Working Paper No. 5 (Washington, DC: PPIAF, 2007); Sarah L. Stafford, "Outsourcing Enforcement: Principles to Guide to Self-Policing Regimes," *Cardozo Law Review* 32 (2011): 2293–2323; Lesley K. McAllister, "Regulation by Third-Party Verification," *Boston College Law Review* 53 (2012): 1–64; Lesley K. McAllister, "Harnessing Private Regulation," *Michigan Journal of Environmental and Administrative Law* 3 (2014): 291–420.

type of private entity to which a regulatory function is privatized: the regulated firms, the beneficiaries of regulation, semi-representative organizations (mainly of the regulated industry) or third parties from the business or civil sector. Section 16.5 traces the logic and rationales that drive this phenomenon, pointing out central promises and pitfalls of privatizing regulation. Finally, the concluding Section 16.6 outlines four possible outcomes of privatizing regulation: reinforcing regulation, underregulation, overregulation and changing the nature and style of regulation.

16.2 THE BLURRING OF BOUNDARIES BETWEEN PUBLIC AND PRIVATE REGULATION

Another appalling case of child abuse in a daycare center is discovered. As the tenth case in a single month, it sparks a widespread protest by parents, who demand tighter regulation of daycare providers. "Where was the Daycares Supervisor?" the newspaper headlines scream. An ad hoc inquiry declares the need for a thorough regulatory revision to ensure the protection of the helpless toddlers. However, instead of increasing the number of public supervisors, policy makers seek new and more efficient regulatory techniques and practices that will assign this regulatory mission to private hands. In the end, private for-profit companies are authorized to enter daycare facilities, exercise search and seizure powers to ensure they meet the required standards, and even set the quality standards for education and care in the facilities. This fictional scenario[9] exemplified the dynamic that is incrementally leading states to assign more and more regulatory roles and powers to private entities.

For years, regulatory power has been one of the most prominent forms of state power. More and more states began using rule setting, rule monitoring and rule enforcement as key policy tools, gradually turning into what Giandomenico Majone coined "the regulatory state":[10] a state with powerful administrative agencies that "command and control" private activity. Worldwide, regulation was perceived and defined as what public agencies do when they exercise sustained and focused control over activities that are valued by the community.[11] The regulatory state arguably reflects the assertion of a new claim by the state for a legitimate monopoly over regulatory power.[12] Thus, states have increasingly enjoyed dominancy, often even exclusivity, over regulatory power.

However, since the 1990s, private actors have been gradually assuming greater regulatory roles. A variety of private entities – such as industry associations, private firms, nongovernmental organizations (NGOs) and private individuals – are integrated by states in regulatory regimes or independently generate their own regulation.[13] Both in global and in local governance, states have lost their exclusive status and are allowing private actors to share

---

[9]   Based on an Israeli case, see: Yael Kariv-Teitelbaum, "The Privatization of Regulation in Israel."

[10]   Giandomenico. Majone, "The Rise of the Regulatory State in Europe," *West European Politics* 17 (1994): 77–101.

[11]   Philip Selznick, "Focusing Organizational Research on Regulation," in *Regulatory Policy and the Social Sciences*, ed. Roger G. Noll (Berkeley and Los Angeles, CA: University of California Press, 1985), pp. 363–67.

[12]   David Levi-Faur, "The Odyssey of the Regulatory State: From a 'Thin' Monomorphic Concept to a 'Thick' and Polymorphic Concept: The Odyssey of the Regulatory State," *Law & Policy* 35 (2013): 29–50.

[13]   Kenneth W. Abbott and Duncan Snidal, "The Governance Triangle: Regulatory Standards Institutions and the Shadow of the State," in *The Politics of Global Regulation*, eds. Walter Mattli and Ngaire Woods (Princeton, NJ: Princeton University Press, 2009), p. 44; Reinhard Steurer, "Disentangling Governance: A Synoptic View of Regulation by Government, Business and Civil Society," *Policy Sciences* 46 (2013): 387–410.

the role of setting, monitoring and enforcing rules.[14] Surely, the concept of private regulation is not new and has existed since the medieval guilds and even before. However, the increasing dominance of private actors empowered by states to fill a variety of regulatory roles is a recent phenomenon that has developed in the context of extensive privatization and globalization processes, and the emergence of new technologies.[15] Having lost their dominance over regulatory power, state regulators have gradually become "less important,"[16] as "just one source of power"[17] as opposed to the new private rulers.

The emergence of private regulatory authority attracted the attention of scholars from diverse fields[18] and more broadly has become a major focus of regulatory scholars. Regulation is no longer defined by scholars as an authoritative set of rules that are monitored and enforced by a *public* agency,[19] but as *any mechanism* of social control.[20] A rapidly growing body of literature describes a fundamental transformation from the traditional "command and control" model of a hierarchical state agency, toward decentralized hybrid and private regulatory regimes.[21] This transformation has blurred the sharp distinction between "public regulation," based on coercive measures carried out by civil servants to advance public goals, and "private regulation," rooted in consent and managed by private entities to unite and promote specific interest groups. Incrementally, public regulators have adopted strategies that assign regulatory roles to private entities, and techniques based on consent rather than coercion. At the same time, many private regulators have emerged or expanded their regulatory scope, often in a declared mission of advancing public goals; some have even gradually obtained coercive powers.

How is this transformation manifested? Which types of regulatory roles are private entities now filling? To paint an overall picture, we first need to clarify what "regulation" means. The definition of regulation has been the subject of numerous discussions in the literature in recent decades,[22] ranging from broad definitions that identify regulation as any mechanism of social control,[23] to narrow definitions that include only the promulgation of an authoritative set of rules that are monitored and enforced by a public agency.[24] Though scholars disagree about the sources, actors and types of activities that "regulation" upholds, all seem to agree that regulatory power includes three central roles: rule setting, rule monitoring and rule

---

[14] Scott, "Regulation in the Age of Governance"; Deborah Avant, Martha Finnemore and Susan Sell, *Who Governs the Globe?* (Cambridge: Cambridge University Press, 2010); Tim Büthe and Walter Mattli, *The New Global Rulers: The Privatization of Regulation in the World Economy* (Princeton, NJ: Princeton University Press, 2011); David Levi-Faur, "From 'Big Government' to 'Big Governance'?" in *Oxford Handbook of Governance*, ed. David Levi-Faur (Oxford: Oxford University Press, 2012), pp. 3–18; Jessica F. Green, *Rethinking Private Authority: Agents and Entrepreneurs in Global Environmental Governance* (Princeton, NJ: Princeton University Press, 2013).

[15] Lobel, "The Renew Deal," at pp. 276–81.

[16] Thomas L. Freidman and Oliver Wyman, *The World Is Flat: A Brief History of the 21st Century* (Hampton, NH: Sound Library/BBC Audiobooks, 2005).

[17] John Braithwaite, "Accountability and Governance under the New Regulatory State," *Australian Journal of Public Administration* 58 (1999): 90–94.

[18] See, for instance: Rodney Bruce Hall and Thomas J. Biersteker, *The Emergence of Private Authority in Global Governance* (Cambridge: Cambridge University Press, 2002); A. Claire Cutler, Virginia Haufler and Tony Porter, *Private Authority and International Affairs* (New York: State University of New York Press, 1999).

[19] Selznick, "Focusing Organizational Research on Regulation."

[20] Robert Baldwin, Colin Scott and Christopher Hood, *A Reader on Regulation* (Oxford: Oxford University Press, 1998).

[21] Lobel, "The Renew Deal."

[22] Levi-Faur, "The Odyssey of the Regulatory State."

[23] Baldwin, Scott and Hood, *A Reader on Regulation.*

[24] Selznick, "Focusing Organizational Research on Regulation."

enforcement. Private entities can fill any or all of these roles. Returning to our fictional example of daycare supervision, the state can rely on private entities for the role of rule setting (e.g., formulating the standards of the quality of care, education, safety, health, etc. in daycare centers), the role of rule monitoring (e.g., supervising daycare providers to check their compliance with the required standards), the role of rule enforcement (e.g., denying licenses to daycare facilities that violate the standards), or all three regulatory roles (e.g., adopting a private regulatory regime that sets, monitors and enforces the standards). This phenomenon can be observed today in various sectors. Over the years, a growing number of private actors have taken on the regulatory role of **rule setting**. Diverse private actors are initiating and designing standards that guide the conduct of rule takers in various regulatory regimes. On a transnational level, new global private organizations are promoting voluntary codes and standards, while the old private standardization boards are expanding their scope and gaining more power as states adopt their standards as mandatory. Hence, private hands are playing a central role in the regulatory realm of rule setting. Still, it appears that states tend to be cautious in adopting private standards as mandatory, except in "technical" areas such as the old *private global standardization boards*.[25] For instance, the International Accounting Standards Board (IASB) develops financial reporting rules used by corporations in over a hundred countries, and the International Organization for Standardization (ISO) and the International Electrotechnical Commission (IEC) account for 85 percent of all international product standards. These specialized global standardization institutes set detailed standards for various products and management systems that are considered essential for creating a unified and efficient global market. The standards are defined as voluntary, but states are increasingly incorporating many of them as mandatory. On the other hand, private "substantial" standards on issues that are considered more value-laden and politically contentious mostly remain voluntary. This is the case, for instance, regarding the rising *corporate social responsibility (CSR) codes of conduct*.[26] These privately designed rules usually include general principles that firms voluntarily accept, aimed at advancing social values such as environment protection, human rights, labor standards and consumer protection. Prominent examples include the International Chamber of Commerce, an international NGO that set 16 principles for environmental management (the *Business Charter for Sustainable Development*) signed by more than 2,300 companies, and the international nonstate network that formulated 6 principles for incorporating environmental, social and corporate governance issues in investment decision-making and ownership practices (the United Nations Principles for Responsible Investment), signed by more than 1,750 companies. Private rule setting can also be found in more hidden structures. On a more local level, as part of the general expansion of outsourcing techniques, many state regulators are now hiring *private contractors* to assist in writing administrative guidelines. Outsourcing rule setting is more

---

[25] Abbott and Snidal, "The Governance Triangle"; Büthe and Mattli, *The New Global Rulers*.

[26] Adelle Blackett, "Global Governance, Legal Pluralism and the Decentered State: A Labor Law Critique of Codes of Corporate Conduct," *Indiana Journal of Global Legal Studies* 8 (2001): 401–447; David Vogel, "The Private Regulation of Global Corporate Conduct: Achievements and Limitations," *Business & Society* 49 (2010): 68–87; David Vogel, *The Market for Virtue: The Potential and Limits of Corporate Social Responsibility* (Washington, DC: Brookings Institution Press, 2005); Michael W. Toffel, Jodi L. Short and Melissa Ouellet, "Codes in Context: How States, Markets, and Civil Society Shape Adherence to Global Labor Standards: Codes in Context," *Regulation & Governance* 9 (2015): 205–223; Rhuks Ako, Patrick Okonmah and Lawrence Ogechukwu, "Corporations, CSR and Self Regulation: What Lessons from the Global Financial Crisis?," *German Law Journal* 11 (2010): 230; Kernaghan Webb, "Understanding the Voluntary Codes Phenomenon," in *Voluntary Codes: Private Governance, The Public Interest and Innovation*, ed. Kernaghan Webb (Ottawa: Carleton Research Unit for Innovation, Science and Environment, 2004), pp. 3–32.

likely to be found in areas that are considered marginal and "technical-neutral" (e.g., the Ministry of Education will more readily transfer the task of writing guidelines for safety in educational institutions to private hands than for the quality of pedagogic plans).[27]

The second regulatory role, the **power to monitor** compliance, is now the most common regulatory role granted to private entities.[28] An increasing number of regulatory regimes are using private entities to perform the task of supervising, monitoring, controlling, testing, auditing or verifying compliance in regulated markets. The most common form is the use of third-party entities to act as "regulatory intermediaries," given their supremacy in operational capacity, expertise, independence or legitimacy.[29] One salient example pertains to *accreditation and certification.*[30] The government or legislature establishes a neutral third body to serve as an accreditation authority, which in turn authorizes private certification entities to perform a comprehensive evaluation of a product, system or process, involving a series of tests designed to verify that it meets the required standards. The European Union, for instance, established an accreditation and certification regime in the EU Legislative Framework – Regulation EC 765/2008. Accreditation and certification schemes can also serve as complementary to public supervision and not only as an alternative. For instance, the US Food and Drug Administration (FDA) enlists independent bodies to accredit private auditors for monitoring food imports, thus complementing the FDA's limited number of inspectors.[31] Accreditation and certification regimes usually grant certifiers, which are often for-profit organizations, very narrow discretion. The certifiers generally run a series of "technical" tests on a product, according to a specified list of requirements.

States can also utilize third parties in monitoring early stages of production. *Third-party verifiers*[32] are private entities that provide an expert opinion to the public regulator on whether the compliance information submitted by the regulated entity is accurate and confirms that the regulated entity is in compliance. It is used, for instance, in mandatory greenhouse gas reporting programs incorporated in ISO 14065:2013, Greenhouse gases. Regulators can also require regulated firms to hire *independent professionals*, such as lawyers or accountants, to audit compliance. This can also be achieved by employing other *independent third-party experts* with special expertise; these are often private for-profit entities. For instance, banks can rely on credit rating agencies to assess their exposure to risk duties. These practices are also referred to as *renting private regulators.*[33]

A more direct way for states to place monitoring power in private hands is the use of *private contractors.*[34] Nearly all government regulators worldwide outsource monitoring tasks to private, often for-profit, firms. These private contractors perform various roles, ranging from

---

[27] Kariv-Teitelbaum, "The Privatization of Regulation in Israel."

[28] See, for instance, regarding environmental protection: Jessica F. Green and Jeff Colgan, "Protecting Sovereignty, Protecting the Planet: State Delegation to International Organizations and Private Actors in Environmental Politics," *Governance* 26 (2013): 473–497.

[29] Kenneth W. Abbott, David Levi-Faur and Duncan Snidal, "Theorizing Regulatory Intermediaries: The RIT Model," ANNALS *of the American Academy of Political and Social Science* 670 (2017): 14–35.

[30] McAllister, "Regulation by Third-Party Verification"; Lars H. Gulbrandsen, "Dynamic Governance Interactions: Evolutionary Effects of State Responses to Non-state Certification Programs: Dynamic Governance Interactions," *Regulation & Governance* 8 (2014): 74–92; Gulbrandsen, "Dynamic Governance Interactions," at p. 20.

[31] Timothy D. Lytton, "The Taming of the Stew: Regulatory Intermediaries in Food Safety Governance," ANNALS *of the American Academy of Political and Social Science* 670 (2017): 78–92.

[32] McAllister, "Regulation by Third-Party Verification."

[33] Seiftei, "Rent-a-Regulator."

[34] Trémolet, *Outsourcing Regulation.*

specific tasks such as gathering information, conducting studies or performing one-time audits, to sustained monitoring. These private contractors can be auditing firms, testing companies, private labs or private inspectors. The role of monitoring compliance can also be transferred to the regulated firms themselves. *Self-policing*[35] describes monitoring power that is partly carried out by rule takers: The regulated firms can choose to conduct self-audits and report to the government regulators if a violation is detected. The government regulators retain the responsibility to impose penalties or demand remediation of the violation, but usually impose lower penalties for self-disclosed violations and reduce public supervision of self-policing firms. This concept was implemented, for instance, in the US Environmental Protection Agency's "Audit Policy" (officially entitled: "Incentives for Self-Policing: Discovery, Disclosure, Correction and Prevention of Violations"). A popular and more comprehensive self-regulation technique, known as *"process-based regulation"* or *"management-based regulation,"* requires regulated firms to develop plans, management system standards and internal practices to become more proactive and responsive to social concerns and thus achieve regulatory goals.[36]

Placing the third type of regulatory power – the **power to enforce** the rules – in private hands is less common in regulatory contexts, as most state regulators opt to retain the power to impose sanctions in cases of noncompliance. Very few of the aforementioned *accreditation and certification* regimes grant private certifiers the power not only to verify or audit but also to deny permits or impose fines. For instance, in some states in Australia, private bodies are authorized by the state (through registration or accreditation) not only to verify that building plans and construction work are consistent with building codes and planning laws but also to issue building permits and sometimes impose fines when they detect noncompliance.[37] More frequently, the power to enforce rules is delegated to private bodies for the specific task of executing enforcement decisions. One prominent form is the outsourcing of enforcement tasks to *private contractors* – for instance, hiring private debt collection agencies or law firms to collect unpaid fines. Enforcement power can also be transferred to *representative organizations* – for instance, delegating the enforcement of worksite safety standards to a committee of union and employer representatives.

The emergence and expansion of these diverse regulatory regimes, techniques and practices have led to a flourish of updated regulatory theories. Some scholars have stressed the new joint role of public and private actors in forming hybrid regulatory regimes, including "meta-regulation,"[38] "decentralized regulation,"[39] "negotiated regulation,"[40] "co-regulation,"[41] "polycentric regulatory

---

[35] Stafford, "Outsourcing Enforcement."

[36] Neil Gunningham and Darren Sinclair, "Smart Regulation," in *Regulatory Theory: Foundations and Applications*, ed. Peter Drahos (Canberra: Australian National University Press, 2017), pp. 133–148; Cary Coglianese and David Lazer, "Management-Based Regulation: Prescribing Private Management to Achieve Public Goals," *Law & Society Review* 37 (2003): 691–730; Sharon Gilad, "It Runs in the Family: Meta-regulation and Its Siblings," *Regulation & Governance* 4 (2010): 485–506.

[37] Jeroen van der Heijden, "Brighter and Darker Sides of Intermediation: Target-Oriented and Self-Interested Intermediaries in the Regulatory Governance of Buildings," ANNALS *of the American Academy of Political and Social Science* 670 (2017): 207–224, p. 211.

[38] Cary Coglianese and Evan Mendelson, "Meta-regulation and Self-Regulation," in *The Oxford Handbook of Regulation*, eds. Robert Baldwin, Martin Cave and Martin Lodge (Oxford: Oxford University Press, 2010), pp. 37–63.

[39] Blackett, "Global Governance, Legal Pluralism and the Decentered State."

[40] Kimberly D. Krawiec, "Cosmetic Compliance and the Failure of Negotiated Governance," *Washington University Law Quarterly* 81 (2003): 487–544.

[41] Anne Wardrop, "Co-regulation, Responsive Regulation and the Reform of Australia's Retail Electronic Payment Systems," *Law in Context: Socio-Legal Journal* 30 (2014): 197–227.

regimes,"[42] "collaborative governance,"[43] "regulatory networks"[44] and more. Others have emphasized the significant new role of private entities in initiating, designing and operating entire regulatory regimes, such as "civil regulation,"[45] "business-to-business regulation"[46] and so forth. Another branch of regulatory literature has focused on the transition of public regulators from the use of coercive measures toward softer techniques of "voluntary regulation,"[47] "industry-based regulation,"[48] "market-driven regulation"[49] and "self-regulation."[50]

Hence, since the 1990s, the boundaries between "public" and "private" regulation have blurred, as private actors fill larger regulatory roles of rule setting, rule monitoring and rule enforcement. While public regulators are gradually adopting softer and voluntary techniques that formerly characterized private regulation, private regulators are expanding their reach and even exercising coercive powers that were formerly the prerogative of public regulators. New entities that project private regulatory authority are emerging; states are developing new regulatory techniques that assign regulatory missions to private entities; and old models of private regulation are being extended and diffused. Thus, the dominance that public regulators enjoyed since the emergence of the regulatory state has eroded. But how should this development be conceptualized? As an expansion or reduction of regulation? As complementary to public regulation or as a substitute for it? As a "publicization" or as "privatization"?

16.3 UNPACKING THE PRIVATIZATION OF REGULATION: PRIVATIZING VIA DELEGATION, REREGULATION AND DEREGULATION

The blurred distinction between public and private regulation and the rise of private regulatory authority, roles and responsibilities are reflected in a myriad of regulatory techniques and practices that are becoming increasingly popular, including mandatory private standardization,[51] voluntary codes of conduct and CSR,[52] private labeling,[53] private

---

[42] Julia Black, "Constructing and Contesting Legitimacy and Accountability in Polycentric Regulatory Regimes," *Regulation and Governance* 2 (2008): 137–164.

[43] Chris Ansell and Alison Gash, "Collaborative Governance in Theory and Practice," *Journal of Public Administration Research and Theory* 18 (2007): 543–571.

[44] Anne-Marie Slaughter, "The Accountability of Government Networks," in *The Globalization of International Law*, ed. Paul Schiff Berman (New York: Routledge, 2017), pp. 471–496.

[45] Vogel, "The Private Regulation of Global Corporate Conduct."

[46] David Levi-Faur, "Regulation and Regulatory Governance," in *Handbook on the Politics of Regulation*, ed. David Levi-Faur (Cheltenham: Edward Elgar, 2011), pp. 1–25.

[47] Colin Provost, "Governance and Voluntary Regulation," in *Oxford Handbook of Governance*, ed. David Levi-Faur (Oxford: Oxford University Press, 2012), pp. 554–568; Eric Biber, "Do Voluntary Compliance Programs Really Improve Environmental Law?," Jotwell (April 28, 2015) (reviewing Cary Coglianese and Jennifer Nash, "Performance Track's Postmortem: Lessons from the Rise and Fall of EPA's 'Flagship' Voluntary Program," 38 Harv. Envtl. L. Rev. 1 (2014)), https://lex.jotwell.com/do-voluntary-compliance-programs-really-improve-environmental-law/.

[48] Neil Gunningham and Joseph Rees, "Industry Self-Regulation: An Institutional Perspective," *Law & Policy* 19 (1997): 363–414; Virgina Haufler, *A Public Role for the Private Sector: Industry Self-Regulation in a Global Economy* (Washington, DC: Carnegie Endowment, 2013).

[49] Vogel, *The Market for Virtue*.

[50] Coglianese and Mendelson, "Meta-regulation and Self-Regulation"; A. Ogus, "Rethinking Self-Regulation," *Oxford Journal of Legal Studies* 15 (1995): 97–108; Margot Priest, "The Privatization of Regulation: Five Models of Self-Regulation," *Ottawa Law Review* 29 (1998): 233–302.

[51] Abbott and Snidal, "The Governance Triangle"; Büthe and Mattli, *The New Global Rulers*.

[52] Blackett, "Global Governance, Legal Pluralism and the Decentered State"; Vogel, "The Private Regulation of Global Corporate Conduct"; Vogel, *The Market for Virtue*; Toffel, Short and Ouellet, "Codes in Context"; Ako, Okonmah and Ogechukwu, "Corporations, CSR and Self Regulation"; Webb, "Understanding the Voluntary Codes Phenomenon."

[53] Christine Parker, Rachel Carey, Josephine De Costa and Gyorgy Scrinis, "Can the Hidden Hand of the Market Be an Effective and Legitimate Regulator? The Case of Animal Welfare under a Labeling for Consumer Choice Policy Approach: Labeling for Consumer Choice," *Regulation & Governance* 11 (2017): 368–387.

certification and accreditation,[54] third-party verification,[55] self-policing,[56] renting private regulators,[57] outsourcing regulatory tasks,[58] "management-based regulation,"[59] "process-based regulation"[60] and more.

Many of these practices and techniques were initially reported mainly in areas where public regulation was absent or weak, as a means of filling policy voids.[61] Civil regulation regimes, for instance, first emerged in areas that were underregulated by states, such as environmental protection and labor rights, adding another regulatory layer of voluntary codes of conduct.[62] Similarly, the use of private third parties to monitor compliance added new layers of auditing and labeling to environmental protection.[63] Many new industry-based and self-regulatory regimes also arose where public supervision was lacking, and were designed to fill these regulatory gaps with private norms and self-policing.[64] Likewise, contracting out regulatory tasks was mostly prevalent in areas neglected by public supervisors, such as auditing financial accounts and quality monitoring.[65] Hence, many of these practices and techniques did not replace public regulators but added another layer that complemented the regulatory regime. Moreover, many of these practices were developed in areas that were considered "technical" (e.g., the quality of products, buildings and food, and financial reports). These areas are far from what are commonly perceived as the core discretional responsibilities of public regulators. It is therefore clear why this movement has been mainly conceptualized as an expansion of regulation that offers the potential for advancing public goals and reinforcing the state's regulatory capacity.

Nevertheless, the growing popularity of private regulation also raises concerns that it will erode the scope and authority of public regulation.[66] Diverse regulatory practices and techniques can be found today in almost every sector and domain of public policy.[67] In many cases, the collaboration of private entities in regulatory regimes ends up replacing public regulators rather than complementing them. That is, instead of a complementing layer, it can become a substitute regime, preempting public regulation. In the daycare example, for instance, relying on private entities to regulate daycare providers might not only complement and reinforce the existing public supervision but ultimately replace it. Moreover, many techniques and practices that were initially promoted for seemingly "technical" issues in resolving global market problems (environmental protection, labor conditions, financial stability, etc.) appear to have slowly spread into more traditional areas

---

54 Gulbrandsen, "Dynamic Governance Interactions."

55 McAllister, "Regulation by Third-Party Verification."

56 Stafford, "Outsourcing Enforcement."

57 Seiftei, "Rent-a-Regulator."

58 Shapiro, "Outsourcing Governmental Regulation"; O'Rourke, "Outsourcing Regulation"; Tremolet, *Outsourcing Regulation.*

59 Coglianese and Lazer, "Management-Based Regulation: Prescribing Private Management to Achieve Public Goals."

60 Gilad, "It Runs in the Family."

61 Steven Bernstein and Benjamin Cashore, "Can Non-state Global Governance Be Legitimate? An Analytical Framework," *Regulation & Governance* 1 (2007): 347–371.

62 Abbott and Snidal, "The Governance Triangle"; Vogel, "The Private Regulation of Global Corporate Conduct."

63 Seiftei, "Rent-a-Regulator."

64 Gunningham and Rees, "Industry Self-Regulation"; Priest, "The Privatization of Regulation."

65 Tremolet, *Outsourcing Regulation.*

66 Neil Malhotra, Beniot Monin and Michael Tomz, "Does Private Regulation Preempt Public Regulation?," *American Political Science Review* 113 (2019): 19–37.

67 Scott Burris, Michael Kempa and Clifford Shearing, "Changes in Governance: A Cross-Disciplinary Review of Current Scholarship," *Akron Law Review* 1 (2008): 1–66.

of public regulation that are considered more local and less technical, such as education, health and welfare. This includes, for example, private certification schemes that were associated with testing product safety, to spread toward testing the quality of care and education in daycares.[68]

It is therefore important to frame the cases in which this phenomenon can be conceptualized as the privatization of regulation, where rule setting, rule monitoring and rule enforcement move from public entities into private hands. The privatization of regulation can take diverse forms, as illustrated in many of the regulatory techniques and practices described so far. It may encompass a formal and deliberated privatization process (e.g., via laws or contracts) or privatization by withdrawal (e.g., reducing the budget of a regulatory agency). It can take the form of "full privatization," where states fully transfer a regulatory role to the private sector (e.g., selling a governmental auditing company), or "partial privatization," where states privatize the operation of regulatory powers but continue to fund it (e.g., outsourcing regulatory tasks) or set price controls (e.g., by awarding restricted franchises to certification bodies). It can be carried out through diverse legal mechanisms, including contracting out, accreditation by franchises, legislative mandate, rent-a-private regulator duties, incorporating private standards in regulations, sale or an informal withdrawal. As noted, privatization can involve any or all of the three central regulatory roles of rule setting, rule monitoring and rule enforcement.

To explore this phenomenon from the lens of privatization, it is useful to classify the array of new regulatory regimes, techniques and practices into three main modes of privatization: delegation, reregulation, and deregulation (see Table 16.1).

Delegation is an active, overt and formal version of privatization, where the state transfers the exercise of coercive regulatory power to private hands. These hybrid regulatory regimes feature varied practices and techniques in which the state subordinates rule takers to private bodies that set, monitor and/or enforce mandatory rules. This is carried out through a range of regulatory practices and techniques, including outsourcing public regulatory tasks, rent-a-private-regulator duties, obligatory private certification schemes, mandatory private standards and legislative mandate of industry associations. For example, privatizing the supervision of daycare by delegation can involve outsourcing the task of conducting routine inspections in daycare centers; accrediting private certification bodies to verify that daycare providers meet the required standards; obligating daycare facilities to act in accordance with transnational private code or standards or to be certificated by a transnational private organization; granting a legislative mandate to a semi-representative organization (of caregivers/parents/educational professionals/etc.) to regulate daycare centers; and so forth.

Reregulation is a less visible form of privatization, where the state reshapes regulatory regimes in a way that reduces the number of public supervisors by relying on private actors, such as consumers or the regulated firms themselves. These increasingly popular regulatory regimes are often described as "market-driven regulation"[69] and new "self-regulation."[70] They include diverse regulatory techniques and practices, including self-policing, process-based regulation and management regulation. Turing again to the example of supervising daycare, privatization through reregulation can take the form of

---

[68]   Kariv-Teitelbaum, "The Privatization of Regulation in Israel."
[69]   Vogel, *The Market for Virtue.*
[70]   Coglianese and Mendelson, "Meta-regulation and Self-Regulation"; Ogus, "Rethinking Self-Regulation"; Priest, "The Privatization of Regulation."

relying on the caregivers themselves by requiring them to self-report on whether they meet the standards, to self-conduct risk management, to voluntarily report cases of violations and so forth. Alternatively, they may rely on the parents by granting labels affirming that a daycare provider meets the state's voluntary standards, by publicly shaming noncompliant daycare providers, or even by supporting class actions lawsuits. As noted, these new practices and techniques may not only complement and reinforce the current array of supervisors but eventually replace them, effectively reducing the number of pubic supervisors "in the field" who are visiting the daycare centers and maintaining close interaction with caregivers.

Finally, regulation can be privatized through *deregulation*. In this passive and often hidden version of privatization, the state privatizes regulation by withdrawal and omission. It can be carried out by cutting the budget of a public regulatory agency, narrowing its powers or refraining from applying regulations in new areas that evoke similar social problems. By reducing public regulation, the state enables – and sometimes even actively encourages[71] – the rise of private regulatory authority to fill policy gaps. Hence, diverse voluntary regulatory regimes emerge as "civil regulation"[72] and "business-to-business regulation"[73] are initiated, designed and operated by private entities. They involve various practices such as voluntary codes of conduct and CSR, private voluntary labeling and private voluntary standards. Privatizing the regulation of daycare providers via deregulation may occur, for instance, when funding for public supervision does not keep pace with the demands of a growing population. Policy makers may argue that there is no need to expand public regulation in the light of private voluntary initiatives, such as a child protection NGO that encourages caregivers to sign a voluntary ethical code or initiate a voluntary "certified childcare" label for daycare providers.

Hence, privatizing regulation describes the spreading phenomenon in which rule setting, rule monitoring and rule enforcement move from "public hands" to "private hands." It may occur by a formal active mode of delegation, by a more hidden form of reregulation, or by a passive and often unintentional means of deregulation. All three modes of privatization can be portrayed as the state's withdrawal from its former role of the "regulatory state." By delegating regulatory powers, reregulating and deregulating, states become less "hands-on" in operating regulatory regimes. They increasingly rely on private entities instead of public supervisors. As section 16.5 will elaborate, all three modes of privatization therefore might promise to reinforce and complement public regulation, but also raise concerns about placing regulatory power in private hands and forfeiting the state's regulatory capacity. For example, relying on private entities to supervise daycare may also lead to preempting public supervisors, reducing their independence and leading to a loss of expertise and weaker connection with caregivers in the field. Moreover, it might stir new problems of abuse of power – for example, when authorizing private certifiers to enter caregivers' homes and to exercise search and seizure powers.

16.4 WHICH PRIVATE ENTITIES ARE ASSIGNED REGULATORY ROLES?

Who are the new private partners in governance? Whose "private hands" nowadays share regulatory responsibility with the state? To evaluate the enormous variety of practices,

---

[71] Adrienne Héritier and Dirk Lehmkuhl, "The Shadow of Hierarchy and New Modes of Governance," *Journal of Public Policy* 28 (2008): 1–17.

[72] Vogel, "The Private Regulation of Global Corporate Conduct."

[73] Levi-Faur, "Regulation and Regulatory Governance."

techniques and strategies of privatized regulation, we must first clarify to whom, or to which type of entities, the regulatory mission is assigned. Abbott and Snidal's well-known typology of the rise of private authority describes the "governance triangle," which distinguishes between three types of actors that can design and operate regulatory regimes: the government, business and civil society.[74] Later on, Abbott and Levi-Faur suggested moving away from the state versus nonstate distinction and focusing instead on rule makers, rule takers and "rule intermediaries"[75] as the three central participants in the act of regulation.

However, from the lens of privatization, a more detailed classification is needed to evaluate the array of privatized regulatory regimes. This classification identifies four types of actors to which states privatize regulatory power, according to the role they play in the regulatory course of action: the regulated firms, the beneficiaries of regulation, semi-representative organizations (often from the regulated industry), and third parties from the business or civil sector. Each regulatory actor has a different set of incentives.

Some states adopt regulatory strategies that collaborate and rely on *the regulated firms* themselves (e.g., in the daycare example: daycare managers and caregivers). Diverse models of "self-regulation"[76] rely on the subjects of the rules to perform regulatory roles, and employ regulatory strategies and techniques such as "process-based regulation," "management-based regulation" and self-policing. Regulated firms are naturally motivated to promote their own self-interest. Consequently, self-regulation is often criticized due to inherent conflicts of interest.

Some governments are developing various new regulatory techniques that heavily rely on the *beneficiaries of regulation* (e.g., in the daycare example: toddlers and their parents). This is sometimes described as "market-based regulation." Beneficiaries are the objects of the rules – that is, the groups whose interests the rules are meant to protect.[77] In some cases, this is the general public (e.g., rules intended to reduce greenhouse gas emissions) and in other cases the beneficiaries are a more specific public group (e.g., stockholders or people with disabilities). Thus, many state regulators seek to replace the traditional use of public supervisors by relying on the beneficiaries for rule setting (e.g., producer organizations have direct representation on the Fairtrade Standards Committee), rule monitoring (serving as "fire alarms" that alert regulators in cases of violation) or even for rule enforcement (class action, shaming, etc.). Beneficiaries are usually large and decentralized groups. Therefore, the challenge of incorporating them in regulatory regimes requires the creation of mechanisms that can overcome the collective action problem[78] and motivate them to participate in regulatory rule making.

Alternatively, governments are adopting various new methods that delegate regulatory power to *semi-representative organizations* (e.g., in the daycare example: a caregivers association). These organizations can be composed of representatives of the regulated firms, the beneficiaries, or collaboration of some of them. The most salient example is delegation to the regulated industry, in what is traditionally called "industry self-regulation."[79] This includes diverse regulatory regimes that are designed, monitored and/or enforced by professional communities and business

---

[74] Abbott and Snidal, "The Governance Triangle." See also: Steurer, "Disentangling Governance."
[75] Abbott, Levi-Faur and Snidal, "Theorizing Regulatory Intermediaries."
[76] Ogus, "Rethinking Self-Regulation"; Gunningham and Rees, "Industry Self-Regulation"; Priest, "The Privatization of Regulation"; Haufler, *A Public Role for the Private Sector*.
[77] Mathias Koenig-Archibugi and Kate Macdonald, "The Role of Beneficiaries in Transnational Regulatory Processes," ANNALS *of the American Academy of Political and Social Science* 670 (2017): 36–57.
[78] Mancur Olson, *The Logic of Collective Action: Public Goods and the Theory of Groups* (Cambridge, MA: Harvard University Press, 1965).
[79] Gunningham and Rees, "Industry Self-Regulation"; Haufler, *A Public Role for the Private Sector*.

networks. There are two basic approaches: public enforcement of privately written rules and government-mandated internal enforcement of publicly written rules.[80] In industry-based regulatory regimes, the government often assigns regulatory power to a semi-representative body of the regulated industry – for instance, a professional association that regulates training, qualification and discipline in the profession.[81] Industry regulators are naturally motivated to promote the interest of the industry; they are inclined to favor the interests of current rule takers over newcomers, and big and powerful rule takers over small ones.

Increasingly, governments are privatizing regulatory functions by delegating them to external *third parties* – that is, to private entities that are not involved in the regulatory relationship. Such third parties can either be from the business sector (e.g., in the daycare example: for-profit companies such as auditing companies of educational institutions) or from civil society (e.g., a nonprofit organization for child protection). Third parties constitute the most heterogeneous group of all, encompassing diverse bodies that have different incentives. They can be nonprofit organizations that, for instance, verify compliance[82] or promote codes of conduct known as "civil regulation"[83], or business corporations that act to pursue profits, such as some certification bodies and auditing companies. Third parties can be single players (e.g., a control company), members of a professional community (e.g., accountants) or part of a global network (e.g., global certification schemes). They can be paid for their services by the government (e.g., outsourcing to audit companies), receive payments directly from the regulated firms (e.g., credit firms) or base their funding on private donations (e.g., civil regulation). Any of these characteristics can divert their incentive in different directions. A for-profit company that financially depends on payments from the regulated firms may be more prone to favor private interests. On the other hand, this tendency can sometimes be offset by professional norms, global reputation or governmental funding.[84]

Hence, it is essential to examine which private entities are assigned regulatory roles, as both the promises and the pitfalls of privatizing regulation stem from the gap – in motivation and norms – between private and public actors. This examination draws attention to the actors' array of incentives and indicates who will most likely benefit from regulation that exceeds or falls short of its public goals. Going back to the three modes of privatizing regulation described earlier – delegation, reregulation and deregulation – each can be associated with a different type of actor to which regulatory missions are assigned (see Table 16.1).

16.5 THE PRIVATIZATION OF REGULATION: CENTRAL PROMISES AND PITFALLS

What drives states to privatize regulation? Clearly, each practice of privatizing regulation has different advantages and disadvantages. However, by tracing the logic and rationales that drive this general shift toward the privatization of regulation, we can identify key promises and pitfalls. Private entities act according to a different set of incentives than do public entities, have distinct motivations and are bound by different norms. This is both the source of their positive potential and a cause for concern when private entities replace public supervisors.

---

[80] Joseph Rees, *Reforming the Workplace: A Study of Self-Regulation in Occupational Safety* (Pennsylvania: University of Pennsylvania Press, 1988), pp. 10–11.
[81] Priest, "The Privatization of Regulation."
[82] McAllister, "Regulation by Third-Party Verification."
[83] Vogel, "The Private Regulation of Global Corporate Conduct"; Toffel, Short and Ouellet, "Codes in Context."
[84] Abbott, Levi-Faur and Snidal, "Theorizing Regulatory Intermediaries," at p. 18.

TABLE 16.1 *Three modes of privatizing regulation*

	Deregulation	Reregulation	Delegation
Method	The state places coercive regulatory power in private hands.	The state avoids applying public regulation and thus enables (and sometimes even encourages) the creation of voluntary private regulatory regimes.	The state reduces the number of public supervisors by designing regulatory regimes that rely on private actors, such as consumers or the regulated firms themselves.
Regulatory regimes	hybrid regulatory regime	civil voluntary regulation; industry-based voluntary regulation	self-regulation; market-based regulation
Regulatory techniques and practices	outsourcing regulatory tasks, rent-a-private-regulator duties, obligatory private certification schemes, mandatory private standards, legislative mandate for industry-based associations, etc.	self-policing, process-based regulation, management regulation, etc.	voluntary codes of conduct and CSR, private voluntary labeling, private voluntary standards, etc.
Which private entities are assigned regulatory roles?	parties from the civil or business sector; semi-representative organizations (industry/ beneficiaries/ collaborative)	rule takers (the regulated firms); beneficiaries	NGOs; semi-representative organizations (industry/ beneficiaries/ collaborative)

16.5.1 *Promises: Justifications and Rationales*

The privatization of regulation spread hand in hand with the rise of what Orly Lobel described as a new regulatory paradigm – "new governance."[85] This new school of thought proposes transforming regulation into a more collaborative, decentralized, diverse, dynamic and flexible practice by involving private entities in the act of regulation. It seeks to replace the traditional state-centered hierarchical model of "command and control" that views the government as solely responsible for achieving policy goals. Instead of the state imposing these on the private sector, the new governance perceives the government, industry and society as entities that share responsibility for achieving policy goals. It therefore encourages multiple nongovernmental stakeholders, including private businesses and NGOs, to share the traditional roles of state regulators.

Hence, the new-governance welcomes diverse methods of privatizing regulatory power as another promising way to share the responsibility of advancing public goals with the private sector and civil society.[86] Initially, the new governance was presented as a new form of

---

[85] Lobel, "The Renew Deal."
[86] Lobel, "The Renew Deal," at pp. 293–300.

governing that minimizes the government's role – "governing without the government."[87] But its main agenda quickly transformed into an empowering project, designed to reinforce the government's role. Decreasing the state's regulatory dominance by sharing this responsibility with other actors[88] was considered a way to expand the public sphere rather than shrink it.[89] This expansion of regulation does not threaten the state's regulatory capacity; on the contrary, it bolsters it.[90]

During the first decade of the millennium, under the concept of "the more new governance, the better,"[91] diverse practices of sharing regulatory roles and missions became widespread. Proponents of "new governance" offer three main rationales[92] for involving private entities in regulatory regimes: increasing their efficiency, legitimacy and effectiveness. Accordingly, these three rationales explain and justify diverse practices and techniques of privatizing regulation.

First, the privatization of regulation offers the potential of increasing governmental *efficiency* by reducing governmental costs and bureaucracy. The same logic that supports the privatization of public services and products underlines the advantages of private actors as flexible agents subject to market discipline, global networks and professional norms. Private actors are expected to act more efficiently by performing the same tasks at lower costs. They are usually subject to competition and are thus expected to be more motivated to act efficiently in order to avoid being replaced. They can decentralize costs among more rule takers by offering their services to other states (e.g., global standardization boards) or by adapting them to needs of the local business sector (e.g., auditing companies). Furthermore, they are considered more flexible since they are not bound by the civil service's rigid employment conditions, such as tenure.

Second, privatizing regulation can reinforce the political *legitimacy* of regulatory regimes. They may be perceived as less intrusive when they rely on the stakeholders themselves, including industry associations and consumers. Private third parties can also enjoy a higher degree of trust as external independent agents, immune to meddling by politicians and subject to global competition or professional norms. Their good reputation can enhance the credibility of the regulation they impose, especially vis-à-vis administrations that have a low degree of public trust or weak local regulatory capacity. Examples include the mandatory use of external private agencies for conducting technical tests and audits in the water and electricity sectors in Brazil, Chile, Argentina and Gaza.[93]

Third, the privatization of regulation is considered a promising way not only to increase efficiency by performing the same tasks at lower costs but also to improve the *effectiveness* of regulatory regimes by better promoting their public goals. Private actors, including consumers and members of a regulated industry (e.g., industry-based regulation), are often more knowledgeable than the state and have greater professional or international expertise. Moreover, the advantage of flexibility allows private actors to more easily initiate and adopt

---

[87] Raw A. W. Rhodes, "The New Governance: Governing without Government," *Political Studies* 44 (1996): 652–667.
[88] Minow, "Public and Private Partnerships."
[89] Jody Freeman, "Extending Public Law Norms through Privatization," *Harvard Law Review* 116 (2003): 1285–1352.
[90] Jacint Jordana, David Levi-Faur and Xavier Fernández-i-Marín, "The Global Diffusion of Regulatory Agencies: Channels of Transfer and Stages of Diffusion," IBEI Working Papers 2009/28 (December 1, 2009), https://ssrn.com/abstract=1557142 or http://dx.doi.org/10.2139/ssrn.1557142.
[91] Jason M. Solomon, "New Governance, Preemptive Self-Regulation, and the Blurring of Boundaries in Regulatory Theory and Practice," *Wisconsin Law Review* (2010): 591–625.
[92] Lobel, "The Renew Deal," 386–390.
[93] Trémolet, *Outsourcing Regulation*, at pp. 6–9.

new techniques to achieve the regulatory goal and to adapt more quickly to change, thus fostering innovation and enabling a dynamic regulatory regime. Hence, private actors can access specialized skills, mitigate the risk of regulatory obsolescence and leverage international experience in specialized areas of regulatory practice.

In the literature on regulation, public regulators are not often portrayed as inherently superior to private entities. Private interest theorists have always been skeptical regarding the capability of public regulators to shape their own preferences and advance the public interest rather than private interest.[94] The theory of regulatory capture[95] has long ago suggested that public regulators themselves are bound to be captured by small interest groups and promote their private interests, due to their expectation of future rewarding jobs in the industry,[96] asymmetrical information and expertise, cultural identification with the regulated industry, or the industry's power to damage the regulators' reputation or to manipulate perceptions and ideas.[97] From this perspective, assigning regulatory roles to private entities should not necessarily be viewed as a problem or anomaly but rather as a possible solution for the concern of regulatory capture. All three modes of privatizing regulation hold the promise of overcoming regulatory capture of public regulators thus *reinforcing* the regulatory regime in advancing public goals. Privatization through delegation to external third parties, for example, can replace public supervisors "in the field" and decrease their ongoing interaction with the regulated industry, thus reducing the opportunities of rule takers to capture them by suggesting, for instance, a future rewarding job or other benefits. Private external regulators that respond to market competition, professional norms or global reputation, and are less culturally identified with local rule takers, may be more immune to the pressures of local interest groups and less susceptible to regulatory capture. Privatization by reregulation or deregulation also reduce the use of public supervisors by relying instead, for instance, on the beneficiaries or the regulated firms themselves, hence reducing the chances of capture by interest groups and distortion of regulation in their favor.

In the daycare example, privatizing regulation by delegating, reregulating or deregulating holds the promise of reinforcing the protection of toddlers. Delegating the role of rule monitoring to private certifiers, for instance, can decrease costs. Private certifiers can be more efficient in monitoring daycare providers not only due to their motivation to make profits and bypass competitors, but also by decentralizing costs among more care facilities (e.g., by offering monitoring services for schools, babysitters or even retirement homes). Moreover, private certifiers can allow daycare supervisors greater flexibility and dynamism (e.g., if the supervisor discovers that most cases of child abuse occur only at the beginning of the year or during afternoon hours, private certifiers can be hired to monitor only during those times). The competitiveness and flexibility of private certifiers can also push them to develop new technologies to maximize profits and overcome competitors (e.g., developing smart databases that cross-reference information about suspicious caregivers). Private certifiers of

---

[94] Jean-Jacques Laffont and Jean Tirole, "The Politics of Government Decision-Making: A Theory of Regulatory Capture," *Quarterly Journal of Economics* 106 (1991): 1089–1127.

[95] George Stigler, "The Theory of Economic Regulation," *Bell Journal of Economics & Management Science* 21 (1971): 3–21; Sam Peltzman, "Toward a More General Theory of Regulation," *Journal of Law & Economics* 19 (1976): 211–240.

[96] Edna E. V. Johnson, "Agency Capture: The Revolving Door between Regulated Industries and Their Regulating Agencies," *University of Richmond Law Review* 18 (1983): 95–119; Toni Makkai and John Braithwaite, "In and Out of the Revolving Door: Making Sense of Regulatory Capture," *Journal of Public Policy* 12 (1992): 61–78.

[97] Daniel Carpenter, *Preventing Regulatory Capture: Special Interest Influence and How to Limit It* (Cambridge: Cambridge University Press, 2013).

daycare can even enjoy greater legitimacy, especially if they work according to a specific checklist with narrow discretion (e.g., marking the number of caregivers and children or checking if there is a fire extinguisher), if they are a part of a strong international professional network or if the public supervisors are considered incapable (e.g., if they are captured by a powerful local monopoly of daycare centers). Privatizing the regulation of daycare providers through reregulation can also reinforce the protection of toddlers. Replacing public supervisors by relying, for instance, on the parents to monitor a daycare facility can decrease costs (parents already visit the facility on a daily basis), increase effectiveness (parents have a wider presence than public supervisors could ever achieve) and legitimacy (caregivers can be more willing to allow them broad access as the toddlers' parents and the ones paying for the service). Alternatively, relying on the regulated industry by instituting a legislative mandate for caregiver associations to regulate daycare centers can also be less costly (at least for the state), more effective (caregivers are more attuned to the field and can better predict which interventions will fit best) and more legitimate (caregivers can be perceived as legitimate professional authorities). Finally, even deregulating the supervision of daycare providers by decreasing the number of public supervisors and encouraging the rise of voluntary private regimes (e.g., a voluntary code of caregivers or a social label of daycare quality) can reduce the state's costs, foster innovation (e.g., encouraging the development of new technologies to fill this policy gap, such as special surveillance tools, an app that alerts in case of prolonged crying, etc.). Such voluntary private regulatory regimes might even be considered more legitimate, as they require the consent and cooperation of caregivers and can therefore be conceived as less intrusive than public supervisors who exercise coercive measures.

Moreover, reinforcing regulatory regimes is not the only promise that privatization regulation offers. Another possible effect, which has received little attention in the literature on regulation, concerns the way in which privatization may *change* the nature and style of the regulatory regime. The advantages of private entities as flexible agents subject to market discipline, global networks or professional norms not only enable them to perform the same regulatory task more effectively but may also change the way in which the task is crafted, defined and measured. It may be suggested, for instance, that the privatization of regulation may transform regulatory regimes to become more attuned to professional, technical and measurable criteria. In light of the ongoing dominancy of private global standardization boards, certification bodies and private labelers, it appears that the use of detailed and specific rules is becoming more and more prevalent. Such rules leave little room for discretion, for both rule takers and private enforcers of these rules. Private regulators may have incentives to promote this regulatory style to gain legitimacy, as it underlines their advantages as part of a professional, often international, network that encourages and facilitates global trade. Public regulators that delegate regulatory functions to private entities also have incentives to adopt this regulatory style. It allows them to limit the discretion of the delegated entities and thus better direct their conduct, decrease the costs of supervising their operation and avoid criticism for relinquishing public power and responsibility. Hence, privatizing regulation via delegation often involves a legal document (e.g., a contract in the case of outsourcing or a franchise in certification schemes) with a clear and detailed checklist of technical requirements to limit the discretion of the delegated entities. Such a change of the nature and style of regulation holds the promise of increasing the certainty and uniformity of the regulatory regime. However, the trend of adopting professional, technical and measurable criteria may also have pitfalls, especially when it comes to regulating "nontechnical," value-laden or politically contentious issues, such as education, welfare or health – areas that may require broader discretion. For instance, relying on private certification bodies instead of public supervisors may favor technical and measurable criteria over substantial ones (e.g., focusing on the proportion of toddlers per caregiver or the number of children's books, instead of the nature of the relationship with the toddlers).

16.5.2 *Pitfalls: Concerns and Limitations*

The initial enthusiasm for the new-governance techniques and practices of privatizing regulation has somewhat decreased after the financial crisis of 2008, which armed its former critics with alleged proofs of their inherited limitations. What started as a local burst of the "subprime mortgage bubble" in the USA rapidly escalated into an international banking crisis that precipitated a global economic recession. This fomented widespread distrust in private regulators and highlighted the essential role of the state.[98] Various practices of privatized regulation were blamed for regulatory failures that led to the crisis.[99] In other sectors, too, the privatization of regulation was deemed responsible for causing regulatory failures.[100] The crisis stirred numerous discussions over the inherent limitations of privatizing regulation.

Thus, the new-governance vision of expanding the public sphere by privatizing regulation faced concerns that the state was losing its regulatory capacity and competency. The financial crisis underlined "the absence of an informed, expertly staffed, and independent institution that evaluates financial regulation from the public's perspective."[101] The more state actors relied and depended on their private partners to perform regulatory roles, the more prone they were to lose their regulatory capacity. Moreover, the financial crisis demonstrated how each of the aforementioned promises – efficiency, legitimacy and effectiveness – can also become pitfalls, especially in the cases of privatizing regulation through delegation.

Privatizing regulation might be less *efficient*, as delegating regulatory powers to private entities can cost more than public regulation. It often involves a high transaction cost: choosing the delegated entity; setting detailed terms to guide its discretion thorough a contract (e.g., outsourcing), franchise (e.g., accreditation and certification) or a legal mandate (e.g., industry-based regulator); supervising its operation to ensure that the private entity meets these terms; and imposing sanctions in the event of breaches and violations. The job of "regulating the regulators" – choosing private regulators, setting the rules to guide their

---

[98]   Dani Rodrik, "Roepke Lecture in Economic Geography-Who Needs the Nation-State?: Who Needs the Nation-State?," *Economic Geography* 89 (2013): 1–19; Ralf Michaels, "The Mirage on Non-State Governance," *Utah Law Review* 1 (2010): 31–45.

[99]   See, for instance: Howard Davies, *The Financial Crisis – Who Is to Blame?* (Cambridge: Polity Press, 2010), at section C; Brooksley Born, "Deregulation: A Major Cause of the Financial Crisis," *Harvard Law & Policy Review* 5 (2011): 231–244; Julia Black, "Paradoxes and Failures: 'New Governance' Techniques and the Financial Crisis," *Modern Law Review* 75 (2012): 1037–1063, at p. 1043; Judith Clifton, Myriam García-Olalla and Philip Molyneux, "Introduction to the Special Issue: New Perspectives on Regulating Banks after the Global Financial Crisis," *Journal of Economic Policy Reform* 20 (2017): 193–198.

[100] Edward J. Balleisen and Marc Eisner, "The Promise and Pitfalls of Co-regulation: How Governments Can Draw on Private Governance for Public Purpose," in *New Perspectives on Regulation*, eds. David Moss and John Cisternino (Cambridge, MA: The Tobin Project, 2009), p. 127; Solomon, "New Governance, Preemptive Self-Regulation, and the Blurring of Boundaries in Regulatory Theory and Practice"; Büthe and Mattli, *The New Global Rulers*; Cary Coglianese and Jennifer Nash, "Performance Track's Postmortem: Lessons from the Rise and Fall of EPA's Flagship Voluntary Program," *Harvard Environmental Law Review* 38 (2014): 1–87.

[101] Ross Levine, "The Governance of Financial Regulation: Reform Lessons from the Recent Crisis: The Governance of Financial Regulation," *International Review of Finance* 12 (2012): 39–56.

discretion, and monitoring and enforcing these rules – can be a complicated and costly task that outweighs the benefits of using private entities.

The privatization of regulatory power may also decrease the *legitimacy* of the regulatory regime. Rule takers sometimes view private regulators as less legitimate, especially when they are required to obey an entity over which they have no influence or control. More broadly, the public may perceive diverse practices of privatizing regulation as a relinquishment of the state's responsibilities.

As for *effectiveness*, the different incentives of private entities might lead them to distort the purposes of regulation due to an inherent conflict of interests. This is the common critique of self-regulation and industry-based regulation strategies, which require the industry or the firms to police themselves, leading to *underregulation*.[102] This critique gained momentum after the financial crisis of 2008, as scholars argued that self-regulation and industry-based regulatory techniques enabled opportunistic behaviors and insufficiently mitigated the risk.[103] The crisis arguably highlighted the absence of expert independent public regulators.[104] It raised concerns that privatizing through reregulation and deregulation disconnects public supervisors from "the field," thus reducing their knowledge and expertise and increasing their dependence on private actors. After the crisis, financial regulation worldwide shifted from private industry-based and self-regulation toward public regulation.[105] The financial crisis also stirred wide criticisms of other forms of reregulation and deregulation, including "management-based regulation" and "meta regulation,"[106] voluntary codes techniques[107] and more.

Furthermore, privatizing regulation may actually exacerbate the problem of *regulatory capture*. This is especially the case regarding privatization regulation via delegation. Delegating regulatory functions to private "intermediators" raises concerns of double regulatory capture.[108] On the one hand, intermediators might be captured by the regulated firms. Private intermediators may have strong incentives to "go easy" on rule takers, especially if they depend on them financially (e.g., if they are hired and paid by them); this can lead to *underregulation*. Indeed, this was arguably one of the causes of the financial crisis of 2008: Credit rating agencies, which served as private intermediators for assessing the risk of financial instruments and bank capital requirements, were accused of favoring the private short-term interests of the banks that paid

---

[102] Gunningham and Rees, "Industry Self-Regulation"; Ogus, "Rethinking Self-Regulation"; Priest, "The Privatization of Regulation."

[103] Clifton, García-Olalla and Molyneux, "Introduction to the Special Issue"; John W. Head, "The Global Financial Crisis of 2008–2009 in Context: Reflections on International Legal and Institutional Failings, 'Fixes,' and Fundamentals," *McGeorge Global Business & Development Law Journal* 23 (2010): 43–112, pp. 93–94.

[104] Levine, "The Governance of Financial Regulation," at pp. 39–56; Head, "The Global Financial Crisis of 2008–2009 in Context," at p. 105; Eric Helleiner and Stefano Pagliari, "Between the Storms: Patterns in Global Financial Governance, 2001–2007," in *Global Financial Integration Thirty Years On: From Reform to Crisis*, eds. Geoffrey R. D. Underhill, Jasper Blom and Daniel Mügge (Cambridge: Cambridge University Press, 2010), pp. 42–57, 391.

[105] Renate Mayntz, "Institutional Change in the Regulation of Financial Markets: Questions and Answers," in *Crisis and Control: Institutional Change in Financial Market Regulation*, ed. Renate Mayntz (Frankfurt: Campus Verl, 2012), pp. 7–28, at p. 14; Clifton, García-Olalla and Molyneux, "Introduction to the Special Issue," at p. 193.

[106] Black, "Paradoxes and Failures"; Cristie Ford, "Principles-Based Securities Regulation in the Wake of the Global Financial Crisis," *McGill Law Journal* 55 (2010): 257–307.

[107] Ako, Okonmah and Ogechukwu, "Corporations, CSR and Self Regulation."

[108] Abbott, Levi-Faur and Snidal, "Theorizing Regulatory Intermediaries," at pp. 29–30.

them in order to be rehired by them, providing lenient risk assessments that eventually precipitated the crisis.[109]

On the other hand, a public regulator might be captured by private intermediators. Private intermediators often replace the public regulator's presence "in the field," managing most of the interaction with the rule takers, thus enjoying greater access to information and gaining greater expertise. As noted, such asymmetrical information and expertise may accelerate regulatory capture.[110] Moreover, public regulators may become highly dependent on the intermediators, gradually relying on them not only to perform specific regulatory tasks but also to assume an active role in designing rules and setting policy goals.[111] Private intermediators might take advantage of their supremacy in expertise and knowledge to manipulate public regulators' decisions in their favor. This can be done by increasing the requirements or applying them to broader sectors, in order to boost profits by expanding the market for intermediators, thus leading to *overregulation*. For instance, it can be profitable for private standardization boards or certification bodies to require additional tests and controls. Similarly, delegating regulatory functions to industry associations also entails the pitfall of increasing the regulatory burden even when it is unnecessary for achieving the public goal. Regulatory scholars have long ago noted the problem of "rent-seeking,"[112] pointing out large and powerful firms' incentives to increase regulatory burden to create entry barriers that ward off potential competitors. Such large corporations, which often play a dominant role in industry associations, standardization boards and diverse collaborative governance institutions are inclined to push these regulatory regimes toward overregulation.[113] The concern of overregulation may be especially troubling when the privatization entails the delegation of coercive regulatory power. Private entities are usually profit-motivated. They are not bound by the norms of public law that can decrease human rights violations. Therefore, the potential for abuse of power may be particularly salient when private entities are granted coercive regulatory powers such as the authority to revoke a business license or to enter, search and seize private property.

Returning to the daycare example, privatizing regulation may leave toddlers unprotected and even unnecessarily increase the regulatory burden on caregivers, especially in the case of privatization via delegation. Delegating the task of monitoring daycare centers to private certifiers may involve high transaction costs (the daycare supervisor will be required to invest in the process of choosing the private certifiers, setting detailed rules to guide their operation, monitoring their activity, imposing sanctions if they exceed authority, etc.). Such transaction costs can make privatization inefficient, especially when the regulatory task is not easy to specify in advance or when it comes to core regulatory missions that are conducted extensively and continually. Private certifiers, which are often for-profit entities that are not bound to any public accountability mechanism, may also be considered illegitimate. Hence, caregivers may resist allowing them to enter and monitor daycares, especially if they exercise coercive powers (e.g., the power of search and seizure). As for effectiveness, private certifiers are often in a conflict of interest that may cause them to distort the purposes of regulation.

---

[109]   Davies, *The Financial Crisis – Who Is to Blame?*, at pp. 123–130; Andreas Kruck, "Asymmetry in Empowering and Disempowering Private Intermediaries: The Case of Credit Rating Agencies," ANNALS *of the American Academy of Political and Social Science* 670 (2017): 133–151.

[110]   Carpenter, *Preventing Regulatory Capture.*

[111]   Yael Kariv-Teitelbaum, "The Privatization of Regulation in Israel," at p. 248.

[112]   Stigler, "The Theory of Economic Regulation"; G. A. Jarrell, "The Demand for State Regulation of the Electric Utility Industry," *Journal of Law and Economics* 21 (1978): 269–295.

[113]   See, for instance, regarding standardization boards: Büthe and Mattli, *The New Global Rulers.*

Private certifiers that operate in a competitive market, in which they are hired and paid by the daycare providers, may be overly lenient in order to be rehired, thus leading to underregulation. On the other hand, private certifiers may push the daycare supervisor to adopt stricter and broader standards (e.g., adding a requirement to have a fire extinguisher or applying the standards to home caregivers of a single baby). Private certifiers' motivation to expand their market in order to increase profits may lead to overregulation. This concern is especially troubling when they possess coercive powers (e.g., search and seizure), which raises concerns about the abuse of power. Finally, privatizing through reregulation and deregulation may also have pitfalls. Indeed, replacing public supervisors by relying on parents, caregivers or a child protection NGO can reduce the state's costs. However, such developments may also be considered an illegitimate relinquishment of public responsibility (e.g., a new regulatory policy that relies on parents to monitor daycares may elicit harsh public criticism). Moreover, these developments may lead to underregulation. Caregivers naturally have incentives to relieve their regulatory burden. Relying on self-regulation practices or voluntary initiatives that depend on caregivers' consent and cooperation may fail to adequately protect toddlers.

To conclude, the privatization of regulation offers great promise for better achieving public goals, but it is also beset with pitfalls. Under certain conditions, it can complement and reinforce regulatory regimes, while in other situations it may distort regulatory goals. It is therefore essential first to identify which type of entity a regulatory function is privatized to, and to clarify the entity's central motivations and the norms to which it responds. This enables an assessment of when the privatization of regulation may raise concerns, as well as an exploration of how to better design the legal mechanisms that facilitate the privatization process. This is especially relevant in the case of privatizing via delegation, which is often conducted through a formal legal mechanism such as a contract (e.g., outsourcing regulation), franchise or license (e.g., accreditation and certification) or legislative mandate (e.g., industry-based regulators). Further research is required to investigate whether the risks of privatizing regulation can be mitigated by legal mechanisms and limitations, such as: privatizing only easy-to-specify regulatory functions that require narrow discretion; privatizing only peripheral functions that are far from the public regulator's core responsibility; incorporating mandatory duties designed to maintain the public regulators' knowledge and expertise (e.g., mandatory reporting duties, public ownership of databases, etc.); applying public law norms (e.g., mandatory cooling-off periods, an obligation to avoid disproportional infringement of human rights, etc.); or implementing partial public accountability mechanisms (e.g., transparency obligations, public participation duties, etc.).

16.6 CONCLUSION: FOUR POSSIBLE OUTCOMES FOR PRIVATIZING REGULATION

The power to regulate private activity using rule setting, rule monitoring and rule enforcing is commonly perceived as one of the central remaining roles of the state in the "post-privatizations" era. Instead of delivering public products and services, states can focus on and specialize in regulating, thus decreasing many of the problems arising through privatization. However, over the past three decades, states are increasingly assigning regulatory roles to private entities, encouraging their ongoing dominance in the regulatory field. States do so by delegating regulatory powers to private entities, adopting new regulatory strategies that rely on private entities instead of public supervisors, and enabling private entities to project regulatory authority by generating their own voluntary regulatory regimes.

One of the main drivers behind this development is the aspiration to share the state's responsibility for advancing public goals. This new-governance school of thought seeks to create true partnerships between the state, industry and society. Hence, sharing regulatory roles with private entities is viewed as a promising way to increase the efficiency, effectiveness and legitimacy of regulatory regimes – a complementary means of reinforcing public regulation and advancing public goals. On the other hand, this new mode of governance also entails the pitfalls of privatization. As the financial crisis of 2008 demonstrated, diverse forms of privatized regulation may lead to substantial regulatory failures. Assigning regulatory roles to private entities that are often profit-driven and are not bound by the norms of public law may hinder the achievement of regulatory goals. The privatization of regulation may not only decrease the effectiveness, efficiency or legitimacy of regulatory regimes but can also potentially erode the state's regulatory capacity.

Is this blurring of public–private regulatory boundaries an incomprehensive oxymoron or a natural development? Should this new mode of governance be conceptualized as publicization or as privatization? Has it extended regulation or reduced it? Does it lead to the promotion of public goals through private measures or does it advance private interests by public means? This chapter does not offer a dichotomic answer to any of these questions. Instead, it suggests that the privatization of regulation may lead to four possible directions. First, it might expand regulation by *reinforcing* the regulatory regime, thus advancing public goals, adding another layer to the regulatory regime and boosting the state's regulatory capacity. Second, it might reduce regulation in favor of private interests, leading to *underregulation* by preempting public regulation and diminishing the state's regulatory capacity. Third, it might expand regulation in favor of private interests, leading to *overregulation*. Finally, it might *change* the nature and style of regulation, transforming it to become more attuned to professional, technical and measurable criteria. This fourth direction is yet to be extensively researched and requires further study.

In which of these directions is the privatization of regulation leading us? The answer lies in the details.[114] Clearly, each case of privatized regulatory regimes requires an in-depth examination to assess its results. The literature is full of examples of privatized regulation, some more successful than others. This chapter therefore only suggests a preliminary framework, identifying how the privatization of regulation occurs – by delegation, reregulation or deregulation – and to which type of private entity a regulatory function is privatized: the regulated firms, the beneficiaries of regulation, semi-representative organizations (mainly of the regulated industry) and third parties from the business or civil sector. Each private regulatory actor has a different set of incentives and conforms to different norms, which shape its tendency to reinforce the regulatory regime, overregulate, underregulate, or change the nature and style of regulation.

Reconceptualizing this phenomenon as the privatization of regulation raises substantial normative questions that require the close attention of future researchers. Acknowledging the increasing dominancy of private entities in filling regulatory roles emphasizes the need to reinvestigate various normative concerns. It opens the gate to further explore its distributive implications, identifying which groups mostly profit from assigning regulatory roles to private entities. It raises the common concern of abuse of power, requiring to assess whether private regulators are more prone to adversely affect human rights. It also raises the need to thoroughly investigate the concern of democratic deficit, exploring alternative mechanisms

---

[114] Cf. Chapter 15 in this volume.

of accountability to which private regulators are subject. Moreover, the perspective of privatizing regulation not only highlights the implications regarding its effect downwards on regulated firms and individuals; it also casts an important spotlight over the need to evaluate its upward implications regarding its effect on the state and specifically its ability to maintain its regulatory capacity.

The privatization of regulation therefore prods us to rethink the roles of the state. It challenges the regulatory state's conceptual claim for a legitimate state monopoly over regulatory power.[115] It is therefore not surprising that when the new school of thought that is driving this phenomenon, the new governance, was first introduced, it was presented as the "post-regulatory state"[116] or the "new regulatory state."[117] Concerns about the state losing its regulatory capacity require us to design better mechanisms to maintain this capacity. First, however, we must clarify the desired characteristics of this regulatory capacity. Do we expect the state to maintain its dominant position as a regulator? Should it transition to a role of regulating private regulators? Or perhaps the state should adopt new roles and responsibilities that further remove it from the description of the regulatory state?

---

[115] Levi-Faur, "The Odyssey of the Regulatory State."
[116] Scott, "Regulation in the Age of Governance."
[117] Braithwaite, "Accountability and Governance under the New Regulatory State"; Leighton McDonald, "The Rule of Law in the 'New Regulatory State,'" *Common Law World Review* 33 (2016): 197–221.

17

Privatization of Accounting Standard-Setting

Israel Klein

17.1 INTRODUCTION

The financial information about a financial entity is asymmetrically distributed among those who contract with it. Whether the entity is a publicly traded corporation or a nonprofit state hospital, those parties of the inner circle of the entity, for example the entity's management, possess information about the financial stability of the entity and its available resources, whereas those of the outside circle, who in many cases finance the entity or cohesively depend on its services, for example the entity's patients/customers and workers/suppliers, lack information about its commitments, available resources or the use thereof.

The unavailability of information to the outside circle goes together with reduced accountability toward parties of that circle. More so, lack of information prevents external parties from regulating the entity and those who manage it; or, to say the least, makes such extrinsic regulation more expensive for those parties due to their need to self-collect undisclosed information.

One way of leveling the information field, thus improving accountability and reducing the costs of external regulation over the entity, is to require members of the inner circle to provide information about the entity's affairs to the outside circle through timely reports. For such reporting to be useful and efficient, and in order to increase the reliability of reported information, reporting is customarily done by requiring entities and their managers to follow a defined set of mandatory norms, "reporting standards," which are established by a standards-setter whose standards are also followed by other entities. The use of standards in the reporting reduces the overall cost of analysis of the information and allows the reporting of one entity to be compared with that of others, thus reducing the cost of analysis even further. In respect of the reporting of entities' financial affairs, the standards being used are generally known as "accounting standards"; and those widely used by entities are known as "Generally Accepted Accounting Principles" (GAAP).

This chapter discusses the privatization of accounting standards and further focuses on the privatization of the GAAP used by state and local governments and entities they own and operate ("public sector entities").[1] In that context, the chapter examines the case of the United

---

[1] Excerpts of this chapter have been drawn from a previous article by the author, arguing that undetected inflation of pension deficits resulted directly from inadequate disclosure standards promulgated by the public sector's private

States and challenges its public sector's existing institutional arrangements for accounting standards-setting; that is, the delegation of standard-setting authority for disclosure requirements to a private organization (privatization), an arrangement originally adopted from the business sector. In this chapter, "delegation" doesn't refer only to the practice of appointing an agent to act on behalf of a principal but rather to a more general practice, prevalent in standard promulgation generally and accounting standards-setting specifically, in which a private entrepreneurship fulfills some of the principal's regulatory duties, although not necessarily duly appointed to do so.

The chapter explains why maintaining the power to prescribe accounting standards in private hands empowers the private standards-setter with sovereign powers extending far beyond the mere regulation of financial reporting. It further argues that while privatization can be justified in respect of the business sector,[2] when it comes to the public sector, delegation of accounting powers from the accountable and legitimate public regulator to an unaccountable[3] and self-agenda-driven private organization can lead to substantive difficulties, both in theory and in practice.

The analysis of cases involving a privatization of regulatory powers can often be separated for (i) a discussion of the delegator's identity, for example a public versus a private agent, and (ii) a discussion of the way in which vested regulatory powers are executed, for example focusing on the political nature of the rules the agent makes. However, the privatization of reporting standards in the US public sector presents a case with inseparable dependency between the two discussions: In respect of the US public sector, under the current *laissez-faire* standards-setting, the content of the standards is unseparated from the nature of their promulgator.[4] Specifically, as discussed in this chapter, having a private player promulgating standards for uncompelled public reporters necessarily results in reporting that serves needs that appeal to a specific type of stakeholder and not to the needs of the general public.[5]

The rest of this chapter proceeds as follows: In Section 17.2, I review the institutional arrangements currently governing reporting for both the business sector and the public sector; the normative framework that established the Financial Accounting Standards Board (FASB) as the prominent accounting standards-setter for the business sector; and the historical circumstances that led to the creation of the Governmental Accounting Standards Board

---

standard-setter, published in Israel Klein, "It's Time to Mind the GASB," *San Diego Law Review* 54 (2017): 565–605.

[2] See Robert Van Riper, *Setting Standards for Financial Reporting: FASB and the Struggle for Control of a Critical Process* (Westport, CT: Quorum, 1994), p. 9 (emphasizing the private sector's experience); William W. Bratton, "Private Standards, Public Governance: A New Look at the Financial Accounting Standards Board," *Boston College Law Review* 48 (2007): 5–49, p. 5; Douglas W. Hawes, "Whither Accounting and the Law? A Comparative Analysis of the Sources of Accounting Authority in the Light of International Developments," *Journal of Comparative Corporate Law and Securities Regulation* 2 (1979): 195–219, p. 210 (arguing that governments operate too slowly in response to changes needed in accounting); Maurice C. Kaplan and Daniel M. Reaugh, "Accounting, Reports to Stockholders, and the SEC," *Yale Law Journal* 48 (1939): 935–980, pp. 935, 954 and n.78 (arguing that delegation is a device that preserves flexibility); Walter Mattli and Tim Büthe, "Global Private Governance: Lessons from a National Model of Setting Standards in Accounting," *Law and Contemporary Problems* 68 (2005): 225–262, pp. 225, 230–232 (emphasizing the private sector's highest levels of technical expertise). But see George Mundstock, "The Trouble with FASB," *North Carolina Journal of International Law* 28 (2003): 813–846, pp. 813, 816–824 (arguing against some of these justifications).

[3] See also *Waters v. Autuori* (1996) 676 A.2d 357 (Conn.).

[4] See Israel Klein, "The Gap in the Perception of the GAAP," *American Business Law Journal* 54 (2017): 581–634, p. 612.

[5] See Israel Klein, "It's Time to Mind the GASB," *San Diego Law Review* 54 (2017): 565–605; James Naughton et al., "Public Pension Accounting Rules and Economic Outcomes," *Journal of Accounting and Economics* 59 (2015): 221–241, p. 223.

(GASB) as an alternative and almost equal authoritative standards-setter for the public sector. In Section 17.3, I discuss the implications for sovereignty of privatizing accounting standard-setting for public entities. I explain how setting disclosure standards affects the ability of the public to control the public entity, its accountability, and the incentives given to the entity's executives to serve the public good. In Section 17.4, I discuss the existing justification supporting privatization of accounting standards-setting; I explain why these justifications, originally developed in the context of the business sector and the delegation of accounting standard-setting powers from the US Securities and Exchange Commission (SEC) to the FASB, do not hold up in the case of the public sector. In Section 17.5, after the full meaning of delegating accounting standard-setting powers and the lack of justification thereof are brought to light, I conclude with remarks about a necessary change in the existing public sector's arrangement.

17.2 THE PRIVATIZATION OF ACCOUNTING STANDARD-SETTING

Except as applied to federal entities, financial reporting practices in the United States[6] are prescribed by private organizations.[7] For the business sector, reporting standards are set by the FASB; for the public sector, the standards are set by the GASB. Both the FASB and the GASB are private entities, organized as not-for-profit Delaware nonstock corporations.[8] Although the two organizations maintain high levels of transparency in their work and meticulously adhere to due process procedures, they are still private organizations and, as such, are not subject to the administrative duties or obligations imposed by administrative law,[9] for example, compliance with the Administrative Procedure Act.[10] Furthermore, a number of attempts to subject the standards to a judicial review, by the use of different tort doctrines, all failed.[11] Nevertheless, the FASB and the GASB possess great administrative and regulatory power over the entire US financial reporting sphere, and the accounting standards promulgated by these bodies have substantial effects on the economy.[12]

---

[6] In contrast to the Anglo-American approach for accounting standard-setting – as prevailing in the United States, the United Kingdom and other countries influenced by the USA, the Continental approach – as prevailing in many European countries and at the level of the European Union – establishes accounting standards through legislation. Cf. John Flower, *European Financial Reporting: Adapting to a Changing World* (New York: Palgrave Macmillan, 2004), p. 76.

[7] Federal entities are implementing FASAB standards, which are set by a federal board.

[8] The FASB and the GASB are held by a shared parent company, the Financial Accounting Foundation (FAF), which is another not-for-profit, non-stock Delaware corporation. FAF, "About the FAF," www .accountingfoundation.org/aboutfaf.

[9] Cf. Omar Ochoa, "Accounting for FASB: Why Administrative Law Should Apply to the Financial Accounting Standards Board," *Texas Review of Law & Politics* 15 (2011): 489–517, pp. 489, 496.

[10] Administrative Procedure Act (APA), Pub. L. No. 79–404, 60 Stat. 237 (1946) (codified as amended in scattered sections of 5 U.S.C.); see also *Arthur Andersen & Co.* v. *SEC*, No. 76C-2832, 1978 WL 1073, at *2 (N.D. Ill. Mar. 1, 1978).

[11] *Appalachian Power Co.* v. *Am. Inst. of Certified Pub. Accountants* (1959) 268 F.2d 844 (2d Cir.); *Credit Union Nat'l Ass'n.* v. *Am. Inst. of Certified Pub. Accountants* (1987) 832 F.2d 104 (7th Cir.); *Waters* v. *Autuori* (1996) 676 A.2d 357 (Conn.).

[12] Cf. George J. Benston and Melvin A. Krasney, "The Economic Consequences of Financial Accounting Statements," in George J. Benston and Melvin A. Krasney, *Economic Consequences of Financial Accounting Standards: Selected Papers* (Washington: Financial Accounting Standards Board, 1978), 159–252, pp. 159–160; Stephen A. Zeff, "The Rise of 'Economic Consequences,'" *Journal of Accountancy* (December 1978): 56–63, p. 56.

17.2.1 *The Business Sector*

The FASB owes its status as the prominent accounting prescriber for the business sector to the SEC.[13] Although empowered with the authority to prescribe methods to be followed in the preparation of accounts, including the form and content of financial statements disclosed according to various legislation,[14] the SEC rarely exercises these powers. Instead, the SEC historically looked to standard-setting bodies designated by the private market, specifically the accounting profession, thus the FASB and its predecessors, "to provide leadership in establishing and improving accounting principles" governing disclosure.[15]

In the 1930s, when the Securities Acts were enacted and, among other things, the SEC was created, the accounting profession was already self-regulating the practices used in preparing financial statements.[16] At that time, these practices were seen as satisfactory;[17] hence, the newly established SEC elected to continue the existing situation and have the private market continue its role in promoting accounting standards. In the 1970s, when the FASB was established as a full-time independent private body, replacing an existing part-time technical committee of the American Institute of Certified Public Accountants (AICPA) – the Accounting Principle Boards (APB)[18] – the SEC's practice of de facto empowering a private organization with arguably administrative authorities was challenged on constitutional grounds by accounting firms.[19] Although that attempt did not succeed,[20] in the years that followed, legal scholars heavily criticized the SEC's practice and the court's inadequate deliberation of the matter.[21] Eventually, among other changes the 2002 Sarbanes–Oxley Act[22] applied to the accounting profession, it explicitly approved the SEC's practice. Section 108 of the Sarbanes–Oxley Act explicitly allows the SEC to recognize[23] private organizations as standards promulgators for purposes of the securities laws. In a policy statement[24] following

---

[13] Statement of Policy on the Establishment and Improvement of Accounting Principles and Standards, Accounting Series Release No. 150, 3 SEC Docket 275 (December 20, 1973) [hereinafter ASR No. 150]; Commission Statement of Policy Reaffirming the Status of the FASB as a Designated Private-Sector Standard Setter, Securities Act Release No. 8221, Exchange Act Release No. 47,743, 80 SEC Docket 139 (April 25, 2003) [hereafter SAR No. 8221].

[14] See Securities Act of 1933 s 19(a), 15 U.S.C. s 77s(a) (2012); Securities Exchange Act of 1934 s 13(b), 15 U.S.C. s 78m (2012).

[15] ASR No. 150; see Donna M. Nagy, "Playing Peekaboo with Constitutional Law: The PCAOB and Its Public/Private Status," *Notre Dame Law Review* 80 (2005): 975–1072, pp. 983–989; see, e.g., Stephen A. Zeff, "The Evolution of U.S. GAAP: The Political Forces Behind Professional Standards," *CPA Journal* 75 (February 2005): 19–27, p. 19.

[16] Mainly through the work of designated committees appointed by the American Institute of Certified Public Accountants (AICPA), and before it, the American Institute of Accountants. See Stephen A. Zeff, *Forging Accounting Principles in Five Countries: A History and an Analysis of Trends* (Abingdon-on-Thames: Routledge, 1972), pp. 119–140; Nagy, "Playing Peekaboo with Constitutional Law," at p. 986.

[17] See Stephen A. Zeff, "How the U.S. Accounting Profession Got Where It Is Today: Part I," *Accounting Horizons* 17 (2003): 189–205, p.191.

[18] See Stephen A. Zeff, "The Wheat Study on Establishment of Accounting Principles (1971–72): A Historical Study," *Journal of Accounting & Public Policy* 34 (2015): 146–191, p. 147.

[19] See, e.g., *Arthur Andersen & Co. v. SEC*, No. 76C-2832, 1978 WL 1073, at *1 (N.D. Ill. Mar. 1, 1978); Nagy, "Playing Peekaboo with Constitutional Law," at p. 987.

[20] *Arthur Andersen & Co.*, 1978 WL 1073, at *4–5; Nagy, "Playing Peekaboo with Constitutional Law," at p. 987.

[21] See, e.g., Ronald E. Large, Note, "SEC Accounting Series Release No. 150: A Critical Analysis," *Indiana Law Journal* 54 (1979): 317–331, pp. 320–321; see also Homer Kripke, *The SEC and Corporate Disclosure: Regulation in Search of a Purpose* (New York: Law and Business, 1979), p. 153; Mundstock, "The Trouble with FASB," at p. 827; Nagy, "Playing Peekaboo with Constitutional Law," at pp. 983–1006.

[22] Sarbanes–Oxley Act of 2002, Pub. L. No. 107–204, 116 Stat. 745.

[23] Ibid. s 108(b)(A), 15 U.S.C. s 77s(b)(1)(A) (2012).

[24] SAR No. 8221.

the enactment, the SEC, after finding that the organization satisfied all criteria stipulated in §108 of the Sarbanes–Oxley Act, reaffirmed the status of the FASB.

Accordingly, the FASB's financial accounting standards are recognized today as generally accepted for purposes of the federal securities laws, and companies subject to these acts are required to comply with those standards in the preparation of their financial statements, unless the SEC directs otherwise.

With a contribution from the AICPA's Code of Professional Conduct section 1.320 – requiring AICPA members to follow FASB standards for all business entities[25] – FASB's SEC-recognized status with respect to the securities law also extends to business clusters in addition to those subject to securities regulations,[26] resulting in the FASB being the prominent standards promulgator for the entire business sector.[27]

17.2.2 *The Public Sector*

Concern over affairs of local government and uniformity of financial reporting began in the twentieth century when early reformers[28] attempted to develop uniform formats for reporting by municipalities.[29] However, public sector financials did not draw broad attention until the mid-1970s and the early 1980s, when big US cities, among them New York and Chicago, facing the risk of insolvency due to dubious financial management,[30] heightened public awareness of local government financial accounting[31] and disclosure practices, making it a national issue.[32]

Following Senate initiatives in 1979 and 1981[33] to place the development of standards for state and local governments under a federal governmental body,[34] local government executives and those organizations already holding stakes in prescribing accounting practices for the public sector[35] – for example, AICPA, which published its own auditing guide for local

---

[25] See American Institute of Certified Public Accountants, "AICPA Code of Professional Conduct" (2014), http://pub.aicpa.org/codeofconduct/ethicsresources/et-cod.pdf.

[26] Petro Lisowsky and Michael Minnis, "Accounting Choices and Capital Allocation: Evidence from Large Private U.S. Firms," University of Chicago Booth School of Business, Working Paper No. 14–01 (2016), p. 31.

[27] See Klein, "The Gap in the Perception of the GAAP," at p. 600.

[28] See generally William C. Rivenbark, "A Historical Overview of Cost Accounting in Local Government," *State and Local Government Review* 37 (2005): 217–227, p. 217.

[29] Martin Ives, "The GASB: A Fresh Look at Governmental Accounting and Financial Reporting," *Journal of Accounting, Auditing & Finance* 8 (1985): 253–268, p. 257.

[30] See Arthur Allen and George D. Sanders, "Financial Disclosure in US Municipalities: Has the Governmental Accounting Standards Board Made a Difference?," *Financial Accountability & Management* 10 (1994): 175–193, p. 177; James L. Chan, "The Birth of the Governmental Accounting Standards Board: How? Why? What Next?," *Research in Governmental and Non-Profit Accounting: A Research Annual* 1 (1985): 3–32, p. 6.

[31] See Rivenbark, "A Historical Overview of Cost Accounting in Local Government," at p. 217.

[32] Allen and Sanders, "Financial Disclosure in US Municipalities," at p. 178.

[33] In 1979, Senator Harrison A. Williams introduced a bill to create a "State and Local Government Accounting and Financial Reporting Standards Council," comprising the U.S. Secretary of the Treasury, the Controller General of the United States, and the Chairman of the Securities and Exchange Commission, or their designees. Drafts of the bill had been circulated while interactions among involved parties continued, which led, in part, to the establishment of a study group on the structure for setting state and local governmental accounting standards. Nonetheless, after complaining about "foot dragging," Senator Williams resurrected the bill in 1981. Chan, "The Birth of the Governmental Accounting Standards Board," at p. 8.

[34] State and Local Government Accounting and Financial Reporting Standards Act of 1979, S. 1236, 96th Cong.; see Chan, "The Birth of the Governmental Accounting Standards Board," at p. 7; Ives, "The GASB," at p. 253.

[35] For the process of developing standards, and a look at those involved, see Allen and Sanders, "Financial Disclosure in US Municipalities," at pp. 177–178 and Chan, "The Birth of the Governmental Accounting Standards Board," at p. 8.

government accounts in 1974[36] – united in an effort to prevent the federal government from being involved in setting accounting standards for local governments.[37] Although the bill failed in the Senate, the credibility of the existing arrangement of standard setting – the National Council on Governmental Accounting (NCGA)[38] – continued to erode,[39] eventually forcing[40] all parties involved to accept a formula that those engaged either from the public sector or from the private sector[41] could live with, and that would foster cooperation.[42] The formula included the establishment of a distinct and new standard-setting board engaged exclusively[43] in promoting public sector accounting though subjected to the oversight of the existing[44] Financial Accounting Foundation (FAF)[45] (which also oversaw and controlled the FASB).[46]

Unlike the FASB, which enjoys an authoritative status over business entities, supported by recognition of the SEC and the agency's cohesive power, the GASB's status results from its standards being voluntarily accepted by state and local governments.[47] Although the GASB is designated by the AICPA as the exclusive promulgator of GAAP standards for state and local government entities[48] – as the FASB is for business entities[49] – public entities are not legally obligated by Congress or any federal authority to implement GAAP, and therefore they can

---

[36] Chan, "The Birth of the Governmental Accounting Standards Board," at p. 9.

[37] See ibid., at p. 10.

[38] The NCGA was a council of volunteers, originally established in 1934 as the National Committee on Municipal Accounting by the Municipal Finance Officers Association of the United States and Canada (MFOA). The council met only two to four times a year, for two or three days. Frank L. Greathouse, "The History and Evolution of the National Council on Governmental Accounting," *Public Budgeting & Finance* (Summer 1985): 23–29, pp. 23–24.

[39] Allen and Sanders, "Financial Disclosure in US Municipalities," at p. 178 (citing Chan, "The Birth of the Governmental Accounting Standards Board," at p. 6); ibid., at p. 24 (describing structural and procedural problems with the NCGA).

[40] See Chan, "The Birth of the Governmental Accounting Standards Board," at pp. 9–15 (describing the grueling process that preceded the establishment of the GASB).

[41] See Helen M. Roybark et al., "The First Quarter Century of the GASB (1984–2009): A Perspective on Standard Setting (Part One)," *Abacus* 48 (2012): 1–30, p. 11 ("The GASB was formed by agreement between the [FAF], the [AICPA], the Government Finance Officers Association, the National Association of State Auditors, Comptrollers and Treasurers, and the seven organizations representing state and local government officials.").

[42] G. Robert Smith, Jr., "The Growth of GAAP," in *Handbook of Governmental Accounting*, ed. Frederic B. Bogui (Boca Raton: CRC Press, 2009): 1–71, pp. 9–10.

[43] See also Roybark et al., "The First Quarter Century of the GASB (1984–2009)," at pp. 17–19.

[44] A recommendation for the establishment of a new Governmental Accounting Foundation (GAF), with a majority of trustees associated with the public sector, was not accepted. See Chan, "The Birth of the Governmental Accounting Standards Board," at p. 11.

[45] Note 8.

[46] Ibid.

[47] Governmental Accounting Standards Board, "GASB at a Glance," at p. 8, www.gasb.org/facts/gasb_at_a_glance .pdf.

[48] Section 1.310 of the AICPA Code of Conduct requires all AICPA members – over 400,000 accountants in 144 countries – to adhere to accounting standards set by the organizations endorsed by the Institute. See AICPA Code of Professional Conduct s. 1.310.001.01 (2014). Similarly, s. 1.320 prohibits an AICPA member from "express[ing] an opinion or stat[ing] affirmatively that the *financial statements* . . . are presented in conformance with generally accepted accounting principles . . . if such statements . . . contain any departure from an accounting principle promulgated by bodies designated by [AICPA Governing Council] to establish such principles . . . ." AICPA Code of Professional Conduct, s. 1.320.001.01. To date, only three organizations, besides AICPA itself, are endorsed by AICPA for the purpose of setting accounting standards for Institute members: the FASB, for setting standards used in for-profit reporting; the GASB, for state and local governmental entities; and the Federal Accounting Standards Advisory Board (FASAB), for establishing financial accounting principles for federal governmental entities. Ibid., s. 1.320.040.01. Other organizations, such as the PCAOB and the IASB, are endorsed for other objectives. Ibid., at 156.

[49] Ibid., s. 0.400.10.

choose[50] to use some *other comprehensive basis of accounting* (OCBOA) for their reports. Accordingly, while a significant number of states voluntarily adopted GASB standards, a significant number of states and governments still use OCBOA instead of GAAP. However, recent research studies[51] show that although the GASB did not receive wide recognition in its early years – during the 1980s[52] – it has been fueled by the support of the FAF,[53] and is conquering the public sector, while winning the ongoing competition with OCBOA.

17.3 ACCOUNTING DELEGATION AS DELEGATION OF SOVEREIGNTY

Financial statements serve a social need for financial information regarding business entities such as companies, and public entities such as counties and state hospitals. Meanwhile, as statements become the prominent information source regarding economic entities, the power to set the standards regulating disclosure also confers the power to determine what is known about the entities' financial actions and what is not; what actions are disclosed as income-generating and therefore are incentivized, and what actions are disclosed as generating expenses and are therefore disincentivized.[54] Overall, beyond the difficulties created by the delegation of sovereign powers affecting public entities' conduct per se,[55] in privatizing accounting standard-setting there is a risk that disclosure be promulgated in a way that fulfills a private party's political aspiration[56] at the expense of the good of the general public.[57]

17.3.1 *Whoever Controls the Standards Controls Information*

In order for economic entities to communicate financial information in an understandable, efficient, and effective manner, financial reporting implements consensual patterns of disclosure.[58] These patterns use defined expressions and phrases determined by accounting standards to communicate financial results. By following accounting standards, entities can communicate information to statements users who may not be fully

---

[50] Vivian L. Carpenter and Ehsan H. Feroz, "Institutional Theory and Accounting Rule Choice: An Analysis of Four US State Governments' Decisions to Adopt Generally Accepted Accounting Principles," *Accounting, Organizations and Society* 26 (2001): 565–596, p. 588.

[51] Governmental Accounting Standards Board, "Research Brief: State and Local Government Use of Generally Accepted Accounting Principles for General Purpose External Financial Reporting," (2008), p. 3, www.gasb.org/cs/ContentServer?site=GASB&c=Document_C&pagename=GASB%2FDocument_C%2FGASBDocumentPage&cid=1176156726669; Emilia Istrate et al., "Counting Money: State & GASB Standards for County Financial Reporting," NACo Policy Research Paper Series (Washington, DC: National Association of Countries, February 2016), www.naco.org/resources/counting-money-state-and-gasb-standards-county-financial-reporting.

[52] Roybark et al., "The First Quarter Century of the GASB (1984–2009)," at p. 14.

[53] Ibid., at p. 12.

[54] See Allen and Sanders, "Financial Disclosure in US Municipalities," at pp. 175–176.

[55] See also Alon Harel, *Why Law Matters* (Oxford: Oxford University Press, 2014), pp. 73–77; Avihay Dorfman and Alon Harel, "The Case Against Privatization," *Philosophy & Public Affairs* 41 (2013): 67–102; *Arthur Andersen & Co. v. SEC*, No. 76C-2832, 1978 WL 1073, at *2 (N.D. Ill. Mar. 1, 1978).

[56] Cf. Ross L. Watts and Jerold L. Zimmerman, "Positive Accounting Theory: A Ten Year Perspective," *Accounting Review* 65 (1990): 131–156, p. 133; Ross L. Watts and Jerold L. Zimmerman, "Towards a Positive Theory of the Determination of Accounting Standards," *Accounting Review* 53 (1978): 112–134, p. 114 (discussing political influences on standard setting in the private sector).

[57] Klein, "The Gap in the Perception of the GAAP," at pp. 584–585.

[58] Ibid., at p. 587.

familiar with every individual entity's actions but are familiar with the standards and their financial definitions, and therefore they can digest information disclosed by any entity that follows the standards.

Two examples of patterns used in accounting-based disclosures are the profit and loss report, which summarizes the entity's operational results, and the balance sheet, which presents its overall financial status. A fundamental question in producing these reports is what should be disclosed and elaborated in the reports and what should be omitted? Communicating every tiny detail regarding an entity's conduct is impractical and highly inefficient. Therefore, not all information is presented in the reports. Many transactions that share common properties are communicated in aggregate numbers; for example, all expenses resulting from renovation of all highways during the reporting period are reported via a single number in the report. However, some information regarding highway renovation, for example contracts not as yet executed, is generally not included in the aggregate monetary numbers of the reports, as that information is determined as not important enough to be included in the limited capacity of the reported numbers.

The accounting standards-setter generally makes the decisions regarding what information to disclose and what to leave out of the reports, what to disclose as a separate item, and what to disclose as part of aggregate numbers. When defining the consensual pattern used for disclosures, accounting standards define the different items that have to be reported and the form to use in reporting the numbers.

Deciding what to disclose and in what form has two far-reaching consequences. First, it affects the ability to control the entity and to monitor its conduct; second, it affects the entity's systems and control. Disclosures constitute what we know about the financial conduct of the entity and its executive; therefore, the information disclosed and the way it is presented directly affects the ability to control and hold the entity and its executives accountable. For example, presenting all the county's administrative expenses in a single figure, without providing a separate disclosure of executive compensation, prevents information regarding the compensation from being publicly available and therefore shields executives from criticism.

Beyond determining what is known about the entity, accounting standards affect systems and control procedures: Fulfilling disclosure requirements mandates provision of reliable information that can be confirmed by different safeguards, such as the entity's external auditor – as in many cases mandated by federal and state legislation[59] – and the press, who might be scrutinizing the information provided by the entity. Therefore, the requirement to disclosure forces the entity to develop systematic procedures to collect the information. These procedures then create control and enhance monitoring by both insiders and outsiders. Thus, to a certain extent, disclosure requirements determine which operations will be monitored and systematically managed and which operations will be left unsupervised. An effective way to restrain unwanted expenses in public entities, for example overspending on entertainment such as expensive basketball season tickets by a public entity's executives, is to require a disclosure of these expenses.[60]

---

[59]   The Single Audit Act of 1984 requires most governmental recipients of federal assistance to have organization-wide financial and compliance audits on an annual basis. Pub. L. No. 98-502, 98 Stat. 2327 (codified as amended at 31 U.S.C. s 7501 (2012)).

[60]   See also David L. Cotton, "Federal Accounting Standards: Close Enough for Government Work?," *Armed Forces Comptroller* 45 (2000): 34–41, at p. 38.

17.3.2 *The Additional Control over Incentives*

Beyond the decision whether to require information to be disclosed or not, the decision how to classify the information disclosed – that is, whether to describe it as generating income for the entity or as an expense[61] – is a decision that determines the effect that the disclosure will have on the entity's conduct.

For accounting disclosure purposes, many of the public entity's transactions can be classified either as generating an expense or as generating an asset.[62] For example, payments made by a county's administration for construction of a new highway can be expensed fully upon payment and accordingly disclosed as use in full of the current year's budget. In the alternative, they can be capitalized as an asset and expensed in small amounts during the years the road is used and thus disclosed as smaller expenditures of future budgets.

Whether to expense or capitalize affects incentives: Entities, and more specifically managers and executives, are measured and evaluated based on performance as deduced through financial statements. In the same way that corporate management that leads a company to report heavy losses will probably be replaced by shareholders, a mayor that causes a city's budget deficit might not be elected for another term. Therefore, executives and managers in public companies and political subdivisions alike prefer statements to project earnings and increased savings. And so, the decision regarding which transactions and under what circumstances are disclosed as generating expenses – or liabilities – and which are disclosed as generating income – or assets – presents executives with incentives and disincentives.[63]

To a certain extent, a governor's decision whether to renovate highways is affected by the way this expensive construction work will be presented in the local governance's financial statements. If renovation costs are expensed in full the year they occur, then a governor of a deficit state would probably be advised by the state comptroller to avoid having such a heavy negative effect on the state's financials; however, if such expenses are capitalized as an asset, and are only expensed during the useful life of the road until next expected renovation – that is, five to ten years – and cash required for the construction can be raised by loans, for which interest payments will also be capitalized with the construction assets, then the road will probably be renovated – among other things, increasing local employment, etc.

All in all, whoever controls information controls, or at least substantially affects, the conduct.

17.4 THE INADEQUATE JUSTIFICATION FOR PRIVATIZATION IN THE PUBLIC SECTOR

For both the business and public sectors, accounting standard-setting went private. During the years since this institutional approach was established, a number of justifications were suggested in support of such arrangements for accounting standards-setting.[64] However, while justification for accounting standard-setting privatization might provide adequate reasoning in business sector reporting,[65] it does not in the case of the public sector.

---

[61] See Klein, "The Gap in the Perception of the GAAP," at pp. 592–593.
[62] Ibid.
[63] Zeff, "The Rise of 'Economic Consequences,'" at p. 56 (discussing the "economic consequences" – the incentives and disincentives – created by financial accounting).
[64] See sources cited at note 2.
[65] See Lawrence A. Cunningham, "The Sarbanes-Oxley Yawn: Heavy Rhetoric, Light Reform (And It Just Might Work)," *Connecticut Law Review* 35 (2003): 915–988, p. 981.

17.4.1 *Extrinsic Efficiency*

The most prominent justification for the privatization of accounting standard-setting focuses on the extrinsic benefits – that is, benefits seen as such from the standard-setter's perspective – that result from utilizing specialization and expertise in the private market in lieu of establishing and developing these assets by the public agency. First, *ex ante*, when launching a regime that promotes cohesive uniformity in accounting practice, the use of existing private market knowledge is a substitute for "acquiring ... expertise through lengthy and costly training" by the governmental authority.[66] Second, *ex post*, maintenance of specialized expertise, as required in order to promote new and adapt existing standards, provided by a private agent is perceived to be "more efficient" and therefore also more likely to occur. The public servant uses the specialized expertise solely for the purpose of regulation, therefore making maintenance of "expertise more costly" than using private actors who "derive positive externalities from [their] expertise" – by utilizing it in other services provided to the private market, for example consulting services.[67]

The positive externalities associated with private standard-setting not only make the private promulgation of accounting standards overall more cost-efficient, and therefore more desirable in broad social terms, they also create better incentives against stagnation.[68] Altering existing disclosure requirements creates expenses for the regulator and does not usually create any observable additional benefit for the regulator. New disclosures, keeping up with market changes, will not necessarily result in an observable improvement in regulatory work. In most scenarios it will only prevent deterioration of the regulatory function. Moreover, the regulator is required not only to invest resources in developing new standards and adjusting existing regulatory procedures to monitor the new disclosures but also to bear the risk of failure of the new revised requirement. In contrast, a private agent derives additional benefits from altered disclosure requirements mainly by advising existing clients who now need to adapt practices. Although a risk of unnecessary opportunistic changes of the prevailing practice must be mitigated, a private standard-setter is expected to be less in favor of unwanted stagnation.

17.4.2 *Intrinsic Efficiency*

Another justification for placing accounting standard-setting out of reach of state agencies is the wish to keep accounting disclosures intrinsically efficient and without unnecessary political biases on reported numbers. When inadequate disclosure exists, investors will request an additional premium for their money due to the excessive risk engendered by suboptimal disclosure because, for example, *ex ante*, not enough information is provided in order to know whether a company is a washout or not; *ex post*, there is not enough information to know how well the company is being managed. So as to reduce their cost-of-capital, firms themselves will invest in producing better disclosures.[69] Because presumably efficient disclosure was already created by the market

---

[66] Mattli and Büthe, "Global Private Governance," at p. 230.

[67] Ibid., at pp. 230–231.

[68] See Hawes, "Whither Accounting and the Law?," at p. 210.

[69] See also Ronald A. Dye, "Disclosure of Nonproprietary Information," *Journal of Accounting Research* 23 (1985): 123–145, p. 142; Robert E. Verrecchia, "Discretionary Disclosure," *Journal of Accounting and Economics* 5 (1983): 179–194, p. 180.

itself,[70] nonmarket regulation, as levied by the SEC for example, would only serve to make disclosures less efficient.

Another risk created by governmental regulation of disclosure is political sway over the content of the disclosure, for example requiring companies that received investment tax subsidies given as small yearly tax benefits to report them as a one-time, larger sum.[71] Such political influence makes reported numbers convey a different story and is not what statements users are seeking to learn – that is, the subsidies' actual effect on the prospective cash inflow: a small amount every year – again, resulting in suboptimal or even distorted and misleading disclosures.

17.4.3 *Extrinsic and Intrinsic Efficiency in the Public Sector*

Extrinsic and intrinsic efficiency justifications can, to some extent, support privatization of accounting standard-setting for the private market. Nevertheless, when public sector accounting is considered, the support value of some of these justifications decreases substantially.

While business firms' financial statements are expected primarily to communicate information to investors making investment decisions and monitoring manager performance, the public entities' financial statements are expected to fulfill the needs of a much larger group of users[72] engaged in activities other than making investments.[73] Among these users is the public entity itself, in fulfilling its duty to be publicly accountable for monies raised through taxes and for their expenditure in accordance with appropriations laws; and the general public and the media, when evaluating the service efforts, costs, and accomplishments of the public entity and in assessing the impact on the country of the public entity's operations and investments and how, as a result, the entity's and the local government's financial condition has changed and may change in the future.

The information required for these activities, among others, as required to induce public accountability and system and control procedures, is very different from the information required for capital investment decisions.[74] For example, an investor in a county's bonds is indifferent as to whether the county budget is spent on a grandiose fireworks show for the Fourth of July celebrations or on cleaning services provided for local schools; the county's residents, however, care a lot about what their taxes are spent on, and might even act according to that information when voting.

---

[70] But cf. Anat R. Admati and Paul Pfleiderer, "Forcing Firms to Talk: Financial Disclosure Regulation and Externalities," *Review of Financial Studies* 13 (2000): 479–519, p. 480; Baruch Lev and Feng Gu, *The End of Accounting and the Path Forward for Investors and Managers* (Hoboken, NJ: Wiley, 2016).

[71] See, e.g., Maurice Moonitz, "Some Reflections on the Investment Credit Experience," *Accounting Research* 4 (1966): 47–61, p. 47.

[72] Governmental Accounting Standards Board, "Concepts Statement No. 1 of the Governmental Accounting Standards Board: Objectives of Financial Reporting" (1987), at i [hereinafter GASB Concepts Statement No. 1]. See generally Chan, "The Birth of the Governmental Accounting Standards Board," at p. 6; Cotton, "Federal Accounting Standards," pp. 34, 38.

[73] GASB Concepts Statement No. 1, at p. 1; see also Governmental Accounting Standards Board, "GASB White Paper: Why Governmental Accounting and Financial Reporting Is – and Should Be – Different" (2017), at p. 2 [hereinafter GASB White Paper], www.gasb.org/jsp/GASB/Page/GASBSectionPage&cid=1176156741271.

[74] See also Yuri Biondi, "Should Business and Non-business Accounting Be Different? A Comparative Perspective Applied to the French Central Government Accounting Standards," *International Journal of Public Administration* 35 (2012): 603–619, pp. 605–610; Robert K. Mautz, "Financial Reporting: Should Government Emulate Business?," *Journal of Accountancy* (August 1981): 53–60; June Pallot, "Elements of a Theoretical Framework for Public Sector Accounting," *Accounting, Auditing & Accountability Journal* 5 (1992): 19–33.

Resulting from the difference between the two accounting systems, the type of already existing expertise in the private market does not necessarily make a positive contribution to establishing a better disclosure regime for public entities, nor is the private market better incentivized by unique opportunities to leverage expertise in other additional lucrative uses. Market participants, and more specifically public entities, their bond holders, and accountants, do not necessarily know better what information is required by the state administration and the general public in order to monitor public entities' spending, etc. Similarly, market participants themselves – in this case, public entities and the general public – are not incentivized to further develop reporting standards. Although better disclosure regarding budget use by counties might reduce existing reluctance to pay local taxes, paying county taxes, unlike investing in stocks, is not subject to the taxpayer's discretion; hence, and although increased transparency might improve collection, on its own it would not incentivize increased disclosure – especially when other opportunistic reasons exist against such increased transparency.

As far as concerns support for privatization as a means to eliminate political influence over the content disclosed, as mentioned, a public entity's reports are necessary for fiscal planning and monitoring by the local and state government. Thus, a political authority, at the level of the local government or beyond, must be able to adapt the disclosures so as to provide the information required for its fiscal and monitoring uses. Thus, to some extent, a "political" interference in the standards – by the state – is inevitable in order to produce the information needed by the state in providing public services through its controlled entities. However, allowing the state to set the standards opens a gate for a different type of political interference: a *negative* political effect, in which politicians use their administrative powers and opportunistically affect reporting for self-political needs, for example showing better results in election year, hiding budget deficiencies, etc. As further discussed in Section 17.5, a political factor can go both ways and therefore justify some "security valve" in accounting standards-setting, for example judicial review over the standards-setting process and promulgated standards in order to prevent opportunistic use of power.

All in all, the institutional approach currently governing accounting standard-setting in both the business sector and the public sector – that is, the privatization of accounting standard-setting – can[75] be justified for the business sector. However, advantages derived from private sector expertise and market optimization simply do not apply to disclosure standard-setting for public entities. More so, as explained below, actions by the strongest and most motivated constituents involved in the process of accounting standards-setting can results with disclosure that contradict the interests of other constituents, less involved in the process, such as states' residents.

17.5 CONCLUDING REMARKS

Following the business sector, accounting standards for public sector entities are also promulgated by a private accounting standards-setter. Placing substantive regulatory powers in the hands of private accounting standards-setters can be justified for the reporting of business entities – who are believed to benefit from better and more suitable standards under such an arrangement. However, privatization for the public sector is inadequately supported by such justifications. More so, due to the effect voluntary adoption has on

---

[75] See Mundstock, "The Trouble with FASB," at p. 814.

promulgated standards, maintaining accounting standard-setting powers in private hands can result with disclosure that serves needs other than those required to keep public entities duly accountable and incentivized.

17.5.1 *The Effect of Voluntary Adoption*

Accounting standards-setting for the public sector is taking place in an environment very close to *laissez faire*. Standards' authority grows bottom-up and standards have to be "sold" to potential reporters (as the standards-setter does not enjoy a formal authority that compel reporters).

Both in the business sector and the public sector, the most prominent stakeholders incentivized to act and affect entities' disclosure are the entity's managers and capital providers – all maintain perpetual contractual relationships with the entity and thus are personally affected by disclosed financial numbers.[76] Therefore, those are the stakeholders the accounting standards-setter consider when promulgating and 'selling' its standards. Other stakeholders, e.g., entity's employees & customers, although highly depended on entities' accountability as resulting from disclosure, are rarely incentivized to act and affect entities' reporting. Therefore, accounting standards promulgated in a *laissez faire* environment will most likely serve the needs of managers and investors. While such standards might fulfill prominent goals of business sector's reporting, e.g., reduce cost of capital and incentive profit-making for shareholders, in the public sector such standards can reduce accountability to some other stakeholders and negatively affect public entities' conduct. In this respect, the identity of the standards-setter, i.e., being a private agent that must earn authority for its releases by appealing reporters, and more specifically reporters' managers and capital providers, has a determinist effect on the content of the standards.[77]

Since state and local governments can choose whether to adopt standards or not,[78] remember, state and local governments are not obligated to use GASB standards and can use OCBOA, a private standard-setter might well be incentivized to relax stringent disclosure requirements, thus appealing managers in order to induce adoption.[79] For example, during the 1990s, it was claimed that the pension disclosures of important public entities were imprecise[80] and therefore "[...] not useful to the majority of users, would be confusing to them, and might mislead them."[81] Consequently, the GASB repealed these disclosure

---

[76]   Cf. Watts and Zimmerman, "Positive Accounting Theory"; Watts and Zimmerman, "Towards a Positive Theory of the Determination of Accounting Standards."

[77]   See Avihay Dorfman and Alon Harel, "Against Privatisation As Such," *Oxford Journal of Legal Studies* 36 (2016): 400–427 (arguing that agent's identity [e.g., public official vs. private organization] becomes crucial for establishing public responsibility).

[78]   See Carpenter and Feroz, "Institutional Theory and Accounting Rule Choice," p. 565.

[79]   See also Dale L. Flesher and Annette Pridgen, "The Development of Hospital Financial Accounting in the USA," *Accounting History Review* 25 (2015): 201–217, pp. 208–209 (describing how states threatening to establish an alternative standard-setter, independent of the FAF, caused the FAF to change jurisdictional limitation between the GASB and the FASB).

[80]   Governmental Accounting Standards Board, "Statement No. 25: Financial Reporting for Defined Benefit Pension Plans and Note Disclosures for Defined Contribution Plans" (1994): 25 [hereinafter GASB Statement No. 25].

[81]   "Based on the results of a survey and comments received on the ED, the Board believes that a standardized measure is not useful to the majority of users, would be confusing to them, and might mislead them." Ibid. at p. 23 (explaining why GASB Statement No. 25 is repealing the requirement to disclose a standardized measure of the pension obligation, which is used to assess pension plan status and make comparisons among plans under NCGA Statement No. 6).

requirements, thus allowing local governments to increase benefits without triggering disclosure that could have drawn public scrutiny and criticism or created control and accountability over those benefits. The general public was then left to face the potentially disastrous consequences only twenty years later.[82] It is worth mentioning that on the same time, a parallel public accounting standards-setter, the FASAB – an authoritative federal advisory board that establishes financial accounting standards for federal governmental entities – acted differently, and promulgated the relevant disclosure for the federal sector.[83]

17.5.2 *Negative Political Effect*

Systematic advantage of private accounting standards-setting inadequately justify the delegation of regulatory powers over public entities; in addition, setting standards in a *laissez faire* environment will most likely result with a disclosure that does not serve public accountability. However, state intervention might create other challenges: Politicians might use administrative powers to interfere in the standards and affect disclosure to serve needs different than those of the reporting entities or their stakeholders; for example – change reporting standards in order to increase current budget on the expenses of future years; prevent disclosure (and monitoring) of unappealing information about public entities, or even affect standards to incentivize certain ideological aspiration and not others.

In that context, accounting literature often mention Nazi Germany as a radical example for a state intervention in accounting norms – the introducing a mandatory uniform accounting system – in a desire to exercise a close control over individual enterprises and to provide for the speedy preparation of over-all statistics for the government,[84] then used for building up military force.[85]

17.5.3 *A Necessary Change*

Many recognition and classification questions are fundamental and unavoidable for all accounting systems. One of the most fundamental question is which transactions that involve an exchange of an entity's resources, such as money or manufactured goods, for other resources, such as services, are considered negative for the entity, and therefore, are disincentivized as generating an expense; and which are considered positive, and therefore are incentivized as generating an asset or even income.

More than fifty years of modern accounting research has taught us that answers to such disclosure dilemmas are never self-evident, and are conceptually dependent on social, normative preferences – that is, they are subjective.[86] At the end of the day, the preferences implemented in the disclosure are those dictated by the accounting standard-setter who

---

[82] Klein, "It's Time to Mind the GASB," at pp. 597–601.

[83] Klein, "It's Time to Mind the GASB," at p. 601.

[84] Foreign Economic Administration: Enemy Branch, "The German Uniform Accounting System as an Instrument of Allied Economic Control" (October 1945), at p. 1.

[85] Flower, *European Financial Reporting*, at p. 238.

[86] See William H. Beaver, *Financial Reporting: An Accounting Revolution* (Englewood Cliffs, NJ: Prentice-Hall, 1981), p. 16; Joel S. Demski, "The General Impossibility of Normative Accounting Standards," *Accounting Review* 48 (1973): 718–723; see also Peter Miller, "Accounting as Social and Institutional Practice: An Introduction," in *Accounting as Social and Institutional Practice*, eds. Anthony G. Hopwood and Peter Miller (New York: Cambridge University Press, 1994): 1–31, pp. 13–15.

controls accounting and disclosure specifications. Different objectives infer different accounting rules.[87]

Thus, since reporting is subjective, ideal reporting might result from a lack of standardization and by allowing managers to customize reporting according to entity's unique preferences.[88] However, not only would such a practice expose reporting to manipulation and fraud, but will also harm financial discourse's efficiency and effectiveness: Statements users will not be able to digest information using a single set of reported numbers but rather be required to consider every entity's self-adjustment; furthermore, reporting will completely lose its comparability among entities, or become extremely expensive as reported numbers cannot be compared without being re-calculated using shared accounting rules. In order to maintain a functioning financial discourse, standardization is required (having said that, keeping accounting discourse intact does not prevent managers from producing additional set of reports;[89] however such reports, prepared according to standards other than those recognizes by the AICPA,[90] will not be accredited as GAAP reports, and will most likely not be comparable with other relevant reporters, hence provide only minimal contribution to the discourse).

Once the need for standardization is agreed, a question remains about the content of the standards. It is important to keep in mind that fulfilling some users' information needs contradicts with fulfilling the needs of other users.[91] For example, investors ultimately care about future cash inflows, generated to serve debt and interest payments on the public entity's bonds; hence, increased investments in non-income-generating infrastructure – for example, paving new non-toll highways – is seen by them as negative spending as it uses resources for purposes not benefitting bond holders. In contrast, the public is mainly interested in the services provided by the entity and hence interest payments for bond holders are seen as negative spending. In contrast, investments in improving infrastructure – and keeping it toll-free – are seen as a positive use of funds. Thus, a profit accounted and disclosed under the investors' perspective is not necessarily a profit under the general public's perspective, and vice versa. The question of whose objectives disclosures serve – that is, the perspective used when accounting for and disclosing transactions – affects information availability and the incentives and accountability to which the disclosures give rise.[92]

As long as public entities are not compelled to the standards, their release and content will be influenced by investors and managers. At the same time, although a nonprivate standards-setter might be less affected by specific constituents (e.g., investors) and thus will likely be more attentive to the general public's information needs, its standards might be rejected by the uncompelled public entities. More so, state intervention – whether by compelling entities to the privately released standards or by direct governmental standards-setting for the public sector – might result in other challenges, such as *negative* political influence; hence, a third option should be sought. One such would be a professional board, with members from the

---

[87] Klein, "The Gap in the Perception of the GAAP," at pp. 613–614.

[88] See also Lev and Gu, *The End of Accounting and the Path Forward for Investors and Managers.*

[89] See also Israel Klein, "How Normative Is Its Normative Status? On the Legal Use and Status of Accounting Principles," 48 *Mishpatim* (2019): 271–331, pp. 326–327 (in Hebrew).

[90] See note 48.

[91] See Klein, "The Gap in the Perception of the GAAP," at p. 587.

[92] See also Yuri Biondi, "Harmonising European Public Sector Accounting Standards (EPSAS): Issues and Perspectives," *Accounting, Economics, and Law: A Convivium* 7 (2017): 117–123, pp. 118–119; Sheila Ellwood and Susan Newberry, "Public Sector Accrual Accounting: Institutionalising Neo-liberal Principles?" *Accounting Auditing & Accountability Journal* 20 (2007): 549–573.

private and the public sectors, which would also enjoy a formal authoritative power over the reporting of public sector entities.

During the late 1960s and early 1970s, unsatisfactory functioning of the FASB's predecessor, the APB,[93] caused the business community to advocate for its replacement.[94] Similarly, dissatisfaction with NCGA[95] resulted in the public sector community, as indicated by Congress in 1978 and 1981,[96] advocating for the replacement of the NCGA with a new federal-level public board. Nonetheless, historical circumstances, including those personally related to the sponsor of the Senate initiative,[97] in the early 1980s caused the institutional arrangement already established in the business sector to be duplicated in the public sector, resulting in a private accounting standards-setters for both sectors.

However, as discussed in this chapter, the reporting approaches of the two sectors differ, as do the incentives involved in setting accounting standards and the desired accountability (in respect of both the standards-setters and the entities). Hence, in contrast to the privatization of accounting standards-setting for the business sector, setting accounting standards for the public sector requires a different arrangement, one that should not be exposed to pressure, either from a limited number of private constituents or from opportunistic politicians. Existing literature contains some suggestions in that direction (e.g., incentivize states to replace voluntary use of GASB standards with mandatory use of FASB standards; conduct a judicial review of accounting standards-setting, etc.), but more is desired.[98]

---

[93] See generally Zeff, "The Wheat Study on Establishment of Accounting Principles (1971–72)" (discussing the crisis in standard setting that led up to the appointment of the Wheat Study).

[94] Resulting in the establishment of the FASB: In 1971, a public committee, publicly known as the Wheat Committee, was formed to study the establishment of accounting principles and to make recommendations for improving the process. See American Institute of Certified Public Accountants, "Establishing Financial Accounting Standards: Report of the Study on Establishment of Accounting Principles" (1972), p. 9; Richard Vangermeersch, "Wheat Committee," in *The History of Accounting: An International Encyclopedia*, eds. Michael Chatfield and Richard Vangermeersch (New York: Garland, 1996), pp. 607–608; Zeff, "The Wheat Study on Establishment of Accounting Principles (1971–72)."

[95] See Greathouse, "The History and Evolution of the National Council on Governmental Accounting," at p. 25.

[96] See Chan, "The Birth of the Governmental Accounting Standards Board," at p. 5.

[97] Sponsor of the Senate initiative Senator Harrison A. Williams faced a criminal investigation and eventually had to resign from the House in 1982. See Joseph F. Sullivan, "Williams Quits Senate Seat as Vote to Expel Him Nears; Still Asserts He Is Innocent," *New York Times* (March 12, 1982), www.nytimes.com/1982/03/12/nyregion/williams-quits-senate-seat-vote-expel-him-nears-still-asserts-he-innocent-text.html?pagewanted=all.

[98] See, e.g., Klein, "It's Time to Mind the GASB" (incentivizing the replacement of the GASB with the FASAB); Klein, "The Gap in the Perception of the GAAP" (subjecting accounting standards to competition and judicial review); Ochoa, "Accounting for FASB."

Index

For EU product safety concerns, contact us at Calle de José Abascal, 56–1°,
28003 Madrid, Spain or eugpsr@cambridge.org.

www.ingramcontent.com/pod-product-compliance
Ingram Content Group UK Ltd.
Pitfield, Milton Keynes, MK11 3LW, UK
UKHW030903150625
459647UK00022B/2836